BATTERY!

*C. Lenton Sartain and the Airborne G.I.'s of
the 319th Glider Field Artillery*

by Joseph S. Covais

C. Lenton Sartain

BATTERY!

FORWARD

When Joseph Covais first told me he wanted to write a history of "A" Battery and my involvement in it I thought it was a good idea, but had some doubt that it was still possible. So many memories had long since been lost or obscured by age. Now that it is finished, I can say that this book truly depicts what "A" Battery was all about. The reader should be assured that what follows is an accurate account of life in our outfit, the product of a great deal of research and commitment.

I am compelled to add that the true spirit of "A" Battery was reflected in its sergeants and enlisted personnel. Those of us who were privileged to serve in the battery were fortunate to be with such men. For me, it was an honor and privilege to serve in A Battery and the 82nd Airborne. The war was a learning and growing experience for all of us. Although we were really just a bunch of kids, we grew up fast. Friendships we made then are hard to put into words now. I only regret that time has taken its toll and that so many of our members are no longer with us to enjoy this story.

Yet, I believe I speak for those that are still around, though there aren't many of us, when I say that Covais has done an outstanding job capturing and preserving the history of A Battery. His father would be very proud of him. I am myself eternally grateful for his dedication and job well done.

C. Lenton Sartain

Judge, retired

Baton Rouge, September, 2010

BATTERY! C. Lenton Sartain, and the Airborne G.I.'s of the 319th Glider Field Artillery.

Introduction:

Among my childhood memories are many of myself, sitting on the sofa with my father, watching the 1960's television series COMBAT!. In spite of his contempt for the absence of realism, Dad was compelled to watch programs like this. As each Episode unfolded, he would periodically instruct me with remarks like, "See that? That's real, real footage, that's not fake." I remember one time in particular, he waved his hand in the air dismissively saying, "Ridiculous. Grenades don't make that big of an explosion." On another occasion he nudged me with his elbow while Cage, Little John, and Kirby crept up on the Germans. Dad pointed at the black and white television screen, turned to me and said, "See what those guys are doing? Bunching up like that? Don't ever do that. They'd all be dead by now if there was a machinegun. Brrriip brriip, just like that, they'd all be dead! Don't ever do that."

Hollywood movies left him in a strange state of bemused disgust. Documentaries were preferred, unless they were British productions, in which case they were sure to be denounced as one-sided propaganda.

One summer afternoon, I was helping my father build a brick retaining wall for some hedges. At this time I was probably ten or eleven years old and he'd recently changed from smoking cigarettes to carrying a pipe. When it came time to relight the bowl he took out a book of matches from his shirt pocket. "Come here," he said, "I want to show you something. If you're ever in combat this is how you light a match. Because you've always got to think about snipers, always, you've got to think about that."

Dad curled the cover of the cardboard matchbook back on itself and tucked its edge under the striking surface. "What do you mean?" I asked. "The flare, they can see that. That's why they say, three on a match - never go three on a match. See, you make that tunnel and the flare from the match is confined. Here, you try it."

My father's funeral was held on June 6th, 2004. Lying in his casket, he wore the decorations and ribbons he'd earned as a Sergeant in "A" Battery, 319th Glider Field Artillery Battalion, 82nd Airborne Division, including the Purple Heart awarded for the wounds he'd received on June 6th, 1944 – exactly sixty years ago to the day. On the table nearby was a shadowbox displaying his military insignia. In it were paratroop and glider wings, the patches of the 17th and 82nd Airborne Divisions, and a circular para-glider cap badge. There was a ribbon bar with an invasion spearhead and stars representing six campaigns. His photo album was there too. Inside were about 150 snapshots documenting his service from 1942 to 1945. The uniform he wore was authentic from WWII, one, unissued from 1945 and fitted out with the insignias from his original, but since discarded, jacket. It was a project of mine to replace the missing insignia and I

Introduction

finished it only a few days before his death.

Over the decades I'd repeatedly suggested to Dad that he write down what happened to him during those years. Usually he responded to the effect that his role was too limited to be of interest, but if I insisted it was something he might consider next week, or next year, or at some undetermined time in the future, maybe "after the holidays." For today there was always other immediate and more important work to be done. Before either of us knew it he was in his declining years and if the time for such an endeavor was available the simple energy to initiate and carry it through was gone.

Eventually I determined to write up my father's experiences in the Second World War as a magazine article, and fortunately did conduct several taped interviews before his death, but this event left me aware that no more questions would be answered or conversations held between us. I was left with a photo album and several cassette tapes of an old man reminiscing over the events of his youth.

I thought the idea would have to be left at that, counted among those never brought to fruition, when I discovered among my father's papers an address directory for veterans of the 319th which had been assembled by former Staff Sergeant and unofficial unit historian, Carl Davis, in the mid-1960s. Now there was the potential that other members of "A" Battery could be found.

I spent the summer of 2004 researching the 319th Glider Field Artillery Battalion and tracking down surviving members of "A" Battery. Each time a new veteran was found and introductions made there were names recognized and experiences rekindled from memories gone cold. A few remembered my father – most weren't sure, but a collective story began to emerge. With each additional call I was left with an increasing sense of respect and awe for the magnitude of what I was discovering. Before long, what started as an effort to casually investigate my father's wartime experiences grew into something larger.

What follows is not a history of the 319th Glider Field Artillery, though the story of this battalion is necessarily embedded here. It is more accurately the collected personal stories of about twenty men who served in "A" Battery of this battalion. Some of these men knew each other well, others were only peripherally acquainted. Each had his own personal version of memories associated with his time in "A" Battery. Their recollections intersect, sometimes corroborate, and sometimes contradict each other. Indeed the only common element in their stories was their Captain, Charles L. Sartain, Jr. of Baton Rouge, Louisiana.

A few months before my father's death I had established contact with Captain, now Judge, Sartain. Dad had kept in intermittent contact with him since the war and described him to me as, "A smart guy," adding, "He spoke French. He's a judge now and I think he still lives in Baton Rouge." Each and every man I spoke to held a vivid memory of Sartain, recalling how their Captain guided and protected them through what was the most harrowing experience of their life. All expressed admiration, frequently followed with a query as to what became of their Captain since they were discharged. Most had some story to tell about how Sartain advocated or had gone to bat for them at some point. Several recalled a casual remark or gesture of kindness which buoyed their flagging resolve and endured in their memory after all these years. "He was a hell of a man, he was the GI's friend," was what I heard on more than one occasion. As my interviews and acquaintance with these men progressed it became more and more clear to me that Charles L. Sartain Jr. was the true focal point of this story.

BATTERY!

Since our first correspondence, Judge Sartain has supported and encouraged my efforts, not to see his own service memorialized, but rather to see the actions of his men recorded for posterity while the opportunity to do so still existed. His generous spirit, honesty, and cooperation have made the difference between a comprehensive story with a unifying perspective, and a mere collection of interviews and photographs. One might say that this is really Captain Sartain's story of the men he led.

It has been my privilege to assemble these reminiscences, and using official battalion records and maps as a foundation, properly arrange them to flesh out the events of over sixty years ago. In my effort to learn all I could about the GIs under Sartain's command, what I found was an overwhelming preponderance of loyalty, guts, devotion to ideals, and simple determination. Echoes of these virtues were heard over and over again in what I read and was told. Modesty governed whenever courage was described, and every one of the men I spoke to was frank about the fear he faced in a combat battalion. Some admitted that they reached a line of exhaustion or terror beyond which they could no longer push themselves. They lost their will on some occasion to go on, or behaved in some manner they would later regret. Some lost their ideals and spent the rest of their lives trying to recapture them.

In cases where the imperfections of human nature came to the fore it has not been my intention to disparage or embarrass, but it would not be serving the collective record of these veterans well to present a sanitized and necessarily distorted version of events as they were related to me. In a few cases I have substituted pseudonyms where I deemed it appropriate to protect the reputations of men in incidents which had no significant historical bearing. When that was done an asterisk (*) appears where that pseudonym is first used. There are certainly places where the exaggerations or inaccuracies of memory have influenced recollections. The men remembered in these stories may not have been quite as valorous, stoic, carefree, or even virile, as they remembered, and the reader is asked to beg their indulgence. Suffice it to say that what follows are my best portrayals of the actual events. In specific and general terms these episodes have all been corroborated whenever I could do so, and the content of conversations include the words as remembered where ever possible.

When it was necessary to reconstruct conversations, I have done so based on what I understand about the individuals involved, their beliefs, personalities, and even patterns of speech.

More than anything I have tried to be fair and let these men describe what happened to them in their own words. Perhaps the best way of conceptualizing this book would be as if to imagine one were sitting with these veterans, now all in or approaching their ninth decade of life, watching a movie of themselves sixty-five years in the past. They provide an ongoing commentary as the events unfold.

Inscriptions seen on some pages are directly reproduced from what was written in the autograph books of Sal Covais, Mahlon Sebring, and "Zemo," the only veteran who requested to remain anonymous. The photographs which appear on these pages are drawn principally from the albums of Charles L. Sartain, Jr., Roland Gruebling, Arno Mundt, Frank Motyka, Mahlon Sebring, Robert Storms, and my father, Sal Covais. I should also acknowledge the generosity shown by Jan Bos of Nimegen, Holland, Robert Dickson, Mrs. Tallmadge Glenn, Lance and Nancy Gruebling, John Manning Jr., Leonard Linton and his daughter Sandy, Joseph Mullen's son, Michael, Robert Rappi, Ed Ryan, and Dayle Tenhet, Robert McArthur's daughter, as well as others. These persons have made available to me photographs, letters, and a wide variety of ephemera so valu-

Introduction

able to any effort at reconstruction of the details comprising what has now taken place a long time ago.

Invaluable help in the processing of photographs, battalion records, and plotting of map coordinates was freely volunteered by Robert Connelly, Michael Giffin, and Torrey Langdon, then cadets in the University of Vermont's ROTC program, and currently officers in the United States Army. The services of Paul Brown and other staff at the national Archives facility in College Park, Maryland should be recognized. Further research assistance was freely given by Matthew Ciocchi. James McCoy's help in the reproduction of original photographs into digitized images was invaluable. David Schmoll volunteered his time with photographs and numerous research tasks this project required. Sid Eells was a key figure in the completion of this book. Not only did he perform the physical lay-out and formatting, but he also helped with the enhancement of photographs, identification of unidentified persons in those images, and the creation of maps. William Wixon deserves mention as the project's first cartographer, while Sara Krumminga changed my undeveloped listing of sources into a proper bibliography. Equally important was the proofreading and editing which Geraldine Quinlan and Dawn Tetrault freely offered. Their perspectives as persons with limited knowledge of or interest in military affairs as they read the manuscript were indispensable. John Adams-Graf's early encouragement of this idea as a potential book is appreciated. George Bevis must also be thanked for his enthusiastic support of this project in innumerable ways. Above all, I want to thank my wife, Donna, for her unflagging support and indulgence of this endeavor, without which its completion would have been immeasurably more difficult.

It would be impossible to list all persons who have helped me in this project, and I apologize for any omissions. Let me say that in the course of the many hundreds of conversations I have had in the time spent to prepare this book, what impressed me was the genuine goodness of the people who answered my questions and responded to my queries. They shared their lives. They spoke with every regional accent native to Americans. Some were retired and some had to take time out from consuming family or work schedules, but all contributed to show me a people generous and kind. They were interested in and proud of earlier generations while busy working toward the future. In the 1940's all these families shared the 319th Glider Field Artillery in common. Today they still share a common heritage and sense of nationality. They are still "All American."

Joseph S. Covais
Winooski, Vermont,
May, 2011

Table of Contents

Part 1   I was born in Baton Rouge 3
Part 2   I didn't know anything about gliders 19
Part 3   There wasn't much room in between 33
Part 4   Now he's another sad sack 45
Part 5   Better coffee in a canvas bucket 59
Part 6   If a bomb hits we won't know it 75
Part 7   Darby of the Rangers 87
Part 8   Some kind of human sacrifice 105
Part 9   I wouldn't take nothing for what I seen 119
Part 10   Under the Ginzo moon 133
Part 11   You couldn't dig a hole in Ireland 147
Part 12   Brass hats were in the area 165
Part 13   Hey, how's the air up there? 179
Part 14   Out and out murder 197
Part 15   Kiss them as they went by 213
Part 16   It wasn't any big deal 229
Part 17   Not my gal! 243
Part 18   Die with your eyes open 259
Part 19   He played to his own music 277
Part 20   They didn't know boot turkey 295
Part 21   Captain, don't leave me 319
Part 22   They must have made a million dollars 337
Part 23   I was ass deep in bullets 351
Part 24   Like a puffed up hen 371
Part 25   Better than a wooden cross 389
Part 26   A bang up good job 407
Part 27   He bawled like a baby 423
Part 28   A bunch of crazy assed guys 435
Part 29   This is risky business 449
Part 30   You couldn't use any sympathy 463
Part 31   We don't swim naked in Louisiana 481
Part 32   Don't fence me in 493
Part 33   The get out quick line 511
Part 34   It wasn't their water fountain to start with 529
Part 35   I remember everything 549
Bibliography i

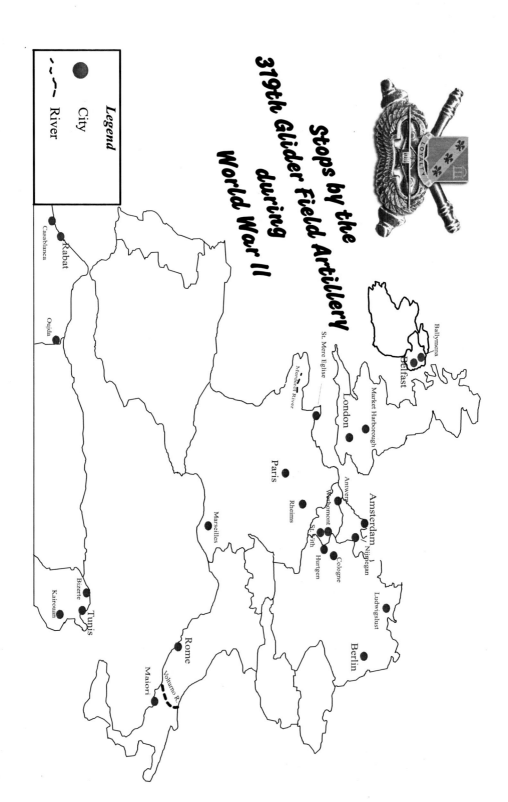

Stops by the
319th Glider Field Artillery
during
World War II

Legend

● City
〜〜 River

BATTERY!

C. Lenton Sartain and the Airborne G.I.'s of the 319th Glider Field Artillery.

"I remember addressing the battery for the last time, telling them goodbye. I hated to leave the battery. I felt like I was a part of them, you know? I did a pretty good job of containing my emotions, but it was very difficult for me, very difficult, so I couldn't say much. I just thanked them. It's difficult for me now to talk about these things without getting too emotional. I just can't do it. Therefore I don't do it."

Sartain sat quietly in his chair, absorbed in his own thoughts. He repacked his corncob pipe, lit it and continued to reminisce. "A" Battery of the 319th was a very, very important part of my early life, it really was, and now, having aged, when I talk about things I get very sentimental. It's very difficult for me to keep my composure when I talk about things I dearly love, you see. And "A" Battery was really something else. I didn't realize it was as special as it was until the damn thing was over with, but looking back over the years I understand that now."

*****

Part 1: "I was born in Baton Rouge."

A disinterested MP brought his jeep to an abrupt stop and announced, "OK Lieutenant, this is your new home." Sartain got out, yanked his barracks bag from the rear of the vehicle and took a second to survey his assignment. Shielding his eyes from the sun, he could see a white frame building with a short staircase leading to the entrance. It was identical to dozens, maybe hundreds, of other buildings at Fort Bragg, North Carolina, except for a lettered sign reading: HQ 319th Glider Field Artillery Bn.: Lt. Col. William H. Bertsch Comdg. Taking the steps two at a time, Sartain entered the battalion headquarters.

Inside a corporal was poking at a typewriter with his index fingers. The man stood and saluted. "May I help you, sir?"

"I'm 2nd Lieutenant Charles L. Sartain, Junior. I have orders posting me to duty with this battalion."

"If you'll wait a moment sir, I'll tell the Major you're here," answered the Corporal, who turned and entered an adjoining room. Reappearing, Sartain was told, "Sir, the Major will see you now."

Sartain knocked lightly on the door jamb as he stepped into the room, still not sure if that was the proper military protocol when entering a superior's office. At the desk sat a middle aged man reviewing a stack of paperwork. Looking up he said,

I WAS BORN IN BATON ROUGE

"Yes?"

Sartain announced himself, coming to attention and saluting. The Major smiled, capped his fountain pen, then stood up and came from around his desk with an extended hand. "I'm Major Todd, Colonel Bertsch's executive officer. Pleased to meet you Lieutenant."

Now Sartain could see that the Major was a tall man of perhaps thirty-five years old, well over six feet and barrel chested, with a ruddy complexion. He had a firm handshake and spoke with a rural, slightly western accent, which the young lieutenant found relaxing.

Todd gestured to a wooden office chair and Sartain sat down. Conversation with the Major came easily. Within minutes the Lieutenant was describing his background, education, and time at the artillery school at Fort Sill. "You say you're an LSU graduate?"

"Yes sir, that's correct, that's correct. Studying law."

"Well, I thought I detected some Louisiana in your voice. New Orleans?"

"Baton Rouge, sir."

"I myself am from Tahlequah. That's in Oklahoma and not that far from Fort Sill. Spent most of my life practicing law in the Indian Nation. It'll be nice to have another legal man in the outfit. I think you'll be surprised how often the law comes up in military affairs. Right now your battery, that's "A" Battery, is out training on the guns. Get yourself settled in and I'll have one of the men bring you out there. I'm sure Captain Kinard will be eager to meet you."

Forty-five minutes later Sartain was driven to a field where teams of men were busily performing the operations involved in loading, unloading, and then reloading each of a half dozen field pieces over and over again. Various sergeants and officers hovered around them, occasionally shouting directions. One of them was wearing a trench coat and officer's insignia, standing alone to one side. His arms were folded across his chest as if supervising the entire activity. Sartain walked directly up and presented himself just as he had done with Major Todd.

"Well Lieutenant, welcome aboard! The 319th needs some training yet, and we can use another young officer like yourself." The Captain spoke with a decided Georgia drawl and continued, pointing, "Now these here guns are 75mm howitzers left over from the last war. See those wooden wheels? Not the latest in weaponry I suppose, but certainly sufficient to teach these boys the basic movements required of a cannoneer."

"Are the men all volunteers, sir?" Sartain asked.

"For the airborne? Not exactly. This battalion was first cadred with regular army personnel from the 26th Field Artillery. That was down at Camp Claiborne in Louisiana, early this year. Back then we had three batteries and were shooting brand new 105s. Nice guns, very nice guns."

"They sent us a pile of boys, mostly from West Virginia, Tennessee, quite a few from Ohio, but mostly Southerners. Then early last month General Bradley announced we were going airborne. The men we had then were allowed to ask for a transfer instead of being sent with us here, but only a few did so. In fact, some others volunteered out as paratroopers and got sent to Fort Benning. Now we're receiving more men, and I dare say they're a good set of boys, but to answer your question, they aren't any of them volunteers for airborne service. The men we're getting now are sent to us straight from their induction centers. Of course some of these men enlisted in the first place and weren't drafted, but no, they didn't none of them ask for airborne as such."

4

BATTERY!

The Captain paused, his attention was distracted by some observation, and then he concluded, "I think they'll make a smart outfit given the chance. Well, Lieutenant Loughmiller is the battery X O and he'll have the men haul these guns back to the ordnance yard in a little bit. Then we can all go get something to eat. Until then you might as well make yourself at ease and enjoy what's left of the day."

Sartain gazed around him, taking in the late summer afternoon. From every direction, near and far, he could not just hear the activity; he could feel it coming up through the ground. Being 22 years old and part of something so vast and full of momentum felt great. That was why, as much as he tried to look serious, it was hard to keep himself from smiling on this September day in 1942.

After a while a whistle blew, more orders were shouted and Sartain saw the men harness themselves to the howitzers. With broad leather and webbing straps across their shoulders, they positioned themselves five to a gun. Besides pulling the fieldpiece, each man was also weighted down with three rounds of artillery ammunition. Actually the rounds were brass casings filled with sand to simulate the weight of a live shell. It was still a load, but the ground at this particular place was firm and reasonably level, which made hauling the guns much easier than it might otherwise have been.

Back at the garrison, Lieutenant Loughmiller dismissed the men and trotted over to Sartain and the Captain as they were entering the officer's mess. "I'm Albert Loughmiller. I see you've met the good doctor here already."

The Captain could see Sartain was confused. "Lieutenant, were you under the impression I was Captain Kinard? Fraid to disappoint, but I'm Walter Bedingfield, the battalion surgeon. My fault, I should have introduced myself properly. The real Captain Kinard will be along directly, I'm sure." Bedingfield removed his trench coat and now the Caduceus on his uniform was revealed. The doctor added, "I'm sure the battery is much better off with Captain Kinard in command. Now you are, if I'm not mistaken, the newest 2nd lieutenant, or the junior junior as we say here."

In September of 1942, the 319th Glider Field Artillery Battalion was commanded by Lt. Colonel William "Harry" Bertsch, Jr., just as the sign at battalion headquarters had said. It's commanding officer was a West Point graduate, class of 1924. 41 years old, prematurely grey, tall and thin, the colonel took immense pride in being a second generation West Point graduate, his father having been part of the class of 1891.

The Colonel's military career began with ten years of service as a lieutenant in the 9th Field Artillery, then located at Fort Lewis, Washington. From 1935 until 1939 his position

Lt. Colonel William H. Bertsch, 319th CO early in the war. Photo taken at West Point .

was that of Assistant Professor of Military Studies at Ohio State University at Athens, Ohio – essentially the executive officer of the school's ROTC program. Bertsch was next sent to Fort Sam Houston, Texas, where he was placed in command of a battery of the 15th Field Artillery. When the 319th was reactivated in early 1942, Harry Bertsch was promoted to the rank of lieutenant colonel and took command of the battalion.

Colonel Bertsch presented himself as distinguished, if aloof, with a keen sense of fraternity toward the regular army and its traditions. The Colonel never spoke to junior officers, and was rarely seen except during actual battalion formations or functions. He took his meals alone and kept his own council. As a lifetime career officer, Bertsch knew the army way for every situation and wouldn't tolerate deviation from it. That he was a stickler for regulations, even a martinet in some eyes, was obvious, but at this stage in the unit's training such a quality could also give one the sense that they were safe in experienced hands.

In any event the majority of operations in the battalion were overseen by Major Todd, whose more easy going style sat well with the other officers, the overwhelming majority of whom came from the National Guard or College ROTC programs.

First Sergeant Jesse Johnson at Fort Bragg. Johnson was one of the original Regular Army cadre when the 319th was re-activated early in 1942. According to Sartain, "He didn't like the gliders and he never volunteered for jump school. He just didn't like anything about the Airborne, as far as that is concerned. He just didn't like anything about it, he really didn't, and he made his dislike kind of known. But everybody just laughed it off." Covais collection.

Captain James B. Wilcoxson served as the battalion S-3, or Plans and Execution officer. As such the position held a bit more clout than some of the other battalion level slots. The Captain was, in many ways, a protégé of Colonel Bertsch and he shared many of the Colonel's personality traits. Insofar as adherence to military protocol was concerned, Wilcoxson could be as inflexible as his superior. His loyalty to the Colonel was unswerving.

"A" Battery's Captain Kinard was competent, serious, but at the same time approachable. Besides Loughmiller, whom Sartain had already met, there were Lieutenants: Green, Vernon Blanc from Florida, Irving Gelb from Albany, New York, Raymond Carey, Franz Johnson, and a Texan named Radcliffe Simpson, fresh out of West Point and spending all his extra time studying army manuals. Headquarters and "B" Batteries had their own compliment of captains and lieutenants whom Sartain would become familiar with too. Cargill from Georgia, Maxwell Torgersen from Seattle, Washington, John Manning from somewhere in New York State, and Andrew "Bubb" Hawkins from Montgomery, Alabama, to name a few. Sartain got to know each of these officers during the coming days, but he also needed to know "A" Battery's assorted sergeants, through whom everything seemed to be accomplished. Primary among these was "A" Battery's 1st Sergeant Jess Johnson, one of the original 26th Field Artillery, 9th Division Cadre. Without doubt, Johnson was regular army, or, as one man later put it, "a straight up and down soldier." He was a powerful and physically imposing man, direct, to the point, gruff, but with a jeweler's attention to the fine balance between the officer corps and the enlisted men. Like the Lieutenant, he was also a Louisiana man, a native of Natchitoches.

The battery itself was composed of six guns, or sections, with their crews. The man in charge of the number one crew was the Chief of Sections, a Staff Sergeant, with the remaining five sections run by "Buck Sergeants," including among others, Albert Hein, Rafferty, Wheeler C. Davis, and Kearney, with their respective gunner corporals.

The communication section represented another sizable portion of the battery's personnel. This section would be responsible for first establishing, and then maintaining, the telephone and radio contact between "A" Battery and the Battalion Fire Direction Center, as well as providing wiremen and radio operators for the forward observers and liaison officers assigned to the infantry units the battery was supporting. Staff Sergeant Harold Peters, a graduate of Georgia Tech, was in charge of this section. Closely allied with communications, and reflecting the artillery branch's technical element, was the instrument section under Sergeant Carl Davis of Mansfield, Ohio. Surveying equipment, aiming circles, compasses, maps, binoculars, were all part of this groups responsibility. The machine gun, or security section insured protection for the battery position with four 50 caliber air cooled guns arranged for defense by Massachusetts' Sergeant Frank Marshall. Whenever the battery posted itself in a new position it would be Marshall's responsibility to establish a network of machinegun nests, covering all likely approaches to the gun position. The motor pool of the outfit, providing the means to transport all these tons of equipment and ordnance, was led by Sergeant Jesse Holman, a cheerful soul from Virginia, fond of chewing tobacco. No less essential was the mess sergeant of "A" Battery, Sergeant William Siegel of New York City.

Staff Sergeant, Harold Jinders of Cincinnati, Ohio, completed the senior NCO corps of the battery. Like First Sergeant Johnson, Jinders was one of the original 26th Field Artillery regulars who cadred the battalion when it was reactivated. In the position of supply sergeant, he negotiated the Byzantine army requisitioning system through which the battery kept itself stocked with all the uniforms, equipment, and multitude of other sundry items it consumed. His long experience with the military system extended far beyond the boundaries of his current assignment. "Jinders was probably the oldest man in the battery, and being a new 2nd lieutenant, he sort of took me under his wing," Sartain would explain in one of our first interviews.

In September of 1942 Lieutenant Sartain would have told those who sat with him in the officer's mess about his youth in Baton Rouge, growing up on France Street, perhaps a hundred yards from the Mississippi River. There he was always addressed at home as Lenton, his middle name, to avoid confusion with his father, Charles L. Sartain Senior. Summers were spent at his grandmother's home near French Settlement, in Livingston Parrish. Lenton, several cousins, and his brother Elwood would get into fights with the French speaking, local boys or they'd climb on the neighbor's hogs and ride them rodeo style.

As the other officers got to know him, they saw that Sartain clearly had a deepsouth manner that was at once gentlemanly and light hearted, with a raffish edge. His great pleasure in telling an amusing tale was obvious. "My grandma had a Grey Parrot, a great big bird. It could curse in three languages – English, French, and Spanish," went one typical story. According to Sartain, the milk-cow got loose and started trampling his grandmother's garden. "That parrot started raising a fuss, yelling, 'Cows in the corn, cows in the corn.' Nobody paid it any mind, so the bird said, 'Goddamn it! Cows in the corn!'"

Sartain had more Louisiana memories to share: Floating lazily down the Mississippi for miles on hot summer days, for example, then hitchhiking back to Baton Rouge with his friends. He could have told the other officers, "You fellas remember Huey P. Long, the Kingfish? Well, my scoutmaster was the guy that shot him down. I think we got the day off for that!"

He may even have told about how a sports injury left him confined to a wheelchair and crutches for nearly two years, and of having to be tutored at home during that time. "Miss Baskin, she'd come by every Monday, Wednesday, and Friday with my schoolwork," he remembered in one conversation we had. "I disliked her because I thought I'd get out of all that schoolwork, but what I didn't understand she'd go over with me until I understood it."

Bored and confined to bed so much of the time, young Lenton took delight in reading. "My daddy kept on bringing me books," he said of those days. Perhaps because he felt as imprisoned as Jean Valjean, Sartain read Victor Hugo's Les Miserables with enthusiasm from cover to cover. His brother Elwood also may have reminded him of Inspector Jalbert as he mercilessly teased his younger sibling, restricted as he was to his wheelchair or crutches. In time, Sartain found ways through sheer force of will to turn the tables and make his tormentor beg for mercy on more than one occasion. It was a difficult period for the adolescent Lenton, but with it came lessons in patience, determination, and discipline, all of which left their mark.

Of course, each new officer in the 319th had his own story of how he'd found himself in the battalion. "ROTC was compulsory at LSU, but I liked it, you see?" Sartain said of his own tale. "So I enrolled in advance military for my last two years. When I graduated they sent me on active duty to Fort Sill. Four or five of my friends from LSU went in to artillery too. Like Armond Butler, from Saint Francisville.

"At LSU the man that ran the ROTC office was a Sergeant Carlson. He would give little talks to us seniors and one of the talks he gave us was, 'Y'all are gonna be graduating very shortly. You'll be getting your second lieutenants bar, you'll be going into the service.' He said to us that, whenever possible, we should sign with a line unit, sign with an artillery unit that is part of an established regiment or division."

"My friend Butler, we went to Fort Sill together too. We were just about to finish up our Battery Officers course at Sill when we saw this notice on the bulletin board. It said, 'Volunteers wanted for 82nd Airborne.' That's when Butler and I went immediately to the desk and said we want to sign up for the paratroopers. They sent us to Fort Bragg, but instead of putting us immediately with the 82nd, they put us in a replacement pool. That was one thing Carlson told us to get out of. So we did. We marched right over to the division artillery HQ at Bragg and said we want to get in the 82nd, how do we do it? Well, write your name and serial numbers here. We wrote it down and we went back to our barracks. God damn, we hadn't any more than sat down and there was a fella knocked on the door, says, 'I'm looking for a Lieutenant Butler and a Lieutenant Sartain.' I said, 'Here we are!' He said, 'Come with me.' When we got to division HQ, they said to me, 'You go to the 319th'. Then they pointed at Butler and told him, 'You go to the 320th.'"

BATTERY!

In truth, though he kept it to himself, Sartain was disappointed to find he'd been assigned to a glider battalion instead of one of the new parachute field artillery units. Still, it was a vast improvement over his initial placement at Fort Sill, where he spent six weeks with a pack-mule artillery outfit. "One of the reasons I volunteered for the paratroopers was to get away from the damn mules! I knew that pack outfit was headed for the Pacific, New Guinea and all that. I didn't want to spend the war following some damn mules through the jungle."

During the last week in September a troop train arrived at Fort Bragg from Camp Upton, Long Island; an induction center for men who came from the greater New York region. The passengers spoke with the thick enunciation of cities along the north eastern seaboard. If you asked who they were, these men could be distinguished from the recruits previously sent to the battalion by the large proportion of names representing Italian or Jewish backgrounds. As the train drew to a stop behind the gates of this massive instillation, word swept through the cars that they were all about to become a part of the 82nd Airborne Division.

"Did that guy say airborne? You gotta be kidding me!" said the recruit sitting across from Salvatore Covais, a 19year old, who'd been producing dies for machine gun cartridges at his Brooklyn job only a few weeks earlier.

Covais was privately thrilled at the idea   of joining what sounded like an elite outfit. He already had some familiarity with military life. At 16 he'd joined the Civilian Conservation Corps to bring in some extra family income. The CCC issued Sal a pair of army dungarees and a train trip across the continent to Camp Cowiche, near Yakima, Washington. Covais loved the hard work, the mountains, and fresh air, but reluctantly returned home at the urging of his parents. Back in Brooklyn again, Sal persuaded an older brother and a cousin to sign up with him in the New York State Guard's 14th infantry, the "Red Legged Devils." Covais enjoyed his time drilling at the local armory but after the State Guard was nationalized in 1940, he was discharged for being underage.

By September of 1942, with the nation fully at war and expecting to be drafted at any time, Covais

Sergeant David Stelow, Artillery Mechanic, Lt. Charles Sartain, Supply Sergeant Harold Jinders and Signal Sergeant Carl Davis. Sartain collection.

9

signed enlistment papers in the hope he'd be able to select a technical service. After a quick induction, Sal received a series of arm bruising inoculations, had a stack of olive drab clothing thrust at him, and found himself on a southbound train loaded with guys who were a lot like him in most ways.

It was without question the start of an exciting adventure. The anonymity the army afforded gave Sal the chance to adopt for himself the name of Theodore, or "Ted." "Well, you know, at the time I thought it sounded more American," he later remembered.

After an entire day and night of rail travel the train finally came to rest within the vast compound known as Fort Bragg. Then a sergeant in jump boots boarded the train, ordered the recruits off and into a large assembly hall. Someone told them to keep their mouths shut and listen for their names to be called. Eventually every man heard his own within a list of others, followed by the notification that they were assigned to one of the various glider infantry regiments or Glider Artillery Battalions. Glider troops eventually came to account for about one third of the personnel in airborne divisions. In just the 82nd, a man could as easily find himself assigned to the 319th or 320th Glider Field Artillery Battalions (GFAB) as well as the 325th Glider Infantry Regiment (GIR) as any other.

Private Ted Covais stalking imaginary Germans at Pope Field, Ft. Bragg, December 7th, 1942. Covais collection.

"I almost died right there. I didn't know they could do that," recalled Eddie Ryan, a twenty year old on that same train who'd been managing one of his father's Sinclair service stations near Poughkeepsie, New York, when his draft notice arrived. "When I saw my first paratrooper down there he looked like a man from Mars – like Flash Gordon. I'd never seen one before. Had the boots and the hat, and so it was a new thing to me."

Another man selected for the 319th described the experience this way, "I didn't really know what it was. All I knew was that they were paratroopers and I wasn't very keen about paratrooping. They brought us into this large auditorium and they started reading off names."

Forget the CCC and the State Guard, now Covais and his fellow inductees from Camp Upton were in the real army.

The men assigned to the 319th Glider Field Artillery Battalion assembled themselves one by one. As each stepped among those already selected, he'd do so knowing that these would be the people he might be spending years with, in very close, constant, and intimate contact. Perhaps it would be the rest of his life. Would there be a friend among all these strangers? An adversary perhaps? In any event there was no time for Sal Covais, Ed Ryan, Milton Sussman, Arthur Brodelle, Bob Storms, Jimmy Rosati, or anyone else to reflect further.

A corporal yelled out, "All right you guys! Grab your barracks bags and follow me. Hey! That means you over there!"

As had been the case with the first recruits at Camp Claiborne, a crash course in the rudiments of soldiering began. It was composed of a continuous regimen of calisthenics, close order drill, operation and nomenclature of the full stock M1 carbine, running in formation, and marches in full gear. Having to march five miles in 45 minutes, or having batteries "A," "B,", and the Headquarters Battery race against each other in close formation marches were common activities.

Silas Hogg, a native of the mountainous regions of eastern Kentucky, had been in the service since 1939. He was one of the original Camp Claibourne group, but the standard of training demanded now that the 319th was an airborne outfit, was raised to a higher bar of performance than had been the case in the peacetime army. Men learned they could meet challenges they might not have thought themselves capable of, in part because they pulled together. Hogg later recalled one such occasion which taught him this lesson, "The Captain came out that afternoon, just before dark. He said, 'We will take every pack and weigh them at 45 pound and you will put that pack on while I'm standing there. You will make a twenty five mile march and if you don't, you will not be here in the airborne in the morning. There'll be some men come and get you and take you away. Where you'll go, I don't know and don't care, because you don't have the guts enough to stay with us. We don't want you.' By God the next morning we weighed our pack and we hit the road. We had gone approximately 20 miles and I was gone, I couldn't go any farther. I knew that I was finished in the airborne. Well, this little Jewish boy, I probably outweighed him by twenty pounds, he was behind me. About three times I started to fall out of formation and he'd grab me. 'You can't do that, Hogg, you can't do it. You still got some left. Get back in formation, come on, come on. I'll pack your pack a few steps.' He'd reach and take part of the load of my pack. That's the way we got through the last five miles. He got me through that 25 mile march, I'll tell you that. I can't remember his name, I just know he was a Jewish boy and a human being."

"They used to pair you off according to size," remembered another man of his early training in "A" Battery. "They'd throw the boxing gloves out there and you had to put the boxing gloves on and have a go at it with the guy across from you. Always one 'pert near as tall as the other. I didn't mind, but this one guy, I think he was a punch drunk ex-fighter from World War One, he'd be hollering, 'Go ahead go ahead, whack him! Whack him, go ahead, kill him!' He'd be walking around with his head bobbing like a punch drunk fighter, which I think he was."

Another man in "A" Battery was Casimir Sobon, a tall and robustly built 21 year old native of Newark, New Jersey, with a passion for athletics, especially basketball. "Of course, I was a fiend for basketball all my life," he remembered of his basic training. "When we were at Fort Bragg we'd go out on these long hikes and come back. All these guys would be moaning and groaning. I would just go in there, take a shower, get cleaned up, go down and get something to eat and go down to the gym and shoot baskets. Nobody else would be down there; I'd be there by myself. Sports, I loved that more than anything. You had to do something to keep out of trouble."

The training was not just physically intensive. There was one or another kind of class or field exercise continuously from 7 am until evening. Meanwhile, inspections, guard or work details and other duties, left the men with little time for themselves. "Don't like it? Go tell it to the Chaplain." became the oft repeated answer to anyone naive enough to complain.

Sergeants did their best to discourage individuality, punish resistance, and weed out knuckleheads who just didn't fit in. At the same time the more promising recruits were quietly noted by the officers as candidates for positions of minor responsibility. Of course the hard training was punctuated by lighter moments. In one of my first conversations with him, "Ed Ryan told me, I remember one particular time. This officer, one of those chicken 2nd lieutenants, was showing us how to handle a rifle and how to prepare it for inspection. Your father knew all about that from being in the National Guard. Anyway this Lieutenant gave it a grab and your dad knew enough to hold on to it a second and then let go. That guy went right on his ass. Showed him what time it was! He never had too much use for Teddy after that."

Going through basic training at the same time, John McNally, another 82nd artilleryman wrote to his girl at home, "Every week, we go out on a field problem. We march for about 15 miles with full pack and at a terrific clip, go into bivouac in the woods, camouflage our tents and go to bed with no lights, no fires. Next morning, we're on our way before dawn." "Sometimes we sing as we march, but not often, as we must save our breath for this double timing. Now and then someone tries to start a song when we are not marching, without much success. It fails because singing has got to come from inside and, as yet, we recruits know in our hearts we are, so to speak, untried and untested. We feel that we are not yet worthy, and so the words stick in our throats."

Besides physical conditioning, various assessments were made of the recruits' skills. Each man's ability to drive a motor vehicle was assessed. Everyone was administered the Stamford-Binet Intelligence Scale, continuing the IQ testing begun during the First World War. Those who scored above 110 were given the option of applying to Officer Candidate School, and some did. Occasionally a 16mm training film was trotted out with the intention of educating the men in anything from the ideals of a democratic society to the dangers of venereal disease. One of the latter varieties featured a hapless enlisted man named "Private Parts" who learns the hard way to

When Silas Hogg joined the Army in 1939, He was a 16 year old from Hard Burley, Kentucky. Hogg was one of the men in the 319th before it became a glider outfit. This photo was taken at Fort Knox, Kentucky, shortly after he enlisted. Courtesy Irma Hogg.

avoid the dangers of unprotected sex.

After a while the training became more specialized. Those with backgrounds in automotive maintenance were taken up by the motor pool under Sergeant Holman's tutelage. Those who were both quick and strong were apt to find themselves as part of a machine gun or howitzer crew. If a man had experience in electronics or showed potential in the use of fine instruments or mathematics, he might be assigned to the signals section, as the communications and instrument sections were collectively known. Notwithstanding all this theoretical selection, there were also an awful lot of guys who couldn't imagine what the army was thinking when they assigned him to whatever job he found himself placed.

At this stage a day's training in the field artillery might involve individual gun crews or the entire battery. Only later on would the entire battalion, with all of its firing batteries and supporting sections be involved. The battery personnel would first locate, then plot out and set up the guns, telephone communications, observation posts (OP), and go through the motions of a typical fire mission. At other times each section might train independently, honing the skills unique to its purpose. The gun sections would concentrate on repetitions of maneuvers peculiar to their work. The machinegun section would be off studying their particular weapons, while the signals crews did likewise with their maps, radios, telephone switchboards, and calculations.

When this section worked its training problems, their job was to first survey a new battery position and plot out the angles from which the guns would be firing. It involved geometry and trigonometry, so being able to work some mathematics was key. The all-important aiming circle; a device from which the battalion's fire direction center determined exactly which way to point the guns, came into use at this juncture. Telephone switchboards were wired up, camouflaged, and manned, or practice with radio communications was conducted as the situation called for. In a joint exercise with the entire battery, wiremen ran telephone cable from each field piece, each machinegun position, and each OP, to the battalion's fire direction center.

One of those assigned to signals was Covais, who said of the training involved for this section, "I liked it because it was challenging. You had to figure things out. Firing line and all that. Fire direction center and how to use a little bit of logarithms, mathematics, and the aiming circle, and I was interested in that. It challenged me a little bit."

Those placed on a gun crew had to first learn every job and its corresponding numbered position, and then become expert in their own. Number one man was the gunner corporal, probably the most complicated position on the crew. The gunner corporal was responsible for setting the gun's elevation. He had to resight the scope mounted on the gun each time the piece was discharged.

One "A" Battery man explained it this way, "See, you line up with the aiming sticks. Every time that gun fired it moved, it bounces around. You gotta realign that up with the aiming sticks so it gets pointed correctly. Yeah, that thing moves, it goes this way and that way. Boom, boom, boom. And so, you've got to re aim it each time before you pull that lanyard. You've got to get the hairline right on the stake."

The number two man on the crew closed the breech and pulled the lanyard, firing the gun. Number three loaded the artillery round into the breech, while the number four man adjusted the fuse on the shell's nose with a wrench designed for this purpose. If necessary, he might be called upon to remove one or two of the five powder bags which were prepackaged into each round. The number five man was there to move the gun trail right or left, depending on the gunner's instructions. In actual practice, when intermittent harassing fire was being delivered for example, the gun could be operated by as few as three men, but at this stage of their education as cannoneers the full crew was maintained.

Many of the men grew impatient with some of the more repetitious and seemingly purposeless activities intended to make working around the gun second nature for its crew. As one commented, "We did things that we never did when we were in combat. Cannoneer Hop is one of them. You go around the gun. That was called Cannoneer's Hop, you go to the right side of the gun and then over to the left side. I didn't know what the point was actually because everyone knew where they were supposed to be. The gunner knew where he was, and the number two man knew where he was supposed to go, and so on down the line. Cannoneer Hop, we used to call it. I could see no use for it whatsoever."

Over the course of the winter the old wooden wheeled guns were refitted with rubber tires, and then the guns themselves were replaced with new 75mm pack howitzers. Originally designed in 1927, the "Pack Howitzer" was intended to be broken down into as many as six parts, loaded on to pack mules (from whence came the term Pack Howitzer), then brought to some otherwise inaccessible location and there reassembled. Measuring only 52 inches from tip to tip, the 75mm pack howitzer was excellently suited for mountain and, coincidentally airborne, use. It had a possible elevation of 5 to 45 degrees, and a traverse of 6 degrees without picking up and resetting the trail. The gun fired a 14 pound shell at a muzzle velocity of 1,250 feet per second, achieving a maximum range of 9,510 yards. As adapted for airborne use with a lighter trail modified from its original design, the gun was a relatively light 1,339 pounds. This meant the 75s could be easily pulled by the 1/4 ton truck, or jeep as it was universally known.

On days that they used jeeps to haul the guns the battery would go out in the morning, then drive back for lunch, and then back out to the field. On the days that they used the slings the men would eat in the field, continue their work, and then pull the guns back to quarters in the evening.

In mid-December, 1942, the battery found itself in the midst of an unexpected snow squall, but the problem for that day had to be worked through and that was all there was to it. Once they were finished and had manhandled their guns back to the road, the boys in "A" Battery realized they'd been under observation the entire time by the division commander, Mathew B. Ridgeway.

"Ridgeway was out in the field on his horse, watching us. He'd inspect us in the field on a horse. In those days anybody with any rank rode horses," remembered then Lieutenant Sartain, "we were pulling those damn howitzers back to the battalion. He was on the side of the road and we saluted him going by. Everybody said, 'Well there's the old man watching us in the snow. He's a good man if he's out in weather like this.'"

Those assigned to the machinegun section under Sergeant Marshall had their own set of exercises and weapons to master. The four 50 caliber Browning machine guns charged with the battery's defense were formidable weapons. Each weighed approximately 128 pounds, was fed by a 110 round metallic disintegrating belt, and could throw up to 550 rounds per minute. These guns could be employed in defense against lightly armored vehicles or slower, low flying, aircraft quite effectively, but in actual practice the 50 caliber needed to be fired with care, in short bursts, to avoid overheating the barrel.

BATTERY!

Opinions about the serviceability of these guns varied. Lieutenant Sartain thought they were simply too massive to be practical. "Why they didn't have the thirty caliber I don't know. The fifty caliber machine gun was worthless, frankly. It's hard to use, it's heavy, and the ammunition is heavy. I don't know why they gave them a fifty caliber instead of the light machinegun, but they had to tote those damn fifty calibers around."

Lester Newman, a young fellow from Alpine, Utah, was one of those in the machinegun section. Newman held these guns in higher regard than Sartain did, but couldn't argue about their being cumbersome to handle. "Well we had a three man crew for that. You know them breeches on them fifty calibers are pretty heavy. One man carried that breech assembly. One man would carry the tripod, then the next guy had the barrel, and we all had to pack some ammunition. They were a hell of a good gun too. It had them double handles on there. Of course you couldn't lay down on that trigger as long as you could on that water cooled machinegun, but we didn't have any water cooled in our outfit, only air cooled."

Raised on a horse farm outside of Poughkeepsie, New York, Bob Storms, known to everyone as "Stormsy," was assigned to the security section from the beginning. "I was supposed to be on the gun crew, but I got on the fifties and all I did was train, train, train. Blindfolded, I could beat anybody taking it apart or putting it together blindfolded. I knowed that gun so much that I could fall asleep and wake up and it wouldn't make no difference."

Of the heavy machinegun, he shared Lester Newman's assessment, "Oh, I don't think you could beat it. For anything, for anything. The thirty might have been a little faster but that fifty, when you opened up with that fifty, I don't care what it was, they all took notice. I don't care what it was. Man, what a gun. That gun could hit a truck motor, go in one side, come right on out the other side and keep right on going. That's a terrible gun, that fifty."

Another man in the machinegun section was young PFC Kenneth Smith. Smith was a six foot, eight inch tall 17 year old from southern Indiana. He'd been part of the first contingent of recruits sent to the battalion in early 1942, and as tall as he was, Smith probably wouldn't have been accepted for the glider service in the first place, but Kenneth had grown a couple of inches since he first showed up at Camp Claiborne. Of course having a man this tall in the battery presented some complications. To begin with, Harold Jinders couldn't get uniforms that came close to fitting Smith. The Supply Sergeant partly solved the problem by having two pair of trousers spliced into one, but the sleeves of his Class A and field jackets would just have to end somewhere above his wrists. If procurement of uniforms for Smith was difficult, marching with him in close order drill was impossible. Being a foot taller than the average man in the battery, First Sergeant Johnson finally gave up and sent Smith to cook's school. "So that's what I did, I went away and learned to cook."

As it turned out, Smitty returned a couple of months later with a T-4, Technical Sergeant's rating as a certified army cook. By that time the battalion had gone airborne and was relocated to Fort Bragg. The outfit had also reconstituted from its original three firing battery organization to only "A" and "B" as firing batteries with a Headquarters Battery for administrative and technical support. Since these batteries all had their own cooks already in place, Mess Sergeant Smith was now a supernumerary and bound to be transferred out to another unit. Smith wasn't very happy about this. When Sergeant Marshall suggested that he'd be a perfect man to help haul those heavy machine guns around, Smitty was amenable to turn in his T-4 stripes for the single stripe of a private first class and reported to Sergeant Marshall.

When the machinegun section wasn't training with the rest of the battery, Smith, Newman, Storms, and others would be at the firing range. Sometimes they would be shooting at fixed targets, but at other times, to simulate more realistic conditions, they might find themselves firing at a derelict truck pulled some yards behind a tank. Alternately, for experience in antiaircraft defense a plane would be employed to tow a target behind. Since every tenth round of ammunition was a phosphorous coated tracer, it was possible for the men to get some idea of how effective their marksmanship was.

Newman found target practice with the 50 caliber a bit demanding, "I went out and fired that fifty caliber quite a few times. It's a hell of a gun and boy, it made a racket. It was noisy, and I didn't think I was gonna keep my hearing if I had to stay in that section very much longer. I'd hate to get hit with one of them."

So went the day in and day out transformation of civilians into capable young soldiers. The average man felt good, grew stronger, and many even began to put on weight. There were, after all, three hot meals a day, everyday, and the food was both plentiful and reasonably good, though this latter quality was quite dependant on how and by whom it was prepared.

As one man in "A" Battery remembered, "We had two cooks. We had a fella from Florida and a fella from West Virginia. As soon as you got in front of that mess hall you knew who was cooking. The guy from Florida, he cooked pretty good. The guy from West Virginia, man I tell you, what a difference."

There was a lot of coffee, a lot of powdered eggs and a lot of mechanically peeled potatoes. Chipped beef on toast, commonly known as "shit on a shingle" or S.O.S., was another common item in the mess hall. This army staple was routinely made with mutton, of various qualities, and was served so often that a chow line joke circulated to the effect that The outfit was really stationed at Fort Bragg, so named to honor all the sheep who had given their lives to feed the troops. In this way the men were fed in the single story mess hall for each battery. Officer's chow came from the same kitchens, but they ate in a separate building adjacent to that used by the enlisted men.

Silas Hogg never did have any complaints about army chow. As he put it, "I thought it wonderful, oh hell yes! I thought it was excellent because as a boy in the hills you got to either; grow it, hunt it, shoot it, kill it, or you don't eat it. I'm a hillbilly. I'm a hillbilly and I can't help it. That food in the army is not any much different from the food you'd grow and eat back in the mountains. Now for a kid who loves cooked squirrel and dumplings, that's good, that's wonderful. You take wild rabbit, you take coon, all them, this is food. So, you learn to survive. A lot of city boys damn sure wouldn't eat it, but I don't worry about that city boy, I worry about me."

Sleeping accommodations for the battery, which numbered about 175 men, consisted of three two story wooden barracks buildings, each with a tar paper roof and external staircase. Inside the men slept on sets of bunk beds and got to know their neighbors. For a few minutes before lights out a man could relax, loose himself in a comic book from the PX, a newspaper from home, read a letter from his girl one more time, or do his best to compose an interesting reply. There might be an opportunity for bunkmates to review some of the day's events or make observations on army life.

Regional differences of habit were quietly noticed. Few of the Northerners from the larger cities had ever seen chewing tobacco, except in Lil Abner comic strips. Having the man beside you suddenly spit out a stream of brown juice while the nearest officer's back was turned could leave some under the misapprehension that they were in the army with the residents of Dogpatch.

Arno Mundt was just barely 19 years old when he arrived in "A" Battery, fresh from his Milwaukee, Wisconsin, high school. Years later he wrote, "Most of my "buddies" were either hillbillies from Kentucky, West Virginia, Tennessee, or a few from Georgia or the Carolinas. The group from the Midwest were all from Wisconsin, Michigan, and Illinois. I soon got used to hearing southern accents and because most of the hillbillies had no education, I spent time writing their letters home for them. Some of them had never worn shoes and their boots soon became their most valuable possession. They would polish my boots in exchange for my writing their letters home."

Meanwhile, those with the most rural and Appalachian backgrounds commented among themselves at the seeming ignorance of the more urbanized men for common manual skills. "Those boys from the city," remarked one, "when it come to work, they don't know too much about it."

Despite these peculiarities, the majority found something to like, and even admire, in men from backgrounds altogether different from their own. Kenneth Smith was typical when he found that he "got along with most everybody." Robert Dickson felt the same way. He was an 18 year old from Belleville, Arkansas, when he joined the outfit. Dickson remarked years afterward, "The main thing is they were all great guys. They were a lot of fun to be around. I'll have to say this for the 319th, basically every man in it was just real good people. Every one of them."

Day by day the battalion was starting to gel. As friendships and respect grew, the guys began to appreciate that they had to look out for each other. Part of the daily routine of the battery at Fort Bragg included an opportunity for officers and senior sergeants to stop by the mess hall in the late morning for hot coffee and biscuits. As a 2nd lieutenant, Sartain was one of those privileged to take advantage of this amenity, and he accepted it as army custom, but nothing worth taking notice of. When the weather started turning cold and rainy, then, aware that the enlisted men were left outside without late morning refreshment, it began to bother him.

One raw day, enjoying a hot cup himself, he asked Sergeant Segal about the arrangement, "These are good biscuits and coffee, you give them to the men?"

"Oh no!" was the Mess Sergeant's immediate answer.

Some regular army habit which everyone assumed to be immutable was suddenly presented. It might have been better not to rock the boat, but for Sartain there was a taste of injustice to it which made the coffee too bitter to be enjoyed the way a southern Louisiana man likes to.

After mulling over the situation for a few days, Sartain approached Captain Kinard on the matter. "Sir, these mornings are getting chilly, and the average poor little ole GI can see his sergeant leave him to go up to the mess hall and get biscuits and coffee. He has to wait, sometimes in the rain, for his sergeant to come back. Isn't there any way we can arrange for the men to get a hot cup of coffee too?"

Kinard listened. He could see Sartain's point and appreciated the lieutenant's good intentions as well as the potential effect on morale, but he also knew that army traditions were not friendly to change. After consideration he told Sartain, "Alright, but it either has to be for everybody or nobody. I'll talk to Sergeant Jinders. See what he says as far as the quartermaster is concerned. I'll talk to Seagle about it too. If he can just as easily serve up enough for the enlisted men, then maybe we'll try it, but if he's going to have to detail another man just to bake biscuits for the whole battery then this won't work."

As it played out nobody got coffee or biscuits anymore. The whole affair was a lesson for Lieutenant Sartain in the nature of army life, the privileges of rank, and the often unfortunate result of trying to do good within a system with limited flexibility.

BATTERY!

Part Two: "I didn't know anything about gliders."

The first anniversary of the attack on Pearl Harbor, December 7th, 1942, began with a signal gun acknowledging the day. The men were assembled in their Class B uniforms, complete with khaki necktie, and brought out to Pope Field for a review before General Ridgeway and an address by him. It was into the afternoon before the battalion was finally dismissed. As the officers made their way toward their mess hall, Major Todd gestured for Sartain to walk with him.

"You wanted to see me sir?"

"I did. You know Sartain, some orders came through for you to go down to Benning for jump school," said Todd.

"Yes, Major, I volunteered for paratroops when I was at Fort Sill. When do I report," the Lieutenant asked.

"Well, that's the thing," explained Todd, "your orders have you going down there on the 15th, but if you do I have to tell you you're going to be assigned to a pool and then transferred out to the 456th or 376th, or maybe even out of the division. The point is that you won't come back to us here, to the 319th, that's pretty certain." Todd gave the news a moment to sink in, then added, "Charlie, I'd regard it as a personal favor if you'd give this some careful consideration. It won't reflect badly on you if you elect not to go to Benning right now. Once we get overseas to where we're going there's sure to be more opportunities to earn your jump wings. I myself would like to see you stay with the battalion. There's been good reports about the way you work with the men, and besides, I think the other officers in "A" Battery have just about gotten over the coffee and biscuit episode."

"I sure learned my lesson on that one, sir," admitted Sartain.

"Well, the army has its ways, you understand. In any event, don't let it bother you Lieutenant. In my opinion you're a good officer and an asset to the outfit. Anyway, you've got a couple of days to think it over. Give it some consideration, alright?"

"Major, I'll do that. And sir, thank you."

The following week several officers did proceed to Ft. Benning for jump school, and, as Major Todd had predicted, they did not return. Lieutenant Sartain was not among them. Looking back with the perspective of over sixty years, Sartain would reflect that, "To remain with "A" Battery was the best decision I ever made, the best thing that ever happened to me."

About this time the first taste of airborne training made itself known. The men were issued the A-9 Flying Helmet, an unlined wool gabardine head sheath not altogether unlike the waterproof women's bathing caps worn at the time. In 1942 the army thought the A-9 might be well suited for airborne troops who would be spending time at high altitudes in drafty gliders and aircraft. The cap was thin enough to wear underneath the helmet without loosening the headband of the liner and exacerbating the problem of helmet loss when parachuting or in crash landings. Intended solely for warmth and not as an impact protection, the A-9 was subsequently found superfluous and discontinued. Next the troops were taken by sections to Pope Field where army carpenters had nailed

I DIDN'T KNOW ANYTHING ABOUT GLIDERS.

together a simulated glider fuselage without wings or outside details. The mock-up was little more than a wooden frame with the interior dimensions of the standard CG4A glider. Since this aircraft was normally loaded and unloaded through its upward hinged nose, these mock-up gliders were left open where the cockpit would have been located. For strictly instructional use the nose would be an impediment and interference. Instructors from the troop carrier command based at Pope directed the men in the elemental components of glider trooping: slip-knots, lashing and securing of equipment, weight distribution, and so on. It was brief, superficial exposure and far from enough to qualify as bona fide glider men. Only after the battalion went through its official glider school training did the 319th add the airborne tab above the 82nd Division patches on their left sleeves.

Christmas Day, 1942 was overcast and dreary. Some of the luckier men who had been with the outfit for several months were gone on two week furloughs. The married officers were off base, home with their families, as were most of those few enlisted men, like First Sergeant Johnson, whose wives lived in Fayetteville. Among those left behind, remaining on base on this holiday, were the loneliest of the men, enlisted personnel and unmarried officers who couldn't get away or had nowhere to go.

Sartain threw on a heavy doeskin mackinaw and took a walk over to the battery's orderly room. He'd been looking out for a package from home and there was the outside chance some mail had arrived the evening before. By the time he reached the building a steady cold sleet was falling. Unbuttoning, Sartain greeted Sergeant Jinders and one of the battery clerks, David Stelow of Hammond, Indiana.

"Well, well, a very, very merry, merry Christmas to you both," announced Sartain, shaking each hand in turn.

"Merry Christmas to you too, Lieutenant," they replied.
Sartain asked after any recent mail.

"I'm sorry sir, there was some mail came in but it don't look like there's anything here for you," said Stelow, leafing through a pile of letters and small packages in a wire basket on the floor next to the file cabinet.

"Lieutenant," said Jinders, "I'm going to make a trip. We've got three or four guys in the dispensary. We were going to pay them a visit. Would you like to go with us?"

Stelow joined in, "Yeah Lieutenant, come on. My

Ted Covais standing in front of the Artillery Dispensery at Fort Bragg, North Carolina, November, 1942. This is the same dispensery which 2nd Lt. Sartain and Supply Sergeant Jinders visited on Christmas day. Covais collection.

mother sent me some candy bars and cookies. We were going to pass some around to the guys in the hospital, you know, to cheer them up. Why don't you go with us?"

Sartain thought it was a great idea. "I will," he answered.

Jinders and Stelow pulled on their long OD overcoats and crammed some candy bars into their pockets. Stelow tucked a parcel under his arm and the three left.

The dispensary was another two storied white building, though much larger than the several dozen barracks the three walked past to reach it. Out front was a sign with the insignia of the 82nd and 101st Airborne Divisions. The words "Artillery Dispensary" were painted between them. Inside a steward took the three to a second floor ward.

"Your man is in the last bed on the right." Jinders pressed a couple of Clark bars into Sartain's hand, "Here Lieutenant, it'll mean more if it comes from you."

The man was Jimmy Rosati, one of the recruits who'd arrived from Camp Upton in September. The Bronx native was sitting up in bed, smoking a cigarette and thumbing through a copy of LIFE magazine. His lower left leg and foot was a bundle of bandages. After a round of Merry Christmases, Sartain, Jinders and Stelow gathered up some chairs and sat down.

Pointing to Rosati's foot, the Lieutenant asked, Rosati, "What the hell did you do to yourself!"

"I dropped a switchboard on my foot. At first I didn't think I hurt myself that bad, but then my leg and all was bleeding like a stuck pig. After a while I couldn't even walk it hurt so much. Unbelievable! So the medics sent me down here. Nice way to spend frikking Christmas, ain't it sir?"

Tossing a couple of Clark bars on the bed, Sartain said, "Well look here Rosati, we brought you a few little nibbles to cheer you up."

"Yeah," said Stelow, "try a few of these cookies I got from home."

Rosati looked into the box extended before him, "What are these?"

Stelow explained, "Molasses cookies and some oatmeal ones too. Those are my favorites so don't take them all, OK?"

Rosati poked his finger around in the box, "Your mother made these? They're all broken, they're all busted up!" He picked up the cookie that was most nearly intact. "I'll take this one," he said, putting it aside and then opening up one of the Clark bars.

Jinders made a face, "You know something Rosati? When some guys, you give them a new pair of shoes, they bitch because they didn't get the box. When was the last time you wrote to your own mother? You should write her a letter today, you know that?"

"Sure, Sergeant Jinders, I'll get on it right away."

"Well, we got a few more men to visit, so you get that lame foot healed up, you see," said Sartain as the trio went on to the next man.

The next man had some sort of severe stomach flu which had more and more men showing up for sick call that winter. "It's awful nice of you guys, and you lieutenant, to come see me. I think I'm just gonna save these here cookies though, the way I've been puking I don't think I could keep them down," he said glumly.

"That's OK. When you're feeling better you'll have a little bit of something for your appetite. In the meantime you get better so we can put you back on that gun crew. That mean Ole Sergeant Rafferty's been asking after you," Sartain told him.

The third man was sound asleep, running a high fever from the same contagion, so Stelow left a handful of cookie fragments and a Baby Ruth on the stand next to the bed. Jinders told the orderly, "When he wakes up tell him Lieutenant Sartain and Sergeant

I DIDN'T KNOW ANYTHING ABOUT GLIDERS.

Jinders were here to see him, would you?"

The fourth man was Charlie Spainauer, a slight, tow headed boy from West Virginia. Sartain, Jinders, and Stelow could see he was pretty sick. Spainauer's complexion was waxy and pale, and he could hardly speak above a whisper.

"Merry Christmas, Spainauer, are you feeling better," asked Sartain.

"The doctor says I'm getting better sir, but I don't know," answered Spainauer. Jinders chided him, "Sure you are, son, you just need some rest. The Lieutenant and Stelow thought you might like a visit today, so we came down here to see you. Stelow's got some cookies from home, why don't you take a few for yourself."

Sartain placed his last Clark bar next to a well worn bible. Spainauer already had a reputation in the battery as a boy who took his religion seriously and undiluted. "Shall I read something Spainauer, this being Christmas day," Sartain asked.

"Lieutenant, that would be very nice, sir. I've tried, but I can't hardly concentrate to read."

Sartain picked up the Bible and opened it. Turning to a random page he began reading, "Charity never faileth: but whether there be prophecies, they shall fail; whether there be tongues, they shall cease; whether there be knowledge, it shall vanish away. For we know in part, and we prophesy in part. But when that which is perfect is come, then that which is in part shall be done away."

"That's from first Corinthians, isn't it," said Spainauer.

"That's correct, that's correct," the Lieutenant confirmed.

Sartain read to himself for a minute. He felt around in the pocket of his mackinaw, took out his pipe and lit it without taking his eyes from the page. Uncomfortable with the silence, Stelow first cast his eyes at his feet, then the ceiling. Jinders looked around the room at the home made Christmas decorations scattered here and there.

Sartain began to speak again, "Then it says here, if I have the gift of prophecy, and know all mysteries and all knowledge; and if I have all faith, so as to remove mountains, but do not have love, I am nothing. And if I give all my possessions to feed the poor, and if I surrender my body to be burned, but do not have love, it profits me nothing."

Placing the silk ribbon bookmark between the pages, Sartain closed the book and placed it back on the table. "We're going to let you get some rest now, you hear? But if you need anything just tell that orderly and he's gonna get it for you."

The three men bade Spainauer a good afternoon but were summoned back as they turned away. "Sir, I'm sorry," Spainauer said faintly.

"What did you say," asked Sartain, who'd returned to his side.

"I'm sorry I'm sick sir."

As the Lieutenant patted him on the shoulder, Spainauer was told, "You just rest up and every little thing's going to be alright. You hear me Tiger? The battery needs every man."

"Thank you sir, I'm gonna sleep some now."

"That's good, that's good," said Sartain, turning to rejoin Jinders and Stelow, who were waiting at the end of the ward.

Other trains kept arriving at Fort Bragg as the balance of 1942 went on. On December 30th, for example, another one pulled in from Fort Sheridan, Illinois. These men were drawn from the upper Midwest. There were Germans from Wisconsin and Iowa. Poles, Lithuanians, and a smattering of Italians came from Chicago, while Michigan's Upper Peninsula contributed a healthy contingent of Vinlanders speaking with the sing-song clipped accent so emblematic of that region. Otherwise, except for the names, these

BATTERY!

men looked like all the others before, about twenty years old and wearing olive drab.

Again the auditorium filled, while sergeants and corporals shouted directions or scolded those who didn't pay close attention.

"All right. The following names are for the 319th Field Artillery, so listen up! Cattell, Lloyd. Girardin, John. Gruebling, Roland. Lewis, Albert. Nemmi, Lester. Mundt, Arno. Olkanen, Jolmara. Plassa, Bartholomew. Porsch, Otto. Radosh, Ralph. Rappi, Robert. Sievwright, John. Spencer, Edward. Stahldorf, Herbert. Tucknaught, Arnold. Wise, Ralph. All you birds grab your barracks bags and follow me!"

The new men were integrated into the battalion, assigned to either battery "A", "B", or the Headquarters Battery as called for. They would go through the same series of exercises and instruction as those who'd arrived earlier. Like them, they would advance through a time of physical exhaustion and sore muscles to realize after a few weeks that the strenuous life wasn't so bad.

John Girardin arrived at Fort Bragg during the last days of 1942. He was plagued by airsickness every time he took a ride in a glidyer – except on the two occasions he rode a glider into combat. Courtesy John Girardin.

There was as well the psychological transformation from a civilian individual to an identically uniformed soldier, one among thousands pulling together for a purpose larger than any one person, eating the same food and keeping the same schedule as the man next to him.

While standing in formation one day early in January, the 319th was informed it would soon be sent to glider school at Laurinburg-Maxton Air Field, a satellite instillation in North Carolina about forty miles south east of Fort Bragg. It was exciting news, signifying as it did the men's true initiation into the elite world of airborne soldiers.

The following Saturday there was a division review. The recent news about glider school gave this occasion an added significance, so there was a little less grumbling than was usually the case when the general wanted to see his troops paraded. After the infantry units passed them by, the 82nd's artillery battalions swung out onto the parade route, marching 16 men abreast. By this time the men from Ft. Sheridan were all assigned out, so there were some new faces in the ranks. Each battery was followed by jeeps pulling their pack howitzers. As they drew closer to the reviewing stand the men could hear the division's band strike up the field artillery's song, "When the Caissons Go Rolling Along." As they past the commanding general, all men did an eyes right and the colors dipped.

I DIDN'T KNOW ANYTHING ABOUT GLIDERS.

By this time General Mathew B. Ridgeway, the commanding officer of the 82nd Airborne Division, had been seen already by all but the newest men, frequently riding around Fort Bragg on a white horse, suddenly appearing unexpectedly during some training activity, or during previous division reviews. This time he was standing stock still on the reviewing platform. The General was wearing a steel helmet with the paratrooper's leather chin cup. Though expressionless, it was plain to see he took enormous pride in his command, and even if it took quite a while, the review was impressive.

Laurinburg-Maxton Air Field was the principle location for glider training throughout the Second World War, but this was particularly so in early 1943. Established and administered by the Army Air Force, the installation included an enormous triangular landing field composed of three intersecting runways, each over 5000 feet long. This design was intended to accommodate the limited tolerance of the WACO CG4A Glider and its normal tow plane, the C47, for crosswinds on landing or take off. Since landings and takeoffs could go in either direction the three runways arrangement offered a possible six directions of approach depending on which way the wind was blowing. Beside this advantage, the enormous triangular field they encompassed made an ideal area of clear and level ground for gliders to land in.

The requisite facilities for Laurinburg's indigenous Troop Carrier Command unit were clustered near by. A sizable number of aircraft hangers, repair and construction shops, mess halls, dispensaries, offices, and a plethora of other incidental buildings were already there when barracks for the newly formed glider wing of the airborne, and the permanent Glider instruction staff, were added. These new buildings were nearly all tarpaper covered structures hastily cobbled together from raw pine lumber produced at on-site saw mills. Altogether it amounted to quite a sizable village.

Tarpaper town that it was, the barracks for classes of glider troops in training would have been blisteringly hot in the summer months, but this was winter. In January the uninsulated structures could barely contain any heat at all. Meanwhile, pot bellied stoves sitting in six foot square sand boxes dried out the green lumber just the same. The results were barracks dripping with sap and groaning, twisting frames, known to sometimes spit out the nails which held them together.

After being trucked from Ft. Bragg to Laurinburg-Maxton the guys in the 319th, "A" Battery among them, would have first gotten themselves settled into their temporary quarters. It was normal for the mess hall to be open when a new battalion arrived for glider school with chow and hot coffee waiting for them, but whether the battalion was this fortunate is not recorded. Afterwards the men were apt to stay up late in their tarpaper barracks writing a quick letter home or speculating on what glider school would entail.

"I didn't know anything about gliders. I didn't know what it was. I'd never seen one in my life and I don't think anybody else had, to tell you the truth," said Kenneth Smith of training at Laurinburg-Maxton.

He wasn't alone. No one in the outfit had ever ridden in a glider, officers or men. Of those who had gotten a look at one, most had only seen them from a great distance. True, a fraction of the men had been taken to the mock-ups at Pope Field late the previous autumn, but that was only the most cursory exposure. Now they were all going to become well acquainted with the real thing.

Early in the morning, immediately after going through the breakfast chow line, the personnel of each battery was informed of the 24 hour schedule they would be keeping for the next three weeks. Day and night, in eight hour shifts, the men would be continuing their basic training, receive instruction in glider school, or be getting some well earned rest. Individual classes in knotting, securing and distribution of cargo, the use of a reserve parachute, or conduct inside a glider, were all given, each being announced by a whistle. After all these classes were attended, the material within them mastered, and two actual flights were accomplished, each man would earn his certificate certifying him as a glidermen.

The men in "A" Battery were then marched to a hanger area where several gliders had been brought outside. They were clumsy looking affairs-decidedly ugly in comparison to the sleek outlines of other aircraft and little more than canvas stretched over frames of steel tubing. Though the nose, floor, and forward edges of the wings were plywood, the overall impression was that the craft was too flimsy to be for real. Divided up into manageable sized groups, men sat themselves down in a semicircle around the glider instructor who placed himself in front of the subject of his lecture. "Because your life and the lives of your fellow soldiers will depend on how well you learn what we teach you here at Laurinburg-Maxton," he began, "You gentlemen best be paying attention to what we have to tell you. Is that clear?"

It was quiet for a few seconds, then he continued, "Alright then, this is the CG4A glider. CG is for Cargo Glider. The cargo, in this case, is you and your howitzer. This aircraft has an overall length of 48 feet, three inches, with a wingspan of 83 feet, 8 inches. With nothing inside it weighs 3,750 pounds. Loaded up this glider will carry just about one ton of cargo to the landing zone. That works out to be about 14 infantry men with their gear or, in y'all's case, three or four of you with a quarter ton truck, an ammunition trailer, or a 75 pack howitzer loaded in through the nose. It'll all be towed

First Sergeant Jesse Johnson and two other "A" Battery men, early winter, 1943. Note the A-9 flying helmet. Sartain collection.

I DIDN'T KNOW ANYTHING ABOUT GLIDERS.

by a C-47, like those you see taking off on these runways. The C-47 will tow you behind at about 150 miles an hour. Any much faster and this thing starts coming apart in the air."

Some of the men glanced nervously at each other. "How fast will these gliders be going when they land," asked one of the officers.

"That's a good question, Lieutenant. A fully loaded CG4A is going to hit the ground at somewhere between seventy-five and a hundred miles an hour, depending on how fast you were being towed, the altitude, wind speed, and so forth. Mostly that's all the business of the pilot, and you won't have anything to do with that. The important part for you is where that weight is distributed and how well it's secured. That jeep or that howitzer breaks loose, shifts around, I'm gonna guarantee; you'll be in a world of hurt when your glider comes to a stop. That is why the bulk of what you learn here will be about how to load this bird correctly so that you and your gun arrive in one piece."

Immediately after the introductory lecture was finished, "A" Battery was marched in formation to a class which taught them how to make the proper knots- especially the Baker-Bolling or slip-knot – and the elemental principles of secure lashing.

Next they were brought to a series of mock-ups in an adjacent field. On the way one of the guys asked to no one in particular, "Hey, what do you suppose the 4A in CG4A stands for?"

"I'll tell you," quipped 19 year-old Robert Rappi, "it stands for fourth attempt."

They were taken to mockups which were quite identical to the interior of a CG4A and a good deal more realistic than those encountered the previous fall at Pope Field. The floors, as on the actual gliders, were constructed of honeycombed plywood, fitted with recessed metal D rings. Marks were painted where the tires of jeeps, pack howitzers, or trailers should be located. Moreover, there would be ammunition, jerry cans of gasoline, tentage, camouflage nets, spools of wire, telephones and switchboards, and other instruments which also needed to be packed carefully. All these items had to be manhandled into position, secured, inspected by glider instructors and officers, then unloaded and the process repeated.

A closer view of a CG4a glider after landing during a practice exercise.
Courtesy Gruebling family.

After about a week of this the men were loading the mockups with proficiency, and they were allowed to try their hand at the real thing. Though the procedure was essentially the same, some new details did come into play. To begin with the nose of the CG4A Glider did not rest flush with the ground. In order to load a jeep, trailer, or gun, it was first necessary that several men go to the tail, lift it as high into the air as they could manage and keep it there. Doing this allowed the nose to drop down closer to the surface of the ground. More men would then uncouple the nose, lift it up like a garage door, and then lock it in place. Once done, a small ramp was pulled out from the open end of the fuselage and the cargo could be rolled inside.

The battery was also trained in loading and unloading the C 47 cargo plane. This was harder work than loading a glider. Everything had to be hauled up a steep ramp leading to a doorway in the side of the fuselage, and then man handled around the corner. Accomplishing this with a trailer or gun wasn't too arduous, but when it came to jeeps quite a bit of elbow grease was required.

Whether the craft was a plane or a glider, all this work of loading, unloading, and then reloading cargo became monotonous. However the men all understood by this time that sloppy loading, or cargo which worked itself loose in flight, would easily crash a glider and possibly bring down its tow plane as well. Consequently the army regarded this portion of the glider training as the most crucial and the men were willing, if sometimes bored, participants.

"There wasn't much unloading," said Sartain of glider training, "well, we might have trained some in unloading them, but our main concern was loading them up right. Of course when you unloaded them all you had to do was pull them slipknots and roll whatever was in there out the front."

As their last week at Laurinburg-Maxton came around, preparations for the actual qualifying flights were made. Strongly implying that such would be available, men were instructed on the wearing and use of reserve parachutes. Then they were taken to a glider which was fitted out with a full compliment of seats as for use by infantry. There was more practice for the students, this time belting themselves to the seats, reviewing the signals the pilot would give when preparing to land, and finally exiting the glider immediately in an organized fashion.

Finally the day for the first glider flight arrived. Since each glider would only hold about a dozen men it was not possible for the whole battery, much less the entire battalion, to fly at once. Instead a continuous relay of several gliders was used. One would be landing somewhere in the triangle field, while another was being retrieved and a third was being pulled aloft by its tow plane. All the while the next group of a dozen men nervously waited their turn to glide.

When it was time for the 5th and 6th gun sections to make their first flight, John Girardin noticed there were reserve parachute bundles lying about on the seats. As they were about to belt themselves in position he asked if they shouldn't put the reserve chutes on at this point.

"Don't bother," said the pilot, "They're only any good as seat cushions."
The pilots, co-pilot, and glider instructor were already wearing actual chutes in accordance with army air force regulations.

Another airman told them to "pay no attention" to the reserve chutes as they were "only filled with straw." Inspection of the pouches revealed that they had been told the truth.

After everyone took their positions and were securely belted in, each flight

I DIDN'T KNOW ANYTHING ABOUT GLIDERS.

started with a gentle tug on the nylon tow rope.

Looking back toward his passengers the pilot, a youngster with a pencil thin mustache, inform them over the roar of the C-47s engines, "See that tow line? There's enough nylon in that 300 foot tow line to make 1,544 pairs of women's stockings. That's one hell of a chorus line pulling this thing. I'll bet you didn't know that!" The pilot went on, speaking to no one in particular. "You guys see that telephone line, twisted around the tow line? That's because this line is nylon and it stretches quite a bit. You put that extra slack in the phone line so it don't get yanked out of the glider. As long as the phone works we've got continuous contact that the Jerries and Japs can't listen in on, which is a good thing."

As the tow plane took up speed on the runway, the men were always surprised to find that they became airborne before the tow plane did. Just about everyone was nervous, even those who flew under the false belief that they could wriggle into a reserve chute and save themselves if something went awry.

Not alone, Kenneth Smith later admitted that at first he was "scared half to death." Another large proportion of the men felt queasy as the glider climbed higher and higher, occasionally lurching one way or another.

John Girardin was particularly unfortunate in this regard. He had a long history of motion sickness as a boy, and even remembered that playground equipment could leave him nauseous, but riding in a glider beat them all. Girardin knew that if the flight lasted very long at all he would loose his breakfast. In sharp contrast was his buddy on crew number six, Robert Rappi, who sat across from him, calmly eating a candy bar.

Although the CG4A was constructed with several small plexiglass portholes, these were intended to provide light inside the fuselage, not a chance for sight seeing. Nonetheless, those of the men who wanted to look toward the nose were able to see their flight reasonably well by the limited view they had through the cockpit.

The pilot suddenly resumed his running description without warning, "See, it all depends on the angle of the dangle. This thing gets too far out of the proper dangle and we're in trouble. That's why we always say, it's the angle of the dangle that counts."

The pilot was talking about the necessity of keeping the glider more or less directly behind the tow plane. If the glider veered too far to the right or left, relative to the forward motion of the plane, it could begin to swing out of control with dire results. Once the glider gained sufficient altitude the tow plane circled until their turn to land came around. Sometimes this could be as short as 20 minutes, at other times a little longer. If the weather was calm the flight could be exhilarating. If the air aloft was turbulent with crosswinds or air pockets, it was less exhilarating, dangle or not. On such occasions it was obvious that flying one of these gliders was hard work. Having no hydraulics of any kind, all controls had to be manually operated in opposition to the force of the air against the glider's body. Depending on conditions, it was not unknown for a pilot to have to stand on one of the various pedals in order to keep it depressed. If the men were sweating out of nervousness or fear, the pilot's perspiration was more likely the product of considerable physical exertion.

Before long it was time to release the tow line and the C-47 brought them around for their landing on the triangle field. More than anything else, what the men remembered of landing was the sudden quiet of the glider once the tow line was released. Their speed immediately dropped, as did their altitude, and the only remaining sound was the swoosh of the glider cutting through the air as it descended. Normally a glider pilot would try to circle the landing zone once or twice before making the final approach, taking care as much as possible to make sure the glider was headed directly into the wind. Fortunately the field at Laurinburg-Maxton was ideal for this sort of aeronautics and a jolting, careening touchdown was made a bit easier by the seat cushions so considerately supplied by the army air force.

These were ideal conditions in which to make a landing, not only because of the large, level, and unobstructed field, but also because the school didn't like to make these flights in unstable or inclement weather if it could be avoided. Despite all precautions, accidents did happen and most of them were minor, but neither were they uncommon. There were bound to be some injuries like bumped heads and bruises, split lips, and maybe a broken arm or leg. After all, in a glider every landing was a crash landing, so there was always reason to be nervous. Overall though, landing with a dozen other men was safer than with a jeep or gun which could break loose and kill someone easily if it did. If there were any injuries in "A" Battery none were serious enough to be recollected.

After a second qualifying flight each man received his Glider Rating Certificate documenting that he'd completed the two flights, was proficient in the loading of aircraft and the use of reserve parachutes. More importantly the men were now given the blue "Airborne" tab to sew above their 82nd Division patches. It was a distinction which everyone was proud of, yet there remained the belief that those in the glider service were treated as stepchildren in the airborne family.

This was an easy conclusion to reach since there were no distinctive jump boots or uniforms like those issued to the paratroopers. Moreover, the absence of hazardous

After qualifying as Glidermen, each man in the 319th received a certificate like this one earned by Mahlon Sebring. Sebring joined "A" Batttery and earned his glider wings during the spring of 1944. Note that this is signed by Lt. Col. Todd. Sebring collection.

duty pay in the face of what was clearly a risky endeavor rankled them particularly. Glidermen gave expression to these feelings of resentment by satirizing the song "The Daring Young Man on the Flying Trapeze" with the words changed. There were several verses, a couple of which went:

Once I was artillery, now I'm a dope,
Riding in gliders attached to a rope.
Safety in landing is only a hope,
And the pay is exactly the same.
We fight in fatigues, no fancy jump suits,
No bright leather jackets, no polished jump boots.
We crash-land by glider without parachutes,
And the pay is exactly the same!
We glide through the air with the greatest of ease;
We do a good job and try hard to please,
The Finance Department we pester and tease,
But the pay is exactly the same!

Once back at their Ft. Bragg barracks, training took on an urgency not previously seen. There were more field exercises with the entire battalion, and more activities which mimicked what actual combat situations would be like, including a live fire obstacle course. Most of the full wooden stocked carbines were taken up and new, airborne versions with folding wire stocks were issued.

"We did some night movements," said Sartain, "Set the battery up at night and simulated fire, no live."

One day the men were driven to a remote part of the base for training in gas warfare. John Girardin was among them. He recalled being instructed by an officer, a southerner with a drawly voice. "I'll always remember him saying, 'Boys, that gas smells like new mown hay. You'll smell it 'cause it smells just like new mown hay.' The officer had the best of intentions, but, I didn't know what new mown hay smelled like," protested Girardin, who'd entered the service from civilian life working at a Rockford, Illinois, machine shop.

Finally, a full scale airborne mission was performed early that spring. The battalion was loaded up on gliders at Pope Field with the army air field at either Lumberton or Florence, South Carolina, as their destination. This involved a ride of about 90 minutes – the first really full duration flight the battery had ever been on.

His glider hadn't been in the air long when Girardin came to the realization that glider flights, and particularly meals before glider flights, were not for him. "I'll never forget that. I was so sick in those gliders and I threw up so much that after we got back for two weeks every time I coughed, I'd cough up blood."

Kenneth Smith had some trouble too. His glider started to encounter some turbulence and its pilot, perhaps anticipating some problem with the angle of the dangle, released the towline and landed in a South Carolina cotton field. A family of barefoot share croppers came out to meet the unexpected visitors. It was the next day before a military truck located them, hitched up their cargo, and hauled them off to the battalion maneuvers, leaving the glider to be retrieved later.

Until someone came after them there was little for Smith or anyone else on that glider to do except answer the question, "How you boys like it in the army?"

On another night the battery was taken, without the 75's, to a series of two and a half ton trucks waiting to receive them. In the moonlight the men could see some of the vehicles were decorated discreetly with names like: "Rocky Mountain Gal" and "Sewanee Sue." "I remember," Sartain recalled, "they put us in these big trucks covered up with canvas so we couldn't tell where we were going, took us way, way out somewhere and dumped us off. They let us out and then we had to find our way back to an assembly area." It was effective practice, particularly since these were areas which the unit was completely unfamiliar with.

Sartain explained that, "You had to read the map, you had to read the compass. You had the maps, you had to check the hills and then you had to find out where the assembly area was. You had it all on your map and you had to make your way to it."

Not long after the South Carolina maneuvers were over and the battalion returned to its quarters, rumors began to circulate. The gist of it all was that the entire division would soon be shipping out. Early in April these rumors became fact when the battery was cut down to its Table of Organization. Supernumeraries, sick men, and knuckleheads in the stockade were transferred out. Lieutenant Loughmiller was promoted to captain and replaced Captain Kinard as battery commander, while Lieutenant Simpson was transferred to the HQ Battery, leaving Sartain as the only 2nd lieutenant in "A" Battery.

On April 12th, when the battalion was placed on alert, things moved into high gear. The men started packing every-thing. As far as their own personal uniforms and gear were concerned they were instructed to pack an "A" and a "B" bag. The "A" bag contained their immediate needs, while the "B" bag held their Class "A" uniform and other articles they wouldn't be needing while in transit.

The men packed all the equipment, including the guns, radios, telephone switchboards, surveying instruments, and everything else needed to operate an artillery battery, into crates. Since field exercises were suspended, time was spent reviewing the Articles of War, map reading, hygiene directives, and first-aid practices. Everyone was instructed to cover the divisional insignias on their uniforms with swatches of OD cloth supplied for this purpose, intended to make identification of troop movements more difficult. Final rounds of physical examinations were given, and other remaining details were taken care of.

Corporal Tom Ludwick of Warren, Ohio, poses in front of one of the quansut huts at Papillon Hall. Note the duty roster posted on the door behind him. Covais collection.

If anybody had business in town, such as a wife who'd moved to Fayetteville, as Captain Manning's and First Sergeant Johnson's had, there

I DIDN'T KNOW ANYTHING ABOUT GLIDERS.

was a very brief chance to say good bye. Some of the men found a way to telephone home for a last sound of beloved voices amid instructions, pledges, and reassurances. Uncertain of what the future held, Girardin mailed his wristwatch home to his parent's in Rockford. If a kid sister had been promised a brightly colored pillow case emblazoned with the words "Fort Bragg, North Carolina," such as were for sale at the PX, now was the time to buy one and send it.

Since it was obvious that the outfit was leaving for some destination as yet unknown, the guys became aware of just how much they'd gotten used to life there. Fort Bragg had been home to these young men for 4 to 8 months. They'd all changed since they arrived there from Camp Claibourne or were herded into the assembly hall and listened for their names to be called out. On that day they were still more civilian than soldier, now the remnants of mufti were almost completely erased from their identity. As hard as much of their training had been, it was about impossible to not feel some element of nostalgia for the endless rows of white barracks buildings, mutton chow, and occasional glasses of watered beer enjoyed at the PX with new friends, particularly when the future was so uncertain.

On or about April 24, 1943, a train pulled out of Ft. Bragg with the 319th Glider Field Artillery Battalion loaded on board. Each man carried his "A" bag and carbine with him and the "B" bags were packed into baggage cars. Piled in among each other and their respective bundles, a man might look back over his shoulder at the place where remnants of his life before the war disappeared forever.

Men had taken on nicknames here to go with their new identities as soldiers. They'd sorted themselves out into circles of friends, some of whom would remain close for decades into the future. By now Bill Bonami and Les Nemmi were comrades, as were talented guitar player Tallmadge "Sam" Glenn and Bill Cooper of Memphis. Robert Rappi, John Girardin, and Bart Plassa, nicknamed "Pop" because he was already nearly thirty years old, were another tight knit group. Ted Covais, the Sicilian from Brooklyn, was at home with Tom "Jughead" Ludwick of Warren, Ohio, Frederick Von-Hassel, another New Yorker, and Roland "The Grieb" Gruebling, a Milwaukee delivery driver for Borden's Milk and destined to be remembered as battery mail clerk.

"See, I always hung out with the guys that I thought were my kind of guy, you know what I mean?" explained Covais, "you get wise guys, rough guys, all kinds. That's why you've got to be careful because it's not of your own choosing. You're put in together, well, like animals, and you don't know their background. But these were decent fellas to me, see, and that's why I hung out with them. The Grieb, Von Hassel, and Tom, we used to call him Jughead. Nice fellas. We were buddies, more than buddies, more than buddies. And the thing is they were German-American, can you imagine? German-American fellas, but USA all the way!"

Thurman King.
1608 Elm St
Cincinnati Ohio

Part Three: "There wasn't much room in between."

In 1932 Grace Line, Inc., launched SS Santa Rosa, the first of four sister luxury passenger ships. She was followed in succession by the Santa Paula, the Santa Lucia, and Santa Elena, all of them making regular trips from the United States to ports in the Caribbean and South America during the 1930's.

Designed by famous marine architect William Francis Gibbs, Santa Rosa had some unique features for her day, including a large swimming pool and gym. All of her first class cabins were outside twins with private bath. With a dining room having a roll back ceiling, her 300 passengers could dine on the promenade deck beneath the tropical night sky. To further accentuate and distinguish the ship as concerned with her passenger's comfort at every turn, the Grace Line always employed waitresses instead of male stewards, believing women were more courteous to the passengers. With New York City as her homeport, her crew would have been American and American men, they thought, made poor servants.

On the evening of April 28th, 1943, the waitresses were all gone. Instead were about 2,500 American servicemen, members of the 82nd Airborne Division, including, but probably not restricted to, the entire 325th Glider Infantry Regiment and 319th Glider Field Artillery Battalion. The vessel was now officially designated as US Army Transport Santa Rosa, operated by the War Shipping Administration. Her 508 foot long by 72 foot wide hull was repainted a dull grey. Cabins were refitted to accommodate 8 to 12officers, while the enlisted men were packed into every other conceivable location.

Pre-war postcard of the Santa Rosa. Ragland collection.

THERE WASN'T MUCH ROOM IN BETWEEN.

Once built for luxury, now the vessel's only purpose was to carry the maximum number of troops, at 15 to 20 miles per hour, safely to the seat of the war.

The long journey had really begun when "A" Battery and the rest of the battalion was loaded on their troop train at Fort Bragg. The men were strictly forbidden to peek out from behind the drawn shades in each car or let them up the slightest bit. A two day, very cramped ride brought them to Camp Edwards, Massachusetts. Other outfits from the division had been shuttling there from Fort Bragg for the last two weeks, waiting and marking time. The 319th must have been among the very last to arrive because within the day, after a stay of only several hours, everyone was reloaded on to another train and sent off in the same direction from which they'd come a few hours earlier.

About noon the next day, April 28th, they arrived at Staten Island, New York. Those in the battalion who called this place home craned their necks in the vain hope they'd recognize a familiar landmark or even a beloved face, but the high security under which all troop movements were made left the former unlikely and the latter an impossibility. Before they were formed up and taken on board, the men had a chance to get one last stateside cup of joe at a Red Cross coffee and doughnut stand set up near the dock. Sartain had been to the city once before. That time he was part of a convention of Episcopalian youth groups held there in 1939; an ecumenical gathering in a troubled, but still peaceful world. Being back again he must have reflected on how much had gone past in the previous three years, for him personally and on the world stage.

By nightfall everyone was squared away somewhere in the ship, their "A" bags, helmets, carbines and personal gear stowed nearby, ready for the voyage overseas. Some time after midnight the Santa Rosa glided past the Statue of Liberty. It was April 29th, 1943, and for those fortunate enough to be on deck it was a poignant moment. Watching this majestic symbol of their nation, as well as all direct contact with it, slowly recede behind the horizon would leave anyone wondering when – if ever, they'd be back.

As dawn broke and the sun rose that morning the men on deck surveyed the view around them. Though most of it was not visible, it was evident that the Santa Rosa had blended in with a large convoy, in fact one with thirty-three other vessels, bound for an as yet unknown destination.

Off to the north lay the battleship Texas. If a man were toward the stern of the ship, he'd see the liner George Washington, now, like the Santa Rosa, a troop transport, behind them. The heavy cruiser Brooklyn was out there too. Once the convoy was safely out to sea, sealed orders were read and the troops were informed of their destination: Casablanca, French Morocco.

With so many troops on board, the Santa Rosa was clearly overcrowded. One man later recalled that "there was barely any room to sit down on deck." In fact, two men were assigned to each bunk. Typical sleeping accommodations were canvas hammocks stacked at least four tiers tall, with as many rows as the location would allow. When Kenneth Smith explained, "You'd stay three days down in the hole and then next three days you'd sleep on the deck. You'd take turns."

He was referring to a system of color coded cards which determined whether a man slept below decks in a canvas bunk, or above decks out in the open, where the air was better but the weather possibly inclement.

Bob Storms remembered sleeping on deck as having its own set of hazards, "Man, when you was above ship and waves come over that boat you was drownded. In some places you wanted to tie yourself there because it'd flush you right off the deck. That ship wasn't big enough for what they used it for. You couldn't move! Everybody was against everybody."

For three days those with yellow cards slept on deck, and then switched with the white card men. Those scheduled to sleep below deck were allowed up for fresh air, but this was itself subject to a four hour rotation.

The officers were under no such restriction, but could come and go as they pleased. They were also quartered in the original staterooms.

Sartain remembered the sleeping arrangements this way, "In a room eight by ten they'd have three, four bunks across and four deep. They were single bunks and you had just enough room to get in your bunk without busting your head on something. I was on the top bunk because of being a 2nd Lt. Down where the men were, probably stacked deeper than that. I know I went down and some of our units were in the forward compartment. You could hear the damn waves hitting the side of the ship!"

Quite a few of the enlisted men were actually quartered in parts of the ship previously devoted to freight. The Santa Rosa's principle cargo before the war had been fruits and vegetables hauled on what her crew would have called a "tarantula run" from South America. Consequently, some of the troops even found themselves stowed in refrigerator compartments.

Girardin specifically remembered having sixteen men in his room, and this was probably typical. The bunks were "four by four, with just enough room to enter and crawl into a bunk."

"We were stacked up there pretty high," recalled Rappi, "guy throws up on the top it comes all the way to the bottom. There wasn't much room in between. The guy above you, if he didn't tighten up his canvas he'd be laying right on you. You get a heavy guy above you he's hanging right close to you. They've got to be tightened up once in a while because they stretch.

With so many men on board, a trip to the latrine, or "head" as the Navy called it, involved standing in a distressingly long line to get to one of the few overtaxed facilities. Recognizing that the ship was carrying approximately ten times the number of persons it was built to accommodate, the navy was forced to adopt a novel, if makeshift, solution.

"Well they used the swimming pool," said Storms, "that was the bathroom! Man you're laying up on the shelf of that, boy that smells sweet. Oh God, I'm telling you, I don't know which was worse, lying out on deck getting drownded with the waves or laying on top of the swimming pool smelling that. You wouldn't believe it unless you seen it."

Ed Ryan's recall of the swimming pool corroborated that of Storms, but in some more graphic detail. "The ship had a big swimming pool out in front," he said. "They covered that over, that swimming pool, and made a latrine out of it. Everybody did what they had to do standing up or whatever in this gigantic swimming pool. About the third day out you didn't have to worry about getting sea sick. One smell of this would make you puke anyway. It was bad. Then when they got sick they puked down there. About four inches of some indescribable shit I'll tell you. Yeah, it was bad."

Other hygiene was problematic. It was possible to take a salt water shower, but of course soap was nearly useless and bodies were left with a salty film. If one was determined to take a fresh water shower there was a brief half hour opportunity in the morning from 0715 to 0745, and again in the late afternoon from 1630 to 1700. For the most part, nobody bothered. Similar restrictions were placed on drinking water, which was intermittently unavailable during much of the day.

One 82nd Airborne Artillery Glider rider, quartered on the George Washington described the standardized naval procedure on troop ships in a letter written on the afternoon of May 6th. The practice was probably the same on the Santa Rosa as well. "A loud speaker system heralds lifeboat drills, dispenses music and miscellaneous announcements. Each time before the announcer speaks, he blows two sharp, staccato whistles into the mike to test the system. I cannot describe the feeling which accompanies the sound of those two innocent whistles, which may herald an attack, report the latest news bulletins, or simply ask, 'Will Pvt. Doak report to the Chaplain immediately.'"

There were several days of rough seas, particularly during the first week. Few of the men had ever been on a ship of any size and only a fraction of those ever out of sight of land. Most of those not already seasick joined the ranks of those who were.

John Girardin, who'd found glider riding such a stomach turning experience, was hardly surprised to find, "I got sick. Most of the time I just stayed on deck. I couldn't take it."

Another land locked unfortunate, nostalgic for firm ground under his feet, was Marvin L. Ragland, an even keeled, deliberate 2nd Lieutenant from Hutchinson, Kansas. He was a methodical young man by nature, with an unhurried, leisurely, manner of conversation. Marvin was trying to finish up his education at Hutchinson Community College when he was drafted in July of 1941. After a stint at Ft. Lewis, Washington, where he received training at a special instrument and survey school, the army decided to educate him further in the artillery branch. Ft. Sill followed, then a 2nd lieutenant's commission in October and assignment to the newly constituted 100th Infantry Division.

When volunteers from the junior officers in his division were called upon for overseas duty in March, 1943, Ragland raised his hand. Before he knew it, he found himself, though as yet unassigned, among officers of the 82nd Airborne Division on the Santa Rosa. There was an immediate difference, Ragland thought, between the relatively casual ranks of the 100th Division and these men. When I first interviewed Marvin Ragland he told me about what he noticed, saying, "For the most part everybody respected each other, but more importantly morale was higher and discipline tighter. It was obvious to me no matter who I was with that these people had a lot of training. It wasn't like going into a brand new division like the 100th Division. Here I was sent to a unit that was already ready to go and had been through a lot of training. I guess I lucked out."

"I got sick I'm sure," Ragland further remembered of the voyage, "I'd never been on the water before and I was sick most all the way over." Most of the time Marvin had little inclination to get out of his bunk, much less leave the cabin where he was quartered with several other transferred officers from the 100th. "I was afraid to eat very much at all, but they kept telling me I'd better try getting something to eat if I wanted to feel better."

This was more easily said than done. Preparing and distributing meals to the nearly 3000 passengers and crew presented a challenge. To help this process along the yellow and white cards utilized in the sleeping arrangements were again put to use. The chow situation left a strong impression on John Girardin's memory, "They gave us a meal ticket," he said. "They'd punch the meal ticket when you went through so you couldn't go back for seconds. I'll tell you though, out of twenty two meals on the ticket, I think I only ate nine of them. I was so sick."

The unusual eating arrangements were remembered by everyone who took a meal on board, not just Girardin, though his description is typical, "They used to cook the food in there too. It seemed like it was the lower deck. I still can see myself lining up and going down the steps and then seeing these big steam kettles there. Then we had tables that were chest high. No place to sit down. Just put your mess kit on the table. Every time you were done the whole line would move and somebody else moves in. They were just like that, there was no sitting. No seats, all standing. They started breakfast at four thirty in the morning and they quit at eleven. Then they would start serving supper at four o'clock in the afternoon and keep going till eight o'clock. I was a sick fella there I was. Oh, man!"

Of course not everyone was made queasy by the odor of food or too seasick to eat. Robert Rappi thought the food served on the Santa Rosa was "pretty good. I'd eat anything in them days. Anything when I was hungry."

Louis Sosa was another 19 year old in "A" Battery. A Tampa, Florida, native of Cuban descent, Sosa was working at a filling station near his home at the time he was drafted. Sosa was assigned as a driver with the signals section. On this voyage across the Atlantic he found that his appetite was fine. "We got fed twice a day and that's it. Matter of fact, one time I slipped down some back stairs and I found myself at the back door to the kitchen. I was watching the cooks moving around and when one of them moved away I jumped inside, grabbed me a couple of chicken drumsticks and took off out the door. If you don't look out for yourself, that's the way it is."

To help pass the time and keep the men occupied, an attempt at calisthenics was made, but space was insufficient, the decks were normally too crowded, and sometimes the sea wouldn't cooperate.

These measures usually proved so unsuccessful that most of the guys had memories much like that of Ryan when he said, "I don't remember them doing anything. The biggest calisthenics we had was playing poker on the decks, but I don't gamble so I had a big time watching the cards going."

Booklets giving phonetic pronunciation of important or common statements as expressed in French or Arabic were distributed, but again the generally overcrowded conditions made it nearly impossible to accomplish any sort of organized classes.

16mm prints of "The Bank Dick," featuring W. C. Fields, along with "Casablanca," starring Humphrey Bogart and Ingrid Bergman were shown over and over again in an effort to keep the troops minimally entertained. It was fun to speculate what the war might be like if this was a preview of who would be there to receive them in Morocco.

Soon after the first showings of Casablanca, Lt. Sartain was busy censoring enlisted men's mail. The army was very fussy about any reference to the location of military units, so strict instructions of what was permissible in the men's letters home were given. Junior officers like Sartain were tasked with reading through all the enlisted men's correspondence and any item deemed as having the least bit of military significance was literally cut out of the letter with a razor. Once expunged, the envelope was rubber-stamped "CENSORED" and signed by the inspecting officer.

Many of the guys had prearranged codes with those who received their mail at home which revealed the soldier's location. Despite these efforts, much of the time simply communicating the news that one was alive and whole was about all that was possible.

John Girardin remembered, "I would try to get around it. See at home I had a nickname; they used to call me Scope. So anyway I would write about Scope once in a while, say maybe, I hear scope was in Africa or something to see if they might understand it, but that was all cut right out of the letter."

Another man used a system by which he would first line up the upper left corners of his letter and one of a map of Europe. Then he would poke a hole through his letter to a point on the map. Since his map was identical to one at home, the recipients could easily determine where the letter was written by following the same procedure. Others offered hints in the most creative ways they could devise at the moment.

Sartain had his own scheme to get news through to his fiancé by making reference to William Reid, Chaplain of the division artillery. "When I'd say that Bill Reid visited us, that meant we were getting ready for an operation," he later explained. "That was my password with Peggy-Lou. Well, I didn't realize it at the time but they always held up our mail for a couple of weeks. It was all over the newspaper before Peggy-Lou got my secret, coded letter telling her we were on our way to somewhere."

As he read through the letters written on board the Santa Rosa, Sartain noticed a flurry of comments along the lines of "When I see Humphrey, I'll tell him you said hello." The clue may have given Sartain a chuckle, but as much as the men's ingenuity might be amusing, the Lieutenant's razor still cut out the offending phrase.

To keep themselves occupied there were continuous and numerous card and crap games. Gambling and poker took up time and kept the money circulating. A man could try to write a letter but conditions conducive to such an activity were hard to find, and there wasn't much you'd be allowed to say in any case. Even the ubiquitous habit of smoking, which did much to help pass the hours, was limited.

"They had the smoking light," said Sartain. "No smoking below deck and on deck only in day light when the smoking light was on. You couldn't have guys at night on the deck striking matches, so they had the smoking light which meant you could fire up and smoke. There were light bulbs around the decks, and if it was on you could smoke. When that light went off the loudspeaker said the smoking light is off, and then it was a court-martial offense to strike a match."

Captain John Manning, aged 27, was the battalion motor officer. He was a big man, over six feet tall and carried over 200 pounds of weight, but having been on the wrestling team at Cornell, was agile as a cat. A native of New York's lower Hudson valley, Manning spent some of the nights in conversation with Dr. Julian Hebert of nearby Troy. Hebert was the battalion's assistant surgeon under Dr. Bedingfield and had a tremendous love of astronomy. Traveling in mid ocean on a blacked out convoy, the stars shone beyond anything most men had ever seen. During the voyage Manning learned from Hebert how to recognize the most common constellations and find his way around the night sky.

Such opportunities to engage one's attention came too infrequently though. The monotony of the trip asserted itself, especially under such tedious conditions. With so little to do, Rappi considered himself lucky to have been given an assignment on the superstructure of the ship. "I used to stand watch all the time, up above where you could see all around, submarine watching. I think it was a four hour shift but only at night. There was fresh air up there. There were quite a few of us that were standing watch. We had earphones on and we used to listen to the guys that were on board ship ordinarily. You'd hear them talking and joking back and forth, telling stories." Positioned aloft, Rappi could see the distant wakes of other ships in the convoy. His job was to keep a lookout for the streak of a torpedo, but if Rappi glanced upward he'd behold the same billion stars Captain Manning and Dr. Hebert were studying, all shifted somewhat from their positions in northern Michigan and featuring new unfamiliar constellations to the south. The ship swayed beneath him and the sailors kept their running commentary through the night. "I never got seasick or airsick neither. I didn't volunteer for it. I didn't volunteer for nothing in the army, but they found me the right spot I guess."

In May of 1943 any Atlantic crossing carried the possibility of a submarine attack by the German U-Boat service's well developed "Wolf Pack" tactics. For the thousands of landlubbers confined on board troop transports, the knowledge that any moment could be followed by a sudden explosion ending with death in the black, immeasurable depths of the sea was always present. Whether by drowning, exposure, or the attack itself, such an event was sure to be a miserable end. Apprehension lingered somewhere in everyone's mind, a backdrop to the overcrowding and boredom. Some were more aware of it than others, while some were just better at concealing their private thoughts.

Though the threat of torpedoes was certainly real enough, only once were the men actually roused to a submarine alarm. About 1:30 am on the night of May 9th, "We got kicked out of our bunks because there was a submarine scare," remembered Rappi. "All we had on was our pistol belt with a canteen of fresh water on it. That's all you put on your pistol belt was a canteen full of fresh water, in case you have to dive off of there, you know?"

With an attack imminent, no one had to be reminded to put on his life vest and few bothered to put on any or much extra clothing. The men concentrated quickly on the upper decks at their prearranged abandon ship positions.

Sartain recalled the scene as he emerged on the deck, "These destroyers were just whipping in and out all around. When they were on to something they had this siren going."

Indeed, given the tightly enforced lights out policy of the convoy, the white foamy wakes created by the destroyers were one of the few visible features of the submarine scare.

The men formed up beside their respective lifeboats, as they'd been instructed to do earlier. Marvin Ragland, the as yet unassigned lieutenant from the 100th Infantry Division, was impressed by the orderly performance of the troops.
Ragland observed that, "They knew who was in command and the sergeants were in control." He found it reassuring to be going into the war with this kind of division, provided one didn't first drown in a torpedo attack.

It was a chilly night, standing around in the dark, floating somewhere between fear, boredom, and exhilaration. Rappi peered over the gunwale and into the blackness. He shivered from the cold, then said to the man next to him, "Jesus, I'd hate to jump in that water tonight!"

The whole affair was a little unnerving, with those gathered in the hatchways listening closely to the muffled depth charges rumbling along the hull, hoping they were finding their mark. Those on deck could see seawater erupting as the depth charges exploded deep beneath the surface.

In the end the warning passed without incident, the all clear was sounded and everybody shuffled back to what remained of their night's rest.
The following day the convoy split up. The largest part proceeded towards Gibraltar, while those vessels carrying the 82nd continued toward the Moroccan coast. By morning of the 10th the African coast would have been visible if not for the fog. It took time to clear the minefields arrayed to protect Casablanca harbor, but once past the destination came into view.

Men of the battalion were keenly aware that the Vichy French Navy had met the American fleet with fire the previous November. Morocco had been a French protectorate since 1912, and with the hostilities between France and Germany ostensibly over, Operation Torch, as the invasion of North Africa was coded, was considered by the Vichy government to be an act of aggression against a nominally sovereign France. The Vichy French Navy made a sharp fight of it at Casablanca that day, so there were numerous wrecks in the harbor. The unfinished French battleship Jean Bart lay beaten and decrepit – dead in the water after she'd duked it out with the American heavy cruisers Brooklyn and Augusta during the seaborne invasion. Besides Jean Bart, there were destroyed cruisers, and abandoned, shot up submarines, along with at least ten cargo and passenger ships. These were the first evidence of a shooting war to the guys in "A" Battery. Even though the fighting had taken place six months before, the signs of raw destructive power were sobering to view.

Coast Guard tugs slowly brought the Santa Rosa to the dock, but no one left the ship until General Ridgeway, whose vessel, the Washington, was already docked nearby, came aboard. The General had first to officially receive the units as present for service. All the while a red fezzed, French Senegalese band played "Ruffles and Flourishes" as the General came up the gangplank, adding to the exotic setting. Once this formality was accomplished the men would be formed up by companies and batteries, then allowed to debark in good military order.

Finally the battalion shouldered its gear, walked down the gangplank and assembled on the dock. Everyone noticed that their legs were wobbly. It was hot, but with a steady seaward breeze, nothing like what most of the men expected. Those who'd been at Camp Claiborne would have remarked that this certainly wasn't as hot as midsummer in Louisiana.

After forming up on the dock a roll call was taken by the first sergeants of each battery. The process of getting everyone sorted out and squared away took a few hours, then loaded down with their musette bags, their overcoats and shelter tent halves rolled on top, the men began a slow march through the winding streets of the city. With all their full field gear on, and still dressed in the OD woolens they'd been wearing when they boarded the ship in New York it was a sweaty hike, but one full of strange and unfamiliar sights. Arab children begged for cigarettes and chewing gum, mysterious hooded figures stood at the doorways to Moorish courtyards, a European woman in heavy make-up smoking a cigarette and speaking in French, palm trees and white stucco buildings. Past all these sights, and many others, the battalion made its way to a bean field on the northeastern outskirts of Casablanca, about five miles away from the dock.

"As good as it was to be off ship and rest secure in the knowledge that they'd crossed the Atlantic safely, many of the men had trouble sleeping that night after retreat sounded. Lieutenant Ragland noticed that he still felt the rocking of the Santa Rosa even as he lay on his cot, firmly placed on dry land.

Arno Mundt, who lay among the pup tents of "A" Battery, gazing at the stars above him, remembered, "My first real bout of homesickness hit me. I was not alone for I could hear some guys actually crying during the night."

Deeper was the awareness that each stood on the edge of some vast and as yet unknown journey, which they could neither exercise much control over nor shrink away from.

As for the Santa Rosa, the transport continued on through the straights of Gibraltar, then back to New York. In all, by the time the war was over she made 21 round trip voyages from New York to Europe, three to Africa, and one each to Australia and India. Santa Rosa was refitted and returned to Grace Lines in 1946. She then continued her prewar "tarantula run" until 1958 when Grace Lines replaced her with a new, larger, and more luxuriant vessel of the same name. After three years lying idle at Hoboken, New Jersey, the original Santa Rosa was sold to Greek interests. Given a facelift and renamed Athinai, she adopted Venice, Italy, as her new homeport, making two week cruises around the Aegean Sea. In 1966 the ship's parent company was disbanded and she languished in a Greek port among dozens of other aging, decrepit hulks for a decade until called out for one last triumph. The once Santa Rosa, was purchased by the production company of the film "Raise the Titanic." She was approximately the same size as that tragic craft and had many similar architectural features. After some superficial adjustment and quite a bit of paint, she was reborn in her role as the ill fated Cunard Liner.

May 11th, 1943, was a day spent getting the battalion in order. Everyone recognized that the men were tired after the long, uncomfortable voyage, and needed a rest. A few days to get themselves settled in followed. The vehicles had to be unloaded from the ships, uncrated, and made serviceable. The guys in the motor pool were kept very busy taking care of this. There was a lot of equipment and gear to be unpacked and distributed as well. The unit's 75mm howitzers were then turned in to the ordnance depot for a compliment of new, short barreled, 105mm guns.

The first of many mail calls to come for the guys in "A" Battery was made, with Roland "Grieb" Gruebling sounding out, "Hey, hey, hey! We've got mail today!" Short notes home informing the folks that you had arrived safe, "somewhere in Africa" were written and collected. A meal eaten in a sitting position away from the odor of the Santa Rosa's swimming pool was eagerly anticipated, and a decent night's sleep were all on the short list of things to do.

Lieutenants Ragland, Vereen, Lewis, and a few other newly assigned junior officers reported themselves formally to Major Todd. The XO interviewed the young lieutenants in turn and familiarized them with the battalion and their fellow officers in the outfit. Colonel Bertsch wasn't around at the time, and when he did later come by the headquarters took no notice of the new faces in his battalion.

During the few days spent there, most of the men appear to have been given a pass to go into the city of Casablanca for a few hours. It was a bit of a let down for a lot of them, particularly in contrast with the film of the same name which they'd just seen so many times. "Humphrey" was nowhere to be seen, nor, for that matter was "Ingrid." It was both amusing and disappointing; with the strongest impression being that the city was dirty and unkempt. The local Moroccans seemed to be either poor, degraded Arabs, often begging or soliciting GIs to trade with them for what little they had to offer, or cynical French colonials who viewed the American servicemen more as sources of income than as liberators newly arrived to help France throw off the yoke of fascism.

The next day, armed with an afternoon pass, John Girardin and a buddy caught a truck shuttling men from the bivouac areas into the city and back. Girardin's companion was one of the old crowd from Ft. Sheridan. Whoever it was, they could plainly see that the town itself seemed overrun with GIs going about their military business or simply on afternoon passes. They noticed as well that the GIs there also had a lackadaisical attitude about military protocols. "Hey" commented Girardin as he nudged his buddy, "you notice these guys aren't saluting officers?"

Evidently, the two figured, saluting officers was a stateside formality which those in this theater of operations were not obliged to concern themselves with, and the two quickly adopted the new custom.

After nearly two weeks of seasick nausea, Girardin was eager for a hearty meal, making the first attraction the chance to get some non-army chow and a glass of the local beer. The food was cheap and good enough, but what followed in the restaurant bathroom left more of an impression. "It was the first time I ever seen a bathroom with the hole in the center and a platform on each side and a tank above for the water. I never seen anything like that in the States."

Once outside, the two continued on their way, laughing about the exotic toilet facilities and blithely ignoring those of the officer class. Then one young 2nd Lieutenant called them to attention, demanding to know why they hadn't bothered to demonstrate the proper respect for rank. John and his buddy could only stammer that they noticed none of the other enlisted men around were saluting, so they assumed such formalities weren't necessary.

The Lieutenant, "one of these 90 day wonders" as Girardin described, took umbrage at their explanation. He produced a notepad and pencil, demanding their names, serial numbers, and outfit. Once the information was given the glidermen were told to back up and try it again. This time salutes with an exaggerated deference were given and the matter was closed.

As men rotated back from Casablanca they brought reports of which places to avoid, which establishments were friendliest to American soldiers, and what was available where. Desperate for food or souvenirs, the men started rummaging through their baggage for things they might as easily part with.

Ted Covais found a pair of brown leather Oxford service shoes in his duffle bag. Since it looked unlikely that this would be an essential item; here in the seat of the war, the idea that they might be used to acquire something akin to the food at home became a mission. When his turn to catch the truck into Casablanca came the next day his hope was for a salami, some real Italian bread, and maybe some olives. In the end Covais traded his shoes to an Arab for two dented cans of sardines with torn French labels. It wasn't a salami sandwich, but it was better than nothing.

Not everything about Casablanca was seedy and rundown. Lou Sosa found a way to slip off and explore a little on his own. In a secluded side lot he found a cow, milked it into his canteen cup, and slaked his thirst for something fresh.

Rappi was another one who caught the truck into town. Sixty years later he remembered, "I went to town once there. There were some nice looking women, the clerks in the stores. I'll always remember that there was one, I think she was French, she was really a beauty. Being a young man, you're drawn to that."

After three or four days the 319th received orders to move on. The larger tents and bulkier equipment had already been loaded directly onto the new trucks without first unpacking them. Captain John Manning, the battalion motor officer, was in charge of the convoy, with the portion of this motor contingent belonging to "A" Battery under Lieutenant Sartain. The motor convoy had already moved out on the morning of the 12th, proceeding ahead to establish the battalion's new bivouac area in Spanish Morocco. The route would take them along the coast road and through Rabat, a "beautiful city" situated on a mountainside, as Sartain remembered.

In the meantime the rank and file of the 319th were issued C rations, and then marched, probably on the afternoon of May 14th, to the rail station in Casablanca. Officers were assigned to passenger cars while the enlisted men found themselves in boxcars. These were the infamous, narrow gauge "forty and eight" cars so familiar to the Doughboys of World War One. As the name described, each held forty men or eight horses, though, with personal equipment, rations, and other gear, only about two dozen men could be assigned to each car. No other accommodation was made for comfort except for the matted layer of dirty straw held inside with a piece of lumber placed across the doorway.

The train left the city in a northward direction along the African coast. With the steady flow of air through the open doors the ride felt refreshing for the first several hours. Once the sun set however, there was nothing to look at and nothing to do but sleep if one were able to do so, and that was problematic.

"We were four days and four nights in one of those boxcars, all sleeping on the floor," said Girardin of the trip, "if you had to pee you had to get up and try not to step on anybody. You go to the door and open the door and pee out."

With no way to cook or even heat food the men became increasingly frantic for a hot meal, or even more so a cup of coffee. In some cars the men scooped gobs of axel grease and lubricant from the gear boxes during the frequent stops, mixed it up with whatever scraps of wood or other combustibles they could lay hands on, and built fires directly on the wooden boxcar floors. Sometimes the cars themselves caught fire. "Every time we stopped all the fellas would get out of the boxcar. They'd take out these little kerosene stoves and try to heat up water for coffee. By the time the water is ready in the canteen cup the whistle blows and everybody had to run back. We never had any hot meals at all."

Following the coast, the train proceeded past the city of Rabat, and then turned easterly toward the interior, in the direction of Fez, and Oran. The still moderate, though warm, temperatures of the coastal region quickly became a daytime furnace well over 100 degrees, alternating with crisp nights which felt downright cold in their exposed accommodations. Numerous stops were made, sometimes for no apparent reason, or at some dilapidated village where the train would be besieged by locals attempting to trade or sell what they had – usually fruit or wine. These brief market sessions actually posed quite a problem for the officers and sergeants, who did their best to prevent the flow of wine into the ranks and the loss of traded off government property and rations to a minimum. Afterwards the men often noticed that they'd been the objects of theft. These incidents steadily sapped the remaining good will between Arabs and American servicemen.

It was a different world, one where the French regard for the lives of the Arabs was not so dear. Ed Ryan saw one demonstration of this on the way. "We'd pulled up to this railroad platform. We had a sergeant, I think from the 325th or something, who was good at this bayonet drill. Some French soldier got off and wanted to compete with him. They boxed around and the American disarmed him. There was a crowd of soldiers and Arabs watching. The French soldier picked up the gun and ran an Arab through with the bayonet just for fun, because our guy had humiliated him."

At one locale the train crawled past another stopped a few yards away on a sidetrack. It was loaded with German prisoners, the recently surrendered remnants of Rommel's Afrika Korps who'd just capitulated in Tunis. It was an unexpected face to face encounter with the enemy. They were a sunburned lot who smiled and waved at the Gis. The Germans were packed tightly in their cars, wearing caps with long visors and a strange array of uniforms.

On the night of the 18th of May the train, which had mostly crawled along no faster than the average man could trot, ground to a stop at a desolate place called Marnia, Algeria. It was a bleak station located about twelve miles outside of Oujda and comprised of no more than perhaps a half dozen buildings. The Red Cross had set up a coffee stand, and the men who'd had nothing other than cold C rations for days, all had a cup full and a doughnut or two. That the Red Cross routinely charged for coffee, doughnuts, or other snacks, antagonized the guys, who were already tired and weary from the endless journey in cattle cars.

The 319th's motor convoy which had left Casablanca a week before was there to meet them too. The glidermen were loaded onto trucks and brought out to a large wheat field situated alongside an olive grove. Since it was dark and already quite late, they threw themselves on the ground and slept under the stars without bothering to pitch tents. Setting up their first bivouac overseas could wait until the next day.

Part Four. "Now he's another Sad Sack."

"In the morning I woke up and I could hear singing and Arabs talking. It was these Arabs cutting the wheat down around that area," Girardin told me of that first morning.

One man in "B" Battery found the whole thing quite interesting and recorded it in his diary this way, "Our government had paid France for the wheat, but in the meantime they let Arabs come in and harvest the wheat --- which they did by hand. The men, about 5 abreast cut it with a scythe and the women tied it in bundles. They chanted all the while and paid no attention to us. Then they put bundles on a donkey and thrashed it by letting horses tramp the wheat out by going in a circle. They fanned the chaff in the wind and had to throw out the horse manure. It was interesting."

After the sun was up and the men could appraise their bivouac area, the battalion began to settle itself in among the nearby grove of olive trees. The men started putting up their pup tents in the little available shade where possible, in an effort to escape the broiling sun. This place was hotter than anyone in the battalion had ever experienced in the United States, so it seemed the only logical, reasonable thing to do.

When colonel Bertsch arrived on the scene at mid-day he was visibly angered by the men's initiative. He made it plain from the start that he would tolerate no relaxation of military precision and ordered all tents taken down immediately, then directed Major Todd to have exact battery streets laid out with surveying equipment. Some of the men rolled their eyes while others cursed and grumbled complaints only audible to their closest buddy. The enlisted men were, by and large, disgusted, but most of the officers still shared Lieutenant Sartain's opinion that the Colonel's strict adherence to regulations would ultimately carry through as resolution in combat.

Camp Marnia, as it came to be named, was the cantonment of all glider troops of the division, as well as a number of British Commonwealth forces, at Oujda. Once the wheat had been harvested from the arable portion of the terrain, what the men of the 325th Glider Infantry, 319th, and 320th Glider Field Artillery found was an inhospitable valley. It was rocky and windswept, baking in the day to temperatures reaching 125 degrees with nighttimes as chilly as 50. Everyone agreed that it was a God forsaken location, and that assessment was only made stronger by the generally dilapidated condition of Oujda, which was over ten miles distant in any event.

Some of the men had a further disappointment

Capt. John R. Manning, CO of "C" Battery. Courtesy John Manning, Jr.

upon their arrival at Marnia. Captain Manning's motor convoy had evidently neglected to place guards over their trucks at night while bivouacking on the way. Although the German resistance in North Africa had been brought to an end, no one considered that the local population presented a considerable threat through thievery. "I lost my uniform and everything, except what I had on," lamented Lieutenant Marvin Ragland. "Evidently the Arabs sneaked in there at night. They said they didn't have any guards out at night. They figured they weren't in enemy territory. Anyway, I didn't get another uniform until I got to England."

Aggravating as it was, the relocation of the camp on that first morning at Marnia may not have been attributable solely to an effort by Colonel Bertsch to gratuitously exert his authority. After all, laying out an orderly bivouac within any grove of trees is difficult at best, and the exact location of the 319th's campground was likely already staked out, probably under the direction of someone beyond Bertsch's control. This was, in fact, the case for the 325th Glider Infantry. Nevertheless, his draconian attitude about disturbing the men had been obvious to officers and enlisted men alike from the beginning, leaving no one with much inclination by this time to see anything but disdain for his men in his actions. As a result, relations between Lt. Col. Bertsch and the men in his command, which had always been cool, began to break down entirely.

Despite the expectation that once overseas he would be more inclined to make some demonstrations of solidarity, Bertsch's habit of removing himself from all social contact with his officers was sustained. The Colonel persisted in taking his meals alone and never associated with his officer cadre unless military formalities called for it. Moreover, the Colonel frequently made remarks showing an open disrespect for anyone who was not a career officer and a graduate of West Point. When Bertsch said, as he did on several occasions, that he couldn't wait until the war was over and everyone else reverted back to their peacetime rank or returned to civilian life, the majority of officers in the battalion took it as a personal insult. With a very few exceptions, these men were ROTC, Reserve, and Officer's Candidate School (OCS) officers. They willingly left their private lives behind to fight fascism and defend the nation. Maybe they did still have the hearts of civilians, but they sincerely believed in their cause, as well as their ability to accomplish it by giving their all, even if that meant their lives. This was the army, and no one expected the commander to treat those of lower rank as his literal equal insofar as military decorum and discipline was concerned. Nonetheless, the Colonel's manner showed that he did not regard them as brothers in arms or as his moral equivalent.

All this came as no surprise for those who'd been with the battalion at Fort Bragg, but new officers just assigned to the outfit had no way of anticipating such a reception. Lieutenant Ragland, accustomed to the relaxed fraternity of the 100th Division, was puzzled, concerned that the problem lay somehow with him. After a few weeks of being completely ignored by the Colonel, Ragland approached Major Todd and asked the battalion exec directly if he was in some way offending Colonel Bertsch or not performing up to expectations.

Major Todd, who found himself in an increasingly awkward position as the intermediary between Bertsch and his officers, answered Ragland reassuringly, "Well, that's just Colonel Bertsch. It has nothing to do with you, son, you're doing just fine." Todd paused, then, sensing that Raglan deserved more of an explanation, added, "He's just kind of a loner."

Ragland recalled another incident from about the same time. The officers of the battalion were gathered for a special dinner for some since forgotten occasion. It was a semi official affair of the sort which Colonel Bertsch would sometimes acquiesce to attend. "We waited and waited and waited. Finally Major Todd said, 'Normally we wait for the Colonel to come in but we're not waiting anymore.' So we started eating and about that time he came in and you could tell he was teed off. I don't think too many people liked him. He just had an air about him like he was better than everybody else, didn't want to hobnob with them or anything."

Camp of the 319th at Oujda, Morocco. The stones which Captain Manning complained about gathering in the desert can be seen lining the lanes between the tents. Courtesy Gruebling family.

Captain Manning, on battalion staff, had been with the outfit from the early days at Camp Claiborne. As the chief motor officer, he had even driven the Colonel's private automobile from Louisiana to Fort Bragg when the change of base was made. Manning respected Bertsch as far as his training of what was largely a gang of several hundred drafted civilians into a disciplined military unit was concerned, but events at Marnia were rapidly alienating him as well. In his position on Colonel Bertsch's staff, Manning usually had intimate knowledge of the Colonel's pet projects, such as the personal shower he had installed at Marnia and the construction of what Bertsch called his "patio" near his tent.

"I was always getting the word as to how some of these special projects should be implemented." wrote Manning decades later. "I remember hauling stones from the hills and placing them in rows to line out the walks and roads of the camps. This in particular ground on me after picking up stones from the field back home. Very necessary for the war effort."

If the officers of the 319th were disaffected by their commanding officer, the feelings of the enlisted men of the battalion began to approach outright contempt. When a pass to Oujda ended badly for two men in the battalion soon after Camp Marnia was established, Colonel Bertsch, who was fond of admonishing his command in formal addresses, called a battalion formation.

"It has come to my attention," Bertsch announced, "that we have these men who were down here all liquored up on this dirty rotten Arab vino. They got in a fight down there and one man lost his eye. Now he's another Sad Sack and typifies to me what a man in my battalion ought not to be. He's had punishment enough. The other man will get the full extent of a court martial. Let this be a lesson to all of you."

The intention was to instill discipline. But the way colonel Bertsch went about it only generated angry resentment on the part of the enlisted personnel. They perceived an element of sadistic pleasure in the Colonel's speech, and if there were any in the ranks who still believed the Colonel to be well intentioned, they now joined those who'd already decided he was uncaring.

Ed Ryan was by this time a Technician Fifth Grade assigned to the headquarters battery. As such he had more contact with the Colonel than did enlisted men in the firing batteries. Sixty-five years after these events had taken place Ryan's memories of Colonel Bertsch were still bitter. "I remember him," he growled when Bertsch's name was mentioned for the first time. "A nasty son of a bitch if you ever bumped into one. Boy, I'll tell you how rotten he was. This is just an example. I was walking by the officer's latrine one day. He came out of the latrine, threw a pack of cigarettes on the ground and said, "Pick that up." That's just one of his little tricks. I used to hang around with a mess sergeant, his name was Alvin P. Larrieu, come from Louisiana. He was a pretty good guy really. Anyway, Bertsch had what they called a CP tent. It was about a hundred yards away from Larrieu's mess tent and I could hear Bertsch holler, 'Sergeant Larrieu, I want my fruit juice!' 'That son of a bitch,' I'd hear Larrieu say, 'If I get a chance I'll give him his fruit juice!' Yep, in the middle of all this mess he wants his fruit juice. He was just plain nasty."

The mess Ryan referred to was comprised of the unremitting heat sapping everyone's energy, the horrible preserved rations, and shortage of coffee and cigarettes, along with a wave of dysentery accompanied by an outbreak of malaria. The tension built. After a few weeks some of the enlisted men in the 319th were nearing a breaking point of frustration. Unyielding and evidently absent of any compassion for their suffering, Colonel Bertsch became an easy object for all the men's pent up rage.

Bob Storms, in "A" Battery's machinegun section, recalled an incident verging on open mutiny. In Africa, somebody shot through his tent. Somebody shot right through his tent but they missed him. Boy the whole battery was up for trouble over that. Oh man, couldn't go to town for a couple, two, three weeks. Nobody knowed who shot what. He caused us a lot of trouble over that shooting deal. After that you wasn't even allowed talking about it because they'd bring it up and court martial you. They said you knew something about it and wouldn't talk."

Ed Ryan corroborated Storms's story and added an additional detail. "They had bullets laying around with his name on them. They dropped them around near his tent too. Well, there's a bastard if you ever saw one. A lot of this stuff hasn't been told before."

Continuing with a general observation of Colonel Bertsch, Storms concluded, "He found fault with everything. None of the officers, nobody, got along with him. He was a hard man to get along with. He was mean, he was just plain mean."

Captain, and later Major, James Wilcoxon, the battalion's S-3, was another difficult individual. He was given a nickname which reflected the attitude toward him in the 319th, where few took him seriously. As Sartain explained, "Fidgety Phil, we called him. He was always fidgeting with a cigar or his helmet or something. He was just real fidgety. You'd think he was going to have a nervous breakdown."

Wilcoxson also generated a significant level of antipathy from the enlisted men by his abrasive manner of conducting himself with subordinates. John Girardin explained the problem with Captain Wilcoxson this way, "Oh, he was a son of a gun. They used to have a nickname for him, Fidgety they used to call him. Fidgety! Yeah, yeah, Fidgety they used to call him. I think he was the worst officer that I remember. All the other ones were pretty good. He was more ornery. I don't know if he was a West Pointer or what but he would stick by the rules and I think everybody really resented that. I mean, everybody was doing their work, nobody was goofing off, but he always had something negative to say about us. I think that was the biggest point."

Battalion officers recognized that the men were putting honest effort into their work, but the Major's manner of humiliating the enlisted men was uncomfortable and embarrassing to witness.

Lieutenant Ragland expressed the viewpoint of his fellow officers when he commented of Wilcoxson, "That guy, he just rubbed everybody the wrong way. He made them feel like they were nothing and you just can't do that. When you have an officer that tries to bully people he's making a big mistake."

Frustrations with superiors are endemic to any hierarchical system, military or otherwise. Those who are a part of it learn to adapt, perform their duties, and grumble when the situation permits. The bivouac at Marnia was established just the same. Once this was done, the battalion and its motor convoy were reunited, giving the men the first real access to their barracks bags. This meant that they now finally had the opportunity to take off their woolen OD uniforms and change into cotton, herringbone twill fatigues. It was a tremendous improvement considering that temperatures routinely exceeded 120 degrees in the sun by midday.

Another change to the uniform of the 319th made its appearance about this time. Circular patches for the men's garrison caps were issued depicting a white glider and parachute superimposed over a blue background. The patches looked rakish on their caps and helped to assuage some of the stepchild status which glider troopers labored under, but only in a symbolic way. In all other respects the appearance remained that of standard ground troops with canvas leggings and field jackets.

Gratifying as the cap badges might have been, they did little to alleviate the dreadful conditions at Marnia. The compound was quickly tramped into a fine powdery dust by the thousands of soldiers marching across the same battalion streets and parade grounds over and over. Dust permeated everything and was made all the more intolerable by the daily gusts of wind blowing off the sun baked desert.

So strong and steady were these winds that the mess sergeants had a difficult time properly cooking rations, let alone bringing them to an appetizing temperature. When the men lined up with their mess kits for chow the contents were disappointing in both quality and quantity. The preserved foods, sometimes mixed with mystery meat of undetermined origin was minimally warmed, then covered with dust and flies immediately after being plopped into their mess kits. By the time they had the chance to sit down on the ground and eat, any semblance of an appetite, except to relieve their hunger, was all but gone.

Malaria began to make its presence known immediately and persisted as long as the outfit remained in North Africa. As a precaution everyone was required to take Atabrine in the form of small yellow tablets. Some of its side effects were serious. Headaches, nausea, and vomiting were not uncommon. In a few cases the drug was known to produce a temporary psychosis. These facts were known to Doctors Bedingfield and Hebert, but there was little need to make matters worse by informing the enlisted men, who were already reluctant to take the pills because of the extraordinarily bitter taste and sickly hue it imparted to their skin. Besides these apparent side effects, there was a common belief among the men that Atabrine caused impotence and this misconception ruined any voluntary ingestion of the drug.

Now He's Another Sad Sack.

"Being the junior junior, I was the Atabrine officer for the battery," remembered Sartain. "Every time the guys would come through the mess line I would stick a yellow Atabrine tablet on their tongue to make sure they swallowed it. OK? Every time, before they could get on the chow line I had to give them their Atabrine tablet. I was the only guy in the battery came down with malaria because I didn't take them." In fact, there were others. The newly promoted Corporal Covais was one in "A" Battery, for example, as was Captain Manning from battalion staff. Fortunately the Atabrine was largely effective and a whole scale epidemic was avoided.

More ubiquitous than malaria was the wave of dysentery which swept through the ranks. Some men claimed that the very soil of North Africa brought it on. More likely was the explanation of the battalion doctors, who said that the high winds and general scarcity of combustibles made it difficult to bring either food or water for rinsing mess kits to a boil, allowing spoilage and bacteria to do their work.

The onset of dysentery was sudden, as Storms could attest, "Yeah, that was outside of Oujda somewhere. We went somewhere, we were walking back, and I said, 'Hey Brodelle.' He said, 'What.' I says, 'It's too late.' He said, 'What happened?' I said, 'Look at my feet.' Holy god almighty, you had a little sharp pain and you look down it was too late; it was running right out of your boots. Oh what a mess! Oh what a time we had trying to get me back to camp. Jesus, I was a mess. When I got back I got cleaned up but there was nothing you could do. They take you, put you in your pup tent and they'd come and wash you, change you, and they'd bring your food to you. You was good there for about three days like that. All you could do was lay there. The whole camp got it. They tried to say it was from the sand and mess kits and like that. They never did find out how come we all got it. We all got diarrhea. I think everybody in camp had it before it got over with."

The latrine itself was a long wooden box with holes along the top, placed over a trench. Many of the men, doubting that they could return to the latrine quickly enough should another attack take hold, simply lingered around the latrine, crowding into the slowly moving shade which its canvas walls offered, never daring to go far.

Though the worst bouts lasted a few days, full recovery came slowly. Many a man learned through hard experience to always bring his entrenching tool along if

Camp of the 319th at Oujda, Morocco. The stones which Captain Manning complained about gathering in the desert can be seen lining the lanes between the tents.
Courtesy Gruebling family.

he was detailed for guard duty or suspected he might not have immediate access to the latrine. As might be expected of such a large camp on the edge of the Sahara, water supplies were limited and of poor quality.

Kenny Smith remembered that "We'd go every day someplace and get a truckload of water and bring it back. We had the cistern truck or what ever you want to call them. You'd put that bag up to the little spigots it had on the bottom and draw water out of them, but it was hot."

After a while some men learned a native method for storing and cooling water so that it would be more palatable for drinking. Thick earthenware jugs purchased from local Arabs would hold the coolness of the brisk desert nights through most of the day if kept shaded within a pup tent or at the bottom of the slit trench which accompanied each canvas home. It was a considerable improvement over the outright hot water which flowed from the metal cistern trucks parked at the end of the battery street. Each man was allotted about one full helmet, or canvas bucket's worth of water to wash, shave, and do his laundry in. In the intense sunlight their green herringbone twill fatigues would dry within minutes and bleach to a pale yellowish tan color within a couple of weeks.

Showers were eventually set up at the water source a few miles away. Periodically the men were trucked to that location for a quick two minute opportunity at bathing. One man in "A" Battery, Arnold Tucknaught, was not overly fond of personal hygiene. Eventually the other men couldn't tolerate his odor any longer, so they carried him bodily to the showers and threw him in, uniform and all.

Sartain had quite a different attitude toward bathing and made special arrangements to accommodate his needs, "Jesse Holman in North Africa, every morning he'd fill the jeep trailer up with water and hide it in back of the motor pool. By the time it was four o'clock in the afternoon the water was just right and I would go take my bath. It wasn't for general distribution. I got in there first." I was about the only officer that knew about it, so I would take my bath and be careful not to soap it up too much, then everybody in the motor pool would take their bath."

Lieutenant Sartain found this way to unwind and revive himself, but a bath, even if taken in a trailer, was not typically available to the average enlisted man. More commonly for them were such diversions as a pass to Oujda, a location largely off limits to American troops except for a few blocks where one could sample the local cuisine, snail soup for example, have a drink of the sweetened French Moroccan beer, or local variety of wine served at bars which were hardly more than a few wooden tables serving their libations from a pitcock at the bottom of large wooden barrels. A few might have had the opportunity to see a belly dancer or purchase some token of their sojourn in this exotic locale.

"The Casbah was off limits to us and seeing all those veiled women gave me no desire to break the rules and see them in another kind of way," said Arno Mundt. "Besides, those films on venereal disease burned a hole in my mind. Any thoughts of a night on the town with wine women and song faded quickly when I remembered the signs of the diseases it was possible to contract."

Those more adventurous souls could visit one of a few houses of ill repute in Oujda. Ed Ryan remembered trying to enter one establishment with his friend, an Ohioan named Cletus McVicker. When MPs at the door demanded that the pair prove they were free of disease by showing the guards their healthy genitals, McVicker inquired, "Can I ask you a question? When you write home to your mother, what do you tell her you do all day?" The two were thrown out as a couple of wise guys, "But we were laughing so hard it didn't bother us that we didn't get in."

Roland Gruebling was another who got a pass to town. While seeing the sights there was a collision between the accepted customs of Milwaukee, Wisconsin, and those of Oujda, Morocco. Seeing an Arab entering town perched high upon his camel while his wife followed, walking submissively behind with a large bundle on her head, Gruebling forced the local fellow to halt. Through a variety of emphatic hand gestures the Arab was forced to dismount and help her upon the animal's back, then take up her bundle and follow as she led the way. Scarcely a block down the street Gruebling saw the Moroccan order is wife off the camel and reclaim his rightful place. Though his impact on Islamic customs was quite short lived, Gruebling felt he'd at least made some effort to further the march of civilization.

Some few of the men in the battalion had a keener appreciation of the indigenous culture. Robert McArthur, a gunner corporal in "A" Battery, was one of them. A native of Marks, Mississippi, McArthur had been a mathematics major at the University of Mississippi on a football and boxing scholarship when Uncle Sam tapped him on the shoulder.

In a letter home Bob described the people and customs he encountered in North Africa, "These Arabs are a very interesting group of people. The way they work, the way they talk and sing, the kind of clothes they wear, and their costumes and the way they live is very fascinating. Most of the boys here think that their ways and customs are crazy and backwards. Well, some of their customs do seem funny but there is always a reason for their customs. Here is one of their customs: married women wear veils over their faces to keep other men from seeing how pretty they are. That's nothing but natural – no man wants other men to run around making eyes at his wife and trying to steal her. This is a very interesting country, Mother. The more I see the more I want to see."

Usually there was no pass, and the GI's only chance to cut loose came from unauthorized, but largely tolerated trading with the local Arabs.

Not all transactions went smoothly. As one man from "B" Battery remembered, "We had a lot of people come through there selling grapes and stuff like that. One day, a guy came in and he kept raising the prices. So we pulled him off his donkey and kicked his rear good!"

It would seem that a high proportion of trading with the local population involved grapes in one form or another. Ed Ryan remembered it well, "We bought wine alright. You'd see this guy with his mule coming across the desert. He's got two five gallon cans on him. They're full of that vino that they make. It's strange vino. Tasted like pepper was in it. They wanted Camel cigarettes and nothing but Camels. After we were there a while, every guy that smiled looked like, they called it the purple death! Their teeth were all purple you know."

One night Gruebling, Jughead, and Albert "Smash" Lewis, decided to celebrate Ted Covais' promotion and recent twentieth birthday by introducing him to the pleasures of intoxication. "We happened to get a jerry can, a five gallon jerry can for gasoline, that type of container. We put some red wine in there. We got red wine somehow, somewhere, I don't know where, maybe out of the sky, but we drank out of that thing."
Reveille came early for the purple toothed celebrant. "Let me tell you, if ever I was sick as a dog I paid for being drunk," recalled Covais of that night. "I didn't know what I was doing. I said, red wine, forget it. I was sick for two days. That was the last time I was ever really drunk."

Bob Storms' proficiency on the heavy machinegun was rewarded with a promotion to sergeant of his own crew. Thinking he'd celebrate his advancement with a little drink, Storms made his way to Marnia station on his own authority. "I guess I got a little drunk and I took off. Oh boy but I had a good time! I jumped on that forty and eight train and I went way up in the mountains somewhere out of the desert. I stayed a couple of days up there. Those were beautiful towns way up in the mountains, oh, beautiful. Those Arab people, they fed me and they gave me cigarettes and then on the second day they made me get on a train and come back, they sent me back to my outfit. I was gone three days. Fourth morning they had roll call, they hollered my name. 'Here!' Everybody turned around and looked. After the all present and accounted for, the first sergeant said the Captain wanted to see me after breakfast. So I went over to see the Captain. He called me in. He wanted to know what happened. Well that time I lied to him a little bit. I told him I went down there and got in that wine and, gee, when I woke up it was nighttime so I come back the next day. He said, 'Hell, that was three days ago.' I told him I got drunk and didn't know about the other two. He said, 'You know I had three jeeps out looking for you. I didn't want to turn you in as AWOL because you'd go to prison for that, and I don't want none of my men to go to prison.' So he let me off with a good warning. He was good, but when I got back I was a Private."

"I thought everything was alright but the First Sergeant, he put me digging holes for three days. The Captain excused me but the First Sergeant, he seen right through it and I dug holes, I'll tell you that."

Whatever holes Storms did dig were shallow, and by kneeling within them anyone observing from a distance was likely to have the illusion that the culprit was standing in a deep pit.

"After supper the First Sergeant come out and he said, 'Well, Storms, I guess you've had enough to learn your lesson. Come on, get out of there.' I wasn't digging. I only dug a little hole and he wouldn't leave. Boy, but he wouldn't go away. I thought he'd go away and I'd stand up and walk out. I'd have still got away with it. I said, I'll be right out, but he wouldn't go, he wouldn't leave. He said, 'I told you to get out of the hole.' So finally I had to stand up. When I stood up he said, 'Is that all you've dug!' Well I dug right on. I dug till about three four that morning and went back the next day again. After I got the hole all dug he made me fill it back in. First Sergeant Johnson, he was a big guy. I never argued with him. He was a good sized fella, but he was fair, I have to say that. He always got somebody trying to get ahead of him a little bit, but he knowed all the ropes."

A few weeks later Storms was told to visit Captain Lougmiller's tent

First Sergeant Jesse Johnson poses with Motor Pool Sergeant Jesse Holman, masquerading as an Arab woman. Casablanca, May 1943. Sartain collection.

again. He may have been apprehensive, but Loughmiller knew Storms was a very capable machine gunner, and besides, there was something likeable about the man which made it impossible to maintain him on a disciplinary status for long.

The Captain told him, "Stormsy, I don't know what I'm gonna do with you. I make you acting sergeant all the time, but I can't make you no rank, you loose it! So I'm gonna make you a combat corporal. The only way you can loose that is if you get in bad trouble, otherwise you can't lose your combat corporal."

"So I hung on to corporal from there till I come home," Storms explained. "Everyplace I went I was acting sergeant. The boys all knowed it so I didn't have no trouble. I had the corporal stripes on, but if we went to town or anything I was acting sergeant all the while. We never had no trouble like that. The boys all knowed it, so that's all there was to it. We put it up and took it down. Man I got off lucky on that one."

With conditions as difficult as they were, the morale of the battalion was strained. The heat, horrible rations, dysentery and hostility toward Colonel Bertsch and his XO converged to make this period a miserable one for the outfit. Chaplain Reid took notice. One day a card was distributed to the men. It was sized to conveniently fit into the pocket New Testaments which most of the men had. Across the top were the words "All-American Troubled Soldier Ticket." Reflecting the issues men had raised with him, Chaplain Reid listed the appropriate bible verse for a long series of quandaries ranging from "Lousy Chow" to "No Mail" and "Tempted." For the soldier troubled with "Wife Problems" Reid suggested reading the book of Mark, verses 9 and 10. If a man found himself with a "hangover" he was directed to Proverbs, 23, 29, while a "3:06 am fire mission, at my command do not load!" called for Luke 12, 39.

If Fort Bragg had turned citizens into soldiers, Camp Marnia was turning them into a lean and proficient outfit, experienced in everything except combat itself. As much as this involved continuous training, the GIs noticed that other Allied troops around them remained inactive during the most blistering afternoon hours. Not so the Americans, whose commanders kept the men on a rigorous schedule, training all day and frequently at night as well. In the incredible heat all men suffered and many collapsed from heatstroke. As might be expected, vehicle engines overheated, while the battery plates of the large SCR-610 radios fused together and the

The "All-American Troubled soldier Ticket" distributed by Chaplain Reid to the men in the 82nd Airborne's artillery battalions. This particular card was carried by Bob Storms. Covais collection.

units themselves malfunctioned.

There were a lot of timed competitions between "A" and "B" batteries to locate a position according to map coordinates, set up the howitzers, establish a secured perimeter, and be ready to register the guns. At other times the timed competitions took place within the battery, each gun crew vying to see who could unlimber and set up their gun the quickest. Occasionally live ammunition was used, but usually these sessions did not involve live fire.

Some training exercises were conducted in coordination with infantry outfits, most generally the 325th, since they occupied the same bivouac. These field exercises concentrated on coordination between the artillery and infantry, but frequently they were not concluded until well after night had fallen.

"I was able to put to use my expanded knowledge of the constellations when we were released by the infantry colonel at midnight some five to ten miles from our camp," recalled Captain Manning, thinking back to his nights sitting up with Dr. Hebert and learning his way around the stars on the Santa Rosa.

Manning went on to observe that "It is often better to travel over the plain at night than to wait for the heat of the morning." In fact, it was cool enough during these night marches that the men needed to wear their field jackets to keep off the chill.

Kenneth Smith well remembered these night maneuvers, some of which were solely intended to instruct the men in finding their way across terrain in the dark. "We did most of our training at nighttime in Africa. Mostly we did night marches. We learned to walk by stars and stuff like that. They'd send us out on a march. They'd put down seven different markers out there in the desert. You had to walk to each one and go to the next one and pick up a marker. What it was doing was teaching us to use the compass and stars and stuff in the sky, you go by that. Well, that was all new to us. A lot of us got lost. Yeah, they'd come out and find us. We finally learned how to travel by stars and stuff."

During these marches encounters with Bedouins were common. Sometimes they too were traveling in the cool of the night, at other times the column would come across a party of Arabs, wrapped in blankets and sleeping on the ground beside their tethered camels and donkeys until barking dogs warned of the approaching troops.

Glider training continued, both to maintain the glider status of those already qualified and to bring new men up to speed. Yet even this aspect of training was affected by the heat. Strong and sometimes unpredictable winds emanated off the desert plain. More dangerous was the way the canvas glider skins had a tendency to come unglued and slip off when subjected to the combination of wind and heat.

Punctuating this strenuous training schedule were an annoying number of reviews. When Sartain commented that "there were all sorts of show off parades and retreat ceremonies," he was right. Formal division reviews were held for over a dozen general officers of the United States Army, as well as an assortment of Allied commanders and foreign dignitaries in less than a month's time. One of the biggest took place when Commander in Chief Eisenhower, as well as Generals George Patton and 5th Army Commander Mark Clark took their turn reviewing the 82nd on June 3rd. After the formation, General Eisenhower addressed the division's officers. Though he did not mention John Girardin by name, the Commander in Chief did criticize what he thought was a lackadaisical attitude on the part of many of the airborne enlisted personnel toward saluting and other details of military bearing. When Patton next delivered his standard speech, the address went over flat. The latter's remarks were laced with swearing and coarse descriptions of what it took to win in battle. Rather than incite the officers to a higher level of morale, the consensus was that Patton came off as one prone to showboating and not to be taken seriously.

Oujda also provided the first real chance for men in the battalion to become acquainted with their allies against the Germans. A lot of the GIs were filled with hubris and quick to adopt a somewhat superior attitude, but Sartain liked the Commonwealth troops in spite of their quirky ways and remembered them with respect. "There was a Scottish regiment and they had this bagpipe outfit. We had a lot of contact with them in North Africa because they paraded a lot and we paraded with them. They had this bagpipe band and we had retreat with them at night. It was quite something. We got a big kick out of them."

There were also New Zealanders and Aussies, and they hated the British troops as well. "We got together a team to play the British in rugby," remembered Sartain. "The 319th's boys didn't know a thing about Rugby but that didn't stand in the way of their confidence. They thought they were pretty good but they got their tail beat. Well, that was the end of that."

In the last ten days of June notice was given that the battalion would be leaving Oujda for another undisclosed destination. As was the case with the change of base from Casablanca to Oujda, this displacement would also be made by different means of transportation according to which portion of the battalion was being moved. Rumors abounded, in spite of the absence of official news, and all signs indicated the destination to be somewhere in Tunisia. Everyone was glad to leave, confident that any place had to be an improvement over Camp Marnia.

All the vehicles, by their nature, were driven in a motor convoy, and this component was among the first to leave. While one might reasonably expect traveling by jeeps and trucks across the desert to be some relief from the broiling heat, those in the motor convoy discovered just the opposite to be true, as Bob McArthur explained in one of his letters home, "I took a little trip last week in a jeep and believe you me it was really hot. This hot weather is not like it is back home. Back in the U.S. we can get in a car on a hot day and ride around and cool off, but it's not that way here. If you get in a car here and start riding, it gets hotter as your speed increases. So the best thing to do is to get in an air tight place and it is cool in there. I see now why these Arabs put on a lot of clothing here in the middle of the day. We all thought they were crazy at first but now we see different."

Next the heaviest equipment and ammunition, including the howitzers, were loaded aboard open flatcars at Marnia Station and departed, as the motor convoy had, in an easterly direction. Those who were detailed as guards soon discovered that soot and cinders from the locomotive rained down on them continuously, making their exposed positions in the sun even more intolerable.

The majority of the guys in the battalion made the journey in one of several relays of flights over the Atlas Mountains, either as passengers in C-47 tow planes or in the CG4A gliders. By now the rumors of Tunisia had been confirmed, with the additional knowledge that the new bivouac would be at a place called Kairouan.

As before, the men assembled their personal baggage: helmet, gear, and carbine, musette bag packed with underwear or sundries, all with their overcoats and shelter halves rolled on top. Since all the guns, vehicles, and equipment had already been removed via rail or convoy, the gliders and tow planes were loaded only with the men and their kits.

"It was our first long glider ride," recalled Sartain of the five hour trip.

For his part, Captain Manning vividly remembered his experience of leaving

BATTERY!

Camp Marnia for the last time, "When it came time for the gliders to move we were headed into a blinding sand storm. One hasn't lived until one rides in a flimsy pipe and canvas glider, staring out at a rope which disappears into a black cloud and seems to have a life of its own."

"We flew across the mountains in a glider over toward Kairouan, and after we got up in the glider we about froze to death going over them mountains. We never thought that would be possible. We had to put our overcoats on trying to keep warm," said Kenneth Smith of the ride.

The trip was also turbulent, the more so as glider and tow plane climbed to higher altitudes to clear the mountain ranges. "Air pockets" would suddenly drop the aircraft by tens or dozens of feet, though passengers remember these abrupt drops in terms of hundreds. Covais was in one of the CG4as and remembered it as the most terrifying non-combat flight of his military service. Despite being belted in, anything not specifically tied down was apt to go flying within the fuselage. Helmets, carbines, eyeglasses, cigarette lighters, all became airborne.

Inevitably, men got motion sickness. As one began to vomit, the odor and sight often caused a kind of contagious phenomena. One member of "B" Battery described that aspect of the ride in graphic detail.

"Yeah, going over all the mountains we'd hit air pockets. I remember that some of the guys were sick. They were throwing up in their helmets. Then we hit an air pocket

Members of "A" Battery in North Africa. They are, left to right: Lloyd Cattel, Charles Shaw, Mess Sergeant William Siegel (later killed in Holland), Roland Gruebling, unknown, and Michael Sinko. Courtesy Gruebling family

and this guy's puke got all over me. That's when I got sick too! It was a mess when we landed. The floor was just covered with filth, but we made it."

BATTERY!

Part 5: "Better coffee in a canvas bucket."

After a journey of nearly 700 miles directly east, the 319th found itself reassembled in the vicinity of Kairouan, Tunisia, about the 25th of June. It was one of the Islamic world's holy cities and the location of numerous burial grounds. Because of this, Kairouan was known to the Muslims in the region as "The City of the Dead," with all the graves fashioned above ground and vented to allow for the departed's soul to escape to Paradise. Unfortunately for the American troops bivouacked in the countryside surrounding these cemeteries, the odor of necrosis escaped just as easily, leaving the atmosphere tainted with foul smells for a dozen miles in any direction.

Notwithstanding, the designated site for the battalion was quite an improvement over Camp Marnia. The battalion was situated within an 80 acre olive grove near an oasis called El Alem, and only a mile or two from the Mediterranean Sea. The grove itself was surrounded by a formidable hedge of prickly pear cactus, approximately ten feet in height and several feet thick. There was also a large building within the cactus enclosure, a mysterious edifice surrounded by a tall earthen wall painted a brilliant white. No one ever saw the single gate to the inside of this structure opened or gained a look within, though an occasional barking dog or indistinct female voices were sometimes heard.

Instructed to make their canvas homes among the olive trees, the guys were relieved to finally be living amidst some shade. "The pup tents went up again. However, I must admit that the officers had larger tents with cots," confessed Sartain, while Captain Manning constructed his bed upon a platform of empty jerry cans. As at Marnia, each tent had its own slit trench in case of air attack, but this time proximity to German held Sicily made a visit from the Luftwaffe a real possibility. The men were consequently told to disperse their pup tents in irregular patterns and take care that no articles likely to reflect sunlight were ever exposed. The weather in Tunisia was just as hot as Camp Marnia, but the shade which the cactus hedge and olive trees offered, coupled with a continual breeze coming in from the shore, made the situation more tolerable. Besides this, the army now realized that a split schedule in which the men were roused at 04:30, began their training at 06:00, and took a siesta during the hottest hours of mid-day, was in everyone's best interest. Many a case of heatstroke was avoided in this way, though it was normally too hot for the men to sleep unless out of sheer exhaustion.

Being desperate for fresh fruit of any kind, the men promptly began eating any prickly pears within reach. There were consequences, as Arno Mundt remembered, "We all learned the fruit had tiny needle like spines which became stuck in our tongues, throats, gums and lips. The Arabs would simply roll the fruit on the ground with their calloused feet and then nonchalantly eat them like apples. The preliminary step of removing the tiny spines escaped most of us and several days of suffering followed. Well once we got used to the fruits we learned to actually enjoy their sweet taste."

Kairouan had other problems. There was a substantial mosquito population which slept within the cactus hedge all day and came out to feast on the warm blooded soldiers all night. There had been mosquitoes at Marnia but the problem was nothing like what was being experienced at the new bivouac. Since the army had a keen interest in keeping the spread of malaria to a minimum, and these buzzing nuisances were the primary conveyance of the disease, netting was eventually distributed, but more as a preventative measure than for comfort.

It wasn't the mosquitoes which the men in the 319th remembered but the crickets. The olive grove at El Alem was infested with a variety of mole cricket or beetle, which lived in the soil and emerged, like their mosquito neighbors, after dark. These beetles were large, numerous, unnerving to discover crawling across one's face or inside one's clothing, and thoroughly annoying.

Private Sosa found the beetles particularly disgusting. "They're sort of like roaches, they were so bad. The roaches were so bad they gave us that chemical stuff, some kind of a pesticide, I forget what it was. Because we were sleeping on the ground they gave it to us to spray on the ground and keep the roaches out. The thing about it is the roaches ate it. It wouldn't kill them." Sosa was determined to find a solution, "So, what I did I struck my tent and pitched me a hammock between two trees. I slept up in the air. You understand what I'm saying? Instead of sleeping on the ground I made me a hammock. I didn't like sleeping with roaches. You have to look out for yourself."

Knowing that these insects would always seek shade, other men found entertaining ways to make use of the mole crickets by exploiting their nature. Ed Ryan explained it this way, "The guys had beetle races and they bet on them. What they do with the beetle, they're big beetles, bigger than a cricket, what they do is draw a circle around a tree. Everybody has one. They put the beetle down and it'd race for the shade. They took little toothpicks and marked numbers on them so you could tell what number he was. One time on inspection I was surprised some of the higher officers didn't bother them, even though they kept the beetle in a matchbox sitting on top of the stuff being inspected." Evidently, as long as the beetle was stowed in the proper place for personal effects the inspecting officers saw no need to confiscate it as contraband.

Major Wilcoxson was ordinarily the inspecting officer and he was notorious-

During maneuvers in the desert, men of "A" Battery pose with one of the local Arabs. They include David Stelow, René Picher, Milton Weidner, Thomas Legg, Harold Jinders, Carl Davis, and others. Sartain collection.

ly fussy when conducting inspections. Whether or not he was aware of the miniature stables is unknown, but it would have been out of character for the Colonel's XO to allow such a frivolous breach of military decorum. Wilcoxson usually shared Colonel Bertsch's affectation for strict military formalities in all ways. Perhaps the Major just couldn't see anything materially wrong with beetle races. "You know," said Ryan, "in a place like North Africa beetle races was big money. Guys had nothing else to do with money so they gambled on that."

In spite of their entertainment value, the beetles could also be quite destructive in their own way, as Captain Manning discovered after a couple of weeks. He'd stored his dress uniform in a canvas bag underneath his jerry can bed, only to discover that hungry beetles had eaten massive holes through the clothing, leaving little more than buttons connected by ruined fragments of uniform cloth.

Corporal Covais had his own close acquaintance with the beetles of Kairouan. With campfires forbidden as a security risk which could reveal a bivouac to enemy aircraft, and the only coffee available as a particularly unappealing variety of instant Sanka, everyone was desperate for a good cup of the beverage in a fresh brewed form. When one of his buddies came into a small quantity of ground coffee through some means better left unspoken, he shared his good fortune with the Corporal and another friend in "A" Battery. That night the three retired to the bottom of a slit trench with a blanket spread over the top. In hushed voices they stealthily fired up one of the small Coleman stoves, boiled the grounds, and then enjoyed their first cup of brewed coffee in weeks. It was delicious, and sweetened with the knowledge that they'd gotten away with a forbidden pleasure.

When morning came another man in a neighboring tent asked, "Hey, did you guys have some coffee last night?"

Covais joked, "Yeah, what's it to you, jealous you didn't get any?"

"No, I wouldn't say I am," answered the man. "Come over here and take a look."

Covais and his fellow conspirators ambled over to the coffee pot being displayed before them. Mixed within the previous night's grounds were the boiled carcasses of beetles.

Indeed coffee wasn't the only thing in short supply. Rations, which had been of a consistently poor quality since arriving in Africa, became markedly meager in quantity as well. Mess Sergeant Seagle was apologetic and, trying to find some levity in it all, told the guys lining up for chow that he'd be serving out meals with a tablespoon for the foreseeable future. The Sergeant's humor may have been appreciated, but it did nothing to satisfy the men's hunger. Many of them were becoming alarmingly thin. Though assigned to another battery, and probably an extreme case, Ryan, for example, realized at this time that he'd lost over 70 pounds since entering the service. Men began to complain openly and Major Todd was made aware of an alarming number of men caught pilfering rations.

As John Girardin recalled, "When we were in the olive grove we ran out of food, you might say. They put guards around the truck or trailer where the rations were kept so nobody would break into them. This went on for a couple of weeks." Girardin further remembered a stop gap measure which was employed in "A" Battery. "Each fella put in so much money so the Mess Sergeant went down and bought one of them bulls or a cow to feed the outfit."

The ever resourceful Sosa, who'd found his own private solution to the beetle problem, knew he'd fare poorly if he didn't exercise some initiative where his chow was concerned. "Our rations was bad! We got a lot of what looked like chili and powdered potatoes. They had some kind of lemonade, powdered eggs and powdered potatoes. It was bad, real bad. I had a little Bunsen burner, one of them little gasoline stoves, so what I did was go off and buy some chickens from the Arabs. I cooked my own food out there. I wouldn't eat that crap from the kitchen. There's no point in making it harder for yourself if you don't have to. So I went out there and got me some bread and butter and stuff and I just cooked my own stuff. I'd take what I wanted from the kitchen and fix up my own."

Poor rations notwithstanding, Kairouan had its amenities. Most days, some fraction of the guys in the battalion were allowed down to the shore to enjoy the water. Eddie Ryan described it this way, "That was pretty good going for us in Africa, at Kairouan. There was shade and we could swim all the time. We had swimming parties on the buddy system, so you had to have somebody with you, but the Mediterranean was right out there."

The most spectacular entertainment event of Kairouan was unquestionably an unannounced visit from comedian Bob Hope and popular singer Frances Langford. Both were already well known celebrities by 1943. Hope, at the time in his early forties, had been a radio and film personality for years, particularly with his radio variety show sponsored by Pepsodent toothpaste. Langford, then 29, had been performing as a dancer and singer since her teens. By the time Hope and Company appeared in North Africa they'd already entertained thousands of American troops at stateside bases, in the Aleutian Islands, and across the British Isles.

Lieutenant Sartain's memory of Hope's arrival was clear, "This C47 came and landed. The airstrips in the desert were on metal mats across the sand. They opened the door and pulled out a folding platform. I thought it was another pep talk by Eisenhower or Patton or somebody; maybe Bradley. Out stepped Bob Hope and Francis Langford. He came out and went to the microphone. I think the first words he said was, 'Has anybody got a glass of ice water?' Something like that."

Standing beside Hope was the first American woman anyone had seen in a long, long time. Langford was a petit five feet tall, delightfully dressed in a pair of khaki slacks, a midriff revealing white halter, and open toed wedgies. Her hair was swept up in a snood and she wore bracelets about her wrists. Many of the men would have recognized her immediately from recent films such as "Too Many Girls" and "All-American Co-ed." Perhaps they'd seen her perform with James Cagney in the 1942 film biography of George M. Cohan, "Yankee Doodle Dandy" before going overseas. Recognized or not, she was an American girl, young, attractive, and entirely adorable. The soldiers applauded, and called out to her. Some whistled their approval. Then Miss Langford launched into a medley of Cohan's patriotic songs from her recent film, beginning with "Over There!"

When Miss Langford, who packed a lot of voice in a small package, was through, Hope took her place at the microphone, "Let's have a big hand for the lady and her orchestra. That's Tony Romano, the fastest guitar in the European Theater of Operations, and Jerry Colonna on trombone."

There was a big round of applause for Langford's backup musicians. This was infinitely more fun than another "blood and guts" speech from another untried general, so the reaction of the men was both enthusiastic and sincere. When Hope commented on Colonna's bushy mustache joking, "You know Jerry, you're the only guy I know who can kiss a girl and give her the brush off at the same time!" Laughter rippled through the audience.

Then, turning back to his crowd, Hope kept the jokes rolling. "When the War Department asked me and Frances to come out here to see you guys they said it was because they wanted to try out a new bomb. Really though, the guys in England, those fly boys, they have it PRETTY rough. All that cool cloudy weather and warm beer. Then the brass told us we were coming down here to get a vacation in the sun. I knew we were in trouble when the pilot showed up wearing goggles and a scarf."

"Seriously", continued Hope, "I like Tunisia. It's like Texas. With Arabs."

Raucous laughter again, from an audience which was by this time quite tired of North Africa. Then Hope resumed, "You know, we couldn't bring Miss Langford all the way out here to see you guys without her singing something special."

"Do you mean my special song, Bob?" She added.

"Yeah," said Hope, "Especially since I can't tell whether those are beads of sweat running down these guys' faces or testosterone!"

"Golly Bob, I know what you mean. With all these handsome young fellas in front of me I can only think of one thing. I'm in the mood for love."
Someone in the crowd yelled out, "You've come to the right place, sister!"

Once the laughs settled down Romano and Colonna struck up the melody of Frances Langford's signature song, she stepped up closer to the microphone, almost embracing it, and in a powerful but sultry voice began:

> I'm in the mood for Love
> Simply because you're near me.
> Funny, but when you're near me
> I'm in the mood for love.
>
> Heaven is in your eyes
> Bright as the stars we're under
> Oh! Is it any wonder
> I'm in the mood for love?
>
> Why stop to think of whether
> This little dream might fade?
> We've put our hearts together
> Now we are one, I'm not afraid!
>
> If there's a cloud above
> If it should rain we'll let it
> But for tonight, forget it!
> I'm in the mood for love.

Hope stepped up to the microphone. "I don't know about you, but after that I'm about ready to blow a gasket!"

The guys went wild, forgetting for the moment where they were and why they were there.

Langford chimed in, "You know Bob, this heat is really getting to me too. Isn't there something we can do to cool a gal down?"

BETTER COFFEE IN A CANVAS BUCKET.

"What do you have in mind, Frances?" Asked Hope.

"Well Bob, I was thinking that maybe it would help if me and the boys all sang together. Maybe something like, well, how about a little bit of White Christmas." Then, addressing the audience, Langford asked, "What do you say fellas, should we give it a try?"

The GIs would have done anything Langford asked by this time, but the moment the first chords were played it became quiet. Singing White Christmas triggered a sentimental wave. It swept through the crowd as soldiers suddenly realized how much they missed the U S A, loved ones, and how very far away from home they were. Everybody tried to sing along, some had reasonably good voices and others, disarmed by their own sudden emotion, could only mouth the words.

The song, according to Ryan who was sitting about a hundred feet from the performers, "Made everybody, well, it bothered a lot of people. It was a real tear jerker. Everybody was dreaming of it. Anything to take your mind off that heat."

The show lasted a little over an hour. Then they said, "We've got to go." Hope went back in the plane followed by Romano and Colonna. Frances Langford was last in, waving and blowing kisses to the troops until the door closed. Just as suddenly as they'd appeared, remembered Sartain, "They pulled the thing up and the C47 took off!"

For those who were there, Lieutenant Sartain and Tech/5 Ryan among them, the visit from Bob Hope was a welcome diversion and one not easily forgotten. Sartain observed that the crowd was large, numbering at least two or three thousand. Yet recall of the Hope visit is noticeably absent from the memories of enlisted men in the firing batteries. Considering that the show itself probably lasted no more than 90 minutes, it is entirely possible that the men in "A" and "B" Batteries were otherwise occupied with some training exercise, while Ryan as a radioman in HQ Battery and Sartain as an officer with some greater degree of autonomy, were able to take advantage of the opportunity offered.

Shortly after the gala event, rumors, then orders began circulating to the effect that an invasion of Sicily was at hand. Every preparation was made to bring all the previous months of instruction in the art of war into use. The most efficient method of reassembling the battalion after a glider landing was practiced to perfection. Accordingly, a memorandum was distributed by Colonel Bertsch's XO, Major Wilcoxson, on July 6th. The directive outlined Standard Operating Procedures (SOPs) under daylight and nighttime conditions. The directive instructed that there was to be a "Sand table briefing and explanation by the battery commander of the planned landing." Colored Flags and Lights were to be used for identification; red for HQ Battery, white for "A" Battery, and blue for "B" Battery. Item number three warned; "Unidentified aircraft will not be fired at by troops unless they attack. At no time will aircraft be fired at when out of range of the individual weapon," while #5 directed that, "Troops should be trained in the use of the Mae West life preserver."

Late on July 7th the battalion was loaded on trucks and taken to an airstrip near Tunis where they bivouacked. The next day was spent loading the gliders. All those hours at Fort Bragg during basic training, everything from forced marches to the hours spent in instruction on weapons, radios, and a thousand other gadgets of war, all the special glider training at Laurenberg-Maxton and Pope Field, the whole shooting match was coming down to this day in Tunisia, loading up for Operation Husky. Officers were briefed, informed that the 319th was going to go in by glider on D+2 and land at Pointe Olivia Airport just north of the beachhead at Gela. This time they were tying down the jeeps, trailers, guns, and distributing the cargo for an actual combat mission.

BATTERY!

A wrecked German JU-88 in the desert near Kairouan. Sartain collection

"It was obvious that the men and officers had been through this before and knew what they were doing," observed Marvin Ragland, who was at this time assigned to work with "A" Battery. "Lt. Blanc was in charge of loading the gliders. He knew all about how you load the weapons, the guns, the trucks, the people and everything. Of course, I didn't know anything about it."

On the morning of July 10th a circular was read to the battalion: At this moment, troops of the division are in combat against the enemy. Last night, at 2340, the 505th combat Team dropped successfully on the Island of Sicily and opened the door for a powerful seaborne Allied Army, now storming the beaches. The remainder of this division will follow as fast as air transport will permit. You are part of a mighty force which will first shatter the Italian Empire and bring ultimate destruction to the Axis. The invasion of Europe has begun. The 82nd Airborne Division is its spearhead!

That night the Luftwaffe made an air raid against the positions around Tunis, hoping they could prevent Allied forces in Sicily from being reinforced by air or sea. The attack was visible from the position occupied by the battalion, though several miles away. The men could plainly see searchlights, antiaircraft artillery and machinegun tracers sweeping the sky. Now and then a searchlight would fix upon one of the German bombers and the men would be left shouting directions to the Akak crews which were, of course, altogether inaudible to anyone but themselves. This raid was the first time the men had seen shots fired in anger and the impression on many was that there seemed to be an awful lot of lead thrown at the enemy with little discernable effect.

Before dawn a storm blew up with hail and strong enough winds to damage some of the gliders. The repairs were manageable and not catastrophic, but when six planes loaded with paratroopers and seventeen other planes were shot down by the US Navy on their way to Sicily, Airborne operations were suspended until further notice. It was a significant loss, and not just in personnel, but in aircraft too. All at a time when there was still a very restricted supply of C-47s and gliders on hand.

Of this event Covais said, "It's very unfortunate. I was at the airport with the glider, ready, loaded with live ammunition, I mean with complete combat gear, when the word came down that everything was canceled out. But those things do happen. Mistakes do happen. They call it friendly fire, but when you get killed it's not that friendly."

By July 13, because it had become obvious that the 319th was not going to be sent in by glider, or by sea for that matter, the battalion was told to stand down, unload the gliders and return to Kairouan. The news was received with a mixture of relief and disappointment after having been brought up to the very point of departure. All the preparation was for naught, though as part of the division's ready reserve the 319th was still awarded a battle star for Sicily.

There was a significant change in the organization of the 319th Glider Field Artillery after the return to the olive grove. Orders came down for the battalion to revert back to its original arrangement of three firing batteries with one HQ Battery in support. Whether this was because a battalion of only two firing batteries was believed too inflexible in its response to the fire missions expected, or whether the change had something to do with the rearmament of the battalion with short barreled 105mm guns, or yet some other unidentified cause, is unclear. Whatever the reasoning behind this decision was, it ultimately must have been intended to increase the efficiency of the outfit. Accordingly, two gun sections were taken from "A" and "B" Batteries each, along with a contingent of men from HQ Battery, to form a new "C" Battery. Thus re-organized, the battalion now had three four-gun batteries where there had previously been two six-gun batteries.

"A" Battery remained under the command of Captain Loughmiller, with Lt. Vernon Blanc as his executive officer and Lt. Harry Warren*, a barrel chested South Carolinian who'd graduated from OCS the previous November, as the assistant XO. "B" Battery was under the command of Captain Robert Cargile, with Lt. Max Torgersen serving as his assistant executive. The creation of "C" Battery would be, as Manning predicted, "An ideal opportunity for battery commanders to shed trouble makers and goof offs from their ranks." With this in mind, as a new battery, having of necessity to build its own sense of unity and team spirit, the battery commander and his executive would need to be chosen for their demonstrated ability to lead and be respected by the enlisted men. After careful deliberation, Captain Manning was selected as Battery "C"s commanding officer, perhaps in part because he'd served successfully as executive officer of "B" Battery early in 1942. Lieutenant Sartain, already recognized as energetic and charismatic, a rising star as it were, was placed as Manning's executive officer.

Reflecting on this years later, Sartain commented, "Todd must have taken a liking to me, making me exec of "C" Battery and putting me with Manning. Little ole second Lieutenant made the Battery Exec, that's not normal, you know? I guess he made me battery exec so he could promote me to First Lieutenant."

Manning and Sartain looked over the roster of their new battery. They had to admit that some of the men "were oddballs." Sartain knew the ones transferred from "A" Battery and could vouch that they were essentially good men who were tough and could work hard. Manning knew many of the "B" Battery men from his stint as that battery's XO, but the others were an unknown quantity. Both officers agreed there was good material to work with if the men were just properly motivated. Indeed, they discovered that they shared a common philosophy about how to go about this, a belief that treating these men with respect while simultaneously making it clear to them that only the highest standards were acceptable was the right strategy. It was a challenge they were eager to take on.

Once the physical organization of "C" Battery was made, John Manning started the career of his new command with a meeting to establish the rules, making clear what he expected of his men and what they could expect in return. The guys were gathered in a shaded area for the first of what came to be known as the Captain's "bull sessions," where a man could speak freely, without regard to rank, and make his views known. A lot of familiar faces were there and some new ones too. Eddie Ryan, the radio operator

BATTERY!

from Poughkeepsie was there, along with Willie Bragg, another radioman from HQ battery. The gun crews of Sergeants Albert Hein and Wheeler C. Davis were taken from "A" Battery. These included Robert Rappi, John Girardin, "Pop" Plassa, and Jolmara Olkanen, a selection in which Vinlanders from the upper peninsula of Michigan were well represented. Kenny Smith, the tallest man in the battalion was there with the rest of his machinegun crew. One Wisconsin native, Alfred "Fritz" Nigl, a "B" Battery man with a beautiful singing voice from Oshkosh, and whose favorite watering hole at home was a tavern called "The Chieftain," was there. Motor pool drivers included Louis Sosa from "A" Battery, a Sioux Indian named Clarence Janis from Lone Pine, South Dakota, and Glendeth Wells, nicknamed "Lost John" because of his night blindness and who was, according to one man in the battery, "a big pain in the ass." There were other colorful characters like Giles Kelly, a man with a constant thirst for alcohol, and Charlie Ipolito, a small time hood who insisted on being called "Charlie Blue" and bragged about his supposed Mafia connections. Silas Hogg, from Buckhorn, Kentucky, was another. He had a habit of gambling and sang the popular song Praise the Lord and Pass the Ammunition, over and over again. There were two Jewish guys from Cleveland, Ohio: Bernard Tansky, who kept a chicken named Nellie tethered to his tent for the eggs she laid, and Milton Susman, a multilingual native of Germany who'd escaped Nazi genocide by the skin of his teeth. Now Susman was back and ready to even the score. That many of the "C" Battery personnel had been selected to get them off the rolls of their previous battery assignments was not lost on the men.

Robert Rappi remembered it this way, "They put all the ding a lings in there and I was one of them!"

Sartain agreed, later commenting, "Like Manning said, we ended up with a bunch of screwballs, but we melded pretty quick, we really did."

The senior NCO and junior officer staff of "C" Battery was, on the other hand, a well selected and competent crew – no screwballs among them. The 1st sergeant was Keith Cormany, a professional wrestler in civilian life and formerly in HQ Battery. The

319th men with locally grown melons in North Africa. Sartain collection

67

chief of the gun crew sections was Staff Sergeant Delos Richardson, a Michigan man from "B" Battery who took his work so seriously that others assumed he was regular army. The security, or machinegun section was headed by Sergeant Spencer, from Janesville, Wisconsin, an "A" Battery man, while Sergeant Alvin "Get out of my Kitchen" Larrieu of New Orleans headed up the mess crew. The medical detachment was represented by Corporal James Jamison and a Hispanic from Houston, Texas, named John Rao.

Among the officers were 2nd Lieutenants Carey and Hull. Carey, from Kingston, New York, was known for his love of children. He had one waiting for him at home whom he'd never seen. On temporary duty from the 456th Parachute Field Artillery was Lt Hull, a small, wiry young man who didn't hesitate to take on things larger than himself. When he learned that Captain Manning had been on the Cornell wrestling team and that Cormany'd wrestled professionally, Hull couldn't help but challenge them.

Sartain remembered Manning, Hull, and those matches this way, "Manning was a big man, about six three six four. I guess he weighed two hundred twenty pounds. He was muscular, very agile. We had a lieutenant name of Hull, a real tough little guy, but very, very good. He was always challenging Johnny to a wrestling match. Johnny would just toy with him."

After the previous months of heat, horrible food, and seeming indifference from Colonel Bertsch, the "C" Battery men sensed immediately that life in a battery run by Manning and Sartain might be different. It wasn't that these two officers pandered for the men's popularity, they didn't. In fact they seemed to demand more, yet they gave more in return.

Neither the Captain nor his XO would tolerate any behavior which showed a lack of spirit or initiative. For example, John Girardin was corrected early on for unmilitary posture. It suggested a hang-dog attitude that wasn't compatible with what was expected in Manning's battery.

On the other hand, the enlisted ranks knew that they could go to their officers and be heard if there was a legitimate gripe, even if there wasn't always a way to correct the situation. Terrible rations were always understood to be something the men would just have to put up with, but after a short while the "C" Battery guys felt they could at least approach their officers about the subject. Robert Rappi, by now the gunner's corporal on his crew, found himself selected to raise the topic with Lieutenant Sartain. Rappi recalled his audience with the XO decades later, "Our coffee was tasting terrible. You couldn't drink it. We bitched to Sartain, he said, 'I can make better coffee in a canvas bucket than those cooks do, but there ain't nothing I can do about it.' That's all he said, he could make better coffee in a canvas bucket." Even if the coffee remained as bad as ever, knowing that the complaint was acknowledged with sympathy made a big difference.

One who wasn't easily impressed with the officer class was radioman Ryan, but Captain Manning won him over despite his skepticism. Ryan expressed the respect which he and the other "C" Battery men developed for their CO. "Manning" he said,, "he was a real soldier, acted like one anyway. He knew everything about the military as far as that was concerned, but he was very just. He was a man that spoke to people like they were human beings, like you were his friend. Everybody admired him so. I never heard of a guy who didn't like him. A great officer and a great human being as well."

Sartain later described how he and Manning motivated their battery. "Those guys were considered as oddballs but when they came to us we didn't treat them as odd-

balls. We just didn't. We just treated them with respect, gave them chores and responsibilities and they just came through, you know? It didn't take us long to get cohesion."

The approach taken by Captain Manning and his XO was a textbook example of
group motivation psychology. Take a collection of individuals who share some identity,
in this case "C" Battery goof offs. Tell them they are potentially superior to a compet-
ing group which has rejected them. Then treat them that way, with all the esteem and
standards incumbent on that status. The usual response would be for the group to adhere
more strongly to each other, then pull together and rise to the expectations of those who
believe in them.

"There was an esprit d' Corps that I don't think was in any of the other batteries," said Sartain. "We were the best battery. We always were on mission first, ahead of
the other two batteries. We beat the other two batteries consistently. Everybody considered us as screwballs, but I think that may have given the whole battery the feeling of,
well we're gonna show everybody, by golly we're gonna show them, and we did!"
Tensions between the men in the battalion and colonel Bertsch seem to have lessened
somewhat during the Kairouan period, offering as it did the diversions of the aborted Sicily mission as well as intermittent tension relieving opportunities like the Bob Hope visit,
beetle races, and chances to swim in the Mediterranean. Just the same, the battalion's
CO remained unpopular, and whether articulated or assumed, this sentiment hovered
about the camp.

As before, details of military protocol continued to be a bone of contention between Colonel Bertsch and his command. Unauthorized seepage of the men out of camp
at night persisted in spite of the rigorous training schedule and the formidable grip of
the cactus hedge, making it one area over which he was growing increasingly frustrated.
Accordingly, the Colonel placed the nearest village off limits to all men in the battalion.
Still, men slipped away at night.

"In the olive grove, that was something. Holy Jesus, that fence was high all
around it," remembered Bob Storms of how he and his buddies made their way out of
camp. "Oh yeah, man! What we'd do is take our knives and cut in maybe two foot or so,
and then you'd go either left or right for three, four feet, and then you chop a little hole
and then go out the other side."

Guards at the two entrances to the grove were firmly instructed that under no
circumstance were they to allow anyone in or out unless they had a pass or could give
the password.

Storms described an incident which took place late one night when a ranking
officer paid Colonel Bertsch a visit, "One of my guys was Gwaltney. He was a big, tall,
bony guy. They put him on guard at one end. The way I got it, the General come and
somebody else was with him and Gwaltney, he was a little queer, he shouted at the driver
for the password. They didn't know it so he told them to turn their ass around back till
they got the password. So they went back somewhere till they seen a soldier and they
got the password. They come back and got it and he let them in." Colonel Bertsch might
have been expected to be furious. Regardless of who this officer was, whether a general
or 2nd lieutenant, the event would have been embarrassing. Gwaltney was summoned
and harshly disciplined. "They turned him in because we all knowed the General," said
Storms. "They turned him in and he pulled a little hard labor for that."

That Gwaltney took advantage of the situation to use the Colonel's own rules
against him was clear. Just the same, disciplining him for doing exactly what he'd been
ordered to do seemed entirely unfair to a lot of guys. It is likely that Gwaltney was put

to work digging holes and then filling them back up again, since this was First Sergeant Johnson's preferred mode of punishment.

Several nights later, Colonel Bertsch was returning back to camp from the off limits village. It was quite late when his jeep driver pulled up to the olive grove with his passenger, who, expecting to see a lone sentry standing guard, instead saw no one except for a pair of legs protruding out from beneath the cactus hedge. With all the recent mischief around the question of men slipping in and out of camp, the Colonel became livid, got out of the jeep, stormed over to the prone man and gave him a swift kick.

The man turned out to be Private Milton Goldfarb of Brooklyn, New York, formerly a sewing machine operator in the canvas goods industry and currently a member of "B" Battery. Goldfarb offered a hasty explanation but Colonel Bertsch was in no mood to listen to excuses. He had the sentry placed under arrest immediately for sleeping on post, then vowed that Goldfarb would be facing a court martial as soon as it could be arranged.

Later the next day Major Todd asked Sartain to come to his quarters. "Charlie, he told the Lieutenant, we've got a man in the guardhouse, a kid named Goldfarb from "B" Battery. Evidently Colonel Bertsch is convinced he caught Goldfarb sleeping on post. Now we're convening a local court martial and I'd like you to defend him, if you're willing."

Sartain asked a few basic questions. The Major answered them. Todd may have reminded Sartain of their first conversation on the day he'd arrived at Fort Bragg. Like I said, there's a need for lawyers in the army, Todd reminded, then added that if Goldfarb were found guilty he would be in very serious trouble. Lieutenant Sartain thought about it. He'd chosen the law as his career, so turning down this chance was out of the question. One simply does not walk away from challenging opportunities like these. Besides, there was also this business of kicking a man who was down, even if he was sleeping. The incident was emblematic of the Colonel's attitude toward the men as a whole. It didn't set well with Sartain, making the decision easier.

"Well Lieutenant," said Todd, "You'll want to get rolling on this right away. I've already sent for a stenographer from the Judge Advocate's office at division, so as soon as I get word about that we can get started."

If the Private's defense council spoke to the man's battery commander, Captain Cargill, he would have been told that Goldfarb was essentially a good man, though perhaps not really cut out for the military life. There was a fraction of the men in every outfit like this. These were the men with the crooked necktie, the lost piece of equipment, or who were perennially out of step when marching in formation. They weren't troublemakers and they did their best to perform their duties, but military discipline and élan were outside of their nature. As one man who knew him commented, "Goldfarb was like a Sad Sack, one of those guys. He wasn't into it too much."

When Sartain met with his client he found a young man of about 21. Milton Goldfarb spoke with an accent which would have reminded anyone of subways, skyscrapers, and block on block of Brooklyn's four story tenement buildings. He also seemed frightened. Sartain asked Goldfarb what happened as he remembered it.

"Sir, I was looking for my flashlight lens. It came off and rolled underneath the bush. I was down under that cactus bush looking for it when Colonel Bertsch came up."

Goldfarb would have been asked directly if he was, in fact, asleep.

"Was I sleeping? Under the cactus bush? Well, sir, I guess it's possible. I mean, while

BATTERY!

I was down there, maybe I did fall asleep for a second, but I really crawled under there to look for my flashlight."

It was apparent to Sartain that the man was probably doing something other than searching for his lens. Years later, when asked about defending Milton Goldfarb, Sartain would say, "He crawled under that cactus bush to relax. I don't think there's any question about it. He wasn't hunting around for his flashlight; he was sleeping under the damn cactus bush." But whatever the case, Goldfarb deserved to be defended, and if he was going to be his defense council Sartain intended to do his best at the job.

Sartain thought for a minute, then spoke, "Goldfarb, you've got yourself in a serious situation, you understand that? This business of sleeping on post isn't just a lot of, you know, silliness." Goldfarb didn't respond, he sat looking at Sartain and waiting for him to finish. The Lieutenant continued, but now with some exasperation in his voice, "I mean, what on earth were you thinking anyway!"

"Sir, I know it was a stupid thing to do. Now I feel like a shmuck." Sartain drilled him. "Listen, you say you were looking for your flashlight or some such nonsense? You stick with that story. Don't embellish it. The prosecution will try to trip you in a lie, so the less you say the better, you see? The lens came off your flashlight, it rolled under the cactus, you went to get it and the Colonel came up and kicked you and that's all there is to it."

Goldfarb listened closely, was quiet for a moment, and then said, "Do you think you can help me Lieutenant Sartain?"

"I don't know, but I'll try," was the answer.

On the morning the court was held everyone involved in the case was gathered under one of the large mess tents. Despite the heat, they were all attired in their best dress khakis, complete with ties neatly tucked into their shirts. The defendant was present, seated beside his attorney. In the case of such Local, or Special, Court Martials, as they were sometimes called, there would be a jury composed of three officers. Defense councils were allowed the privilege of challenging and, in effect, rejecting any two of these, with their places filled by alternates. Once selection was finished, the most senior among these would act as presiding officer of the court, calling witnesses, ruling on objections and so forth. On this occasion the presiding officer was Captain Walter Bedingfield, the battalion surgeon whom Sartain had mistaken for the CO of "A" Battery nearly a year before.

"I challenged the first couple of officers and that's how Bedingfield ended up being chairman and presiding officer of the Goldfarb case," said Sartain, describing the courtroom strategy he was developing. In later trials, "If I represented a man at a special court in another battalion and particularly at General Court Martials, I always challenged the top two people. That gave us an even playing field."

Captain Biddingfield was the senior officer, so he was the presiding officer of the court martial. "I can visualize the panel with Biddingfield and all. I don't recall who else was in it but I recall Biddingfield. They could have been Captains, junior grade to him. He happened to have been the senior captain and he loved the authority. He loved it. You'd have thought he was Chief Justice Oliver Wendell Holmes! Bedingfield was an authority on what ever he thought he was an authority on. He would call the witnesses up, he'd swear them in. I was impressed with him."

In the normal sequence of a court martial the prosecution would first call its witnesses, with an opportunity following for the defense to cross examine. Next the defense called its own witnesses and the prosecution had its own chance to cross examine in turn.

The first witness called by the prosecution was Colonel Bertsch. "He had to testify about getting out and satisfying himself that the man was asleep on duty and all that humbug," remembered Sartain of the trial. "It did a little more to irritate the court martial, but that was alright. I left him alone. I didn't ask him one question."

The prosecution next called the Colonel's driver. His answers were vague and lacked dedication. Still Sartain declined to cross examine.

"Then Goldfarb took the stand," remembered Sartain. "He explained how he was looking for his flashlight, how it'd fallen and come apart and all that foolishness. Very sincere, he was very sincere. Made a good witness. Of course the prosecution didn't have his heart in the case to begin with."

"Then I called Bertsch's driver. I could call him under cross because he was a prosecution witness. I felt like I had a good chance of him not remembering anything being definite, so I called him on the cross. And sure enough he came through just like I thought he was gonna come through."

Sartain began by asking the driver if he could tell for a fact that Goldfarb was asleep when he drove up to the olive grove with Colonel Bertsch.

"No sir, I couldn't say for sure that he was," was the answer.

"You mean you didn't hear any snoring or see anything indicating he was sleeping?"

"No sir, I did not."

"How long," Sartain asked, "Would you say you had been there when Colonel Bertsch got out of the jeep?"

"Well sir, I would say he got out as soon as we came to a stop."

"And how long did it take before Colonel Bertsch kicked Private Goldfarb and placed him under arrest?"

"Only a couple of seconds, sir."

Commenting later, Sartain would say, "You know when you represent anybody in court you've got to know when to quit. And you never ask anybody a question unless you've got a pretty good idea what the answer is. I learned that with these lawyers I'd worked for."

Concluding arguments were delivered and the court recessed. A short while later everyone was reassembled. Goldfarb was visibly nervous but Sartain felt confident about how the verdict would go. He was correct in feeling this way because when Captain Bedingfield read the panel's findings, Private Goldfarb was found not guilty of all charges against him. Colonel Bertsch's face flushed red and twitched with rage.

Looking back on the case years afterward, Sartain made this observation, "They just didn't like the Colonel. It was the Colonel's word against everybody else's and so they really put the screws to the Colonel. The battalion in those days was fed up with hauling those damn rocks and straightening those tents out with an aiming circle to please ole Harry Bertsch. They were not about to back ole Bertsch up when he complained Goldfarb was sleeping on duty. Everybody had the red ass at the Colonel, and that's why we turned Goldfarb loose! Any other impartial jury would have found him guilty. I don't think the court martial would have put up with just anything, but I think if Bertsch, if he had just waited a little while to be sure Goldfarb wasn't moving and he was, in fact, asleep, OK. But no, he drove up and saw those feet out from under the cactus bush, he got out and he kicked him on the foot, that was it."

It was a humiliating outcome for Colonel Bertsch. He'd intended to make an example of Goldfarb but somehow his plans were turned upside down by a volunteer 2nd lieutenant.

Sartain was already known and well liked by the men in "A" Battery who'd known him for months as their "junior junior," the one who would willingly pick up cigarette butts up off the ground with them at Fort Bragg when placed in charge of details assigned to police the area. The guys in "C" Battery felt the same way. They were glad to have Sartain as their Exec once that battery was formed. He was one of the only officers they knew who'd never cut into the chow line ahead of them, instead always taking a place at the back. Now Sartain's popularity spread through "B" Battery and the rest of the battalion as well. He was already known as "an A-1 man" and now had a new reputation as "a defense lawyer for the average GI" as well.

The next day Colonel Bertsch had Sartain brought to his quarters. The Lieutenant entered, came to attention, and saluted. Bertsch made no sign of acknowledgement.

"Lieutenant, that was quite a display you pulled yesterday," he said flatly. "I suppose you fancy yourself some kind of lawyer. Another Eugene Debbs perhaps?"

Sartain would only have been able to say, "Sir, as Private Goldfarb's defense council I was obliged to defend him to the best of my ability."

"Well," harrumphed Bertsch, "in my opinion you're using your meager knowledge of the law to undermine the discipline of my command, do you understand?"

Sartain gave no reply. Colonel Bertsch added coldly, "You're dismissed." Lieutenant Sartain saluted, turned on his heel and walked out.

BATTERY!

Part 6: "If a bomb hits we won't know it anyway."

Never anticipating anything but a swift conviction of Private Goldfarb, Colonel Bertsch could do little to save face once the Not Guilty verdict was reached. If the embarrassing episode had taken place some weeks earlier it is doubtful the Colonel would ever have allowed Sartain to be appointed executive officer of "C" Battery. But such was not the case, and now, in the absence of some egregious error on the Lieutenant's part, there was little he could do about it except hope that some opportunity to even the score would present itself.

After the Goldfarb trial, training continued, now with three firing batteries. As had been the case at Camp Marnia, there were constant drills and competitions between batteries and among the individual gun crews, much of it at night. There was also a greater proportion of live fire practice than before, in anticipation of an inevitable invasion.

On one occasion shells fell among a Bedouin camp in the desert, resulting in a tragic mishap. Sartain's memory of the event was that, "We were having an artillery shoot and one of the rounds went astray. It killed two kids. So the 82nd or somebody settled with the family for the two children. I think it was 35 dollars per child, can you believe that?"

Whatever the actual details were, the incident was sobering. It was among the first of countless instances to follow in which blameless civilians were caught in the middle of a war where much of the time no distinction could be made between combatants and innocent bystanders.

In late July life at the Kairouan olive grove came to an end. The conquest of Sicily was nearly complete, but the efficacy of the invasion's airborne component was less than desirable, not from the standpoint of the performance of the troops themselves, which was admirable by anyone's standard of measure, but rather in the implementation of the principle of vertical envelopment. In other words, did large scale airborne operations really work? Despite the best of efforts, paratroopers had been dropped in small, wildly scattered and isolated groups instead of as cohesive units within an at least somewhat localized area. Repercussions of the disastrous error in which hundreds of airborne troops were shot out of the sky by the Allied Navy and land antiaircraft batteries during Husky continued. The feasibility of airborne operations on a divisional level was brought into serious question, with Eisenhower himself disinclined to support any drops larger than battalion size. In the looming invasion of Europe, use of the highly trained 82nd as part of a seaborne amphibious invasion of the Italian mainland became a more realistic option.

To accomplish this, a change of location became necessary and the pup tents were taken down. "After a period of training at Kairouan," wrote Captain Manning of this time, "We went by truck convoy through Tunis to Bizerte. At Bizerte we camped on the shores of the sea. Naturally, yours truly insisted on pitching the officer's tent on the highest and windiest bluff. Everything tasted like sand because it was sand."

IF A BOMB HITS WE WON'T KNOW IT ANYWAY.

Though Bizerte was fully ten miles to the south, their relative proximity to the city did have an advantage in the form of Arab vendors selling fresh fruit. Once camp was reestablished, training exercises immediately focused on those details particular to amphibious landings. Sosa, as a member of the "C" Battery motor pool especially remembered preparation of the jeeps and trucks. "They taught us how to waterproof the vehicles and then run them out there in the water and see if they really were waterproofed. The distributor head had to be covered with some kind of blackish stuff to keep the water out, the spark plugs and the wiring, you know. Then you run up a pipe for the exhaust system. That's about it. It worked fairly well, it worked to a point, but most of the time they weren't really waterproofed. It wasn't really successful but we did it anyway. A lot of the time you run the engine out there and they quit. Then you have to run a cable out there and off of one of the trucks and pull it out. They never did run too good after that."

Readying the howitzers was less involved, but still required pounds of Cosmoline for each piece, every ounce of which attracted a coating of sand on the wind swept beach.

After reveille one morning the men of each battery were taken to the water's edge. A buoy floating several dozen yards off shore was pointed out to them. According to Silas Hogg, an officer said, 'You see that?' We all looked at it, said, 'Yeah.' He said, 'Now you're gonna swim to it, swim around it and come in. If you can, that's what you're gonna do every day till we move.' Well hell, I was a little ole boy from the mountains, I couldn't swim halfway across the Atlantic. So, that's what we did."

In "A" Battery First Sergeant Johnson had a dilemma. "Yeah, Johnson. Johnson didn't know how to swim," remembered Casimir Sobon. "We being in the Mediterranean there, on the beach, swimming and all, they used to tease him all the time. He was a good sergeant, but he was scared in the water and he would holler, get out of here get out of here!"

Casimir Sobon of Newark, New Jersey. An excellent athlete, Sobon was a star player on the Battalion Basketball and baseball teams. He was attached to the Signals Section of "A" Battery.

Johnson wasn't alone in his fear of the water. Arno Mundt had deliberately volunteered for the army to avoid the navy. No doubt there were others, but they each overcame their fear, at least enough to take them out to the buoy and back.

A simulated amphibious landing was finally conducted in conjunction with the 325th Glider Infantry. The troops were trucked to Bizerte harbor where they were loaded aboard LCIs and LSTs. Once on board the mock invasion force was taken a short distance into the Mediterranean, then landed at a predesignated coastal location. Lieutenants Sartain and Torgersen were waiting for them there. "We went on some kind of training problem. It had to do with, well, I don't know what it had to do with but it had to do with observation or something about a seaborne landing exercise. I remember while we were on that trip me and Torgerson went by and looked at

Carthage," said Sartain.

This opportunity to engage in a little tourism was not unique. Periodically larger groups of personnel from the battalion were loaded into trucks and convoyed to the beaches around Souse and Sfax, the latter being selected for officers. These had been resort areas of the French colonials and other Europeans before the war. Many Vichy French who had the means to do so elected to wait out the hostilities in North Africa.

Lieutenant Sartain remembered the beach at Sfax vividly, "Everybody liked to go swimming there. We liked to watch the gals there change into their swim suits, their bikinis. They'd get under a blanket wrapped around them and their clothes would drop to the ground. Then they'd drop the blanket and they'd have on a damn bikini. We never could understand how they could do it under a blanket. These would be natives, but they weren't the Arabic ladies. They weren't the typical Arab woman because the typical Arab woman would never put on a bikini. There were a lot of European ladies over there, a lot of them. I don't know who it was but we enjoyed watching them."

Sfax was also one of the locations where locally produced goods of higher quality could be bought, and the prices were cheap – even in 1943 dollars. "There was a lot that done that," Sartain said, looking back on those trips to Sfax. "I could kick myself in the butt from when we were in North Africa and not buying one of those Persian rugs that were for sale for basically nothing. All these guys were buying them up like mad and sending them home. For fifty dollars you could buy a Persian rug that nowadays might sell for three, four thousand dollars."

Invariably these excursions involved singing at least a few verses of a ribald song circulating freely at the time. The lyrics of "Dirty Gertie from Bizerte" included:

Dirty Gertie from Bizerte
Hid a mousetrap 'neath her skirtie,
Strapped it to her knee-cap purty,
Baited it with Fleur-de-Flirte,
Made her boyfriends' fingers hurty,

Lieutenant Marvin Ragland led one of these expeditions of enlisted men to Souse. "The Colonel had me in charge of the convoy going down, two, three, maybe four trucks of men. I think Lieutenant Warren brought up the last vehicle. We went down there for that weekend and came back. When we got back Major Todd said, you're supposed to report to division headquarters. So I did. General Gavin was the one I reported to. You know, Ridgeway was CO, but Gavin was the one I reported to there."

He said, "We've got a complaint about you."

I said, "What's that?"

He said, "You took this convoy down to this area? General Patton was in his vehicle going the other way and no body saluted."

I said, "Well, I don't remember seeing that."

Gavin just said, "That's the report we got, so you're going to have to go back to your battalion and they're gonna give you some disciplinary action."

I went back to the battalion and Major Todd said, "Yeah, we've got to send in a report of what we're gonna do. I'm gonna send in the fact that you need more training in being in charge of convoys and so we'll just give you more training to do that."

"That was the end and I never heard any more about it. General Patton was mad because no body saluted him as he drove by, but Todd didn't seem to take it too seriously. Even Gavin, I had the feeling he wasn't too fired up about it."

As August, 1943, came to a close, the 319th Glider Field Artillery was again placed on alert. Men were restricted from leaving on passes and extraneous equipment was packed up in anticipation of an expected march order. On the morning of September 6th that order arrived and the seaside camp was rapidly taken down. The battalion moved into Bizerte itself, by late afternoon taking position alongside the docks where transports lay waiting to receive them.

That night the Luftwaffe launched a bombing raid against Bizerte harbor, knowing that a seaborne invasion of the Italian mainland was imminent. Since this location would be a major staging area for that force, the Germans were attempting to sink or disable as much of the gathering flotilla as possible before it was even under way. The guys in the 319th had seen air raids a couple of months previous while they were assembled for the Sicilian operation, but those raids were really more an exciting spectacle, quite some distance away with no real threat of harm. This time they were in the middle of it and that was a different experience. The night sky was full of searchlights, tracers and explosions from American antiaircraft fire, as well as the sounding of sirens and drone of Junkers JU-88 bombers.

In a mad scramble, everybody took cover as best they could. Several of the "C" Battery gang dove under the nearest vehicle. Corporal Girardin remembered, "We went underneath a truck. This guy says, 'Hey, you guys are under an ammunition truck!' We said, 'What's the difference, if a bomb hits we won't know it anyway!'"

It quickly became evident that the principle danger was not so much the enemy bombers as it was the fallout of spent machinegun bullets and shrapnel of aerial bursts. As Captain Manning remarked with irony, "Our first contact with war operations consisted in ducking the dropping flak from our own anti-aircraft batteries which were supposedly protecting us from German attack." A few men in the battalion were lightly injured by this shower of lead, while the rest of the men took the threat of death or harm from friendly fire as an insult to their martial spirit.

The raid did little to bolster the opinion the artillerymen had held of navy gunnery since Sicily. Failing to observe a single Luftwaffe bomber brought down, a lot of guys agreed with Ed Ryan when he complained that "Our navy couldn't hit the broad side of a barn if they were inside with the doors closed."

The next day Colonel Bertsch with the largest part of the battalion was loaded onto an LST or Landing Ship, Tank, probably LST-355. This included all of the vehicles, 105mm howitzers, machineguns, and other bulkier equipment.

Over a thousand flat bottomed LSTs were constructed during the Second World War, mostly at shipyards deep within the continental United States, hundreds of miles from any large body of water. These ships, measuring fifty feet across and 328 feet long, were capable of delivering tanks, trucks, halftracks, and any of the numerous other vehicles modern warfare demanded with up to 150 personnel. Carrying a crew of about 125 officers and sailors, a fully loaded LST could bring its bow up to an unimproved beach, pulling only eight feet of draft, open the bow doors and allow fully operational vehicles to drive directly into the shallow surf from its two decks. An enormously successful design, and one without which none of the Allies amphibious landings in Europe or the Pacific theaters could have been accomplished, no LSTs were ever named, instead bearing only their numerical designations.

The commanders of the 319th's firing batteries, accompanied by a cadre of their command structure, together with Major Todd and a group from battalion headquarters, meanwhile boarded on three smaller LCIs, or Landing Craft Infantry, being operated under lend lease agreement by the Royal Navy.

BATTERY!

With them on these craft were Company "H" of the 504th PIR, as well as elements of both the 80th antiaircraft and 307th Engineer Battalions. T/5 Ryan was aboard the LCI with "C" Battery's CO and his Exec.

Ryan was surprised to see a group of about twenty African colonial soldiers on board too. "Big tall black guys," he said. "They had rifles with triangular bayonets with three or four round loaves of bread on them. They were leading sheep right onto the boats. They were very black, wore turbans on their heads with shorts and were supposed to be real vicious."

Silas Hogg, on the same LCI with Ryan, remembered them too. His description was that, "They was real tall, about 6 foot 6 and carried big knives on their hips. They didn't have to have a gun, they could cut your head off in one swipe."

Known among sailors as "Elsies" or "Spitkits" the LCIs which the battery commanders boarded were a mere 158 feet long and at their widest measured 23 feet of beam. LCIs could approach a beach to within 5 feet, 4 inches of depth before grounding, at which time a pair of ramps on either side of the bow would be lowered for troops to disembark. Though capable of carrying up to 75 tons of cargo, the LCI was intended to bring just fewer than 200 infantry directly on to the beach, unload them and pull away within ten minutes, utilizing a dropped stern anchor to pull the craft away from shore and back into deeper water. The 24 man crew of a Spitkit would bring their passengers to their destination at a speed of about 15 knots, and while certainly never intended for ocean going duty or deep water sailing, the thousands of LCIs used during the war all had to be navigated across the Atlantic and Pacific Oceans in order to reach their respective theatres of operation.

The three Spitkits departed the harbor of Bizerte on the morning of September 8th. A few miles off shore the vessels came to a halt and drew within close proximity to each other. A public address system on the central vessel crackled and came to life. Over the loudspeaker broke the words, "Gentlemen, you have been selected to be among the spearhead for the invasion of the European mainland."

The address continued but the essence was already clear. Up to this point some of the men believed the gossip that this was to be the true invasion was only a rumor, maintaining the whole affair was just another simulated amphibious landing or something else tedious and inconsequential which they would not be allowed to write home about. Now they knew differently.

The next day, September 9th, the LST followed. Presumably there was a similar address given to the troops on board once the harbor was cleared. They may also have been told of the collapse of the fascist Italian government under Marshal Badaglio that very day. What the men in the battalion did not know at the time were the details of the original plan for their part in Operation Giant II, a swift move to seize Rome. As originally envisioned, the Giant II plan called for two parachute regiments of the 82nd to drop on and take the airport at Rome. In the meantime, the 319th would arrive by LST, travel up the Tiber River to Rome and support the troopers.

When Italian support proved untrustworthy this operation was canceled. Now, with the 319th and other supporting units already seaborne and under way it was decided to include them as an augmentation of Operation Avalanche, the seaborne invasion of the Italian mainland at Salerno. The battalion would land at the small Italian coastal village of Maiori to support the 1st, 3rd, and 4th Rangers under colonel William O. Darby at Chiunzi Pass.

Darby's Ranger Force, which included two groups of British Commandos and

IF A BOMB HITS WE WON'T KNOW IT ANYWAY.

a smattering of other American units, had landed before dawn on September 9th, about twenty miles north of the main Salerno landings. His mission was to seize the pass at Chiunzi and occupy the Sorento heights. From there the Rangers could cut highway 18, the principle German supply line leading from Naples to the Salerno beachhead and prevent the enemy from threatening the Allies' left flank.

While at sea, the LCIs and LST were redirected to report to the command Ship Ancon in the Gulf of Salerno where they would receive further orders from General Mark Clark, commanding the invasion force. ANCON was a large ship, bristling with antennas and radio equipment to coordinate the entire Salerno invasion, which had also begun early on the 9th.

About mid-day on September 10th, the LCIs pulled up alongside the vessel and the battery commanders went aboard for their briefing. "C" Battery's Captain Manning was astounded by what he saw on the ANCON. "It was almost like walking down the streets of a small city back home. They had shops of every description. Seeing the ship and all these things after our time on the plains of North Africa almost made us forget to attend the briefings."

While the battery commanders received their orders and news of the Italian defection at General Clark's headquarters, the enlisted personnel on the LCIs were treated to a shower of apples and oranges from the ANCON, whose sailors threw them down to the men on the deck of the landing craft. Ed Ryan remembered that one navy cook started tossing pork chops down as well. British naval ships had a reputation as being dirty, and the decks of the LCI were covered with a thick slimy layer of mud, sheep dip, vomit, and seawater, mixed together into a pasty mess. Men were fighting over the pork chops, picking them up off the deck and eating them. One sailor called out, "My God, they're eating them right off the deck!"

The battery commanders received their orders, then rejoined their men on the landing craft. Word spread among the men that they'd been ordered to proceed directly to Maiori, where they'd join Darby's Ranger Force and place themselves under his command. As the LCIs pulled away a navy submarine surfaced nearby. In a few minutes the

Postcard showing the beach at Maiori where the 319th landed. The seawall along which the advance group dug in is visible. Ragland collection.

sub's deck was covered with sailors in dungarees and chambray shirts who hollered out to them, "Win the war over there!"

The Spitkits were amidst an enormous armada of naval vessels of all kinds, and as long as they remained squarely within this flotilla there was safety in numbers. However, as they traveled northward along the Italian coast toward Maiori they drew away from the herd. In the late afternoon's setting sun an alarm was sounded at the sight of enemy aircraft. Immediately all land soldiers were ordered below deck to allow the British sailors unrestricted use of their antiaircraft machineguns. This was much more disconcerting than submarine alerts on the Santa Rosa ever were. The hatches leading on to the upper deck were sealed, leaving the men confined below to consider what drowning in the Mediterranean Sea, trapped in the hold of an LCI on a September afternoon in 1943 would be like. So much for being in the airborne!

After waiting out the air raid below deck the racket of the Elsie's 20mm machineguns ceased and the men were allowed back up into the open air. It was a relief to be up on top again, especially since everyone was back in their woolen OD uniforms and loaded down with a full compliment of field gear. Now the sun was down and flashes of artillery fire along the Salerno beachhead glimmered intermittently along the horizon.

As the landing craft approached the coast near Maiori some of the men could discern that the vessels seemed to be homing on a light shining from a tall structure, perhaps a church steeple. It was the dark of night, well after 10pm, and though Darby's Rangers were supposed to already be in possession of the village, this was still a combat zone. Everyone was well aware that the Luftwaffe was active and besides, mistakes happen easily in wartime - this might not even be the right location. Drawing closer, a beach of about 1000 yards wide could be made out. Other naval vessels were in the water nearby but that was not a guarantee that the men on the LCIs wouldn't come under fire once they started down the ramps.

It was a silent approach with not a sound coming from the shoreline, and then the men heard an anchor drop from the stern of each Spitkit. In the LCI carrying "C" Battery's advance team the next sound was the grinding of the hull as it scraped against a submerged sandbar and came to a halt. Immediately the ramps were dropped into an undetermined depth of water. The skipper of the LCI told the men on his craft, "Go and get them!" The men aboard found that they'd been let off in nearly three feet of water and had perhaps twenty yards to reach the shore. The other two LCIs seem to have come in closer before dropping their ramps. The beach at Maiori had a fairly steep grade, so those craft were able to come very close to the water's edge and debark the men without getting their feet wet. Wet or dry, eventually everyone scurried on to the sand and across the beach to a retaining wall several dozen yards inland.

The GIs were both relieved and a little surprised at the complete absence of enemy presence, or, for that matter, Rangers. Captain Rogers, the battalion communications officer had his .45 automatic drawn and was directing men up the beach, pointing his weapon one way and another as he did so. Somebody remembered hearing Major Todd remark to him, "For God's sake Rogers, put that thing away before you shoot someone! At the wall the men were assembled. "They said to dig in," Ryan told of the event years later. Entrenching tools were unsheathed and put to work in the darkness. "It was sandy and I was digging in on this beach. The guy next to me was filling my hole up faster than I could dig it," he added, evidently still annoyed.

When a plane, presumably German, flew over the village and dropped a flare, everyone remained still, as they'd been taught to do. After the flare burned itself out there was a lot of hushed chatter about an air raid or artillery barrage which could reasonably be expected after being sighted. Sergeants told the more talkative to shut up and get back to work on their foxholes. Though nothing followed, all those on the Maiori beach were left feeling very exposed, even in the dark.

While "C" Battery's headquarters crew was entrenching itself along the retaining wall a lieutenant came up to them. "He wanted volunteers to go up in town," Ryan said. "I didn't like where I was so I volunteered. Took about seven or eight of us. Banging on doors and stuff to find out if there were any Krauts." There weren't, but the patrol did come across some Rangers and a German 88mm gun mounted on a flat-bed truck, plainly knocked out by Darby's men the day before.

Over among the "A" Battery crew, Lieutenant Ragland took a similar group up from the wall to probe the village. He made contact with the Ranger Force too. Word was sent back to Major Todd that the village was clear and held by Darby, so the battery advance crews left their foxholes and climbed over the wall.

Captain Manning wrote, "We gradually felt our way across the highway and into some garden-vineyard areas. After everyone was accounted for, we decided to wait for morning to assess the situation."

Once Major Todd established communication with Darby's headquarters he was instructed to send parties from each battery out of Maiori and up into the mountain range to scout out battery locations and points of observation. In "C" Battery it was decided that Lieutenant Sartain should be the one to take a radio crew and reconnoiter the new positions, while Captain Manning stayed in the village and made a rendezvous with the battery as soon as the LST carrying the trucks and guns arrived.

With a few Rangers as guides, the group started out of town. Radioman Ryan was one of those selected for this party. With him went Ed Conover, a guy from Mount Holly, New Jersey. "I had to lug this stuff around. Conover, he had a Thompson and was supposed to protect me," explained the radioman.

In fact, most members of the airborne field artillery felt under armed with what the army gave them as a personal weapon. The .30 caliber M-1 Carbine had a poor reputation. To begin with it was universally regarded as underpowered and unreliable in all but ideal conditions. Another common complaint was that the weapon was inaccurate. The airborne version with its folding wire stock and pistol grip was all the more difficult to fire with any reliability, earning it the nickname of "M-1A1 Malfunctioning Stock Carbine" by many airborne troopers who carried them.

As one battalion man put it, "If they got a little dirty or you got to shooting it too much or too fast they would jam."

Ed Ryan agreed, saying, "They weren't any good. A little speck of sand and they would hang up."

Another 319th man was more blunt when he said, "I'd have been better off using a .22! That folding carbine was a piece of junk!"

Almost immediately some of the men in the 319th started to re-arm themselves when the opportunity came to do so. Ed Ryan may have been among the first, "We started up the mountain that night. On the way out of town I picked up an Italian carbine. It was lying by some dead Ginzo soldier that must have been killed by Darby's men. I kept it, it was better than mine. I hid it and brought it with me. Ammunition was no problem since cartridges of all kinds were plentiful and some Kraut ammo fit it."

Through the night the scouting party made its way up a winding mountain road. As they climbed higher and higher, they began to hear the distinct report of machinegun

BATTERY!

bursts intermittently echoing among the hills. They were already familiar with the sound of the American .30 caliber light machinegun. German weapons were immediately recognized by their buzzsaw rate of fire. Along the way officers made frequent reference to their maps, conferring with the Rangers who were guiding them as to where they were and what these areas looked like in daylight.

It took time, all night really, to reach the heights on the ridge, and hauling up the SCR-610 radio was a heck of a job. Once on top, the Rangers explained the situation. Their positions here on the mountain were thinly held, but in the light of day the view was magnificent. Ahead was the plain of Naples extending for miles. Artillery would have unlimited targets in view to choose from, in addition to the highways leading from Naples to Salerno and all the enemy vehicular traffic they carried. Behind could be seen the entire bay of Salerno with all its current naval activity. Battleships, cruisers, LCIs, and LSTs, you could see them all from up here.

The Rangers themselves seemed like a rough and tumble lot but definitely a high morale unit of the kind the airborne men were used to. Darby's men were combat veterans of North Africa and Sicily who wore short, spats like leggings. After talking with the 319th team some more, the Rangers added that with so much ground to cover German raiding parties and infiltrators were impossible to keep from working their way behind the forward positions. This meant that movement outside of Maiori after nightfall was still dangerous and one had to be careful whenever traveling between the village and the mountain tops.

After digging a foxhole into the gravelly pumice stone, Sartain made note of suitable locations on his map for the battery just behind the ridge, then settled down and caught an hour or two of sleep in the time remaining before dawn.

Meanwhile, for most of the battalion September 10th had been spent aboard the slower moving LST as it approached its rendezvous with the ANCON, where contact was made after midnight of the 11th. Colonel Bertsch received his orders from General Clark to proceed immediately to Maiori. The LST was underway before dawn and by early that morning was in the vicinity and approaching the seashore village. Numerous other naval ships were in the bay. Several of these were LSTs loaded with the 307th Airborne Engineers and 80th Anti-Aircraft Battalions. The British Monitor HMS Roberts, looking out of place with her archaic 19th century design, was there too, as well as the American light cruisers Philadelphia and Savannah.

By 09:30 the 319th's LST was in the midst of these ships, actually a half mile or less from Savannah, when a flight of 12 Focke-Wulfe 190s were seen approaching from the north. They were doing their best to drop bombs onto the cruisers. Both Savannah and Philadelphia turned all their antiaircraft guns against the Germans, as did those mounted on other auxiliary smaller vessels in the immediate area.

One of the dropped bombs narrowly missed the USS Philadelphia. The explosion momentarily raised her entire stern out of the water, then slammed it back down again. Savannah was lying still at sea, awaiting fire missions on inland targets from artillery and naval forward observers when the raid started. She immediately rang up all the speed she could and got underway. After all, moving targets, even big ones, were harder to hit.

Bob Storms was situated among the battalion vehicles on the LST when the air raid started. Her 20 and 40mm guns were going like mad. He remembered the incident clearly, "We were getting attacked by planes. We were loaded on this boat to make the invasion. I was on a truck, big ten wheeler loaded with ammunition, and up on top of the cab I had a fifty caliber mounted on it. So when I seen the plane coming I jumped under the truck. It was a fighter plane coming down through and he was dropping bombs at the ships. I don't know what I thought I was gonna do because if it hit the truck I'd never knowed it."

None of the Focke Wolfes scored a hit, and with all their bombs expended there was little else they could do but return to base to re-arm. At first thinking the danger was passed, another aircraft was then spotted by the soldiers and sailors. John Girardin remembered that the single German plane, later identified as a Dornier-217 twin engine bomber, "Was way, way up there. Everybody was pointing, saying, hey, do you see that? Can you see that plane up there?"

"He was up so high," continued Storms, "Everybody was hollering fire, fire, fire! I said, it's not for me to fire at. He's way too high. This one plane that was way up, he was coming along and it looked like something, like smoke, left the plane. I thought it was way past the ship, then the smoke made a big arch and come right on back at the cruiser Savannah. It hit number three gun turret and boy, people flew all over."

In observing that the smoke trail literally turned around in mid air, Storms was correct. What he'd seen was an FX "Fritz" radio controlled bomb. The Fritz was, in fact, the first guided missile, and the Savannah was the first naval vessel to be struck by such a weapon. For the British and American servicemen who saw them in flight it was quite an amazing thing to see.

The missile penetrated 34 inches of steel, exploded below deck and blew up an ammunition magazine. From the LST the men in the 319th could see that the turret had been literally blown on its side and flames were racing across the ship. The series of explosions left gaping holes in the hulls bottom and sides. Two hundred and eighteen sailors were killed outright and dozens, if not hundreds of others were wounded.

Flying at about 18000 feet when it released the missile, the German Dornier was well above the ceiling at which most anti-aircraft guns mounted on ships, not to mention 50 caliber machineguns, could have any chance of hitting their target. This meant that the Germans were able to launch their new weapon from a comfortable and safe distance from its intended target, having to only worry about Allied fighters. The design was revolutionary. Put to immediate and widespread use it could have had a catastrophic effect on naval operations. Fortunately for the navy, the army overran a Luftwaffe airfield near Fogia a few days later and uncovered a cache of nearly 2000 of the innovative projectiles.

Lieutenant Sartain was sitting atop Mount San Angelo, discussing targets with a British naval forward observer from the Roberts when his attention was drawn to the German air raid. "I never will forget, like I told you, sitting on the top of that mountain and watching that USS Savannah get hit. There was a naval gunfire officer sitting right next to me when that happened. You could hear it but it took a while for the sound to get to us. You could see the fire mushroom up and then the ship put the buzzer on. Then they kept making a circle. About three destroyers showed up and stayed with them. Eventually they got the fire out, but I think they had to tow the ship off."

In fact, the steering mechanism was damaged and nearly 20% of the ships lower compartments flooded. It wasn't until nearly 1800 hours that evening that the Savannah was in any condition to limp off to a dry dock in Malta.

Back on the LST there was a good deal of commotion. Charlie Spainhour, from Battery "A," felt this would be a good time to hold a prayer meeting. Several gathered together, kneeling in a circle on the deck, asking God for protection and courage in the face of death. Because it was never too late to get right with the Lord, a few joined in this time who'd had nothing to do with religious services before.

Some of those who'd insisted that Storms open up on the DU-217 with his .50 caliber machinegun began to hurl accusations. "They try to tell me I'm a coward because I wouldn't fire. I refused to fire, you know. So they turned me in to the Captain. Somebody turned me in.

He said, "So what the hell you refused to fire your gun? I know you're not that kind. What happened?"

"I says, Cap, that guy's up there fifteen, twenty thousand feet, my gun won't reach him. Why should I burn a barrel out just to send up a lot of bullets?"

He said, "Well, I see your point there."

I said, "Them guys don't know what my gun can do. All they want is me to shoot all the time. No sense shooting at a plane up there."

"Oh," he says, "No, they didn't tell me that."

"A" Battery's Captain Loughmiller would have been on one of the LCIs and already on shore at Maiori by this time, so the Captain whom Storms had his audience with was probably an officer from the Headquarters Battery, or an "A" Battery lieutenant; perhaps Vernon Blanc or Harry Warren. Whomever it was they could see the logic in the machine gunner's actions and the matter was left as it was.

With the landings disrupted by the havoc on the Savannah, and obliged to stand by until the anti-aircraft and engineer battalions were debarked, it was nearly 2300 hours before the LST was cleared to make landing at Maiori. Even though American troops, including advance elements of the 319th had been landing there for the past two days, the average GI on the landing ship was ignorant of this. Viewing the retaining wall as they drew closer, men mumbled amongst themselves about German machineguns set up along the top. Yet the shore was utterly silent except for the sound of a couple of barking dogs.

The LST came to ground on the steep Maiori shoreline and opened its bow doors. In a matter of minutes the beach became a flurry of activity. There were trucks, howitzers, jeeps and officers directing men and material to and fro. Private Sosa drove his jeep off the ramp and on to the sand. Storms, Girardin, Rappi, and Kenny Smith were all there too. Some men noticed Colonel Bertsch with a cluster of battalion officers, hovering over a map spread out on the beach. With them was a tough looking character hunkered down, a cigarette gripped between his lips as he spoke, pointing to locations on the map. It was Colonel Darby.

Shortly the conference broke up and Colonel Bertsch with his battery commanders departed the beach on a forward reconnaissance to the area proposed for the 319th's gun positions. Unloading the LST entirely and getting the battalion organized took a few more hours. While this was being done each battery's vehicles were collected at a holding area until radio communications instructed them to move out.

About 0130, Batteries "A" and "C" were ready to go. The order was received and the column started off, first threading its way through Maiori and then slowly ascending the same mountain road the scouting parties had taken the night before. Aside from jeeps pulling trailers, the convoy mostly consisted of two and a half ton trucks either loaded with supplies or pulling the 105s with their crews riding in back. "When we went into Italy we had a two and a half ton truck pulling us," said Corporal Rappi. "A jeep pulled that 75 mm gun, but we had a six by six pulling the 105s. Going up that road from the beach into the Italian country, the curves were so short that the trucks had a hell of a time getting around some of them corners. Very narrow roads and sharp corners, they had to go back and forth to get around some of them."

There was a real chance one or more of the trucks might slip off the edge and perhaps down the mountainside. At one point Girardin was handed a flashlight and told to walk several feet in front of the truck he was in and indicate with his flashlight where the edge of the road was. "The trucks didn't have any headlights, just those slits, those cat's eyes. So I had to walk in front with the flashlight and guide them." This was how the convoy made its way to the base of the mountain.

About 0330 hours Battery "C" stopped while Battery "A" continued up the road. They seemed, in the darkness, to be amidst a grape vineyard on the mountainside, at a spot where a small shelter was built. Adjacent to this shelter was a spring which fed an irrigation system among the grapes. Beside the spring began a trail leading up to the spine of Mount Saint Angelo, where a fight was developing over control of the heights.

Sartain had already come down from the OP established the night before. When the battery arrived he was impatient to brief Manning on what he'd seen and assume his duties as XO. He told him excitedly, "You can see the whole German army from up there, Johnny, traveling along highway 18 from Naples. Trucks, armored vehicles, all kinds of nonsense. All the way from Vitri, on our right, past Sarno, to Nocera, to Tore Anunziata, that's twenty miles away, it's nothing but gas dumps and bivouacs, motor parks, there's even a damn hospital with a red cross painted on the roof!"

Manning was anxious to get up there and see for himself. It sounded like an artillery officer could have a field day just firing on targets of opportunity, and he wanted to be there at dawn to get started. Looking over to his driver, Manning said, "Wilson, would you get us some coffee?"

Sartain pulled his pipe out of his shirt pocket, opened the silver lid which was affixed over the bowl, and lit his tobacco. He puffed up the fire in his pipe, then snapped the lid down. Sartain urged his friend to go, assuring him that he'd take care of setting up the guns. "It's quite a climb up there John," he warned, and added, "but it's worth it."

Wilson brought over two canteen cups with lukewarm, day old Sanka. Manning and Sartain took them and drank. The two officers were in deep conversation over what each had seen since leaving Bizerte, especially since the landing. All the while the members of "C" Battery were manhandling their 105mm howitzers into position, putting up camouflage nets, digging pits for the ammunition, setting up the aiming stakes, and digging their own foxholes. The same was happening with the guys in "A" Battery, which had stopped at its gun position about two miles further up the road. At 0430 hours, according to the battalion's daily journal, both Captains Loughmiller and Manning radioed in that their batteries were in position and ready to accept their first fire mission of the Second World War. Manning turned and, with his collection of wiremen, a lieutenant, and FO team, disappeared up the trail.

BATTTERY!

Part 7: "Darby of the Rangers."

Darby's landing at Maiori caught the enemy off guard, but the Germans opposing the Ranger force were rapidly positioning themselves to retake the Sorrento Heights
if possible. At very least they intended to prevent a thrust out of Chiunzi Pass which
would threaten their rear at Salerno. The 1st Panzer Grenadier Regiment and the re-
nowned Hermann Goering Parachute Division were chosen for this assignment. All day
long on the 10th and 11th, German pressure increased as they continued to concentrate
their firepower in the valley beyond the heights. Large numbers of mortars, 88mm guns,
and Nebelwerfer rocket launchers began to pepper the hilltops, as well as the countryside
between the heights and Maiori.

Though the Rangers had achieved their D-Day objectives, and were in fact the
only invasion force to do so, Darby lacked sufficient strength to take the town of Nasara
astride Highway 18 and cut the Germans off. Indeed, the Ranger force lacked heavy
weapons and was thinly stretched across the heights from Vitri pass to the tip of the peninsula. With so few men at his disposal, Darby's line was porous, even if he did hold the
high ground and passes.

At 0430 hours on September 12th, according to the battalion's daily journal,
both "A" and "C" Batteries radioed that they were in position and ready to accept their
first fire missions of the war. "B" Battery, possibly delayed at the beach waiting for its
equipment to be unloaded, followed the other two batteries by about 90 minutes and
reported itself ready to go at 0600 hours.

Meanwhile, Manning and his team were making their way up the trail, which
was in places so steep that one was really climbing, pulling oneself along with both arms
and legs. While ascending the mountain a party of German infiltrators made an attack
at the crest. As they were climbing, the glidermen heard hell break loose between the
Germans and Rangers above them. Manning recalled that "Just before we arrived at the
observation post area it had been over run in a surprise raid. We had to work our way
through bodies to get our posts set up."

Once on top the 319th, crew was welcomed to the fight by the Rangers who
looked forward to the badly needed artillery support. Until dawn there was little else to
do.

The Captain improved the time with a couple of hours sleep. "I remember establishing a foxhole for myself on our side of the ridge, wrapping up in a blanket at the
bottom of the hole and going to sleep for the night," wrote Manning. "In the morning
I noticed something draping over the edge of the hole. I moved cautiously to see what
was going on. In the night we had been sent some Gurkhas as reinforcements, and I was
being guarded by one with one of the longest knives I had seen yet!"

The "Gurkhas" which Manning refers to here are puzzling. Darby mentions
neither British nor French Colonial troops with his Ranger force. Yet both Captain Manning and Ed Ryan clearly remembered some group of dark skinned colonial troops on
the LCI and atop the Sorrento Heights. Ryan's description of their bayonets as long and
needle like are consistent with the French LeBelle rifle widely issued during the First
World War and carried by their native regiments during the Second. It is most likely

that these men were part of the (French Expeditionary Force (CEF), which was known to have participated in the fighting in Sicily and on the Italian mainland. The CEF included Senegalise, Moroccan, and Algerian regiments, as well as at least one Moroccan Mountain unit. Records about the CEF are sparse, but normally state that none of these troops were on the Italian mainland before November, 1943. That elements of specialized mountain troops would be incorporated into the force composed of American Rangers and British Commandos is not implausible, especially considering the terrain they expected to be fighting on, but has not been confirmed independently.

As morning came on Manning could see for himself what Sartain had told him. The valley below stretched for miles and was an artilleryman's dream. He immediately began to confer with the Ranger officers and a British naval observer about which targets were priorities. The enemy was up early too and already had the range. A Nebelwerfer battery let loose, sending three dozen rockets in ten seconds streaming toward the American positions.

Ed Ryan had been up on top since the night of the 10th and well remembered the rocket attack. "The first time those rocket launchers fired on the hill at Maiori I was sitting in the OP. These things come screaming up the hill. It sounded like a cow dying! Everybody got their military book out trying to figure out what it was."

Not so the Rangers, who'd already been exposed to the unnerving, whine of the "Screaming Meemies" in Sicily. The Nebelwerfer was an electrically ignited array of either six 150mm, or five 210mm rocket tubes mounted on an artillery chassis or on the back of a vehicle. It could fire high explosives, smoke, gas, or illuminating rockets as called for. Though without a doubt destructive, this weapon incorporated an additional element of terror by the unearthly pipe organ whine its rockets produced, giving it a psychologically demoralizing value which conventional artillery could not match. Capable of delivering a high number of rounds clustered in a small area very quickly, the Nebelwerfer did have one serious drawback for its user in the distinctive smoke trail leading directly from a rocket in flight back to its launch site. This made the Nebelwerfer batteries particularly vulnerable to counter battery fire if they were not moved at once after each discharge.

The observers atop Mount de Chiunzi immediately radioed the map coordinates to the 319th Fire Direction Center. At 0745 hours "C" Battery executed the first fire-mission of the war for the battalion when it cut loose with 85 rounds directed at the rocket battery. The gunners of "C" Battery fired their howitzers at a furious rate of about one round every 45 seconds for their first fire mission. Fifteen minutes later a 65 round barrage on a troop bivouac was ordered. At the same time as "C" Battery's second fire mission, "A" Battery fired their first shots, a 21 round concentration on a crossroads junction.

Battalion records regularly refer to the Sorento heights which lay before the 319th as "the mask" because it effectively blocked from view everything beyond the crests, including all their targets. So mountainous was this countryside that standard methods of laying out the guns and range tables were inadequate to the topography. Assuming that the 105mm howitzer was placed on reasonably level ground, the gun had a maximum elevation of 548 mills, or about a 55 degree angle. Yet the crests before them had in most places an elevation in excess of 50 degrees, meaning that just clearing the top presented an immediate challenge.

The men on the gun crews saw at once that setting up a GP at this location could be a problem. "We just looked through the tube. That's the thing you do when you get into position, you look through the tube and bring it up until you can't see the mountain anymore," explained gunner Rappi during one of my first interviews with him. "If you can't see the mountain then that was minimum elevation, but that wasn't the right way to do it. That's not a very accurate assumption because the projectile has an arc to it and you got to give it a little more elevation. They gave us an elevation that was below the minimum. Our battery called back in but they said fire anyway. It hit the top of the mountain and a big boulder started rolling down! There must have been a ravine ahead of us that it got hung up in. I don't know why they fired below the minimum elevation."

In fact, experience would show that in order to reach many targets a quadrant elevation as high as 700 mills were required. To gain an even higher elevation, crews had to dig pits beneath the gun trails.

So it began, Batteries "A" and "C" delivered thirteen concentrations of fire that day. Their targets included enemy artillery, a truck convoy, a locomotive with four cars attached, bivouac areas and truck parks. The high angle fire was a problem to be overcome and concentration points needed to be registered, but the battalion was off to a good start. Fire missions quickly became routine and the gunners were in no doubt of their work, especially as observation of their hits came rolling in.

Rappi reflected the confidence the gun crews had when he said, "That gun would shoot quite a ways. 105 probably shot farther than the 75, but it was very similar. We got accustomed to it. It was a nice gun. In fact, I think we could get rid of the number five man because, as a split trail, it could handle the recoil better. You were closer to the aiming stakes. It's usually the first two three rounds that you fire, then it really sinks in, the trail sinks in."

Highway 18 curved around the base of Monte Chiunzi and St. Angelo on the side opposite the sea. It was thus generally in dead space for conventional naval and artillery fire as it went through Pagani, Nocera Inferiore, Nocera Superiore, and Cava. Mortars were designed for this kind of problem, and Darby did have a unit of 4.2 chemical mortar troops with him, but they were completely dedicated to firing on the wide gaps between Ranger strongpoints.

Looking back on the eventual answer to the battlefield conditions facing them, Captain Manning said, "One of the problems we tried to solve was being able to hit the target areas on the forward slope. The 105's had five powder bags in each shell, and Sartain came up with the thought that we might be able to drop the rounds closer to the ridge by removing some of the powder. The bags were of different sizes, so we had lots of possibilities to work with."

Sartain agreed when he commented on this same issue, saying, "We had to do something to get those shells over that ridge in front of us. We didn't have the high angle firing tables with us, so we just played with it until we had enough to get it over that hill."

Back at "A" Battery, Captain Loughmiller was also experimenting with different powder bag combinations, and no doubt Captain Cargill's "B" Battery was as well. All three batteries were learning to cope with the challenges unique to their location in relation to targets. When "B" Battery dropped a short round among the hilltop positions of the 1st Rangers, their Captain Sam sought out Manning, knowing he was an artillery officer from the same battalion. The Ranger Captain "told me very succinctly what my fate would be if one of those rounds hurt some one." Though the threat probably had some genuine anger behind it, the Rangers and the 319th worked well together.

DARBY OF THE RANGERS.

Contact with the Rangers, particularly if it involved Colonel Darby, often produced colorful stories. According to "A" Battery machine gunner Bob Storms, Darby came through the battery position and took notice of his battery's gunnery. Recalling it from memory, Storms said, "What was his name? Darby of the Rangers. We fought with his bunch there one time. He liked our guys to fight with too! He was watching our guys; because you got so much mountain and hills you can't always shoot an artillery piece. Well, he got the biggest kick out of our bunch. He'd hear our guys say, they want charge three and two cans of rations or charge four and one can of ration. So he come up and asked our officer, what the hell is this charge so and so and so many cans of rations? The guy said, 'I'll show you.' He showed them what place they want to hit. Well with the regular charges you're either over or under. So you fill up a ration can of powder and dump it in there extry and it'll be just enough to do just what you wanted. He used to say that was the damndest bunch of fighting he ever saw, but it done the job."

Ed Ryan said he also heard references to the use of loose powder over his radio up on the mountain. Yet it is worth noting that neither he nor Storms was on a howitzer crew at the time. Darby did visit the 319th's CP, and no doubt the challenges of effective firing over the mask were discussed between Colonel Bertsch and the Ranger force commander. That a demonstration was made of the mix and match solution for Darby's benefit is reasonable and would have been easy to arrange, but did 319th gunners really add loose powder to their shells to achieve the exact charge for their targets? Robert Rappi was a gunner throughout his time in the battalion. While he recalls handling individual powder bags in Italy, his opinion is that use of loose powder would have been unlikely. Sartain's comment on this particular question was stronger when he said, "We never cut that bag and measured that powder in a ration can. No no no."

Suggesting this was never the practice, at least in "C" Battery. In the end the story might be an exaggeration or it could have been describing a genuine adaptation used by that battery on that day. The one certainty is that Darby seems to have been the kind of man who attracted legends regardless of the literal objective facts.

Over the passing days many check points were registered upon, after which it became possible to deliver accurate concentrations almost anywhere within the zone of fire. Manning's final evaluation was that "we were successful to some extent, but did not perfect the exercise to the level Colonel Bertsch expected. He would have liked full charts of powder selections and resultant ranges!"

September 13th began with all three batteries firing from daybreak. A motor park, an ammunition dump, and another rocket battery were among other targets. Early on "A" Battery's GP started to be the object of sporadic mortar fire, accented at points with 88mm shells. As late morning approached the shelling increased.

According to the battalion's after-action report, "On one occasion, several stacks of ammunition were set afire. Lieutenant Warren, Battery "A," together with Sergeant Carl Davis and four other enlisted men distinguished themselves by seizing fire extinguishers and putting out the flames. So well was the battery dug in that only four men were wounded as a result of the enemy fire."

Corporal Mundt was one of them. "I can't remember the shell that got me and three others, but the red hot feeling running through my chest was unmistakable. One of the other guys had fallen on his back, the shrapnel ripped through his face and took one eye out." The men were taken by ambulance to a PT boat which whisked them out to a British hospital ship lying off shore.

It eventually became impossible for Captain Loughmiller's crews to continue at their guns. Their last fire mission for the day was registered at 0910 hours.

Sergeant Bob McArthur looked back on the barrage in a later letter home, observing, "Believe me, when they get the range on you there's nothing you can do but leave in a hurry. Everybody in my battery has been run out of our battery position by German artillery. These damn Germans can really use artillery too!"

Something was afoot. Enemy fire was heavy, getting louder, and signs were that at least one force of unknown strength had somehow worked its way behind the mask. About 1130 hours Colonel Darby appeared at the battalion command post, perhaps to determine why one of Bertsch's batteries had gone silent. No doubt Colonel Bertsch and the Ranger force commander discussed the problems "A" Battery was having and the overall pressure the Germans were exerting that day.

About this time, Lieutenant Lewis took a crew of "A" Battery FO and communications people up the mountain to the 1st Ranger's position. Covais was among those chosen, and given the events at the battery that morning, thought it a good break. Since none of the guys with Lewis had been up the mountain before, a group of 1st Ranger Battalion men were also there to guide them up the trail. By the time the contingent left the battery position the heights were also starting to take mortar fire. Halfway up the mask Covais had a close call. Artillery rounds and mortar bursts were landing at irregular intervals as they climbed, throwing pumice stone, dangerous chunks of granite, and bits of grape vineyard across the mountainside. The next round Covais heard came screeching down from straight above. This time it had a different quality, gaining in intensity a split second more quickly or perhaps a half octave higher in pitch. The Corporal threw himself to the ground just as the shell exploded less than twenty feet behind him. Under normal circumstances a strike this close would at least cause some injury from concussion, but the slope on this part of the trail was so near to vertical that the entire blast was directed downhill. When he got back to his feet Covais looked behind and saw that the two Rangers bringing up the rear and next in line were lying with their faces to the sky, quite dead.

The situation became more unsettled. Shortly before 1600 hours a message was received that a force of between 150 and 200 German infantry were approaching the "B" Battery position from its rear. Appearances were that the Germans had busted their way through the pass. A few minutes later another report came in to the battalion command post. This time a prisoner, evidently a member of the Hermann Goering Division had just been taken at one of the outposts. Colonel Bertsch issued a march order to "B" Battery and had them reposition themselves in a location from which their fire could be brought against the enemy's breakthrough.

Next, "A" Battery was attacked from the rear by the enemy raiding party. With the battery emplaced so near to Chiunzi Pass, the enemy were upon them immediately on forcing their way through the defile. The men were already down in their foxholes when they realized they were taking small arms fire as well as artillery. Unfolding their stocks, they began to return fire with their carbines. The defense was a rare example of artillerymen actively defending their gun positions with personal weapons during World War Two. If it were not for the arrival of a strong force of American infantry sent to intercept the Germans, the outcome could have been a disastrous one for the battery. As it was the attack was beaten off, but at the cost of one man killed and another wounded.

When the Germans penetrated to the rear of the mask that afternoon, they threatened not only the "A" Battery gun position, but the battalion machinegun crews and the forward observers' Ops on the Chiunzi heights as well. For a while it looked like the enemy was seizing the pass and turning Darby's flank. Storms remembered the attack on that day and the confusion of battle for those in the midst of it, saying, "I was way over on the left there. We had an attack from some Germans. Yeah, they had quite a battle that one afternoon. You couldn't see or know what was going on, they just push it, a lot of firepower both ways. They finally gave up and went out of there."

Corporal Covais had only just reached the summit after his hair raising climb when machinegun fire began spraying the area. Decades later Covais said, "I was up there at the forward observation post with a group of other guys. They were off a little distance and everyone was engaged in digging holes, digging foxholes. I had my binoculars out, viewing the enemy, and I heard machinegun shots being fired from behind. I was digging my trench with my shovel but I didn't get all the way down the way I should have when I heard this firing. What it was, the Hermann Goering Division got behind our lines. So I had to make a quick decision. I was sticking out there like a sore thumb. I figured, if they shoot my head off I'm dead, if they shoot my feet off I've got a chance to live. So I put my butt side down into the hole with my feet sticking up in the air, like that, and I put my head below the level of the ground, and I thought, well, I'm not gonna move my feet, so maybe I won't be noticed. That's how I survived that. It seemed like an eternity, but who knows, it's hard to say."

After the attack on "A" Battery was repulsed, Loughmiller's men got some relief from the day's artillery as well. Not so for those on the ridge-top. The Ops of all three batteries were getting a steady rain of fire, "a real shellacing," as one put it, throughout the late afternoon and it became necessary for the FOs to be pulled in or constantly relocated. There were also a few more men wounded, including Captain Loughmiller while he was making observations from the crest.

Early that evening Darby directed Colonel Bertsch to detach one of his batteries to accompany some of his Rangers on a mission near Vitri, where the Germans seemed ready to break through the pass located near that town. "A" Battery was selected and prepared itself to displace, but just as they started loading the German artillery opened up again. Though with difficulty, "A" Battery hitched up the guns amidst bursting shells and made it out. By the time the battery reached Maiori the German threat had been blocked and Darby ordered Loughmiller back to his previous gun position. The directions were followed and the battery was re-established in a new GP about 3/4 of a mile further from the pass and closer to the other batteries. The new position allowed "A" Battery to bring fire to bear on the pass itself, as well as Mount Saint Angelo. It also offered a better chance for Loughmiller's battery to defend itself should the Germans come pouring through again.

It was an exhausting day for everyone in the battalion. Manning's battery alone fired an impressive 573 rounds, spread over six large fire missions. Before it was through the battery had destroyed a Nebelwerfer battery, torn apart a truck park and a motor convoy, and exploded an ammo dump camouflaged in an orchard. Bob Cargile's "B" Battery fired 272 rounds at similar targets and was relocated after its GP was threatened. Loughmiller's "A" Battery was mauled, with six or seven men wounded and another killed, it's CO wounded, ammunition catching fire, and the GP both shelled and attacked by infantry, but it held together and still had plenty of fight left in it. To finish it off the battery packed up, drove to Maiori, then came right back and set up all over again.

"A" Battery's Sergeant McArthur was perhaps in a fortunate position, able as he was to have the satisfaction of striking back with his 105mm howitzer when he saw buddies killed and wounded. Firing salvo after salvo into the enemy provided a vent for the emotional stress of combat which would have built inside him. McArthur understood this and made his thoughts clear when he commented on the deaths of two local boys in a long letter home, "I'll tell you one thing; I have more than evened the score for those men's deaths with Jerries a hundred times. The implements of war that I have for my use have given the Germans great misery. I know it doesn't bring those men back. It wouldn't if I killed the whole German army, but it does get something off my chest. It also redoubles my determination to fight this thing through."

The situation on the American side of the mask continued to be problematic for the next 36 hours. Even after the main body of German infiltrators was driven out with heavy losses, small parties continued to cut telephone wires, take pot shots at GIs, and cause enough disruption to prevent much of the supplies from getting through.

"My battery was cut off from the rest of my outfit by German infantry for two days and nights. We fought the whole time without food or ammunition. We could get no communication from the others. Things were pretty tough," wrote Sergeant McArthur of "A" Battery. Then he added his observation of the American fighting spirit, "When men stand up under things like that you can say they are made of good stuff. That's the strange thing about Americans though; we really don't start fighting until we're in a fix. The attack on the 13th tried to penetrate Darby's left flank and a limited breakthrough was achieved. On the 14th, an attack on the right, against the position on Mount Saint Angelo, was made and driven off after some furious fighting. Though German reconnaissance patrols, snipers, and small raids continued for some time, the American side of the Salerno Heights never saw another German force of as great a size as that which attacked "A" Battery. "That was the Hermann Goering Division. They were paratroopers too, they were German paratroopers. We wiped them out. We just turned the howitzers around and shot right into them," said another "A" Battery man, his respect for the enemy evident in his words.

German infiltration of the American lines remained a problem with German soldiers being discovered as they tried to mingle with Italian refugees. Some of these appear to have been deserters and stragglers, while others were undoubtedly gathering intelligence or bent on sabotage of the American rear areas as much as possible.

After Captain Wimberley interrogated one such enemy prisoner on the afternoon of September 23rd, a directive went out to all batteries that "German soldiers are stealing Italian clothes and using them as a disguise to infiltrate through our lines. All batteries and CPs are to stop and question all refugees passing through our lines."

Measures were taken to apprehend infiltrators where ever they might be discovered and public gatherings of any kind were a good opportunity to do so. For example, the next Sunday a squad of men from "C" Battery were sent to a church just outside the village of Maiori. "We were looking for Germans. There was a mass going on and we walked right down the aisles with our guns. I think we found one. A lot of those Germans were wearing civilian clothing," said one of the men who was there. Most were taken captive in uniform, either probing the American defenses or attempting to take prisoners of their own.

Casimir Sobon remembered a couple who were caught skulking about behind the "A" Battery forward observers posts on Mount deChiunzi. "We got a couple of young kids, prisoners, and we were interrogating them. They were typical German young guys, with just the shirt on. Real, real cocky. They believed they were winning the war. They said, 'No doubt, we're gonna win.' They said, 'We're in New York, we're bombing New York, we're winning the war over there! You couldn't tell them, no, you're nowhere near

New York, you're not even getting out of Europe. No, no, no, no, no!"

By the 16th "A" Battery had expended hundreds of rounds of ammunition, but its supply hadn't been replenished since the attack by the raiding party. Someone ordered the drivers to crank up the jeeps with trailers and bring as many 105mm rounds back from the beach as they could manage. Since the FO men Lieutenant Lewis had brought up on the 13th came back down to the battery that day, Covais made his way with Fitzsimmons, one of the "A" Battery drivers, to help load.

These runs down the mountains and into the village of Maiori were not without danger, but there was only one way back to where the ships were unloading supplies. The route was several miles of narrow winding and minimally paved road, the same one taken after the battalion landed on the beach. Much of it was now congested with men and vehicles from all the units under Darby's command. At any point the road could be subject to air attack, snipers, and persistent shelling from German artillery. This was, after all, what was already known as "the Battle of 88 Pass."

The beach was changed too. It was covered with supplies of all sorts stacked up beyond the high water mark. Men were lifting these goods up from the beach to the top of the retaining wall where others loaded it all into trucks or trailers. Several naval warships were firing continuous salvos into the valley beyond the mountains, and Focke-Wulfe 190s still made their presence known at unpredictable intervals.

As soon as the trailers were full, the little "A" Battery convoy made its way back through Maiori, back toward the gun position. Part of the road was lined with infantry-men from the 143rd Regiment, 36th "Texas" Division. The 1st Battalion of this regiment, as well as "A" Battery of the155th and the entire 133rd Field Artillery Battalions were part of the Texas 36th Division. They wore as insignia a light-blue arrowhead with an olive green letter "T" superimposed over it and sewn to their left shoulders. These troops landed at the southern tip of the Salerno beachhead on the 9th with the rest of their division and got ensnarled in intensive combat. The units assembling at Maiori were then detached and rushed up to reinforce Darby at Chiunzi pass.

The 143rd was holding Mount Soretto, the promontory on the west side of Chiunzi Pass, and the "A" Battery ammunition convoy was evidently among members of this regiment as they maneuvered their way toward their positions.

Suddenly the distinctive brrip brrrrip of German machine-pistols sounded from somewhere above, spurts of dust and gravel flew up from the road-bed and men everywhere ran for cover. Fitzsimmons pitched the jeep over to the uphill side of the narrow road. The artillerymen leapt out and crouched against the mountainside while several more bursts swept the roadway. Somebody said something about snipers. Then someone else started yelling for a mortar team.

When Covais told about the incident he said, "There was a big embankment there and I just crawled alongside the embankment and cowered there for a while. I heard a couple of big explosions, boom, and boom! I waited, nothing happened. Then I went up further on the road, and I saw, unfortunately, a whole string of guys that were wounded and dead. I was gonna help them out you know. I remember one of these persons sitting up against the embankment, young fella, with his rifle between his legs, with his eyes closed. I went up to him, I said, hey buddy, can I help you? Hey, are you alright? Are you OK? And he did not respond. It was then that I knew that he was dead. So, I just backed off and let him be in peace."

These were the last words said to someone's son, or brother, maybe their husband. They never would have known the details beyond "Killed in action near Maiori,

Italy, 16 September, 1943." Covais's memory of this Texan's death was more complete than that of his family. It lingered with him until his own decease, just as someone remembered this soldier as a vivid, living person they still loved until their own final day. Covais reflected further and said, "They finally got these snipers up there. What had happened, why this person got killed, and others got killed too, is that they were using mortars. Now, in mountainous country it's tough to figure out elevation. You're down here trying to shoot up there in the mountain peaks and all that. They miscalculated the range, the distance. Well, it's very hard. Mortar shells have a high trajectory. They come right down and wipe a few guys out. Unfortunately those things happen. Things happen like that all the time."

As the Texans wound their way further up toward the heights they came across "C" Battery, stopped and took a break by the water trough.

The battery was between fire missions, so Rappi sauntered over to investigate. One of the Texans noticed his distinctive carbine and it generated some conversation. According to Rappi, "This soldier had an old time bolt action. He didn't have an M1. He seen that I had a carbine, he said, do you want to trade? I said, sure! I give him the carbine and he give me the Springfield."

When Kenneth Smith wasn't on the heights with his machinegun he was kept busy shuttling fresh ammunition from the beach, in this case to "C" Battery, or even between batteries, with his own memories of traveling over the Italian countryside. "At first it was kinda scary but we got used to it," Smith recalled. "I know once when "C" Battery was out of ammunition, I had to go over to "A" Battery to pick up some. Well they was being shelled while I was up there. The Captain got on me for driving up there and saying that I was giving away their position, that I had to get that ammunition and get on down the hill. Other times I'd take the truck and go down to the beach and get ammunition and bring it up to each gun. There was one bridge there we had to cross and some German had an 88 up in the mountain. Every time you'd get near that bridge he'd shoot trying to get you. It didn't bother me too much. I'd go there and I'd wait till somebody else went by, he'd shoot, and then I'd take off. He knocked it out two or three times. We never did find out where the shell was coming from."

If Smith got used to it, other men found driving the gauntlet on the Chiunzi road too much for their nerves. When one man's reluctance to expose himself to the fire on the road presented itself, Sosa took advantage of the opportunity. "I was a driver for communications at first," he remembered. "Then something happened while we were in Italy. The Captain's driver was supposed to go down to the front and pick up the Captain. He didn't want to go. He was scared. I told the driver, hell, I'll go get him. So I cranked up my jeep and took off down there. When I got down there I come to a dead end. I turned my jeep around facing back on the road there and I got jumped down in a ditch. I didn't know anything at all except that we were in the area somewhere and the Captain was there and I was supposed to pick him up."

After a short while Captain Manning came up, recognized his jeep and got in with Sosa. Driving off, Manning turned to the Private and asked him what happened to Wilson, his driver.

"I don't know sir," said Sosa, who let the answer hang in the air without taking his eyes from the road. Then Louis sensed the time was ripe and added, "But if you need a driver, I'm available."

This was a job Sosa'd wanted for some time, knowing that drivers for officers had to be on hand 24 hours a day, but were otherwise exempt from the duty roster and largely autonomous. As the Captain's driver, Sosa would answer directly to Manning without having an NCO intermediary breathing down his neck or being obliged to work in close cooperation with other guys.

"I was kind of a loner, you might say," was Sosa's own self description. "I didn't want to work in the communications section. So when we got back the motor pool Corporal told me, 'OK, you're the Captain's driver.' I said, fine. It all went on from there, just like that."

The navy was vigorously employed in firing on land targets all along the Selerno landings. Near Maiori the gunboats included the Philadelphia and Savannah until the latter was disabled on September 11, as well as other warships, some from the Royal Navy.

One of Darby's men remembered, "We also got great fire support from a British monitor, HMS Roberts. I never saw the Roberts, but I can still hear the noisy travel of her 15-inch shells as they went through Chiunzi Pass. She certainly, and the navies generally, never received proper recognition of their importance at Salerno."

Each of these vessels charged with fire missions on land targets furnished what was called a Shore Fire Control Party, composed of a Naval Liaison Officer (NLO) who worked in close conjunction with ground artillery FOs. The SFCP was furnished with Army radio operators and wiremen, making them forward observation teams for their gunship batteries.

Blending army and navy together did come with some adjustments. Sartain remembered one such area when he said, "We couldn't understand them. They used mills instead of degrees, and they used the metric system instead of; yards. Like we'd say, up 200 and right 200, meaning yards. Well they used all mills and meters."

Covais remembered a US Naval SFCP with "A" Battery.

Over at "C" Battery's OP, Ryan recalled another group, probably from the Roberts, "There were a couple of them from that British ship, they came up and did the observing too. I admired the one guy's rain coat. It was camouflaged with a bump in the back for your knapsack. The officers were up there but I never saw the enlisted men."

Manning remembered the Royal Navy NLOs as well when he wrote, "One interesting experience was my contact with a British naval gunnery officer. He had been sent to act as an observer for one of their large warships in Salerno Bay. He and I worked out patterns of targets and he took over on the ones we could not nullify. It was very impressive to hear those big rounds come whistling in."

Evidently the cluster of Royal Navy sea-dogs and glider artillerymen got along well. The British sailors received US Army rations and interacted freely among the Americans.

Of one occasion where they traded newspapers Ed Ryan said, "I remember particularly the one guy had never seen the funny papers. Somebody had an American newspaper up there. He went ape over the funny papers and all the rest of that stuff."

A more official recognition of the close cooperation between the Royal navy personnel and those of "C" Battery is seen in the battalion journal of September 25th, which states that until further notice there will be "3 officers, 12 EM from British Naval Bombardment detachment attached for rations." Three guys from the HQ Battery were also sent along with the British, and it is likely that the naval party had been ensconced at the Battalion HQ from early in the fighting until then. Now the British were working out of the "C" Battery position, bivouacking and taking their meals with Manning's men when not up on the mountain top.

BATTTERY!

Manning's friendship with the Royal navy officer included something which would become closely associated with the "C" Battery commander through the rest of the war. "He gave me his issue winter coat when he returned to ship. It served me very well through the war and afterwards."

The coat Manning refers to here was a Royal Navy Duffle Coat, an astonishingly thick Khaki woolen affair, made with a hood, fastening with four sets of wooden toggles and rope loops. At an altitude of between 2600 and 4000 feet at any given point, the exposed Ops were windy, cold places at night and generally subject to turbulent weather, including violent hail storms. The GIs didn't have their overcoats with them. Maybe The NLO who'd enjoyed an American comic strip or K-ration lent Manning his coat. They may have shared a cigarette, talking about their lives, either in the Royal Navy or of growing up in New York's Hudson Valley, of a family feed business, a wife named Marge waiting at home, and a love for horseback riding. The duffle coat became a trademark of Manning's.

Sartain remembered it too, "Johnny Manning was the only one that had that type of a coat. He wore that coat all the time. They're heavy, they were knee length. Of course on Johnny it hit him above the knee, but it was big enough to where it was comfortable on him and he was a big man. I think he swapped something for it."

Whether British or American, the naval gunfire had a nerve shattering effect on the men along the crest of the mask. To clear the ridge, cruisers like the Philadelphia had to keep their guns elevated at the maximum angle or aim their projectiles directly through the notch at Chiunzi Pass. Occasionally these giant shells struck the hilltops, killing and wounding our own men in enormous blasts. At the very least the freight train-like screech of the shells as they passed perhaps only yards overhead was hard to take for hour after hour, but there was an additional quality to the naval fire.

"What used to scare me the most up on the mountain," said Bob Storms, "Was when the rings would go off of the shells. They'd flip and oh boy, they'd scare you to death when they went by."

Ed Ryan spent his share of time on the mountain and made the same observation. "We were firing those naval guns. The projectile would go over our head but the rotating band would come loose. As it went through there it would come loose. These rotating bands would swing up through, right over your head. Zing zing zing! It would scare you worse than the projectile would."

For those who participated in the fighting on Mounts Sorreto, Chiunzi, or Saint Angelo it was a battlefield which was never forgotten. From the top of the mask could be seen Mount Vesuvius to the north as it released a continuous cloud of smoke, while at night its fires displayed themselves as long as there was darkness. The entire Mediterranean stretched behind them to the horizon and all of Italy before. So high were these observation posts and defensive works that artillery projectiles could regularly be seen with the naked eye as they sailed past. GIs on the crests had the unusual experience of looking down to watch P-38 lightnings as they strafed and bombed German positions. In fact the details of American fighters and light bombers were clearly visible from an altitude 3000 to 4000 feet above the sea as they passed over the crest toward their targets. The battalion machineguns were apparently also placed on the heights, suggesting that security for the gun positions was either truncated or the responsibility of Rangers or other units as they came on the scene. Bob Storms's machinegun was, for example, up on top, as was Kenneth Smith's weapon.

"One time in Italy," remembered Smith, "I was on the machine gun and a Ger-

Darby of the Rangers.

man transport plane come over. There it was, getting over the top of the mountains. They called me on the phone and said don't you dare shoot, you'll give away our position. I could have shot that plane down with that fifty caliber. It would have been real simple, but I didn't. I don't know where he came from, but I could see the pilot in the plane, that's how low he was. If I had to do it over now I would have shot him. I was probably scared to, but wouldn't that have been something?"

Hauling the machineguns up to these locations was a considerable problem; likewise food, water, telephones and ammunition. Jeeps were, of course, completely out of the question, so everything had to be manhandled or another way found for transportation. Many local Italians were hired very cheaply, though in their malnourished state allowing them to carry rations was inviting theft. "It was a nice hike," remembered Sartain. "We paid these little bitty natives, little boys, a nickel to carry a five gallon can of water up that mountain."

Other men recall using mules procured from the local inhabitants to carry supplies up the trail from the battery gun positions. Horses were tried too, but as the trails became narrower and higher these animals were apt to become skittish. Ryan related one such episode, "I still feel bad about this. We had a big white horse that we took with the mules. He wouldn't go any further. The guy with me, I think it was Big Myers, he knew about horses and said, 'You won't get him to go any further.' I said to him, What the hell are we gonna do? We had no choice so we pushed him off the cliff."

Given the difficult access, it is not surprising that water and rations were in short supply for those on top. No mess kit of hot S O S was ever seen up there, and when K-rations were gone men supplemented their edibles with grapes growing on the terraced vineyards near the crests. Other men remember one old Italian gent scurrying from foxhole to foxhole, handing out balls of mozzarella cheese.

Nonetheless, for all the problems the altitude of the mask presented, it was well worth the effort for the artillery. Over the time that the 319th was established at Maiori the Battalion Fire Direction Center zeroed in on over 100 pre-registered concentration points. These were especially useful for intermittent harassing fire delivered through the night. For instance, the night of September 20 was typical, calling four fourteen road junctions to be fired on with two to four rounds each, commencing at 2000 hours.

Italian POWs were frequently employed as adjunct medical helpers. This prisoner poses with Carl Davis (left) and David Stelow (right) of "A" Battery. Sartain collection.

If movement at night was difficult

for the Germans, daylight deployment or activity of any kind became impossible as soon as the logistics and physics of artillery fire in mountains were brought under control.

Key to that success was the use of communications between the forward observers and Captain Wilcoxson at Battalion Fire Direction. Given the rugged terrain, radios were expedient, of course, but radios also presented a problem because their signal could be used to triangulate the operator's location. As one "A" Battery man put it, "In three minutes they could pick up a radio signal and put a shell right in your pocket."

Radio transmissions could be, and were, intercepted. Ryan remembered one transmission of sensitive information. The man on the other end claimed to be Tony Simon, another "C" Battery man whom Ryan was friendly with. Since he'd just had a conversation with Simon the previous day about coon hunting with his pet dog near Poughkeepsie, Ryan asked, "What's my dog's name?"

"Homer," answered the radio.

"And what does Homer do," continued Ryan.

"He hunts coons," was the immediate and correct answer.

Because of these problems with radio communications there was a concerted effort to run and maintain telephone wires from each OP to the Battalion Fire Direction Center when possible. Marvin Ragland said, "After several days they had the telephone up there in that area. If they had time they could get a line up there, but it didn't last long because they dropped some rounds in there and cut the wire. So most of our conversation would have been by radio I think, at least initially."

For the wiremen on the FO teams, keeping the telephones in operational condition was both a laborious and dangerous task. "Then they tell you one of the phone lines or something got blown up," said Sobon of "A" Battery. "There you are, go ahead, go out and fix it. So, you got a line is out, you grab a hold of the wires, you walked it. You got another guy with you to stand guard. It's in the middle of the night, dark as hell, and you can't put a light on, put a light on and that'd be the end of you."

There was no way of knowing whether the break was the result of a shellburst or deliberately cut by a German patrol. The latter was a favorite method of snatching a prisoner. Cut the telephone wire, then lie in wait for the repair crew that was certain to appear. Ambush the party, take one or two prisoner and kill the rest.

One unexpected quirk of communications caused a directive to be issued early on. Confusion of the word Italian with the word Battalion suddenly became more than an annoyance when trying to understand radio signals which faded in or out and were often full of static. A directive was given through the Ranger Force HQ that in all future communication Italians were to be referred to as I-ties.

With virtually unlimited visual access to the German rear areas, the 319th FOs honed their shooting skills even sharper. According to Sartain, "It was real sport to register different concentration points. You'd figure out how long it took that shell to reach the junction, you see? Then you see a convoy coming way down the way and you kind of time it. You say, 'Fire!' And they'd fire, then you're waiting for the convoy and the shell to arrive at the same time. You knew you were pretty close because; you're watching the convoy and when they start to scatter you knew they could hear that shell coming down."

From his experience with "A" Battery, Ragland described the same practice, saying, "We were up there where we could see anything coming down and we could fire on targets of opportunity. In fact, this one time I had this crossroads zeroed in. I seen this vehicle coming down and I sent down word to get ready to fire on that intersection.

I said, I'll tell you when to fire. Well, here come this vehicle, and when I thought it was about time I said fire! Well in the meantime this guy had been there before I guess, because he stopped in the shade of some trees. After the rounds had all hit and everything he took off. It's kind of hard to run down a vehicle that's on the move, you know. Anyway, I missed him."

PFC Casimir Sobon was up on Mount de Chiunzi too, probably an enlisted assistant on Ragland's FO team. He remembered another detail, saying, "We seen they had a hospital down below there. We seen the nurses walking around in the yard, we could see the doctors walking around, and we could see the ambulances coming and going. We had the binoculars, we were up on the mountain, they were down below. At the same time we could see the Germans firing their shells out of the hospital grounds. But you know the Americans; you can't fire back at a hospital."

Ragland corroborated this recollection, and described what happened by saying, "Down below the hill area we were in, there were some pretty good buildings there and they had red crosses on the top of them, like a hospital. You weren't supposed to fire on a hospital, but captain Blank said he seen some German military vehicles coming in, go in that area and stop. I think one of them was a tank. Captain Blank said, 'That's no hospital.' We fired on it anyway. Well it happened to be a supply area. They had ammunition and everything in there and he knocked a lot of that out."

The presence of the 319th, along with the other batteries whose fire was directed through the battalion FDC, became a problem for the enemy and they retaliated with counter fire. At certain times the Germans would focus on observation posts, at others they would attempt to zero in on the batteries themselves, though necessarily handicapped in doing so without observers of their own.

Consequently the battery positions did come under occasional shellfire, especially "A" Battery, but the constant, relentless barrage was for those on the mountains. Manning wrote that, "Somehow it became possible to endure their artillery, but when the multi-barreled rockets started it was a different story. We tried to target the rocket launchers, but they were mobile and were kept parked under bridges or overpasses between firings. We were blessed with some replacement officers who had to take turns at the OP. One stood up and focused his glasses on a rocket launcher location. They spotted him and we had to carry him off on a stretcher."

The officer was probably Lieutenant Edward R. O'Brien. He was actually a member of the 456th PFAB, as was Lieutenant Hull. "A" Battery had a couple of lieutenants from the 376th PFAB assigned to it and "B" Battery probably had assigned FOs from outside the unit as well. Both O'Brien and Hull were temporarily on duty with the 319th, gaining some valuable experience and both gave their lives in later campaigns.

Ed Ryan was there but remembered the wounded officer as being unpopular with the "C" Battery enlisted men. Rightly or wrongly, the theme of enlisted complaints suggests the Lieutenant had a brusque manner with the men. The guys in the 319th all appreciated, and were accustomed to, officers who treated them decently. They resented the few who flaunted their status. The fact that O'Brien was from another outfit and brought with him the rivalries which are incumbent between neighboring military units probably contributed to the tension. Ryan commented wryly, "When he got hit everybody was happy. They couldn't get anyone to carry him away. Nobody wanted to carry him off the hill."

Rockets were terrifying with their devilish whine, and ability to fall in tight clusters. On one occasion a Nebelwerfer attack produced a gas scare when a barrage loosed an inert yellow smoke. At once a cry of "Gas!" ran through the Rangers and FOs on the crest. It was a false alarm, probably only smoke intended to obscure the view from the heights, but the GIs reaction hints that the rocket's effect was as much psychological as physical. Without question, artillery could really tear men apart both flesh and mind, and for long periods like the 21st to 25th of September, hammered viciously at the American positions.

Marvin Ragland freely admitted "One time when I was up there they started firing on the area and I ran down the hill a little ways towards the unit. After a while it quit so I came back to the OP."

Notwithstanding, it was generally possible to determine rather quickly if a shell posed an immediate threat or not. This wasn't nearly as true with mortars, which the Germans used with more frequency as they pressed their attacks on the heights. "If you didn't know the sound of a mortar the first time you heard it," the men would say, "You'd recognize it the second time."

Bob Storms put it his own way, "Oh yeah, you got shelled, and then they'd send these darned mortars over every once in a while. That's the only thing I dreaded was mortars. The shells, that wasn't too bad because they go up and they arch and past you, they go whistling right on by. But the mortars, they go up and come right down. You can't get away from that. Mortars, I hated mortars."

Sartain's comment about these weapons was in agreement. "All the FOs got to where they could tell whether a shell would land near by. The hardest thing to tell was where a mortar was gonna be. You could hear it go off, you know, and then it'd go up and you didn't know where the damn thing was going to land until you could hear it coming down. If you could hear it coming down you were OK. It was when you couldn't hear it coming down. That was trouble because it was coming down on you."

Rockets, mortars, and artillery weren't the only things to worry about on the crests of Chiunzi and Saint Angelo. Small arms fire, grenades, and, machineguns took their toll too. On Mount Saint Angelo with the "C" Battery FO team, Ryan found himself pinned down one afternoon. "I remember them trying to crawl up the hill, coming at us. They had leaves sewn to their uniforms and stuck in their helmet nets. Oh yeah. One of them almost got me. He had me pinned down. I couldn't even move and he was shooting at me. This Captain Sam of the US Rangers, big guy with a handlebar mustache, he crawled up along side me, a little higher than me. He said, 'Stick your head up one more time.' I did and, spling, he got him. He said, 'That was a close one.' I said you don't have any idea how close it was."

It would always remain a source of pride for the battalion to have fought against the Hermann Goering Panzer Division. The airborne men took note of their distinctive cuff titles and had a respect for the elite status their German counterparts had earned. But the 82nd and the Hermann Goering Panzer Division were already acquainted, having first butted heads in Sicily, where the division fought them to a stand-still, saving the invasion's beachhead in the process. By the time Darby's force landed at Maiori, the Hermann Goering Division was refitting near Naples, and when they realized that elements of the 82nd were facing them again, were eager to even the score.

Just as much the 319th men felt pride to have been shoulder to shoulder with Colonel Darby and his Rangers. The glidermen admired their aggressive and unorthodox style, which was exemplified in their leader. Anecdotes about Darby and his men multiplied as the time passed at Maiori.

One story came from a 319th radio operator who listened in on a conversation between

Darby and some of his Rangers. They were trying to use a captured German fieldpiece to shoot over the mask. "Our Rangers took a German 88. Darby was up on the ridge line, talking on the radio with them. I heard Darby say, 'Now point that gun this way.' Darby's got an OP on the hill and he tells them to bore site it. 'OK', he says, 'Fire a round.' Well the thing exploded near Darby, the gun wasn't elevated enough. He hollered over the radio, 'That was right up my ass! Yu'd better adjust that thing or I'll come down and kick the shit out of somebody!'"

Storms was likely speaking for the whole battalion when he described Darby and his command by saying, "He had some bunch of fellas. They were aces. Oh man! Your never backwater with them, never backwater. They'd push, then they rest a little bit and go right on pushing. I'll tell you, they don't give an inch. Up on the mountain you hit SS once in a while, everything comes to a halt. They're rough to fight, those SS, but when that happens they're the boys to have with you, that Darby bunch, they were a good bunch."

Storms is probably referring to members of the Goering Division when he mentions SS, and the misidentification might have been fostered at the time since the Goering Division had been issued SS camouflage smocks and helmet covers, but the kudos to the Rangers and Darby were unambiguous.

Even at that the nature of war is confusing, and mistakes between American units did take place. Beginning September 18th there was a replacement or rotation between the Rangers and the 325th GIR. Relief of one unit by another is a likely opportunity for mistakes and Covais remembered one vividly. "I was in the foxhole. Night time, everything is quiet, and you've got to listen very carefully. Anyway, I had a lieutenant with me. I was in one hole and he was in the other. I heard a thud, like ploomb, which I thought was unusual; never heard that thud before. So I ducked, and the thing went off. Baloom! It was a grenade. Whew! So then, I heard another one, and I ducked again, and the thing went off. Again, Baloom! Then we heard a machinegun, one of ours. The Lieutenant says, 'I'm gonna go around the back and see what's going on there.' So the Lieutenant went on around, and I hear him say, 'Hey! You son of a guns, what are you doing there!' It was one of our own American machine gun crews, or from another unit, I don't think it was from our battery. But, the guy says, 'Hey, Lieutenant, we didn't know, we thought you guys were Germans!' We were so far advanced they thought that we were Germans and we thought they were Germans too. It was night time and very difficult to see, so, you've got to listen very carefully. In war, hearing is very important! It can save your life."

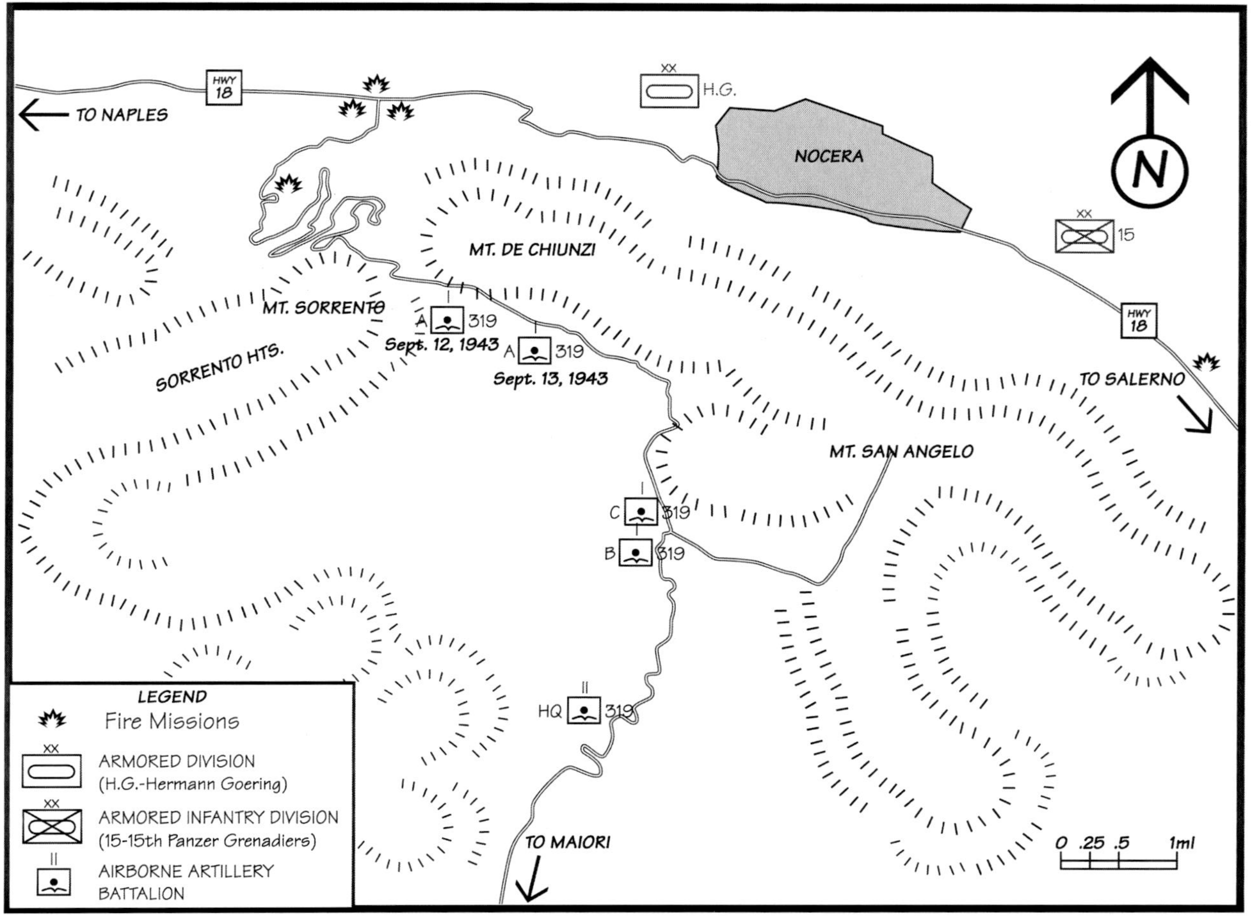

319th GFAB positions in Italy between Maiori and Nocera, September 1943.

LEGEND

Fire Missions

ARMORED DIVISION
(H.G.-Hermann Goering)

ARMORED INFANTRY DIVISION
(15-15th Panzer Grenadiers)

AIRBORNE ARTILLERY
BATTALION

TO NAPLES

SORRENTO HTS.

MT. SORRENTO

Sept. 12, 1943

Sept. 13, 1943

MT. DE CHIUNZI

MT. SAN ANGELO

NOCERA

TO MAIORI

TO SALERNO

HWY 18

HWY 18

H.G.

0 .25 .5 1ml

N

BATTERY!

Part 8: "Some kind of human sacrifice."

On September 18 one of the "C" Battery men up on the mountain was lightly wounded. After a first aid dressing was applied, he was sent down to the aid station where medics Jamison or Rao could look after him.

Captain Manning turned to Ryan and asked, "Do you know anybody that we can pick up down there?"

Ryan thought a moment, then answered, "Let me go down and find out."

Ed Ryan grabbed his Italian carbine and scrambled down the trail to the Battery GP. After a brief explanation First Sergeant Cormany picked out a good robust fellow who always enjoyed getting in a scrap. He told him to get his gear on and go back up the trail with Ryan. "This guy down there used to clean out bar rooms and everything, real tough," remembered Ryan. "I brought him up. He wasn't up there an hour and he started crying for his mother and everything else."

This sometimes happened with men when first exposed to intensive fire but most got a grip of themselves and adjusted. This man didn't. Instead he got worse, really coming apart. After a while it was clear things weren't working out and Manning called Ryan over to his foxhole.

The Captain told him, "I think you made a poor choice."

Ryan had to agree. He made his way over to the hysterical man, told him to get back down to the battery and send up someone else.

Though the reactions to combat in their varied forms had been described since antiquity and recognized universally by military medical services since World War One, it was not easy to predict how well individual men would manage. One important part of the response to combat stress was dependant on the internal temperament of the individual soldier. Those free of pre-existing conditions such as depression or anxiety, with even dispositions were at an advantage.

Lieutenant Ragland represented this group well when he remembered, "I was always kind of a slow individual, easy going, and didn't get too fired up about anything. Of course you're a little up tight when you're in there, especially if they're firing at your area. I know the other officers that I was with, they couldn't understand why I wasn't over there wringing my hands, sweating or something. They couldn't understand that, but I guess it works out."

Ted Covais was probably much more typical of the majority of men in his level of reaction to battlefield conditions. He reflected back on it and remarked, "I did not smoke until I was in Italy, to calm down, from combat stress. One day the shelling had been heavy and getting close, dangerously close. I figured, well, I'll try a cigarette in my foxhole and recover, and maybe calm myself a little bit. Psychologically, that's what I did."

Covais was displaying the first levels of neurotic responses to battlefield trauma. Combat stress reactions began with anxious attunement to one's surroundings, frequently accompanied by sweats, dry mouth, or an escalation of habits such as smoking or chewing gum. The classic hallmark was a hyperawareness of the sounds signaling small arms fire, artillery, and air attack.

SOME KIND OF HUMAN SACRIFICE.

"You get jumpy," is how one man in "A" Battery described it.

This constant, unremitting vigilance was actually essential to survival. A soldier in the front lines needed to be very aware, or, as Marvin Ragland put it, "Not so scared that you're gonna run off and hide, but scared enough that you'll be alert so you won't make foolish mistakes and try to be a hero."

Two other factors determining how individual soldiers would react under fire were the duration and intensity of combat. As the length of time in combat grew or its volume increased, most men in front line units started to develop further neurotic complications. These could include disrupted sleep, fatigue, nightmares, difficulty concentrating, assorted skin rashes or intestinal problems, a proclivity toward emotional volatility, depression, and slight tremors. For the vast majority of these men the reactions would recede once the proximity to danger was eliminated and a chance for rest had elapsed. However, a significant proportion would continue to show these symptoms in a residual form for long periods.

The fourth factor in men's performance was the degree to which they felt part of a strong social network within their military unit. The knowledge that one could depend on his buddies, and that they in turn were counting on him, held enormous sway. Army medical records showed that, overall, with every four wounded men removed from the line there was an additional fifth psychiatric casualty. Yet units with low morale had disproportionately high numbers of psychiatric losses, in some cases as high as 50%, or equal to the number of physical casualties. Raw replacements inserted into existing organizations also fared poorly if they were not able to quickly see themselves as part of some close group. Units like the 319th would have done well, having had the benefit of extensive training together as a body, their specialized status as glidermen, and general élan of airborne forces.

The social environment of an outfit could even influence the symptoms by which the inevitable pressure of combat stress was articulated. In elite units men who reached moderate to severe levels of decompensation were most likely to display conversion disorders. These psychological disorders take place when the true unconscious urge is expressed overtly through disabling the nervous system. Spontaneous paralysis of limbs, sudden blindness, deafness, or other stroke-like, incapacitating effects, seemingly beyond one's conscious control, were the most common symptoms. Indeed, wartime analysis of psychiatric casualties resulting from the battles of Salerno and Anzio did show significantly higher rates of conversion disorders among the Rangers and Airborne troopers than among GIs in ordinary divisions. Because these highly trained units placed such a premium on courage and steady nerves, behaviors normally associated with fright, like crying, hesitation, or malingering were psychologically less acceptable to these men.

Combat stress reactions during the First World War were normally referred to as "shell shock," a name which reflected the belief that army doctors were witnessing the effect of close proximity to blast concussion of artillery bursts on the brain. The term itself served to restrict the interpretation of the syndrome to one which was essentially physiological and not psychiatric. However, as the conflict continued it became increasingly obvious that men need not come in contact with high explosives for their mental integrity to begin deteriorating. Those who succumbed also included many who were in support units or other positions relatively safe from blast concussion of any kind.

At first these cases were regarded as either shirkers or mentally fragile prior to military service. From this perspective the psychologically disabled soldier appeared willing to collude with the enemy by offering himself as a mental casualty in order to escape from danger. Because of this widely held belief the treatment of "shell shock" victims was unenthusiastic, lest it be seen as indulging weakness.

Over time the massive scale at which the syndrome occurred in its varying degrees forced the acknowledgment that healthy men were susceptible as well.

The recognition that the symptoms were a normal response which would develop in even the best of soldiers given enough exposure was widely established by the time World War Two began. It was further accepted that there would be some limit to each man's personal resources, beyond which lay his breaking point. When that time came for soldiers in the American armed forces, medics would assign the man as suffering from "exhaustion" and have him removed to a field hospital. Exhausted men were as likely to have been ordered off the front-line as to have reported themselves as unable to continue. Experience showed that in the majority of cases a brief rest, a hot meal, sometimes a sedative, and the assurance that his symptoms were not unusual, was enough to return the man to duty.

In a very few cases the reaction to combat was extreme and approached a kind of battlefield psychosis. Men in this condition were completely out of control and posed a real liability, exhibiting most of the previously mentioned symptoms but in their most acute forms. Sometimes they would become frozen, experience visual or auditory hallucinations, or others would dash about in the open, exposing themselves to fire. Though such men were typically aware of their surroundings and thus not truly psychotic, their behavior was sufficiently irrational or out of control as to render them entirely unfit for service.

Kenneth Smith's older brother Ned was a medic with the 331st Infantry, 83rd Division. He described his experience with a man confined to a room because of combat psychosis in this way, "I went in there and he was clawing the bricks in the wall and everything. Tearing up his fingers and everything. He just went haywire. He didn't know where he was at, he didn't know who he was or anything. So I just slapped him, laid him over and said, wake up! He didn't wake up, so I knew he was gone. I went back to Major Snyder and told him, dope that guy up as high as you can. Dope him, 'cause we've got to get him out of here, and that was the end of that."

If such a man were forwarded to a more centralized Corps or army psychiatric hospital, it was unlikely he would return to service in combat zones again, being for all practical purposes a casualty.

Whomever the "C" Battery man who lost his nerve on the mountain was, it was probably the same soldier Sartain was talking about when he said, "That was the only man that I can recall of the whole outfit that ever totally lost it, you know what I mean? He was nuts, he wasn't putting anything on. Well, you don't know what brought it on, whether a mortar attack or something, you really don't know. The whole operation was really stressful."

In spite of all this, most of the GIs – especially those on the gun crews -- settled into some kind of routine. Activity helped to discharge tension, and Manning's battery was certainly active. As he later wrote, "Our odd-ball battery location turned out to be the most advantageous relative to the target areas so "C" Battery got a large number of the firing assignments."

Sartain described his battery's GP this way, "In Italy the battery was set up on the back side of a mountain. It was in a nice big vineyard. We rolled the guns down right off the road in to the vineyard. We cut the wire holding up the grapes, put the guns in there and just put the wire back. We'd pull away the wire, shoot, then put the wire back and camouflage the battery. We had grapes all over the place."

The artillery shells for the 105mm howitzers came packed in clusters of three each, wired together and buffered with pine slats. A considerable number of these discarded pieces of wooden packaging accumulated quickly once the fire missions started. The men had use of a few for incidental fires to brew a cup of coffee perhaps, but there were a lot of little Coleman stoves around and a mess truck was parked down the road to take care of any real cooking.

Local Italians, on the other hand, were desperate for fuel and began appearing at the battery gun positions in small groups. They brought with them tomatoes, onions, eggplant and other vegetables to swap for the little sticks of wood. The trading was brisk and amiable. The Italians saw the Americans as liberators, all of them being fed up with Mussolini and his fascist German henchmen. Others, a lot really, had relatives living in the United States.

A significant number of the men in the battalion also came from Italian backgrounds and could speak the language. In "A" Battery, Ted Covais and Jimmy Rosati in the instrument section, were examples. Though native born Americans, they needed to speak Italian if they expected to have a conversation with their parents. A few, like John Girardin, had even been born in Italy, though the Venetian dialect he spoke was unrecognizable to the local inhabitants.

Sartain said of these men, "When we got to Italy and they could start talking Italian to the natives they were in hog heaven!"
Even those who spoke Spanish, in "C" Battery Sosa and Rao, could get by without difficulty.

Everyone was happy with the transactions, particularly the GIs who were starved for fresh food of any kind. Besides tomatoes and other garden vegetables traded to supplement the soldiers' rations, there was at least as lively a business in wine. Rappi commented that there was more around than the officers were aware of. The beverage was abundant and prices were cheap. Even at that it was considered great fun to put one over on the Italians if it could be so arranged.

Ed Ryan remembered one method, "We had message books, pads with official military business only printed across the top. Guys would hand them one of these slips and sign any old stupid name to it."

Within days of setting up, the battalion officers were being approached by local civilians presenting what they thought were vouchers signed by Lieutenant Donald Duck, Captain J. Edgar Hoover, or Supreme Allied Commander Dwight D. Eisenhower.

As time at the mountain position passed a few brief periods of quiet came along. The guys in "C" Battery noticed that the wooden irrigation channels fed by the spring and winding their way through the vineyard, would also make excellent bathtubs. GIs would seize the chance to clean up with a refreshing bath, much to the amusement of the senorita who continued to work the vineyards nearby.

The operation of the winery had an Old World atmosphere to it, with the sequence of tending the vineyard, harvesting the grapes, and processing them into wine evidently unchanged for thousands of years. Guys in the battalion had heard of grapes being stomped by hand, or foot as the case might be, but now they could see it for themselves. Closer to the village the GIs saw youngsters, mostly girls, jumping and tromping about in wooden vats filled with fruit. When they got out their skin was died purple to their knees.

"The Italian people are very friendly, more so than we expected," one man wrote home.

Most of the men really liked the Italians too, who welcomed the Americans in spite of the enormous hardships the war had brought upon them.

Storms recalled two with particular fondness when he said, "I had two young Italian boys, one was Angelo and the other was Pasquale. They were only around ten or twelve years old, and they used to come up about two three times a week. They'd come down off the cliff and they'd spend all day and gather up some women and children and old men. Then they'd sneak back through the lines again. They'd come through at night. I used to try and give them something to eat and then get a little sleep. You fed them, they'd just throw it up. I took them down and the doctor said there wasn't too much he could do. He gave them something to take but they wouldn't take it. You try to feed them and they throwed up a lot. But they brought a lot of people back through us up on that cliff."

After he was finally relieved from the top of Mount Saint Angelo, Ryan was able to spend some time at the battery and mingle with the locals too. One of them, the vineyard owner's foremen, had a conversation with him. "I bumped into the Italian who engineered the landing, made contact with the Americans. He gave them all the clues and was really a spy, but I don't think they gave him much. He spoke good English. He said, 'I worked in New York City, I peddled bananas on the street. Used to have to get up five o'clock in the morning, go down to the market, get the bananas and then go out and sell them. Sometimes you got stuck with half a load of bananas.' He said, "I came back over here. I've got these two women. I got the wife that does everything, and then this other woman that picks all of the fruit, brings me the wood for the fire, and all the rest. So, he said, I've got it made.'"

The owner of the vineyard made it a point on almost every day to visit the American artillerymen and their guns on his property.

Sartain remembered seeing him, hunkered down several yards behind the guns, with his index fingers stuck in his ears. "He was a short guy, and if a shell came in he'd jump right in the foxhole with the men! He'd watch the gunners for a while, then once the fire mission was finished, stroll over to visit with Sartain. He owned much of the mountainside and all of the grape stomping, which men saw further down the road toward Maiori, was part of his winery operation."

One afternoon the vineyard owner approached Sartain, who was seated at a camp table with a cup of coffee, examining maps and marking them here and there with a pencil. The owner began speaking, making gestures suggestive of eating. The Lieutenant couldn't understand any of what he was being told and called for John Rao, one of "C" Battery's two medics and a reasonably good Italian speaker. "Rao," asked Sartain, "what's this guy saying? "

"He says he wants to invite you to his home tomorrow for Sunday dinner, sir," Rao explained. "He says you should bring the Captain with you."

"Well", Sartain answered, standing up and extending his hand, "That's very nice, very nice. Tell the gentleman I'll be happy to be his guest, unless something comes along to prevent it, you understand. Tell him I'll try to bring Manning with me."

Before Rao could translate, the Italian smiled broadly and said in heavily accented, broken English, "Thassa good, Capitano Manning, si, si!"

"Find out from him where he lives and when Johnny and I should be there,"

Some Kind of Human Sacrifice.

Sartain said to Rao as he shook the Italian's hand.

On Sunday, as it turned out, Sartain and Manning were both able to take a brief absence from the battery. Though their Class "A" uniforms weren't available, each man had a fresh shave and put on a khaki necktie.

About noon Manning had Sosa fire up the jeep to take him and Sartain into Maiori. Sosa found the house easily. Manning was learning that this was one of Sosa's best traits as his driver, an ability to relate a map to the landscape and intuitively sense where a road would take him. The jeep came to a halt in front of a rowhouse near the shore. After Manning told him to come back for them in two hours, Sosa went exploring.

Knocking on the door, the two were greeted by the owner and his wife. They were ushered inside the home, which was cool with subdued light. It was not elegant but handsomely appointed with large, dark pieces of furniture and oil paintings on the walls. In the foyer was a sideboard displaying family photos; the vineyard owner and his wife, two adolescent girls, and a young man in uniform.

The vineyard owner's wife called two names up the stairs. A pair of teenaged girls with deep brown eyes and olive complexions glided down the steps, allowed themselves to be introduced, and offered their hands modestly. The group retired to a parlor where Manning and Sartain took seats on the first upholstered chairs they'd seen since leaving the states. After the wife and daughters excused themselves, the Americans were served wine from a crystal decanter. Next the vineyard owner passed around a box of cheroots for the men folk to smoke. A toast was offered to the name of Franklin Roosevelt by the host, but since no one was sure who was running the newly allied Italian government the gesture was difficult to reciprocate.

In an adjoining dining room the meal was taken, with several courses served on china and eaten with large silverware utensils. First a soup, then followed by chicken and pasta with vegetables. A salad, served last to cleanse the palate finished the main courses. Afterwards the daughters cleared off the table and brought back a strong expresso coffee. It was poured into tiny china cups with a sliver of lemon on the rim. The Italians added a dash of anisette to theirs and the two officers did the same. For Sartain, the Louisianan whose love of strong coffee was seldom shared, it would have been delicious. A platter on the table held a variety of cookies. Some covered with sesame seeds, a few others made with a filling of fig preserves.

The meal was delightful. The surroundings were clean, immaculate really in comparison to camp life, the food was obviously prepared with care, and everyone was polite. It reminded the two Americans of what normal life was like, away from tired, whiskered men, and howitzers, and observation of artillery concentrations on enemy targets.

"A bit of a language barrier, but we all came through," wrote Manning of the visit years later.

Sartain was left with an equally positive impression, "They were OK, the Italians, they really were. How they ever let Mussolini take control of the country is beyond me."

Sosa brought the two officers back to the GP before nightfall. After dark there were too many things that could go wrong in a combat zone. Enemy patrols, snipers, or even nervous American sentries; most of the time though things were reasonably safe within the battery perimeter. This was especially so for C" Battery which was highest up and thus most within the dead zone for German artillery.

BATTERY!

Capt. John Manning, Commander of "C" Battery, beside his "Command Car" in front of his quarters in Naples. Courtesy John Manning, Jr.

Most "C" Battery men remembered their battery GP as receiving little artillery fire while at Maiori. Rappi didn't think he was ever in direct contact with anyone wounded or see any dead while at the position.

Girardin's memory of shelling at Maiori was similar, adding that, "The only thing I remember scared everybody was this one time, all at once we hear this funny whistling noise. It sounded like a large projectile coming down. You could see it. Everybody thought it was a large bomb. Turns out it was the empty gas tank off a P-38 fighter!"

About the 20th of September Ryan was finally pulled down off the mountain he'd been on since the night they landed at Maiori. He needed to take a break badly. Manning told him to take a couple of guys with him and go into the village. There's a lot of wounded men in a field hospital at the church downtown. Check on our guys down there. While you're at it see if you can't find some more canteens and whatever else would be useful to us at the OP, he said.

Ryan had Ed Conover with him. On the way they grabbed Willie Bragg, an older guy from Tennessee, and the three headed off for Maiori. On their way they came across a "little town with cobblestone streets. It had a grocery store, little hotel there too." Ryan went in but there wasn't much left except a small wedge from a wheel of cheese. "It was round with a net around it." He bought what there was and asked after more. The shopkeeper responded that he'd have more cheese in another few days but warned Ryan he could only save it if it was paid for up front. The price of an entire wheel was haggled over and finally settled. "I gave him sixteen dollars to get me more cheese," Ryan said.

It seemed like an exorbitant price, but one takes what one can get when the circumstances call for it.

A little while later, in the village itself, they passed an empty lot where prisoners were being collected and questioned. Ryan, with Conover and Bragg, stopped to look at the Germans up close. "They were paratroopers with uniforms a lot like ours, except their jump boots laced up the side. They had that Hermann Goering armband on," remembered Ryan.

A cluster of intelligence officers were interrogating one of the captured enemy. They calmly posed each query in German but the prisoner only glared back at them. Bragg leaned toward his buddy and remarked, "That one looks like he was weaned on lemons."

Another question was presented to the prisoner, who this time spit in the officer's face. A one sided scuffle erupted while another guard briskly told the spectators, "Alright you guys, beat it!"

It was easy to locate the field hospital, the Church of Saint Domenico, a prominent building at the center of town. Its steeple was the one from which a beacon shone on the night they landed in the LCIs.

Ryan went up the steps and into the church. "They had the pews cleared out. It looked like some kind of human sacrifice," he said years later. "Wounded men were laying on stretchers and cots, covering the floor and much of the altar. Here and there nuns were ministering to them. You couldn't look anywhere without seeing bloody

bandages or someone moaning in terrible pain. Over them all a suffering Christ looked down from the cross he was nailed to, bleeding and wounded as well."

They approached a medic. The men he was looking for, Ryan was told, were already evacuated to a hospital ship. Turning to leave, he saw in one corner the weapons and equipment of the casualties. Bragg and Ryan started sorting through the pile. Conover said he'd wait outside. Ryan started setting aside selected items; a 45, a few canteens, a pair of binoculars, into a little grouping to one side. His buddy finally nudged him and said, "Come on, let's get out of here."

Lieutenant Ragland was another from the top of the Sorrento heights who was finally given a few days to recharge himself. With almost no water up there, living like a prairie dog scurrying from burrow to burrow, screaming meemees, and small arms fights which erupted with no predictable pattern, these men coming down off the mountains were unshaven,

Lieutenant Marvin Ragland, Corporal Thurman King, and Milton Wiedner pose for their photo. Maiori, Italy, September, 1943. Ragland collection.

exhausted, and covered everywhere with a layer of pulverized granite dust. Ragland was given a jeep and told by Vernon Blanc to head into Maiori, get cleaned up, find something other than Sergeant Siegel's cooking to eat, and take Corporals King and Wiedner with him.

Maiori was a busy place. GIs, were everywhere, driving trucks or jeeps, receiving freight from LSTs loaded with supplies, or seeing to any of the other thousand tasks an army performs. Sometimes they had Italian prisoners in tow, supervising the POWs to assist in what ever ways manual labor was needed. Their whole status was a little confusing. Were they willing prisoners or disorganized allied personnel? There was no question that the Americans were in charge, but the Italians were obviously in sympathy and required little in the way of guards.

The people of the village did their best to adapt and use the situation to their advantage where possible. Fascism and years of war had been hard on the economy, but now there was more money around than there had been in a long, long time. Most shops were open, even if there wasn't a lot for sale.

Ragland, King, and Wiedner first stopped at a barber. The man's son, not more than twelve years old, did the rough cut. Then Papa took over and completed the haircut with a pair of long pointed scissors. Finally he lathered up the man's face, drew his straight-razor across the large strop hanging from the chair, and gave him the closest shave he could remember.

The haircut felt great, and the three were starting to feel like human beings again. A hot meal was next in line. Not as refined as that enjoyed by Manning and Sartain, but still fresher than something which was cooked in the United States months previous. Ragland bought a couple of postcards at an apothecary with boarded up windows. Before they left the three men posed together at a makeshift studio run by an enterprising Maiori photographer.

Another time, Captain Manning told Ryan, "Grab a few guys, go get as many Italian prisoners as you can and have them unload this ship at the dock in Maiori." Selecting a corporal's squad, Ryan and his press gang took a jeep into town. They would need some manpower for this kind of assignment but couldn't find more than a few Italians who weren't already busy loading or unloading something. Then one of those he'd recruited told him he knew where there were perhaps twenty Italian officers with nothing to do. The Americans need only follow him.

This they did, and the Italian led Ryan's squad up to Mount Falerzio overlooking the village. Many natural caves dotted the hillside. They had been used as a sanctuary by brigands and refugees over the centuries. Ryan sent his prisoner into the hideaway to inform his friends inside that their presence was wanted at the docks. A murmur of protest echoed from the group within, evidently annoyed at being interrupted from what ever they were doing.

It has been said that the German's uniform is designed to appeal to men, while the uniform of the Italian is intended to appeal to women. As the Italians came out of the caves this dictum would have come to mind. They were dressed impeccably, with flared breeches and tailored, open lapelled tunics. Their uniforms were adorned with art-deco eagles, fascines, and oak wreaths surrounding Roman numerals. Every boot was highly polished. They assembled in the sunlight, slapping the particles of sand from the seats of their breeches and adjusting their caps. Several were taking out sunglasses; a few others combed their hair, mustaches, or goatees. There were one or two with trench coats draped cape-like over their shoulders and more striking sophisticated poses, often smoking cigarettes in bakelite holders.

Under the accepted articles of war, belligerent armies exempted captured officers from manual labor. The Italians probably didn't realize they were supposed to help unload a LST until they reached the ship and were ordered to serve as stevedores. "So we got a bunch of these Ginzos and put them to work," said Ryan. "They were hollering and mad and sweating!"

The unloading continued for some time, accompanied by sustained protests and considerable gesticulation. To Ryan and his crew it was obvious these men were officers, but nobody cared. Every time one of them approached with another vociferous complaint, Ryan would just repeat, "No capishe!" and shove him back to work with his carbine. Somehow word got out that a squad of GIs had put a group of Italian officers to work unloading a ship. "We were just about through the unloading when some colonel comes down saying, 'Hey, you can't do that! These guys are officers!'"

On September 24th Colonel Darby ordered all units to pack one day's worth of rations and supplies in preparation for an advance. Word was going around that the Ranger force would be moving out any day. Charlie Spainauer, the "A" Battery clerk who'd led the `spontaneous prayer meeting on the LST, continued with "A" Battery until he was reported sick a couple of weeks later. While in the infirmary at Maiori, Spainauer heard the rumors too about the 319th moving out. Everybody knew that men left behind in hospitals were likely to be sent to any old unit as replacements when they felt better. Spainhour was determined not to let this happen to him. After beseeching the doctors to release him, he collected his things, laced up his canvas leggings in spite of the dizziness and nausea which plagued him, and slipped out a side door.

That afternoon of September 27, 1943, Spainhour made his way slowly up the mountain road. On the way he found himself passing "C" Battery's GP, where he stopped to refresh his canteen at the spring, rest, and visit with some of his old "A" Battery friends, now serving under Captain Manning. Rappi spoke to him before he left. John Girardin was another who saw him there. "We were all bivouacked there along the mountain, dug in. He went right by us."

When Spainauer reached the "A" Battery position Covais was there. He was glad to see Charlie and they shared a short conversation. Then, just as twilight was coming on there was an unexpected mortar attack. When it was over Ted was among those who saw Charlie's shredded body as the life left his eyes forever. There was a lot of blood and the sight really put the gunner corporal on McArthur's crew over the edge. He cracked up, went hysterical and had to be evacuated in the same vehicle with Spainauer's body. The chain of events left Covais feeling disturbed for a long time. He saw the death as at once ironic and also laden with destiny. Apparently being "good" didn't count for much and had nothing to do with whether one lived or died.

"I remember Charlie Spainauer. He was a good man, very religious. Charlie was very good in fire direction center. Laying out the artillery direction. He got hit by a mortar shell that came in and landed right by his foxhole. He didn't make it. It's just sad," said Covais years later.

Bob McArthur mentioned the incident when he wrote to his family in Mississippi, telling them about the human toll of war. "When bullets really get flying lots of men get sick. Lots of men get scared half to death, lots of men get shell shocked and go crazy. Yes, some men go crazy. I know that because my gunner went crazy. I have seen all that. Not only have I seen other men scared, but I myself have been scared half to death. I have seen men riddled with rifle and machinegun fire, cities destroyed by bombs, ships bombed and sunk while men screamed. I have seen my own friends that were shell shocked, and believe you me, that's really something. I believe it's worse than being hit. Some of them get over it and some don't."

Word of Spainauer's death filtered back to his "C" Battery friends.

"The next thing you know," said Girardin, "Two hours later, we heard a few noises. We didn't know what happened, but somebody come back and said "A" Battery got hit by mortars and he was the one that got killed. I remember him, he was a nice fella he was."

Spainauer was the last man in the battalion killed at Maiori. 36 hours later the 319th received its march order. All the FOs were brought down from the heights, hauling their radios and telephones with them. At the battery gun positions they started folding up the camouflage nets, pulling up the aiming stakes, and readying the howitzers to be hitched up and hauled away.

With Darby's line as thinly held as it initially was, and remaining outnumbered throughout most of the fighting around what became known as "88 Pass," the support offered by the 319th in defense of the American positions was incalculable. Because 319th gun crews found ways to reach the dead zone on the opposite side of the mask by utilizing different combinations of powder bags in their shells, the Germans were never able to either assemble sufficiently large concentrations of troops, or bring them to bear against the Americans on the heights without inviting a withering barrage of 105mm shells. That portions of the battalion had even taken part in the defense of their gun positions through a small arms engagement with enemy troops was remarkable as well.

More influential on the course of the greater battle of Salerno was the way the battalion maintained a stranglehold on any German traffic on the highways between Naples and the German forces opposing the British and Americans further down the Italian coast.

As Lieutenant Ragland put it, "We stopped that traffic pretty cold after two or three days."

As a result, the fire missions of the battalion made a shift over the weeks from convoys, troop concentrations, and identified artillery or rocket battery positions fired during daylight, to interdicting and harassing fire on road junctions executed at irregular intervals during the night. Over the time at Maiori the battalion records show scores, possibly hundreds, of trucks and armored vehicles destroyed, dozens of enemy artillery, mortar, and rocket batteries neutralized, and innumerable personnel killed and wounded.

For some of the targets out of their range the 319th's fire was augmented by naval gunfire and mortars, as well as 155mm batteries, but these fire missions were all coordinated through the 319th Fire Direction Center and observed by battalion FOs. In the end, the resourcefulness of the battery commanders as they adapted to difficult circumstances and found ways to still reach nearly all targets within the range of their 105mm guns, demonstrated ingenuity, initiative, and spirit.

The men in the outfit had given a good account of themselves and could rightly claim the title of "veteran" now. Though battalion records are inconsistent with each other, and with other accounts, the casualties of the battalion were about fifteen men wounded, one of whom later died of his wounds, and probably three killed. The majority of these losses were in "A" Battery. ""A" battery took the worst beating, I think, of the three batteries," said Corporal Kenneth Smith. ""A" battery got shelled a lot. I guess they's more out in the open."

SOME KIND OF HUMAN SACRIFICE.

Casualties among FOs serving with the 319th from other artillery battalions in the 82nd, such as Lieutenant O'Brien with "C" Battery, were not counted as 319th losses even though the men were on duty with the outfit at the time they were injured. At least two, and possibly a third, additional casualty was from men who cracked under the stress of combat conditions. For the rest who came through with body and soul intact there was a sense of relief that they'd been tested and found able to withstand the battlefield's challenges.

The earlier tensions between Colonel Bertsch and the battalion in North Africa were expected by many to become irrelevant or petty once the fighting in Italy began. Surely the commander would find a new object for his abrasive nature in the Germans, and demonstrate his antipathy toward the enemy with the same enthusiasm he applied to his standards of military performance within the unit.

"We all thought he was going to be a terrific CO in combat," said Sartain. His words reflect the consensus among the men in the unit at that time. They adopted the belief that from here on out there was a clean slate between them and their Colonel now that they faced the common enemy.

However, within a few days of landing at Maiori it became evident that there might not be a renaissance of admiration between Colonel Bertsch and his command. Under normal conditions battalion commanders were expected to periodically visit all components of their units. Naturally, to do so involved being in exposed or front-line positions from time to time. The first thing that guys in the 319th noticed was Colonel Bertsch's rare appearances at the battery GPs , and nearly complete absence of visits to the observation posts on the mountain tops.

"In Italy," explained Sartain, "It was generally Major Todd who came around. You'd see Wilcoxson sometimes but Bertsch stayed in the rear in his dugout." Other veterans of the outfit volunteered the same observation. When Colonel Bertsch was mentioned during a conversation about the fighting in Italy, Robert Rappi's immediate comment was, "Yeah. He was the Colonel when we went to Maiori. He was hiding in a hole someplace I think. He was a West Pointer too!"

While another remarked, "He always had the biggest foxhole with a strong cover and he never left it."

Others corroborated Rappi's memory. PFC Sobon had seen plenty of fire with the "A" Battery observation teams on Mount de Chiunzi. When the subject of Colonel Bertsch was raised, his response was direct and immediate, "He was about as yellow as anybody I know. He's the guy, when you're in training, he's Rah Rah, you better learn to kill or be killed, it's gonna be one or the other. Soon as he got into combat he never got out of his hole. He couldn't stay in any kind of combat. Big hero!"

Marvin Ragland remembered that Colonel Bertsch did go forward once, and battalion records confirm this when the 319th first arrived at Maiori. "They tell me Colonel Bertsch and some of the other staff, they kind of acted like they were at Fort Sill. Then the rounds started coming in and they abandoned that position in a hurry. I understand that Colonel Bertsch never went forward again. I guess that scared him off."

Captain Wilcoxson also attracted the ire of the men, even though his presence at the gun positions was more frequent. Sartain explained why when he said, "If you were in combat you could tell whether a shell was coming in or whether it'd go over you. You could tell that. You could hear these shells coming in, but man, Wilcoxson, he was gone. When he'd hear some shells coming in he would scoot. If he was walking down the lane and a shell would come over he would just absolutely go hog wild. He was lining the first ditch he could find. He'd hit the hole. The GIs really got a big charge out of it. Everybody would laugh behind his back and call him Fidgety Phil. The men would laugh out loud at him. They'd holler, 'Give us another one!'"

It isn't surprising that anecdotes circulated which involved Colonel Bertsch and Colonel Darby together.

Ed Ryan remembered one this way, "We were shooting the naval guns from out in the bay on to the Germans that were down in the valley. So all of a sudden comes a march order. Gonna get people out of there. Bertsch was gonna retreat, go back to where the boats were. Of course we didn't know about this, we were up on top of the mountain. He was gonna leave us dry up there. The guy that was the head of the Rangers, Colonel Darby, he was there and he was a character himself. He was an effeminate guy, you know, talked with a girl's accent. He might have been girlish there but he was tougher than a son of a bitch. Boy he was tough! Bertsch was leading elements of the battalion down the road. He caught Bertsch, and boy they told me that this effeminate guy screamed up one side of him and down the other. Was gonna have him busted or whatever it was."

This story is probably not false, but is likely an exaggeration. It is corroborated by other men in the battalion, though not as eyewitnesses. No mention is made in the battalion records of any retreat ever being ordered. If any such event did take place it was likely on or about September 13, the day when a large force of German infantry attacked the batteries directly and Colonel Darby was also present at battalion headquarters. More plausibly Colonel Bertsch suggested a withdrawal and Darby reacted by vociferously rejecting the idea out of hand, with the episode being then embellished in each successive recital. Even if completely untrue, the story says much about both the attitude of contempt which the rank and file of the battalion held toward the Colonel, as well as their admiration for Darby as a leader.

Whether justified or not, the judgment of the men in the 319th was that Colonel Bertsch in particular, but also Captain Wilcoxson, were reluctant under fire.

"The men could see it," observed Sartain decades later with pity, adding, "Accordingly, he lost all respect from his men."

In fairness, a commanding officer's responsibilities are often best served from a rear area where reports from all pertinent sources can be received and evaluated quickly. A CO who is seldom where his subordinates can reach him, or who limits his knowledge of the tactical situation because he is viewing the battle from isolated vantage points is not serving most efficiently. By the time the battalion departed Maiori the 319th was responsible for coordinating the fire of eleven different batteries through its fire direction center. This would have required considerable control and synchronization. The Colonel's presence at the Battalion CP at most times may have been proper, but those in the ranks already held Colonel Bertsch in low esteem. They were consequently disinclined to be generous or interpret his actions in a favorable light even if some other explanation was available.

Operation Avalanche wasn't the immediate success General Clark hoped for. Instead of holding the passes at Vitri and Chiunzi for a few days, Darby's force was locked into a continuous battle for nearly three weeks. The same was true for the British X Corps and the American VI Corps at the southern end of the Salerno landings. The British X Corps, which controlled the invasion force landing west of Salerno, was unable to begin its drive to the Plain of Naples until 23 September and did not succeed in reaching it until five days later.

SOME KIND OF HUMAN SACRIFICE.

With more troops under his command, Darby's forces now included the 143rd Infantry Regiment, the 325th Glider Infantry regiment, the 505th PIR and elements of the 504th PIR, along with his own three Ranger Battalions. The Ranger commander became more aggressive, coming down off the heights and pressing the Germans. On the 24th a sharp fight erupted over Caba Bridge. Lieutenant Simpson could see the battle from his mountain top OP as if it were a vast sand table of miniatures.

The minute to minute observations reported the bridge changing hands repeatedly through the day. In some ways it was similar to following a ball game over the radio, except the stakes were much higher. At 1032, "Our front parties extend past Cava Bridge about seventy feet. Gap blown out on north end of bridge." Then, at 1045, "Enemy troops still active on Cava Bridge." By 1115: the Americans were evidently holding the bridge again when it was reported, "North end of Cava bridge strafed by hostile aircraft." Finally, at 1730 a message was received from Lt. Simpson, "Observed many of our vehicles crossing Cava Bridge."

By September 27 the Ranger force under Darby was still crowding the Germans. From the heights Lieutenants Blank, Simpson, and Lewis could see it all. Two large tanks parked at a church near Sarno, a patrol of about thirty Germans, the positions of the 325th's 1st Battalion. At 1500 word was received from Lieutenant Simpson, the liaison officer with Darby's HQ that "Anthony," the code name for the British breakthrough to the plains, was set for that night. Colonel Bertsch immediately called in officers from all his batteries to be at his CP at 1600. Lieutenant Hawkins from "B" Battery, Lieutenant Lewis, Lt. Sartain, and Captain Loughmiller from "A" Battery represented the 319th's firing batteries. Captain Gilmer from the 155th, with Lieutenant Derryberry of the 133rd Artillery Battalions were there too. Bertsch informed them of Anthony and their roles then dismissed them. The meeting lasted eleven minutes.

After a series of coordinated barrages on the enemy that night, the attack was resumed early the next morning of the 28th. Observers, as they had the day before, immediately reported the progress as seen from the heights. The Germans seemed to have conceded the Salerno line. They were making for Naples and points north, trying to break contact when possible. At 1115 hours, "four tanks crossing railroad bridge" and "apparently meeting no resistance." At midday another report described "continuous convoy of vehicles of every description apparently British moving west on Highway 18 as far as Angri."

About noon on the 28th a British Liaison officer arrived at the battalion CP. It was a Captain McClain of the 74th Medium Regiment Royal Army. The British 26th Armored Brigade, regiments of lancers in Sherman tanks, would be coming up Highway 18 to meet the battalion as it descended from Chiunzi Pass. News also arrived that afternoon instructing the battalion to return to the 82nd's command as of 0600 the next day, September 29, and be attached in support of the 505th PIR.

The Captain stayed the night with the 319th. Given his disposition, one might speculate that Colonel Bertsch would have felt an affinity toward the more class conscious British officers. If so, the Colonel would have enjoyed having the guest take his evening meal with him and his headquarters staff. Perhaps finding himself hoping some of Captain McClain's habits would rub off on his own subordinates.

BATTERY!

Part 9: "I wouldn't take nothing for what I seen."

March order arrived at 0755 the next morning, September 29th, but it wasn't until afternoon that the 319th formed up in convoy on the road leading out of the valley and over Chiunzi pass. As the battalion ascended the men could see more and more of the Salerno battlefield of which they'd been a part. Near the top was a two storied stone building, half carved into the limestone cliffs of the notch. That was "Fort Shuster," or "Shuster's Mansion," a kind of combination OP, advanced command post, and field hospital. It was so named for the battalion surgeon of the 3rd Rangers, Doc Shuster, who'd treated many wounded there. The windows were all blown out, some said from our own naval artillery's shells, and the stonework was flecked with chips and scars from shrapnel, machinegun fire, or direct hits, but the building itself was standing intact.

At the crest the men who weren't on observation teams finally saw what they'd been hearing about, and shooting at, for nearly three weeks. The convoy, with some British tanks in tow, moved slowly, with frequent stops, so there was time to look out on the panorama before them. Mount Vesuvius, the villages of Sarno, Pagani, Vitri, and Nosara. Along Highway 18, passing westwardly from Vitri and through Nosara was the rest of the British 23rd Armored Brigade and elements of the American 36th Division. Kenneth Smith glanced down from the truck he was riding in. On the side of the road lay a dead German soldier, the first he'd seen so far. The corpse had a horrible head wound crawling with flies. "When we went over the mountain to advance I seen him lying on the side of the road. Kind of spooky, seeing a man laying there with his head half blown off," he said.

As the battalion came down the reverse slope of Mount de Chiunzi, the only route was a narrow lane with numerous switchbacks owing to the exceedingly steep grade.

Sobon remembered an unfortunate incident which exposed the tensions between American and British forces that were rapidly developing. "When we were finally going down the mountain in Italy," he said, "On this one road that was open, as we're coming down this British tank moved over to get out of the way and it went over the cliff. It was a pretty good drop off this cliff and these guys got killed. We didn't know anything about it until we got down to the bottom, that's when we seen them around there and what happened. The British told us this GI truck coming down wouldn't move over and, I guess, well that road was too narrow for two vehicles, especially a tank, to pass. I said to those British guys, well, if I was driving a tank I would never move over for a truck if it was that risky. But they're mad, they're mad as all hell, they're mad at you, you did it, they said. They tried it I guess, and they found out you can't do it. They moved over and realized the ground gave way, it wasn't that strong, and that was it."

Once it had descended to the plain below, the battalion got into line with the British and Texans. Though the Germans were falling back all along the front, they were keeping up a sporadic shell fire on the advancing column. Fortunately their fire was unfocused and no one in the battalion was made a casualty. Late that afternoon the 319th went into position near the village of Sala. The situation was very fluid, with no clear line of demarcation between territory still held by the Germans and the edge of the allied advance. For the first time in weeks no fire missions were called.

Still, the Germans had only just vacated the area and were not far off.

When "A" Battery's XO took Ted Covais with him to scout the fringes of their advance, the two had a close call. "I'm talking to Lieutenant Blanc," Covais recalled, "And we're standing up by a wall, just talking like maybe a foot and a half away. All of a sudden I hear, Pzing! Like a bee. The bullets were whizzing right by, like a bee, you know? When you can hear that you know you're close! It was a sniper in the woods. We went down right away, because when you hear that pzing, pzing, you've got to be alert, ready to hit the ground. We hightailed it out of there in a hurry."

In the morning the outfit reverted to division control. Colonel Lewis of the 325th, designated as General Ridgeway's proxy for the time being, ordered the 319th to proceed to a bivouac area in the vicinity of Castellamare with the 504th. As the American column proceeded through each tiny hamlet along the way they were met by groups of cheering civilians, obviously overjoyed to finally be reached by the Allied advance. Here and there surrendering Italian soldiers would emerge from hiding, sometimes calling out, "Hey Joe! Don't shoot! I got an uncle in Brooklyn!"

As they advanced across the plain, Mount Vesuvius loomed larger with every mile. The British X Corps drew off and skirted around the base to the East, while the 504th and 319th turned West and captured Castellamare. The battalion was closed in its assigned area by late afternoon, September 30. As good as it felt to be on the move and victorious, foxholes still had to be dug before anyone could rest.

Ryan and another man decided to reconnoiter the next village up the road, before darkness set in. He remembered what happened in great detail. "Me and this guy Larkin Reed, he was from Hollywood, we went walking up the road up to this little town. We went in, we weren't looking for trouble. We met these Italians cooking in the street. So we paid them to make us something to eat. We got a bowl of chicken. I knew to look for a priest if you want to find someone who speaks English, so they got the priest.

In his album, Roland Gruebling captioned this Naples photo "Hospital Raiders". Courtesy Gruebling family.

BATTERY!

I was talking to him and eating chicken. When I got to the bottom of the bowl the head and feet were in there too. The priest asked, 'Aren't you hungry?' Then I thought I saw a Kraut run across the alleyway. I asked him, 'Any Germans around?' 'Oh yes,' he said, 'Come up in the church tower.' We did and could see about 200 bivouacked on the other end of the town. 'You should go capture them,' he told us. Reed says, 'Yeah, let's capture them.' I said, 'Keep your mouth shut.' Then I said to the priest, 'Would you come with us and tell the Captain what you showed me?' So we took the priest back to Captain Manning. The priest asked him, 'Are you going to help?' He asked him what he'll do about it, what orders he'll give to the men. Manning said, 'Yes, I'll give the march order. Get this outfit ready, let's get out of here!'"

"C" Battery pulled up stakes and made for a more secure location where infantry support was known to be close at hand. In their haste to break off contact with the enemy the Germans were making a hurried retreat, with small units sometimes over-run by the more mobile Americans and British. When this happened, the policy was to avoid pitched battles since these pockets of resistance could be neutralized with minimal casualties later.

During the night of September 30 -October 1, the battalion was attached by division order to the 504th Parachute Infantry. The men were told to abandon their freshly dug foxholes and get back in the trucks. They left their bivouac area shortly before midnight, September 30 and before daylight October 1st, occupied positions in the vicinity of Torre Annunziata, actually a suburb of Naples.

When the convoy stopped on the edge of town everyone was dog tired. The town itself was a wreck. Over the preceding weeks battalion observers had watched from the Sorrento heights as American and British bombers made raids which slowly reduced most of the town to stone and masonry rubble. At night the flames of burning buildings could be plainly seen through their field glasses. Torre Annunziata was a ghastly ruin now, but what really grabbed hold of the men was the stench of rotting corpses which filled the air. Unlike larger urban centers which had underground facilities or bomb shelters of some kind, this sad town on the outskirts of Naples had little to offer its inhabitants other than the cellars of their homes and apartments, leaving many of them dead beneath the ruins.

Even in the darkness, clusters of civilians or Italian POWs could be seen from the motor convoy as the 319th rolled through town. They were digging out the dead and the dying. Some were German casualties, but the majority were civilian residents. Refugees were all over the place. One man in "C" Battery looked around from the back of the truck he rode in and saw an old woman running aimlessly back and forth, screaming into the night and pulling out her grey hair by the roots.

Torre Annunziata exemplified so much of the civilian misery the guys had seen since landing in Italy. When Bob McArthur was finally able to write a long letter home later that month, he described the things he'd been through. Responding to his brothers' wish that they could see action in a combat zone like him, McArthur had to caution them, "I have seen civilians by the hundreds leave the area where the war is going on. Some were a few weeks old babies in their mother's arms. Some were just old enough to walk. Some are pregnant women, some are old men and old women, grey headed, and they had everything they owned on their backs. Some of them had no shoes. Most of them had very little clothing, and it was really cold at night up in those mountains. None of them had any food and God knows how long they had been without it. On those people's faces was written the horrors of the war. Until a person has seen these things he doesn't really know what the war is like. I have seen little children run down a rocky road with their little feet already cut to the quick, but they kept on going. It makes a man sick to his stomach to see these things. No, I know you don't want to see all this."

The determination was already made that the 82nd would not be lingering once Naples was taken. The airborne troopers were to continue another twenty miles north to the Volturno River, behind which the Germans were retreating. However, this was only expected to go on until General Clark and the British could regroup and establish themselves along the south bank. The division would then return to Naples and begin occupation duty. Each unit in the division was thus accordingly assigned a portion of the city for which it would be responsible. The 319th, in consideration of its role at Chiunzi was given the fashionable Vomero district, which overlooked the bay. Manning later described it as "a classy residential portion of the city." As a special distinction, "C" Battery was also selected to lead the division artillery into Naples as the convoy penetrated the city proper.

Silas Hogg wasn't impressed with the honor, "They told us one morning, you will get the honor of taking Naples. Honor of taking Naples, my ass! We took Naples alright, for a whole bunch of men killed."

It took most all the morning to work these plans out and distribute the orders, but around noon word came down that Naples was secure to enter. Everyone climbed back in the trucks. No one was sorry to leave Torre Annunziata with all its offensive smells and suffering humanity, but it wasn't until they were well away from the village that the guys in Ed Ryan's truck started to complain that the odors of decay seemed to be traveling with them. Noticing that their uniforms were soiled and the bed of the vehicle was wet with gore, the men deduced that the truck they were riding in had been drafted that morning to transport decomposing bodies to a collection point at another part of the town. In the process the benches and floor of the truck were smeared with the partly liquefied entrails of the dead.

Ryan remembered, "I had my barracks bag with me, it was lying in the juice. Normally the barracks bags were carried in a separate truck; unless you've got some loot in there you need to keep an eye on. What a mess."

The 319th, with "C" Battery in front, did lead the 82nd's Artillery into the city. "Entering Naples was something else," remembered Sartain. "The natives were out in force. We got kisses, bananas, apples and flowers. As battery commander, Captain Manning's jeep was indeed at the head of the artillery column. His driver, Sosa, could claim for the rest of his life that he'd driven the first jeep into Naples, saying, "At least I didn't see anyone ahead of me."

Ryan looked back on it the same way, "I expected resistance but it didn't happen. There was a whole bunch of Italians there, tens of thousands of people. We were grabbing girls and kissing them. Some Italian guy jumped up on the truck. When this GI turned around this guy kissed him on the lips. Boy was he pissed. He kept saying, can you imagine that son of a bitch, kissing me!"

The crowds eventually thinned out. With all the vehicles streaming with flowers the outfit made for a curious procession. Each of the men had his own cache of foodstuffs crammed into his musette bag or the pockets of his field jacket. A few had been lucky recipients of bottles of wine. All had been kissed as many times as their libido or tolerance dictated.

Though the enemy had evacuated the city there were scattered reports of snipers as well as apprehension over booby traps or other surprises left behind by the Germans, but the 319th found the Verumo quiet and safe as far as anyone could determine. In fact, the neighborhood was made up of very comfortable homes and apartments of more affluent Neapolitans, and included a first rate night club, all situated along a broad avenue known as the Via Taza. Many of the residents had already fled the city, perhaps because they were fascists, but more likely simply to escape the air raids and approaching battle front. Consequently many homes were already vacant.

While the men slept on the sidewalks that night, battalion officers scouted through their neighborhoods for suitable accommodations.

"We took over a vacated estate, complete with a Lancia sedan, for Battery "C"", explained Manning.

This billet selected for "C" Battery's enlisted men was a three story mansion situated at a fork in the Via Taza as it came up from the lower portions of the city. Rumor was that it had been the home of a big shot in the fascist movement. Who's ever it was, the home was as different from sleeping in a foxhole as could be imagined.

Corporal Kenneth Smith thought the accommodations were splendid, saying, "At Naples the Germans and Italians, the ones that lived out there took off when we came in and took over their homes. We lived in a real good, you might call it a castle. That was a beautiful place. The owner of the house had to be a millionaire. He was a fascist, he believed in Hitler and Mussolini. We were up real high and we could look out over the Mediterranean and see all the ships out there."

The home chosen for "A" Battery's billets was every bit as nice. In fact, none of the guys in the battery had ever lived in such a luxurious building. Captain Cargile's "B" Battery and the Headquarters Battery were similarly quartered nearby in the Verumo.

Before anyone had a real chance to settle in and get cleaned up the first order of business involved sweeps of the district to confiscate weapons. Not all of what was collected was turned in to the authorities. A lot of the guys in the 319th took the opportunity to arm themselves with handguns for their own personal use. German automatic pistols

American troops advance through Naples, early October, 1943. Covais Collection.

were already a favorite battlefield souvenir, as was the Italian Beretta. These latter were considered sportier than the German pistols but keeping a supply of the ammunition was a problem. Those men more pragmatically minded chose revolvers since these were unlikely to jam the way automatics had a habit of doing. Covais pocketed a small, nickel plated revolver with a collapsible trigger. Rappi acquired a British Webly. Ed Ryan got one too.

Remembering the acquisition he said, "They had a big shake down in Naples. This Ginzo guy came up and he said, would you buy a pistol if I gave it to you? I said, yeah, I'll give you something for it. So he handed the Webly to me. He had some kind of relative took it away from a Limey before that. I liked it because it couldn't hang up. I give him ten bucks. I could have just taken it away from him."

Bob Storms and his crew found themselves searching the residence of a well known and high ranking Fascist official. Surrounded by mobs of vengeful Italians looking to vent their misery on the regime which had led them to this, Storms and the other GIs became uncharacteristically destructive. He recalled, "As a matter of fact, in, what the devil was that Italian guy's name there, he was a stinker anyway. He was in the Italian army. Anyway, I got in his home. He had a beautiful home there in Naples. That was quite a place. Everything was marble in that house, the hallways and the steps and everything. Beautiful marble Oh, his wife had some clothes. We throwed them all out the window to the peasants. They grabbed them. We throwed everything out of the house we could throw and then we hand grenaded the house."

Then he remembered a funny story. "We were on the second floor and I went in there with my crew. Boy I heard the guys hollering and screaming in the bathroom. I grabbed my gun and run in there. Who the hell was it, Leggs or one of them hillbillies that I had. I think it was Leggs, he wanted to blow up the toilet. I heard him hollering like hell. I run in there, I said, what's going on? Well, they got the regular commode, and then a little one, and then you got your shower. What it was the one in the middle's for the women. It was the first one I ever seen. Leggs wanted to blow it up with a hand grenade. I said, what's the matter? He said, every time I sit down it sticks me in the ass! He wanted to blow it up because the water was shooting up. So finally I figured out what it was, I said, no, no, no, Leggs, you got to sit on that other one. This one's for the women to flush themselves out. You try to explain that to a hillbilly, you got some problems!"

Occupation duty had only just started when the battalion was called into action again. This time the 319th was selected to support the 505th Parachute Infantry in their drive to secure bridgeheads over the Volturno River. The mission was understood to be of a limited duration, so each battery designated a few men to leave behind as guards for the new billets.

"We didn't want any rear base people coming in and taking our place while we were gone, you understand," said Sartain.

The next day, October 4th, the outfit was on their way again, its vehicles in among those of the British 23rd Armored brigade.

"Our goal was to secure a crossing over the River Volturno," remembered Captain Manning. "We were integrated with some Brits - and continually had to wait while they made tea!"

It was frustrating to be held back just when it felt like they had the Germans on the run. The guys in the outfit had been around British troops in North Africa, and in the context of training just thought their habits were amusing quirks. The Allied drive from

BATTERY!

Naples to the Volturno and beyond however, was the first time they needed to cooperate closely with Commonwealth troops under combat conditions. The juxtaposition of British patient doggedness against the comparatively over eager Americans with their naïve enthusiasm for a fight, wasn't always smooth.

In "A" Battery, Corporal Covais, for example, was perturbed, even years afterward, saying, "At the Volterno River we had to stop because the British had a timetable. They would not move forward. They do things their way, they move slowly, by a timetable."

Above all it was the seeming obsession with tea which drove the Americans crazy. Sosa had respect for the Brits as soldiers, but the fixation with tea puzzled him. "Good fighting men," he said. "Especially some of the tank outfits, but no matter where they go the first thing they do is jump out of their tank, make a fire and start making tea. Crank up a cup of tea, they would say. Tea tea tea, boy they love that tea."

Storms, when asked about the move up to the Volturno, had his own memory of the British customs regarding their favorite beverage. The "A" Battery machine gunner said, "We had a lot of trouble with them every time we tried to move. They could be fighting on the front line and everything. When it comes tea time, if they're in the middle of the road or I don't give a damn where they are or what they're doing, everything stops! It's tea time, and when its tea time, I don't give a damn what happens, they have their tea, and that's no lie! They get their little five gallon cans out, pour water in there, and build a fire. They come with sugar and milk already in it. Whether you like it or not, that's what you drink. You stop, you build your fire, the Germans look over there so they have tea, and we have tea too. You keep your eye on them. The minute somebody starts drifting away from the fire, look out, you're gonna get shelled pretty quick. I guess the Germans liked it too because they didn't have to fight while they were having tea. Now I can see why they took so long to do anything. They'd be fighting that war yet if it wasn't for us."

Sartain's view on the whole question of tea time was more balanced, but essentially echoed those of the enlisted men. He said, "We couldn't understand why they'd stop in the middle of a battle at 3 o'clock in the afternoon and make their tea and all that humbug. You know? Some of our guys would comment at them and they'd say, 'What's your rush? What's your hurry Yank?' I didn't agree with it. I thought the damn war ought to be won. We were impatient, we were all gung ho. We didn't know sheep shit from shinola anyway. We had to learn the hard way. But the British had been over there, they'd been fighting for three years. They weren't going to win the war overnight. They were going to win it, but not overnight. They were very good, very good."

By the time they reached the vicinity of the Volturno it was after sunset and the weather, which had been mild for so long, was turning inclement.

After dark the outfit got to their new position. Steady rain was falling. Foxholes were dug anyway and immediately developed standing water. Exhausted, the guys spread shelter halves over their slit trenches and tried to sleep until each was roused by a Sergeant warning them, "You guys keep awake. You better be careful, stay awake. Make sure you don't have any Germans around here, crawling around, because they'll cut your throat. They'll crawl up to you and slit your throat!"

It was an eerie way to begin at a new position, but there was evidently some genuine reason for the men to be warned of this danger.

In his postwar memoir, Captain Manning also made reference to this issue when he cryptically commented, "When we reached our security checkpoint we found that the entire squad had been knifed during the night."

The description, and the context in which it was given, are vague. To further obscure the question, no official battalion records are extant for this period which might shed some lightand leaving the mystery unsettled. Ultimately it is left unclear whether Manning was writing about men from the battalion, if he witnessed this first hand or was himself passing along a rumor. What ever the truth was, the message made it clear that the 319th was back in the thick of it again.

That night the rain kept coming, growing heavier with each hour. The temperature started to fall too. It had been a long time since the guys were in weather this cool. "It rained, and I mean it really rained hard," said a man from "B" Battery. "The first thing I knew the water was running in and we were up to our knees in water." It was the same story in "A" and "C" Batteries as well.

As Ryan explained, "That was bad up there on the Volterno. It was awful wet and it was very cold. The only medicine for the cold was to heat up Italian vino. That would help. The way you could get warm was you'd stay in the foxhole till the water warmed up from your body."

Sartain had his own introduction to life on the Volturno, which he recalled with some amusement years afterward, "I remember in the night I had to get up out of my foxhole to relieve myself. It was dark as pitch. I got lost and I just lay back down on the ground and waited till daylight. I wasn't going to meander around and get shot. Man, if you moved at night you had it. When morning came I wasn't ten feet from my foxhole."

As the rain continued the following day, and the day after that, trucks and tanks ground the earth into a soupy morass. According to Kenny Smith, "You couldn't drive the trucks or nothing because you'd get stuck every time."

Another man remembered one tank hopelessly mired to its fenders, "They had three jeeps trying to tow it but it didn't work. They gave up when the jeeps broke their axels."

Yes, the Germans were retreating, but they were also doing so on their own terms, insisting that the Allies be kept on the south side of the Volturno as long as possible. The river was part of the so-called German "Barbara" line, kid sister to the more substantial Gustav line further North, but formidable in itself. Although the Volturno was not very deep, it was broad and getting deeper with every passing day now that the rainy season was on hand. The Germans also had the

This photograph is believed to show members of "A" or "C" Batteries while the 319th was supporting the 505th PIR on the Volturno River, early October, 1943. Sartain collection.

advantage of some very prominent high ground on their side of the river, allowing them splendid observation of the Allies on the southern bank. It was a situation in many ways exactly the reverse of Maiori.

Speaking of the terrain on the Volturno, Sartain remarked, "It was flat. It was very very flat."

Manning agreed, going on to observe, "Our positions were quite out in the open and received a fair amount of fire. We lost some men at the Volturno. There were no hills for OP's so we had to get right up into the front lines to direct fire."

Over the following four or five days, until about the 8th of October, the battalion supported the 505th PIR in it's objective to secure important bridges over the Rogi Lagni Canal in the vicinity of Villa Literno and to seize the town of Arnone. This latter city was located on a bend of the Volturno with significant railroad and highway bridges crossing the river at this site.

On the morning of October 6th "E" and "F" Companies of the 505th occupied the town of Arnone. Forward observers of the battalion were in amongst them. With the absence of high vantage points, structures of any height became the best, if not only, suitable locations for FO teams. Manning remembered one at Arnone in particular. "For battery "C" we chose the top story of a 3 story jail. It soon became a target in itself."

This building was located near the foot of the highway bridge. When the Germans launched a counter-attack to retake the city that afternoon, the 505th men holding the town were forced to retire in the face of a fierce artillery barrage followed up with enemy infantry crossing over to the southern bank in force. The "C" Battery FO team became trapped inside the jail, prisoners after a fashion, and cut off.

If control of the city was to be regained, it was imperative to prevent those Germans who'd entered Arnone from being reinforced. All three batteries brought their guns to bear on the town and the northern bank of the river with a ferocious barrage of their own. After action reports submitted by the paratroopers laconically commended the 319th, stating simply, "This fire was very effective." Once the battalion's 105s had the enemy pinned down, the stranded observers in the jail took advantage of the chance to make their escape back to the 505th's defensive positions.

During the action, lacking any elevated point of observation, Manning climbed atop a British tank and had Ryan hoist a radio up to him. "He got hold of the radio and was standing on the front deck of this tank, calling artillery fire from it. I said to him later, that was a pretty dangerous thing to do. His answer was, 'You've got to get this thing over with.'"

Earlier in 1942, while Manning was XO of "B" Battery, he developed a friendship with one of his junior officers, Lieutenant Benjamin Fitzgerald, of Fort Collins, Colorado. The young Lieutenant admired Manning's way of leading the enlisted personnel and the respect with which he treated those he was responsible for. A protégé of Manning's, and the Reconnaissance Officer of "B" Battery on the morning of October 6th, Lieutenant Fitzgerald had taken an FO team out early that day. They occupied a small farmhouse on the outskirts of Arnone until the enemy launched their concentrated artillery and infantry attack, forcing the party to abandon their advanced position. Though snipers and machineguns were peppering the building, Fitzgerald provided covering fire to allow the men under him to make their escape. The Lieutenant continued to serve as a one man defense, occupying the enemy until his men reached a point of safety.

By late that day, directing his battery's part of the battalion counter-fire, Fitzgerald was using a church steeple as his OP. It was an obvious observation point and as sure to attract fire as it would be useful in directing it. The expected rounds of 88mm artillery didn't take long to arrive. One made a direct hit on the steeple. Fitzgerald was found dead in the rubble and his radio operator was severely wounded.

Lieutenant Fitzgerald would become the first man in the 319th to be awarded the Silver Star, albeit posthumously.

The next morning the Germans made another attempt to retake Arnone. This time they were crossing over the railroad bridge on the town's western side. The enemy was spotted by members of "E" Company of the 505th and the 319th responded again with their howitzers. As the paratroopers later reported, "the fire was accurate and caused the enemy to withdraw."

In the month since leaving Bizerte the men had been in constant movement, getting little sleep and often little to eat, all aside from the continuous stress of combat. Already in a physically exhausted state when they reached the Volturno, the men started to succumb to the miserable conditions in which they were fighting. Malaria, pneumonia, and trench foot were among the maladies which appeared. Tech-Corporal Ryan came down with a serious case of pleurisy after a few days. With even the most shallow breaths causing a searing pain through his lungs, he was unable to keep going. Ryan was not the only one who reported to Doctor Bedingfield from "C" Battery that morning. Since it was impossible for ambulances to get anywhere near the gun positions without becoming mired in the mud, a jeep was scrounged up to bring him and a few other sick men back to Naples and deposit them at an army hospital.

"The hospital in Naples," he said, "it'd been bombed and one thing or another. There was no electricity and no working elevator. I was up on the fourth floor so they had to yank me up there. No beds, just a Terrazzo floor. Laid out two three blankets on it and there you were. The medics brought food around. They made it in tin cans with wires on them and had to carry it up from the kitchen."

Ryan quickly developed a respiratory condition on top of his pleurisy. He was pretty sick, and on the scale weighed 128 pounds, having entered the service at a portly 212. Clearly his health was severely compromised and needed attention. Ryan regarded the nurses and medics with respect but had a poor opinion of one battalion doctor. He complained, "That Hebert is the one I remember the most. He was no hero. One time I was mighty sick. I was down in this place in bed. Anyhow, he was banging this nurse in the next room and when I'd cough he'd tell me to shut up. I remember that. He didn't like to be interrupted."

Meanwhile, the fighting along the rain sodden Volturno dragged on. "One guy on the gun crew volunteered to go up there as a forward observer," Rappi recalled while thinking back on the campaign. "He was kind of an outlaw, a criminal type, but he was a good guy. He was comical and fun to be around, a good egg too. He'd come down from up there with the infantry and tell us about it."

Rappi was probably talking about Arthur Pease of Chicago, Illinois. Pease was one of the men transferred from "A:" to "C" Battery and certainly would have fit in with the other "C" Battery eccentrics.

Since the gun positions were quite hazardous already, it would have been unusual for a man to put himself in harm's way by asking to be assigned to an FO team. Most motor pool and gun crew members felt much like Lester Newman when he remarked, "Forward observers, I wouldn't have wanted to have been in the forward observers. We never got too close to them guys and we didn't want to get too close to them either!"

BATTERY!

But Pease's nefarious civilian life seems to have left him with an appetite for danger. Mahlon Sebring wouldn't get to know Pease until he joined the 319th as a replacement several months later, but he remembered him too. "He was a character. I don't know for sure what he done. I know what he told us, but I don't know if that's true or not. He said that he had an uncle that done something to his family. So one night he rented a moving van and went over his uncle's house and he moved every god damned thing out of his uncle's house and sold it. He said, 'I got the money in the bank, so when I get home I can spend it.' Every time he went into combat he signed an affidavit that he was going in under his own free will. I wondered what the hell was going on, so I asked him. He said, 'Oh, I was in prison, then I had a chance to go in the service and I took it. I don't have to go into combat; they can't force me to go in.' But he always went in."

Though the story about selling his uncle's furniture left the guys feeling there was a lot more which remained unsaid, it didn't matter. Everybody liked Pease in spite of his mysterious past.

Over the subsequent campaigns of the battalion, Ted Covais was often with Pease at the infantry positions and remembered him well. "This guy Pease was a former convict. He volunteered, and he went to jump school too. Some guys, they don't have to be prisoners or have a record, but you just can not work with them because they're just troublemakers, they're just wise guys, and I always avoided people like that. You've already got enough stress in the army. But Pease was no problem, we worked well together."

Pease became a permanent part of the "C", and later "A" Battery, signals section. Apparently he enjoyed the front line where he could indulge his appetite for thrills and adventure.

Summing up the fighting on the Volturno, Manning said, "We continued to pound the mountain on the other side of the river with all the fire we could. When the infantry went across, they still found an awful lot of resistance. In the end we were able to hold the crossing but not the advance. Other troops came forward through our lines and we were returned to Naples."

History has not been kind to General Mark Clark, and the bitter fighting that took place along the Volturno through the month is part of the reason. Several attempts were made to cross the river but it would ultimately take almost two more weeks before Clark was able to gain a firm foothold on the northern bank. In the meantime the Volturno was a dreary and vicious action in which men were continuously killed and wounded in an environment more akin to Flanders in 1916 than to most World War Two battlefields. Still, Clark's reputation with the common soldier was better than it now is with historians if Ed Ryan is any indication. "They were trying to get across the water there and the Krauts was giving them a hard time," he recalled. "He got in big trouble over that, but I remember you could actually see Mark Clark hiking back and forth in the mud, right in with the men trying to get something done. That's more than Ridgeway would do."

On October 8th the 319th received its march order to return to Naples. The Volturno had been dreary and depressing, so it already felt good to be leaving. As the battalion was packing up, preparing to depart, official word came down that Colonel Bertsch was leaving and wouldn't be coming back. There'd been a rumor afloat that this could happen since the outfit left Maiori. Part of the story involved a scathing report by Darby when the battalion was returned to the division about the Colonel's performance. When the Colonel stayed in Naples while everyone else went on to the Volturno, the pessimists pointed to Bertsch's absence as just another way of avoiding front line combat, while the optimists took it as a good sign. Now it was official, Major Todd would be taking command. Everybody's spirits soared and the prospects for an enjoyable occupation looked brighter than ever.

While the change was a major event for the battalion, it wasn't disruptive. Sartain explained why, "There weren't any real changes because Todd was the go to man already. He was running things already. The only difference was that everybody breathed easier."

Colonel Bertsch was always isolated and discouraged contact with his subordinates whether official or informal, making himself in effect a supernumerary, so his personal presence in his command was correspondingly limited.

As the battalion unloaded on returning to the Vomero the men were directed back to their billets and officers to the private apartments that had been reserved for them. Though they'd only occupied these quarters for a few days, it felt like a homecoming of sorts. It was also clear that this time they'd have an extended, and well deserved, rest.

The city, the bay, the sea, and the Isle of Capri visible off shore all made for a beautiful sunset every evening. Bob McArthur certainly thought so, and expressed his feelings now that he had a chance to write home. "I thought that the cities of Africa were pretty, but after seeing Italy I guess I can't say that any more. I guess they were just strange cities in Africa, but they are really beautiful in Italy. Out of all the places I have been in Italy, Pompeii and Naples are by far the prettiest places. No city in the USA has anything on Naples. Naples is located due north of Mount Vesuvius and the city itself is stretched along one of the prettiest harbors I have ever seen. Out in the harbor a few miles an island sticks up out of the sea and it is the island of Capri. Pompeii is another pretty city. Naples and Pompeii run together and no one can hardly tell where one ends and the other begins, with the exception of a few signs. I have seen all of these in pictures of geography books while in grammar school, but I am actually seeing them in reality now that I am here. This is really a beautiful country over here. You can see that I am just a small town country boy who is really seeing the sights. I've always loved to travel and have always wanted to see other parts of the world, but it took a world war the second to get me here."

Sartain remembered his apartment house as similar to a city rowhouse, with the lower floor situated a few feet below street level. "They were the best quarters we had during the war," he said. "A four story complex, very nice apartments, like a modern day condo, you know what I mean? Our land lady was named Christina, she's the one that took care of us."

"We were responsible for the operation of the night club, the "Orange Garden." Our landlady and a girl named Adrianna Cappocci were very instrumental in our getting the right contacts for that job," wrote Manning.

The nightclub featured a marble dance floor, well stocked bar, and a balcony from which lovers could view the lights of the city below and the stars above. Except now it was an officer's club for the 82nd Airborne and there was no electricity in Naples. In fact, the retreating Germans had done all in their power to wreck the city and turn it into a humanitarian calamity for the Allies instead of a logistical asset. Hundreds of rubble blockades had been constructed across the streets. Water and sewer lines were blown apart, and the electrical power plant as well. Over 100 vessels had been scuttled in the bay to inhibit any supplies from entering the city by sea. Prisons were emptied, leaving the inmates to run free and prey upon innocent civilians. Booby traps and time bombs were also placed in locations where the Germans expected ranking Allied officers to be concentrated.

The Engineers worked night and day to bring the city back to life, but it all took time. As a stop-gap measure, some limited electrical power was drawn from generators in abandoned Italian submarines. Bull dozers cleared the streets while channels were marked out to allow supply vessels to enter the harbor. Airstrips were quickly brought back into use and the first liberty ship of food docked on October 5th. By the end of the month over 7000 tons of supplies were being unloaded each day.

In the meantime, unlike the Italians who lived in the countryside and could cultivate gardens or keep farm animals, the residents of Naples were hungry and becoming more desperate. Food shortages continued for a long time after the occupation began, and Allied soldiers were rightly seen as the best source of an immediate meal.

Bob Storms remembered what it was like, "You go down the street with a couple of apples or a couple of oranges in your hand that you got out of the mess kit. You look behind you, there'd be a whole string of people begging. Oh, my sister's gonna have a baby, all the reasons they should have the food. It was something to see. I'd never want to go through it again for any money, but I wouldn't take nothing for what I seen."
Captain Manning witnessed one demonstration of hunger which he'd never forget, "I remember seeing a skinny horse go down trying to pull a cart up one of the cobblestone hills. Three hours later there was only a pile of bones."

To maintain order the occupation troops were kept busy supervising the breadlines and several sources of potable water which the engineers had restored to use.
Lieutenant Ragland described it this way, "When the Germans left Naples they ruined a lot of things. The battalion had to run bread lines and water lines because they were short of bread and water. Then they'd have to have somebody kind of watch it so it didn't get out of hand and fight over the stuff. One of the guys said some lady come up there and said she was pregnant; she ought to get in front of the line. They found out she had a pillow stuffed in her. Then another time they had a little row going and I guess somebody fired a pistol in the air to get their attention, but it didn't take long till they got those things lined out."

"Night and day there was a steady line of people there with pots, pans, anything they could get to carry drinking water in to have for the house," said Storms of the civilians he saw. "They'd be in line night and day. You could walk down through there and pick out what you thought was the most beautiful girl or woman and take them for a walk. All you had to do was put her a few people ahead on the line. Because when a soldier puts you in line, there you stayed. We was the law. It's hard like that when people have to live under Fascist rule and then we come in."

On October 15th the electricity was restored throughout the Vomero, but because of a widespread suspicion that undiscovered bombs, hidden in numerous locations by the retreating Germans would be detonated by the electrical current, precautions were taken.
"I was there when they turned the lights on in Naples," said Rappi. "We all had to get the hell out of town that time in case there were bombs, if the current was hooked up to a bomb. We went out in the country and watched the whole show. You could see everything out there. Nothing went off. Nothing happened."

While part of the actions of the battalion appears aimed at pulling down the institutions of the defunct fascist regime, vastly more energy was directed at helping the average Italian, who elicited the sympathy of the American GIs. Restoring, and then maintaining, order, were the principle duties of the occupation. Kenny Smith thought it a lark most of the time, and was no doubt typical of how the other men felt about their responsibilities. He said, "We were pulling guard duty in Naples, but it wasn't much guard duty. I'd get in the jeep with a couple of men and drive around town. We could do just about anything we wanted to. We wasn't on no time schedule or anything like that."

This was all very easy. "Like a vacation," as another man put it. Given the surroundings, field exercises with the howitzers were impractical. Still, the men needed to be kept in shape and under discipline.

Manning remembered that, "Our training consisted primarily of long hikes and calisthenics."

Another officer described the routine similarly, "Fall out in the morning and do calisthenics, maybe a little close order drill, we did that all the time too."

Once Ed Ryan was returned to the outfit after his bout of pleurisy he got a tour of his new quarters from his buddy, Larkin Reed. The Californian confided to his pal that as luxurious as the "C" Battery accommodations were, he'd found an even better location in the cupula situated on the roof.

"See, if they can't find you then they can't volunteer you for duty or details. So we slept up there where no one could find us," Ryan clarified.

About this time the troops who'd been engaged at Maiori were reassembled at an airfield outside of Naples to be reviewed by General Clark. The 319th was at one end of a line of men, nearly a mile in length, drawn up for review, but most of them were from the Texas 36th Division. As the General's car, with the other accompanying brass on board, pulled on to the landing strip, officers brought their commands to attention with the order, "Ten-hut!" Company and battery commanders echoed the order, which was then taken up by their sergeants in turn. The preparatory command of "Present!" followed by the command of execution, "Arms!" could be heard as it rippled down the entire length of the formation. Mark Clark's vehicle rolled slowly down the line while the band of the 36th Division at the opposite end struck up the Gene Autry tune, "I've Got Spurs That Jingle, Jangle, Jingle."

BATTERY!

Part 10: "Under the Ginzo moon."

The "Giardino Degli Aranci" or Orange Garden" became the officer's club for the 82nd Airborne in Naples. With all the pent up tensions of operations Husky and Avalanche, everybody was looking forward to getting the establishment opened and blowing off some steam in a civilized setting. It was only a short time before the Garden of Oranges was ready to receive customers. Off-duty officers started dropping in, alone or in groups, sometimes escorting army nurses or civilian ladies. Among the first gatherings was a spontaneous get-together of officers from the 319th. This time, for the first time in a while, they were shaved, bathed, well rested, and wearing their Class "A" uniforms, with all brass highly polished.

The gathering took on the atmosphere of a celebration, not just of the unit's outstanding performance since landing at Maiori, but of Colonel Bertsch's departure too. Captain Manning was there with Sartain, their friendship now solidly forged by the accomplishments of their stepchild battery. Lieutenant Hull, still on TDY from the 456th, was there as well, along with several officers from the other batteries, who joined or left the group as the evening progressed. Bottles of wine were ordered and uncorked, their contents poured into 75mm shell casings sawn off a few inches from the base and buffed to a gleam. "We used to take them and polish them and make tumblers out of them," said Sartain. "We'd use them for the salutes, you know? We'd pour drinks in it and salute and all that foolishness. It's called a Pop Blast."

"Well, here's to all you gentlemen, you've all done a swell job," went the first toast. Pop Blasts were touched together and the contents emptied. Sartain leaned back in his chair, fished out his pipe and puffed it up.

Manning held out his hand, saying, "Charlie, let me see that light, would you?" Cigarettes appeared, along with a cigar or two, and the table became enveloped in tobacco smoke.

"I want to make a toast", announced Manning as he raised his brass tumbler, "This time to my battery's Chief of Sections, Sergeant Richardson."

To Sergeant Richardson, repeated each man as he took a drink. If Captain Loughmiller or Vernon Blanc was there they'd have proposed a toast to "A" Battery's Chief of Sections. Anyone from "B" Battery would have followed suit for their own chief as well.

Sartain remembered the evening. "We all celebrated when Bertsch was pulled out. There were five or six of us, there was a lot of wine. We toasted everybody, GIs and everybody. I'm sure we had a hell of a good time."

As the pronouncements of generous good will made their rounds "B" Battery's Bubb Hawkins added his own, saying, "Boys, y'all don't forget Fitzgerald in all this."

The Lieutenant's name was spoken softly by each brother officer. Drinking in his memory had a solemn quality about it, causing the table to go quiet.

Then one Lieutenant broke in, "Here's to Major Todd, upending his tumbler." Someone else added with enthusiasm, "And good riddance to Harry Bertsch!" Laughter, then an animated discussion of the 319th's former commander followed. A few offered their own narrations of incidents in which the Colonel hadn't lived up to their expectations. One, in a voice accented by the Corn Belt, contributed, he kind of reminds me of what the hat-rack said to the hat. You go on ahead and I'll hang around back here.

More laughter, then someone grumbled, "I just can't believe they promoted him up to Div Arty, I just can't believe they did that," as he exhaled a cloud of cigarette smoke through his nose and rubbed out his cigarette.

"Come on man", answered another, "That's because he's West Point, and these West Point boys look out for their own, you see?"

The comment brought nods of agreement around the table. Manning made the observation that, in fairness, since Maiori, Colonel Bertsch probably had more experience coordinating the fire of multiple batteries than anyone else in the division. Not everyone at the table was mollified.

"That may be so, but I still think he's yellow", muttered one as Lieutenant Radcliffe Simpson joined the gathering.

Simpson was a 1st lieutenant in the headquarters battery now, so the bars on his epaulets were silver. He was also the only other graduate of West Point besides Colonel Bertsch in the battalion. With the less inhibited direction the discussion had taken since the first round of toasts, reference was made to his recent promotion.

Sartain looked back on the conversation, "The regulars, these West Point guys, got a promotion every six months. When Radcliff got his promotion he jumped everybody when he got his first lieutenancy. I have no problem with that now. I did then, oh yeah man. Oh yeah. But he was OK, he was a nice guy. He kept telling us to relax. Just relax, don't get up tight about us regulars getting promoted. You guys are gonna go home to your wives and children. We're gonna have to wait fifteen years before we get to be captain. Well, that wasn't the case, but it was in peace time. You know these guys in peace time; you could be a first lieutenant for years. All of us guys that were not regulars, we kind of understood this was their profession."

Everybody felt they'd gotten things off their chests by the time they made their way back to the apartments. Regular army or not, a sentiment of camaraderie bound them together as they walked back in the cool Neapolitan night.

The enlisted men were enjoying their time in Naples every bit as much as the officers. They didn't have access to anything so refined as the Giardino Degli Aranci, but there was a sanctioned nightspot called the "Allied Club" where drinks and dances with Italian girls could be had at popular prices.

Rappi put it most directly when he made the comparison between Naples and what they'd just left on the Volturno, remarking, "That was a nice switch. We lived right in town. You could go out and get anything you want to drink and there are a lot of women around. They didn't mind us fraternizing until we got to Germany."

With the possibilities what they were, it became important to look good. "So every day you wanted a shave you went down the street and sat there on the curb and one guy would shave you and another guy polishing your shoes. But the money was so little that you could afford it. You could have a whole pocket of money and not have nothing according to our money," explained Bob Storms.

Garrison caps were allowed if a man was off duty, and for those who were on friendly terms with their battery supply sergeants, a taste for Class "A" blouses shortened to waist length, inspired by British battle-dress jackets, became fashionable. The key was to first arrange for your current uniform to be declared unserviceable because, say, a fountain pen had leaked through the lower pocket for some odd reason. Once this was accomplished and a new Class "A" blouse was issued, an Italian tailor would rework the "unserviceable" tunic for a pittance and you still had a regulation blouse for purposes of inspection.

After the completely foreign people of North Africa, the Italians seemed refreshingly familiar.

While off duty one day, Casimir Sobon was surprised to see some neighborhood boys playing basketball in an empty lot, just as he'd been doing not so long ago. "So I played basketball with them," he said. "I never thought they knew what basketball was in Italy."

With fraternization in full swing, many of the guys "went native." Edwards, Josephs, and Roberts became Eduardos, Giuseppe's, and Roberto's overnight. Those who were uncommitted at home and many who weren't, found close, if temporary, attachments with the young ladies of Naples.

"I had a girlfriend in Naples," said Ryan. "What a time. The Italians make rings out of silver money and I had this Italian guy made a ring. We're out there under the Ginzo moon and she wanted to wear it. Then I couldn't get it away from her. She kept yelling something. I couldn't understand what she was saying, so I asked Rao, 'What's with her? Rao spoke fluent Italian. He says, 'She's nuts, you gotta get away from that.' Two guys had to hold her down while I pulled it off her finger. It's in the family yet."

Rao's ability to speak the language was a real advantage at such times, but he couldn't resist the chances it offered to play a little mischief. The mansion in which "C" Battery's enlisted personnel were quartered still had a housekeeping staff. Every morning a trio of Italian women entered the building as had been their custom for years, passing on their way the ground floor office where Captain Manning and the first sergeant had established the battery's orderly room.

"Manning would always say to them, good morning ladies," remembered Ryan. So they asked Rao, 'How do we answer him?' The medic listened and carefully instructed them in how to properly address a gentleman in English on such occasions. The following morning Ryan, Rao, and a few of their cronies made it a point to linger around the Orderly Room. When the three women approached, Manning greeted them with his customary, 'Good morning ladies.' They were ready this time. They smiled at him and proudly answered, 'Fuck you Captain!'"

October 10th, 1943, Corporal Covais on duty on a naples sidewalk. Covais collection.

"It was a long time before anyone in the battery could salute Manning without cracking a smile," said Sartain. "I mean, there'd be this smirk on their faces and you just knew what they were thinking."

Despite these intermittent miscarriages of romance or language, relations between the men in the 319th and the residents of Naples went exceedingly well. True, many of these friendships were driven by the need of the people to trade what they could for food of any kind. As Sartain recalled, "A loaf of bread could get you anything you wanted."

Notwithstanding this, the conviviality between soldiers and civilians was genuine, even with its pragmatic beginnings. Lots of men in the battalion came to remember their hosts with fondness for decades to come. Manning recalled one occasion demonstrating this bond when he "took some of the people who had been so helpful to us down to Pompeii to see some relatives and get some fresh vegetables. In return they gave us a tour of Pompeii. The old Lancia was quite well loaded on that trip."

Kenny Smith, the tallest corporal in the 82nd Airborne, was befriended by an Italian baker and his daughter. "They lived down the hill from where we lived, just two or three blocks. I run around with them for about a month. It was just him and his daughter. He said he was a baker, but he didn't have no flour to bake bread with. I said, 'Well I'll get some.' I was seeing his daughter at the time. In them days you couldn't be too particular, but she was nice looking. I'd like to go back there and see them. She's probably an old lady by now."

That Smith would somehow procure sacks of flour and pass it on to his Italian friends was not a secret, nor was it particularly troublesome to his Captain. Indeed, Manning was glad his command could help out the civilians, even if it meant exercising some unorthodox initiative. According to his memoir, "C" Battery's commissary was "a department of our battery which operated very efficiently due to a super-scrounger named Corporal Smith. He "assisted" in the off loading of many ships coming into the harbor.

John Girardin knew of another arrangement concerning purloined foodstuffs, this time involving Bart Plassa, a member of his gun crew. "Pop Plassa, he was a baker by trade. I remember when we were stationed there in Naples he got involved with a baker. He got together with him and he used to bake our bread for us. He'd go out to the warf and trade certain items for flour and yeast, things like that. He would make bread for us. We were the only ones, Battery "C," to get fresh bread."

To say that Pop Plassa traded for the yeast and flour is almost certainly a euphemism for theft. It was, of course, how all these sacks of flour came into the hands of Smith, Plassa, and no doubt others, in the first place. Theft was ubiquitous throughout the army, especially between units and branches. Getting caught was considered the only real crime as long as one wasn't stealing from another guy in the outfit.

Take the example of cigarettes, which were more of a staple than bread to the average soldier. For some time smokes were in short supply and their quality poor. In the field this would have been an inconvenience the guys would just have to tolerate, but in Naples cigarettes were the coin of the realm and could be traded for anything.

Louis Sosa quietly considered the situation, calculating what could be done and how one would need to go about it. Having access to Captain Manning's jeep, he hitched up a cargo trailer and recruited the help of a couple of associates from the battery. They went down to the docks and scouted around until they saw crates of cigarettes being loaded onto British supply trucks. Following one as it departed, Sosa drove along behind until the time was right. Suddenly accelerating, he cut the truck off, jumped out and thrust a souvenir pistol in the driver's face. Sosa told him not to make a move. Meanwhile the others jumped in back and took what they came for. After they'd filled up the trailer with crates of cigarettes, Sosa and his confederates disappeared like the gang of bandits that they were. The heist only took moments, and when they got back the smokes were distributed among the guys in the battery.

"We wouldn't have hurt them, but they didn't know that," said Sosa, looking back on the caper decades later.

But what goes around comes around. Sartain himself remembered thievery against the battalion as well.

"I forget who it was who had the jeep stolen at the port in Naples," he said. "You couldn't leave your jeep unattended. If you did you had to fix it, you had to open the hood and take the rotator cup off. Even then you'd have to be careful because the base section boys would come by in another vehicle. They would pull up and latch a rope on to it and just take off with it. Pull it away. Well, the navy boys would steal it too. They'd take it to the side of the ship, drop a cable and lift it up and put it on the ship. In the navy they're painted grey. Then they'd drop it back down. You're looking for your jeep, there's a brand new jeep painted grey, it can't be yours. What happened to yours? Well, it's gone!"

Kenny Smith's scrounging efforts on behalf of his baker friend finally caught up with him. Referring to a modus operandi which was apparently well established, he said, "I was following the truck, and it stopped. That's when I jumped out and got a hundred pound sack of flour and they caught me. They caught me putting it in the jeep. Hell, they had a truckload! I was just 18, I didn't know any better. We was young back then, didn't think too much about it."

The British MPs who'd spotted Smith tossing hundred pound sacks of flour into his jeep didn't see it the same way though. Maybe the British military was just fed up with all the missing flour, not to mention a recent and very brazen armed robbery of a supply truck loaded with cigarettes. In any case they weren't very happy.

When the battalion was notified that one of their men was being held in the British guardhouse, Sartain went over to fetch him. The British Provost Guard Officer was in a sour mood, but led Sartain to Smith's cell. The young Hoosier was scared and relieved to see a familiar face.

"In fact, my Captain told me, he said, 'Now don't worry Kenny, I'll get you out of this.' I said, 'OK,' and I just forgot all about it. That's all there was to it. We never did talk about it after that." But he was some man, a good Captain, an A-1 man, I'll say that. He was young at the time too."

Though Smith, in his memory didn't recall Sartain as being a 1st lieutenant at the time, the relief he felt was obvious and no doubt attributable not only to Sartain's reassuring words, but to his already growing reputation as the enlisted man's friend. "I remember Kenneth Smith stealing that sack of flour from that British depot," recalled Sartain. "It was a major international deal at the time. We got involved in it, said what's this all about? I told them, what are you going to do with a guy that steals a sack of flour, you gonna put him in the brig? You're gonna dishonorably discharge him for making bread? It was very innocuous. It would have been a general court martial and I would have defended him, since he got to pick his lawyer, but we got out of Naples before it all came up. Then everybody dropped it. We left before they could do anything about it. I think it was part of a grand strategy with the Americans and the British and all, to leave all of that malarkey alone."

The 319th's performance in the fighting from Chiunzi to the Volturno was praiseworthy and already well established. Yet a greater acknowledgment of their efforts was demonstrated when a Presidential Unit Citation was awarded. About the first of November the battalion was drawn up for this special occasion. "There was some kind of function, a ceremony. Gavin and Ridgeway showed up," recalled Sartain.

With everyone at attention, assembled in close order, the citation was read aloud: "As authorized by Executive Order 9396, the following units are cited by the War Department in the name of the President of the United States as public evidence of deserved honor and distinction. The 1st and 3rd Ranger Battalions, with the following-attached units: 2nd Platoon, Company A, 307th Airborne Engineer Battalion; 319th Glider Field Artillery Battalion, Company H, 504th Parachute Infantry Regiment, Headquarters Battery, 80th Airborne Antiaircraft Battalion, Battery D, E, F, 80th Airborne Antiaircraft Battalion, and Medical Detachment, 80th Airborne Antiaircraft Battalion are cited for outstanding performance of duty in action during the period 10 to 18th of September 1943."

This was the first award of its kind given in the European Theater. The men were beaming with pride, "But," added Sartain, "that citation was originally only for the Rangers. Then Todd got wind of it and thought we should get it too, so he went through what ever channels he had to go through to get us on it. You know, Todd had a lot of savvy that way."

Of course Naples was still within a war zone and not all that far from the front lines. As much like a vacation as the occupation duty often seemed, any day, particularly around twilight, was apt to be interrupted by an air-raid which would send everyone scrambling for the nearest bomb shelter.

Sartain remembered his as being attached to the back of the officer's apartment building. "It was a big cave cut out of the hill. When we heard the air raid siren go off we all rushed into the air raid shelter, soldiers and civilians too. They'd bring a bunch of lanterns and candles and all. So after a while we hooked us up a generator to a light bulb. A lot of the civilians would show up with something to eat and maybe some bottles of wine. Man, it was a big party. It got so we liked the air raids, we didn't care if the air raid was ever over!"

Considering the convivial atmosphere, well remembered anecdotes were bound to take place.

Sartain recalled one with much pleasure in the telling, "My friend Butler from the 320th visited with me a lot. They were in a building not too far away. This one time he was in the air raid shelter with us. Butler had this goose he picked up somewhere. He kept the goose on a little rope, tied to something in his quarters. He kept feeding it, kept feeding it. I think he was going to have a roast goose for Thanksgiving dinner. Goose pate, you know? Well, this private came in the air raid shelter and saluted. He said, 'Lieutenant Butler sir, your goose is loose.' Well we all went looking for the goose, everybody, even the natives, they all scoured the neighborhood, but we never did find it."

Exposure to German air attacks were something every man in the 319th would remember as part of their time in Naples. "One night we had a German plane coming right down the road," remembered Casimir Sobon. "Sirens started wailing and a plane came down. He dropped one bomb about three blocks up, another bomb about two blocks up, and a third bomb landed right in the street, right smack in front of our building

BATTERY!

where we were staying. The concussion just traveled through the building. If you were sitting down it lifted you right up. The women were down there with their babies and all, screaming! Christ. It was amazing but there wasn't that much damage.

However, most of the time German bombing raids were a very serious component of the occupation, and one which kept the men busy. Smith described why, "Every night up there Germans bombed that place. They'd come over Mount Vesuvius and drop bombs all over the city. We'd have to go around and check on the people there and help them out if they needed to be helped."

Civilians weren't the only casualties of air raids, as Bob Storms could well attest. "One night I was out there and about twenty to seven or something like that the Jerries used to come over and bomb. We heard them coming so we run in the air raid shelter. I just got nicely in there and he dropped the bomb right outside of the air raid shelter. Landed right outside the door. Last I remember I was going around the post like a pinball machine. Then when I come to, I heard everybody hollering and screaming. I waited till it quieted down and then I hollered for some help because I couldn't see or didn't know where I was. They come and got me and took me up to the hospital way up on the hill there in Naples. I was blind for a while. They operated on my eyes. It was mostly cement and concrete blowed in there and they had some job picking it out. Anyway, they saved both of my eyes. It took a few weeks but I came out 20 20 with my vision. I was so lucky on that. One night they blowed up one side of the hospital. We had good doctors and good nurses. They used to go down in the bottom to the air raid shelter. But us ones who couldn't be moved, that nurse used to stay in the room with us. We'd beg her to go down but she wouldn't, she'd stay right with us."

Storms spent the balance of the occupation in the hospital, recuperating from his wounds. Most guys of course were unscathed by the air raids. They carried on with their duties and recreations.

One of the favorites in the latter category included a visit to the Isle of Capri. Contests were held between gun crews to determine which could most correctly answer technical questions and have the cleanest howitzer. The winning crew would be awarded with a 24 hour pass to Capri.

Sartain remembered his own trip to the resort island with Captain Manning. The two hired a fishing boat to take them to the island, with a bit of a sight seeing excursion along the way. "Johnny and I decided we'd take a weekend off and go to Capri. So we landed over there and checked into our hotel."

After the pair were settled into their room an exploration of the island was the first item of business. In the plaza was a shop selling ice cream. It was made from goat's milk but was ice cream nonetheless, and the first either had tasted in many many months. Manning had heard about the funicular railway, a narrow gauge car pulled to Capri's highest point by cogs and cables. The two officers bought a ticket for the ride to the summit. From there the view was spectacular, with the turquoise Mediterranean Sea, the city of Naples, and smoldering Mount Vesuvius all forming a picturesque Italian panorama. "We wanted to go to what they called the Blue Grotto over on the other side of Capri," continued Sartain. "It was a restaurant with two big rocks right outside, always in photographs. So there was this little Italian with a mule and a two wheeled carriage, a buggy, and he'd take you around the island. I forget what the price was. It was drizzling and when we got to the restaurant Manning takes off his raincoat and puts it over the damn mule. I said, 'Manning, what you doing?' 'Well,' he said, 'At the cost of that damn mule I don't want him to get pneumonia!' We were feeling no pain anyway. He put the raincoat over the mule. So we paid the guy to wait for us and we went into the restaurant. You know, in Italy I couldn't wait to get meatballs and spaghetti sauce, but I never did get it. The natives didn't eat it that way." Sartain clearly remembered their menu selection that night, "Manning ordered mussels. I said, 'I don't eat mussels.' He said, 'Well, you eat oysters?' I said, 'Yeah.' In Louisiana, if you didn't eat oysters you were in real trouble. He said, 'Well, you'll eat these.' Anyway, the whole time the head waiter kept coming over, kept coming over, and saying, 'Coat, Coat, mule!' I'd say, 'OK, OK, OK!' When we finished eating Manning takes the coat off the mule, puts it back on and we go on back to the hotel down on the plaza."

Manning and Sartain certainly enjoyed themselves at Capri. But playing the tourist and dining out with a few drinks to wash it all down were among the more innocent of pleasures available to the men in Naples. The city, particularly the area near the docks, offered numerous opportunities for horizontal refreshment with prostitutes. Even on the first night, before proceeding up to the Volturno, the inexpensive price of love for sale made itself known.

Ed Ryan recalled that while waiting with the halted convoy along the Via Taza he and his buddies were approached by an Italian who asked them, have you had any yet? The guys were at first puzzled and asked, "What are you talking about?" The Neapolitan gestured toward a woman leaning in the doorway of the closest building, "Here she is," He said.

"They were giving them away for a C Ration," Ryan remembered.

Once back from the Volturno, things really got under way. In the bordellos near the waterfront, prostitutes could be bought for as little as a dollar until the air force came in and ruined everything. They shut the houses down and when they reopened all the prices were higher.

Carl Davis in Naples 1943. Covais collection.

"I think they wanted to keep out the riff-raff," as one battalion man later complained.

In fact, with an estimated 42,000 prostitutes in the city, the military took over supervision of the red light district in an effort to protect soldiers from crime, theft, fights, and disease.

This last item remained a serious problem. "Short arm" inspections were routine and there was a liberal distribution of prophylactic kits. Medics in every unit became known as "shanker mechanics" and were frequently sought out for impromptu examinations by men who suspected they were infected.

"Rao, our medic, the minute we settled in guys had him checking their privates," said Ryan. "That's the bull dog he caught, is what he'd say, because it hangs on and won't let go." Going on to described one such unfortunate, Ryan continued, "I remember we had a fella, a nice guy, he was built like a real man, but he never had any sex before. So they took him to town and had him one. The poor guy, he caught the worst kind of gonorrhea. When he'd piss he'd be crying like a baby."

Despite the temptation and only nominal expense involved, many men found that the risks and precautions were enough of a deterrent to discourage visits to common prostitutes.

"I tried one once and never again," said one "C" Battery man. "They give you some kind of stuff you shove up your dick to make sure you don't get the clap and stuff. Then you pee brown for several days. I said, to hell with this shit! So I never went back. Too messy and your fingers get all stained brown. God damn!"

With the disrupted social mores of wartime superimposed over the pressure on civilians to trade what ever they had, sometimes only sexual favors, for food and protection, many soldiers found intimate liaisons with local women easy to establish, even though they were not prostitutes as such. In any event, rates of infection continued to be high. By the time the 82nd left Italy for Ireland in mid-November, the division had one of the highest rates of venereal disease among the units in the theater.

Vice, in all its permutations, is an inevitable companion of war. Away from the restraints of home and isolated from the morally reinforcing presence of women, men who are young, lonely, uncertain of their future, and perhaps a bit frightened, will feel the urge to explore all of life's earthly pleasures while they still can.

One who ran afoul of these temptations was Lieutenant Harry Warren of "A" Battery. He was a 29 year old from the Carolinas who'd already served some months as an enlisted man at Fort Lewis, Washington, when he entered OCS. Commissioned a 2nd lieutenant in November, 1942, Warren then joined the 319th shortly before the battalion arrived in Casablanca. He must have given indications of an officer with potential, because he was placed as assistant XO of "A" Battery. When Warren courageously extinguished a fire among the ammunition stacks at his battery's gun position during the German attacks on September 13th, he garnered a recommendation for a Silver Star. Harry Warren was, in fact, almost certainly the first man in the 319th to be so recognized. However, as the campaign advanced his battery commander and fellow officers became concerned. When the opportunity was there for Warren to drink he did so, and ordinarily to excess.

"The way I understand it," remembered Ragland, "He was an alcoholic. One time he was a forward observer and it wasn't working out. When they sent him forward he would just get the shakes because he knew he couldn't handle it without his drinks. That's the story I got anyway. He had a drinking problem he couldn't control. He seemed like a pretty good guy as far as I know, but I never got all the details."

After the breakout from Chiunzi was accomplished it was noticed that Warren would make a habit of scouting each town and village for alcohol as his battery passed through, and once the occupation of Naples began, his compulsion to imbibe was unlimited by short supply. Only his capacity to function while on duty remained to restrain him. Drinking in moderation was the norm among most officers when off duty and the circumstances were appropriate. However, Warren was clearly unable to manage himself and headed for trouble. In the free wheeling and sometimes licentious atmosphere of occupied Naples, it was only a matter of time before things would start to come apart.

Sartain remembered the situation years later, making the point that controlling his alcohol consumption wasn't Warren's only vice, "He had an alcohol problem and he had a woman problem. Thought he was a ladies man, that's all he could think about. Then

Warren brought this prostitute to the officer's quarters. That's what really turned Todd against him."

That officers drank was known, and that officers sometimes engaged the services of women of easy virtue was also tacitly accepted, but all these activities had to be conducted in a discreet fashion.

"Sure," said Sartain, "there were a few guys who'd sneak women into their rooms, and then they'd have to sneak them out again. But when Warren just holed up with this tramp, parading her around the whole weekend, oh man, you can't do that, you know?"

About the middle of October Major Todd, having been made aware of Warren's conduct, summoned him to his office. The Major administered a severe reprimand, a tongue lashing to the effect that this nonsense had to stop. No more prostitutes in the officer's quarters, no more drunken binges with Warren bringing discredit to himself, the battalion, and the service. Todd could have summoned a court martial, local or general, and really left a black mark on the Lieutenant's record, but the Major was himself no teetotaler- far from it, he understood the relaxing effect an adult beverage could bring a man. After conferring with Captain Loughmiller and careful consideration of Warren's potential, Major Todd decided against such action. Warren's superiors sincerely hoped this incident would put the fear of God into him and make him get control of himself.

On Sunday, November 7th, the officers of the 325th Glider Infantry hosted a party at the Giardino Degli Aranci to honor brother officers who'd served with them at Maiori. Accordingly, all those of the 319th, along with those of the 307th Engineers, 80th Anti-Aircraft, and "H" Company of the 504th PIR, were invited. When Captain Loughmiller arrived, having strolled to the nightclub with Lieutenant Warren from the 319th's officer's apartments, the party was already well under way.

As they entered the building the two were immediately immersed in all the elements common to a party of the time. Lipstick, cologne, big band music, and cigarette smoke. Officers in pinks and blouses were dancing with their dates, who seemed to be equally composed of local Italian ladies and army nurses. Small square tables surrounded the marble dance floor. Each had a white table cloth, an ash-tray, and a pitcher of ice water. Most of those who weren't dancing at the moment were smoking and nursing drinks or clustered in small groups around the periphery of the room.

Loughmiller and Warren joined a few other battalion officers who'd dragged a couple of tables together. A red jacketed waiter took their order, then returned with the drinks. Anyone watching closely would have noticed that Warren seemed uncomfortable, self conscious, perhaps trying too hard to pace himself in light of his recent reprimand from Major Todd. An army band was playing "Robbins and Roses" while a local female vocalist did her best to sound like Helen Forest, albeit with an Italian accent.

Somebody said, "Hey, did y'all notice Colonel Bertsch over there?"

Gee, added another, "I'm surprised he hasn't come by to say hello."

As a waiter passed nearby, Warren gave up trying to sip his drink and knocked it back in one swallow. Holding up his hand to get the waiter's attention, he ordered another scotch and soda, adding, "Make it a double", as the waiter turned away.

Two hours later the band had advanced the tempo to a frenzied rendition of "Beer Barrel Polka." The dance-floor was crowded. Captain Loughmiller had been keeping an eye on Warren all the while and was aware he was drinking, but seemed to be maintaining himself reasonably well. In any event, Warren wasn't causing any trouble so he left him alone. When Loughmiller next glanced in the Lieutenant's direction he was slumped in his chair, slack-jawed and face to the ceiling, evidently passed out. The Captain could see he'd had enough, nudged another 319th officer and leaning close, told him, "Warren's drunk. Help me get him out of here."

The two got up and positioned themselves on each side of the sleeping Lieutenant, shaking him to get his attention.

"C'mon Warren, wake up, wake up," Loughmiller told him, but the man's head simply lolled around limply on his shoulders.

One Italian girl, an officer's date named Julia, was watching, amused by all this revelry. Thinking she might get in on the fun, she dipped her hand in the pitcher on the table and flicked drops of ice water into Warren's face. The drunken Lieutenant had been slowly rousing himself, but at this point, startled, an impulse of rage took over. Warren stood up suddenly, broke free, and took a swipe at the girl with his fist. Fortunately his aim was poor and Julia lurched backward. The blow was powerful, but only grazed her chin. A cluster of officers were on Warren immediately, restraining him.

"That's enough Warren, you're going home now!" The Captain commanded. Warren stared back at him blankly, weaving, and answered through labored breaths, "I will not."

Loughmiller spoke again, this time enunciating each syllable,"That is an order, Lieutenant."

Warren only shrugged off the hands holding his arms, turned, then staggered onto the dance floor and disappeared among the couples gathered there.

The incident put a damper on the evening, at least for those in the battalion, who started to gather up their dates and make their way toward the exit. There were going to be repercussions from this latest installment in Warren's alcoholic history, Loughmiller could see that. His mind was already on the further disciplinary actions which he knew he'd have to initiate in the morning, but at the moment, the Captain thought it best to leave Warren alone and let him settle down on his own. Loughmiller took care of the tab, then on his way outside, came across Warren standing near the doorway.

"C'mon Warren," he said, "Let's go home."

The Lieutenant had a strangely vacant look in his eyes. He didn't answer, only pushed his way past his CO and reentered the club.

Inside again, Warren picked up an unattended drink and sat down alone at a table next to the one occupied by Major Gardiner of the 325th. The party had peaked and the band started playing some slow numbers. The Major was talking to an army nurse. She'd seen the earlier spectacle and now felt the Lieutenant at the next table staring at her. When "Begin the Beguine" started, she suggested to the Major that they dance. Warren got up too, sat at the Major's table and ordered another scotch.

From the dance floor, Gardiner kept his eye on Warren, who in turn continued to watch the Major's partner. Gardiner and the nurse worked their way near Captain George Mc-Cawley of his regiment.

The Major nodded in Warren's direction, then said to McCawley, "Don't let that guy out of your sight."

Warren meanwhile kept up his drinking. When he attempted to get the attention of a passing waiter his movements were so unsteady he nearly fell out of the chair and upset the table. Gardiner and McCawley exchanged glances, then watched in disbelief as Warren arose, stumbled, caught himself and staggered toward a string of tables occupied by the 325th's CO, Colonel Lewis. Warren swept several glasses and an ash-tray to the floor, climbed onto the Colonel's table, lay down and passed out.

Gardiner and McCawley excused themselves from their dance partners and strode over to the Lieutenant. They enlisted the help of another 325th officer, Captain Hall, and with some considerable effort, were able to get Warren upright with an arm over each man's shoulders. They carried Warren outside and summoned the Major's vehicle. With the help of Gardiner's driver the three were able to get Warren into the back seat, and McCawley got in next to him. Major Gardiner sat in front and instructed his driver to take them to the quarters of the 319th's officers. On the way there Warren came to life. As with his performance on waking up earlier in the evening, Warren's first action was to throw a punch. This time he made contact, giving Captain McCawley a clout on the jaw. The two 325th Captains already tired of Warren, responded by forcibly restraining the Lieutenant until he stopped resisting. This time Warren was subdued for the night and deposited at the officer's apartments. He lay in the doorway for some time when, in a disheveled state, he slowly rose and went off to bed.

The next day Captain Loughmiller talked over the previous night's disorder with Major Todd, who had by this time already caught wind of the incident. Clearly the events called for a General Court Martial, involving as they did ranking officers of other units in the division. Major Wilcoxson was called in as the investigating officer and a few days later formal charges were submitted to the Judge Advocate's office.

On Wednesday, November 17th, the court was convened. Lieutenant Warren heard the charges against him: Drunk and disorderly in a public place and failure to obey the orders of a superior officer. Represented by Defense Council, Captain William F. Jones, he pleaded not guilty to both charges.

The Prosecutor, Captain W. H. Holz called his witnesses. These included Lt. Col. Bertsch, now the Executive Officer of the Division Artillery, "A" Battery's Captain Loughmiller, and Captain George McCawley of the 325th Glider Infantry.

The court convened at 1pm. After opening statements, Captain Holz called his first witness to the stand. Colonel Bertsch was sworn in identified himself. And he was then asked by the Judge Advocate if Lieutenant Warren came to his attention at any time during the night of November 7th.

Warren's former commanding officer testified, "Well, towards the latter part of the evening, I don't remember what hour it was, I glanced over to my left and I saw Lieutenant Warren standing there, facing a young woman. As I continued to look he attempted to strike her. He actually swung his fist to her face but she dodged and he failed to hit her. Then two or three officers took hold of him and held him."

Warren's Defense Council, Captain William F. Jones declined to cross-examine Colonel Bertsch and he was dismissed from the witness stand.

When Captain Loughmiller was called, he too testified to the events of November 7th. Warren's Defense Council then asked Loughmiller if his Lieutenant fully understood his order to leave the nightclub.

"Would you say that he fully comprehended the order as it was given to him?" Loughmiller had to answer," I don't think he did. I honestly don't believe he did."

The testimony of Captain George McCawley was probably more damaging. When asked, as other witnesses had been, if the defendant had come to his attention during the night in question, he replied, "We had eight or ten tables in a row across the front of the dance hall, one of which belonged to Colonel Lewis, and Lieutenant Warren occupied the top of four of those tables for a short period of time. He laid down there apparently to rest."

Next McCawley was asked how he would describe Warren's condition. He said simply, "I would say it was a deplorable condition for an officer to be in in a public place."

The only witness offered by the defense was Major Raymond M. Britton, the division's Adjutant General, who testified that Lieutenant Warren had been recommended for the award of a Silver Star for gallantry in action in the recent Italian campaign. The Major added that the award of this decoration was being held in abeyance pending the outcome of the trial.

A statement written by Warren was then read to the court and admitted as evidence as follows, "On the night of November 7, 1943, I attended a dance at the Al Giardino Degli Aranci in Naples, Italy, in the company of Capt. Albert E. Loughmiller. We had been drinking and apparently I imbibed too heavily for I remember nothing of the events with which I am charged. Such events perhaps occurred for which I am duly sorry and only too willing to offer any apologies to those whom I offended."

After a secret ballot of the jurors, all fellow officers from other 82nd Airborne units, the verdict was given. Warren was found guilty of being drunk and disorderly, but not guilty of willfully disobeying a superior officer. Warren's recommendation for the Silver Star was reiterated by the court. On the other hand it as well acknowledged his recent reprimand for reasons of similar misconduct during the preceding weeks. They concluded that Lieutenant Warren "seems to be a good officer, but tends to lose control of himself when under the influence of intoxicants. This trait is one which accused is capable of controlling."

The court ruled that even though, "the battery commander, the investigating officer and the battalion commander recommend that accused be eliminated from the service, this recommendation cannot be concurred in as it is felt that accused can be of some benefit." It was deemed that dismissal from the service "would be too drastic under the circumstances." In the end, Warren was made to forfeit $100 of his $165 monthly salary for a period of four months.

The entire court martial took less than an hour. The veracity of the charges against Warren never seemed in doubt and his only words of defense were little more than an admission of guilt. That Warren was able to preserve his commission as an officer seems remarkable, especially when considering that all three of his direct superiors felt he should have been "eliminated" from the army. The decision to retain him clearly says much about the keen need for experienced officers who'd demonstrated that they were capable of bravery in combat at that point in the war. Though Warren's antics on the night of November 7th did reflect poorly on the battalion, it was he as an individual who was dishonored and not the unit as a whole.

Word began to circulate well before the court martial that the division would be pulling out of Naples. When the battalions guns and larger vehicles were taken away to be loaded onto Navy transports the men knew their turn would be coming soon. As with the trip from New York to Casablanca, "A" and "B" bags were prepared. Finally the order was given that November 18th would be the departure date. Good-byes were said between GIs and their Italian friends, some of whom cried to see their American soldiers leaving them. Last visits were made to those still in hospitals.

Bob Storms was still recovering from the wounds to his eyes when a few guys from "A" Battery paid him a farewell visit. "They said they were getting ready to move out. I said, 'What do you mean?' They said, 'We're packing up, we're leaving Italy.' 'I said, 'What!' He says, 'Yeah, we got your stuff all packed. What do you want to do with it?' I said, 'Put it on the boat. Get a hold of the Captain, I gotta get out of here. I'm not loosing my outfit. Tell the Captain to get a jeep up here tomorrow, I'm going too!' So they said they'd be back the next day with a jeep and they did. I got some clothes and I got out of there. I found out later on that's why I lost my Purple heart because I didn't get discharged, I just took off. But hey, I stayed with my outfit anyway."

Storms knew that if the 319th pulled out of Naples with him left behind he'd be reassigned to a new unit full of strangers. For the average soldier in an outfit like the 319th with strong unit cohesion the thought of being a replacement in God-only-knows what battalion was unthinkable.

On the morning of November 18th the battalion was taking care of its final preparations; while there was still time, Captain Manning left Sartain in charge of the battery. He had one last mission to take care of before leaving the city. Manning went back to the estate, climbed in the Lancia and ordered Sosa to follow in his jeep. Parking near the hospital, Manning had Sosa give him the jeep rotor, then told him to keep a guard on the sedan.

Inside he found the men he was looking for, Ed Ryan and Willie Bragg. Ryan's pleurisy had reasserted itself and Bragg was having a flare-up of malaria. Now the two were lying side by side on the floor with a few blankets as a mattress. The Captain brought a few loaves of bread and probably a carton or two of cigarettes with him. After distributing the gifts, Manning explained that the battalion was leaving Naples that day. Then he added, "Listen to me, I'm not authorized to get you guys released. The doctors won't let me take you with me, but," Manning paused, looked around to see if any medical personnel were watching, then produced the jeep rotor from his pocket. "Here's the rotor to my jeep. It's down at the corner. If you two can find your way out of here in the next few hours, get in my jeep and make your way down to this dock that's where the battalion's ship is boarding. That's all I can do." Manning handed them a slip of paper with the dock number and the words USS Joseph T. Dickman, written on it. "If you don't make it, I want you to know it's been my privilege to serve with both of you men. Good luck." Captain Manning looked Ryan and Bragg in the eye, shook each man's hand and left.

At the corner Sosa was waiting with the Lancia. There was no time to waste now. Meanwhile, back at the Vomero the 319th was lined up along the street, each man loaded down in the same way they'd been when they stepped onto the shore at Casablanca. Of course they were veterans now. Those of them still unscathed had seen the face of war in Italy, stared it down and come through, if not unchanged, then at least intact. Sartain remembered that morning clearly. The 319th was assembled along the Via Taza. He was wearing the aviator sunglasses he'd grown so accustomed to. "We were all lined up ready to go. We were across from the building where the battery was living. This girl sticks her head out the window, third floor as I remember. She starts yelling, 'Pete, Pete, Pete! my baby no via da sada! My baby's not leaving today!' She was the girlfriend of "A" Battery Staff Sergeant Harold Peters. Peters didn't crack a smile, but everybody else just roared. What she was doing up on the third floor at 9am I don't know, but that's neither here nor there. Then I gave the order, everybody right face, march, and we marched away, down to the docks."

albert Lewis aot.
2369 N 9 th
Gary
Indiana.

146

BATTERY!

Part 11: "You couldn't dig a hole in Ireland."

Sick as they were, Ed Ryan and Willy Bragg had no intention of being left behind in Naples. They bundled up their belongings and, when the medics weren't watching, slipped off the hospital ward, down a back staircase, and out a side door. Manning's jeep was just where he'd told them it would be. Once the rotor was replaced they threw their musette bags in the back, cranked it up, and took off for the docks.

They'd become friends, these two, though at first regional differences separated them. "Willy Bragg was a real Reb from Tennessee," explained New York stater Ed Ryan. "He was an older guy. His wife's name was Mildred Nunly, she was just a teenager. Yeah, he was a real Southerner. I remember he told me that at Picket's Charge, Picket kept on coming at the Yankees even though his head was blown off by a cannon ball. He was like a lot of those Rebs. They didn't have much use for us. They'd call you Yank. Oh yeah, they'd call you Yank. That happened all the time, but some of those guys got to be great friends after we were in combat together. They all became great friends of ours once the shooting started."

At the docks, a sailor gave the two directions to the pier from which the battalion's ship was being loaded. Because sunken and submerged wreckage still cluttered the shore, the Dickman was anchored several hundred yards out in the bay. Bragg and Ryan abandoned Manning's jeep in haste. Explaining their situation, they jumped aboard an amphibious DUK which was shuttling some remaining supplies out to the Dickman. The DUK's pilot told them they were lucky, the rest of the 319th was already aboard the ship.

As the DUK left the dock and drew closer, Ryan could see the Joseph T. Dickman was a single funneled transport, painted a brooding dark hue and draped with heavy rope nets along her hull. Another DUK was already tied up alongside while crates were being hoisted from it on to the ship. Once their DUK was secured the sailors told Ryan and Bragg it was their turn to scramble on board. When Bragg went to reach for the Jacob's ladder the sailor warned him, "Hey soldier, you better loosen that chinstrap." If you fall in the water it'll break your neck.

Bragg glared at him, hesitated, then unclipped his helmet. Ryan remembered the climb. "Willy Bragg was in front of me. It was our first experience with that landing net. We had to crawl up that thing. If you ever missed a beat you'd go in the drink and that'd be the end of you. When he got to the top some sailor reached for him, but Bragg said, 'Take your hands off me!' Then he almost fell off when he went to climb over the edge. Two or three sailors had to catch him and pull him on to the ship."

The Joseph T. Dickman, APA-13, wasn't the most inviting of vessels. Built as a passenger liner, like the Santa Rosa, this ship was ten years older and never as elegant. She was longer by about 30 feet, with the same beam and, like Santa Rosa, also traveled at a top speed of a little over 15 knots. Originally named the President Roosevelt, the liner was acquired by the War Department in 1940, renamed Joseph T. Dickman after the First World War general, and manned by a Coast Guard crew. Having made dozens of trips loaded with British and American troops since mid-1941, the Dickman was by this time a seasoned veteran of the Mediterranean campaigns.

The 319th found the Dickman to be a lot less crowded than the Santa Rosa was, there was no three day rotation between canvas bunks and the deck as sleeping quarters for example, and many of the bunks remained unoccupied. Unlike the Santa Rosa, with her standing-room-only eating accommodations and continuous chow line, the guys in the outfit found that they could take their meals with the crew, sitting at tables. But although there was more space, the vessel was also much dirtier. When the officers entered their cabins they were disgusted by the sticky floors and grimy walls, having become habituated to their clean and comfortable accommodations in the Verumo. A detail of enlisted men was accordingly drafted to clean the officer's quarters before they were suitable to move into. One battalion man wrote in his diary that the ship was "old" and "full of cockroaches," while another simply remarked, "It was nothing like the Santa Rosa, I'll tell you that."

Nobody was eager to go below decks. The weather was pleasant and with so many fond memories of Naples it was much more appealing to watch the activity in the bay, smoke cigarettes, and take a last look at the city. Loading all the other troops and equipment took all day. The only excitement of any consequence came when two one-man Italian submarines suddenly surfaced a few yards off and opened their hatches. Their tiny crews surrendered to the amazement of the sailors operating utility vessels in the bay and the amusement of the men observing from the deck of the Dickman. Mount Vesuvius, meanwhile, had come back to life in the days before the departure. The sight of the volcano with its vast plume of smoke made the view all the more impressive when the 319th's ship finally weighed anchor and made for open seas. Years later Captain Manning wrote, "I well remember pulling out of the Naples harbor late at night, with Pompeii glowing in the background."

The Dickman and other transports loaded with members of the division were headed for Ouran, Algeria, and presumably balmy weather, but once the convoy was in deep water the winds picked up and the seas became stormy. The only redeeming factor of the rough weather was that it helped keep enemy submarine activity to a minimum. Everybody was forced to remain below decks and this only made for an all the more uncomfortable voyage. John Girardin, to no one's surprise, was "sicker than a dog" within a few hours, soon to be followed by scores of other unfortunates.

Corporal Kenneth Smith, perhaps out of boredom, but more likely seeing an excellent opportunity to scrounge, volunteered to work in the ship's galley and help prepare a special Thanksgiving meal. "I was the one that cut it up. We got in to a lot of bad weather coming back to Ouran. We got into some rough water we had to by pass and go around. I volunteered to cook. I was cutting up duck I guess, a bunch of ducks and the weather was so bad the ducks would slide off on to the floor. You'd just pick it up and keep a-cutting."

A few days later the convoy steamed into the harbor of Mers El Kebir, Algeria, just outside the city of Ouran. The Dickman drew up to a dock but no one was allowed off the ship. Rumors abounded; the division's transports were waiting for additional ships to form a larger, and safer, convoy as protection from German wolf-packs, the division would be sent through the Suez Canal to open a new front against the Japanese in Burma, or that Roosevelt and Churchill were debating whether to initiate the next invasion in France or the Balkans.

Whatever the truth was, the battalion would have to remain idle until the next phase of operations was decided. Until then, once a day each battery was trotted out to the pier for an hour's calisthenics, then loaded back on the Dickman. There otherwise remained little to do besides gamble, smoke, and nap.

In "A" Battery, Roland Gruebling started a fad for canteen etching. Using some sharp tool, a soldier could easily perform a 20th Century version of scrimshaw on his soft aluminum canteen. Gruebling decorated his with his name and army serial number, then started listing the names of each foreign country he'd been in. Ross Marsico, a Technical Corporal in the Signal Section, did the same and then proudly added, "West Virginia. The Chemical Center of the World," to display his home state affiliation.

The rumor of a complete Thanksgiving dinner, scoffed at by all those who weren't friends of Kenny Smith, turned out to be true. On that day, November 25th, the men were handed a small menu card as they entered the mess hall. On the cover was printed the words: "Thanksgiving, 1943 On the Blue Mediterranean." Inside was a verse from Deuteronomy, reminding the reader to give thanks to God for his blessing. Most of the men were incredulous as they read the menu, "Long Island roast turkey, sage dressing, giblets gravy, candied sweet potatoes, green asparagus tips, cranberry sauce, fruit cake, candy, and ice cream." No one had attempted to feed the men so lavishly since before they'd left the United States nine months ago. It was a fantastic treat, but one which convinced the glidermen that they were in the wrong branch of service.

The battalion's officers were fed separately, sitting down to their meal at smaller tables in the wardroom. Officers of the Dickman joined them, eager to have stories of the fighting for Chiunzi Pass and along the Volturno told by those who'd been there. The airborne soldiers and deep water sailors passed a convivial evening. Before they all returned to quarters each signed the other's menus as a memento.

A limited number of enlisted men were granted a day pass into Ouran before their holiday meal that evening. "A" Battery's Sergeant McArthur was one of them. That night, back on the ship, he wrote home to his mother in Mississippi, telling her: "Well, here it is Thanksgiving Day once again. Last Thanksgiving Day was in Fort Bragg, North Carolina, and I believe I have more to be thankful for this Thanksgiving than last one. I am thankful that I am able to be sitting here all in one piece, writing to you, because I did have some mighty close calls. I guess I was lucky and maybe the good Lord had something to do with it too. I spent today in a beautiful city all by myself. I saw two picture shows and a floor show. Most of the day was spent at the Red Cross Club reading. It was the first day that I have really had to myself in over ten months. I really enjoyed it, but I really think I deserve a day off."

The next day things went back to normal and the special chow disappeared. Lieutenant Sartain was quickly growing weary of the cuisine, which was at least in part composed of Royal Navy stores. He remembered, "They gave us pickled herring twice a day, every day, every day." Even the Navy's traditions regarding liquor consumption grew tiresome for him. "We had a rum ration. The officers and the whole crew, they got their rum ration," Sartain said, adding with disgust, "You had to drink the damn stuff straight. No Cocoa Cola or anything!"

At least a few of their men found another source of alcohol while the officers of "C" Battery suffered under the regimen of rum without mixers. According to John Girardin, "We had all our barracks bags in the hold of the ship. After I got out of sick bay, Pop Plasa came to me, he said he was crawling around in there looking for something or other and he put his hand on one of the bags. It felt like a bottle of liquor. We didn't have any locks at that time on these bags, so he put his hand in and came out with two bottles of Old Crow. Remember Old Crow? So he took them. Come to find out this barracks bag belonged to the captain of Headquarters Battery. Well, it wasn't right. The officers had all the good liquor, we didn't have anything. Anyway, Rappi and a couple of us fellas drank them up. We were drunk. We weren't alcoholics, but anything we could do to make us happy, we did."

On the night of November 29th the Joseph T. Dickman made for the open sea again, where they found the weather even worse than after leaving Naples. "The incessant movement of the ship was almost too much to bear," recalled Corporal Arno Mundt, who'd returned to "A" Battery a few weeks before, despite the shrapnel lodged in his heart. "Even the sailors got sea sick. My daily meal ticket revealed I didn't eat for three days."

With all the zigzagging necessary to avoid submarine attacks, it wasn't until December 2nd that the convoy reached the vicinity of Gibraltar. However, passing through the straits was deemed too risky during daylight hours because of the confined nature of the passage and the sympathies of the Franco regime in Spain toward their brother fascists. The Dickman, and other ships of the convoy, put in to shore on the African side, waiting for nightfall. Ed Ryan was on deck, watching with interest as full masted sailing ships were loaded with onions a short distance away. Then another curious sight caught his attention. "There was an Arab girl. She pulled her dress up over her neck. She was a skinny thing, fourteen, fifteen, showing herself and dancing around for the amusement of the troops, I guess. It didn't get much response from the guys on the deck, most of us were pretty well disgusted with the Arabs by that point anyway."

After dark the convoy reformed. Guided by minesweepers and other escort vessels, it prepared for this most dangerous run. There was little room for evasive action. The Germans needed only to listen closely for the sound of Allied ships, then, whenever lights along the ostensibly neutral Spanish Moroccan coast were blocked by the silhouette of a blacked out vessel, it became an easy target for waiting U-boats.

On board the Dickman extra precautions were taken. Everyone donned their Mae Wests and assembled at their evacuation stations. The voice of Lt. Commander C. W. Harwood, the ship's captain, came over the public address system. He informed his passengers, "Any man that lights a cigarette on this deck tonight, if I am alive in the morning I will personally blow his head off." Silas Hogg bristled under the order, grumbling to his buddies, "I been smoking since I was a little kid, and here a guy tells me I can't smoke a cigarette!" Sixty-five years later Hogg was still insulted, but admitted finally, "We slipped through. You know, that Straights of Gibraltar was the most fortified piece of water in Europe. Them other ships were mine cutters, cutting them mines loose and pushing them away. I watched this in the dark. Gibraltar was the most heavily mined piece of water in the world but we slipped through anyway."

Having made it through the straights and into the Atlantic, APA-13 plowed steadily westward when the Dickman and a few other ships of the Attack Transport class broke away from the convoy and headed for the mid-Atlantic. While the division was obviously not going through the Suez Canal to the Indian Ocean, rumors continued to propagate. One version of the scuttlebutt maintained that the 82nd was returning home to go on an enormous War Bond drive. This scenario would inevitably involve photo essays with Hollywood starlets, cocktail parties, and a quasi-celebrity status for even the lowest buck private. It was a hard rumor for the realists in the battalion to accept, yet no one could deny that with each passing hour they were nearer to home than they'd been since landing at Casablanca.

Bob Storms looked back whimsically on the journey, "Whew, was that rough!

Man that was in December or something. The ship bounced all over and everything. Oh that was rough! We were out there, I don't know, three, four days, five days, whatever it was. All of a sudden the whistle whistled and everybody said, so what! Somebody got on the speaker and said, now remember this time tomorrow. Everybody said, so what! You'll find out tomorrow but not today. That was the end of it. The next day they blowed the whistle again. They said, remember this time yesterday we told you to remember? Everybody said, yeah, so what! Well, he said, 'Don't get no ideas of jumping ship, but just at that time you was a hundred and fifty miles out of New York harbor, but you're a helluva lot farther now.' Holy Christ! 'But don't jump,' he says, 'because there's no ship routes around here.' He says, 'You're a helluva lot farther today than you was yesterday.' That's why they wouldn't tell us where they was then, because half the ship I think would have went overboard."

While the Dickman was probably a good deal more than 150 miles out of New York harbor, most sources agree that the small convoy was slightly more than half the way home when it turned around. The most plausible explanation for this maneuver was an effort to deceive German intelligence into believing, as so many men in the battalion did, that the division was headed for home or the Pacific. Such was not the case. The Dickman and a few other attack transports with it, eventually rendezvoused with an east bound convoy and fell in with it.

Meanwhile, the voyage dragged on. Though still sick with pleurisy when he boarded the Dickman at Naples, Ed Ryan was feeling better. "C" Battery's medic, John Rao, aware of the introduction of penicillin for venereal disease, recommended to him, "Line up for the pills in the morning, they'll probably do you some good." They did. "So I'd stand right in line with the guys that had the gonorrhea," said Ryan. "By the time I got to Ireland, I was feeling alright." So great was his recovery that Ryan found himself off the sick list and detailed for work. "I was on submarine watch. They took me on guard up in the prow of that ship. Supposed to be looking for submarines. Rough experience too because it's in the fall and it's cold in the North Atlantic. The spray was coming up. Boy I was never so cold in all my life. The navy had coffee for the sailors, they wouldn't give us any."

Time passed slowly, and all the more so with the cold weather discouraging anything more than a quick cigarette on deck before returning below. "The threat of torpedoing was very real," Arno Mundt remembered of the U-Boat risk. "At that time they were very active sinking many boats in the area. We were on black out from dusk to sunrise every day. I spent the evenings keeping the sailors on night watch company and spent so much time on the deck one of the sailors asked me if I wanted to transfer to the navy. Seriously I wanted to be on deck in case of a torpedoing because staying three decks below the waterline didn't appeal to me."

Gambling remained one of the few available amusements for officers and men alike. Lieutenants Ragland and Sartain both remembered long poker games. The latter observing, "There was a lot of poker on the ship. We had no poker chips so we played with whatever foreign money we had." Since American airborne troops were well paid, and foreign currency had little value compared to the dollar, the games took on a surreal quality with heaps of what amounted to Monopoly money piled up in the center of the tables.

Shooting dice, or "craps" as most men called it, was a favorite gambling game of the enlisted men. More than a few became addicted to the game, with dire consequences. Casimir Sobon remembered some of these unfortunates when he said, "We had guys from I think every state in the union. A lot of them came from West Virginia. Some of them couldn't even sign their names, but they were great in shooting dice you know. For a lot of them there was no such thing as odds. Three to two, two to one, stuff like that. They'd just bet straight money. Make the eight, make the ten! Straight, no odds. A lot of them, if a guy really wants to take advantage of them, that was it. I seen them come on the ship with a bag full of money. They'd get into these card games and crap games and before we landed they was flat broke, borrowing money."

Ryan found his own way to profit from the vice without getting directly involved himself. "I had a big time watching the cards going, but I don't gamble. I would loan them money and if the guy won something I got half, if he didn't I got the money back anyway."

Captain Manning had one recollection in particular, "My main memory of the trip is of PFC Silas Hogg, one of my men who was always in and out of trouble, but still a capable soldier. Hogg got involved in crap games on ship and won heavily. Then he got concerned about having all that money. He asked me to keep it - and not to let him argue me into giving it back to him."

Hogg also remembered the incident decades later. He commented, "That was me, I used to be a good gambler. I shot crap all the time. Of course, knowing me, I got in a game and that particular night I had every pocket full. I hit it good that night, I won a fortune. I gave it to the Captain to send home. Oh yeah, we got with it sometimes. You look around you there'd be three or four games going, any one you choose, Buddy. Oh man, they were stealing from each other like it's going out of style."

Hogg wasn't above using loaded dice himself, and explained how it was done. "See, you got to keep four in one hand. You got your fingers educated for it. Some time you turn them loose and you throw three and that won't get it. What you got to learn to do is control four dice in one hand. The little finger and the one next to it must be able to control two dice. The other three fingers have to control the other two. Once you got up on it, got your fingers trained to it, hell, there was no sweat to it you could throw the crooked, you could throw the straight. If I couldn't hit them one way I'd hit them another."

According to Manning's memoir, "About two days later Hogg was constantly at me to return his loot, so he was quite prophetic in his thinking, but I managed to keep it until we arrived in Belfast and then had it sent home to his family. It took a couple of months for him to settle down."

Now into their third week on the Dickman, the men were "starting to go stirbugs" from confinement and the lack of anything to help pass the time. "On the ship, just for fun as they was running along they had a question and answer thing by the navy over the public address system," recalled Ryan. "Some naval officer was doing this. They'd ask him questions. Somebody asked him about Einstein's theory of relativity. He said it was the same as throwing a baseball and having the baseball turn inside out without breaking the stitching on it. I think he thought he was a brain, I don't know."

Submarines continued to threaten the small convoy, even after they were joined up with a larger group and were clearly headed back toward Europe. On one occasion, as they were drawing nearer to the Irish coast, U-boats made a serious attempt at the American vessels. Storms later said of the incident, "Before we got to Ireland we got scattered one time. I guess on account of a Wolf Pack or something. They got a couple or two, three ships or something, and then them sub chasers come around and run them off or some damn thing. They said something about Wolf Packs. Whether we got tangled up in them or we were trying to avoid them, or what ever it was, we never found out. But we finally got to Ireland anyway." Other men on the Dickman recalled the attack and the salvos of depth charges which followed until debris, including a mattress, came floating to the surface.

On December 9th the Joseph T. Dickman finally sailed into the harbor at Belfast, Northern Ireland. The port was packed with troop transports, freighters loaded with war material, and naval gunships of every kind. Assembling on deck, the guys in the 319th looked around at the grey city and shivered in the cold. In the dim afternoon light of this overcast northern latitude, the easy life in sunny Naples seemed, and was, very far away.

With the battalion formed up, one last man was brought out. It was the "C" Battery soldier who'd come apart on Mount Saint Angelo back in September. Sartain would never forget the sight. "I remember him getting off the ship in Belfast very vividly," he said later. "We didn't know where he was. Bedingfield kept two guys with him down in the hold so he wouldn't hurt himself. Then they brought him up out of the hold with two medics in a straight jacket. He was crying for Johnny Manning, kept calling for Manning. 'Captain Manning, Captain Manning, don't let them do this to me!' He went completely, totally berserk. It shook everybody up. He never came back to us after Belfast."

It took time to unload the ship, and the battalion had to wait around the docks before they could be loaded into the trucks which were sent for them. Three weeks on the Dickman without any real bathing facilities left the guys dirty, tired, and disheveled in their wrinkled uniforms. Meanwhile, squads of local girls gathered around, inspecting the newcomers. Arno Mundt noticed that in comparison to the Italian girls they "all were red haired and pale as ghosts. After months in the Mediterranean zone, we were very darkly tanned. They thought we were Italian prisoners of war."

Finally the order was given to get in the trucks. A journey

Probably taken in Northern Ireland, Sergeant Thurman King of "a" Battery poses with his M1a1 folding stock carbine at port arms. The Folding stock carbine was issued to airborne troops and the 319th received theirs before leaving for North Africa. In spite of this, a few men remembered carrying the full stock carbine as late as the Normandy Invasion. Sartain elected to carry a full stock carbine throughout the war, but "normally left it in the jeep with Sosa." Sartain collection.

You couldn't dig a hole in Ireland.

out of Belfast and through the Irish countryside came to an abrupt halt after a few hours. The men were ordered out. In the darkness it was difficult to discern more than an indifferent collection of dreary utility buildings placed on a muddy field within some sort of stone enclosure. Formed up again, the battalion was marched to a nearby mess hall. Ed Ryan still remembered the meal decades later, "We got in about twelve at night. Hungry. We were hosted by the 9th Division. They gave us a great meal, which was bully beef with milk in it. What a bunch of crap that was. Oh it was lovely. Warm bully beef with milk. That was enough to make you heave. We couldn't wait till Larrieu took over the kitchen."

Once the bully beef was consumed the men were apportioned out among about a dozen Nissen huts. A British forerunner of the larger American Quansut hut, the Nissens held about thirty men each. Each end of the hut was fitted with a door and two small windows, the floors were plywood, while the walls and ceiling were formed from a continuous curved sheet of corrugated metal. Efficient and easy to construct, the huts were also uninsulated. The battalion first encountered these remarkably ugly buildings in North Africa, where they were intolerably hot. Here in Northern Ireland, the huts were instead intolerably cold and damp.

Describing the new quarters, Kenny Smith said, "We didn't have no heating to speak of. Just little tiny stoves about the size of, probably a half foot in diameter and three foot tall. You'd put coke in there and catch it on fire, but it didn't put out much heat."

The sleeping accommodations were "those small bunks," according to Gunner Corporal Rappi. "It was built like a box and they put straw in there. There was no mattress, there was just straw in there."

The next morning the 319th was drawn up at its new bivouac. John Girardin and his "C" Battery buddies who'd helped themselves to the bottles of liquor at Ouran,

Ed Ryan and other members of the "C" Battery Signal Section in front of their Nissen hut at Camp Ballyscullion. Ryan wears coveralls and a helmet liner. Standing in the doorway at back is Joseph "Dirty Joe" Meaghan. Courtesy Ed Ryan.

BATTERY!

saw Captain Rogers of Headquarters Battery. With his men at attention, the Captain was dressing down his battery, barking something about two missing bottles of Old Crow. "He lined his guys up and was asking about it. He said if he ever found out who took his Old Crow he'd have the man court martialed. Nobody knew who did it." Girardin, Rappi, Plassa and Olkanen knew. They exchanged smiles and glances, but kept their mouths shut.

The men were informed that they were now encamped at Castle Ballyscullion, a couple of miles from the village of Bellaghy, and about 45 miles southwest of Belfast. Castledawson, where division headquarters was located, was only a few miles away. Ballymena, perhaps ten miles distant, was the nearest town of any consequence. Judging from the enormous building stones scattered about the grounds, there must have been a true castle at Castle Ballyscullion at one time, but that was a long time ago. All that remained intact was a stone wall, nearly ten feet in height and crowned with shards of broken glass. The rest of the compound was composed of mud and the Nissen huts occupied by British troops until a few weeks before the outfit's arrival.

With a sun that didn't rise until nearly 9am, permanently overcast skies, and an impenetrable darkness which descended by 4pm, most guys in the unit agreed with Tampa native Louis Sosa's first impression of Ireland as, "Wet, dark, and cold." Notwithstanding all this, many of the men had Irish backgrounds and everyone felt good about being somewhere where English was spoken, even if the local dialect was hard to understand much of the time.

One of the Irish-Americans in "C" Battery was Ed Ryan. He and his buddies were itching to explore their new surroundings. "We were in these castle grounds," he told me during one interview. "Walled in, no passes. About the second night we went over the wall to this town, Bellaghy. It was probably two miles in the dark. We heard music from a hall there, upstairs. We walked through the door and this guy there was taking tickets, he said something about the money. Guy says two and six, what ever the hell that is. We were in combat clothes from Italy yet. He was scared of us, so we went right in to the dance. They had food there too. We stayed almost till dawn eating sandwiches and chasing girls, then we went back and sneaked over the wall back to camp again."

Though Ryan may have been among the first to go over the wall, he was followed by scores of others in the following days. "A" Battery machine gunner, Bob Storms, had his own memory of how this was accomplished. "Like when we got in Ireland, the army put us in this place and it had a high wall all around. So we thought, oh, this is gonna be nice to get out. Well, you go to get over that wall, they got all kinds of whiskey bottles and wine bottles broken in concrete with the broken part up. Hey, you don't crawl over these walls." But Storms was no more willing to be penned in by the wall at Castle Ballyscullion than he was by the cactus hedge at Kairouan. "First thing you got to do," he explained, "Is find a rock and then a couple of good guy's shoulders you could stand on. You rub that place down real smooth up there, then you mark it. Then you take turns pushing one another up over the wall. They kept us in there for a while before they let us go into town. By then we know the towns pretty good."

Until field exercises could be arranged, and before general passes into the surrounding villages were issued, there was little to do besides the unending duties necessary to the operation of any military encampment. John Girardin's memories of these chores include details that would have been familiar to all those in the enlisted ranks. "They used to make us go out with a wheel barrow and shovel water from the puddles

155

into the wheelbarrow," he remembered. Then, on guard duty each guy would try to be dressed as neat as possible, hoping to be picked for best job, such as keeping the stove going in the mess hall all night."

In fact it was only several days before exercises resumed. As "C" battery commander, Captain Manning, wrote later, "After we got into our routine we went into intensive training, mostly long hikes in the area and convoy trips to artillery ranges laid out in the moors near Londonderry. It was a very open, rural area lightly populated. Our travel was entirely by truck convoy since no airport facilities existed at our location." Having not fired their howitzers since early October, gunnery practice was a necessary, if uninspiring, activity. The only unusual feature of these exercises was the tendency which the peat laden Irish countryside had for catching fire where ever a high explosives shell burst occurred.

Manning's comment about the widespread use of marches as training is quite true. Given the food shortages experienced by the United Kingdom during the war, a strenuous effort was made throughout England, Scotland, and Northern Ireland, to maximize crop yields from all possibly arable land. Consequently, the military was under orders to avoid damage or disruption to farmers or their crops whenever possible. This meant that normal field exercises, with their digging of thousands of foxholes or gun emplacements, and generally running roughshod over the countryside, such as were conducted at Fort Bragg or in North Africa were out of the question.

It took a little while to fully appreciate the restrictions under which training had to take place. Storms remembered this period and how the army's activities sometimes overstepped the line. "We got there to do training and stuff," he said, "But you couldn't dig a hole in the ground nowhere. You could march and do training like running and marching, but you couldn't stop in the fields and tromp down their fields or nothing. They wouldn't allow that. You couldn't dig a hole in Ireland. Like a foxhole or nothing. You'd make believe like you were taking a town, but we got in a lot of trouble with that. We scared the people a lot too! We'd go in and capture a house. The poor women, they wet their pants, then they'd turn us in. We got in a lot of trouble for that and couldn't do that no more. That's why we left Ireland kind of early. It was more of a place for rest anyway."

As Storms suggests, local residents and farmers placed complaints with the military authorities over trampled gardens and nervous milk cows who's udders had dried up. Often these complaints were accompanied by lists of damages for which the farmer would be reimbursed. Restricted as they were to marches, a fifteen mile hike became almost a daily routine. However, the unusually late sunrise and early sunset presented opportunities for the more fatigued enlisted personnel. "We'd go on a march every morning," recalled one "C" Battery man. "Lieutenant Carey or Poole or one of them is leading a march, but it's still dark, so the last ten fall out without him knowing it. Then by the time they're on their way back it's dark again. You could see them coming because the Lieutenant would have a flashlight, so you just slide right in at the tail end of it."

Robert Rappi recalled one method of working off excess energy for those who were not so fatigued, "Billy Cadle, him and I used to wrestle all the time, me and Billy. We'd tear up things. Them bunks were just made out of wood and had straw in the bottom, but he hit his head on a nail there one time, so we quit that bullshit!"

To funnel antics of the sort Rappi described in a more constructive direction, the battalion organized a basketball team to compete against other US Army units stationed in North Ireland that winter. Players were recruited from the four batteries. Among them were Casimir Sobon, Staff Sergeant Harold Peters, and First Sergeant Jesse Johnson from "A" Battery, all well over six feet tall. The most talented player was Tom Soule from "B" Battery. "Kenny Smith used to play," mentioned one man of "C" Battery's contribution. "He was a center. He wasn't that great, but he was tall." According to Sobon, there were also other advantages. "It was great for us," he said, "because we didn't have to stand inspection on Saturdays. We didn't want to stand the inspections, so that was one way of getting around it. We took trucks into Belfast, to the American Red Cross canteen. We went in on a Saturday and if we won we'd stay in town and play on Sunday. We used what we had. We had shorts, but where we got them from, I don't know. But everybody had shorts. We won every time we went up there because we didn't want to come back. It was a pretty good basketball team for a bunch of guys that never played together before."

History has not recorded the name chosen by the battalion's team and none of the players can think of it today. "I can't remember what we went by," recalls Sobon. "All I know is we were 82nd Airborne. We just went in there, whatever name was put down, that's what we played."

They might have been the Ramblers, the Snowbirds, Awe-nuts, the Section Eights, the 4F Commandos, or the Hellcats. All were teams fielded by units of the 82nd, as were the 507th PIR's "Spiders" and the "Red Devils" of the 508th.

Evidently, Sergeant Peters was first selected as team captain. There were still several weeks to go before the championship, but during the first games the team was going nowhere. "He had it about two weeks and Major Todd come to me and said, you're taking over," remembered Marvin Ragland. "Well, that was just down my line cause I'd been involved with a lot of that in school."

Things started to gel. Then, after a couple of victories it began to look like the 319th might actually make it into the finals. Sergeant Johnson was one who took the

Basketball team of the 319th in Northern Ireland. Team members included Casimir Sobon, Harold Peters, Jesse Johnson, Marvin Ragland, Tom Sowell, Paul Lubianetski, Victor Buinowski and James Rosati. Kenneth Smith can be scene in the back towering over everyone. Lt. Ragland took the picture. Ragland collection.

games very seriously. He also had a temper when the opponents made a move he didn't like. Sobon recalled a specific game, "Johnson got hot headed every once in a while. We were playing one team one time and he was ready to take this guy, really take him over. Some guy from the other team says, hey, you better watch out, that guys an officer. You know what? Johnson doesn't care what the hell he is; he doesn't care what the hell he is! He's gonna take care of him, he's gonna take care of him."

Summing up their season, Ragland said, "Yeah, we did alright in Ireland. We had our first basketball tournament up there two weekends. Let's see, we won the tournament the first weekend, and the second weekend we lost by two points in over time to the engineers or something. I think it was the 82nd Airborne engineers unit, but it was fun. The 319thers probably ran afoul of the Amertex, an engineer team from outside the division and the previous year's champions. The contest that year came down to the Amertex versus the Spiders. Let it be recorded that it was the Spiders of the 507th PIR who achieved the title of "1943 Basketball Champions of Northern Ireland."

Basketball certainly wasn't the only amusement for the glider troopers. A couple of weeks after the battalion moved into their Camp at Castle Ballyscullion regular passes into Bellaghy and even weekend passes to Belfast were being liberally granted. As one man put it, "they let us loose quite a lot there in Ireland." Then it was Christmas again. One year ago many of the men were on furloughs home from Fort Bragg. Others, like the guys from Fort Sheridan, had only been inducted into the service for a few days. They hadn't even heard of the 319th, gliders, or Fort Bragg for that matter. A year before young men their own ages but from other regions of the United States seemed foreign.

Now they'd all seen the deepwater Atlantic, Casablanca, and the deserts of North Africa together. Combat at Chiunzi Pass and mud on the Volturno, Darby's Rangers, Colonel Bertsch, then six weeks in Naples. A lot had gone by since then to reflect upon.

Now they were part of a GI family as well. In many ways the two, their family at home and their family in the service, were comparable, with lots of the same likes, dislikes, sense of belonging, and tensions of any extended family repeated in olive drab. One of the guys at Camp Ballyscullion commented on this in a letter written about this time, saying, "There is real pleasure to be sitting in an ale house and have one of the boys in the battery walk in. It's like meeting one of your family. By now, we've taken each other's measure, so to speak. We know each other so well, we can act like a family acts. We are no longer an alphabetical list of men."

Sgt. Tom Sowell in basketball uniform of 319th GFAB. Photo courtesy Thomas Sowell.

If the mess hall at Camp Ballyscullion was anything like others of the 82nd Airborne that year, it would have had some makeshift holiday decorations, like stars snipped from tin cans, perhaps even a wreath or Christmas tree. An extra indulgence of coffee and doughnuts were probably on hand too. Most men had also received some parcel from home with favorite foodstuffs and toiletries. On Christmas Eve Ed Ryan was having a "celebration" with some of his "C" Battery chums in their Nissen hut. Then an unsought guest dropped in. According to Ryan, "They had a Chaplain. On Christmas Eve he come down to the huts. He comes down and gets us out of there to go and sing carols in this town, Bellaghy. We're supposed to go door to door singing christmas carols. What a mess. We were singing carols. Every time we went to a house the Northern Irishmen would come to the door and give us booze. By the time we got done we were all drunk. Can you imagine that. They loaded us up on the truck like firewood to take us back out of there," he said, then concluded, "You've got to watch out for those Chaplains."

Shortly after New Year's Day, 1944, and continuing for the next month, many battalion men who had weekend passes took the opportunity to see Irving Berlin's review, "This is the Army." Traveling by train from Castledawson to Belfast, or riding along in military vehicles, soldiers could soon find themselves walking the sidewalks of an English speaking city with familiar sounding names. That felt good. However, if you weren't with someone who'd been there before, the wartime blackout imposed upon the busy metropolitan life was disorienting at night. Men noticed that it was easy to get lost since the only lights were, as one man put it in a letter home, "weird green flashes from the streetcar power lines."

The Irving Berlin review came to Belfast from Glasgow, where they'd performed to a packed house. Since arriving in Liverpool in late October, 1943, "This Is the Army" toured first through London, then Manchester and Birmingham, before going on to Scotland. The show, really a review featuring a play within a play, interspersed with dancers, comedians, and other variety acts, was an updated version of Berlin's First World War review, "Yip, Yip Yaphank!"

Yaphank, New York, was the location of Camp Upton, a vast Army induction center in eastern Long Island. As a sergeant stationed at the camp during World War One, Berlin had persuaded his superiors to sponsor a semiprofessional re-

Men from "C" Battery pose by their Nissen hut. Left to right: Billy Cadle, Bart Plassa, Robert Rappi, Jalmara Olkonen, Arthur Forsman, Paul Massie, and John Girardin(kneeling), at Camp Ballyscullion. Photo courtesy John Girardin.

view for the benefit of the troops and public morale. Yip Yip Yaphank, actually Berlin's story of his life as a recruit, was the finished product, featuring Berlin's catchy numbers and entertainment savvy.

Camp Upton was again processing thousands of recruits during the months leading up to World War Two, but on an even larger scale than a quarter century before. Irving Berlin, by this time a well known entertainer, visited there in May, 1941, and conceived of reviving Yaphank to help in the mobilization effort. Berlin envisioned a cast of actual soldiers receiving army pay, instructions, and discipline, performing side by side with contracted civilian talent. All proceeds generated by the review, as well as Berlin's own personal royalties as the composer of the music, would be donated to the Army Emergency Relief Fund. When the War Department approved the plan, Berlin got to work at Camp Upton at once. With a cast that included over 350 actual servicemen, the play, now titled "This is the Army" opened July 4th, 1942 on Broadway. After a successful run, followed by an equally popular stateside tour, the company was pared down to 150 Army personnel and embarked for England on October 21, 1943.

The plot of "This Is the Army" revolves around Jerry Jones, a New York City dancer. Jerry gets drafted, is sent to Camp Upton, and stages Yip, Yip Yaphank in much the same way Berlin did in 1917. But this time Jerry goes overseas, is wounded and looses a leg. Twenty-five years later Jerry's son, Johnny, an entertainer like dad, is drafted and charged with putting on a morale boosting review of his own. The show which the guys saw during those January nights in Belfast was the product. Complete with tributes to the navy and air corps, "This is the Army" appealed to the common citizen soldier's experience. Robert Rappi went to the show and clearly remembered Berlin dressed in a First World War uniform, standing beside a pup tent and singing his signature, "O, How I Hate to Get up in the Morning."

Others remembered some of the variety acts which punctuated the play. One of these was the "Fan Dance." As one 319th man explained, "They had these chorus girls, ten or more gals with the fans, doing the Fan dance. They would dance around and keep that fan in front of them. The finale was at the end when they'd drop the fan and they didn't have on any brassieres or anything up top, but we only got a glimpse of them, that was it."

Sergeant John McNally of the Division Artillery's Headquarters Battery, and also bivouacked at Camp Ballyscullion, was in the audience one night too. He later wrote, "There is a kind of magic about Irving Berlin. He's a small man with a cracked voice, but he has a humbleness that's close to greatness. Standing alone on a bare stage in an odd-looking uniform, he brought home closer to us than it's ever been before. He seemed surprised when, after asking us to join him in singing "White Christmas" there came an outpouring of sound from all over the theater. I don't think he realized that every soldier in this war knows the words to that song."

Sergeant McNally may have been right. Irving Berlin's music, simple and witty as it was, had a way of coming easily to memory. For men who'd scooped water into wheelbarrows, stood many hours of guard duty, or chaffed under the restrictions of military discipline, the title song's lyrics were a perfect, yet cheerful, expression.

A bunch of frightened rookies were listening filled with awe
They listened while a sergeant was laying down the law
They stood there at attention, their faces turning red
The sergeant looked them over and this is what he said

BATTERY!

This is the Army, Mister Jones!
No private rooms or telephones
You had your breakfast in bed before
But you won't have it there any more
This is the Army, Mister Green!
We like the barracks nice and clean
You had a housemaid to clean your floor
But she won't help you out any more
Do what the buglers command
They're in the Army and not in a band
This is the Army, Mister Brown!
You and your baby went to town
She had you worried but this is war
And she won't worry you anymore

"This is the Army" continued its tour to the Mediterranean and Pacific theaters of war, raising millions of dollars for the AERF by the war's end. On October 22nd, 1945 on the island of Maui, Hawaii, the cast, including Berlin, performed for the last time.

North Ireland also offered another opportunity for GIs to purchase regional specialties and ship them back to the States. Members of the 319th sent home carpets from Morocco and Algeria, jewelry from Naples, and from Ireland, linen. In Naples Lieutenant Ragland bought several pieces of jewelry for his mother in Kansas. Yet, he remembered his thoughts in Belfast when he observed Lieutenant Gelb buying the local specialty. "He was buying a bunch of this Irish linen, real high priced stuff, and sending it home. I remember thinking, why would a person do that?"

Linen wasn't the only local specialty. Sartain speculated in another one of Ire-

"A" Battery men including Thurman King and David Stelow at Camp Ballyscallion, Northern Ireland. Sartain collection.

You couldn't dig a hole in Ireland.

land's products and explained what happened this way, "I had a friend in the 2nd Division, they were in Ireland too, right on the border at a town called Innesscillen. He called me up, said, 'Hey I've got a connection to get real Irish whiskey. Come on down.' So I took up a collection among the officers and some of the enlisted men too. Collected one pound notes. Even Todd was in on it. I don't remember if we took Manning's jeep, but Sosa was driving. We went to the side of the mountain on the border and met this Catholic priest. We gave him the money, he took his cut. About three hours later these little donkeys come over the mountain loaded down with crates of whiskey. As many as would fit in a jeep. We drove back. It was Teacher's Irish Whiskey. When we opened the bottles it was half watered down. They had those bottles sealed back up so you couldn't even tell. Man, they about skinned me alive. But it was good, and you didn't need a chaser for it since it was half water already."

Though the battalion men sometimes were a nuisance when they tromped through gardens or pulled prankish stunts, like upsetting Bobbies on their bicycles just for laughs, relations between the fellows in the battalion and the Irish people went exceedingly well. Silas Hogg said, "OK, to me the people were good, they were nice. They were glad we were there, glad we were trying to protect them. I dated a girl there, cute little thing. Don't remember her name. If my wife hears me tell you this she'll kill both of us."

Social contact between the servicemen and the local girls seems to be something both parties were eager to establish. Arno Mundt noticed that, "it wasn't long before they were clustering around the gates at the end of the day. The guys who got passes were in no lack of dates."

"I had a girlfriend in Ireland too," said Eddie Ryan. "Another fella came from

Another group of "C" Battery men outside their Nissen hut at Camp Ballyscullion. Left to right: Roland Gruebling, Harold Peters, John Orrell, Harold Mell, Edward Prohazka, and Anzile F. Price. Courtesy John Girardin.

BATTERY!

New York City and he gave me the address of his father in Porter Down. I went down to see his father, an old man named McGee." Looking for the address his buddy'd given him, Ryan stopped to buy milk from a vendor he saw on the sidewalk. "I was drinking from a dog cart in front of this house. This guy yells at me from the upstairs window, 'Don't you ever do that!' He said, 'That's only for babies.' They still had the unpasteurized milk. It turned out to be old man McGee. I used to visit him in Porter Down, he prepared meals for me and I gave him tobacco."

During one of their visits old man McGee had an idea and asked Ryan, "How are you doing in Ireland? You got a girl? You can't be here without having a girl. I'll get you one." Telling Ryan to wait, McGee left the building, then returned in a few minutes.

"She was across the street, all dressed up. Vera Baxter. She was a dark haired, pretty girl, a nice girl. She worked in Robb's mill where they made linen. I've always been interested in how things work. She took me all over and showed me how the mills worked."

Vera and Ed saw each other frequently and she brought him home to meet her family. "She had a younger brother. He thought I was a big time hero. He was doing all kinds of math. A different system there. What impressed me was they were so far ahead of us as far as education was concerned. The old lady was a typical Irish looking thing, constantly stirring a pot of something."

Because public relations were a subject of keen interest to the military, chaperoned and controlled venues where soldiers and local females could meet were encouraged. Captain Manning and his Executive Officer, Sartain, were charged with arranging a dance for their battery at one point, probably the 319th's other batteries had dances as well. Manning wrote his recollections later, "The closest town of any size was Ballymena. It was the site of the Adair Arms, a pub hotel which welcomed our business. For some reason the higher army authorities thought we should improve the morale of the troops by having a big dance. The manager of the Adair Arms introduced us to a lady named Dorothy Pearl Armstrong and her sister as likely contacts to round up girls for a dance. As transportation was needed, Sartain and I were assigned as convoy officers. It is hard to think that you are seriously contributing to the war effort when you are in a jeep heading a three truck convoy loaded with girls across a dark moor. To compound the issue, a lone gunman with a rifle rose out of the mist and hailed us. He turned out to be a representative of the Irish Republican Army. We finally arrived at a small airfield hangar which had been set aside for us, and got good marks from the troops for throwing a party."

The army also kept social contact between officers and enlisted personnel to a minimum, with separate clubs for officers and NCOs. The NCO clubs were off limits to other enlisted ranks, unless an enterprising buck private borrowed the service uniform of a friend who carried sergeant's stripes on his sleeves. While the Adair Arms in Ballymena was the favored off duty club of officers, enlisted men found pubs and taverns of their own. One of these was Mrs. McNichols' Tavern in Bellaghy. Featuring a pub downstairs and a diner upstairs, men could satisfy both their hunger and thirst at one location.

McNichols' was a favorite of Ed Ryan and some of his "C" Battery signals section crew. He remembers Delbert Jackson drinking, sitting there at the bar, and typically drumming out Morse code with his fingertip. On one occasion Ryan was there with his buddies, Willie Bragg and Joseph, "Dirty Joe," Meaghan. Ryan excused himself to visit the toilet, an outhouse in the back lot behind the tavern. "You had to go off the back porch to the out house," he explained. "I saw a chicken all plucked and hanging on the wall. I got back and Dirty Joe went next. Later, Mrs. McNichols runs in yelling, 'Me chicken is missing!' Dirty Joe asks her, 'Whom do you suspect.' He had a raincoat on and stole the chicken off her back porch. While we were in Normandy he got a letter from her. She knew who stole the chicken and wished him no good luck." Another trick the guys would play on the proprietress involved milk, a drink the men were eager to buy, but which she refused to sell by the glass. "You could buy a cup of tea from her. She'd have a milk pitcher in the middle of the table for the tea, so we drank the pitcher dry before she'd get there with the tea."

Despite all their misbehavior, we're left with the impression that Mrs. McNichols must have liked the "C" Battery guys. She certainly trusted Irishman Ryan enough to pull him aside one night and say, "I want to talk to you. Could you please get me a machinegun?"

A couple of Mrs. McNichols' confederates then had another proposal for Ryan, "These guys there offered to set me up if I'd desert the army to train their people." Evidently Mrs. McNichols was an active supporter of the Irish Republican Army. Considering the way Manning's convoy of girls was stopped by the gunman on the way to the dance, there is little question that there was a significant IRA presence in the area.

On February 3rd a division review was held in a cold, driving rain. Some of the men took it as a bad sign that their outfit would soon be on the move again. They were right. First rumors, then orders started circulating to prepare to make a change of base. The battalion was unhappy about leaving Northern Ireland. Many of the guys had found a second home among the Irish people and, even though they wanted to get on with the war, were reluctant to leave. Suddenly, on February 12th, the 319th was again loaded into trucks, taken to a rail station and boarded a train for Belfast. There the men were placed on "an old captured German ship," actually a Dutch ferry which had seen hard and continuous use since the war's early days. Which ever it was, the ferry took the battalion to Glasgow, Scotland, where they disembarked, marched a short distance to a rail yard, and boarded a train.

Ed Ryan missed the boat. He'd granted himself a brief pass to visit Vera and mr. McGee in Porter Down before the unit left Ireland, but when Ryan returned to camp he found the outfit was gone. A moment of realization told him that his AWOL status was sure to be discovered and there would be serious consequences when that happened. Then Ryan heard some noise coming from the mess hall. Inside Mess Sergeant Larrieu and a kitchen detail were still there, packing up their equipment. Lucky for him, Ryan was friendly with the sergeant, who put him on his list of battery men detailed to pack up the mess equipment and follow the outfit later.

BATTERY!

Part 12: "Brass hats were in the area."

At about the same time as the change of base from Northern Ireland to England came a significant adjustment in the organization of the battalion. Once again the 319th was configured with two firing batteries, supported by a Headquarters Battery, as it had been until just after Husky, the Sicily operation. With the disappointing results of the Sicilian drops and confusion which followed it, the future of airborne operations called for major reconsideration. Indeed, Eisenhower doubted that employment of airborne troops in anything larger than battalion sized units was worthwhile, stating plainly in his after-action report on Operation Husky, "I do not believe in the airborne division." Throughout the balance of 1943 the question was debated between airborne proponents and those, like Ike, who believed large scale parachute and glider drops to just be too unwieldy.

On December 6th, 1943, a vast simulated airborne invasion was conducted stateside to test the feasibility of large operations once and for all. Known as the Knollwood maneuvers, the entire 11th Airborne Division was loaded on hundreds of aircraft and gliders from five airfields in the Carolinas and Georgia. Joining up as one vast armada, the force flew off the Carolina coast, over the Atlantic, then turned around and rendezvoused over the predesignated drop and landing zones located near Pinehurst, North Carolina. Their objective was to seize the Knollwood airfield in the face of the 17th Airborne acting as an opposing force, and attempt to resupply themselves over the following days.

The 11th dropped its sticks of paratroopers right on schedule, in tight clusters, at or very near to the intended drop zones – same for the glider component of the simulated invasion force. It was all, as the saying went, "on time and on target." The Knollwood maneuvers were a clear success, so much so that everyone had to admit division, and even multiple divisions, sized operations were demonstrably feasible, provided sufficient planning and precautions were taken.

One of those present at Knollwood was the 82nd's commander, General Matthew Bunker Ridgeway. On his return to the European theater, word was soon circulating that yes, the division would definitely be going into France as an intact airborne unit – not piecemeal as independent battalions or landing either amphibiously or at captured airstrips. Even with that question settled, there still remained real problems associated with any airborne drop. Unfavorable weather conditions, enemy countermeasures, faulty or incomplete intelligence, were all factors which would be exerting themselves when D-Day finally arrived, and all would conspire to disrupt and erode unit cohesion and combat performance.

To mitigate these unavoidable factors, the battalion's organization was simplified and the return to a two firing battery structure was the result. Better, it was reasoned, to try to reconstitute two firing batteries in a post-drop confusion than three. Experience had also shown that in support of a standard three battalion regiment, with one of these battalions held in reserve, it was most efficient to coordinate the fire of two batteries with each of the two battalions in the line than to try to do so with three batteries.

Altogether this meant that "C" Battery would be disbanded. The gun sections would return to their respective batteries of origin, as would the members of the motor pool, machinegun, and signals sections. Yet the battery's command structure of Manning and Sartain, which had proven so effective, would remain intact. The pair was given command of "A" Battery, perhaps because of Sartain's familiarity with its men, but also because Captain Loughmiller was evidently transferred out of the battalion, possibly to take command of some other field artillery unit in need of a combat experienced officer. Although these changes were almost certainly made while still at camp Ballyscullion, it is not exactly clear when the restructuring took place. The firing range at Londonderry was the last time "C" Battery performed as a unit. For all practical purposes, once the 319th disembarked at Glasgow, Scotland, on or about February 15th, 1944, it was organized with John Manning in command of "A" Battery and Bob Cargile continuing to command Battery "B," while Captain Rogers carried on as CO of the HQ Battery.

The train from Glasgow wended its way through the Scottish and English countryside to Leicestershire, finally stopping at the town of Market Harborough. Trucks brought the men of the 319th from there, westward through the small village of Lubenham, and a couple of miles beyond turned into the drive leading to a stately manor. The place was called Papillon Hall. It was an estate of about 100 acres featuring a large three story, ivy covered manor house built in the early 17th Century. The grounds included a barn, stables, several outbuildings, an orchard, and finely manicured gardens with a bewildering series of hedges and intersecting paved walkways, all enclosed by a serpentine brick wall. Still impressive, the grounds and house must have been lavish in their heyday, before being taken over by the military. Now the stables and main house were refitted as barracks, with further accommodations in the form of Quansut huts placed behind the house and about the grounds. This was to be the battalion's new home.

"A" Battery was housed, like "B" Batttery, in Quansut huts fitted out with double bunks, while the HQ Battery lived in Papillon hall itself. The junior officers of the battalion, everyone below the rank of captain, were placed in another Quansut located directly behind the main building. This hut had partitions built inside, affording each lieutenant a cubicle of his own and a modicum of privacy.

The signals and security sections of each battery were quartered in the brick stables, either four or six men to the stall, depending on who is asked. Being some short distance from the rest of the battalion and the officer's hut, many thought these the best accommodations of all. Corporal Bob Storms explained it this way, "I didn't stay in the building itself, I was in it a lot of times but we stayed in some barracks outside where they had a barn out there. We were happy though, we got away with a lot out there. They didn't bother us."

Quickly nicknamed "Pap's Hall" by the guys, a variation on the local moniker "Pamp's Hall," the house seemed literally to ooze history. The most recent owner, a Captain Belville, had decorated the walls of the ground floor vestibule with scenes of a bullfight, evidently a nod to his involvement in the Spanish Civil War and the wife whom he'd brought home from that land. However, Senora Belville was not the first Spanish lady to occupy the building, nor was she the most notorious. At the turn of the 18th Century, David Papillon, the great-grandson of the French Hugenenot builder of the structure and a devotee of occultism, is said to have kept a Spanish mistress in captivity on the grounds. The mistress disappeared mysteriously shortly before Papillon married in 1717, though local residents claimed since to see her ghost walking between the manor and the gatehouse late at night. Papillon's instructions, supposedly enforced by means of a curse, were that certain items, among them the mistress's slippers, were never to leave the building without dire consequences. Since that time, history did indeed record unexplained mishaps whenever the slippers were taken away from Papillon Hall. Fires, lightening strikes, workmen killed by falling masonry, and docile carriage horses suddenly running amok, were a few of the uncanny events which occurred periodically whenever the warning was ignored. When a new owner began repairs and remodeling in 1903, a woman's skeleton was discovered behind a brick wall in the attic, confirming the most macabre of the long held legends.

At the time the 319th arrived at Papillon the slippers were firmly ensconced in a cubby high above the main fireplace, protected by an iron gate, but with all the legends attached to them they were only more desirable as a souvenir. Though not quartered in the building, one "A" Battery man remembered them distinctly, "If you'd monkey with them red shoes why you'd die or something. I went to look for them and some guy had them in his barracks bag. But the officers got after him. I guess he hung them back up. It's just like a bunch of GIs to do something crazy."

Now back in the HQ Battery and living in the hall itself, Ed Ryan remembered more of what happened when the slippers disappeared a second time. "Well," he said, "The slippers hung up over the main fireplace in the biggest room in the hall. Nobody was supposed to touch them and if somebody did touch them they were supposed to have all kinds of hell break loose. So anyway, a guy stole them and they couldn't find them for a long while. Sure enough the guy got in a hell of a jeep accident and got his face all cut up. He was a handsome guy too. So there went the slipper deal."

Without doubt, Pap's Hall and its surrounding grounds were a spooky place after dark, particularly for those who pulled guard duty in the middle of the night. Silas Hogg thought the building to be creepy, the quintessential haunted house, and finally made up his mind to search it from cellar to ceiling with a Thompson sub-machinegun to satisfy himself. "I'll put it to you this way," he explained. "I went all over that castle to find out if they was any booby traps or anything in it. The only thing I found in that castle was a big water tank on top of it, that's all I found."

Bob Storms wasn't quartered in the main building, but he remembered it clearly. "I was living out there in the stables and then that big house I got to go in," he said. "Oh man, what a place. Oh my God almighty! What'd I say, 31 bathrooms in there or 36 bathrooms? Thirty something bathrooms in that house. Boy, that place, you could lean against the wall and sink right in there five six inches. There was silk and velvet all satin and all like that. You had the satin room, the blue room, the velvet room. That place was fabulous! Oh my God, that was like a castle itself. They had hallways up through the walls, then you could go to one room without the regular hallways. You go up through the walls, you know," he continued, then added some GI speculation as to the purpose of the customary servants passages he was describing. "They said years ago, when the rich were there, the maids would go up and take care of the big shots."

Storms also described the surrounding grounds, as well as what happened when he first explored them on his own, saying, "Outside in the back I got lost. They had one of them mazes you could get in. I had to holler so somebody could come get me out. Once you learned it was alright, but without thinking I walked in there and went around a few loops and I couldn't get out. I had to stay in there till someone could come and get me."

Roughly situated northwest of London between Birmingham and Nottingham,

BRASS HATS WERE IN THE AREA.

Lubenham was the closest village to Papillon Hall. Theddingworth lay a few miles to the west and Ashley was a few miles to the north of Market Harborough. Sartain remembered Lubenham as, "a very quaint little village. It didn't have more than three or four dozen houses." This sleepy hamlet had only one main thoroughfare, with several side streets leading off from it, but beginning in 1940 camps of the Royal Air Force (RAF) and Women's Land Army (WLA) were constructed on its outskirts. The RAF site was almost a village in itself, with barracks, kitchens, a chapel, cinema, and mess hall. The WLA facility was established to house some of the thousands of town and city girls recruited into uniformed battalions to replace the shortage of farm laborers across England. Together now with the American 319th, Lubenham came alive in a way it had never seen before, or ever would again.

The battalion established its infirmary over a garage in Lubenham and, as one village boy later recalled, "Many is the time us lads caught oranges, thrown from a window by an American who for one reason or another found himself in the sick bay." Just outside the village, on the way to Market Harborough, the battalion quartered all its senior officers; Major Todd, Majors Wilcoxson and Wimberley, along with all the captains, in a small hotel. First and second lieutenants, along with chief warrant officers remained at Papillon, essentially available for duty 24 hours a day. The arrangement was another expression of the cast system practiced between junior and senior officers.

Of course this cast system was seen most prominently between officers and enlisted men, though the segregation was often beneficial to both parties. Sartain explained some of its details when he said, "We had an understanding that Lubenham was for the GIs, you see? And the officers, with transportation available to them could go into the pubs in Market Harborough. The GIs could walk to Lubenham. That was just the general understanding. Most officers stayed away from Lubenham. That way the GIs didn't have to worry about their behavior in a pub. If they got out of hand the MPs would take care of that. Of course Sergeants Johnson and Jinders let us, the officers, know that was a gentleman's agreement. Well, it was just an understanding. Nothing written, but that was the understanding. So the 319th officers stayed out of Lubenham."

Once the outfit was settled in at Papillon most of the men had Class "A" passes to go off base. This meant that they were free to leave the bivouac any time after retreat and stay out until midnight, though in actual practice answering to morning roll call was usually adequate. "Unless someone else answered for them," said Sartain. "You know they might be in bed sleeping it off from the night before. When Sergeant Johnson told me, all present and accounted for, that accounted for could cover a lot of things. I always made it a point to be present for the men first thing in the morning, but if one of the enlisted guys wasn't there we didn't make a big fuss over it. Of course, if he didn't show up after a few hours we had to send somebody out looking for him." The understanding made life easier on everybody and provided Johnson with a ready pool of names for unpleasant details, guard duty, and other onerous assignments. The guys, in turn, accepted this and appreciated being trusted.

In fact there is ample evidence of the ways in which the officers trusted that the enlisted men could take care of themselves and offer their views on the operations of the battery as well. This was at least the case in Manning's battery, as it had been when he and Sartain were in command of "C Battery. "They had a lot of stuff going on that we officers didn't know anything about," said Sartain later, "And I think that was good, that was alright."

Periodic meetings of an unusually democratic quality resumed for the officers and noncommissioned staff. "That place was one place where Captain Manning used to have his bull sessions," remembered Storms. "He told us there, as long as we was inside at that place we didn't have to salute any officers unless we got the word that other officers were coming in from somewhere else. Then you saluted every officer you see. But otherwise for everyday you never, as long as it was just us alone there, we never saluted an officer. As long as we yes or no sired them, even the sergeants we were very polite to. Well, you figure we'd pass one another twenty times a day sometimes and not salute, so that's one thing they were good at. But if you went to town or got out on the street or when somebody come there to inspect something or look the place over, you throwed your arm out there. We went all the way for something like that."

Storms's memory of these gatherings was told with a conviction which seems to originate somewhere in truth, but Sartain wouldn't agree that battery men were ever excused from saluting at Papillon. Sartain did clearly remember "bull sessions" with his NCOs though, when he said, "I had regular routine meetings with them. It got to where they could say what they wanted to. I relied on their opinions. We had a terrific group of noncoms. Sergeants and corporals. A real terrific group."

For those who toed the mark and behaved themselves, life at Pap's Hall was good. "It was great," said Gunner Corporal Robert Rappi. "We could go to town all the time. Sometimes they had trucks, but me and Kenneth Smith used to walk. It wasn't that far. Kenneth, he was the six foot eight guy, he could reach over the whole crowd and hand our beer glasses to the bartender up above the rest of them. We'd have to be in at a certain time, but there'd be MPs patrolling the road, so we'd have to dive in the woods every once in a while so they wouldn't catch us. We'd run down town and run back."

The pub on the outskirts of Lubenham was named The Coach & Horses. The establishment in Theddingworth was The Crown, in north Kilworth was The Swann, and in market Harborough stood The Bells. These were typical English working man's pubs where a dark and, by American tastes, bitter, room temperature beer was served, hard liquor being impossible to acquire most of the time. According to "A" Battery machine gunner, Lester Newman, "You could buy a drink, but then they never had that much to drink. You know, like hard liquor, they never had any of that. You could drink a beer, which was nastier than heck. It was warm beer, and it wasn't all that tasty either."

At these taverns the guys could relax, have a drink and play darts, quoits, or billiards. As was the custom, the bar rooms were reserved for the men, while an adjoining room was open to men and ladies alike – the latter drinking a mixture of beer and lemonade known locally as a Shandygaff. Most men became introduced to fish & chips, with more than a few growing fond of the dish as an alternative to army chow.

Coffee was another matter, as one "A" Battery man later complained, "You go in and ask for a cup of coffee and they pick up a bottle of what looked like chocolate milk. They'd put about a tablespoon in a cup and fill it up with hot water. It sure as hell didn't taste like coffee, I don't know what it was, but that's what they served you for coffee."

There were other unusual local customs. "Usually here you put your money on the bar and the bartender takes your money till you're ready to leave and you take the change with you. There they didn't do that. They want you to keep your money and pay them drink by drink," observed one 319th man of the practices he witnessed.

Most popular of all with the troops was The Paget Arms, located within the village of Lubenham itself. The owner, Mr. Abraham Tarry, assisted by his daughter Vida, had a way of keeping a good supply of beer and spirits despite the frequent shortages of the time. It wasn't long before the guys in the outfit were regular customers, adding their own initials and airborne insignia to those already carved into the wooden table tops by men from the nearby RAF installation.

Like all other pubs during the war years, The Paget Arms closed at 10pm, when Mr. Tarry would announce, "Time's up gentlemen, glasses please!"
With a couple of hours remaining until they had to be back at Pap's Hall, the guys in the 319th had one more alternative, a small dancehall tucked away in the Lubenham village office building known as "The Sweat-box."

The town had a meeting hall where they held these dances," remembered one "A" Battery man of the Sweat-Box. "I remember it was full of bats. The goddamn things almost tore your head off! I think once a week they would have dancing. There was a local British air force base near there and all the young ladies from this air force base were invited. I remember the land army, but this was the air force. We went there and these young girls, women from the air force, were there to provide dancing partners. We had a nice time, had little cookies, food there, and things like that. It was very nice. We enjoyed that."

"I didn't dance, so I didn't go," Ed Ryan recalled, "but it was just a 25 by 25 outfit. They used to have Limey bands in there. They called it the Sweat-Box. Most of the guys went down there. I didn't go, but I know that one night J. C. Harrison, he was drunk, he was mad and he was gonna clean it out. He was gonna throw a smoke grenade in there. Holy Jesus, good thing he didn't because the damn thing was one of those that burn you bad. Good thing they stopped him in time."

Ryan remembered other mischief, like the time Delbert Jackson dropped his pants and defecated in the middle of Lubenham's main thoroughfare. These juvenile pranks were usually harmless enough but clearly posed a nuisance to the residents of these formerly quiet villages. Commenting further on the high jinx of the GIs, he remembered, "Bragg and I knew two girls in Theddingworth, they lived over the pub. We called them the Stone Heart Sisters because we could never get them out alone. Their bedroom was right over the pub, so one night Willy was trying to get this girl to come out. He was tossing stones at the window, bigger and bigger ones until he broke the window. She screamed, then her father came flying out with a shotgun looking for us."

Evidently Willy Bragg wasn't the only man tossing stones at windows. According to Bob Storms, "Between market Harborough and the other village there was a tavern. I used to stop there and the woman in the tavern never charged me. But sometimes her husband was there and he charged me for drinks. When I come back I'd throw stones at the bedroom window. She'd come out and come down. I'd tell her, hey, your old man charged me for drinks last night when I come out. She'd give me my money back and I go on home. Well I'd come on back in town and then go back to my place. It was a pretty good trip going back and forth."

Considering the frequent, and sometimes more serious disturbances caused by the young GIs, some villages did their best to discourage visits from the Americans. However, Bob Storms somehow seems to have ingratiated himself with the residents of one such community. "I was in a village, I had the whole village to myself," he said. "It was built like in a circle. There was all green grass in the middle, all private homes. The girls there used to go with our guys when they went in town in Market Harborough, but they wouldn't let the girls bring them home. I used to know a lot of the women there. I used to go over there and kid with the women. I'd say, 'Why don't you let some of our guys come out to go with your girls?'

BATTERY!

"No!"

I'd say, "But you let me in."

"Yeah, but we know you Bob."

I said, "But you didn't know me at first."

"Well, we got used to you now."

They wouldn't let no other soldiers come in town. I don't know why, but they wouldn't let another soldier in."

Most officers were not much different than the enlisted men. They were almost all young guys who enjoyed going to pubs and dance halls too. Manning and Sartain, Lieutenants Simpson, Sharkey, Poole, Hawkins, Carey, Torgerson and others, all enjoyed each other's company over a pint or two, or three, of the local malt beverage in the establishments they frequented. Even Lieutenant Ragland, normally a stay-at-home sort of guy, went along on a few occasions. He explained, "I wasn't a party man. A couple of times in England they got me to go with them and have a drink, but first thing I knew they was hauling me back to the barracks."

These outings for officers meant having a driver take them to their destination of choice and then wait to bring them home later. As Sartain said, "I went into Market Harborough because I had a jeep. Market Harborough was a lot larger by most standards. It had two pubs and a theater. You could go to the movies and they'd show old American films. I'd tell Sosa where to drop me off. When I was going out and socializing, something like that, Sosa would drop me off and I would give him a time to pick me up. What Sosa did between the times I have no idea."

Sosa didn't mind, but he didn't just wait around either. Every trip Manning or Sartain made into town gave this enterprising driver an opportunity to make contacts of all sorts. "Yeah, sure," he remarked about these occasions, "You're just standing around doing nothing. If I decided to do a little sightseeing I'd crank up the jeep and go, what's wrong with that?" These jaunts gave Sosa the chance to acquire things not available to the average GI in the battery, "Like jump boots, I had some. They weren't issued to me but I got some. You know, there's ways of getting things if you look around a little bit. It's not bad." Sartain didn't pry, but he was well aware Sosa wasn't idle while waiting to bring him back to Papillon Hall. "Sosa was something else, man," he later said. "Sosa was a good man and he had a bunch of contacts in England that I didn't know anything about. He took advantage of his situation, he had his own agenda, I'll tell you now, but he was just something else."

Leicester, fifteen miles to the north, was a favorite destination for those who wanted a more cosmopolitan atmosphere than Market Harborough had to offer. "A" Battery's Lieutenant Harry Warren quickly became a regular visitor there. If Ragland wasn't a party man, Lieutenant Warren still was, and Leicester offered both more opportunity and anonymity while indulging his pleasures. During the stay in Northern Ireland the Lieutenant had managed to avoid getting himself in further trouble, but if that was because he'd curbed his behavior, his old habits were creeping up on him now.

On the afternoon of Saturday, February 26th, Warren made another of what were already regular trips into Leicester. He was alone, without the company of other "A" Battery or battalion officers, perhaps preferring it that way, perhaps because other officers were reluctant to join him. As one put it, "You didn't want to go because you never knew what you'd get mixed up in."

Warren's driver, motor pool Private Victor Ziska of "A" Battery, dropped him outside the Bell Hotel in Leicester's Humberstone Gate. The Lieutenant instructed Ziska to pick him up in front of the Grand Hotel at 11:30, then proceeded to a local pub for a meal and refreshments.

About 10:00pm Warren, aware that he had imbibed past his limit, left the pub and made his way to the Bell Hotel. He was hoping to find transportation to the division parking lot and make contact with his driver, who wasn't due to meet him for another 90 minutes. Private Herbert Johnson, an MP, was walking his beat past the hotel when he saw the Lieutenant leaning against the building. Johnson recognized Warren, evidently from previous visits to Leicester, and approached him. Warren explained his situation and Johnson suggested they go together to the division parking lot to locate Ziska and the jeep. From his staggering gait it was obvious that the Lieutenant was in no condition to find his way there alone.

At the parking lot the two were approached by MP Corporal Richards, who had charge of the squad responsible for the lot and its immediate area. Johnson explained to the Corporal that Warren needed some help looking for his driver. Richards understood immediately. He'd seen more intoxicated officers than he cared to during his career as an MP, and he was tired of showing respect for rank when the man wearing the uniform was in his cups, so to speak. "Can I see your identification, sir?" He asked.

Warren was wearing Manning's duffle coat, the one the British naval officer had given to him at Maiori, and while he fumbled with the wooden toggles Richards sucked his teeth impatiently. He didn't really need to see Warren's ID, but if he was going to have to nurse-maid this Lieutenant, it was worth making the man squirm a little. When Warren finally did produce the requisite papers, Richards barely glanced at it under the beam of his flashlight, then handed it back. "Alright Lieutenant, why don't you wait here with Johnson and I'll go see if I can't find your driver for you."

Richards walked off, no doubt cursing under his breath. Then he saw another jeep pull into the lot and come to a stop before him. It was Lieutenant Colonel Schell-hammer, the personnel officer for the entire 82nd Airborne Division. Richards smiled to himself and approached the passenger. "Good evening Colonel," he said, saluting. Schellhammer nodded and replied, "Evening Corporal. Everything in order here to-night?"

"Everything's in order sir, pretty quiet really, except there's a Lieutenant over there who's a little, well, feeling no pain, if the Colonel knows what I mean, sir," the Corporal answered.

Schellhammer remarked, "Is that so."

"Yes sir," Richards said, then added, "Would the Colonel like to see him?" The Colonel would, and Richards directed Schellhammer's driver to the place where he'd left Warren with Private Johnson.

Schellhammer found Warren sitting on the bumper of a civilian vehicle. Johnson eyeballed the situation and decided this would be a good time to absent himself. The MP slipped off silently to his beat near the hotel. The Colonel asked Warren to identify himself and explain what his business was in the parking lot. Doing his best to steady himself, Warren rose and walked up to Colonel Schellhammer and gave his name, blurting out that he was just trying to locate his jeep and driver. The Lieutenant's heart must have sunk when he saw the oak leaves on Schellhammer's uniform. Coming to the at-tention of a superior officer of this rank was the last thing he needed at this moment, and of all the possible brass to encounter, none could be worse than the division's G-1. "Alright, what's your driver's name," the Colonel asked.

Warren couldn't remember. Then he turned suddenly and started toward the rows of parked vehicles. Warren was saying something about being sure he could find his jeep, but from his stagger and slurred speech it was apparent that the Lieutenant was in no condition to go anywhere by himself. Schellhammer got out of his jeep and strode over with an apparent intent to investigate, maybe even help Warren out. In the darkness of the parking lot, he knew the Lieutenant would at least need a flashlight. He handed Warren his own but the officer simply stood there, weaving to and fro. When the flashlight dropped from his benumbed hand, casting its errant beam like a little solitary searchlight, Schellhammer knew he had to take some action. Trucks loading up with enlisted personnel going back to their quarters, officers, and small clusters of civilians were all in the immediate vicinity or walking past the embarrassing spectacle. Warren was attracting attention and it didn't look good.

Schellhammer ordered the Lieutenant to sit in a nearby parked jeep and remain there until he returned, telling him he was going to procure transportation to take him to the Provost Marshall's office on Saxby Street. Both parties understood that this meant charges would be filed. Schellhammer's jeep drove off and Warren sat there in the dark. He must have had the growing realization that his military career was dissolving before his eyes. When Schellhammer returned with another jeep a few minutes later, Warren was gone.

The next day a call came in to Major Todd's office reporting that one of his Lieutenants, a Harry Warren, had been in Leicester the night before, drunk and disorderly in a public place, apparently out of uniform, and had disobeyed a direct order from Lt. Col. Schellhammer, the Division G-1. It was, by now, a familiar story. Todd directed Major Wilcoxson to investigate the incident, which he did, finding that there were grounds for the charges and recommending once again that Warren be dismissed from the service "for reason of moral turpitude." Another General Court Martial was scheduled.

It is reasonable to assume there was some discussion between Manning and Sartain of this latest incident, perhaps with Warren included. They were, after all, his immediate superiors. They'd inherited the 2nd Lieutenant when they took over "A" Battery from Captain Loughmiller and were naturally aware of his reputation from previous events in Naples, so the news that Warren was up for another court martial couldn't have come as a shock. Likewise, Warren had seen the way Sartain won a hands-down acquittal for Goldfarb in Africa, how he'd gone to bat for Kenneth Smith in Naples, and for other men too. Warren may have even come to wish he'd had Sartain defending him at his first court martial. Now he was in trouble again and needed help. At some point Warren asked Sartain to serve as his defense council. Sartain really had little choice but to accept. Regardless of his own assessment of him as an officer or individual, Warren was still one of his own and deserved a proper defense.

On March 6th, 1944, Warren's second court martial was convened at division headquarters. There were some familiar faces among those present. Lieutenant Wilson Holz, the prosecutor in Warren's first General Court Martial, was back to prosecute this next trial. Lieutenant Karl R. Price, Warren's Assistant Defense Council in Naples, was also there and serving in the same capacity as before. This time though, Warren had Sartain as his choice of Defense Council.

Members of the court included the 319th's S-3, Major Jerry Wimberley. He requested to be dismissed for previous knowledge of the case and was excused by the president of the court. Then, as was his habit when representing a defendant, Sartain peremptorily challenged the most senior officer, Captain Ogden of the 325th Glider Infantry. Ogden was excused as well. The charges against Warren were read, violation of the 96th Article of War, to which he pleaded not guilty. The trial was ready to begin. The prosecution was the first to present its case. Holz called Private Johnson to the stand, leading him through a recitation of his encounter with Warren outside the Bell Hotel. When Holz asked how it was Johnson judged the Lieutenant to be drunk, the MP answered, "When I walked with him, sir, he staggered and I took it on myself to help him along, he was staggering pretty heavy, sir." The testimony satisfied Holz, who stated he had no further questions.

Sartain then cross examined Johnson. "Did he acknowledge knowing you, -were you recognized by him?" Sartain asked.

Johnson said he did.

For emphasis, Sartain asked again, "He did recognize you?"

Again Johnson had to answer, "Yes, sir."

Sartain then asked Johnson, "Did you warn the accused that brass hats were in the area?"

"Yes, sir, I did," was the reply. It was perhaps not the answer Sartain had hoped for, as the question seems intended to suggest that Warren may have been taken off guard by Colonel Schellhammer's sudden appearance if he had no prior warning.

Regrouping, the defense council attempted to next disarm the question of Warren's dress, a subject he knew Holz was bound to introduce. He asked the MP the condition of Warren's uniform. "The Lieutenant didn't have an overcoat like you usually see the officers have," Johnson told the court. "It was more or less a mackinaw, three-quarter length, it had a hood and had wooden toggles."

Again not the answer Sartain was hoping for. He must have thought to himself, damn that crazy British coat of Johnny Manning's! He'd have to be more careful about how he worded his questions. Sartain then continued, "Was it properly buttoned up?"

"Yes, sir," was the answer.

Good, good, Sartain thought, now keep on this line of questioning. "Was his cap straight?" The answer was again affirmative. "Did he have his tie tucked in?" Again the answer was yes. Now with some momentum behind him, Sartain went on to ask, "Was his clothing torn?"

Johnson answered, "No, sir, I didn't notice it."

Very good. Sartain felt he'd established that Warren was at least coherent and presentable. Even if a little unsteady on his feet, he didn't sound out of control at this point. Feeling a little bolder, Sartain's next question was, "What was his manner of speech?"

"Well," said Johnson, "I would say his manner of speech was that of a drunken person, he stammered and stalled between his words."

At this point Sartain must have known he'd asked one question too many. He'd been warned about this. "The key to a good defense lawyer is to know when to ask your questions," Sartain remembered years later. "When I was just a little ole freshman at LSU I worked for these lawyers in Baton Rouge, Huckabay and Daspit. Daspit's an old south Louisiana family, and Elton Huckabay, he just coached me along. You've got to know when to stop, he told me, and you never ask a question if you don't already know the answer. Well, after a batch of them I got to be pretty good at it."

At the moment though, there was nothing for it except to engage in some damage repair. "Did he answer your questions intelligently?" Sartain asked.

"Yes, sir," answered Johnson.

That was better. If he could establish that Warren was able to understand and be understood, then who was to say just how slurred his speech was. "Did you have any difficulty understanding him?"

"No, sir, didn't have no difficulty."

Sartain then asked, "In your conversation with the accused, did you hear him use any profanity or obscene language?" The witness did not. "Did the accused show the proper respect to Colonel Schellhammer?"

"Yes, sir, he did," Johnson answered.

Sartain probably felt that he'd made a nice recovery when he asked, "Did you notice whether at the time you were accompanying the accused to the parking lot, did any passers-by notice is condition, that is, were any passers-by attention attracted to him by the reason of what you say would be symptoms of intoxication? Did you see anybody turn around and stare at him?"

"Yes, sir, I did, now that you brought it up, a few soldiers turned around and noticed it."

Well, Sartain wasn't about to bring it up again. Having determined that he'd taken this witness as far as he could, Warren's defense council told the court he had no further questions.

Wilson Holz next called Corporal Willy Richards to testify. After Richards first identified Warren as the accused in question, a formality required of every witness, he then incorrectly described the Lieutenant as belonging to the 456th Parachute Field Artillery. Richards was then directed to explain how the accused came to his attention on the night of February 26th, which he proceeded to do. Holz now asked, "You stated that he was drunk. What caused you to have that opinion?"

"He was staggering and I could smell alcohol on his breath," answered the Corporal.

Holz then moved on to Warren's dress. "Was Lieutenant Warren wearing his uniform?"

"Yes, sir," answered Richards, "he had a short coat, I never saw one like it in military line, it had a piece of wood on it and it had about 1 inch of string and cord which ended in the center."

Holz must have believed he'd made clear that Warren was both intoxicated and out of uniform. Now he would demonstrate that his behavior had reflected poorly on the Army by asking, "Was anyone aware of the accused's condition besides military personnel at the parking lot?"

When Richards answered, "Yes, sir, there were civilians there, civilian people at the time," Holz felt he'd made each of his points and concluded his questioning.

Now it was Sartain's turn. It was looking unlikely that he could dismantle the image of Warren as drunk, but an essential part of the charge was the public exhibition of that condition. Sartain asked the witness if it was late at night when these events took place. It was. The defense council continued, "Was it very dark that night?"

Richards replied, "Yes, sir, it was dark."

Well, that left the suggestion that Warren's conduct wasn't exactly a public display. Pleased with raising this fact, Sartain went on by asking, "Did you hear, at any time, the accused use obscene language or any profanity?" The Corporal did not. "Did he act disrespectful to you?" Again Richards answer was negative, Warren did not treat him disrespectfully.

Returning to the subject of Warren's appearance, Sartain next asked, "Was his uniform in any way torn or disorderly?"

"If it was," answered Richards, "I didn't notice it, sir." Richards then added, "Sir, about this organization business, I remember now it is "A" Battery, 319th Field Artillery, I had some other boys in my mind about this other organization."

There being no further questions, Corporal Richards was dismissed from the witness stand. Lieutenant Colonel Frederick M. Schellhammer took his place. The Colonel needed scant direction from the prosecution and touched upon each area of concern without being asked. "During the entire procedure," Schellhammer testified of Warren, "his actions, though not loud and boisterous, were those of a man who seemed to have lost control of his ability to take care of himself. He staggered and his speech was incoherent and that led me to believe that he had been drinking unduly. During this time there were also approximately one hundred men of this division and men of other units, and civilians in the parking lot, and they were all aware that he was intoxicated."

Holz then brought up the subject of Warren's uniform. Schellhammer explained, "At the time I spoke to him he was wearing a top coat which to the best of my knowledge I would describe as an arctic top coat. It had a peculiar type of frog button. The insignia was evident on his cap." After Schellhammer affirmed that the parking lot would be considered a public place, Holz was finished.

Colonel Schellhammer's testimony was incriminating, especially given his rank and position in the division's command structure. Sartain would have to be very careful. With a witness like this, any appearance of disrespect, sarcasm, or undue hubris on his part could easily backfire. Still, he had to soften the Colonel's testimony in whatever way possible.

Sartain began by asking Colonel Schellhammer if Warren spoke to any civilians or if any civilians spoke to him that night. The Colonel said he saw no verbal communication between the accused and civilians. Sartain then asked if, in Schellhammer's opinion, Warren stood up because he recognized his rank.

"Yes, I believe that is why he stood up," answered Schellhammer.

Then, to further advance the perception that Warren was conducting himself properly in the presence of a superior, Sartain asked, "Did he act disrespectful to you?" Schellhammer's terse reply was a simple, "No."

Good enough, Sartain must have thought, and better to let this witness leave the stand than risk his making any more damaging statements.

The prosecution rested its case. Now it was Sartain's opportunity to present witnesses for the defense. There was only one. Private Victor Ziska of his own "A" Battery was called to the stand. Sartain asked Ziska to describe the events of February 26th.

"Yes, sir," the driver said, "I was told to pick up, that is get my dispatch and pick up, Lieutenant Warren at three o'clock and take him to Leicester, which I did. We got into Leicester about four o'clock and Lieutenant Warren told me where to park in the GI parking lot and I dropped him off at the Bell, I think, and he told me to stop at the Grand Hotel at eleven-thirty. I came back at eleven-fifteen or around there, and at about eleven-fifteen Lieutenant Warren came out and we were on our way."

"When you picked the accused up in front of the Grand Hotel," Sartain asked, "Did he need assistance to get in the vehicle?" Ziska said he did not. Sartain repeated the question for emphasis, "He didn't need any assistance and he got in the vehicle by himself?"

Again Ziska answered, "Yes, sir."

Ziska was then asked if he had any conversation with Warren at the time he was driving him home. "Just as usual, sir," he answered.

To this Sartain replied, "Was there anything wrong with his conversation, was it incoherent?" Ziska answered that it was not.

Because the prosecution showed no interest in questioning Ziska, he was released and allowed to stand down. It is usually not advisable for a defendant to testify in his own defense, but this trial would be an exception. It was Warren's idea," Sartain later said. "I told him, you're taking a very big chance. They're going to ask you questions I wouldn't ask you. I tried to talk him out of it but he insisted." Sartain acquiesced, then called his client to the stand. "Lieutenant Warren," he began, "Explain to the court the circumstances of your actions of February 26th, evening and night."

Warren took a deep breath, then initiated his answer, "Well, I was with these people, they were civilians and I had been in a pub before I arrived at the Bell Hotel. At that particular time, that is before that, in a pub, I was before a fire and I got warm and I felt myself getting wobbly, I was wobbly and not in very good shape to walk around, that is walk around the motor park and look for the jeep. I asked Private Johnson to escort me to the motor park and at that time he told me that Colonel Schellhammer was in the area. I was more groggy than drunk when I ran into Colonel Schellhammer there and I borrowed his flashlight, and I was pretty cold and had on my gloves and that might have accounted for my dropping the flashlight. I went directly back to the Grand Hotel when I found that my jeep wasn't there and then went home."

Now Sartain's aim was to let Warren tell the court how he specifically restrained himself. "Did you stop drinking because you felt yourself getting shaky," he asked.

"I did," said Warren.

"Did you feel an impediment coming into your speech?"

Warren answered, "I could."

Sartain then ask Warren directly, "In your own opinion do you think you were drunk?"

"No," he answered, "I wasn't, not so as to know not what I was doing."

Sartain sensed this was the point where he should cease questioning his client. Then, when Holz declined to pose any questions to Warren, Sartain was inwardly stunned. He could scarcely believe the prosecution would let an opportunity like this pass unexploited. But any elation Sartain may have felt was short lived. The court had a question of its own. Who gave Warren a ride to the Grand hotel? Warren didn't know, except that they were American officers.

Lieutenant Warren's inability to answer must have inspired Holz, who suddenly decided to resume his queries. "How much would you say you had to drink before eleven o'clock that evening?"

"I don't know if I can answer that one or not," admitted Warren.

It was a wonderful answer for Holz. The prosecutor tasted blood and pushed on, asking, "Can you make any estimate as to how much you drank that evening?"

"You mean insofar as pints or quarts," asked Warren.

"Yes," said Holz flatly.

"I'm afraid I can't. No, I'm afraid I can't," Warren confessed

This series of weak answers surely left Holz confident that his case was made. He announced to the court that he was through questioning the Lieutenant. Sartain jumped back in, making one last attempt to mitigate the damaging testimony of four witnesses, one of whom was the defendant himself. Rising to redirect, Warren's defense council asked, "There seems to be quite a bit of confusion about that over-coat you wore. Will you explain to the court so that there will be no doubt as to your being out of uniform?"

"This coat belongs to an English naval officer," Warren said, "It's an English naval officer's coat. It has a hood on it so we borrow it and use it when we ride in a jeep for any length of time as protection from the wind. We use it in place of the short coat, just for protection from the wind when we ride in a jeep."

Sartain had done what he could and the trial was essentially over, except for tying up loose ends. Some discussion concerning whether or not Warren's prior court martial had found him guilty of disobeying an order took place. Both Warren and Lieutenant Price, his assistant defense council in that and the current trials, testified that he was acquitted on that charge but found guilty of being drunk and disorderly. Sartain and Holz each made brief closing statements, and the court recessed.

When the court reconvened their verdict was given. Lieutenant Warren was found guilty of being drunk and disorderly in a public place. That was no surprise to anyone, except perhaps the Lieutenant himself. The most surprising element though was the punishment. Despite having been twice brought before a General Court Martial, and twice having had his own superiors recommend he be eliminated from the service, Harry Warren was fined $100 and released. "I don't know what that court was thinking," remembered Sartain, "It was a real shocker. Everyone was surprised except Warren, he was disappointed, he really thought he was going to get off."

Perhaps it was poignant to see this officer in such a compromised position. There may even have been an unspoken consensus of pity among the members of the court. In any case Warren escaped with what can only be described as a slap on the wrist. Looking back on the trial years later, Sartain observed, "Afterwards Todd and Wilcoxson really had the red ass over the verdict. Todd wasn't mad at me though. He was a lawyer. He knew my job was to defend him. A defense lawyer gets his client off and Todd understood that. He figured, well, peace be with him, you know."

Even though Todd understood the limitations of the court, he also knew that as battalion commander he could exert some influence and have his problem Lieutenant transferred out. He must have initiated the process immediately, since Warren's name never appeared again in battalion paperwork after the end of March, 1944. "Major Todd must have gone to some higher ups because soon after Warren just disappeared," said Sartain. "Nobody said anything. Nobody said, Major, what happened to Warren, he was just gone and we never heard from him again."

BATTERY!

Part 13: "Hey, how's the air up there?"

There wasn't really time to ruminate over Harry Warren or his fate. The day after the trial, Sartain was up early and on his way to jump school. In anticipation of the invasion, the parachute infantry regiments would want artillery observation teams jumping with them on location and ready to direct fire at once. This meant that a cadre of 319th Liaison Officers and members of FO teams were called up to become jump qualified. Having already made clear when he entered the service that he wished to become a jumper, Sartain was among the group, as was Marvin Ragland, Max Torgerson, Bub Hawkins, and a number of others, among them Sosa. "Since I was his driver, he couldn't go anywhere without me," he remembered. "So, I went to jump school myself."

According to Sartain, "This was the first authorized school where you stayed with your unit. It was a four day deal. A day of plain class work, a day of packing chutes, stuff like that, then the jumping aspect was over in two days." Ashwell, the division jump school in England, was operated out of the 82nd's airfield at Cotesmoore. Because of the pressure to prepare for the coming invasion, it was more rapid compared to the standard stateside course at Fort Benning. There was no tower from which simulated landings were made. Instead, trainees barely had a chance to lace up their jump boots before they were harnessed in their chutes and climbing aboard a C-47. Sosa agreed that the instruction was accelerated. "That was the quickest school of one kind or another. We took some minimal training," he said, "They gave us the principle of stand up, hook up, and out the door."

By war's end about 30% of the men in the 319th became jump qualified through schools established in England or France, and it is doubtful that any who earned their parachute wings ever regretted becoming part of this select airborne brotherhood. Their motives for doing so were varied. Of course one reason was the inherent danger of the glider service. After each crash landing into a combat zone there was always a new crop of volunteers for jump school. As one "A" Battery man put it, "The glider troops were anxious to get into the paratroops because in a glider you're a big target and you don't have no parachute." Another incentive was a monthly bonus of $50 jump pay. But the real attraction was the élan of jumping, together with the privilege of wearing sterling silver wings and distinctive boots. "I wore the glider wings most of the time with the unit since it was a glider unit. I wore the jump wings if I wanted to impress someone," is how Sartain put it.

Much like a cap and gown, graduates were also issued the classic Model 1942 jump suit with its snap closures and endlessly expanding pockets, even long after this uniform was obsolete and discontinued for use among the parachute units. For example, when Ted Covais became jump qualified in March of 1945, he was issued one of the old style jumpsuits. However, he remembered, "I would not wear that, except just wear it on occasions. I didn't wear it because I didn't want to be set apart from the other guys. We're all in one outfit, one outfit, you know what I mean?"

Though the procedure of parachuting had been performed many thousands of times and had become routine in the airborne, the prospect of exiting a plane in flight was accompanied by a natural anxiety. Sartain's observation was that the first time was by far the hardest, with successive jumps becoming much easier. "It takes a lot less courage to go out that door than hang with that infantry," he said afterwards.

There were always a few men whose composure seemed altogether nonplussed by the prospect of parachuting. Marvin Ragland was one. His even temper kept him calm, even during his first jump, about which he later commented, "Well, it didn't bother me. I didn't mind it. It was just something different that I'd never done."

At Ashwell, that March the qualifying jumps were made in one day, without weapons or combat gear. Nor was there any distinction made among the trainees regarding rank, they were all virgins to the parachute as far as the instructors were concerned. Sartain remembered that once his group was loaded and on their way, the jumpmaster turned to the students and shouted above the roar of the wind and engines, "Give your soul to the Lord because your ass belongs to me!"

In the interest of time, the pre-Normandy jump qualifications were abbreviated from the usual five jumps. "Actually we only made three jumps to qualify, all in one day. Hook up, stand up and made the jumps and that was it," said Sosa. Parachute school at this time also dispensed with the customary night jump, though later schools returned to this requirement. Covais was obliged to jump at night in early 1945, and found it especially challenging. "You had to do five jumps, did you know that? That's five jumps. Four daytime jumps and you've got to do one at night. Everybody's got to do a night jump, but you can't see nothing," he remembered. "The night jump is a doozie, a real

doozie. You can't see the ground. You don't know where you're going to land. Could be on high tension wires, could be in the water and you drown yourself. It's a matter of where you land. Maybe lights in the distance, but in the military nobody's putting a light out for you, and that's it."

In spite of anyone's apprehension, the moment came when the call of "Stand in the Door" was heard. There was no time left to think now, only shuffle to the open door and step off the fuselage into mid air. A scant two seconds later the man would feel a massive jolt as his parachute deployed, then the glorious sensation of relief and floating, descending slowly to the landscape below. "It was wonderful," said Sosa, "You jump at about a thousand feet. It's quiet coming down. I loved it. I really liked it. It's quiet up there."

Sartain in A-2 jacket with canteen cup : *taken outside of paps hall barracks. Sartain collection.

Another distinction was granted

for airborne officers about this time, whether they had been through jump school or were simply glider qualified. All were now authorized to wear leather flight jackets. Sartain remembered being measured up for one by Supply Sergeant Jinders, then receiving it a week or two later, already fitted out with a nametag and division insignia sewn to the left breast. "We didn't wear them in combat," he said, "And we couldn't wear them when we had to wear the Class "A" uniform, but we wore them all the rest of the time." The jackets the 319th officers received were the Type A-2, in this case made by the DuBow Company of Chicago, Illinois, chiefly a manufacturer of baseball mitts before the war. The A-2s were made of dark brown horsehide with knitted woolen cuffs and waistband of a reddish brown hue. The "A" Battery officers loved the jackets and posed proudly for individual and group photos in them on the day they arrived.

After jump school, the next round of specialized training came during the last week of March, 1944. The 319th was trucked to a training area, probably the one located in a rugged region of Wales, at Sennybridge in Northumberland. "I remember we went down to a shooting range, an artillery range," recalled Sartain. The British called these ranges "practice camps," and this one was designated number five. They offered the chance for battalion sized field exercises with live ammunition in an otherwise crowded England.

As Sartain looked back on these training activities, it was clear that competition between the firing batteries was keen, and battery pride enduring. "I don't know about the accuracy," he said, "We all got the same information from fire direction, but yeah, I thought Battery "A" was a better battery. "B" Battery was OK, but "A" Battery just had a better gun section. Quicker. When we went down to the artillery range in Wales, before Normandy, we just out shot them going and coming. I think it was probably the result of their FOs and their batteries. I would give a command to set it up, I'd say, 'Fire when ready.' They didn't have to report, they didn't have to wait, they didn't have to report ready and then wait for the order to fire. I said fire when ready and they would fire. Well, "B" Battery, for some reason, Max Torgerson and those boys always waited until the gun crew says ready and then he says, 'Fire.' We just beat the hell out of them."

Part of the exercises in Wales involved problems in which the batteries needed to go cross country and be set up at a given map coordinate by a certain time. The going could be rough on the steeper slopes, as Captain Manning and his radio operator, Bob Miller discovered. Sosa was driving the two in the Captain's jeep when it started to slip sideways on one of the steeper grades. Manning and Miller were certain that the jeep was about to turn over and land on top of them. They both bailed out and tumbled down the hill to the bottom, landing in a heap. Sosa had confidence in his vehicle however. He knew what it could do and stuck with his jeep until it reached the top, where he waited triumphantly for his passengers to catch up with him.

While at the Welsh range, the outfit was housed in a set of old British barracks. In itself, that wasn't anything novel, but the method of waking the guys in the morning was. As one battalion man explained, "They had loudspeakers up in the air that played reveille early in the morning. We weren't used to that. So one guy, when it started to play, he just reached up with a pair of snips and snipped that wire right off. Went back to bed. All those wire section guys, and radio guys, they've got a pair of dykes right on them, you know? All he did was reach up right out of the bed and snick! That did it."

Some men from the battalion, the machine gun section of "A" Battery for example, stayed at Papillon Hall to hold the fort while everyone else was away. Bob Storms was one of those who remained behind, ever vigilant and watchful. "They went away somewhere," he said, "I don't know where the devil they went to. I think they were gone a week or something, training somewhere and some of us stayed back to watch the camp. We had a good time for a week. Yeah, all the time they were gone we had a hell of a time. We went all through the house. We had girls in the camp and everything else. We had them all lined up, ready. If they'd have known we had girls in bed in camp they would have shot all of us. Oh boy, if they'd have knowed it they'd have hung us!"

Storms was right, at least inasmuch as the party he describes would have provoked, if not a firing squad, then some serious disciplinary action. To guard against just such an unfortunate and deplorable event, precautions were taken. The solution was to maintain a continuous set of guards at the gatehouse where the driveway from Papillon met the road. It was their job to see to it the guys back at the house weren't taken by surprise. As it turned out someone in the battalion was considerate enough to send a jeep in advance of the main convoy, so there were no unnecessary unplesantries. "We stayed behind, we had fun. Them other guys had to go out. They were training and shooting I guess, where ever they went,"concluded Storms.

The 319th received its first influx of new men, replacements for those lost through general attrition or casualties in North Africa and Italy, when the battalion returned from Wales. "A" Battery got its share and one of them was Mahlon Sebring. A tall Michigander, Sebring was a young guy of the hale-fellow-well-met variety, gregarious and talkative. He'd been working at the enormous Willow Run B-24 factory outside Ypsilanti when his draft notice arrived. Because of his war effort work installing hydraulic pumps for flaps and machinegun turrets, Mahlon could have gotten several six month deferments, but decided against it. The army was going to get him eventually, and besides, he wanted to do his part.

By April of 1944, Sebring was at a "repo depot" with a lot of other green troops waiting for their assignments when, "One night a guy come through with a clipboard. He said, 'Anyone want to join the 82nd Airborne?'" Sebring stepped forward, as did nineteen year old Orrin Miller of Messina, New York, and a number of others. "I knew I would be with some experienced people," he remembered years later, "That's the reason that I volunteered to be with them, some people who had already seen some combat." Miller went through basic training at Fort Bragg, and it was there that he'd seen his first airborne troopers. Their jump boots, swagger, and confident bearing made an impression on the teenager, who fully expected to become cannon fodder for the invasion of Europe. Orrin felt so fatalistic that he even got a tattoo on his upper arm of a cross with his army serial number. Now, months later, in a replacement depot, Miller could see that expectation coming true right before his eyes, when the opportunity to at least have a fighting chance presented itself he seized it.

Miller, Sebring, and about twenty others were among those eventually assigned to "A" Battery, 319th Glider Field Artillery. Remembering his first days in the outfit, Miller said, "They didn't put us in anything for two or three weeks. Then we got assigned with the motor pool or the gun crews, or the forward observers, driver crews or whatever." First put on one of the gun sections, Miller was quickly redirected to Sergeant Holman's motor pool, or ammunition section as it was often called. "I worked on the farm and drove a truck. I had that kind of experience, and apparently that's what they were looking for."

On the day Sebring had to stand for his first morning roll call with the battery he did so with a rookie's enthusiasm, looking forward to establishing friendships in his new home. Naturally, given his height, Mahlon positioned himself next to the tallest man, a veteran of Africa, Italy, and Ireland. It was military custom when assembling for roll call that the tallest man locate himself at the extreme right of the line, with stature descending to the left end. This made for a more uniform appearance and had the practical advantage of facilitating close order drill.

The replacement looked his neighbor over. The sleeves of the tall man's field jacket had fraying cuffs which ended some inches above his wrists. Its color was bleached out to a sickly yellowish tan while his trousers were spliced together and had numerous little repairs. "His name was Smith. We lined up and I was right next to him," Sebring remembered. Then he turned to the veteran and jovially said, 'Hey, how's the air up there?'

Smith didn't turn, or acknowledge Sebring in any way except to mutter through his chewing gum, "How is it around my ass."
Sebring was crestfallen by Smith's response. "Hell, I was six foot three, but I got what I asked for, I guess."

As the springtime weather came on, life at an estate like Papillon Hall, nestled in the gentle English countryside, became downright pleasant for the guys in the 319th. Lieutenant Ragland, who'd been transferred to the HQ Battery during the reorganization, bought a bicycle for transportation and to enjoy the scenery at the same time. Sosa, as Captain Manning's driver, had numerous opportunities to explore the English countryside in what amounted to his own jeep. "I tooled all over the country," he said.

The basketball team, whatever their name was, resumed the schedule of games they'd participated in in Northern Ireland. There were other sports activities too. Baseball, football, and soccer, to name a few. Somewhere behind the barn a backstop was set up so that men could practice target shooting with small caliber weapons.

One evening after retreat a cluster of battery men were casually kicking a football around in a pasture beyond the stables, but there weren't really enough of them to form teams. Then Bob McArthur, who was by this time a staff sergeant and chief of the gun sections of "A" Battery, came around with a pair of boxing gloves. He challenged the group, saying, "Anybody want to put the gloves on?" Among the more sports minded fellows in the battery, it was general knowledge that McArthur used to be on the University of Mississippi boxing team.

Casimir Sobon was there, and despite, or because of this, couldn't resist calling out, "Yeah, yeah, I will! I will!" McArthur tossed Sobon the gloves, a small crowd of spectators gathered around them, and the sparring began. Sobon had some height on the sergeant, but McArthur had the edge in boxing experience. He was able to dodge Sobon's first swings and landed a few punches. Sobon was a quick study though and a powerful, athletic guy. In a short time he was giving every bit as good as he got.
The Private and the Staff Sergeant went round and round until McArthur had to say, to Sobon's great satisfaction, "Y'all are pretty good, you know that? Were you a fighter?"
Naturally the most popular sport of all was getting to know the English women. As one battalion man put it, "Everybody dated English girls but there wasn't enough to go around." There was, however, the nearby encampment of the Women's Land Army. This WLA encampment helped greatly with the shortage of females, but they were usually tightly supervised and always under a code of military discipline in any case.

After retreat flocks of "Land Girls" would bicycle down to the guardhouse at the end of the driveway to rendezvous with the young troopers coming off duty. Lester Newman recalled his relationship with a particular Land Girl this way, "I went out with one. They had a camp right by our place, right where we camped. I had one girl I used to talk with quite a bit. We used to meet out on the road and walk around for a while. We'd walk up and down the roads talking. Just keeping company, but it was never anything happen with it, never even wrote to her or anything like that. I can't even remember her name."

Some of the guys developed closer relationships, not just with other Land Girls, but with local girls and their families too. "Of course I got going with a girl that lived outside of Market Harborough," said Storms. Pat Hammond, from the village of Ashley, was the fortunate lass. On one of their earlier dates, Bob and Pat were at a Market Harborough diner. Between the sharp rationing of food and the overburdened demand for meals placed by a multitude of Allied servicemen, eating out in wartime England was often a disappointing experience. Service was slow, "So I put on an apron and started waiting tables. Why not! The people, when they seen a GI waiting tables, they loved it. From then on you could always tell when they made up a plate for Pat and Bob, oh man."

Storms soon became a welcome and familiar visitor at the Hammond home. With pass in hand, he could take the regular shuttle of trucks bringing men between Papillon Hall and Market Harborough, then ride a train five miles north to Ashley. Pat's parents liked Bob too, and not just because he always brought scarce and rationed foodstuffs from Mess Sergeant Siegal's kitchen. The home cooked meals and cozy atmosphere were a comfort for any soldier far from home. Storms was even allowed to spend the weekends, sleeping on the sofa whenever he stayed for the night.

But as nice as these visits were, transportation back to Pap's Hall before getting your name listed for some dreary detail was often a problem. "I used to either get her bike or her father's bike to come home with at night," Storms later explained. "He had to give me a note that it was OK for me to have it."

Early on the morning of April 17th, Corporal Storms was peddling his way

Able Battery men visit with one of the local British children during a field exercise in early 1944. Second from right is Lytle, while Carl Davis is supporting the baby. Sartain collection.

through Ashley in the hours before sunrise. Bicycling all the way back to camp in time for roll call, a distance of well over ten miles, would be a hard ride. Just as he was getting clear of the village, Bob suddenly realized he'd just ridden past the local constable. A stray soldier cycling his way out of town at this hour couldn't go unquestioned and the Bobby called out to him, "Hey there, I want to see you!"

Maybe Storms forgot momentarily that Mr. Hammond had given him a note before he left, perhaps it was the thought that he'd certainly miss roll call now, or maybe, it had simply been a conditioned response to a policeman's attention. What ever it was, Storms gave flight. "Well, them cops don't have no guns, but they got a club, and they can throw that just about as good as a gun. He knocked me ass over tea kettle and down the bank." By tossing his baton into the turning spokes, the constable had snagged his prey as effectively as any cowboy with a lasso. Storms was just getting up when the constable approached and recognized him as a familiar face in the village, a friend of the Hammond girl.

He shook his finger and scolded him, "You damn fool, Stormsy, what made you do that? I didn't know it was you or I wouldn't have hit you!"

Storms slapped bits of dirt and vegetation off his uniform and said something about just kidding around. He unbuttoned his breast pocket and took out Mr. Hammon's permission slip. He handed it to the constable, who read it aloud, "This is to certify that I, Frederick Hammond, have lent this cycle to Robert Storms, American Forces, stationed at Lubenham. F. Hammond."

The constable looked up from the note, folded it back up, and said, "You know better than to run away like that."

Storms shrugged his shoulders and grinned. He apologized, "Yeah but I had a couple of drinks and I was feeling funny." Then, explaining that he'd miss roll call, Storms climbed back on the bike and peddled away.

Like Storms, others developed friendly bonds with the English. One "B" Battery man who had been active in his Milwaukee Boy Scout Troop, became involved with the Lubenham chapter, and through the scouts, grew to know their families. Ed Ryan remembered his friendship with the local game warden, "I was up there in a pub and this Limey found out I like to hunt. He says, I'm gonna show you something you've never seen. He took me into the cellar where he had a cage of ferrets. I picked one up and knew just how to do it. I hunted with him with the ferrets afterward. He was named Stan Levitt. Great sport he was. They had no fences, they had hedges instead. He'd lend me a shotgun. We'd walk on either side of the hedge while his sheep-dog poked around in the hedge. The sheep-dog looked like a black and white Collie, not one of those hairy things. When it found one, the rabbit would have to come out one side or the other. Black powder weapons, I wasn't used to that."

"There was a family that kind of took me in over there," said Sartain. "I met them at a pub in Market Harborough. I'd visit with them. They would invite me to dinner and whenever I could I'd bring them stuff from the mess hall they couldn't get. Butter, chocolate, things like that. Then we'd go to the pub together because we could walk, just a couple or three blocks. Their name was Wallace. I met them through their daughter, Joan. I called Mrs. Wallace, Queenie, Queenie Wallace, I called her and she corresponded with my mother in Baton Rouge all through the war. Joan was married to a British soldier who was in Libya or someplace over there. They had a cute little nine months old girl named Helen."

Don Johnson was a Lubenham boy of about ten years old, whose father collected refuse from the kitchens of the RAF and 319th camps to feed Abraham Tarry's pigs. He remembered the Americans fondly in later years, saying, "I made several friends among the GI's because I called at the kitchens with dad every week. They were a smiling, fun loving people who were generous and friendly, especially to a small boy, such as myself. I received many unasked for luxuries, which made me the envy of my friends. Chocolate, sweets, cheese, gum, and oranges. All foods which were in short supply at the time. I was also given stripes and airborne insignia to show off to my friends. Dad was given cigarettes; Lucky Strike and Camel, which had never been heard of in England pre war." Mr. Johnson also recalled one mystery when he added, "It seemed to me at the time that all the GIs were called Joe. I never thought to question that!"

"We had an excellent relation with the English people. Perfect, perfect," was Sartain's assessment of the contact between his men and the local residents. He admired the British. They'd been five years at war, with all its inevitable social and civic changes, from inconvenience to upheaval, yet they never seemed to loose their gritty patience. "The English people were just staunch, staunch. They were excellent," he would say.

If there were some rumblings of discontent, it would have been among the battalion officers, concerning coffee. During that spring at Papillon Hall, Lieutenant Sartain was in the habit of maintaining a pot of brewed coffee for his convenience and that of his fellow officers. Coffee was, after all, the grease which kept the army's gears moving night and day. The pot was probably kept in the junior officer's quarters, available to any and all who wanted a stimulating, yet relaxing, beverage. Being a South Louisiana man, Sartain naturally considered himself a connoisseur of coffee and an authority on the proper way it should be brewed, though there seems to have been some difference of opinion among those who were exposed to his handiwork. Sometime that spring, Lieutenant Frank Poole of the HQ Battery poured himself a cup, took a drink, and after the first swallow, twisted his face in a bitter grimace.

On the spot, Poole decided to bring the question of Sartain's coffee to a public referendum. Taking a piece of ruled notebook paper, he scrawled across the top, "Impressions of Sartain's Coffee," then added, "It stinks," signed his name and pinned the declaration to the bulletin board. The first blow against the tyranny of Sartain's coffee had been struck. Next Lieutenant Sharky, another HQ Battery officer, came in for a cup when he noticed the complaint tacked to the wall. Sharkey considered the notice for a few seconds, smiled broadly and scrawled, "No doubt was good before it went in the pot, but when it came out, what the ... !"

A little while later someone else added, "Sartain's claim to fame, he did Satan's color in a little coffee mug." When Captain Manning

Class "A" uniform pose of Roland Gruebling on July 26, 1944 in England.

wandered into the officer's quarters sometime that day he may have already poured himself an inky cup of his own when he saw the petition pinned to the bulletin board. Seeing that a kind of coffee revolt was breaking out, about to tear the battalion's officer corps asunder, Manning knew that a diplomatic intervention was called for. He uncapped his fountain pen and wrote, "Take the easy way out now. We have to be polite," then signed J R Manning.

Finally, before the day was through, the last contributor wrote, "One drink of his brew is enough to take you to paranoid paradise."

The officers were clearly crying out for relief, but acknowledging that his taste for strong coffee was not universally shared was a hard lesson for Sartain. "We had a little Bunsen burner, what we called a GI stove," he later confessed. "I would make coffee, drip it, a little two cup coffee pot, a little coffee drip one. My daddy and my father in law to be always kept me supplied with Community Coffee. Our Louisiana coffee, but I did make it too strong trying to impress them. I got to where even I couldn't drink it, then I had to slack off. I'd make it for general distribution the way even I couldn't drink it! Well, they learned later on. And I finally got several of them to like my coffee."

When the 82nd began arriving at its encampments in and around Leicester, a situation quickly emerged which would eventually have far reaching implications throughout the army. The matter concerned the inconsistency of segregation in the military of a nation dedicated to equality. Throughout the Second World War the army maintained separate units for white and black troops. Most of these units were designated for support or construction purposes and were largely led by white officers. Naturally there was discontent among these stepchild outfits. The army exacerbated the situation by refusing to recognize that the racial tensions within the service were, at least in part, caused by the disproportionate number of black units serving in menial and background roles. Since few of the white soldiers had experience in an integrated culture firmly anchored to equal rights, the segregated army system didn't seem unusual, though many thought the black soldiers deserved the chance to test their mettle against the enemy.

As soon as airborne troopers entered Leicester on passes in mid-February, they were angered to see numerous black GIs escorting the local English girls. The black troops, mostly members of a quartermaster unit of the army air force, had already been in Leicester for many months, during which they dated English girls freely and encountered only a fraction of the racial prejudice seen in the United States. As Sartain recalled, "The general attitude among the British, the feeling in a lot of England, was that this was what the Americans were all about."

This would have been a naïve understanding of the reality of American race relations in the 1940s. Many members of the division, perhaps half, were from southern states where Jim Crow laws kept the races apart in nearly every public circumstance. In the world they had come from, intermarriage was illegal and the sight of white girls in company with black GIs was disturbing and offensive. Men from the northern states, while not accustomed to a recognized system of segregation, were rarely indifferent either. Most were similarly taken aback and didn't approve of what they saw.

Almost immediately, white paratroopers challenged the black GIs, taunting them, hurling insults, and picking fights. In fact, brawls would have broken out between incoming paratroopers and any troops already stationed in and around Leicester, if only to establish turf and compete for English girlfriends. The fact that the 82nd encountered black soldiers in Leicester only added exponentially to a fire already waiting to explode. Sobon remembered it, saying, "The guys went into town and they seen all these colored soldiers there with the white British girls. These Rebels, they didn't pull any punches. They called them everything they could think of."

Sartain saw it too. He commented later, "When we first got to England they could not take a black soldier holding hands with a white woman. They just took them on."

The African-Americans responded in kind, and more serious fights started breaking out. When a few members of the all-white 505th Parachute Infantry were stabbed and beaten later that month, a regrettable outbreak of widespread violence erupted. The sentiment for revenge in that regiment was strong enough among enlisted and officers alike, that in retaliation the lieutenant colonel of one battalion, Herbert Bacheller, granted every man under his command leave, with the understanding that they were to go into Leicester and even the score.

Race riots with numerous injuries and some loss of life followed. In the morning one officer from the 505th noted "several" blacks hanging by their necks, dead, from upper windows of the Bell Hotel in downtown Leicester. Finally General Ridgeway stepped in, patrolling the streets of Leicester himself to insure that order was restored. Viewed as embarrassing and injurious to morale, the details of the events were kept unpublicized beyond some internal reports or in the transcripts of General Court Martial trials which resulted from the turmoil. Normal wartime censorship of all civilian news sources in the American press also kept the story out of public discourse, though rumors spread throughout the troops stationed in England about the riots in Leicester. "It was a biggy," remembered Ed Ryan, "And they don't say much about it, particularly nowadays."

It will never be known just how many battalion men joined in with Bachellor's troopers on that night, but their involvement in this fighting appears to have been peripheral and limited to a small number. In fact, all but one battalion man interviewed recalled this riot as something they were told about and not eyewitnesses to. However, one member of "A" Battery remembered being an active participant. He told his story, making no apologies and offering no excuses. "They didn't like whites, we didn't like blacks, it's just that simple," he said. "And they messed our men up. We paid them back the next night. We tore them a new ass. We paid them back for what they did to our men the night before and they found out that they had met their match. They was a lot of men got hurt too, but we went in that night in full force. Six, eight, ten in a group. The only thing you had to do was holler airborne, and there would be 25 more there. That's all you had to do. Just holler, airborne!"

Despite the accounts to the contrary, this man didn't witness hangings when asked about them. He said, "Nobody got lynched, nobody got lynched. They got the shit kicked out of them with fists and beer bottles, but lynched-no, no, no. If somebody'd got lynched it would have been an all out bloody war then. Made no difference which side you got lynching on, there'd been a bloody war."

Afterwards the army attempted to settle things by designating alternate days for white and black troops to have passes into Leicester, but the system didn't really work. There were a lot of units in the Leicester area. Coordinating who was allowed in town on what days inevitably became confusing and got fouled up. When that happened fighting would recommence, even if there'd been no intention of starting trouble. One day later in the season some guys from the 319th found themselves mixed up in one such brawl. Ryan was one of those there. "I remember how it started and everything," he said. "I was right in the middle of it. It was up at a Red Cross, and they had food there. There was a bunch of blacks in there. They were supposed to get out and let the white guys in. So these last two or three of them, when they did finally come out, a bunch of Texans there, they kicked them down the stairs. Long flight of stairs down there. When they got outside the blacks got their friends together there and boy it was something else, I tell you. They had about maybe two hundred of them in it. I was up in the back of one of our trucks that was trying to take off. I was sitting there trying to kick them off with the heel of my boot!"

Storms was another who'd taken a truck into Leicester that day. He and some buddies were isolated in a movie theater when the fight at the Red Cross canteen broke out. "When we came out what the hell, everything was busted up! I said to the fellas, 'Hey, let's get the hell out of here,' but we got in fights anyway. Then you get your uniform all tore up and you have to go to the Red Cross to ask them for another one."

In the end a white MP from the 82nd lay dead from a stab wound. The whole affair exposed the darker side of American society, reflected through its armed services. Military authorities eventually moved the black unit located in Leicester out of the city, but the issue never ceased to be the source of disruption for the provost. Colonel Bacheller, after being transferred to the 508th PIR, was himself slated to be brought up for a court martial, but his death in Normandy prevented this. Sebring expressed a concise sentiment that was common throughout the battery when he concluded, "It was nasty the way that happened."

Sartain felt there had been a breakdown of discipline in some of the parachute units. "I just didn't care for the bravado attitude, you know? Discipline wise they were always in trouble in town. They started more ruckuses in town. That's why they got Leicester and a couple of other towns put off limits to the 82nd."

The fact was that brawls were part of army life. Millions of young men in their prime were being trained to kill the enemy, and some of what they were taught spilled over into fights between men in the same outfit who were normally friendly. "I can remember," said Silas Hogg, "Standing there in formation. They stand there real low talking. I can whip you, you son of a bitch. You wait for formation to be over and you show it. As soon as the first sergeant said, dismissed, pow pow pow! The fists started flying. No, absolutely, no apparent reason. They didn't have a thing agin each other, nothing. They just wanted to show they were better than the guy next to them." Hogg paused, then added, "I was mean. I don't sound like that now, but I was a mean son of a bitch. I'm glad that I got it out of me though. I

Tom Ludwick and Ted Covais gather around an aiming circle during one of the field exercises in preparation for the Normandy Invasion. Speing, 1944. Covais collection.

don't sound like that now, do I?"

With each passing week the tension mounted. There was a constant honing of the fighting edge and level of preparedness. Though they were veterans of the bitter fighting in Italy, and that campaign continued, the guys all comprehended that once the cross channel jump was made the fighting on the Western front wouldn't stop until the Nazis were vanquished from Europe. Everyone knew this was forever to be "The Invasion," the one the world would remember for decades into the future, but that event was going to require a gargantuan collective effort to achieve.

The first step called for training, training, and more training. Reconnaissance Selection and Occupation of a Position (RSOP) exercises were one common activity and were as likely to take place in daylight as in the dark of night. They involved bringing the battalion to an assigned position, unhitching and rapidly digging gun emplacements, then concealing them with camouflage netting and other visual obstructions.

Though use of live ammunition was reserved for firing ranges, the crews would still go through the steps of "registering" the first gun on a hypothetical target. Once accomplished, the command would be given, "Record base deflection!" This was followed by, "Record elevation!" With all six guns thus registered, mock targets would be called in from the fire direction center. Robert Rappi, then a gunner corporal, remembered the process by rote, even sixty years later. "They give the command, Fire Mission! Then you hear, Battery Adjust! Base deflection left 20, or right 40. Then they'd give you the elevation, whatever the target calls for. Then they'd tell you how many rounds they want you to punch up. And that's it. When you're done, you go back to Base Deflection."

Just as important was practicing the whole process in reverse, displacing the batteries quickly and removing them to new positions. While gun crews and drivers were occupied with these tasks, liaison and FO teams honed their radio operations and methods of reporting targets. In the interim, men in the fire direction centers worked on their duties processing fire missions efficiently and accurately, while wire crews trained on laying telephone lines so that communications within the battalion, as well as with the units it was supporting, would be established rapidly and carry on without interruption.

Lieutenant Ragland was involved in some of these latter exercises. Remembering one aspect of wire communications which attracted his attention, he explained, "With artillery, we have not only radio, but we have wire communications, and they wanted to use both of them. So what they did was have a big spool of wire mounted on the back of the jeep. As the jeep is running down the road they have a crew behind them pulling that wire off and putting it off to the side of the road. Finally they get up to the observation post, hook up the telephones, and they can practice firing. Well then when they get done they want to pick all that wire up! The end of the axel where the spool is, has a crank so the guy could turn it. So the guy in the jeep, he drives slow and then another guy comes behind and turns and winds that wire up so they can use it again."

Late one afternoon, as the battalion was finishing up its field exercises for the day, Ragland was observing this chore with some other officers from the headquarters battery. The telephone-wire spool mounted on the jeep brought to mind the bicycle he'd just bought. Ragland reflected on the work, and then an idea came to him. Approaching Todd, the Lieutenant saluted and said, "Major, I think I could fix that so it would work a lot better, but we'd have to alter the jeep." Todd liked pragmatic innovations and Ragland's suggestion had his attention.

"What do you have in mind?" he asked. As Ragland explained his idea he seemed so calm and sure it would work that the Major immediately gave his permission saying, "Well, I think we can get that okayed."

"What I did was take a jeep to the bicycle shop and they mounted a spoke sprocket on the end of the axel where the spool of wire is. Then, in the back of the jeep, above the rear wheels, that flat fender there, we took part of the frame of a bicycle with the pedal sprocket and mounted it on there. Then we run the chain from there over to the sprocket on the back of his jeep, where the spool was to pick that wire up. Man, that guy could just set in that truck and wind that thing. They could pick that wire up in a hurry, only he did it by hand while he was sitting. Anyway, the engineers let us do that and it worked pretty good in training. The only thing is it didn't work in combat because when it come time to move you just got up and moved, you didn't worry about picking up any wire, you just left it where it was, but in training situations it worked pretty good!"

Though much of these operations involved setting up the battery for simulated fire or practice on the howitzers, the outfit was also introduced to another weapon altogether new to them– the bazooka. The M1a1 bazooka, or anti-tank rocket launcher, was a weapon developed by the US Army and introduced in 1942 with widespread success when used under the right conditions. Though itself quite portable and weighing only 15 pounds, its rocket grenades were heavy, restricting the number which could be practically carried. Though tested to a range of 400 yards, the bazooka was also impossible to fire with any accuracy except at extremely close range. Eighteen bazookas were distributed to the 319th. They were intended to be kept at hand in the event of the gun positions being overrun or threatened with capture in a German breakthrough.

Much of the other training was of a more elemental nature. Replacement Orrin Miller recalled his first months in "A" Battery as, "A full schedule of mostly marching and calisthenics and obstacle course." Nonetheless, rural Leicestershire in springtime was as pleasant a setting for a fifteen mile march as could be imagined. At one spot along the usual route a local sheppard-ess was remembered by the soldiers who passed her. She would always be encountered taking her sheep out to pasture in the opposite direction, with her sheep dog keeping the flock together in a way not so different from the way their own sergeants did with them. Invariably and very politely, she would call out to the column, "Lovely day, isn't it?"

Of course the central object of all this was the anticipated glider landing in France, and since nobody'd even been around any gliders since North Africa, bringing everyone up to snuff was a priority. New men, like Sebring, Newman, and Miller in "A" Battery, and others too, needed to become glider qualified. For their part, the veterans in the outfit were also required to maintain their qualification as glidermen with a flight at least every 90

Interior of CG4-A Glider looking toward the cockpit.

days. Now that the battalion had access to the Cotesmoore airfield, all this could be accomplished.

The men took their flights in CG4A gliders from Cotesmoore and, after a nominal circling of the immediate area, landed again on the same airstrip. Much like the flights taken a year before at Laurenberg-Maxton, it was a thrill for the novices and old hands alike, though the latter did their best to appear nonchalant. What was new to the 319th was the variety of glider on which the battalion was practicing its loading and unloading. "We used those British gliders, damn Horsa gliders," said Sartain. "The British loved them. It was much larger than the American glider and it was made of plywood. You could carry a lot in them, but they were too big. Then, for the equipment to be unloaded, the tail had to be torn off and everything unloaded from the rear, you see?" Sartain was right. The entire tail section, which included two jump-seats, had to be disconnected from the fuselage on landing. During the loading and flight, bolts kept this portion of the glider attached. Once on the ground, a battery powered switch, much like that used in the bazooka, would ignite primacord packed in between the tail section and the fuselage. The explosion was enough to separate the tail, but it was still necessary to manhandle it clear of the glider. Though some Horsas, the improved second model, were equipped with a hinged nose section much like that used in the CG4A, all the gliders retained the removable tail to help expedite unloading. The arrangement, like so much else about the British military, struck the Americans as peculiar and awkward.

Orrin Miller remembered the Horsas too, saying, "We took training in the British gliders, the big ones. They were just like a large airplane with no seats or nothing in

Laying telephone wire during a field exercise before Normandy. The man standing in the foreground is Thurman King from Cincinnati, Ohio, a Sergeant in the Signals Section. Sartain collection.

them, just a round hole in them with places to tie down your equipment, that's about it. We had tool chests in them too. Metal tool chests for the guns and so forth. No, no seats, no belts and no parachutes. You're in there to go. As a matter of fact, for seats I sat on the ammo boxes."

Actually, there were a series of folding benches with rudimentary seatbelts, along the inside walls of the Horsa's fuselage, as well as two more jump-seats located in the tail. But the thing that impressed everyone about the British Glider was its size. The Air Speed Horsa, named for an ancient Anglo-Saxon warrior, with a fuselage of 67 feet in length, was more than half again as long as the American CG4A, though the wingspan was only five feet wider. More contrasting was its height, which at 21 feet was nearly twice that of the Waco. This greatly enhanced hold meant that the Horsa could carry a half ton more than its own weight of 7500 pounds. Whereas the Waco was limited to one gun, jeep, or trailer, with perhaps five men and some extraneous supplies at most, the Horsa could carry both Jeep and trailer or gun, along with ammunition, its entire crew, and driver. Given the still existing constraints of size and weight, the 75mm pack howitzers were again used in these exercises. Since the Horsa was fitted with a set of large barn-like doors on the side of the fuselage, everything was brought aboard this way, checked for proper distribution, and tied down. Unloading was simply done in reverse, as was the practice when unloading the similarly sized c-47 transport.

The British had, of course, already conducted several missions using the Horsa since late 1942. The Americans also had a little experience landing them in combat in Sicily, although the consensus circulating among them was that the Horsa was a death-trap. Too large to land in all but the most ideal fields, too heavy to glide in at a reasonable speed, and its plywood construction ill-adapted to the crash landings which were an inevitable part of all glider missions. Several trips to Cottesmore for training sessions in loading the Horsa were conducted that spring, but to no one's disappointment, the battalion wasn't given an opportunity to actually take a flight in one before the invasion.

In the interim training went on, as did the daily routine of garrison life at Papillon Hall. Then, early in May an issue which had been a minor, but persistent irritation in the 319th came to a head. All the fuss revolved around major Wilcoxson and army regulations regarding the use of the knitted woolen caps issued to the men for cold weather. As Sartain explained, "It was chilly in England year round, but wool knit caps were to be worn only under a helmet liner or you were out of uniform. Anyone Major Wilcoxson caught not in proper attire he would assign extra duty to, KP, garbage, stuff like that. It was hard for the men to understand because the little wool knit cap was very comfortable, you know? Without making a federal case out of it, they just like to wear it."

Among the first to run afoul of the regulation was Delbert Jackson, a radio operator in what was then "C" Battery. One cold morning while at Camp Balliscallion, Jackson was manning a large transceiver fitted out with headphones and a Morse code key. Of course it was impossible to wear a helmet with the headphones on, so Jackson wore only his knitted skull cap. This wasn't a problem for the "C" Battery officers, but one of the brass hats on staff, possibly Wilcoxson, noticed the infraction and Jackson pulled some extra duty as a consequence.

Throughout the outfit's time that winter in Northern Ireland, and continuing after the change of base to Papillon Hall, violations of the knit cap rule continued to the annoyance of Major Wilcoxson, although no one else seems to have been bothered by the practice. In fact, uniform infractions of all kinds were of particular interest to the battalion executive officer. For example, one sergeant in the HQ Battery remembered,

HEY, HOW'S THE AIR UP THERE?

"We weren't supposed to wear jump boots. This Wilcoxson, he got on everybody for wearing jump boots, but he was wearing them himself." Never one to shy away from a critique of his superiors, Ed Ryan, now again a member of the HQ Battery, remarked of Wilcoxson, "Oh yeah, another bad ass. After we arrived in England he had something against these woolen hats. He was another along the lines of Bertsch."

Then, early one morning as the staff officers approached the gatehouse from their quarters in Lubenham, Major Wilcoxson found that the two stone cherub statues flanking the lane leading to the manor house were each wearing a knit cap. Of course they wore no helmets and Wilcoxson interpreted the act as a personal affront, which it was. He ordered the caps removed at once, but it was already too late. The gag persisted each morning and the more furious the Major became the more statues were discovered out of uniform. "Sometime during the night someone would put a wool knit cap on each angel," remembered Sartain. "This would send our battalion exec up the wall! He would remove the caps each morning and each night they would reappear. He put a guard on the cherubs at night over those wool knit caps. This was really a burden on the men on guard duty. If that wasn't a bunch of shit!"

Tensions over the knit caps mounted, taking on the character of a covert operation each night. Though he undoubtedly had several accomplices, one HQ Battery man appears to have been the ringleader who brought the caper to a head one morning in May. "Laurence O'Dowd, he was in my section, he was the one who put the hats on the statues," Ed Ryan revealed years later. "Nobody hated officers like O'Dowd did. He must have had forty or fifty of them on the statues. When Fidgety Phil came out that morning he went ape. He blew his cool right then and there."

Howard Fichtner, a chief warrant officer with the battalion, later wrote of the event, "The officers tramped up to Paps Hall that lovely morning to see all the woolen caps decorating the statuary. I thought Major Todd was going to have apoplexy, not because he was mad about it, but rather because it was so damned funny and the guy couldn't show how amused he was by it all."

"The next day everybody got reamed out. They sent down a notice that you weren't allowed to wear those skull caps anymore. They issued you skull caps, then they tell you that you can't wear them," recalled a bemused Casimir Sobon of the episode. "The only thing that saved everybody is we were just before the invasion of Normandy. We were told, you're only lucky that you're going soon, but that's not the end of this yet, wait till we get back!"

Once again, as had been the case while acting as Colonel Bertsch's exec, Todd found himself mediating between pragmatic realities and the letter of military discipline. The men were justifiably exasperated with Wilcoxson's rigidity regarding so innocuous an item as wearing knit caps as part of their field dress; however, in the interest of discipline it was also important that his Major not lose face. "Finally Major Todd called us battery commanders in," Sartain remembered. He said, 'OK guys, cut this out.' No questions asked. No more wool knit caps and no questions asked. That was the end of that escapade. That's all Wilcoxson had to do, all he had to do. Knit, knit, knit! Yeah man, Wilcoxson was something else."

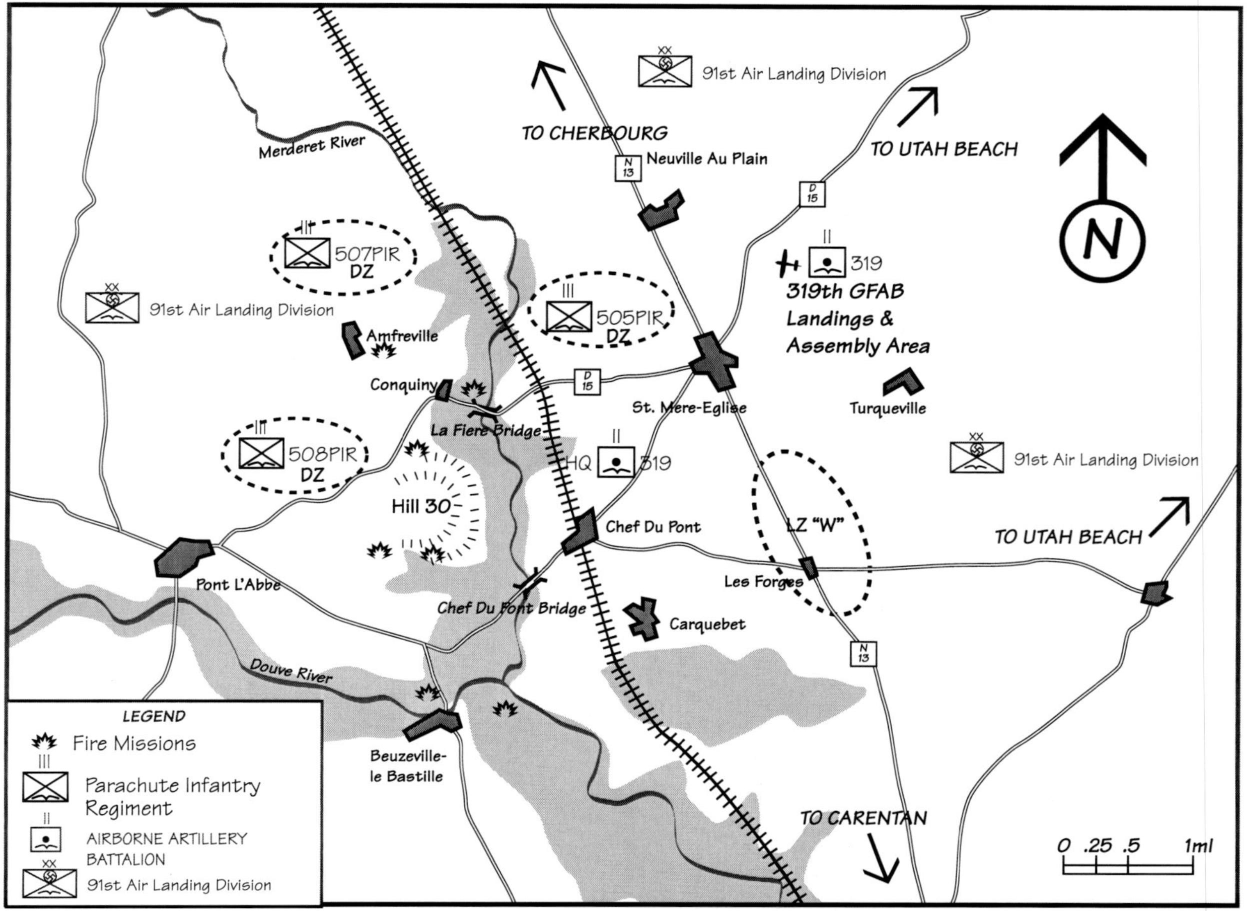

319th GFAB positions in Normandy, June 6-16, 1944

LEGEND

Fire Missions

Parachute Infantry Regiment

AIRBORNE ARTILLERY BATTALION

91st Air Landing Division

Douve River

Pont L'Abbé

508PIR DZ

91st Air Landing Division

Merderet River

507PIR DZ

Conquiny

Amfreville

Beuzeville-le Bastille

Hill 30

Chef Du Pont Bridge

La Fiere Bridge

TO CHERBOURG

505PIR DZ

Neuville Au Plain

91st Air Landing Division

Carquebet

Chef Du Pont

HQ 319

319

St. Mere-Eglise

319th GFAB Landings & Assembly Area

TO UTAH BEACH

Les Forges

LZ "W"

Turqueville

TO CARENTAN

91st Air Landing Division

TO UTAH BEACH

N

0 .25 .5 1ml

Part 14: "Out and out murder."

By the last week of May preparations for the invasion of France, the glider component of which was codenamed "Operation Neptune," were complete. It remained only for the go ahead order to be issued and the vast air and sea borne armada would be set into motion. When the division issued a directive on May 28th that all units be packed and ready to move out, it was clear that the progression of events was fast reaching a point of no-return. Last minute checks of equipment, issues of rations, clothing, gear, and ammunition were made. Just enough time was left for one last trip to a favorite pub, or one last desperate meeting with those whom the men had become endeared to, while Chaplain Reid compiled a list of next-of-kin from each of them.

New "special" leggings, shirts, and trousers were given out to everyone, and of them Sartain said, "We were issued new uniforms for each operation. The ones for Normandy were brown and they were impregnated. When I say impregnated, I mean they were treated with a chemical that was to help if there was a gas attack." The chemical agent applied to these uniforms made them stiff and added a texture which some later described as "greasy." It robbed the woolens of their normal insulating properties. "Man," remembered Sartain, "they were stinky and hot. They were very very uncomfortable."

Each man was given a strict list of what he would take with him. No more and no less. "In the airborne outfits you flew in as light as you can," said Casimir Sobon of the directive. "At first they said you could take a blanket with you. Then the order came down, no blanket, no nothing, you're going just the way you are, that's it."

As it turned out, the men were limited to a raincoat, one shelter half, an extra pair of socks, an extra pair of underwear, toothbrush and shaving kit. As had been the case on other occasions, an order was circulated to remove all divisional patches from field jackets, a task which led one man to complain loudly, "Why the hell don't they give us zippers for these things!"

On Tuesday, the 31st of May, the 319th left Papillon Hall by truck for Market Harborough, where the battalion then boarded a train for the pre-invasion security camp. This compound was a sealed complex of hangers, Quonset huts, and pyramidal tents for the troops waiting to take part in Neptune and the parachute drops. It was situated adjacent to the Membury Airfield, in Berkshire, southern England. Surrounded by barbed wire, the men were forbidden to write letters home or communicate in any way with anyone not in their own unit, let alone outside the compound.

As the battalion arrived the guys could see many of the gliders they would be taking and the C-47s that would tow them across the English Channel. Covais never forgot the sight, and later said of it, "When we got to the airport, the planes, thousands of them, it seemed like thousands of them were lined up ready to take off. It was impressive. It's still vivid in my mind."

Since meals, guard mounting, and other incidental chores of garrison life at the security camp were handled by the indigenous air force personnel, the men in the 319th were able to concentrate on activities directly related to the mission. First and foremost the Horsa gliders needed to be loaded. Classes were then given on how to most efficiently get the one or two rubber life rafts in each Horsa out of the glider and inflated if they had to ditch in the English Channel. The guys looked at each other, wondering if anyone seriously thought there would be time to get a life raft out of a glider as the sea poured in through every hole. Somebody started a rumor that the wings of the gliders were filled with ping pong balls to keep them afloat in just such an exigency, but only the more gullible and frightened believed it. Mae West life preservers of a bright yellow color were another item shown to the men, with lessons held on how to inflate them by use of two CO_2 cartridges.

Next, everyone's kit was checked, inspected, and checked again. American flags, printed on cotton muslin and measuring about four by seven inches, were handed out with instructions to sew them to the upper right sleeve of the field jacket. Then each gliderman was given 200 Francs of invasion money, a map of Normandy, a pair of hand grenades and a bandolier of carbine ammunition. At least one man in the outfit found an extra bandolier, emptied out the cartridges, and refilled the pouches with cigarettes.

Another item given to the men was little metallic clickers, which later became a symbol of the airborne invasion of Normandy. Popularly known as "crickets," the clickers were intended as a means of distinguishing friend from foe during the initial stages of the operation when speaking the sign and countersign aloud would be too dangerous.

Sartain well remembered another feature of the security camp. "When we finally got to the airfield there was a big Quonset hut and I guess maybe twenty feet by forty feet of a sand table of Normandy, showing where the drop zones were and the landing zones. I forget what scale it was, but it had every tree and farm house and road, elevations and everything else on it. It was thought to be exact in every detail. All the officers and NCO'S, down to and including corporals, were allowed to study the sand tables at their discretion. Large aerial photos were hanging on the wall too. The only problem was that the aerial photographs were taken at high noon, so they didn't show the height of the hedgerows. You'd look at the aerial photographs and those hedgerows looked like those little jumping hedges in England. We thought maybe they were two or three feet high, but no way man, they were eight and ten feet high!"

During their off duty hours, many of those authorized to view the sand table took the opportunity to go back and study it in seclusion, perhaps hoping secretly to see their future revealed in the scale model. Corporal Covais was one of those who went back during those days spent waiting. Ed Ryan did likewise, and said, "Everybody at that time wanted to make sure they knew what they were looking at. They weren't fooling around then. I went back to the sand table two or three times so that I'd make sure."

One night Covais entered the hut. It was late and there were only a few other men there. One of them was crouched down, viewing the modeled terrain from the shallow angle he might see it from if already on the ground. It was Ed Ryan, Covais's old pal from induction at Camp Upton. Their assignments to different batteries soon after joining the 319th hadn't allowed much opportunity for the two to talk since then. Ryan stood up, walked over and extended his hand. "So Ted," he said, "Congratulations, I heard you got married. Just couldn't wait, heh?"

Covais answered, but seemed distracted, "Yeah, thanks. Me and Cathy took the train to Peekskill and eloped." Then he added, "We're a long way from Yaphank now, aren't we?"

"No kidding," Ryan replied, "freaking' 88 Pass. That was some hairy shit." Then Ryan changed the subject and reminded Covais, "Hey, remember the time you let that chicken shit lieutenant fall on his ass? I thought I'd die laughing."

Covais had to chuckle, but whimsical pranks seemed a long way off and his laughter felt forced. In fact, maybe it was just the impending operation, but Covais seemed like a much more serious guy now than Ryan remembered him being at Camp Upton. "What do you think, Ryan, we gonna come through this thing alive, or what?"

"Sure we are," said Ryan. He flicked his cigarette butt onto the concrete floor and ground it out with the toe of his boot. "Fucking –A! Especially now that we're rid of that no good S O B Bertsch." Ryan lit another smoke, then asked Covais how he liked serving under Captain Manning. "He's a swell guy, ain't he? Not like some of these other dodoes." Covais had to agree.

The two looked over the sand table together, taking different vantage points and commenting on this terrain feature or that, until one of them decided to go. Shaking hands they wished each other Godspeed and a safe crossing. "Good luck, Ryan," said Covais.

"Yeah Teddy, same to you. Next time we'll have cognac and crepe suzettes."
"Sure," Covais answered, and stepped outside. Ted noticed how cool it could be in England, even in June. In a nearby hut he could hear the sound of a Hollywood movie being shown, then looked up at the stars which were just beginning to appear through the lingering twilight. They were beautiful, so very beautiful.

Movie projectors were running every night at the security camp, and the division band was working overtime too. There was also a lot of unusually good food, what the guys called "PX chow." Inevitably these meals of ham and eggs or lamb chops generated wry comments about "last meals" and "being fattened up for the kill." Not so, their officers assured them. Every detail had been accounted for, every contingency factored in, and every precaution made to optimize their chances of safety and success.

All through that first week of June, briefings intensified, plans were formulated, adjusted, and reformulated. On the 4th, for example, the glider-artillerymen watched as the many hundreds of olive green planes and gliders which surrounded them were painted with a series of alternating two foot wide black and white stripes on the fuselage and wings of each aircraft. The measure was just one manifestation of the debate waging at Supreme Allied headquarters as to how to best avoid having the gliders and troop transports of Neptune shot down by their own navy. The "invasion stripes" were one precaution settled upon. There was also an agreement from the chief of naval operations that no antiaircraft fire would be permitted during the times which the several waves of airborne assaults would be passing overhead. This decision carried with it a considerable risk. Any German air attack on the invasion fleet which might strike during these periods would be facing an array of defenseless vessels, but a repeat of the debacle experienced during the Sicily invasion had to be avoided at all costs.

Essentially, the mission of the 82nd was to land astride the Merderet River, some miles inland from the seaborne landing site at Utah Beach and protect the right flank of the invading forces. To accomplish this the division would have to first seize the vital crossroads at the village of Saint Mere Eglise, and then secure the area encompassing the villages of Amfreville, Chef-du-Pont, Etienville, and Neuvilleau-Plain. The bridges over the Merderet were to be taken intact to allow a forward movement to the west, across the Cotentin Peninsula, while the bridges over the Douve River would have to be destroyed to block any German counterattack from the south. The division would disrupt and stop German counterattacks directed toward the Utah Beach area. Ultimately the intention was to cut off and take Cherbourg. In so doing, they would gain a much needed seaport on the French coast, through which the larger Allied advance into France could be supplied.

These objectives, and the other tasks assigned to Operation Neptune, would be achieved through a relay of six glider missions beginning in the predawn hours of D-day and continuing at intervals until the morning of D+1. Each mission was named for a different American city: Chicago, Detroit, Elmira, Galveston, Hackensack, and Keokuk. The 319th was scheduled to go in with Elmira late in the evening of D-Day. Mission Elmira was itself divided into two waves, with each wave composed of two serials. The first serial of Elmira's second wave, though made up almost entirely of the 319th, also included elements of the 307th Airborne Medical and 307th Airborne Engineer Battalions. Towed by the 436th Troop Carrier Group, this serial was composed of two CG4A and 48 Horsa gliders, loaded with the battalion's 12 75mm pack howitzers, 31 jeeps, about a dozen trailers, over twenty-five tons of ammunition, and an equivalent load of other equipment in the form of radios, bazookas, tentage, camouflage nets, rations, water, gasoline, 50 caliber machineguns, and a myriad of other articles deemed necessary to the combat performance of the battalion.

The 319th's commander, Major Todd, in company with a reconnaissance team, would depart with Mission Detroit, listed to leave from Ramsbury Airdrome just before 2am. One of "A" Battery's officers, Lieutenant Irving Gelb, with a contingent of 13 enlisted men, was selected to go in with the gliders of the 320th GFAB. This outfit was scheduled to depart in the second serial of Elmira's second wave, from Welford Airdrome, immediately after the 319th left the airstrip at Membury.

Lieutenant Ragland and Captain Hawkins, having qualified the previous March as paratroopers, were originally chosen to jump with the 507th and 508th Parachute Infantry Regiments respectively. The two regiments were designated as the 2nd Airborne Infantry Brigade, and the 319th was assigned as their artillery support. However, Ragland's memory contradicts this information. He maintains to this day that he actually jumped with the 505th parachute Infantry and there is some documentation that this may be so.

Whatever the case, these men, with a small number of enlisted assistants, left the battalion to be with their invasion commands a few days prior to the invasion.

Captain Sartain and Lieutennt Ragland during a field exercise. They would form the Command structure for "A" Battery from Normandy to the End.
Sartain collection

BATTERY!

Major Todd explained to Ragland that since he was now jump qualified, he'd be parachuting in with the infantry as an integrated FO. "So, about a week before D-Day they sent me down there and I got to know a few of them," said Ragland as he described his time with the paratroopers. "The commander of the battalion, I think it was 3rd Battalion, said he'd like for me to instruct his officers on how artillery FOs worked. So I did a class on that for their officers with a chalkboard and all that. They said, 'Well, that's about the same thing we do when we have an observer for our mortars.'"

In spite of all the preparations, what the men, and all but the highest ranking officers for that matter, were not told was the prediction by the Chief of Allied Air Command, Sir Trafford Leigh-Mallory, that half the paratroopers and an astounding 70% of the glider troopers might be killed, wounded, or seriously injured before their units had a chance to assemble on French soil. They did not know either, that the commander of the American ground forces, Major General Omar Bradley, and overall Allied Commander Dwight D. Eisenhower were quite aware of this and willing to accept these casualty rates. They had made up their minds to carry through with Neptune in the full knowledge that the operation could mean feeding their airborne divisions into a slaughterhouse, because without it the beach assaults had only a limited chance of success.

In addition, the aerial photographs and sand table the men were shown were not accurate in some very important respects. They did not reveal, for example, that large areas bordering the Merderet and Douve rivers had been flooded to a depth of three, four, and five feet, enough to drown even an uninjured man loaded down with many pounds of equipment.

Similarly, these photographic aids failed to reveal the hundreds of thousands of Rommelspargel, Rommel's Asparagus, which had been planted in fields the Germans expected the Allies would try to utilize in a glider assault. These obstructions, personally designed by Field Marshal Erwin Rommel, who was charged with construction of the defenses of "Festung Europa," consisted of poles, not unlike telegraph poles, or iron railroad rails, planted vertically at intervals of about 75 feet apart. These offered deadly obstacles in themselves, but the asparagus were then wired together and fitted out with explosive charges which were set to go off should anything become entangled in them.

Sergeant Bob McArthur, later described the asparagus fields he inspected this way, "Every field that a glider can half way land in has anti landing obstacles in them. Anti landing obstacles are nothing but huge poles that are ten to fifteen feet high and about a foot in diameter. They're sticking out of the ground all over the fields like fence posts. One of these posts can tear a glider all to pieces. Those fields that didn't have the posts stuck all over them had mines planted in them." At a density of over 1000 per square mile, it would be virtually impossible for a glider to land without encountering asparagus if the landing field were already prepared with them.

As originally planned, the invasion would take place on the 5th, but poor weather conditions forced a 24 hour postponement. When meteorologists predicted a window of adequate calm for June 6th, there was nothing left to do but go. At about midnight of that day the men of "A" Battery were all sacked out on their cots. Most were asleep, but those few who lay awake considering what the future held for them suddenly noticed a growing drone of aircraft above them. The unmistakable sound grew steadily until more and more men sat up and nudged the men on either side, saying, 'Hey, do you guys hear that?' In a few minutes the air became saturated with the drumming of C-47s reverberating overhead. They were all awake now, and all knew what it was. "When the paratroopers took off, all we heard all night was shwew, just airplanes, aircraft flying overhead, all over. The skies were just loaded with planes," remembered Covais of that night. "You could just imagine, when they got to Normandy what would happen."

The next morning word circulated quickly that Mission Detroit, with Major Todd and his party, was already gone, that the paratroopers had landed the night before, and that seaborne forces were hitting the Normandy beaches at that very moment. Though it had been done dozens of times already, everything was checked again, this time more out of the need to expend nervous energy and keep the men occupied than for the needs of preparation. There was an issue of three "K" and six "D" rations per-man. Then, in the early afternoon the batteries were drawn up in formation. In "A" Battery, First Sergeant Johnson said, "We're having a early supper today, boys, because you're gonna be traveling tonight." The men were led off to a mess tent where a meal of pork chops, potatoes, and spinach was served.

Early in the evening the 319th, 16 officers and 321 enlisted men, was drawn up in formation again. Cigar in mouth, Fidgity Phil, the Battalion XO, gave them one last look over and a few words of encouragement. Dismissed, the men suited up, reformed, and were marched out to the airfield. Their gliders sat waiting with the nylon towlines already attached and meticulously laid out on the tarmac in a zigzag, back and forth pattern. With the sun just beginning to settle, the light was softening as the men were dispersed in small groups at the Horsa preselected for them. Small clusters of glider and tow plane pilots stood by, going over the final details of their jobs.

The ranking man among each group of glidermen began drawing up a listing of all those who would be aboard, should some unthinkable disaster, such as being blasted out of the sky, be waiting for them. Meanwhile, a supply of Mae Wests was passed out. As taught earlier, the men knew that if the glider had to ditch in the English Channel, they would need to get out of their heavy equipment or it would surely drown them in spite of any life vest. Accordingly, they removed their equipment, put on the yellow life vests, and then pulled their equipment back on.

As he climbed into the glider, Gunner Corporal Rappi was struck by the strong aroma of the spruce plywood from which it was constructed. At some point in the future, working in the lumber mills of Alaska, this moment would come flooding back to him whenever the scent of freshly sawn spruce filled his nostrils. For the present though, he took one of the two seats situated in the tail and clipped his safety belt to a cable running along the interior of the glider for this purpose. Private Densil Rogers, the jeep driver settled in the seat across from him, while Sergeant Wheeler Davis, Vic Buinowski, and a few others on the gun crew took positions toward the front, beyond the jeep, howitzer, and other cargo.

Captain Manning got into another glider. Along with him went his driver, Sosa, and his radio operator, Bob Miller. Staff Sergeant Frank Marshall, Chief of the Security Section, climbed in too, as well as Bob Storms and a few assistant machine gunners. The last man aboard was Corporal James W. Jamison, a medic with the battalion's medical detachment. Manning remembered Jamison from the "C" Battery days in Italy and, having confidence in his abilities in treating wounds, specifically requested that he be assigned to "A" Battery for this mission.

And so it went. As the men got themselves situated at each of the forty gliders used by the 319th, a jeep with a major riding in it came down the runway. At each glider he addressed the troops and pilots, reading to them a statement from General Eisenhower. "Soldiers, Sailors, and Airmen of the Allied Expeditionary Force. You are about to embark upon the great crusade, toward which we have striven these many months. The eyes of the world are upon you. The hope and prayers of liberty loving people everywhere march with you. Your task will not be an easy one. Your enemy is well trained, well equipped, and battle hardened. He will fight savagely. But this is the year 1944, the tide is turned. The free men of the world are marching together to victory. I have full confidence in your courage, devotion to duty, and skill in battle. We will accept nothing less then full victory. Good luck, and let us all beseech the blessing of Almighty God upon this great and noble undertaking."

The glidermen and pilots were informed of the sign, "Flash," and countersign, "Thunder." The pilots were now given one final instruction: Once the coastline of Normandy is crossed, continue for three minutes, then cut your glider loose from the tow plane. At this the Major left and went on to the next Horsa, where the speech and instructions were repeated.

After a while the engines of the 436th Troop Carrier Group's C-47s started sputtering and wheezing, then sprang to life. The night before these same aircraft had transported plane loads of 12 to 15 paratroopers, known as "sticks," of the 101st Airborne to their drop zones in Normandy, and many of the planes had the bullet and shrapnel holes to prove it. Now they were hauling glider Field Artillery of the 82nd Airborne to Landing Zone "W," a collection of Norman fields along the N-13 Highway to Cherbourg, outside of the town of Saint Mere Eglise.

Taxiing on to the runways one by one, the towlines uncoiled and became taut. Within the gliders the noise of so many engines revving up was thundering all around. Some men, the calmer ones, looked out of the Horsa's small portholes, but some others glanced nervously from face to face, seeking reassurance. At 2037 the first combination of transport and glider went hell for leather down the runway. As with all gliders, the Horsa was the first to become airborne, being fully 10 to 15 feet off the ground before the C-47 touched off from the surface. As overloaded as the glider was, the runway was just barely long enough. Another followed about a minute behind, so that while the growing flotilla circled Membury Airdrome, it required nearly an hour for the entire serial of fifty to assemble in formation at flight altitude.

When this was accomplished the gliders turned southward in the dimming light, flying four abreast in a column several miles long. By this time the serial from Welford had joined them, essentially doubling the size of the task force. Gruebling later wrote his folks at home in Milwaukee, "Wish you could have seen the take off. All the planes had their red, green and amber lights on, all in formation. Looked like a big Christmas tree floating through the sky. Two of us stood up all the way over, looking out of the port hole compartment, watching the escort of fighter planes we had, and I mean we had an escort."

Because of their much higher speed, the fighters flew in a graceful series of arcs, back and forth, above and below the gliders to be sure they did not leave them behind. Captain Manning was similarly impressed by the sheer magnificence of it all. Years later he recalled, "It was a sight to remember. The sky was like a 5 mile wide thruway - jammed with planes, and planes with gliders in tow. It was almost dusk as we flew over the White Cliffs of Dover. At any other time it would have been very scenic."

Now crossing over the channel, Corporal Arno Mundt, whom one "A" Battery man described as "always having his nose in some book," was thinking of the historical implications of participating in an invasion from England to Normandy. When Mundt shouted something to the other guys in his gun crew about 1066 and the Norman Conquest, they glared back, nonplussed, and told him to shut up.

OUT AND OUT MURDER.

Reactions to the tension of the flight were as varied as could be imagined. Some men noticed squadrons of B-17s overhead, returning from missions against the German lines of supply and transportation located miles inland from the beachhead. The most anxious among them were manic, almost giddy at the sight, mistakenly proclaiming it as proof that any opposition was surely pulverized.

Oddly, John Girardin, for the first time he'd flown in a glider, wasn't airsick. However, many nervous stomachs fell prey to the apprehension of the occasion and, as Ryan commented about their last meal before the flight, "The moment the glider was in the air they spit that spinach all over the floor." Sosa, who'd been sitting in his jeep since takeoff, got up, staggered to the back of the glider and vomited the two pork chops he'd eaten for supper into one of the buckets provided specifically for this purpose. When he got back to his jeep, Louis lay down across the front seats and fell fast asleep.

First Lieutenant Laurence Cook of Memphis, Tennessee, was the grandson of a Confederate artilleryman. Cook was among the replacements who joined the battalion the previous March. He remembered, "I was sitting in the front seat of the glider, but I was beginning to get seasick so I got up and stood beside the co-pilot all the way across the channel."

Captain Manning took up the same vantage point in his glider, as did Corporal Covais in his, explaining later, "I didn't want to miss anything, so I got up and stood between the pilot and co-pilot."

Rappi remained calm and even found the trip enjoyable. "Well," he said of it afterwards, "being a young person, I was 21 years old, sometimes you think it's fun. You take things differently when you're a kid."

Yet, not all the young men felt the same. When Silas Hogg was asked his private thoughts nearly 65 years after the invasion, he answered, "Really? You want to know? If I'd be there the next day. If the job I was supposed to do got done, and if it did, would I be in one piece, and if I was in one piece would I be in a good piece. If I was, what would I do. Would I be able to go ahead and carry on? I'm like everybody else, I'm selfish. I wanted to live. You follow me? I didn't think I was gonna survive. No, hell no. I looked back behind me and I saw nothing but the sky full of planes and gliders. Not knowing or having any idea where I was going, or what I was gonna do when I got there, I knowed whatever it was I had better do a good job if I wanted to come home. I was like everybody else, I was scared."

As mission Elmira's two serials approached the Norman coast they were picked up by the Germans, who could easily see their targets catching the last rays of light as the sun dropped below the horizon. They rapidly trained their longer range anti-aircraft guns on the gliders and opened up. Suddenly the skies around the gliders and tow planes started to erupt with dozens of bursts of flak.

"The antiaircraft fire came up even while we were still over the channel," recalled Louis Sosa, who roused himself once it started. "As a matter of fact, it's a strange thing. You see on television these air force movies? The akak up in the sky? Well, I found out what that was when we crossed the English Channel in the glider. All that akak was popping around all over the place. It sounded harmless and at first I didn't think it was so terrible, as bad as it looked like in the movie. They sound just like little firecrackers, absolutely harmless. But they're not harmless, no. As a matter of fact, I found later on that I had a crack in the jeep, on top of the gas tank on the driver's side. Something hit it, right on the left hand corner. I didn't see it till much later. Yeah, that akak was up there, popping all around us. Sounded like firecrackers. That's a weird experience."

BATTERY!

Since this second wave of Elmira came through on the exact same heading as the first had two hours previously, the Germans had their range, were fully alert and ready to receive them. Most of the aircraft were catching shell fragments. Two of the tow planes from the Welford serial were hit hard and plummeted into the Channel, taking their gliders with them. Standing behind the pilots, Covais had a ringside seat he would never forget as his glider passed over Utah Beach. "It was getting pretty dark by the time we got over the Normandy coast. I could see the cruisers and battleships firing salvo after salvo right on to the shoreline. I'm looking down from the glider. Unprotected, no parachute, nothing. All of a sudden, as we crossed the beach, we went into a whole barrage of antiaircraft fire and machinegun tracer bullets. It looked like Christmas just burst open. All kinds of lights. All I could see were the lights. All kinds of stuff. So, I said, well Lord, please, just let all of us come through."

In his own Horsa, Lieutenant Cook had a similar experience, saying of it afterward, "I saw the coast and they told me I better get in the back and get tied down. I got back in and I couldn't get my belt fastened, so I put my foot against the seat across the aisle. The coast looked like the depths of hell. There were tracer bullets going every which a-way. The flares had it lit up. They were firing at everything."

Staff Sergeant and Chief of Gun Sections, Bob McArthur, found the experience similarly unsettling, and later commented, "From the time we left the channel on the French side until we landed those gliders, we were riddled and re riddled by machine gun fire. Before I landed I saw more bullets shot at me than I thought was in the whole German army. I've often wondered what those boys in the air force felt like when they were getting shot at. Now I know, only I didn't have the flak suits and armor to protect me that they have. I guess the air force men are wondering why the glidermen feel like that now. If any of them will come around I'll tell them."

At the same moment, Gruebling could see it was time to take cover. As he put it, "We hit the coast and then hell broke loose. Flak and tracers coming up. That's when I hit my seat, strapped in and huddled up like one of these monkeys: speak no evil, see no evil, etc. What a helpless feeling. Sounded like hail stones hitting the glider."

Gruebling's observation of the sound wasn't unique. Many men noticed the way machinegun rounds and shell fragments could be distinctly heard as they tore through the Horsas, splintering the plywood and sending long wooden shards flying through the interior. One man remembered later, "The shells passed right through our plywood glider. Several men were hit by anti-aircraft fire. Men were praying out loud and I joined them. We said one "Hail Mary" after another." Pandemonium started breaking loose as gliders were jostled by blast concussion and the men inside were wounded or killed where they crouched among the cargo or sat belted in their seats. In Captain Manning's glider, a string of machinegun fire ripped across the fuselage. One man lurched in his seatbelt, coughed up a mouthful of blood, and was dead, just like that.

Statistics later showed that this second wave of mission Elmira received the worst drubbing of all the glider serials that were sent into Normandy during Neptune. Fully two thirds of the C-47s took a substantial hit from either antiaircraft or machinegun fire, and it is reasonable to assume that the proportion among the gliders was similar. It was fortunate that Landing Zone "W" was located only six miles past Utah Beach. Had the distance been much further, accumulating damage to the gliders and tow planes would surely have caused many to break apart in the -air or lose control and crash.

As it was, the three minute duration of the flight over the German occupied portion of Normandy seemed interminable. The Troop Carrier pilots, despite orders to deliver the gliders to the landing zone at a slow speed and generous altitude, gave their engines more thrust and headed for the treetops in an effort to evade the tremendous fire they were taking. The pilot of the plane towing Manning's glider got on the phone line. He sounded frantic and warned the glider pilot that he was going to cut them loose himself if they didn't release their glider right away. Hoping to maintain some control over the situation, the glider pilot agreed to release as soon as he could spot a minimally large field. Traveling at an altitude of approximately 500 feet and at a speed of about 125 miles per hour, glider pilots had a good idea of just how many seconds it would take a fully loaded Horsa to impact the ground. With this in mind, the co-pilot took off his wristwatch, handed it to Manning, and shouted to him, "When you see us let go of that line, you start counting the seconds, you hear me?" Taking the watch, Manning stepped back to take a seat. Realizing there wasn't any time to belt himself in, the Captain wrapped his arm firmly around Bob Storms's shoulder and held on.

When a glider is released from its tow line, the background roar of engines and the general noise of the wind and propeller wash rushing past suddenly stops. Noticing the sudden quiet, the guys in the Horsas knew they had begun their final descent. Manning was calling out the seconds, five seconds, ten seconds, fifteen seconds, seventeen, twenty, twenty-one. Everyone braced themselves in the darkness, their frozen faces and white knuckled hands illuminated for brief moments when the flash of explosions penetrated through the portholes or front cockpit. Twenty-eight, twenty-nine, thirty! As the impact started, some clenched their teeth and squeezed their eyes shut, others cursed, cried out for God's mercy, their mothers, or just howled in terror.

After action reports of the division later stated that the gliders of Elmira began landing at 2305 hours amidst, "severe enemy small arms and mortar fire. Reorganization commenced immediately but was handicapped by intense enemy fire." In fact, the largest concentration of gliders missed the landing zone by about 5,200 yards, coming to rest about two miles northeast of Saint Mere Eglise. Some landings were among the forward outposts of the American 4th Infantry Division, some were right on top of the German defensive positions as they stood on the night of June 6th, and others lay somewhere in between.

Manning's glider made its first contact with the Norman countryside about midway across one field, then careened through a row of trees and finally came to rest astride a hedgerow on the opposite end. The glider was more or less in one piece, if one didn't consider the wings, but the occupants and cargo were all jammed to the front in one disorganized heap. The pilot was badly injured, hanging half suspended in the hedges. The co-pilot was dead.

Manning later wrote that he "Came to on a pile of rubble still holding the watch. I found my right hand to be cradling my partially disconnected thumb. Naturally, I bypassed my medical packet and wrapped the thumb in a dirty handkerchief. I found that I could hardly move my back, dragged out my 45 Colt and tried to take charge."

Manning could see that four or five of his men were killed outright and as many others badly hurt, among them Medic Jamison who was alive but unable to render medical attention to anyone. Meanwhile, Sergeant Marshall took a couple of men and had them establish that there were no Germans posing an immediate threat. Bursts of machinegun fire were breaking out here and there, and some desultory mortar rounds were starting to fall too, but this particular glider didn't seem to be attracting direct fire. Marshall's scouts came scampering back, reporting that though the enemy was heard in the area, they seemed nearly as confused and disorganized as the Americans. Marshall also made contact with a couple of other gliders which they knew landed in adjacent fields or even saw at the opposite end of their own.

Now that some security was established, it remained to remove the dead and get help for the injured. One of Marshall's men reported that Doc Hebert was ensconced in a hedgerow across the field. "Go," Marshall ordered impatiently, "Tell Hebert that Captain Manning's hurt bad and needs some help." In the meantime Marshall got the men started, knocking the tail off the glider and unloading enough cargo to try driving Manning's jeep and the machinegun trailer out of the hind end.

It wasn't going easily, with the Horsa pitched at an awkward angle across the hedgerow. Remembering the job they were having, Sosa said, "The tail end of the glider set up about four feet in the air. Couldn't get it down, we had a hell of a time getting out of it and bringing the machinegun section and all with it. The trailer or something got jammed up in there and my jeep was spinning its wheels on the floor. We finally managed to get it out, the equipment and everything, but if we'd been under direct fire we'd have been deader than hell."

Meanwhile Marshall's runner came back, but without the doctor. "Where's Hebert, where the hell is Hebert," Marshall demanded.

"Hebert says he can't come, he says it's too dangerous."

Sergeant Marshall was furious. "Tell Hebert to get his ass over here. Tell him Manning's hand is tore off and Jamison's probably dead!"

It took a while, but Marshall got the jeep and trailer, along with its 50 caliber machinegun on the anti-aircraft mount, out of the Horsa. It was well after midnight when Sosa finally drove off with Manning in the passenger seat and a few other injured men in the trailer. Leaving them all at a quiet hedgerow corner some distance off, Sosa returned to the glider for a final run with Marshall and the remaining men. By this time Marshall's runner had come back a second time, still without Doctor Hebert, and the Sergeant made no effort to hide his disgust. All the way back he repeated to no one in particular, that son of a bitch, that son of a bitch, over and over. This time they put Storms in the passenger seat. After discovering him pinned behind the trailer after the crash, it was becoming apparent that Bob certainly had at least some cracked, and maybe some broken ribs on top of the obvious contusions he'd suffered.

Captain John R. Manning commanded "A" Battery during Operation Neptune – the glider invasion of Normandy. He was severely injured in the crash landing. This photo was taken in Leicester, England, early 1944, shortly before the invasion. Courtesy Manning family.

OUT AND OUT MURDER.

"We went maybe a couple of hundred yards, and then slipped up under over-hanging hedgerows, more or less," said Sosa. "I camouflaged my jeep and my trailer so you couldn't hardly see it. Then we scattered out in that ditch. They were shooting all around us." Sosa then went back to where his Captain was lying. Someone must have administered a morphine surret to him because the way Manning's hand was mangled no one would be able to stand this pain and still be coherent without it.

"Are you alright, Captain, can I get you anything?" Asked Sosa.

"No," Manning answered, then added, "Where's your Tommygun?"

"All busted up in the crash, sir," Sosa answered.

Manning thought about how proud Sosa had been to be issued the submachine gun. Now his enterprising driver had no personal weapon. Manning held out his .45 toward his driver. "He sat there and gave it to me, he said, here, you take it, and gave it to me."

Through the chaos, every man in every glider had his own personal invasion that night. Covais had his story, and told it this way: "We smacked right into the trees at least a hundred feet up and we splattered right down. We had both our wings sheared off, and when that happened, man, the whole top of the glider came off with it. We pancaked right down. We splattered, we splattered. And when we splattered out, whew, everything lit up." Although he never did learn of these anti-glider devices, at the time or afterwards, Covais's description of hitting "trees" and the explosions immediately following them, suggest impact with asparagus.

Covais continued, "I could hear the machineguns firing all around us, bup bup bup bup bup bup. My knee was banged up and I had a bad cut across my forehead and left eye. I was bleeding like a pig, but I was lucky."

"I had this Lieutenant with me. We got into a ditch, a depression off to the side, but you could see everything was broke up, the whole glider broke up. They were shooting at us from under the parachutes, the Germans were, they had machinegun nests set up under the parachutes that our own paratroopers left there when they landed. As a guy would try to crawl away they would fire. I figured, well, here we are, this is it."

"Then this Lieutenant says to me, 'Hey, I forgot my binoculars. Go back out there and get my binoculars.' The glider was under machinegun fire, bup bup bup bup bup, all over the place! It was very rough. I said, 'Lieutenant, let the binoculars remain where they are. We'll go back later and get them, we'll recover your binoculars.' He didn't want to hear it and I finally said to him, 'You know Lieutenant, if you want your binoculars you'll have to go get them yourself.'"

"You know, I would have been dead just to get his binoculars back. It's danger-ous, very dangerous, a lot of confusion, paratroopers all over the place, a lot of activity going on. You don't know who's who. It's dark, confusion reigns, and you can get killed very easily. Anyway, I made it out of there alive."

"What a place to land," was Rollie Gruebling's comment, "in between our lines and the German lines, with mortar and machine gun bullets going back and forth. The air was so full of lead that if you took too deep a breath you inhaled the stuff. Four of us hit a ditch and had to stay there till noon the next day because every time you popped your head up the machineguns would start talking. Then we didn't know which were our lines, in the front or in the rear of us. You can tell the sounds your rifle makes and you sure can distinguish the German, but the frenzy was all around us so we had to stay put. Each glider fought a war by itself. Artillery men turned into infantry men. In all I didn't know a ditch could be so heavenly and protective."

BATTERY!

Before Rappi's glider came to rest in one field it flew through two rows of trees lining a road, probably the D-15 highway leading north-east out of Saint Mere Eglise. The force of impact was so strong that his safety belt snapped the steel cable to which it was attached. The next thing he knew, Rappi was yards away from his seat, lying between the jeep and the bench along the side of the glider's fuselage. Fortunately, they didn't seem to be in the middle of any machinegun crossfire, as others had found themselves. He remembered, "We crawled out of there. Old Sergeant Davis had a broken leg. That's the last we seen of him. Nobody else got hurt. Everybody else was alright except Davis." Despite the light casualties to the personel, the glider was a wreck and the equipment packed inside took a beating. One of the bulkheads crushed down in between the front and the back seat of the jeep," Rappi explained. "We couldn't get it out of there. Then the elevating arc on the gun was bent, so the gun was no good either."

Lieutenant Cook's glider was among the few which landed in one piece, wings still attached, and without casualties. "When we landed the glider was in fairly good shape," he explained, "But the front nose wheel came up under my leg. My leg was a-resting on it when we stopped. I heard something outside, running around the plane. I knew the damn Krauts, the Germans, were out there, but it was my job to raise that door and look out. When I did I expected I'd get cut in two, but there was about seven or eight cute little calves out there running around."

Lieutenant Cook assembled his group while other gliders were still passing overhead, careening across fields and slamming into trees. "I counted about eight planes that crashed in the same field I was in, but we was the only one that landed at least half way right. You just didn't know what was happening. I know I got out and started walking down the road, when a damn shell landed right across the road from me on the other side of the hedge. It felt like it was right in my pocket. I hit the ditch and the damn ditch was full of water! That was my first taste of combat."

Cook's landing was about as ideal as any were that night. More typical was the experience of Mahlon Sebring when his glider crashed. "Jesus," he said of his own landing, "I know we came in pretty dang fast. The damn glider just collapsed and you went sliding down the road with plywood strapped to you, or you strapped to the plywood. So there was a lot of skin lost. I had a lot of black and blues and scabs for a couple of days."

Silas Hogg's landing was among the more harrowing. He said later, "The glider I came in on, it hit, and it hit with such a force that it drove the pilot through the top. The pilot was crushed, you couldn't even recognize him. We hit the ground so hard that we ricocheted across a road. The left wing hit a tree, pulled us to the left. We're still in the air. Now get this, we got shoved to the left, we hit another tree on the right and that swung us back to the right."

Judging from his description, the trees which Hogg remembered may also have been those lining the D-15. Then a second tremendous blow occurred. "Another glider come in right at exactly that second and it crammed straight into us. That's when Porch and Sergeant Wade both were killed. They were both killed when the two gliders collided. It just came in, hit the ground, ricocheted and hit our glider."

The two Horsas were crushed together in a terrible heap of plywood, jeeps, guns, and dead, wounded, or dazed men. "When I come to, well I hear, 'Get off of me you son of a bitch! Get off of me you son of a bitch!' I was knocked out and laying on top of Bob Carte. I just wonder if ole Bob's still living," said Hogg, looking back on that night over sixty years later.

OUT AND OUT MURDER.

As all these events were taking place, the pilot of Sartain's glider could see that the place his Horsa would be making its forced landing in was far too small for this procedure. Without question, he was going to overrun the open field and collide head on with the trees and hedges. Fortunately he could discern a country lane which cut through the hedgerow looming ahead. It offered a gap to aim for. Through the pilot's skill, or luck, or a combination of both, the glider ran straight up the middle of the lane and when the Horsa finally came to a stop it had traveled quite a few yards. Like nearly every other glider that night, it had lost its wings, but the fuselage was intact and upright with no one injured beyond the usual bumps and scratches.

Sartain and his men, ten of them with the pilots, scrambled out and collected along a nearby hedgerow. Because this glider didn't carry any jeep, trailer, or gun, there was no need to expend time breaking off the tail section. The essential cargo was unloaded into a pull cart and they were off.

Sartain directed his people to proceed up the lane cautiously. They hadn't gone far when the sound of nearby motorcycles was added to the background chatter of machine guns and anti-aircraft fire echoing across the countryside that night. Taking a few men with him, he went to investigate. He soon found a large farmhouse with its barn and outbuildings all enclosed by a substantial stone wall. The complex was evidently some sort of German command post, judging by the number of dispatch riders and small vehicles which constantly arrived and exited the yard like bees at a hive. Approaching to within forty yards of the wall, but staying well concealed among hedges and outbuildings, the glidermen could hear the Germans shouting orders excitedly. "The home was occupied by at least a platoon of Germans, but it sounded to me like they were as screwed up as we were," he said.

With all the coming and going the German position was generating, it was likely their glider, and perhaps them with it, would soon be discovered. Expecting hell could break loose at any moment, Sartain had his German P-38 drawn. He'd acquired this pistol in Italy and carried it in combat from that point on because, as he said, "That damn .45 automatic they gave us was useless, unless you were in a closet with whoever you were shooting at." Then all the traffic stopped. It sounded like the vehicles had driven off and none were returning. Sartain and his men waited and considered in whispered voices what to do next. At that moment there was a noise. Someone was out there, calling out in a heavily accented, hushed voice, American, American! It was the Frenchman who lived in the house. "How he knew we were out there I'll never know, but he told us the Germans were all gone." Thankfully Sartain could still remember a little of the French he'd grown up around when he'd spent summers with his Mother's family in rural Louisiana. From his conversation with the Frenchman, the Battery X O got a fix on where he was on his map. "I knew we were somewhere south of Saint Mere Eglise and our LZ (landing zone) and the assembly area," he later remembered. "The spot was near a little hamlet named Etienville. There's two villages with that name, but this was the smaller one and the farmhouse was on the map.

"We worked our way from hedge row to hedge row with the use of the cricket. Along the way we picked up about 6 more 319th members. Then the German traffic on the road got pretty heavy, both vehicles and on foot. You could hear them coming, so every time something came by we jumped into the hedges and knuckled down, just let them pass, you see?"

Rather than run the risk of getting tangled up with a strong force of the enemy, Sartain decided to wait until daylight before proceeding further. German vehicles, motorcyclists, and bodies of infantry continued to pass, but after a while there was a long period of quiet. Then Sartain heard footsteps approaching. This time though they did not sound like the hobnailed boots and shoes worn by the Germans. Sartain could see it was a group of about a dozen men, probably Americans. Using crickets and the password, the two groups accepted each other as GIs and met by the roadside. Then Sartain recognized a voice. It was unmistakable, and in the moonlight the Lieutenant could now plainly see he was face to face with, of all people, the imperious Colonel Bertsch. Sartain had not seen or spoken to his adversarial superior since Naples, and suddenly encountering him in these circumstances was a bit of a surprise. It may have been for Bertsch as well, but while the Colonel obviously recognized Sartain, he would not acknowledge him as an officer whom he knew well and who had served under him for a year.

There was a quick exchange of information, after which Bertsch ordered Sartain's party to fall in behind him. He said, "Are you ready to follow me, Lieutenant?" Sartain answered, "Yes, sir." But thought to himself, "I'm not following that bastard anywhere." "Bertsch turned on his heel and walked off. Sartain remained in place. "He had about a dozen guys with him," Sartain recalled. "He thought we were going to follow him, but when he walked off three or four of his people stayed behind with us."

When dawn broke on the morning of June 7th the men could see the true scale of the carnage from the night before. Wrecked gliders were everywhere, and in the daylight one could see that nearly all were literally demolished. Indeed, a survey of the gliders afterwards determined that 97% of them were damaged beyond salvage. Equipment lay scattered all over the ground. Unserviceable jeeps, trailers, and howitzers littered the crash sites as well. There were also more grisly things to be discovered. Numerous bodies of dead paratroopers were seen hanging from trees, and all efforts were made to cut them down as soon as possible.

There were a lot of casualties from the 319th and 320th out there too. On the way back to his glider to retrieve usable cargo the next morning, one "B" Battery man saw a disturbing sight. "A beam from a glider had broke lose and run through a tree," he said. "This guy was impaled on the part that broke off the glider. He was just hanging on that tree with that thing through him. That was sort of a dirty frightful thing."

Another 319th veteran of North Africa and Italy remembered how a recruit had asked him if he would let him wear his flying helmet, one of those issued at Fort Bragg to provide some warmth during high altitude flights. By the time of Normandy, most all the seasoned troopers had discarded these helmets as useless baggage. They certainly didn't offer any protection whatsoever. This anxious recruit only knew it was a "helmet" and, frightened at the prospect of gliding into combat, asked the old timer if he could wear his. The veteran answered, "Sure, you're welcome to it." The next morning, while recovering equipment, "we picked up a parachute and he was laying under it. His head was just smashed flat. He still had the flying helmet on. That always kind of bothered me."

One of the privates in "A" Battery was Bronx native, Jimmy Rosati, part of the instrument section. When his glider came down, it passed through some trees and the tail was broken off. Rosati happened to have been in the tail end of the glider when this happened and suddenly found himself tangled among the branches, perched high above the ground. Scratched and bruised, Rosati wasn't really hurt badly, but he was stranded until he could be rescued the next day.

When a tally could finally be made, it was found that two officers and fifteen enlisted men had been killed outright in the landings. Four more officers and 68 enlisted men were wounded and selected to be evacuated off Utah Beach, while an additional two officers and eighteen enlisted men, though wounded, were judged able enough to stay with the battalion aid station until they could return to duty. Altogether this meant that of the 337 men of the battalion who flew into Normandy with Mission Elmira, 50% of the officers and 113, or about 35% of the enlisted men became casualties. It was perhaps not the wholesale slaughter which Leigh-Mallory had predicted, but the death toll and loss of equipment, just to deliver troops to the field of battle, was staggering.

Afterwards, a few months before his death at age 83, Sosa stated ruefully, "Now that I look back at it, it's a wonder that as many of the GIs that went over there on D day did survive, because it was out and out murder. Life at that time was so cheap. It didn't mean anything. It's strange how people in power lead us to slaughter. You know what I'm saying? I'll see that for the rest of my life as a slaughter of human beings at war with each other. They get so uncivilized."

BATTERY!

Part 15: "Kiss them as they went by."

Between midnight and 0500 on the Morning of June 7th the effort to reconstitute the battalion had more the appearance of chaos than deliberate action. Depending on where their glider had come to rest, those who came in with Elmira spent these hours looking after their injured comrades, scurrying about in the darkness in search of friendly troops, or hidden in some hedgerow somewhere in Normandy. Among the heaviest concentrations of landing sites locating friends was a little easier, but when gliders grounded too close to German positions, or apart from the main clusters of landings, problems beyond those presented by crashing in the dark had to be faced.

Early on, Captain Manning's band made contact with Jesse Johnson, and several men from his glider. "A" Battery's first sergeant had been fortunate enough to make his landing in one of the two CG4As used in Elmira's second wave, and his landing had gone as well as any that night. The two united groups formed the command structure around which more "A" Battery men, continued to rally. The rest of the men were elsewhere, killed, wounded, pinned down by contact with the Germans, or had dropped too far from the main group to assemble with them. "We found ourselves near a farm lane which appeared to lead in the compass direction of Saint Mere Eglise, our focus point, so we proceeded down it," Manning later wrote. "I set up a command post and we gradually rounded up about half of our battery."

There were a lot of the enemy around, and while some of them were evidently confused by the paratroop and glider landings, really not looking for a fight if it could be avoided, others were more aggressive. Sometime during the night, for instance, Kenneth Smith and several other battalion men were searching their way through the dark, like so many others when they came upon a group of paratroopers setting up a 30 caliber machine gun at a road junction. "Their officer got three of our men to stay there and take over that gun. They tried to get me but I told them I had work to do," he remembered. "One of them was from Ohio, one from West Virginia, and another guy, I can't think of his name." In the Norman "bocage" countryside, with its little fields completely enclosed by tall earthen banks, crowned with thick foliage, visibility was limited to the closest hedgerow and the sound of small arms fire could be strangely contained. The result was that vicious firefights erupted suddenly, in isolation, and without warning. Smith explained, "We found all three of them the next day. They were dead. They was killed right there."

First Sergeant Jess Johnson had his own surprise encounter with the enemy. Before he met up with Captain Manning's group, Johnson was scouting about on the outskirts of a village near the landing zone, perhaps Saint Mere Eglise, perhaps Beuzeville au plain. Turning a corner in the moonlight, Johnson found himself standing a few yards from a German soldier. The German threw up his hands and shouted "Kamerad!" Johnson replied, "Kamerad my ass!" and cut the German down with his Thompson submachine gun. According to Sartain, "That was Jess Johnson's claim to fame. He never got tired of telling that story, but what else could he do, nobody was taking prisoners that night, nobody. Yeah, and he never went anywhere without that Tommy gun. It was a worthless weapon, but he carried it everywhere he went."

When Silas Hogg was asked how close he came to getting killed or captured that night, he answered, "Well, if there's one hole and two people jumping for that one hole, that's how close I come. I come close enough that I holed up with a .45 Thompson machinegun. I fired over 500 rounds that one night and I threw every hand grenade I had. I was sitting there waiting the next morning for the Germans to come and pick us up. Yeah, uh huh, awful close. Handshaking close."

As dawn began to break, men who weren't pinned down by German fire or utterly lost, started making their way toward their best guess of where the rendezvous point was. "As soon as it got light we found a road," said John Girardin. "Pretty soon some officers with a bunch of GIs come by there and they said, fall in. So we fell in. We went down this road, an old farm road like, and we come to a German antitank gun. It was still smoking but it looked like it was just abandoned, at least I didn't see any dead bodies. We went right by there and went to a holding area out in the farm fields. They had all these GIs there, but we didn't have a gun, so we didn't really have a fighting force. We didn't know what we were doing; nobody knew what the score was. Tell the truth, I think we scared the Germans more than anything else."

Girardin's group seems to have been one of those picked up as the batteries moved on from the landing area where they'd spent the night, to a rallying point not far from Beuzeville au plain, about three miles north-east of Saint Mere Eglise, and behind the front lines of the 4th Division.

An Aid Station was set up there beside an orchard and began processing the casualties. Under a tentfly marked with a large red cross, compression bandages and sulfa were applied as medical personnel quickly distinguished the fortunate and lightly wounded from the more serious evacuation cases, and those least fortunate ones, who had little or no chance of surviving. From "A" Battery, sixteen enlisted men were tagged to be evacuated back to England. Among them were Sergeant Davis, Corporals Covais, Lewis, and Motyka, Privates First Class Prohaska, and Rogers, as well as Privates Derwister, Duplechain, Forsman, Grigus, Price, Rosati, Russ, Stolldorf, and Tobin. When the doctors took a look at Corporal Bob Storms, they wanted to add him to the evacuation list, but he refused, fearing that he might get reassigned as a replacement to some strange outfit. What, they asked, was he going to do in the front lines with cracked ribs? "My boys can take care of me at the machinegun," he explained to the doctors. "I have men enough for the gun. I got two good ears and that's all that we need out there." So they wrapped ace bandages around Storms's torso and sent him on his way.

The battery's CO was eager to get back to the outfit if it was possible, but when surgeons took a look at mannings hand it was clear he was headed for England. According to his post-war memoir, "My thumb injury received a quick stitch or two, a heavy dose of sulfa, a bandage, and a ticket to be put on a hospital transport. With the way Manning's right hand was mangled, it was clearly impossible for him to remain in the field, but apparently, he also resisted being placed on the evacuation list. The larger than life rumor which circulated among the "A" Battery men was that their Captain put up quite a fight. As Rappi remembered, "The story was it took six men to put him aboard the boat, he didn't want to go."

Meanwhile parties of men from the various batteries of the 319th and 320th continued to trickle in. Ed Ryan's glider had taken a particularly hard landing the night before, leaving more killed and injured men among the occupants, than those who remained in one piece. By morning the survivors were slowly picking their way along one lane searching for a collection point. "We were out there, dragging stuff around in these stupid carts, a lot of headquarters stuff," he recalled. "Dirty Joe Meaghan, he was kind of spearheading the deal. He may have been a pain in the ass, but he had balls. We had a guy in the battery, a clerk, he wasn't a fairy, but he was an effeminate guy, and he's with us too. Then we saw a few Krauts cross the road up ahead, so Meaghan says, hand me the typewriter, meaning the machine gun. So that's what the guy does, he hands him an actual typewriter! Dirty Joe says, 'Not that, you stupid bastard!' We all start laughing. And this guy says, in that whiny voice of his, 'Well, I didn't know what you meant!' We started laughing, I'll never forget it, out there with the Krauts all around us, we're all laughing."

Back at the assembly area the odor of dead bodies was noticed wafting on the summer air. The smell was distinct, and those who'd seen combat in Italy recognized it immediately. There was also intermittent sniper fire. One man who was there remarked, "I remember that because I could hear the doggone zing." The sniping made organization harder to accomplish, but no one in "A" Battery was hit and it had little results aside from the effect on nerves. Major Wilcoxson and whatever staff he could gather up were busy all the while, sorting things out, trying to establish order and make contact with Major Todd and the division. Meanwhile, much of the initiative came from the ser-

geants, who could plainly see what immediately needed to be done while the battalion brass decided on what to do.

In "A" Battery, Sergeant Rene Picher took the lead. A French Canadian, Picher enlisted at Springfield, Massachusetts, in February of 1941, and had been with the outfit since before it went airborne. According to one "A" Battery man, "He was a guy that really enjoyed living. Very talkative and diminutive, but he fancied himself a ladies man and a cook. He evidenced all the characteristics of a true animated Frog. French, French, a hundred percent French."

Of the Sergeant's actions on June 7th, Sartain commented, "Picher picked up a bunch of guys and they took off to the gliders to get the equipment. He took the lead in getting some of our guys, and what jeeps we could get to run, back around to pull our guns and jeeps out of the gliders. Picher

Sergeant René Picher, Able Battery's Chief of Sections during Operation Market-Garden. He took over the job from Sgt. Bob McArthur, when the latter received a battlefield commission. Summer, 1944. Covais collection.

basically took the lead."

Rappi was one of those Picher took with him, as well as Flavious Carney, the battery gun mechanic and a few other men. They first returned to Rappi's crashed glider. With a lot of manpower and the help of some axes, they were able to extricate the howitzer and haul it back to the collection point.

Now acting sergeant of his gun section, Rappi remembered, "The gun we got out, but the elevating arcs were bent. We weren't much good without our artillery piece, so the gun mechanic and I went around looking for parts and we found them. The paratroopers dropped theirs in pieces." It is possible that Rappi and Carney came across some of the bundles intended for two pack howitzers of the 456th Parachute Field Artillery which jumped with the 505th the day before. These were the only two fieldpieces dropped by parachute during the invasion, and the 456th men were able to reassemble just one of them. "A lot of them bundles went into the water," continued Rappi. "There were water holes around there, kind of swampy, but we found a pile of gun parts. We found the elevating arcs and took them and made a usable gun out of it. I know I had my gun all fixed and ready to go!"

Sartain and his group had a long way to travel from where they'd spent the night. By the time they were able to locate the reconstituting battalion, it was late afternoon, and Major Todd had himself only just arrived to assume command. The "A" Battery XO immediately reported in to his battalion commander. Todd was already informed of Captain Manning's injuries, so Sartain's presence was especially welcome when the Major told him, "Charlie, I have to talk to you. Manning's been severely hurt. In fact, he's already been evacuated to the beach. You're taking over command of "A" Battery."

Sartain had questions, but Todd didn't have many answers. "It's pretty much a SNAFU situation," he told him. "I understand Gelb and Carey from your battery are OK, but a lot of our other officers are casualties. Dick Johnson, from your battery, is wounded. Dietrich and Dorges from headquarters are both dead."

"Who else," Sartain asked.

"Radcliffe Simpson," said Todd with emotion welling in his voice. "Apparently he thought he was going to storm some Jerry machinegun and got caught in a crossfire. At least that's the story I heard. Well, anyway, he's not expected to live." Todd paused, then said, "You'll have to do something about an XO for "A" Battery, but right now we've only got three or four tubes in the whole battalion, so at the moment it's a moot point. In any event, you know what to do, Lieutenant. Get your battery organized and get some of these damn guns into working order."

About that time an unexpected convoy of jeeps pulling trailers piled high with ammunition and other equipment drove up to the battalion command post. Marvin Ragland, whom no one had seen since several days before the invasion, was leading the way. It was all desperately needed material and a real shot in the arm for the 319th.

Ragland got out of his jeep and bounded over to Major Todd and the other officers. "You look surprised to see me, sir," he said. Given the way the parachute drops had gone, it had been anyone's guess whether Ragland was dead, alive, or captured. Naturally, everyone was curious about his experience jumping with the paratroopers. Guys crowded around him and started posing questions. "I was the last one out of the plane, and I was glad to get out," he told them. "There wasn't anyone there to push me, but when you're going over that area with the enemy fire and akak you're glad to get out," then, tapping the small bible in his shirt pocket sent to him by his mother in Kansas, he added, "I guess it worked. Anyhow, I landed in with a bunch of cows. But we started locating each other and that didn't go too badly."

Then one of those listening to Ragland's story asked him, what about after the drop, what happened to you that day? Ragland filled them in, "Well, it's like this, you do what you think you need to do until somebody comes along and tells you what to do. When it come daylight there was a bunch of us assembled after the landing and the first person I recognized was General Gavin. He came walking up and wanted to know who I was. I told him I was a forward observer from the 319th and I came in with the infantry. He said, 'Well, we gotta set up a security area, there's a man down there with a 50 caliber machinegun, you go down there and be with him and help him.'"

Soldier's General that he was, the guys loved these Gavin stories. By the war's end it seemed like every man in the division had his own personal Slim Jim anecdote to trade with those of his buddies. Ragland told the others that he remained with the machinegun position into the night. The next morning, when he returned to the division CP to check on reports of how the landings of the 319th had gone he spoke to the General again. "Gavin said to me, 'We've got some vehicles here that came in on gliders. They belong to your 319th unit.' Then he showed me a position on the map. He told me, 'I want you to take these vehicles down there.' So I went down there where he told me to go."

Thus the battalion started to come together, shake off the confusion of the crash landings, and prepare to face the enemy. Picher's group, and others, continued to recover equipment and scour the countryside for salvageable gun parts. Now that he was the CO of "A" Battery, and Sosa was his driver, Sartain decided to see what he could find on his own. He told his driver to crank up the jeep. The pair went up and down country lanes, occasionally being stopped by paratroopers or 4th Division men who warned them they'd be entering German held territory if they went any further. When they saw a glider Sosa would pull off the road and go cross country so they could investigate. In one field Sartain and his driver pulled up to a mostly intact Horsa, but it wasn't until they were fully upon it that they could really comprehend what they were looking at.

The glider was sprayed with bullet holes from head to tail. A German machinegun position must have been only yards away when it came to rest and the effect of its fire covered the ground. In the growing twilight, Sosa remembered the spectacle, "There was one glider, you could see where the guys were actually running out and they had all been killed. There must have been 12 or 15 of them, all in a row, all laying dead there on the ground. That was horrible. They came running out of that glider, and they were all laying deader than hell. Laying dead just stretched out one alongside the other one. That's a hell of a sight, man."

"While we were there, grave registration showed up," added Sartain. "I forget what unit they were from. Wasn't the 319th obviously. It was probably the 325th. The division was primarily concerned about injured soldiers. When they examined everything and found they were all dead, then they went on to the next glider."
The whole scene was eerie and left the two feeling like intruders at some very private gathering. "I didn't stop that long to look at them," concluded Sosa. "We turned around and left."

The work of assembling the battalion went on, but one thing everyone needed desperately by the time darkness fell on June 7th was rest. It is safe to say that no one had slept at all the night before, and with the tremendous build up of tension leading up to the invasion, sleep during the final nights at the security camp had been fitful at best.

KISS THEM AS THEY WENT BY.

For those who were alive and in one piece, the relief and exhaustion of surviving the invasion took over. The deep slumber of one who realizes he has passed through a long anticipated ordeal descended over them all.

Early the next morning, June 8th, communications were re-established with division headquarters. At mid-morning Major Todd traveled there to report his battalion as ready for action, albeit with only seven serviceable guns temporarily operating as a single battery. While the Major was gone, parties made a final visit to the crash sites to reclaim any remaining material and bury the dead. In the meantime the rest of the unit prepared for the anticipated march order.

Even as the recovery parties at the gliders were making their last sweep, more lost men came straggling in. "Well, you know we had a lot of guys that couldn't get back to the battery that were dropped or landed so far from the assembly area, a lot of guys," was Sartain's recollection. "I remember when we finally got the four guns together we had about twenty guys missing. Then one or two at a time started showing up." Casimir Sobon and another "A" Battery man were among them. "Everybody was spread all over," Sobon said. "We were there for about two or three days when we caught up with somebody else. All we heard was some people talking and digging and stuff. I couldn't see anything, so I was with another guy and I said, 'Come on, I'm gonna go over there and find out who that is.' I went over there and there they were, they were other guys from our own outfit. These guys said, 'Where the hell have you been?' They were ready to send a telegraph home. Missing in action, you know. I said, Christ, don't ever do that! Don't ever send a telegram home for me unless you identify me positively." When Sobon got to the bivouac of the battalion he started asking after the other guys in "A" Battery, especially Ernie Mazur, his best buddy. Somebody told him Mazur was at the aid station, and about to be evacuated. "Mazur, we were pretty friendly he and I. They had him rigged up on a stretcher on the top of a jeep," recalled Sobon. "It didn't look like he had any outer injuries of any kind, so it might have been all internal from the crash landing. That's the last I seen of him. He was still alive. Later I found out he died."

When Todd returned he called a meeting of the battery commanders. Given the heavy losses among the officers, a final run down of the battalions present table of organization was reviewed, then Todd briefed them all on the current state of affairs. At division he'd been given orders that the 319th would be moving out immediately to the vicinity of Chef-du-Pont. There it would support the efforts to secure the bridges over the Merderet River at that location and at La Fiere, about two miles to the North. The battery commanders were dismissed and, at 1154 that morning the battalion moved out.

It took less than two hours for the 319th to reach its new position and get its 75s set up. Their orders were to support the 508th PIR and other units which were forcing their way across to, or were isolated on, the western bank of the Merderet. In the state of flux which still existed, the battalion was barely able to organize a liaison party of Captain Wimberley, Lieutenant Blank, and an enlisted support team, when the first fire mission came in.

About 400 troopers, mostly from the 508th's 2nd Battalion, but including members of every parachute regiment in the division, and some 101st Screaming Eagles too, were dug in on a piece of high ground near the confluence of the Merderet and Douve Rivers, designated Hill 30. Lt. Colonel Thomas J. B. Shanley was in charge of the isolated contingent, and he had no intention of relinquishing the ground under any circumstance. The hill was located close to the west bank of the Merderet, just north of the causeway leading north-east, over the river to Chef-du-Pont. As long as it was held,

BATTERY!

the Americans controlled the causeway and it would be impossible for the Germans to regain control of the Chef-du-Pont Bridge. Hill 30 also threatened the German strongpoints on the western end of the causeway at La Fiere, a short distance up river to the north. Thus situated, Hill 30 was key to the Germans if they were to ever drive the invasion back toward the English Channel. But these points were equally indispensable to the Americans if they were going to break out of the beachhead and cut across the Cotentin Peninsula, as planned, making Hill 30 a point which had to be held.

With only two light machineguns, a Browning Automatic Rifle (BAR), and one bazooka, to compliment their small arms, the beleaguered troopers on Hill 30 were in desperate need of artillery support. During that afternoon of June 8th, they were being attacked on three sides with their backs to the river. Having only just established their gun positions, no forward observers from the 319th were as yet able to make their way to Hill 30. This also meant that no radio or telephone communications with the battalion had been established either. Radio communications with Colonel Lindquist at 508th Regimental HQ had been made though, and Shanley's men were informed that the 319th was at hand.

Relaying their targets to the 319th through their Regimental CP, Shanley's men on Hill 30 began calling in their requirements. The first target, at 1832, was two tanks of the 100th Panzer Replacement Battalion. Though these tanks were modified French Renaults mounted with 37mm guns and far inferior to the German's current state-of-the-art armor, they were still formidable weapons against the lightly armed paratroopers on Hill 30. Thirteen rounds were fired by the 319th. One of the panzers took a direct hit and the other retired to a safer position. A little over an hour later one of the 508th officers on Hill 30, Lieutenant Albright, observed German infantry massing for an attack only a couple of hedgerows away. Albright radioed the information to his regimental HQ across the river. Within a few minutes a 48 round barrage followed. According to the regiment's postwar history written by one of its officers, William G. Lord, Albright "called for the guns of the 319th Glider Field Artillery to fire a concentration for him. Delivering effective fire, these guns broke up all semblance of organization among the enemy in the area."

This was close in firing of a kind that called for pinpoint accuracy if it was to be effective without killing and wounding their own men along with the enemy. Not all the troopers on Hill 30 were aware that the 319th was within range, so their fire came as unexpected to those privates not in the command structure. As another one of the 508th men on Hill 30 recalled, "...artillery began falling in the next hedgerow. We were bewildered because we were unable to decide whose artillery it was. Were the Germans shelling us and falling short, or were the Americans firing on target? Luck was on our side, it was our artillery firing with deadly accuracy. The shells exploded all around our position and the German attack never came."

Beginning at 2000 the battalion fired concentrations on targets all around Hill 30, then its barrage slowly crept up the west bank of the Merderet in the direction of La Fiere. Changing its coordinates every twenty minutes or so, tanks, infantry, and machinegun positions were all pounded individually and in combination. Darkness, and the absence of FO teams in place with the 508th, brought concentrations on identified targets to an end after the expenditure of 113 rounds of ammunition, though intermittent harassing fire continued through the night.

That next morning a single 75mm pack howitzer and crew from the 456th Parachute Field Artillery Battalion was attached to the 319th. This allowed the battalion to resume its normal configuration of two firing batteries, although with only four guns in each. As an independent firing unit once again, it was determined that the position of XO for "A" Battery would be filled by First Sergeant Johnson. With the acute need for trained forward observers resulting from the loss of half the battalion's officers, none could be spared for this job and Johnson was, in any case, quite capable of performing its duties.

Elements of the 505th PIR and 325th GIR had finally secured the western end of the bridge and causeway at La Fiere by mid-day of June 9th, aided, in part, by a barrage from the 319th and other divisional artillery. Though that crossing was still under long range German artillery and machinegun fire, it was determined to send the balance of the 508th across the Merderet by that route to relieve the regiment's 2nd Battalion on Hill 30. Along the way the 508th troopers saw the devastating effect of barrages placed on enemy positions the day before and that morning. According to Lord, "The effectiveness of our artillery could be seen at the west end of the causeway, where a small group of buildings was almost obliterated. Dead Germans and Americans lying a few feet from each other testified to the bitterness of the battle that was fought here."

All day on the 9th, the 508th Troopers had to battle their way to their brothers on Hill 30. The Germans resisted stubbornly and it was slow going. The 319th did their part with continuous fire missions along the west bank of the Merderet and around the hill. When the Germans were seen massing for a counterattack against the newly won La Fiere bridgehead in the early evening, the battalion let loose with a punishing 270 round barrage, followed by another of 120 rounds an hour later.

Shortly after that, according to Lord, "Lieutenant Albright was again directing the 75mm pack howitzers of the 319th Field Artillery from Hill 30. This time a battery of enemy infantry howitzers was the target. They had moved up a sunken road to within a few hundred yards of the hill." This particular fire mission was interrupted because the 508th relief column was arriving on the scene and taking the Germans from their rear. The siege of Hill 30 was broken, and the 82nd was firmly established on the west bank of the Merderet River.

Rappi remembered that day's work. "They said fire at will. Well, we were firing everything! Anti-tank, smoke, shells, high explosives, everything, because we don't carry that many shells, you know. We were shooting everything," he said. His memory was accurate. Battalion records indicate that by midnight of June 9th, well over 700 more rounds of assorted artillery shells had been expended.

1st Lieutenant Howard Dibble, an assistant surgeon of the 319th went along with the first patrols to establish contact with Hill 30. According to a later citation for the Bronze Star, Dibble, "moved forward along roads harassed by sniper and enemy mortar fire to render immediate medical aid to 34 casualties who had little in the way of such care since being wounded." Sartain remembered him years later, saying, "Dibble was a good guy, but I don't know how he became a surgeon because he was all thumbs." Lieutenant Dibble, a native of Wisconsin, remained with the 319th through the war.

While the 319th's two batteries were sending their shells over the river, the seaborne element of the outfit joined the battalion, arriving at 1520 that afternoon. Despite the airborne designation of all units comprising the division, each had component parts which could never be delivered to the field of battle by parachute or glider. These included heavy trucks, mess kitchens, and 3/4 ton weapons carriers, along with larger stores of ordnance and rations. Consequently, Force "C" of the division, as these troops were known, under the command of Brigadier General George P. Howell, landed on

BATTERY!

Utah beach on the afternoon of June 8th. Force "C" had set sail from Bristol on June 6th and waited at sea until the time was right for them to make landfall. For the 319th, this included about 45 men, 15 of them from "A" Battery, who carried with them a load of ammunition much too heavy to have been brought in by glider.

Orrin Miller was one of them. As he described it, "Before the invasion, they pulled me off of the gun crew because somebody took sick in the motor pool. I was on the six by six truck, in the motor pool at that point. We had to waterproof our trucks so that they could go through the water. We had to extend our exhaust pipes up so that they would extend out of the water, then we had to put a kind of a putty around all of our spark plugs and wiring so it wouldn't get wet. It was probably a good week's job getting that vehicle ready. You had to do the job good enough so that it wouldn't stall out. If I'd have stalled out in front of the other ones, we'd all be in trouble."

When the battalion's seaborne element was ready to disembark from its LCTs on the afternoon of June 8th, the situation on Utah was still unsettled. Desultory artillery fire continued to land in no predictable pattern and occasional strafing runs by Luftwaffe fighters, despite the overwhelming Allied air superiority, still occurred. Miller remembered that the LCT wasn't able to come right up on to the beach, in fact, it was necessary for it to "stay out in the water quite a ways before they just drop the front of it down. Then you have to drive off into the water and up to the beach. The water was probably six to eight feet deep when we first went off. We had to locate our battalion and get oriented with them to get the supplies that we had on the vehicles to them. Of course they were short of ammo, and that's what we had for them."

It took the balance of June 8th to get all the LSTs off-loaded, the vehicles de-waterproofed, and everyone on the beach. The landing was an eye opening experience for the motor pool guys, many of whom were, like Miller, new replacements. He remembered Utah Beach as, "Very very disrupted. There was gunfire all over. Stranded vehicles, everything was a complete mess. There was dead people around because they hadn't had time to take care of any of them."

The next day a team from the battalion made their way to the beach to guide the seaborne element back to the unit at Chef-du-Pont. With the two firing batteries consolidated at this point in time, Sartain was able to accompany Lieutenant Connelly, the battalion S-4, or supply officer. His memory of the scene at Utah clearly corroborated Miller's, saying, "The beach was a mess, with burned out vehicles and tanks all over the place. I recall several German fighters making runs on the whole beach, but not close to me."

With contact established, Sartain and Connelly led the trucks back to the battalion. The journey wasn't without incident. On the way a pair of German fighters strafed the ammunition loaded column. "We all had to hit the ditches," Sartain said, "But none of our vehicles were hit. You'd see the German aircraft, and then right on their tail would be our own after them."

On the 10th the attack on the Germans was carried through the front lines of the 82nd by the 90th Infantry Division. For the guys in the 319th this meant a welcome break. Most of the men took the chance to soak their chemically impregnated uniforms in whatever ponds or flooded areas they could find in an effort to wash the anti-gas agents out of them. "The men were also given the go-ahead to write letters home and mention that they were still alive and "somewhere in France," but no description of the action they had seen was permitted.

Efforts to build up the number of operative guns continued and "A" Battery returned their borrowed howitzer from the 456th, having salvaged another one of their own to replace it. The 188th Field Artillery Battalion, a North Dakota National Guard outfit, was also attached to the battalion that day. For the time being, the 155mm guns this unit was equipped with would have their brawny artillery managed through the fire direction center of the 319th.

From the 10th to the 12th of June the 508th advanced it's patrols, feeling its way from the consolidated Merderet Bridgeheads to the banks of the Douve on its left flank, and a mile or so west, beyond Hill 30 and the causeway at La Fiere. On one of these patrols, Ed Ryan was with the liaison team assigned to Col. Lindquist. Liaison teams would normally be composed of an officer, a sergeant to assist him, a radio operator, and perhaps one or two extra men to help out as needed. Their job was to stick with the infantry CO, available for any on-the-spot fire missions the commander might call for, or to serve as an ad hoc FO team when no forward observers were available or had OPs already established. Making their way up one road, Ryan thought he could just hear the faint clanking of a tank. "I told Lindquist, there's a tank coming," he remembered. The Colonel answered gruffly, 'You can't hear a tank coming in this country, it's too swampy.' A moment later the point men called out, 'Tank!'"

Everyone hit the ditches which lined the road. "This Mark II comes along with all these Krauts on top, yakking among themselves. They had no idea we were there. One of our guys throws a Gammon grenade in the bogey wheel and they shot the ones on the tank," Ryan explained. Disabled, and surrounded by infantry close enough to toss grenades, the Germans were hopelessly trapped. It was a golden opportunity to take prisoners. After one or two very long minutes of quiet, except for the idle of the engine and pinging of hot metal in the June sun, a GI stepped boldly in front of the tank. He spoke German and demanded that the crew surrender. Instead there was a burst of machinegun fire from the Mark II and the American fell dead. Ryan recalled what followed, "Well, they finished off the tank. Weird thing was that when the medics looked at the GI in the road there wasn't a mark on him. They figured he died of a heart attack."

These few days before the battalion became involved in the efforts to force a crossing over the Douve River, also gave the guys a chance to supplement their K-rations. At one barn, close by the village of Chef-du-Pont and not far from the battery gun positions, there was a group of French women cooking up quantities of hot food. Guys in the outfit could go there, stand in line, and get their mess-kits filled with something that wasn't army chow for the first time in a long while. The luckiest ones were able to lay hands on a piece of gooseberry pie, locally called a Mirabelle. Since Bob Storms was still nursing his cracked ribs at the machinegun position, his crew took along his mess-kit and carried it back to him full.

If farmers were driven away from their homes by the tides of war, unchaparoned chickens were another prize well adapted to the average GI. "This guy in the battery got this chicken and kept it on a string," remembered Sartain of one of his men. "He was going to have the first fried egg he'd had since he left the states. The chicken got up in a tree and laid eggs. Of course they broke and the chicken wouldn't comedown, so they had fried chicken instead."

On Sunday, June 11th, the 319th was visited by Chaplain Reid of the division artillery. Nondenominational religious services were held for the battalion, one battery at a time. Reid, who'd jumped in with the first paratroopers on D-Day, apologized for the damp sheets of "Hymns from Home" he circulated among the men. They were, he explained, still wet from his splash into the Merderet. In fact, Reid swore that when he finally made his way to dry land he found a fish in his pocket, but no one believed him. It didn't matter. Chaplain Reid was the first Chaplain to set foot on French soil and the men took pride in that fact, even if that soil was at the bottom of a river.

Chaplin Reid wasn't the only division level personage who came calling that day. About 1400 Col. Andrew March, Chief of the 82nd's Artillery, and his XO, Lt. Col. Bertsch, arrived at the battalion's CP to brief Major Todd on his unit's role in the next stage of the battle for Normandy. With the division's line now advanced, the battalion was directed to displace to new gun positions beyond the Merderet, from which a crossing of the Douve could be supported. After his superiors left, Todd called a meeting of his battery commanders to brief them on the latest developments and order a reconnaissance of new positions. At 1700 the battery commanders, with skeleton survey crews, departed to scout suitable gun positions.

Sartain described the process of displacing the battery. "We would reconnoiter a new position in the daylight," he said. "The battalion would take a reconnaissance. Colonel Todd or somebody and then "A" Battery and "B" Battery, myself and or Hawkins or whoever had "B" Battery at the time. We'd pick out where the battery was going to be. I'd have MacArthur or one of the top sergeants with the battery look at the position and figure out where each gun was going to go. You had to find an area where you could put all six guns and get a shot off without taking the top of a tree out. That's the way it was."

"I'd stay at the new position with Miller. He had the radio. He had the radio in the jeep and he had the hand held radio you see. But most of the time when the battery was changing position it was radio silence. I would say that was standard operation procedure."

"At night we would move out, we would mark the route with different people

One of the very few photographs known to have been taken in Normandy. This view shows officers attached to "B" Battery. They include Andrew "Bub" Hawkins, Marvin "Shorty" Ragland, Captain "Old Folks" Cargile, Laurence "Cookie" Cook, and Max "Torgie" Torgersen. Note that because Hawkins and Ragland dropped by parachute into Normandy, they are wearing complete or partial jumpsuits. Ragland collection.

Kiss Them As They Went By.

from the unit and Sosa would go back and lead them back. I would say he did this dozens and dozens of times. Sosa was very, very reliable in combat. I liked the sort of juvenile attitude he had at times, but he was always a good driver in combat. He followed instructions and he was very good at leading the battery back to a new position. I don't ever recall Sosa or anybody ever making a wrong turn coming back, and 99 percent of the moves were at night."

The displacement that followed on June 12th would be an exception to this rule, with the battalion moving out at 1130 that morning. The new gun positions were located about a mile southwest of Hill 30, approximately midway between the Merderet and Douve Rivers. By 1500 the batteries were settled in on some of the only higher ground in the immediate area, among orchards and fragmented, incomplete squares of hedgerows around the fields.

The FOs who'd been directing fire along the Merderet line, among them Lieutenants Cook, Gelb, Gutshall, Hawkins, Ragland, and others, all noticed the difficulties which the relatively level ground, compounded by numerous small fields surrounded by hedges of up to 40 feet in height, posed for observation of targets and the efficacy of artillery fire. Ragland described the problem this way, "At Fort Sill, and when you're in training, you set up on this hill and pick out targets to fire on. The funny thing is, when we were in Normandy you didn't set up on a hill. It was all flat and there were all these hedgerows and everything. If the infantry wanted me to set a fire mission on something, they had to show me on the map. I couldn't see it. He might say, put some on this crossroads which is over yonder here. I would just call in the coordinates to the fire direction center in the battery and they'd put fire there. In Italy that was a different story because we were up high enough we could see the enemy positions."

About this time, to allay the problems of limited ground visibility in Normandy, small Piper Cub, L-4 planes, were flown over from England to aid in artillery observation. By June 12th there were three airfields established on the peninsula to accept these

Though this photograph wasn't taken during the Normandy campaign, it does illustrate the "Grasshopper" Piper Cub observation planes which came into use during this time. Sartain Collection.

aircraft as they flew over, though once on the scene they hardly needed a proper runway to land or take off. Known as the "Grasshopper," the L4 was a high-wing monoplane which weighed a scant 740 lbs. With a 185 horsepower engine, it had a maximum speed of 85 MPH and a range of 185 miles. Arranged with two seats, one behind the other, the L-4 could be flown from either position.

Two L-4s were allotted to the battalion, essentially one to each firing battery. A division HQ operations order dated June 24, 1944, stated in part, "When not engaged on fire missions, observers in air will maintain air reconnaissance for enemy battery positions, vehicular movements on roads, troop concentrations or movement, and other signs of enemy activity," and that, "Observers will report all signs of enemy activity or occupation to battalion. Battalion S-2 will forward this information to Division Artillery S-2. The effect of our fire will be reported in detail."

The pilot most closely associated with "A" Battery was a mustached 1st lieutenant named Wimberley M. Morgan, flying plane number 57J-112. A native of Leesburg, Florida, Morgan was, according to Sartain, "A big ole long, lanky guy. He was crazy." Manning, who'd had some experience in the L-4 with Morgan before the invasion, simply described him as "One who loved to be flashy."

Lieutenant Cook was among the first FOs from the 319th assigned to make air observations, searching for targets of convenience and adjusting the effect of fire missions. When asked if he was happy with the assignment, Cook answered, "No, I was kind of put into that. Well, it was scary as hell! Of course I always wanted to fly the GTB line, the go to target and go back line. When we'd go over that front line we'd get shot at, bullets in the wings and everything. I know my first flight out; it was late in the afternoon near dark. I saw on the ground, near a clump of trees, I thought they had one of these kerosene lamps cooking supper. I told the pilot and the pilot took one look at it and said, 'Hell!' He took a dive! It was a machinegun firing at us. That's the first fire I seen, so it seemed close. But I knew what it was from then on."

Cook made his first flight on June 12th. Five days later Sartain gave it a try and quickly became a devotee of air observation. "I really liked it! Those little Piper Cubs were something else. You could really direct artillery from them," he said later. "All you had to do was be very sure to stay out of small arms fire. They would take a pot shot at you once in a while with an AKAK gun. But once they did you got their position and you could blow the hell out of them. We got lost one time and I looked down and there were all these German soldiers in their foxholes hunched down. I patted Morgan on the shoulder and pointed down. Man he almost did a backwards flip getting back out."

Sosa remembered another occasion when "A" Battery's commander was engaged in air observation. "One time Captain Sartain was up there in the airplane firing the artillery," he commented years later. "I think he may have made a direct hit or something. He said, 'God Damn!' He was cussing. He was so happy he was cussing. Well, that tickled the hell out of me. I think somebody talked to him about that, chewed his ass out as soon as he got on the ground because of using profanity. We weren't supposed to do that."

Sartain said when told of Sosa's memory of that day, "I probably made a statement like, 'We got those bastards!' Something like that. You know, I was excited. When you get excited you get carried away and you cuss."

Laurence Cook would eventually make hundreds of sorties in the Piper Cub, becoming one of the most experienced officers in the division where air observation was concerned. "The Piper Cub didn't hold much gasoline. An hour up an hour down, all day long," he remembered. "I'd have a map in my lap. I keep up with it all the time. That's how I identify my target. And then I have radio contact with my battery fire direction center. We were looking at things on the ground, weren't looking at the air much. We were searching the ground, that's where we found our targets. But we had to keep look-out for enemy planes too. If we were spotted by an enemy fighter plane we'd go down to the tree tops."

Enemy fire was not the only danger. The 508th's historian, William Lord, recorded another episode involving air observation planes during the battle for Normandy when the 3rd Battalion's 81mm mortar platoon, "gained dubious fame as the first group of mortarmen to destroy an aircraft in flight in France. Unfortunately, however, the aircraft was a low-flying American artillery observation plane. Flying directly above the mortar positions while a barrage was being laid down, the plane was hit by a shell which destroyed part of its wing and sent it crashing to the ground."

If he'd heard of the incident, Cook would not have been surprised. He had his own brushes with friendly artillery rounds too. "My plane was never hit," he said, "But we had some close calls. You could see the artillery shells coming through the air. The firing from our guns, at the right height you could turn your head and kiss them as they went by. You could actually see them if you turned in the right direction and follow

the shell. You could see it in the air. I thought I was going crazy! Then I said something to one of the other observers in the other plane, and he said, yeah, he seen that too, but he didn't say nothing about it because he thought he was going crazy!"

Between enemy fighters, anti-aircraft fire, and his own artillery projectiles, Cook knew that being shot down was always a distinct possibility. Nevertheless, he wanted to maximize his chances of survival with a reserve parachute. Cook explained his actions this way, "The pilot didn't wear a parachute, but I wore a parachute. I didn't feel like I wanted to go down in a crash if I had a chance. I was gonna jump out even though we's only two three hundred feet up most of the time. Some of the paratroopers weren't but dropped at 200 feet in Normandy. They said you couldn't tell the difference between the chute opening up and hitting the ground."

Lt. Laurence Cook in his A-2 leather jacket, spent many hours forward observing from aircraft during the Normandy campaign. Sartain collection

Evidently, Morgan reveled in dare-devil stunts with the Piper Cub, deriving some delight in the nervousness of his passengers. In Cook's case he would insist that the artillery observer take the controls from time to time, just for fun.

Taking off and landing in small Norman fields, even in the L-4 could be, and was, hazardous. Sosa well remembered seeing one of the planes caught up in telegraph wires. "How they got those guys out of there, I don't know," he remarked.

Early in July, Morgan's Cub, with Sartain as his passenger, clipped some tree tops on takeoff. When the observations were finished and the two returned, Sartain was summoned to Major Todd's tent. He told me, "Charlie, you like being head of a battery?" Sartain said he did. "Well you're gonna either be an aerial observer or you can be a battery commander," Todd told him. "If you want to continue to be battery commander, you have to keep your ass out of that airplane."

While the 4th and 90th Infantry Divisions continued pushing northwesterly toward Cherbourg, the 9th Infantry Division and 82nd Airborne renewed their attacks to the southwest. The plan was for the 508th to make a crossing over the Douve during the pre-dawn hours of June 13th. The objectives were the villages of Coine and Baupte, where a link up with the 101st Airborne Division was to be made.

For the 508th, the site of the destroyed bridge at Beuzeville la Bastille was the planned crossing point. The bridge had been blown by the Germans on the morning of the 10th in the expectation of just such a crossing. In fact, it was Lieutenant Cook, observing the explosion from his OP with the infantry outposts who accordingly reported the fact to the battalion.

By June 12th the 508th, with FO teams supplied from the 319th, was poised on the river's east bank. Ed Ryan and Bernard Tansky, formerly members of Captain Manning's "C" Battery and now in the battalion's HQ Battery, were part of the FO teams assigned to the 2nd Battalion of the 508th. This regiment and the 507th were collectively designated as the 2nd Airborne Infantry Brigade, under the command of General George Howell. Ryan remembered that day. He said, "Me and Tansky were waiting at the side of the road. This General Howell, he came up to us and said, 'Hello Corporal!' Tansky said, 'Hello General!' Tansky was cooking a chicken in his helmet. Tansky was always cooking something. Then Howell asks him, 'Corporal, what are you cooking?' This Howell was a very romantic looking character. He had red parachutes painted on either side of his helmet. When he was tanned up he looked like a movie star."

Howell chatted with the two, declined a bite of Tansky's chicken, and may have noticed Ryan's Italian carbine. In any event the General was reminded that the 319th was one of the few units in Normandy to have seen combat before. "Then he asks me, 'What kind of weapons do you expect here?' I think he knew we'd been through things in Italy and had some experience. I told him what the Krauts would have waiting for us. Howell says, 'We're gonna cross this river. I'm gonna show you how were gonna do this.' He's got this stick and he draws a map in the dirt, kind of a three arc thing going across. He asked me, 'What do you think of that?' I said, 'It'll never work.'"

Frustrated by the jaded attitude of the artillery veterans, Howell moved on. Ryan described what happened next. "There was a couple of Kraut prisoners a few yards down the road, two or three of them," he remembered. "They asked for cigarettes and the paratroopers gave them some. When the General saw that he started yelling, take those cigarettes away from those men, you're supposed to be killing them!"

BATTERY!

Part 16: "It wasn't any big deal."

At one minute after midnight, on June 13th, the attack of the 508th on German positions located on the other side of the Douve began. One company of that regiment crossed the river in the vicinity of the destroyed bridge at Beuzeville la Bastille, rowed across in small pontoon boats provided by the 307th Airborne Engineers. Though they quickly encountered two tanks after deploying on the shore, and dispatched them with bazookas, no other enemy attempted to dislodge them from the western end of the causeway. The Engineers immediately began to rebuild the bridge sufficiently to bear infantry and light vehicles.

Beginning at 0200 hours a massive preparatory barrage of artillery fire was launched through the 319th's Fire Direction Center. The participating battalions included the 319th with its 75mm howitzers, the 105mm howitzers of the 320th, and the mighty 155mm guns of the 188th Field Artillery, as well as artillery from the 90th Infantry Division. The barrage, said to have been personally directed by Major Todd, pounded the southwestern banks of the Douve, shaking the earth and sounding, to the engineers and 508th troopers who were hugging the river banks like "one continuous explosion." This fifteen minute barrage and the assorted other fire missions which followed it over the coming ninety minutes, fairly destroyed the village of Beuzeville-la-Bastille and any prepared defensive works which the Germans might have assembled there to resist the crossing.

Forward observers and liaison officers from the 319th, with their respective teams of enlisted men, were in place with each of the 508th's Battalions as they began crossing the Douve at 0400 hours. Lt. Ragland was assigned to the 1st Battalion, Lt. Gutshall was placed with the 2nd Battalion, and Lt. Irving Gelb of "A" Battery accompanied the Regiment's 3rd Battalion.

The 1st Battalion was the first to cross, seizing its objective of the village of Coigny by 1600 and destroying twelve foolishly unescorted Renault tanks along the way. The 3rd Battalion followed the 1st and then proceeded in a southwesterly direction, taking the regiment's right flank. This group encountered harassing fire from snipers, some of whom turned out to be unenthusiastic members of enemy tank crews who's panzers were destroyed or unserviceable, but otherwise did not come upon serious resistance.

The 2nd Battalion was meanwhile proceeding swiftly south toward Baupte, where they were to link up with the 101st Airborne Division. All went surprisingly well until within two kilometers of the village, where they ran smack into a significant German force with no apparent intention of retreating.

Radio Operator Ed Ryan was part of the FO team with Lt. John D. Gutshall, embedded with the 508th's 2nd Battalion as it approached the village. "We ran all the way to Baupte. There weren't any Krauts until we got there," said Ryan of that day. Describing the normal course of events when encountering a stubborn enemy position, Ryan's account of the procedure may well have been about what took place on the late afternoon of June 13th. "The doefeet were on the move and of course the FO team stays right with them," he said. "Two columns of infantry go up a road. They'd run into resistance, the point would. He'd holler he'd want the bazooka up front. Then he'd want the machinegun up front. Then the next thing he'd want is artillery up front. So everybody ran up and did their job."

That is just what happened to the 508th's 2nd Battalion as it approached the village that day. Patrols determined that the northern edge of Baupte held a well positioned defensive perimeter supported by tanks and artillery. At 1615, the 2nd Battalion attacked, but met with only limited success. A German counterattack followed and it became clear that artillery would be needed to dislodge the enemy from Baupte.

Sartain's battery of the 319th had already crossed the Douve by this time, and was in position by 1805 hours, while the rest of the battalion was en route. The batteries of the 320th had crossed as well and were also ready to let loose with their 105s. At 2045 the first of three "A" Battery fire missions began. The targets included troop concentrations, infantry moving on roadways, and other defensive points. Altogether it amounted to another 118 rounds beyond the hundreds fired early that morning.

As dusk began settling in, the 508th troopers resumed their attack and started driving the Germans from the village. Apparently the 100th Panzer Replacement Battalion, a unit previously engaged on Hill 30, was occupying the town with a sizable number of supporting infantry, including at least one battalion of the German 1049th Infantry Regiment. The 508th's 2nd Battalion had a couple of 57mm anti-tank guns from the 80th Airborne Anti-Aircraft Battalion with them, and a vicious fight erupted in the gathering twilight. Lt. Gutshall's FO crew found themselves right in the thick of it, as paratroopers and Germans fought their way door to door through the streets of Baupte.

"That little town, it had one main street in it," remembered Ryan. "These German tanks, Renault tanks, came down the street. Six of them shooting in every direction. Our guys with the anti tank gun got one. One of them, I'll never forget it, he was bitching that they kept putting him and his anti-tank gun right up front, so he taped a bayonet to the muzzle. They shot those tanks up. It was a real mess.

"I remember this Kraut soldier laying in the gutter with his hand shot off. He was just screaming and moaning. He kept saying, 'Hande, hande!' He was maybe seventeen, you know. I thought about going over and shooting him, but I couldn't do it."
"Then, can you believe it, in the middle of all this mess I have to take a crap. So I run up behind this house and there's a privy in the yard. I got in and when I was done I pulled up my drawers, but when I started to open the door a Kraut with a burp gun took a shot at me. Brip, brip! I tried to step out again and it happened again. Brip, brip! That Kraut had me trapped in the shithouse. My friend Henry Broski is outside. I yelled to him, some Kraut has me trapped in the privy! He says, OK, swing that door one more time. So I did and, sping! He got him. He saved my life."

By the end of the day the 508th's 2nd Battalion was in control of Baupte, along with a vehicle park full of German trucks, munitions, gasoline, and rations. Numerous Renault tanks were destroyed and the 100th Panzer Replacement Battalion ceased to exist as a fighting formation.

West of Coigny the Douve River takes an abrupt turn to the north. Thus, at the same time that the 508th had crossed the river and was advancing in a generally southwestwardly direction, the 325th Glider infantry and 505th PIR were still on the northern bank and attacking due west toward Saint-Sauveur-le-Vicomte, an important road juncture upstream on the German side of the Douve. All day on the 14th, the 508th having made contact with the 101st Airborne south of Baupte, continued to simultaneously press the enemy westward. Supporting fire from the 319th was maintained at a level every bit as intensive as that at the opening of the offensive over the Douve the day before. For example, in addition to numerous limited fire missions of two or three dozen rounds on specific targets scattered throughout the day of June 14th, there was a massive 334 round barrage hurled at enemy infantry positions at 10:30, and another 251 round bombardment at 1950 placed on a German mortar battery. Thankfully, "A" Battery was once again at its full six gun strength, having been delivered another salvaged 75 pack howitzer that morning from division ordnance.

Meanwhile, as the fire missions continued, trucks brought a steady supply of fresh ammunition to the gun positions. "As soon as you'd get a fire mission, then the ammunition crew goes into work," said Mahlon Sebring, one of the gunners manning the howitzers during that period. "They come along, dumping off ammunition, rolling it off the back end of the truck. It comes cased up three to a pack, wrapped up in wood with wire around it. You take an axe and cut the wire and knock the wood off and it's in cardboard tubes."

Having secured the southern flank of the front at Baupte, the division's attention was now concentrated entirely to the west, to carry through with the intended cut off of the Cotentin peninsula. This phase of operations called for the 507th to advance its line to Vindefontaine, a town situated on high ground beyond a southern tributary of the Douve River. In preparation for this next offensive, the 507th relieved the 508th late on June 15th. The 319th, as was customary for supporting artillery, remained in place, lending fire to whatever infantry unit was rotating through its sector of the line.

On the 16th, in preparation for this attack, and to alleviate depleted supplies, orders were received that the battalion would "collect all abandoned ammo, turning same over to nearest unit which can use it, or to division ammo dump" and that the battalion was also to "collect hand grenades and turn them over to infantry units or to division ammo officer." Sartain remembers that it was about this time that another housekeeping order came down, instructing the men to turn in all serviceable life vests. "Well, you know that Mae West is only serviceable if you haven't pulled the CO2 cartridge on it. But when that vest is inflated it makes a pretty good pillow, so anyone who hadn't inflated their Mae West already did so then. I don't think we turned in a single one of them."

All the while, fire missions intended to soften up the German defenses were continued at a high volume. Each day was a full day's work, with many of the gunners stripped to the waist as they fired their howitzers in the June sun. Neither did darkness bring an end to the cannoneers labor, as the bombardment of targets would go on through the night.

"A" Battery fired 289 rounds on June 16th and another 391 on the 17th, much of the latter in counter battery duels. German counter battery fire had become an increasing problem since crossing the Douve, in part because of additional German divisions rushed in to contain the American toehold in France, but also because the enemy wisely anticipated probable future locations of American batteries and already had these spots zeroed in. To mitigate this problem, Major Todd directed that imitation gun positions would be set up before any actual displacement in order to test the new position's security. On the afternoon of the 17th, in expectation of the coming offensive movement, Major Wilcoxson reconnoitered new locations to which the battalion could be repositioned after the front lines moved ahead.

These new gun positions had to be chosen carefully. Private Orrin Miller was one of the guys detailed for this job. "At night they would take four or five of us out of each gun crew and we would go up and set up a mock gun with camouflage nets and put up a log for a gun barrel to make it look from the air like it was set up," he recalled. "Then they would observe that the next day. If it got hit with gun fire, artillery shells in that area, then they wouldn't move us up. I did that one time three straight nights in a row before they'd allow us to move up. Every time we set one up we'd be getting shelled the next day." Miller was almost certainly remembering the nights of the 17th, 18th, and 19th of June, culminating in an actual displacement of the battalion on the 20th.

The anticipated attack of the 507th was scheduled to begin just after midnight on the morning of June 19th. First, though, leading elements had to be brought into position on the opposite side of the flooded tributary. For this mission, Lieutenant Marvin Ragland was designated as the reconnaissance FO with the 507th's 1st Battalion. Late that night he found himself posted with a platoon of troopers, ordered to accompany them as they forded the river and establish a beachhead before the main elements launched their attack. "We had to cross this river," Ragland remembered. "I don't know if it was a river or just a flooded area, but it was above waist deep. We crossed it at night under a harassing fire." The river was, in fact, over five feet deep in places and at least 50 feet wide. It was necessary for Ragland to help his enlisted crew wade across, holding their radio equipment above their shoulders as they groped their way through the darkness, under fire and in water up to their necks.

"Well, the funny part of it is, we got on the other side and the lieutenant with the infantry group, he had to report back to his commander," Ragland recalled. In the darkness, soaking wet and cloaked in the undergrowth along the riverbank, the infantry officer radioed into his battalion that his pathfinder group had successfully reached the opposite shore.

"I don't remember the commander's name," said Ragland, "But he asked him if he knew where he was at and where he was supposed to go." The paratroop officer had to admit to his superior, 'No sir, I don't know where I'm at.' The voice which came back was likely that of Major Benjamin "Red" Pearson, CO of the 507th's 1st Battalion. Pearson, clearly angered by the inadequate reply, demanded to know if any other officer was there. 'Well, there's some Lieutenant here from the artillery,' the 507th Lieutenant answered. Pearson ordered, 'Well put him on!'"

Ragland recalled his conversation with the Major. "I got on the radio and he said, 'Do you know where you're at?' I said, 'Yeah, I know where we're at.' 'And do you know where you're going?' I told him, 'Yeah.' He said, 'Well, you take over.'"

Though he didn't know any of these 507th men, orders were orders and Major Pearson was very clear about what he wanted. Ragland looked around him and noticed one man with a Thompson submachine gun. "Well, you've got that automatic weapon," Ragland said. "Why don't you lead the way and the rest of us will follow along." Ragland's party felt their way forward a couple of hundred yards when the point man heard a noise and let loose with a burst from his Tommy-gun. Then a concealed voice called out from the bushes, "Joe, is that you?"

Joe was the hapless lieutenant whom Pearson had relieved of command. The voice was that of another officer from the same company with whom Ragland's group was supposed to rendezvous. With the two groups united, Ragland could see that "Joe" now had his bearings and returned the platoon to his leadership.

After creeping ahead another half mile, the force reached its objective, a crossroad on the way to Vindefontaine. Now it was Ragland's turn to radio his superiors. "I called in to Major Todd and said, 'I'm here in position but I can't really help them. My map got so wet I can't read it.' He said, 'Well, just come back and get another one.' So I did."

Ragland made his way back across the river to 319th Headquarters, obtained fresh maps, then recrossed the river for a third time that night. This time he had his maps safely stowed in his helmet, and found his way back to Joe's platoon in time for the launch of the attack.

All that day and into the night Ragland directed artillery fire, keeping right up with the attacking troopers as they advanced through a fusillade of artillery, mortar, small arms, and machine gun fire. "One of their officers suggested that I climb up a tree to get a better look, but I told him that wouldn't be a very good idea." For his performance during the attack on Vindefontaine, Lieutenant Marvin Ragland was later awarded the Bronze Star for Valor. The decoration came as a surprise to him. Even decades later, Ragland was reluctant to overstate his actions on that day in June, preferring to simply comment, "For some reason or other, during that whole riggamarole, they decided that I should have a Bronze Star. Well, I don't know, I was just doing what I was getting paid for. It wasn't any big deal."

Before the day was through "A" Battery alone fired an incredible 555 rounds at such diverse targets as fixed defensive positions, "enemy strongpoints," artillery, tanks, and infantry formations. "That's a long, drawn out haul sometimes," remembered Orrin Miller, who'd been reassigned back on a gun crew. "We actually burnt the barrels right out of our guns. I don't even know how many rounds, and the shells were so hot that the ejectors wouldn't eject them all the way. Then you had to reach in there with your hands and finish pulling the shell case out of the barrel."

Another effect of prolonged, continuous firing on the 75s was remembered by Kenneth Smith, who observed, "You'd fire the gun and it'd kick back and stay back. We'd have to shove it back up, it got so hot. The springs got so hot it wouldn't recoil." Indeed, beginning with the evening of the 13th and for the entire time leading up to and including the offensive, the battalion's batteries barely stopped firing for more than a few hours at any one time. Deafened by the muzzle blasts, the cannoneers worked their pieces as if in a stupor. Rappi, acting sergeant of his crew, was so exhausted he lay on the ground, dead asleep within a few feet of his men as they loaded and fired their gun, then reloaded and fired again and again and again.

In the colossal arm-wrestle over the Cotentin Peninsula, it was becoming clear to the Germans that if they were unable to keep the Americans from cutting their way from the channel to the Atlantic coast, they could not prevent the capture of both Cherbourg and several of their divisions. Consequently they fought savagely to hold Vindefontaine and the highways which it lay astride. The battle for the town was, for the 507th, every bit as fierce as the fight for Baupte had been for the 508th, but by the end of the day its capture left the path to the sea almost within sight.

At sundown on the 20th, the 319th began displacing to its new positions beyond Vindefontaine. Since the Germans were in the habit of destroying all bridges as they retreated, engineers were obliged to construct temporary spans over the same river in which Lieutenant Ragland had gained so much wading experience a couple of nights before. The bridges were, however, makeshift, and it was necessary to disassemble the howitzers and take them across in pieces. The whole process required time. "B" Battery crossed first, and was in position before midnight, but it wasn't until 0730 on the morning of the 21st that "A" Battery was ensconced in its new emplacement and ready to fire.

IT WASN'T ANY BIG DEAL.

Over the following several days the 319th took a more defensive posture in consideration of the nearly 25 mile wide sector of the front line which the 82nd was charged with holding. Restrictions were placed on the number of rounds the battalion could expend due to shortages of artillery ammunition. Meanwhile, enemy artillery became more aggressive than ever. For example, at 1700, on the afternoon of June 22nd, the battalion CP came under a severe barrage. One shell landed only 40 feet from Captain Wimberley's tent. Amazingly, no one was hit, but forty minutes later it was "B" Battery's turn to take a pounding, this time with casualties, but no loss of life.

When a communication from the division's G-4 was received at battalion HQ wanting a rundown of exactly how much transportation would be required to bring the battalion to a port or beachhead, the rumor that the unit might soon be relieved circulated quickly. The hope of immanent relocation back to England amounted to nothing. On the 23rd, each man in the battalion was issued a new shirt, trousers, and pair of socks. It wasn't really a consolation for remaining in the line, but at least this time the clothing didn't have the chemical impregnation of their previous wardrobe.

Captain Hawkins of HQ Battery, who'd been missing since he paratrooped into Normandy with the 508th on June 6th and was assumed killed, suddenly appeared at battalion HQ at about this time. He'd been taken prisoner immediately after his jump and was held until it became clear that Cherbourg would be invested by siege. At that point he, and a substantial number of other captured paratroopers were released. "Well, they had to," commented Sartain. "They didn't want to mess with them and they didn't want to get in trouble shooting them, so they turned them all loose. Hawkins was one of them. A lot of 508th guys too."

The battalion had now been in Normandy for over two weeks, and in the breather after the taking of Vindefontaine an issue generating some internal tension within the 319th presented itself for Major Todd's consideration. The matter revolved around Doctor Hebert and his supposed failure to come to Captain Manning's aid on the night of June 6th. At the time, Sergeant Marshall made no effort to conceal his anger and disgust at what he considered to be an outrage against one of the most beloved officers in the battalion. Within a few days gossip about Hebert and Manning spread through the battalion like wildfire. "The word got out about it and from then on everybody in the battalion, officers included, gave Hebert the cold shoulder," remembered Sartain of the episode. "The privates had to salute him because he was a Captain, but nobody would sit with him at mess, nobody would give him anything."

As the story went, Doctor Hebert flatly refused to risk enemy fire, despite the full knowledge that Captain Manning lay grievously injured directly across the field. True or not, the actual facts of the incident made little difference given Manning's massive popularity with officers and enlisted men alike. Indeed, no one appears to have made much of an attempt to withhold judgment or consider Hebert's situation on that night. When Manning resisted measures to evacuate him to the beach the following day, his actions only served to make the Doctor's performance look all the more despicable. Then Doctor Dibble's efforts a few days later to reach the wounded troopers on Hill 30 contributed to make Hebert, by comparison, even less worthy of respect.

Though Sartain could understand that the Doctor was himself in a dangerous position, it was also difficult for him to remain objective, even years later. As he put it, "Guys were crawling across the fields to help everybody get out of the gliders and everything else, but he was holed up in his little niche across the field. It was a fairly nice sized field, no question about that, and everybody was being shot at, but he wouldn't do

BATTERY!

it. He didn't want to expose himself, so the men got even with him."

Major Todd finally brought the matter up at a meeting of the battalion's senior officers. After the current affairs of the outfit were covered, Todd asked before dismissing the group, "Alright gentlemen, what gives with Captain Hebert?" The question was met with quiet, though a few officers glanced furtively at each other. Finally the Major broke the silence and said, "OK, cut it out. What gives with Hebert?"

Sartain remembered what happened next. "Somebody told him that Hebert wouldn't crawl across the field to tend to Manning. So Todd said, 'OK, that's it.' So even Todd put the cold shoulder to him, you see."

Whether the reaction of the men in the outfit was justified or not, Doctor Hebert became persona non grata, an outcast, ostracized, a nonentity within the battalion. "It really affected him," said Sartain, reflecting on the event later in his life. "It finally got so bad that he ultimately prevailed upon Todd to transfer him to division medic and get him completely away from the 319th. He got transferred later to a divisional medical unit. Whatever really happened, it'll be something he'll have to live with."

On the evening of June 28th the 319th was subjected to one of the heaviest bombardments of the Normandy campaign. This time the positions of "B" Battery and the HQ Battery were hit especially hard, with casualties in both. In the HQ Battery the loss was more severe, with Lieutenant Blank and four enlisted men wounded, as well as the death of two of the outfit's most well-liked men. Ed Ryan remembered it, "We had such intense artillery fire that day. I never saw the cows get down and crawl before, but they did there, it was so bad. Keith Cormany, him and Lieutenant Poole, they both got killed. They was laying in a ditch in Normandy, I saw them there. Lieutenant Poole was a runner you know, he ran against Glenn Cunningham for the championship of the world. Frank V. Poole, he was an athlete, he didn't know anything about smoking and drinking, but he was a nice guy. Keith Cormany, he was a professional wrestler in civilian life and he could lick any man in the battery. He was our first sergeant when we had "C" Battery with Captain Manning. A great guy. His wife at home had just had a baby. We took up a collection in the battery and sent her $500. She said she couldn't accept it and sent it back, so we bought a savings bond in the kid's name instead."

In at least one case the German shells were not deadly at all. William Lord, in his history of the 508th recorded that during one barrage at the end of the month, there was "the discovery of a German artillery shell which contained not explosives, but merely notes in Polish encouraging the Allied war effort. The resistance movement in German-occupied countries was effective in one case at least." The Americans also loaded some of their artillery shells with leaflets encouraging German soldiers to desert, though there is no record that such rounds were ever fired by the 319th.

That same day the restriction on what information could be written in letters was relaxed. Most everybody made a point of describing to those at home some of what they'd been through, particularly the experience of a combat glider mission. Staff Sergeant Bob McArthur's letter to the folks in Mississippi, headed with the stiplified "Somewhere in France" was typical, and said in part, "Once again I landed all in one piece and once again I had some very close calls. I guess I'm just the luckiest guy in the world because if I hadn't been, I couldn't be sitting here in France writing you now. We landed here in France on D-day behind enemy lines, but I'll tell you one thing, those Jerries strictly paid for everything. We caused more confusion behind enemy lines than the Germans have ever known. I'll tell you something else, these Jerries here in France are easier whipped than those in Italy."

IT WASN'T ANY BIG DEAL.

There was some truth to McArthur's observation about the enemy. Many of the German troops the Allies encountered, particularly during the first two weeks of the Battle for Normandy, were German in name only. One case in point would be the 795th Georgian Battalion, one of the units dispersed in the area where the 319th's gliders landed. This unit was composed of Soviet prisoners who'd chosen service in the Wehrmacht over the abject misery in which captured Red army soldiers were kept. Foreign conscripts from Eastern Europe actually composed a large proportion of the Axis troops manning the coastal defenses of the Atlantic Wall. These so called "Ost Battalions" were led by German officers and sergeants, but were otherwise composed of Poles, Ukrainians, or members of other ethnic groups under Nazi domination. Truly German units, such as the 100th Panzer Replacement Battalion, were often made up of poorly trained middle aged men or teenagers. These units were frequently armed with obsolete and inferior equipment; much of it, like the Renault tanks, captured from Germany's defeated neighbors. The one handed German soldier in Baupte whom Ed Ryan recalled was, by his description, "a kid of sixteen or seventeen." Even some of the best German units in Normandy, like the paratroops which faced American airborne men at Saint Mere Eglise, had an average age in their ranks of less than 18 years. Notwithstanding all this, there were well trained veteran divisions on the field in Normandy too, and young troops, when adequately armed and trained could perform very well in combat. Having been raised since early childhood in an atmosphere of Nazi indoctrination, they often fought with a fanaticism which counterbalanced their inexperience, particularly when placed in elite units such as Flaschirmjaeger (paratroop) or Waffen SS Divisions.

On the last day of June the battalion received seven replacement officers from the base camp at Papillon Hall. With the high proportion of officers who were casualties in the initial landings compounded by losses during the subsequent fighting, the acute shortage of officers and trained FOs had become a serious problem. To help the situation, several Lieutenants from the 456th had been on temporary duty with the 319th since the landings, and Sergeant Johnson was still serving as "A" Battery's XO. Among the three 2nd lieutenants assigned to "A" Battery were Marvin R. Fellman, from Pipestone, Minnesota, and Joseph Mullen of Kentland, Indiana. The two had been part of a second installment of replacements sent to the 319th immediately after it departed for the Security Camp. Kept at Papillon Hall to learn the ropes while the rest of the unit was in Normandy, these men would fill what were expected to be depleted ranks of the outfit when it returned from France. In the case of these seven officers, however, they were needed immediately, and were accordingly sent off to fill the gaps in the 319th's command structure at the Normandy front.

Marvin R Fellman was born in Red Lake Falls, Minnesota in 1919. Growing up in the nearby village of Casnovia, he worked in the family grocery store. Marvin attended high school in Pipestone, then spent one year at Macalaster College in Minneapolis, but was obliged to return home to help run the family store when his father became ill. Fellman began his military service in April, 1942, at Fort Sill, Oklahoma, where he completed his basic training. Because Fellman had some college experience, he was immediately considered eligible for Officer Candidate School and was commissioned as a second lieutenant in November of that year.

Joseph Mullen entered the service right out of High School. Because of his superior score on the IQ test at the induction camp, Joe was selected for Officer's Candidate School, despite his youth, having only been born in September, 1925. After receiving his 2nd lieutenant's bars, he started his military career in the Army Air Force where he began receiving training as a pilot at an air field in Texas. Early on, however, Joe thought it would be a great idea to take his trainer on a low altitude pass over the swimming pool at a nearby girl's college. If the co-eds were impressed, the army wasn't. The exploit brought Mullen's pilot career to an end and he was transferred to the field artillery. By the spring of 1944, 19 year old 2nd lieutenant Joe Mullen was at a replacement depot in Wales, where he became friendly with Marvin Fellman.

Lieutenant Fellman almost certainly became Joe Mullin's closest buddy in "A" Battery, but by the time he could be interviewed for this book, a stroke had sharply limited Fellman's ability to communicate verbally. Nonetheless, when he heard the name Mullen, he recognized it immediately. Fellman's voice swelled with emotion and he somehow found the words to speak, saying, "He was a good kid. He was a heck of a good guy!" Lieutenant Cook became another close friend of Mullen's, and when asked about him commented, "Oh yeah. I remember him very well. He was the finest little boy I ever knew. I thought the world of him. He was young, but he was a good fighter."

When asked about Lieutenant Mullen, Sartain remembered him vividly and held many of the same opinions. "Mullen, yeah, Joe Mullen," he said. "He came to us as a 2nd lieutenant of course, but he was a gutsy little peck of wood, he really was. He was short and he smoked a cigar all the time. Always had a cigar stuffed in his mouth and the cigar was as big as he was! If that wasn't an incongruous looking situation. Little ole Joe Mullen with the damn cigar in his mouth. He was a little tiger."

As June drew to a close the battalion was informed that they were now qualified, through an act of Congress, to receive an additional $35 per month as glidermen. Of course the news was well received. After all, not drawing any extra compensation for what was clearly every bit as dangerous a job as parachuting into combat, had long been a bone of contention among those in the glider service. It is doubtful, though, that there was much celebration. Combat since the landings had been non-stop and the casualties high. German artillery had hit the 319th right between the eyes and killed some of its best men during the days immediately preceding the news. Additionally, the guys were exhausted from the almost incessant cold rain which had been falling since the night of June 19th. Sleeping in a foxhole flooded several inches deep in water was nearly impossible, and limited the response to hazardous duty pay to an unappreciative grumble of, "Yeah, well it's about time."

On July 2nd orders came through promoting Major Todd to lieutenant colonel. The promotion was welcome by everyone, not just because they felt Todd well deserved the rank, after all, he'd been in command of the battalion since October of 1943, but also because, as Sartain said, "We were afraid they were going to ship in a lieutenant colonel from some other unit. Maybe that's why they waited on Todd's colonelcy, it was a battlefield promotion. But Colonel Todd was a good commander, really good. He was low key but he knew what was going on at every level in the battalion, and he was constantly looking out for the welfare of his men."

Sosa saw Todd from the perspective of an enlisted man, but his assessment was just as positive. "Damn good man," he said. "He was tall, kinda beefie, red faced. To me he looked like a cowboy, but just as nice as he could be. The Colonel, I don't know how he treated the battery commanders, but when it comes to talking to enlisted men, he was real nice."

With Todd's command of the battalion now a permanent position, the discontent with Major Wilcoxson was brought more to the fore. The discussion of this point seems to have circulated independently among officers and enlisted men without each being aware of the other's feelings, but the parallel gripes were the same. In simple terms, the men felt that Wilcoxson lacked intestinal fortitude in combat, particularly given the level of dissatisfaction he expressed with everyone else's performance. Respect for him suffered accordingly. Dislike of the Major had been building since Fort Bragg, then Maiori ruined his reputation as a combat officer, and the fiasco surrounding the knit caps on the statues at Papillon Hall destroyed any residual respect in the battalion, branding him as a martinet of the worst kind. If Major Wilcoxson had a chance to redeem himself in the eyes of his command during the fighting in Normandy, the consensus is that he clearly did not take advantage of the opportunity.

Condemnation of the battalion's XO was universal, and more than 60 years later veterans of the 319th expressed their anger without prompting. "He was not only a pain in the ass but he was trouble all the time," said Ed Ryan. "He wasn't what you'd call a leader of men like Colonel Mendez from the 508th, or Captain Manning, or anything like that. Those guys were real people, but not this idiot."

Rappi simply commented in his taciturn way that Major Wilcoxson was, "a terrible sort."

When the Major's name was mentioned, Silas Hogg became enraged, and poured out a lifetime of pent up bitterness. "Out of combat the son of a bitch never let you rest a minute," he spat. "In combat he hid, I mean actually hid, H I D! Actually got under something! He hid, and just as quick as we'd get out of combat he'd show himself and he'd give us hell because we were resting. I remember, I remember good! Yeah, and he scratched his ass all the time."

Sartain looked back on Wilcoxson with a mixture of bemusement and disgust, saying, "Well, Wilcoxson didn't have any guts, and he was a real chicken kind of a guy. When he'd hear some shells coming in he would scoot. He had about as much courage as Bertsch did, which was none." The resentment toward Major Wilcoxson was building and building for a long time, just festering. The guys hoped the Major would somehow just go away, in much the same way Colonel Bertsch had gone. Yet, under the circumstances of combat in Normandy, Fidgety Phil was the Battalion XO and there was nothing which could be done about it, at least for the time being.

The battalion had already displaced on July 1st to new positions further west in preparation for the next move against the Germans. This offensive action was planned for the morning of July 3rd. its ultimate objective was the town of La Haye du Puits, which would have effectively placed the right flank of the VIII Corps, to which the 82nd was now attached, on the Atlantic shore and facing south. First, though, the high ground of Hills 131 and 95, which guarded the roads leading to the town, would have to be taken.

Hill 131 was the highest point for some distance in the surrounding bocage countryside, much of which was nearly underwater from days of heavy rain. On the morning of July 3rd, low, water saturated clouds which were dominating the sky left its summit obscured from view. The gloomy weather only served to give the prominence a menacing, ominous appearance. According to plan, Hill 131 would be attacked by the 505th and 508th together. With the 507th held in reserve, the 325th would assault Hill 95.

The 319th, along with all the 81mm mortars of the 508th and other artillery from the VIII Corps, opened its barrage on Hill 131 at 0615 hours, firing 255 rounds at enemy positions obscured in clouds. The Germans countered by dropping a few shells in the forward positions of the American lines, a ruse which gave the impression that

BATTERY!

friendly artillery was falling short. Naturally, the American batteries would cease firing, recalibrate their guns and double check their coordinates, all in all disrupting the effect of the preparatory barrage. Despite this subterfuge, the leading elements of the 505th and 508th reached the crest of Hill 131 by mid-morning, and from that vantage point they could see the Atlantic Ocean.

The Germans counterattacked fiercely through much of the day, trying to retake the hill. Close artillery support from the 319th was required the entire time. Fire missions followed at frequent intervals: a crossroads, 44 rounds, a bridge, 72 rounds, response to mortar fire, 42 rounds, enemy infantry, 102 rounds with "good effect, machine gun nest in house, 76 rounds, and others. The day's work outstripped the fire missions against Hill 30, Baupte, and Vindefontaine. Altogether "A" Battery alone fired an impressive 590 rounds before, after midnight, they were ordered to displace again, with the howitzers in their new gun emplacements well before dawn.

Ed Ryan was posted as a radioman with Captain Hawkins, the liaison officer with the 508th. "The thing I remember was some hot combat," he said. "On hill 131, on a dirt road going up, they had a stone building there with a bunch of Krauts in it. They tried getting at it with an anti tank gun, but it didn't work. Finally some guy with a bazooka went and fired at the building. It blew all the shingles off the top. Man, I never saw slates fly like that. What was left of the Krauts inside surrendered."

"We'd been told there was to be no vulgarity on the radio," Ryan continued. "Some infantry got on the radio frequency and asked if they could fire on the hill too. Hawkins gets on the radio. He was kind of hot tempered, and yells, 'Anybody can fire on this fucking hill!' He said that. He was a total rebel, that Hawkins."

By evening Hill 131 was secure, but the assault on Hill 95 had not gone as well. Finding its left flank exposed, the 325th was diverted toward the east, while two battalions of the 508th were ordered to assault Hill 95 on the morning of the fourth.

During the change of position that night, Colonel Todd relieved Lieutenant Ragland from his assignment as one of the liaison officers with the 508th, effectively allowing him to sit out the rest of the fight, and replaced him with Lieutenant Raymond Carey from "A" Battery. The decision was not made from any deficit on Ragland's part. On the contrary, he, and other battalion officers, had been up front with the infantry, directing artillery fire since the landings, and doing an admirable job of it. That was nearly a month ago. These men deserved a rest. With the addition of seven new replacement officers, Colonel Todd could finally afford to pull them, here and there, from the FO teams and place them on a much needed rest status at the battalion's HQ for a few days relief.

As the 508th 's attack on Hill 95 got under way on the morning of July 4th, it was met with a terrific pushback of artillery, machine gun, and mortar fire. From the start, it was a tough day for the 319th. The assault had only just been launched when a mortar round landed square among the liaison team from "A" Battery, wiping them out. Lieutenant Carey, along with Corporal Eugene Smith and Private Theodore Ratlief were all killed. When the news came in, Colonel Todd had Ragland summoned to him and explained what happened. "Well," he said, "I guess we'll send you forward again to be an observer."

"Ragland was stunned by Carey's death, as were others. Sartain remembered Carey as, "Quite a guy. He loved children and would play with the children in Italy. Carey's wife had a baby while he was overseas, but he never got to see her."

Years later Ragland was still troubled by Carey's death, having only traded places with him a few hours before. "I told my wife once, I think Lieutenant Carey must have taken my place," Ragland said regretfully. "He wasn't there but half a day and he got killed. You just don't know."

Ragland collected up a liaison team and reported in to the infantry pinned down at the foot of Hill 95. "Later that day they started moving forward," he continued. "There was some rounds come in. Some guy was a sniper back in the hill someplace. They picked off a couple of infantry guys. Then the rest of us started out and they threw in some mortar rounds. Anyway, a couple of more guys got hit. There was a blast and I hit the ditch. I did get skinned up on the arm, a flesh wound on the arm, but mostly I got a concussion out of it. The first thing I knew the rest of them were gone. So I got up and started out and got to the road and here come a jeep. For some reason this driver, I don't know who he was, decided he better do something, so he took me back to our battalion aid station. Colonel Todd got a hold of the doctor and said, get him patched up. And so I got wounded that same day, the same day Lieutenant Carey got killed."

Hill 95 was like some kind of giant meat-grinder. Shortly after Lieutenant Ragland turned up at battalion HQ, bleeding, dazed, and disoriented from blast concussion," A" Battery's Lieutenant Irving Gelb, assigned as FO with the 508th's 3rd Battalion, was brought in too, wounded, another casualty of Hill 95. All the while the 319th kept up an unrelenting fire on the enemy. Before the day was through, "A" Battery alone fired an astounding 617 rounds from its pack howitzers. Independence Day turned out to be their heaviest delivery of fire so far in the campaign.

In the face of determined German counterattacks, July 5th wasn't any quieter. The 319th fired without cessation from 0800 to 2300, with 963 rounds let loose by the battalion, including 308 rounds directed at a spirited German counterattack, a 128 round barrage dropped on an enemy motor park, setting numerous vehicles afire, and a 156 round barrage to finish off the day. July 6th, on the other hand was relatively quiet, with only a couple of hundred rounds fired. The tide of battle for La Haye du Puits was al-

"C" Battery men, including Lieutenant Ray Carey who was later killed in action in Normandy, cleaning weapons at Camp Ballyscullion, Northern Ireland. Sartain collection.

ready decided. Other divisions of the VIII Corps carried the attack home and on the 7th the town was in American hands.

The battle for Hills 131 and 95 were the last serious combat for the 82nd in Normandy. The battalion remained in position, taking on fire missions in a more casual way, since the weight of the offensive had now been transferred to other divisions. Once again, rumors began to circulate that the 319th would soon be relieved from combat, a story which gained credibility when the battalion was notified of the location of mobile showers on the evening of the 9th. Stronger confirmation followed in the form of a directive the next day that excess ammunition was to be turned over to division ordnance. Then, at 2300 official word came down that the outfit would be relieved as of 0800 on the 11th.

If anyone surveyed the guys that morning as they made their way to the rear, they would have seen a lot of exhausted young men with faces drawn and whiskered, hands grimy with grease, their fingernails blackened from digging out hundreds of fox-holes and gun emplacements. Their uniforms were torn, wrinkled, faded, and mud spattered, with frayed edges. Some of their helmets had the paint burned off the top from being used as cooking pots or vessels to heat up water to shave with. Bits and pieces of German equipment could be seen tucked in their gear or dangling from belts. Some had souvenir German helmets with them. Others had picked up pistols, caps, or odd pieces of regalia. Little German issue kerosene cook stoves were a popular acquisition, especially for those who were on FO or liaison teams, spending three or four days at a time in forward outposts, away from any mess kitchens. There was also an expression of relief and growing realization that, for now, they'd made it.

The guys were taken to a processing point where they were told to put their personal belongings in a sack furnished for this purpose, then get in line for the first real opportunity to wash with soap and water in six weeks. Casimir Sobon remembered it as "a big trailer truck with showers in it. You went in one end, you took your clothes off, threw them on a pile, went through, took a shower, came out the other end, and they issued you new clothes. So when you went back to England you looked like you were in the parade."

Though they retained their helmets, garrison caps and gear, there were brand new shirts, trousers, socks, underwear, and field jackets for everyone. The best part, and quite a surprise, was the issue of jump boots to every glider rider. The hated canvas leggings, a constant reminder of their step-child status in the airborne division, were never to be seen again.

As the cleanup continued there was plenty of hot water for a close shave. It was great to be clean again and the weariness from lack of sleep even felt more remote. Everyone was collecting up their gear, combing their hair or enjoying a cigarette when a couple of stragglers made their appearance, looking like Rip van Winkles in olive drab. "Dirty Joe Meaghan and I were the last ones to be relieved," claimed Ed Ryan. "They told us we had to report down to a place where we'd get our new fresh uniforms and some other stuff. We went down there and everybody's ready to go. They've already got their new uniforms and they're all showered. Anyway, the Colonel's down there. Todd says to us, 'You two clowns got down here late. Now I want you to go to the end of that column and don't you ever move off it.' Here we are, we looked like shit. We came right out of the foxhole. What a mess we were, terrible, you could smell us for a mile."

The guys got a real night's sleep and, about noon the next day, set off for Utah Beach. On the way Sartain had Sosa make a detour into Saint Mere Eglise. A liquor store was said to be in business there and it would be nice to pick up a bottle of bourbon for a celebratory round of drinks once the unit was back in Lubenham. They passed through shattered villages and countryside won with the blood of thousands of American soldiers. Radcliffe Simpson, Ray Carey, Frank Poole, and a lot of others were gone forever. Johnny Manning, and dozens of others just in "A" Battery alone were hospitalized. Who knew if any of them would really recover. If Sartain thought about whether it was worth the cost in his countrymen's lives, he may have felt ambivalent. Though his pride in the accomplishments of the battalion, the division, and his own battery were irrefutable, his feelings toward the French people were certainly mixed. Too often French civilians seemed to not fully appreciate what the soldiers had sacrificed or appeared preoccupied with preserving their material possessions while strangers to their country had freely given so much. Even after sixty years the mixed emotions wouldn't go away. "In the smaller villages the French were pretty nice, but in the larger towns they weren't," he said in one interview. "I made a mistake and I never made it again. In Normandy one of our guys, could have been one of the mess sergeants, killed a cow and just cut off the hind quarters. The farmer came up to me just raising hell. I said, 'OK,OK, how much.' He gave me a figure, probably fifty or sixty American dollars and I paid for it out of my pocket. I told Sergeant Johnson what I'd done and he said, 'Well that's not right.' Without me knowing about it, he took up a collection and they paid me what ever I paid for that damn cow. I guess this farmer had a right to complain about somebody else slaughtering his cow, but that's the last I ever felt sorry for the French and it's the last time I ever paid for anything dealing with the French. They were ungrateful and they took advantage of the GI when he went through. You'd go through some of these towns and they still had World War One debris! That's correct. I'm telling you, no where else in Europe did they have World War One debris like that. Buildings just left. And they still screwed up!" As it turned out, Sartain remembered, "The liquor store was a little bitty joint. There was no bourbon, so I bought a bottle of cognac."

The 319th bivouacked about five miles from Utah that night. At mid morning on the 13th they left for the beachhead, but since the loading of vehicles would require special handling, this last leg of their movement was made on foot. They hadn't gone far when many of the men started to have second thoughts about their new jump boots. As Rappi recalled, "A lot of the guys had sore feet before they got to the boat. The shoes were too small or something. We had to walk to the boat with them on." Brand new as they were, and not at all broken in, a march in their fresh jump boots was the worst thing they could have done. By the time they got to the shore much of the battalion was hobbling along with blistered feet.

Once on Utah Beach the men could see their transport, LST-212, grounded some distance off shore. It was low tide, so the men were loaded onto Higgins boats and taken out to the ship where they climbed aboard. Of course there was quite a bit of material to be loaded too, and the tide needed to come in, so it was nearly 1800 hours before they finally pulled away from shore. In the meantime the guys hung around on deck, smoking and talking over the campaign. The navy had the ship's radio tuned in to the uptempo jazz program hosted by Axis Sally, or, as some called her, the Berlin Bitch. The music playing over the loudspeakers gave the scene a festive atmosphere. As one man remembered, "The Berlin Bitch, she had this radio show every night. She was always telling something. They put her on the PA system of the LST leaving Normandy. She's saying, 'There's a thin trickle of troops heading down to the shore, the 82nd is leaving beaten." The guys in the 319th Glider Field Artillery Battalion knew better.

BATTERY!

Part 17: "Not my gal!"

LST-212 arrived at South Hampton, England, the next day, July 14th, 1944, at about 13:00. After the 319th disembarked, they were marched through town to the rail station. Along the way they found the streets lined with mobs of British civilians who cheered them and clapped as they passed by.

Loaded onto a train, the unit reached Leicester a few hours later and was then put on trucks for the final leg of their journey back to Lubenham. It was late by then, approaching midnight, and with so much lost sleep and fatigue from the campaign, most of the guys were in deep slumber by the time the convoy reached Papillon Hall.

After the men dropped out of the trucks and shuffled into their old quarters, they awakened the next morning to find there were a lot of new faces. These were the men brought in to fill in the expected gaps generated by the combat in Normandy. In "A" Battery they included Robert Dickson and Ethred "Duel" Elmore, both teenaged farm boys from Arkansas. Joe D'Appolonio was there, fresh out of his Youngstown, Ohio, high school. Another was Carl Salminen, also a teenager, in this case speaking with a distinctively Scandinavian accent and hailing from the farther reaches of Michigan's Upper Peninsula. Theodore "Ted" Simpson was a youngster from the St. Louis area, trying his best to conceal the fact that he'd had some college education, especially from the parochial NCOs who enjoyed making examples of "college boys" like himself. There were a few NCOs among them as well, like Sergeant Gost from New York City and Sergeant Jones*, who'd been transferred from the artillery school at Fort Bragg. They'd all been waiting at the repo-depot for several weeks when a sergeant with a clipboard walked into their barracks and wanted to know who'd like to volunteer for the airborne. Dickson remembered how it went. "They came by and asked for volunteers. One guy raised his hand and said, 'Once before we volunteered to be truck drivers and they put us behind wheelbarrows. We don't volunteer for anything now. You'll just have to pick us.' So they started calling off names. They put us on a train and there must have been about fifty of us. After we were on the train Lieutenant Fellman came in to the car and said, 'I can tell you all right now that you're headed for the 82nd Airborne!'"

Carl Salminen was there on the train too, as was D'Appolonio, Gost, Simpson, and all the others. Later Salminen remembered, "Well, at first it kinda gave all the guys the willies. You know, that's a paratroop outfit. We didn't know about gliders, we'd never heard about gliders. Anyway, we landed in Market Harborough and then from there truck convoyed to where they were stationed at in England, at what they called the old Paps Hall. And, heh heh, that's the way the history goes."

When he was asked what he remembered about being assigned to the 319th, Ted Simpson clearly remembered Lieutenant Sartain being at the train station to receive them. "I remember how impressive he seemed when we got off at the station at Market Harborough," Simpson later said. "He was the one guy I saw that looked like he knew what he was doing. Here were a bunch of rookies just off the train. I remember him walking around in an encouraging way to the soldiers he didn't know, and I remember what a commanding performance and appearance he gave. He was a very, very proper airborne lieutenant. I was struck by his obvious know how of his position and his responsibility."

At Pap's Hall the new guys were issued folding stock carbines and circular Paraglider patches to sew on to their caps. Years later, Ted Simpson recorded his experiences in the 319th on paper for his children and grandchildren. Recalling the cadre left behind at Lubenham to train the new men, he wrote, "What I didn't know was that this small contingent, all wearing the 82nd patch, comprised a selection of warriors who were handpicked to chaperone and train us at Papillon Hall until their less fortunate comrades returned, much later, from a jump into France which they were now awaiting at the airport. We missed going ourselves by that narrow margin."

While the rest of the battalion was soon laying down artillery in France, the new guys were put through their paces at Papillon. "Right away they started basic training for us in the airborne outfit," Salminen continued, "like they train them in the marines. You go through the same doggone thing as the marines do. Marines always say how tough of an outfit they are, they're no tougher than the airborne guys. I had one week in artillery training, which really didn't amount to that much. You couldn't possibly remember everything about the aiming circle and all that. Anyway, then they put me to driving a truck all day. Other guys, when they went to do their physical training exercises and calisthenics or whatever you want to call it, and double timing out there, I was out with the truck someplace. I had to do this in the evenings with the sergeant. All alone out there double-timing, that was life. That's about it, you know, but after we were there for a while I got pretty proud of the outfit."

Elmore found the training quite manageable. "It wasn't too bad on me because I was raised on a farm," he said. "The only thing that bothered me was, hurry up and wait."

There were also some of those at Papillon who'd been injured in the glider landings or wounded in the subsequent combat in France, but whose wounds were light enough to return them to duty at the unit's base camp before the battalion came back from Normandy. Among these were Lieutenant Johnson, Staff Sergeant Jinders, Sergeant Picher, Corporals Covais and Motyka, along with Derwister, Prohaska, Rosati, Sykes, little Tobin, and a half dozen others.

Those who'd been casualties in the landings and selected to be evacuated now had the chance to tell their buddies what happened to them. They told how they'd been taken by jeep to Utah Beach early on the 8th of June, where they were laid out on their stretchers awaiting transport back to England. There was still a great deal of confusion there at Utah, they said. The beachhead was still within the range of German artillery fire and Luftwaffe fighters who dared to make a pass over the massive concentration of troops and ships, made their presence known too. Covais remembered that, "they put me on the beach on a stretcher. There was one German plane came over, a couple of them, and decided to strafe the beach. The only ones that had guts enough to do that, because we mastered the skies! He came in with guns blazing and I said, Lord, save me from this one. It didn't come close to me so it was OK, I was lucky, but I heard later that one of our officers was wounded on the beach too and got killed that way, lying on his stretcher." Other battalion men had heard this rumor as well. Covais thought the unfortunate officer was Lieutenant Simpson, others a Lieutenant Dietrich from HQ Battery. Records do give Simpson's date of death as June 8th, but do not give further details as to whether he was literally killed by strafing on the beach or if he died of the wounds received from the German machine gun he rushed during the pre-dawn hours of June 7th.

BATTERY!

Later on the 8th an emptied LST was ready to take a boatload of wounded back on its return trip to England. Each relay of wounded men from the 319th would have been placed together as they were left at the beach, waiting their turn for evacuation. Probably these men were also positioned on the same transport vessel and then treated at the same hospital once they reached England. Captain Manning recalled the transport he, and probably most of the others, took as, "a large freighter which had brought over supplies for the landings. The side walls of the hull were hung with hammocks and we were each assigned one. While we waited for the ship to fill up we went through three bombing raids, but with only minor damage. The trip across the channel was a bit rough as the ship was riding quite high in the water. The seriously wounded men had a very hard time of it."

Manning, and all those on the ship with him were taken to a large hospital at Malvern, in southwestern England. His thumb was re-attached to the rest of his right hand and skin was grafted from his leg. The Captain was really chewed up and a series of skin grafts were necessary. Manning also had some serious back injuries and it took the help of regular physical therapy to start to improve. This would take time though, and Manning remained hospitalized through most of July.

After the dressings were removed from Corporal Covais' face and the caked up, dried blood washed from over his left eye, doctors found his wound was not so serious. Really, he'd been a fortunate recipient of a standing order that all men with head-wounds be immediately evacuated. After several stitches and a week recovering, Ted was sent back to Papillon with some of the other less seriously wounded. "When I got back they put me on a detail of men picking out the barracks bags of those that were deceased, remembered Covais. "We had to pick them out, the barracks bags of the guys that were killed. Then they looked through their personal belongings. They took out the government property and anything that might have been, you know, embarrassing, but it was tough because we knew these guys and now they were dead, they were just gone."

Three members of the 319th pose with British soldiers outside the Paget Arms pub in Lubenham. Courtesy Market Harborough Historical Society.

NOT MY GAL!

Once settled in, everyone was eager to get back to their favorite table at Mr. Tarry's Paget Arms pub or to see a girlfriend and her family. In fact, while the reception for the guys was enthusiastic at South Hampton, it was undoubtedly more heartfelt on their home ground. Sartain remembered that "it was like old home coming, both in Lubenham with the GIs and in Market Harborough with the Officers." Indeed, some of the guys were surprised, both at their own joy in seeing the local English and in the emotional welcome they received from their normally reserved hosts.

"You know, after you're there a while you get to know the people," said Casimir Sobon, "You get friends and all, just like you do here or anywhere else. They ask you, where's so and so, where's so and so? It's a hell of a thing to tell them they're gone because they became friends with them too." Other "A" Battery men felt the same way. "When I come back it was just like coming home," said Bob Storms as he looked back on it all after more than sixty years. "The people were crying and everything," he continued, then the emotions overcame him and tears of his own began to flow. Finally he regained his composure, wiped his eyes and said, "The last time I left, I never got to go back there. I miss those people. Yep, that was just like being home."

Among the first formal acts of battalion business upon returning to Papillon was a ceremony honoring those in the battalion who'd lost their lives in Normandy. This was quickly followed by a visit from General Gavin, who presented the 319th with its second Presidential Unit Citation. Being twice selected for this prestigious award added a little

General Gavin presents the 319th with a battle streamer for the Normandy Campaign sometime during the summer of 1944. Sartain collection.

BATTERY!

more swagger to the outfit's already high morale.

As complimentary as another unit citation was, the week long furlough granted to every man who'd participated in the Normandy invasion during the last weeks of July was more welcome. For men who'd been under constant military supervision since landing at Casablanca over a year before, a full week without reveille, fatigue details, or someone who outranked them seemed like paradise. Many traveled to London, where entertainment in all the forms desired by soldiers away from home could be had in abundance. In many cases this amounted to no more than cigarettes and beer at a pub with their buddies where no one would bother them, or perhaps a shadowed female figure in a doorway asking, 'Got a match, Yank?' Others preferred to sight see more of the countryside, and took advantage of the extensive network of Red Cross canteens to accomplish their goal. With so many Americans stationed in England, others had relatives and friends from home to see.

Covais, for example, had a cousin stationed at an army air force base near London and took the opportunity to visit him. Cousin Jack was part of the ground crew for a squadron of B-17 flying fortresses. "I think I might have spent a week or ten days with him. He worked; I'd get up and work right along with him. I mean, to me, I wanted to do that. It was a war effort. Rather than doing nothing I'd rather do something. It was a new experience, and it brought me close to these bombers. I had the good fortune of loading some bombs for Adolph. I was happy just loading the bombs up, and guys would write things on the bomb, you know, this is for you there Adolph or something like that, Shickelgruber, whatever, here's one for you!"

Part of the ground crews' work involved replacing shattered windows or sections of the fuselage, along with cleaning out the thousands of spent machine gun casings which littered the decks of the fortresses after a bombing run. In their off duty hours, many of the ground crewmen would fashion discarded fragments of the B-17s into pieces of trench art. Lamps, scale models, or portrait frames. Covais constructed one of the latter from pieces of plexiglass portholes, aluminum sections, and spent 50 caliber machinegun casings. "I got pieces together and I molded and cut it with shears and used a file to take the rough edges off the plexiglass, you know, rounded out the edges. When you cut something like that you have sharp edges. I mean, it was done in a crude way, but other guys were doing it and I figured well, I'd do something."

Mahlon Sebring had a brother stationed in England, also at an air base. Sebring took advantage of the furlough to see him and his new bride. "He married an English girl and I spent a week with her family after Normandy," he remembered. "It was a large family. One thing that stands out in my mind there, one night everyone had gone to bed and we were talking. All at once the lights went out. I wondered if a bomb somewhere knocked them out. She said something about the electric. Believe it or not, up over the front door was a little box. You put two shillings in it and the lights come back on. Well, she couldn't reach the box and I didn't understand in the dark English money pretty good, but I had a whole pocket full of it. Every time I bought something I give them a bill. You know they had three pence and six pence, and farthings and half crowns, and I thought, what the shit! Well, I hadn't figured it out yet, but she knew the sizes. She searched around in my hand and got two shilling pieces and put them in, and the lights come back on. So, the light bill's always paid, you can't screw the electric company!"

Scotland was another favorite destination for the men when an extended furlough, like the one issued after Normandy, was granted. Captain Manning took a trip there, stopping in Glasgow, Edinburgh, and Loch Lomond. Lieutenant Ragland also toured Scotland. "They had a studio in this town," he recalled, "they had this kilt. You could go in a dressing room and put one on and have your picture taken." That was what Ragland did, posing bare legged in kilt and jump boots.

Sartain took his furlough in Scotland too, with a few officers from the 320th, his friend Butler from the ROTC program at LSU among them. They checked into the Bear's Foot Hotel in Glasgow. "There was a dance hall in Glasgow right next to the hotel, a very large dance hall. The girls there were very highly chaperoned. It was kind of like a USO deal. You could go in and when you went in you bought tickets. Then when you'd see a girl you wanted to dance with you'd go over and give her the ticket. It was their way to make money to support their activities to support the troops. I met one girl there that I, if it hadn't been for me and Peggy Lou being so tight, I probably would have pushed it a little bit further," he reminisced. "She was well educated, most attractive and good company. A very attractive blonde."

"There was always this guy in a black trench coat and hat watching over her. I never could figure out if it was her body guard or a relative and when I asked her she just laughed. I always wanted more information on her because she was so heavily chaperoned. We made arrangements to go to Loch Lomond. We took a bus from Glasgow to Locke Lomond, and how she got rid of the chaperone, I don't know, but we had lunch there and got on the bus back to Glasgow. The next night I went to the dance hall again and there was the guy with the black trench coat and hat. She still insisted I give her a ticket when we danced. I went to the Isle of Skelt with her, that was one day, and we looked around Glasgow, but there wasn't much to do there except drink.

Later I invited her to come down to Market Harborough, you know, with a friend because I knew she couldn't come alone. Finally she wrote to me and said she couldn't get away. I don't know if she thought I was trying to lure her into a den or what. She knew that Peggy and I were gonna get married, and there wasn't anything improper, but we were kind of close and all of that business. I probably, well, it was never very very serious, she was just an excellent companion. We corresponded all through the war. She even wrote to my family and Peggy-Lou. But after I came home I got rid of all her letters. No point in kicking a sleeping horse in the tail, you know?"

For his furlough, another "A" Battery man thought he would consummate a love affair he'd initiated at home in the States. "We had a corporal that was going with a girl when the war broke out," remembered Sebring of this man's story. "She was a nurse. She went in the service as a 2nd lieutenant and he went in as an enlisted man. They were sweethearts, you know, going together. Right after Normandy they gave us a furlough. He said he was gonna try and see the Captain and get a jeep to go see her. We started kidding him and saying, 'Hell, she won't have nothing to do with you. She's an officer. She won't monkey around with an enlisted man, that's forbidden!' He said, 'Not my gal!' Well he went to see her and he came back all kind of broken up. Damned if she wasn't going with a Captain."

Recollecting what he did with his own furlough, Ed Ryan told yet another story of lost love. "Some people I knew in the U S had relatives in Charlton-Come-Hardy. I thought I'd go see them," he said. "On the way there I'm riding a bus when I saw this old lady fumbling for money, so I threw some change in the box for her. She said, 'You're nice, maybe you'd like to meet my daughter. Why don't you come to the house.' So I did. Mary Justine was short, with light brown hair and had a beautiful face. She was on the quiet side, more on the quiet side, but she was an opera singer in Manchester, what they called light opera." Eddie and Mary Justine hit it off, so to speak, and over the following weeks they saw each other whenever circumstances allowed. Before he knew it Ryan felt like he had a steady girl and she broke off her engagement to a Canadian soldier.

One time Ryan took the bus to Mary Justine's home on the chance of seeing her, if only for the day. There was no opportunity to send a letter beforehand and telephone calls were, of course, out of the question. When her mother came to the door she told him, "she's not here. She's up in Lincolnshire doing her part in the Land Army, but you can get there on the bus and see her." Riding the bus from town to town in wartime England had its obstacles. For security purposes no destinations were marked on the buses and the drivers were told not to answer questions about bus routes or schedules. The driver would only tell him, "Get on Yank, I'll tell you when to get off." After a journey of twenty-five or thirty miles, Ryan found himself deposited with some vague directions at a dirt road leading to the village he was looking for. By this time it was dusk and the prospects for finding anyone or anything were beginning to look bleak. "Finally," Ryan recalled, I saw a Limey walking down the street. I said to him, 'I've got a girlfriend working on a farm.' He said, 'Only one place that could be, she's working at a nunnery.'" Mary Justine had mention to Ryan that she was a practicing Catholic, but she was evidently more devout than he'd realized.

It was dark by the time Ryan reached the convent and knocked on the door. An older nun answered and listened to his story. : Yes, Mary Justine was there, but he wouldn't be able to see her tonight. Was he hungry? He was, and was led into the kitchen where the nun served him a gooseberry pie. "You can sleep here on the floor tonight," she told him, "but you'll have to be up and out by daylight." Lying on a pad of blankets, Ryan fell fast asleep.

Before dawn he was roused and handed a mug of tea. "Then Justine came in and the nuns let her go off with me for the day. That's the day we went to Stratford-on-Avon, Anne Hathaway house, all that jazz. It was a lot of walking and riding on busses. I caught the same bus back and it took me till the next day to get back to Pap's Hall."

Another one of their dates was remembered by Ryan. "One time she was gonna sing in Queen Anne's hall in Manchester. That's a big deal down there. She said, 'I'd like you to come but I got no way to get you in.' I took the train to Man-

Marvin Ragland models a kilt while on furlough in Scotland, July, 1944. Courtesy Marvin Ragland.

chester and went to the Red Cross. I told them I'd like a ticket to get into the opera. They looked at me and said, you gotta be kidding! I think they were afraid I'd start trouble. I almost did too. During the intermission some big tall South African was pushing people around in the bar. I pushed him back. Anyway, I did get in and she sang on stage. I'll never forget it, she sang Deep Purple, she dedicated it to me."

"So I had a real girlfriend there. She was a nice girl. She took me to all the places in England, and we talked about getting married, but she was Catholic and I had no religion, so we dropped the subject. Besides, if you wanted to get married, there was a lot of things involved. You had to get permission and they usually tried to discourage you. The last time I saw her the outfit was getting ready to leave for Holland. We had orders to keep our mouths shut so I never told her I was leaving. When I left her at the train station she was crying, but I didn't say anything. She wrote me when we were in Holland but I didn't answer. I didn't know if I'd ever be back there again. To tell the truth I didn't think I'd survive. One time, many years after I was home I got a Christmas card from Canada. I saw that card from Canada and there was no name on it, but I recognized the handwriting. Well, that was a long time ago. It was one of those things, during war time you get very involved with people very quickly. Eventually it goes away."

It was true. The lives of millions the world over were being swept up in a contest which had little respect for the desires of individuals. Instead, lives were continuously ruined or ended in the most abrupt, sudden, and often ghastly fashion. The pressure, especially for the young, to enjoy life to its fullest while one still could do so made it easy to fall in love or surrender to the passions of the moment. It was all a natural response to a future which was both uncertain and frightening. Psychological studies in recent years have confirmed this as what might be called the "Tunnel of Love" effect. Simply put; proximity to danger heightens emotional reactions.

Whatever mechanism of mind and emotion was at work, its power made it perhaps too easy for some men to forget commitments at home, if only for a single night. Toward the end of his life, one "A" Battery man who was a husband in 1944 and who would

be happily married for over fifty years afterwards, felt the need to reveal a long held secret to his son. One night that summer, he told his son that he and his best buddy were in the company of two girls from Market Harborough. The night was unusually warm. Perhaps they'd been dancing at "the Sweat Box" or some other crowded nightspot. Then their dates let slip that there was a municipal swimming pool located in a gymnasium on the outskirts of town. Of course the building was locked up and the two couples were obliged to climb

Triple Date. Frank Motyka and James Fitzsimmons pose with their dates on a spring afternoon in 1944. A third GI was presumably taking the photograph. Covais collection.

in through a window to gain access to the pool. There, in the darkness, all four shed their clothes. Without their uniforms the soldiers became unregimented young men, undefined by rank or training. The girls seemed to also take on some condition of timeless beauty in their nakedness. Together and in pairs the four played and swam nude in the cool, barely illuminated water, until approaching daylight reminded them of the world they'd escaped from for a few hours.

Indeed, there seems to have been a lot of activity at night between battalion men and English girls. Sosa commented that once the pubs closed at 10pm, "The haystacks would come alive. Yeah, the haystacks were crowded every night. Guys would take their raincoats with them even if it wasn't raining, so they'd have something nice to lay on in the hay with the girls."

One "A" Battery driver remembered taking two battalion officers into the town of Black Pool. "They were on leave with these two nurses. They were American, they were nurses I guess," he said. "I had a girl too. Mine was British. Good looking girl had red hair, freckled face, kinda chubby. I told them, 'Look, why don't you guys just take the jeep. I'm gonna meet this girl and I'm gonna spend the night with her, why don't you guys just go ahead and take the jeep.' Rather than having me driving them around. They said, 'OK!'"

Reflecting on the qualities of the women of various European nationalities, he observed, "They're all the same. There's no difference, they're all the same. All except for the British girls, they didn't like to screw laying down. They said they had to screw standing up. They said it wasn't proper. You're not a proper lady if you lay down and screw, especially when it's not your husband. I guess that makes it OK to screw standing up, but that don't work too well. I don't know why but that's the way it was."

Whatever the sexual allure of a haystack under the moonlight or some other secluded point of rendezvous may have been, most of the relations between the soldiers and the British girls were of a more innocent nature.

Rappi recalled one Lubenham girl fondly, saying, "I had a pretty steady girl there. I don't remember her name anymore, but she was cute. I used to go to her house all the time and they'd make me a meal. That was pretty nice of them. They had a garden right in the back of their house. It was a very small one but they grew vegetables in there."

There was a tacit understanding in most all cases that these relationships were, by their nature, transitory. "I never did write to her," Rappi added. "The English women were alright, but I liked those Italian women. Of course, I was young in them days and everything looks pretty good then."

Bob Storms reminisced about the summer of 1944 with Pat Hammond and her family in Ashley. "All the time I could get out of camp I spent out there," he said. "It was just like my home town. One time her aunt comes from London on the train and she had two girls, two cousins with her. I went down and met them at the station. The one girl had one leg shot off on account of a bombing. Then while she was in the hospital they blowed it up and she lost her other leg just below the knee. She was in a wheelchair. They stayed there about a week or two and I spent a lot of time with her. Oh boy, I used to raise hell with that one girl with her legs off. I'd put a blanket out on the grass and I'd carry her out on the blanket and then we'd roll and wrestle around. Her mother'd come out, 'Bob, your gonna hurt her, don't do that! I'd say, 'Ma, that's what's the matter with her. You're babying her too much! She's no different than you or I, she wants to have some fun too!'"

NOT MY GAL!

The guys had a lot of pent up steam to blow off and Storms's horseplay was one example, but sometimes their manner of doing so took the form of more serious mischief. One battalion man recalled a typical episode, "The RAF was having a dance. We couldn't get in. So we were standing out in the street and told these British paras they couldn't get in either. They busted the door off and went in. Because we were standing out in the street laughing the local cops quizzed us. We told them we were from the 320th. That's what we always told them when any of us got in trouble with the Limey cops. They'd ask what unit we come from. We'd say, the 320th. I guess the colonel up to the 320th was nasty. He'd keep his men restricted to their quarters. That kept the 320th guys out of the way and we could do things by ourselves most of the time, which was good."

On other occasions the release of tension was more serious, even dangerous. Covais was sergeant of the guard one night at Pap's Hall when the alarm was sounded. A drunken trooper was in the main building, throwing furniture through windows, pummeling his fellow soldiers, and causing quite a disturbance. He was out of control and going to hurt someone. Covais entered the room, intending to quiet the man down. Instead a struggle erupted and the trooper snatched the .45 from Covais's holster, cracked him over the head, and barricaded the two of them together in the room. When Covais came to he heard the officer of the day, a lieutenant, pounding on the door. "Watch out Lieutenant," Covais yelled out. "He's got a gun! He's right on the other side of the door!" The Lieutenant, aiming deliberately low, fired. The slug hit the drunken trooper in the hip with such force it threw him across the room. That settled the man down and brought him a transfer out of the 319th. For his part, Covais received a half dozen stitches on his head and a good lesson in how to handle a drunk.

On August 2nd, with everyone returned from their furloughs, the battalion passed in review with the rest of the 82nd before the Supreme Allied Commander. Eisenhower addressed the troops, congratulating them on their second Presidential Unit Citation and promising that more fierce fighting awaited them in the future. When it was time for the individual units to pass in review, Covais, having experience in carrying the "A" Battery guidon, was selected to bear the National Colors for the 319th as it marched past the General. It was an act which he took pride in for the rest of his life.

The weather was unusually hot for England, and the site chosen for the review was a newly laid asphalt airstrip outside Leicester. "I skipped out of going on the parade," Orin Miller remembered. "When those fellas come back they had tar up all over their boots and up about a half an inch all around the edges. It was so hot with that tar and marching on it, they just sunk right in. What a mess they had getting the tar off of their boots. But I just skipped it, that's all. Took a chance and skipped it. Nobody missed me."

As the summer advanced more trappings of airborne status were conferred on the glider troopers in the 82nd. They'd already been granted hazardous duty pay and jump boots before leaving Normandy. Then, in mid-August the army bestowed on them sterling silver glider wings. These were intentionally designed to look just like the parachute wings worn by the jumpers, except that the parachute device was replaced with a head-on CG4A glider. Each man in the 319th wore his new wings above his medal ribbons and on top of an oval of wool felt, colored red for field artillery.

Often during the balance of July, August, and early September wounded men from the battery were released from the hospitals across England. When Sartain was notified of this, he would arrange for Sosa to go pick them up and bring them back to Pap's

BATTERY!

Hall. "See I was a pretty good man with a map," Sosa explained, "And I'm a damn good driver, you understand what I'm saying. So, the Captain or the 1st sergeant would call me in and show me a spot on a map. They'd say, "There's a hospital over there, go over and get so and so and bring him back. So I really saw the country. England is beautiful. I liked it very well."

On one occasion it was Captain Manning who needed a ride back to the battalion. The Captain wasn't really altogether healed, but remaining in the hospital until one was completely ready for duty brought with it the chance that a man could be reassigned to a new unit. A lot of men actually went AWOL from their hospitals and returned to the 319th on their own, out of fear that just this would happen to them. "By wheedling information from nurses Haines and Hagen-- from Utica, New York -- I was able to slip out of the hospital after a month," Manning later wrote. "I had heard that the battalion was back at Lubenham, and wanted to make contact. I did not want to be re-assigned to a repo-depot. Colonel Todd pulled a few strings and got them to process my release back to the 319th when they felt I was ready for discharge." Manning's arm was still in a soft cast, and would remain so for a few weeks longer.

The expectation was that the Captain would resume command of "A" Battery, but this was not the case. Instead Manning was placed in the position of Assistant S-3, a job which normally served as a liaison between the battalion and the infantry unit which it was supporting. Sartain learned that he would be in permanent command of "A" Battery.

"There was a lot of paperwork in the mill during and after Normandy because of killed in action and the promotions which resulted from that," said Sartain. "At supper one night, Colonel Todd said, 'I've got an announcement to make. One of our officers has been made a Captain." Afterwards there was a brief ceremony and the double silver bars were pinned to Sartain's uniform. The next day he packed up his belongings

Lt. Gutshall, Capt. Sartain and Lt. Ragland at Pappillion Hall August 1944. Note the new M1943 jacket and trousers with the Sateen finish. Ragland Collection.

at the junior officer's quarters behind Papillon Hall and moved to the billet for senior officers outside Lubenham. There were other changes. Lieutenant Ragland was assigned as XO of "A" Battery, a position he would hold for the balance of hostilities. Lieutenants Laurence Cook and John Gutshall were also transferred from HQ to "A" Battery, making up the officer cadre which would carry the Battery through the coming campaigns.

Changes were afoot in the enlisted ranks as well. Corporal Covais received a promotion to sergeant, as did Robert Rappi, for example, and there were numerous others who added a stripe to their sleeves. Sartain later explained how these decisions were made, "I never let a vacancy go more than overnight, but every time I promoted somebody I did it with the complete concurrence of Sergeant Johnson. He clued me in on who was deserving, particularly in the gun crews. I wouldn't promote anybody in the signal section without getting Carl Davis to concur with Sergeant Johnson. Johnson and Ragland, they'd say, Simpson is ready to be made a corporal, or so and so is ready to be made a sergeant. Picher is ready to take over the sergeant's place or something like that. I would want to promote somebody who was deserving and who the rest of the men would recognize as deserving. That's just the way it went."

Sobon was another man selected for an NCOs warrant, but his veteran's attitude toward inexperienced officers seems to have gotten in the way. Sobon described why, saying, "When we come back from Normandy invasion and all that other crap, then they replaced the guys that were gone. They had me put in for sergeant or some damn thing, some promotion. So we got a shave tail lieutenant that just came in, never was anywhere in anything. He come up to me and he says to me, I gotta see what you can do before you get this. I told him what he could do with his rank. This guy hadn't seen nothing but he was gonna see what you could do. That was enough, I didn't need it. Didn't need the responsibility. Somebody else could take it."

Though he may have been talking about another officer, Sergeant Rappi shared Sobon's attitude toward freshly minted 2nd lieutenants who, in their view, didn't exhibit the proper deference toward enlisted men who'd fought their way through both Italy and

One of the Battalion's CG4a gliders being loaded just prior to the Market-Garden operation. Courtesy Gruebling family.

Normandy. Rappi remembered one in particular. "Lieutenant Mullen," he commented, "he come in as a shavetail. Yeah, I remember him, I can remember him in England. He said to us, 'When I blow this whistle, I want you to come running, and bring the fences with you!' He'd just got out of O C S, so that wasn't a very good entrance for him."

Given vacancies in the other batteries of the 319th, Sartain was also informed that he should select his two most deserving senior NCOs to be offered commissions. "The word came to us from Colonel Todd to recommend people for battlefield promotion. Bob Macarthur was number one and Carl Davis was number two," said Sartain. McArthur accepted the promotion, albeit reluctantly because it meant being transferred out of the battery. That was standard policy when an enlisted man received a commission. "He got his lieutenancy," Sartain hastened to add, "but thereafter he never forgot his enlisted buddies and constantly visited them." Sebring remembered him transferring out, and said of it," I remember when he left we kind of hated to see him go because he was an all around guy." Everybody in "A" Battery felt the same. Rappi remarked years later, "Sergeant Macarthur, he went up to the HQ Battery. He'd always come over to our barracks and shoot the breeze with us like he used to when he was head sergeant of the guns. He made lieutenant and he was an enlisted man's friend."

When Sartain approached Sergeant Davis he gave the offer some hard thought, then declined. "Carl Davis said no, he turned it down," Sartain later revealed. "He told me, Captain, I would prefer to stay where I am and what I am. Carl Davis was a very dependable member of the battery and was head of the signal section then. He didn't want it known and I have kept his secret until now."

Staff Sergeant Harold Peters was chief of the instrument section and under Carl Davis. "Peters," explained Sartain, "was the third man on the list for promotion to 2nd lieutenant. We had two spots we could fill, and so Harold Peters was picked for the second spot. I thought he was going to be a good man, but he turned out very disappointing."

The problem was not in Peters' execution of his responsibilities as an officer. No, it was agreed that Peters knew his duties and performed them all with competence and proficiency. The issue turned instead on how he was perceived to have changed after receiving his commission. Sartain described what happened, "Once he got his lieutenant's bar he totally ignored his old buddies in the battery, you see. There was no reason for him to not at least have some contact or visit with the guys he'd been in the trenches with for two years or longer. There wasn't any reason for that. I sensed it once Peters got his promotion. I sensed it and said to myself, you know he's let this 2nd lieutenant bar go to his head."

Rappi expressed the same opinion, but from the enlisted point of view when he commented, "Sergeant Peters never came back to visit us at all. That lieutenancy got to his head." Covais always maintained that Peters' promotion was the product of a sycophantic attitude. "This guy was what we used to call a Brown Noser, you know what that means. I can remember he used to ask the officers if he could dig their foxholes for them, that sort of thing."

Sosa evidently saw some of the same behaviors and was similarly put off by it. His blunt remarks, when asked about Peters were in many ways those of a man who has reached the conclusion that the time for sensitive feelings is long past. "He was a brown noser and he was full of bullshit," Sosa said. "Talked a lot of bullshit. Yeah, he talked a lot. He wasn't a bad fellow though. He came into our quarters once or twice, just standing around talking bullshit. Pete, we called him Pete, Lieutenant Peters. He was pretty good about socializing with us, as far as that goes, but he was full of shit."

While accepting that they were under military discipline, the citizen soldiers in the 319th also had a highly developed sense of the respect with which enlisted personnel deserved to be treated. NCOs who pulled rank or officers who flaunted their authority were only tolerated as far as order demanded. In at least "C" and "A" Batteries, Manning and Sartain's personal leadership styles both fostered and mirrored this attitude. Reflecting later on this social tradition within the battery, Sartain observed, "I could personally associate with the troops. They could keep their place, I could keep mine. I had no problem with that. Cook could, most of our officers could. They didn't go around with their nose stuck up in the air because they were captain or first lieutenant or 2nd lieutenant. But Peters literally divorced himself from his men, his old buddies. It wasn't a good thing. He didn't bust the unit up, but when the guys would pass him on the street they'd have some bad thoughts in mind. Anyway, we had a nice ceremony, battery ceremony – no a battalion ceremony even though it was "A" Battery, and I pinned the 2nd lieutenant's bar on each one of them, McArthur and Peters. Shook hands, all that foolishness."

Now that the outfit was back in England, discontent over Major Wilcoxson reasserted itself. Everyone knew there would be another mission soon and with the events of the Battle for Normandy fresh in their minds, none relished the idea of having to put up with the Major through another campaign. Meanwhile, Wilcoxson's strict adherence to the minutest details of military formality served to further antagonize the officers and men alike.

Toward the end of August two sergeants in the HQ Battery hatched a plan to embarrass the Major. Sergeant Knecht and his buddy typed up a petition calling for the removal of Major Wilcoxson as battalion XO on the grounds that he'd shown a marked absence of courage in Normandy. Kept a strict secret from the officers, the petition found immediate and widespread circulation. "After we went through all that crap and come back to England again they wanted to get rid of him, they really wanted to do something. Yeah, everybody signed it," recalled Casimir Sobon.

Sobon's memory was accurate. Silas Hogg remembered signing the circulated petition too. "I don't know who made the petition, but it got typed up and it flat told that he done nothing in combat, but hide. He was no assistance to any man in combat. Everybody in that battalion, now get this, in that battalion, the 319th, signed that petition. The first sergeant, they all signed it. Absolutely! Everybody signed it!"

At the end of the week Knecht slipped the petition in with other battalion mail headed for division headquarters, then he and his confederate sat back to watch the conflagration. They didn't have to wait long. On the following Monday morning the battalion was out, engaged in a field exercise, when word came in that the unit should get back to Papillon at once, with every last man confined to quarters. Colonel Todd was quite upset. It was one thing to tease Major Wilcoxson by putting knit caps on statues, but a petition advocating the removal of a senior officer was going too far. He questioned the captains and lieutenants but the men's security had been tight and none of the officers had an inkling of what was taking place. The next day, two majors and a clerical team from the division inspector general's office arrived at Papillon and set up shop, interviewing every man whose name appeared on the infamous document.

Ryan's attitude typified what the inspectors found as they worked their way through the names on the petition. "He asked me if I signed it. I said yes. He said, 'Where'd you get it?' I said I was in the shithouse and somebody passed it to me. He said, 'Who was it.' I said, How could I tell, you know?"

The inspectors surmised that the petition had originated with some person, or persons, in the HQ Battery. They asked Knecht if he started it. "I didn't want to lie so I didn't answer them," Knecht said later.

Then they called in his buddy and asked him, "Did Knecht start this petition?" He said to them, "I don't think he's capable of it."

The investigation into where the petition had originated just couldn't make much headway. The major's and their typists left unfulfilled in their objective and filed a report. Then, one morning a few days later the battalion was called into formation to be addressed by General James Gavin, now commanding Officer of the 82nd Airborne Division." This time he wasn't there to commend the outfit or present any awards. Storms simply remembered it as "a big bull session, a big shindig." It was really more significant than that. Gavin, Jumping Jim, he was on the exercise platform, walking from one end to the other, one end to the other, "madder than a firecracker," remembered Silas Hogg. What transpired was remarkable, and the whole experience made an impression on all those who were there, including Ed Ryan. His memory was that, "Gavin had all the officers leave and he had everybody gather in a circle around him. It was just him and us. He told us what it was, it was mutiny and under normal circumstances we could all get shot. He wanted to know who had anything to do with it and nobody would answer. He'd walk right up to one guy after another, looking at us with those beady black eyes. He'd say, are you going to talk to me, are you going to talk? I was like other guys, I had respect for him but I wasn't going to give him anything to go on. Boy, I never seen him so mad. I thought I was gonna put in life in jail by the time Gavin got done talking."

As serious of an infraction as the petition was, sentencing every man with a signature on the paper to hard labor at Leavenworth, a court martial for the whole battalion and perhaps an execution of the ringleaders could have been pursued under military law. The problem was that it was clear the guys in the 319th felt compelled to take the measures they had for reasons which held some merit. Compounding the dilemma for Gavin was the injurious effect which taking wholesale disciplinary actions would have on the morale and combat efficiency of the division as a whole. The 319th was arguably the most experienced artillery outfit in the 82nd, with two Presidential Unit citations. With the knowledge that another mission was at most only weeks away, Gavin really had little choice. As Ed Ryan put it, "The guys, knew that Holland was coming up so there wouldn't be much they could do about it." Hogg told how the assembly ended. "Finally Gavin stopped," remembered Hogg. "He said, I could have every son of a bitch in front of me shot, but I'm not going to. I need you. I'm gonna get rid of the Major. You won't see him here anymore. Maybe I'm gonna give you one a lot worse than him, but you won't see him anymore to bother you."

General Gavin was true to his word. A few days later Major Wilcoxson received a "promotion" to division artillery and quietly left the 319th. For the enlisted men it was an unabashed victory, but the officers were delighted as well. They were also both surprised and proud of the bold, successful initiative of their men. Sartain expressed it in plain terms when he said, "You know, among the battery, among the men, they had a lot of secrets among themselves that we officers didn't know anything about. They did, but that was OK." Not one single officer knew anything about the petition, but all the officers agreed with it. We got a big charge out of it, we'd giggle about it in the mess hall. Had any of the officers known anything about it there would have been very serious consequences. As it was, it was a very big deal. Colonel Todd almost lost his job over it, but I think he handled it well, he seemed resolved to keep his mouth shut and let nature take its course. Best thing that ever happened to the 319th was getting rid of Bertsch and getting rid of Wilcoxson. " Though the petition flew in the face of military discipline, the enlisted guys had faced down the system and removed a field officer all on their own, something that wasn't supposed to happen in the army.

It wasn't long after the Wilcoxson episode was over when the alert for the 319th's next mission was sounded. This operation, planned for September 2nd, was canceled when Allied forces overran the intended landing zone located in Belgium. It was actually the last of at least 17 airborne operations which were prepared, but never undertaken since D-Day. Nonetheless, a fortnight later the men were alerted again. This time the destination was Holland.

Unlike before the Normandy invasion, everyone sensed the outfit wouldn't be coming back to Papillon Hall again. With the Nazis on the ropes it looked like the war could be over before the New Year. The people of Lubenham felt it too. The knowledge that the 319th was leaving what had been its very pleasant home for the past seven months lent an emotional element that was bitter-sweet. On the morning of September 15th, the guys passed through Lubenham to Market Harborough one last time. Don Johnson, the Lubenham boy who'd become a mascot of the guys at Pap's Hall, remembered the event as a man in his later years, "It was a sad day," he wrote, "when the 82nd Glider unit marched to Market Harborough enroute south. We were waving goodbye to people who were open and friendly, especially if you had a sister. They had brought life to Lubenham such as we had never known before. It has never been quite the same since."

BATTERY!

Part 18: "Die with your eyes open."

The 319th's next mission was a strategic gamble, one which could end the war in a matter of weeks if successful. The plan, originally conceived by British Field Marshal Montgomery, called for the newly created 1st Allied Airborne Army, comprised of the American 82nd and 101st Airborne Divisions, as well as the British 1st Airborne Division and the Polish Independent Parachute Brigade, to seize a corridor across eastern Holland up to the German side of the Rhine River.

Code-named Operation Market, and scheduled for Sunday, September 17th, 1944, the airborne mission would drop the 101st Airborne closest to the British front lines, then located just outside the Dutch frontier. Their job was to capture a series of bridges and secure the first section of highway leading northeast toward the city of Nijmegen and then beyond to Arnhem.

Meanwhile, the mission of Gavin's 82nd was to first occupy the high ground around Groesbeek, near the German border. The Groesbeek heights were really the only prominent ground in Holland and commanded any approach leading to the ultimate objective of the bridges at Nijmegen. Gavin was also tasked with taking several bridges, including Europe's largest single span located over the Waal River at Nijmegen. Of course, all these objectives required holding the highway leading up from the positions of the 101st as well.

While the Americans were establishing a secured route of advance, the British 1st Airborne Division, with the Polish Parachute Brigade, would be dropped in a position from which they would seize and hold the bridges over the lower Rhine at Arnhem, a full 65 miles behind German lines. In theory, with two American airborne divisions paving the way, the land invasion led by the British XXX Armored corps would race up the highway to their airborne troops at Arnhem within a few days. If all things went as planned, there would be a British armored corps in Northern Germany before the enemy would have time to react. Once established at this point, the Allies would be in easy striking distance of the German industrial heartland and in a position to force the enemy's capitulation.

Operation Garden was the codename given to this overland part of the mission. Thus, together with its airborne component, the invasion of Holland would be collectively known as Operation Market-Garden. The idea had some merit, bypassing, as it did, the entire Siegfried Line, the series of formidable German defensive positions which held their frontier to the south. On the other hand, there were significant problems with Market-Garden which left many of those involved in its preparation uneasy. To begin with, only a few days had been allotted to assemble all the intelligence necessary for this undertaking of such a vast scale. Consequently, little was actually known about the German troops who would be on the ground to meet the Allies. Market-Garden planners seemed satisfied with the assumption that they would be demoralized, second rate units already retreating in disarray. With the three airborne divisions strung out along a narrow corridor running deep into Nazi held territory, the failure to seize any one of the vital bridges intact would place any troops beyond that point in serious jeopardy. Airborne troops, after all, did not carry heavy weapons with them and would be dependant on unreliable airdrops for supplies of ammunition or rations. The highway which the British tankers would be traveling on was also only a two lane road and really inadequate for the task for which it was intended. Furthermore, the American divisions were required to occupy enormous expanses of terrain, with that assigned to the 82nd being in itself over thirty miles from one end to the other. With no alternate routes of advance, Montgomery's plan left little room for the confusion of battle or the inevitable and unforeseen developments of the battlefield. Just the same, given the rapidly deteriorating defensive posture of the Wehrmacht, the risks were deemed acceptable in the face of what could be gained, provided everything worked precisely as planned.

By the time preparations for the invasion of Holland commenced it was clear that the fight against the Nazi regime had also taken on a more urgent and earnestly humanitarian feature. Liberated inhabitants of France and Belgium were revealing the wholesale disappearance of enemies of the Germans, mostly Jews, but also gypsies, homosexuals, labor unionists, communists, and anyone else whom the Nazis deemed incompatible with their vision of a socially cleansed Europe. These populations were whisked away, never to be heard from again. At the same time, Soviet troops overrunning German held areas of Eastern Europe were already discovering the first of what would prove to be hundreds of concentration camps. Some of these installations were designated as work-camps; others were simply intended for extermination. All were brutal and relied on the utter dehumanization of the prisoners to maintain order.

Before leaving Papillon the battalion was drawn up and the mission's objectives were explained. Orders were also issued to prevent men from falling into the German's genocide program should they be taken prisoner. In "A" Battery, Robert Dickson

The day before the flight into Holland, waiting "A" Batttery men pose at the airfield. Left to right: Gus Kokas, Roland Gruebling, Tom 'Jughead' Ludwick, Ted Covais, Harold Mell, Felix Ferrante, and Milton Lessler. Courtesy Gruebling family."

recalled what they were told. "When we went to Holland they got us out in formation. They said, anybody that has a Jewish background and got any identification as to being a Jew will have to get it gone. There were a lot of people in my outfit that were Jews, but they had to leave all their identification at headquarters. They couldn't have it on them because if they were captured they immediately would be killed or put in a concentration camp."

After the formation was dismissed one of the men approached Captain Sartain. It was Bill Siegel, the battery's mess sergeant and a Jew. Siegel, having owned a small diner in New York City during peacetime, took great pride in providing decent chow to his new patrons. Normally a cheerful guy, Sartain could see clearly that the Mess Sergeant had something serious on his mind. "Captain," he said, "I've been with this unit from the very beginning. I can't go home and tell my children that I never went into combat with the battery, that I never made an airborne operation. Sir, can I go with the battery into Holland?"

Sartain considered Siegel's request. Normally, as had happened in Normandy, Siegel and his mess truck would have rejoined the outfit with the seaborne element a week or so after the airborne operation. It seemed though, that there might not be another airborne mission. Perhaps the open acknowledgement of what was happening to his fellow Jews across Europe lent added meaning to this mission for the Mess Sergeant. Whatever the reason, Sartain couldn't refuse him and said, "That'll be just fine. Tell Sergeant Johnson I said you're coming with us and he'll get you situated."

"Thank you Captain," Siegel answered, "This really means a lot to me."

If Sergeant Siegel was eager to go, there were others who didn't quite share his ardor. For example, Sartain remembered another man who came to his quarters soon after his conversation with Siegel. "He came to see me before the Holland invasion and said, 'I just can't make this next operation.'" Sartain knew the man as an old member of the outfit, but one who'd also developed a bad reputation as unreliable in combat. "I asked him why and he told me, 'I'm just not comfortable with it.'" There would have been explanations which Sartain might have felt some sympathy for, but coming so soon after Siegel's request to take a position of danger, this answer particularly riled him. Sartain felt his face flush with anger as he responded, "Well, you just get comfortable, because you're going." Even after over 60 years had passed, Sartain grew irritated at the memory. "Never will forget him. I was gonna make that little bastard go into Holland with us. See, you couldn't just let anybody that had any qualm about going in transferring into another position. You'd have, not a rebellion, but you'd have quite a few characters who wanted to get out doing that. So I kept an eye on him at the airfield and all of that humbug. Then I got busy with other things and lost contact. I didn't see him, didn't see him, then when we made the operation I found out the son of a bitch wasn't with us! He avoided it, I don't know how, but he disappeared. Went to some other unit, I don't know. Somehow he got away, and I never saw him again, never heard of him again."

As was the case with Operation Neptune, there was an issue of a brand new combat uniform for every man in the battalion before leaving for the security camp. Unlike previously, this time the clothing wasn't treated with the detested anti-gas agents which made the Normandy uniforms so uncomfortable. These new uniforms were, in fact, altogether different. Because the 82nd and 101st were the only divisions in northwestern Europe issued this clothing at the time, the airborne troopers assumed it was simply an updated version of the khaki jumpsuits worn by the paratroopers in Sicily, Italy, and Normandy. They were not.

DIE WITH YOUR EYES WIDE OPEN.

First field tested by the 3rd Infantry Division while fighting at Anzio the year before, the Model 1943 Field Uniform was part of a complete revamping of the army's clothing which would not take full effect until the spring of 1945. The new system relied on the layering principle for protection and warmth. The jacket consisted of an olive green cotton sateen outer shell, built with two expanding breast pockets and two lower pockets below the waist. The whole was fully lined in poplin, had a drawstring at the waist, and covered button closures throughout. Deliberately oversized, the M-43 was intended to employ an alpaca lined inner garment with knitted cuffs and collar, along with the five-button, high neck sweater, for winter use.

A matching pair of generously cut, olive green trousers were issued to complete the uniform, with the intention that they would be worn over the mustard colored woolens which had been in use since the 1930s. In the case of the airborne divisions, these trousers were also altered at their parachute rigging shops by the addition of large canvas cargo pockets at the thighs. These pockets were patterned after those on the old khaki jumpsuits, being of roughly the same dimensions but constructed from stocks of British canvas.

This time divisional patches remained on the left shoulder, in addition to a large American flag on the right. Helmet nets with elastic bands were passed out to officers and those enlisted men who would be operating with the infantry. Together with the jump boots, it was a very different appearance which the 319th had from its previous combat uniform, but one which would typify their appearance for the rest of the war and the American soldier for the rest of the century.

On September 15th, with the next mission set to initiate within 48 hours, a new battalion XO had to be assigned immediately to replace Major Wilcoxson. Major Frederick Silvey, XO of the 320th, and a native of San Antonio, Texas, was chosen and took his place with the 319th late that morning as the outfit was packing up. Silvey was well known to the officers in the battalion, and well liked too. His reputation as a field officer who didn't shrink from frontline combat had earned him a decoration for gallantry in Normandy, and that carried a lot of weight with the battalion's personnel. "Major Silvey was a good man, a good man. He was always visiting the batteries both in and out of combat. He was rather low key, like Todd, but very positive and very good," was Sartain's appraisal of him years later.

With Silvey now on board, the battalion assembled to leave for the Holland invasion. This time, unlike with the Normandy operation, there was a relaxation of the order prohibiting cameras, giving one of "A" Battery's sergeants, probably Carl Davis, with a viewfinder ample opportunity to indulge his interest in photography. Before leaving Pap's Hall for the last time, he asked the "A" Battery officers to pose together. In front of the mansion's goldfish pond they lined up, Lieutenants Gutshall, Cook, Mullen, Fellmen, and Ragland, all in a row, with Sartain, their Captain, at one end.

At 13:00 hours the battalion moved out, leaving Papillon hall behind forever. This time each battery had a different destination airfield from which it would be flying. By late afternoon they were in place: HQ at Cottesmore, "A" Battery at Barkston Heath, and "B" at Fulbeck Airfield – all in Lincolnshire. The guys were fed a hot meal that evening. It was a beautiful night and, at least in "A" Battery, they slept under the stars on folding cots set up in a field adjacent to one of the hangers.

The 16th of September passed slowly. Once again they were in a secured camp, restricted from doing much else besides checking gear, smoking cigarettes, waiting, and rechecking. "It was kind of boring, it really was," commented Sartain of the wait. If anyone was apprehensive about the invasion, they might have referred to the "All-American Troubled Soldier Ticket" which Chaplain Reid had distributed in North Africa. Under the heading of "Next Mission," they would have been directed to Ecclesiastes 7:8 and read, "Better is the end of a thing than the beginning thereof, and the patient in spirit is better then the proud in spirit."

Kenneth Smith had a fatalistic attitude about the mission which was typical of the veterans in the outfit. He said, "Every time we went into combat I knew that had to be the last time I'd have to worry about it, because I'd probably get killed, but I never did. I just kept coming back one more time. It was the same with all of us. We knew one day we weren't gonna get home. It's a lot of luck."

Bob McArthur, Able Battery's former chief of sections and now a 2nd lieutenant in HQ Battery, wrote home to his mother that night. Though trying to allay her fears, his words suggest what was almost certainly on most of the men's minds as they considered the coming operation. "If you want to know where I am just listen to your radio news and read the headlines in the paper," he wrote. "But don't worry about me, Mother, I'll be ok. After you go through so much of this stuff you get to where you never think about being killed or anything like that. It never crosses my mind so don't let it worry you. And anyway Mother, you can't fight a war without loosing men. Men have already died, more men will die before this thing is over. If this war calls for me to give my life, then I'll just be one of them, but I have no fear of that Mother. I've seen too many men die to be afraid to die. This will probably be the last letter you get from me in a long time, but don't worry, I've got all the confidence in the world in this thing."

The "A" Battery guys watched as a regiment of British paratroopers waddled out to their C-47s early on the morning of September 17th. The transports were part of the 61st Troop Carrier Group. On this day it would ferry two serials of the British jumpers to their drop zones near Arnhem, with a trip for "A" Battery to the glider landing zones around Groesbeck scheduled for sunrise the next morning. Once the C-47s were

Taken just before boarding gliders bound for Holland, "A" Battery officers." Left To Right: John Gutshall, Laurence Cook, Joseph Mullen, Marvin Fellman, Marvin Ragland, and Captain Charles L. Sartain. Sartain collection

aloft, the 319th started getting their things ready. As had been practiced so many times before, the battery busied itself in transferring its guns and equipage from the trucks and on to the gliders, which had now been towed to their stations along the airstrip. That the gliders waiting for them were the American CG4A and not the British Horsa, did much to buoy the spirits of the men. Whether their dread of a Horsa flight was from previous experience or acquired secondhand from their veteran buddies, no one wanted another repeat of the Normandy crash landings.

Lieutenant Gutshall had meanwhile been selected from "A" Battery to go in with the advance contingent of the 319th. He, along with Colonel Todd, Major Wimberley, Lieutenants Peters, Procopio, and Kondradick, as well as Sgt. Brown from HQ Battery, collected themselves at Balderton Aerodrome. They were to glide in to Holland simultaneously with the parachute drop of the 508th and receive the battalion with prepared surveyed gun positions when it glided in the next day.

That night the battery again bedded down on cots set up in the open air, but sometime around midnight the stars disappeared behind a heavy bank of clouds. Then a light rain began to fall. The guys tried to ignore it, but before long the drizzle became a downpour. By one's, then two's, and finally whole squads, the men got up cursing in their soaking wet blankets. "All night long it rained cats and dogs," Sartain said later. "It rained on everybody. We were sopping wet, so we turned our cots up on end and went into a hanger. Slept on the floor and everything else." If anyone checked, Chaplain Reid's All-American Troubled Soldier Ticket also had a citation specifically intended for wet blankets, though there is no evidence that anyone read it that night. The citation was Psalm 69: "Save me Oh God, for the waters are come in onto my soul. I sink in deep mire where there is no standing. I am come into deep waters where the floods overflow me."

By sunrise on Monday, September 18th the rain had stopped, but foggy conditions over the landing zone in Holland resulted in a four hour delay of the scheduled take off time. Nonetheless, events had passed the point of no return. As one "A" Battery man later remarked, "After they issued us ammunition and food we knew we were on our way."

The guys gathered in small groups around their glider stations, smoking, talking together, or reviewing the loading manifests and double-checking the lashings one more time. These last activities were really done to expend nervous energy, for all these duties had been performed many times already.

The CG4A was designed for a pilot and co-pilot seated side by side in the cockpit, a shortage of trained pilots called for the recruitment of instant aviators from among the artillerymen. Prior experience or knowledge of piloting an aircraft was unnecessary. Generally being the ranking man among those who would be riding in the glider was enough to be awarded this job. Thus Captain Sartain, as well as Lieutenants Ragland, Cook, Fellman, and in all likelihood Mullen too, were all drafted as co-pilots. If an officer wasn't available, sergeants would do, as Robert Rappi and Motor Pool Chief Jessie Holman, as well as others, discovered. As Rappi put it, "I happened to be the ranking member of the tribe." If one had even the slightest exposure to aircraft, this was also considered sufficient reason to be promoted to co-pilot status.

Sebring found this out when he was told, "You worked on bombers so you have more airplane experience than anyone else here." His civilian job installing wiring on B-24 Liberators was enough.

In the short time remaining before take-off, most of the pilots gave their new partners a crash course, introducing them to the various controls and giving them an ad-hoc lesson in flying a glider. "The pilot gave me instructions before we left Great Britain," Rappi recalled. "He said, you see that rod over there right next to you? Well, when I holler, spoilers, you pull that all the way back. Then let it back easy, real easy, or else we'll balloon. Whatever he meant by that, I still don't know."

Sartain didn't have time for a glider lesson. Instead he received a G-2 briefing that morning on what the paratroopers had encountered so far in Holland. According to G-2, indications were that the airborne drop had been a complete surprise, leaving the Germans in a state of "extreme panic." Elements of the German 84th Division had been positively identified, along with sundry ersatz battalions, but these were collectively described in the report as "a mixed lot with no real backbone." So far the principle enemy resistance encountered was centered near the city of Nijmegen and the village of Mook, a hamlet located south-west of the battalion's landing zone outside Groesbeek. Of particular concern was a dozen square miles of forest situated near the LZ, just over the German border. Known as the Reichswald, this area was suspected to be concealing a German force of unknown size, which could pose a potential threat of some significance.

Afterwards, while Sartain's men were waiting at their stations, he went from one group to the other, briefing them as he had been briefed and stressing what he felt was important. Sartain remembered it. "The G-2 briefing didn't get down to the troops," he said. "We had all of these recruits who'd never been on a glider mission before. I told them, don't hang around that glider, once it lands don't sit around thinking about what you're gonna do. You'll get shot. Get out of that glider and assemble. We drilled that into them time and again. Get away from that glider and take the pilot with you." By this time the Captain had evidently been informed of more complete information about the enemy troops in the Nijmegen area as well, and he passed this intelligence on to the men in his command.

Mahlon Sebring described his battery commander's talk to the cluster of men at his glider. "Captain Sartain, he laid it on the line to us at the airport before we went into combat. He told us everything that he thought we ought to know. He said we might have a lot of trouble with tanks. There was some big SS tank outfit in that area and they couldn't find them, so we might run into a lot of tanks in this wooded area. Then, when he got done he said, alright, there it is, you've had it."

At 11:05 the order was given for the men waiting at Barkston Heath to take their places in their gliders. Altogether there were 40 of them, with 31 to "A" Battery and the remainder loaded with personnel from division artillery. The gliders were attached in pairs to the tow planes. The arrangement was typically to have one glider loaded with the 75mm pack howitzer and its five man crew, towed in tandem with its jeep and three other men in the other glider. In this way, when released, each gun and its transportation would be landing simultaneously and in close proximity to each other.

The synchronized take-off time from all three airfields was 1135. As with any large scale glider operation, it took most of an hour for all the Troop Carrier Squadrons from Cottesmore, Fulbeck, Barkston Heath, and other airfields to unite at altitude and begin their journey over the channel toward Holland. It was a massive serial, altogether composed of over 450 gliders carrying the 319th and 320th Field Artillery, a battery of the 456th Parachute Field Artillery, and assorted other units ranging from quartermaster troops to medical detachments, along with Division Artillery Headquarters. On the ground, boys in the village of Lubenham heard the drone of aircraft and, shielding their eyes, looked up to see their American GI friends being towed above them.

DIE WITH YOUR EYES WIDE OPEN.

Once the serial set course, Lieutenant Ragland was informed of some surprising news by the pilot of his glider. "When we got ready to load up the pilot asked me, 'You the senior person in this group?' I told him I was," Ragland explained. "So he said, 'You ride up front with me then.' Well, we just got in the air when he said, 'Here, you take it, you fly the glider.' I said what! 'Yeah, he said, we're short of copilots. All you have to do is hold the control steady and don't cross your rope with that other glider. When you get over the coast of Holland I'll take over.'"

Ragland was lucky that he didn't find himself trying to control the glider in a sudden burst of turbulence because keeping the glider under control wasn't really a job for a novice. Other gliders did have problems. That flown by Flight Officer Benson J. Reed, with Lieutenant John Eskoff as his co-pilot, and four other men from the HQ Battery found it veering and banking wildly when it was caught in the prop-wash of several British bombers which passed a few hundred feet below. When it looked as if the glider would cross tow-ropes with another glider flying alongside, Flight Officer Reed cut loose from the tow plane to avoid bringing down other aircraft with him in one tangled tragedy.

Dropping out of formation to the English Channel, Eskoff's glider hit the water at about 70 miles per hour. By this time those inside had already kicked the windows and doors open or taken axes and cut holes in the ceiling. Good thing, because the glider immediately flooded and, loaded with a trailer and more than a ton of equipment, began to sink. All five men escaped, with the most serious injury being a broken nose, and they were immediately picked up by the Royal Navy. Though Eskoff was in no way responsible for what happened, a misconception persisted among many enlisted men in the battalion that he'd deliberately released the tow rope to avoid combat in Holland.

No other incidents occurred while over the channel and North Sea. Conversation was nearly impossible in the noise, so the men mostly kept to themselves, occupied with their own thoughts. Lester Newman tore a hole in the side of his glider so that he could observe what was going on. "I was looking out a side window. Well, there was no window there, you put your fist through the damn glider and get you a hole big enough to see through. I'll tell you one thing, them gliders; you could rip a hole in them big enough to see a long ways."

It was generally believed prudent to empty one's bladder before landing, and that was a personal chore which many also took care of during the flight. As Sebring explained, "You go to the back and pee, or else open the door and pee out the door. But some guys was pretty scared and they didn't wander around much."

As the airborne armada approached the Dutch mainland, it started to receive fire from islands off shore and anchored barges mounted with anti-aircraft guns. Those who hadn't already done so, took precautions. Corporal John Girardin, for example, lay across the hood of the jeep in his glider. Others who'd been walking freely took seats and belted themselves in as soon as the concussion from exploding akak began to buffet them.

This was Carl Salminen's first combat. He later remembered what it was like in his glider, riding with Sergeant Holman and a wire corporal. "When we started getting over the shore of Holland, that's when the German akak started to open up. I could hear this little snapping sound. I asked, 'What the hell is that snapping sound?' Well, of course the pilot didn't know. The Sergeant says, he says, 'That's bullets coming through'. I counted sixty snaps, and one come up right behind me. It went through the jeep floor right behind my back. I don't know what would have happened if it would have come under me because the gas tank is underneath the seat. I kind of wondered at the time how scary this would be, but not like it was for Sergeant Holman or that other guy, the telephone operator or lineman, what ever he was. They had flown into Normandy of course, so they were scared. They were like a sheet. But for me, it didn't effect me because I was, you might say, a rookie."

After passing the coastline the anti-aircraft fire continued, though mostly in a scattered manner, waxing whenever the serial passed over larger towns or military installations. Most all of the gliders took some hits. Lester Newman recalled that, "We had a machinegun go the whole length of it but nobody got hit." The tail of Lieutenant Cook's glider was similarly ripped up by machinegun fire, but again no appreciable damage was done. This was typical, since the bullets and fragments would pass through the canvas skin without doing any harm unless it happened to hit someone or something which might explode. Nonetheless, the danger was real enough.

Sitting in the plexiglass bubble of the cockpit, Sebring found the whole thing sort of unnerving, saying afterward, "You sit up in that plastic nose and see all that flak antiaircraft fire coming up, you wonder how the devil you'll get through it."

Captain Manning was with the headquarters contingent that had flown out of Cottesmore and, like most of the officers, was drafted as a co-pilot. He agreed with Sebring's thoughts as his glider drew flak, writing later of the flight over Holland, "We could see the dikes and roadway systems very clearly - and they could see us! We received a lot of flak, but our glider only had superficial hits. It was very uncomfortable being such an obvious target, but the daylight helped us make out the landmarks."

The question of a glider mission in daylight was one hotly debated before Market-Garden. Obviously, gliders would be large and slow moving targets for German gunners in daylight, but the carnage caused, in part, by the night landings in Normandy couldn't be ignored. In the end the two deciding factors were the weakness of the German Luftwaffe by the late summer of 1944 as compared with earlier that year, and the shortage of experienced glider pilots who could handle nighttime landings. The GIs in the 319th had mixed opinions on the point. Clearly any glider silhouetted against a bright sky was an easier target, but some agreed with Covais when he asserted, "Holland was better because Holland was daytime. You can see where you're going. I mean, if you're gonna die, die with your eyes open, see where you're dieing."

Another mitigating factor in support of a daylight mission was the strong presence of the air force all the way from England to the landing zone. Escorting squadrons of American P-51 fighters went to work immediately, diving after any German gun positions which dared to fire upon the glider fleet. As Sartain put it, "As soon as they would open up on us, right away one of our little fighters would take them out."

The 319th's destination was Landing Zone "T," located about a thousand yards northeast of Groesbeek, and LZ "N" on the town's southern side. What the guys in the gliders didn't know as they flew over Holland was that the landing zones were largely in the hands of the Germans. With the division so thinly spread, Gavin had been forced to take a gamble and concentrate his efforts on seizing the bridges over the Waal River at Nijmegen. If the enemy remained disoriented long enough, their confusion might allow a string of outposts from portions of the 505th and 508th regiments to keep any Germans away from the critical landing zones.

The enemy proved to be more resilient however. They anticipated that zones "T" and "N" would be the logical sites for expected glider reinforcements, and on the morning of the 18th, mounted their first organized counterattacks against isolated American strongpoints along a line from Mook to Groesbeek. Though composed of a hodge-podge of standard Wehrmacht units, Luftwaffe ground troops, and even some landlocked sailors from the Kriegsmarine, the GIs were forced to relinquish ground to the enemy's pressure. As the Germans swarmed out of the Reichswald and filtered onto the LZs, they brought with them a formidable array of firepower, including over 60 twin-barreled, 20mm anti-aircraft guns, quickly digging them into fixed positions to await the expected glider force.

General Gavin withdrew the 1st Battalion of the 508th Regiment from the Nijmegen front and forced marched them back to the same landing zones where they'd dropped by parachute the day before. Their counterattack came just in time to regain enough control of the LZs to make the landings possible. Had they arrived less than an hour later it would have been a disaster for the gliders.

As it was, much of the fields were still being cleared and contested, even while the glider fleet was arriving. As Lester Newman peered through the hole he'd punched in his glider's canvas covering he could plainly see German anti-aircraft gunners abandoning their pieces and running for safety with American paratroopers in hot pursuit, firing as they went. Some guys saw at least one glider already crashed and burning on the ground. Other sights from the air were mysterious. Mahlon Sebring saw figures in white robes moving about on the LZ. Puzzled at the time, he later learned these were nuns from a nearby convent carrying pitchers of water for the incoming troops.

The glider "Flak Happy" and its HQ Signals Section passengers at Cottesmore Airfield on the morning of September 18, 1944. They are, Left to right, kneeling: T-4 Ed Ryan, First Sergeant Irving Rosenwasser, George Barron, and Dimitrios vassal. Standing, Left to right: glider pilot William Marks, Corp. Ernest Osborne, Seymour Englander, and Motor Pool Sergeant Jarret Fury. Englander would become the last man in the 319th wounded in Holland. Of Osborne, Ryan later said, "None of us liked him. In England we got drunk one night and tied him to a railroad track. Then a train really was coming, so we had to go back and cut him loose."photo courtesy Ed Ryan.

BATTERY!

In spite of this, most of the German 20mm guns were still manned and firing furiously. Ed Ryan was in the co-pilot's seat of a glider named "Flak Happy" and described the final approach this way, "We were low, about six hundred feet all the way. The bullets were hitting the wings of the aircraft. You could hear them going tack tack tack. I could see the gun go off and right up at me. The glider pilot, he said to us, 'You guys have had combat before. I'll do what you tell me to do. I want you to understand that. You take over when you want to cut loose or whatever you tell me and we'll do it.' I said, 'OK'. So I had an air photo and I could see where the landing was supposed to be. I saw that yellow "T" on the landing field and told him to cut the cord." Ryan was referring to a large "T" fashioned from panels of yellow canvas measuring about three feet wide by twelve feet long, laid out by the paratroopers to identify the landing zone.

However, not all the glider pilots were as communicative as Ryan's was. Rappi thought of the instructions he'd gotten before take off about pulling the "spoilers" to keep the glider from "ballooning" and waited for the pilot to give him the order. "Once the AK started coming through our glider he didn't say nothing," Rappi remembered. "He didn't tell me nothing, he forgot all about them spoilers! Never told me nothing. I was waiting for his command, but he never gave it."

The time was 1445 hours, and the skies above landing zones "T" and "N" were full of gliders, tow planes, and flak of every caliber. One of the battalion's gliders took a direct hit from a flak shell. "As we come in circling around the field, I had a glider on my right. I looked around and then looked back and it wasn't there. I saw men flying through the air. He got knocked out of the air right there," said Lieutenant Cook.

Robert Dickson actually witnessed the hit, and the sight never left his memory. "A glider flying beside the one I was in exploded," he later said. "It was loaded with gasoline with about four men in it. It was full of gasoline. Flak hit it, it exploded. That was, boy, that made you hurt all over. Just to see it, because you thought, well, I might be next." Dickson continued his description, stressing how the training and unit cohesion got the men through. "Everybody was scared to death," he said, "but they kept their cool and did their job. That was the good part about it. Everyone knew what they were supposed to do and they did it. Nobody backed up on anything."

Captain Manning's glider had its own close call. "We spotted a crossroad near Groesbeek, and cut loose. Just in time, our tow plane went down in flames a few minutes later," he wrote. "We dropped into a large field in a rather steep glide - and dug up about ten bushels of potatoes as we plowed our way to a stop."

As his glider came over the landing zone, Carl Salminen was sitting in the driver's seat of his jeep. "The only safety belts I had was that steering wheel," he said, describing the final moments of his first combat landing. "I took my arms from underneath the steering wheel and anchored myself in case, if the thing goes over, I'm staying with it. I depended on the ropes would keep. All the communication from the C47 was the red light and a green light. Red light is just get ready. They unlock the nose three minutes before landing. When the green light came on that is when they uncoupled the tow rope to the plane. That's when they said, down we go!" Gliders were cutting loose and landing all over now. Salminen's came to rest in a wheat field, but most ploughed through turnips, beets, and like Manning's, potatoes.

In another glider, Sebring had a set of headphones on, assisting in communication with the tow-plane. As the concentration of flak got thicker, the C-47 increased speed to a dangerous degree. The glider began shaking violently, as if about to come apart. And its pilot told Sebring to inform the tow-plane of this fact. The answer was,

DIE WITH YOUR EYES WIDE OPEN.

"You're coming with us, so hang on!"

Then a burst of flak nearly cut the tow line in two. It was just as well, since they were over the landing zone anyway. Releasing the towline, they went in a steep glide toward a line of trees. When Sebring looked to his left he saw the pilot was frozen, making no effort to correct their descent. Someone had to act fast, so Mahlon grabbed the steering yoke and pulled back on it for all he was worth. The glider responded just enough to clear the treetops, then lost its forward momentum and pancaked into the next field. This glider sustained enough damage that the mechanism which lifted the nose and allowed the jeep or other cargo inside to be rolled out the front was broken, hopelessly jammed shut. Fortunately the glider had also cut a shallow trench which gave the guys a little cover from the machinegun fire spraying the field. Sebring and the other guys scrambled out of the glider's side door and flattened themselves in the trench until paratroopers drove off the enemy machine gunners, then went to work with axes to chop away enough of the fuselage to get their jeep out. They had only one man injured. "My buddy got his bladder busted in the landing. His name was Harry Kerr. He was from Anderson, Indiana, and he was a pretty sick guy for a few days. Of course, if he'd gone back to the back end of the glider or open the door and relieve himself, why that probably wouldn't have happened."

With their glider pretty well torn apart, the guys in Sebring's crew were able to pull out the howitzer, but their tow jeep was nowhere in sight. Finally a jeep with Red Cross markings came close enough to be called over. The gunners told the driver to hitch up their gun and haul it to the rendezvous point. "I can't do that, I'm a Red Cross," he answered. Sebring raised his weapon and said to him, "You want to die right here, or hook on to the gun?"

It was 19 year old Joe D'Appolonio's first glider ride or taste of combat. However, as he later said, "At that time, at my age nothing bothered me. I wasn't afraid of dying or anything. There was no fear in me at all because I didn't know any better." But when the tow line to D'Appolonio's glider was released, he was alarmed to see how quickly it descended toward earth, and the landing itself was jarring to say the least. The glider's nose plowed into the ground, leaving the tail suspended in the air at a 45 degree angle. Joe and the others in his glider had to kick out the side door and jump down to the ground. There was small arms fire all around them and it was evident that their landing site wasn't really secured. Then Joe had his first face to face encounter with the vaunted enemy he'd trained so long to fight. "We were all pumped up about, oh boy, these guys are all six foot two and 250

Joseph D'Appolonio of Youngstown, Ohio. He was one of the replacements waiting in Lubenham when the Battalion returned from Normandy. Joe was said by the men of "A" Battery to be a tremendous shortstop. Covais collection.

pounds," he later recalled, "But the first German, the first one we saw was surrendering and he was just a little guy."

Nearby there was a farmhouse from which a cluster of Germans were emerging with their hands on their helmets. Paratroopers were rounding them up, shouting at them, 'Hande hoch, hande hoch!' D'Appolonio's group went over to investigate. "They were at this farmhouse. We went down to this house, we rushed down there and all these Germans were surrendering. A lot of them were scruffy. Some of them, they were pretty rough. Most of them that I met were younger."

Then there were some shots which clearly came from a sniper aiming directly at the Americans around the house. After a scramble for cover, D'Appolonio remembered what happened next. "There were some trees around there and I guess he was up in a tree shooting. I just spotted him. I think they left him behind. I shot at him with my carbine and I hit him in the stomach. He was up in a tree and it was all coming out of his stomach. Oh man, I didn't know what the heck to think. It was a young guy."

Though the enemy was loosing his grip all over the LZ, Ed Ryan's glider, with a half dozen other guys from HQ Battery's Signal Section, landed right among the German positions. "We landed in a turnip field," he remembered. "First of all the fence post in the field came up through the floor. Another thing was that they were firing on us pretty good, small arms. We get out and we're lying on the ground, trying to hide behind a turnip. The Krauts were firing on us. They had a machinegun nest right over in the corner. So one of our guys says to me, he says, 'What are we gonna do?' I says, 'Let's attack them.' He said, 'You're kidding!' I said, 'No, let's try it. That's an old trick. When in doubt attack.' So the seven or eight of us got up and we ran at them. The Krauts threw the machinegun away and ran! Boy they had us dead to rights too."

Yet some of the other gliders came down as nicely as could possibly be expected. Covais' experience was that, "It was a beautiful landing. Wide open fields. It was a pleasure. I mean, not that the war was a pleasure, but it was a lot better than D-Day, oh yes indeed, yes indeed." His landing seems to have been particularly smooth, but Covais also must have witnessed some of the Germans retreating pell-mell from the landing zone. "We piled out," he continued. "We got all the equipment out and we met the Germans head on. Right there we surprised them. There was a real surprise right there, more so than most."

Sergeant Rappi and his gun crew also had a smooth landing, and it was followed by a treat they'd have never expected in a million years. "It was a beautiful afternoon. The jeep come over and hooked on the gun. We all climbed aboard the jeep and on the trail of the gun, which we weren't allowed to do in the states, ride the gun, but everybody got aboard and we got the hell out of there. Then we seen where there was kind of a road going out of there, so we took it and got to the main highway. There was a house, up on the corner right by the highway. We drove up to the farmhouse and as we were pulling up there Colonel Todd come riding by in a jeep. He'd already been in there a day or so. He put his hands over his head with clasped palms, he was shaking them at us. Like to say, good job or something. Then a woman run out of the house with her apron up in the air. She had beer bottles in there, six or seven of them. Beer bottles! We stopped there for a while and had a nice cool drink. Good cold beer!"

Captain Sartain's glider landed reasonably well, though his driver, Corporal Sosa, got bruised up pretty badly. Just the same, Sosa sped off with his Captain, Bob Miller, Sartain's radio operator, and the glider pilot, to the battalion rendezvous site on the road between Groesbeek and Nijmegen. When they arrived Sosa overheard some trouble involving one of the guns and took it on himself to correct the problem. "The truck driver for one of the howitzers, he went off and left his guys, gun and all," Sosa later explained. "So I turned around and went back and I told them, hook that gun up to the jeep there. So they hooked it up to my jeep and then all them guys piled into my jeep. I couldn't move, just sat there spinning my wheels! I had a helluva time making them get off because there were bullets flying all around the place, you see?" It was true. This glider had landed in a portion of the LZ which was still being contested. Machinegun bullets and mortar rounds were peppering the field all around them. Sosa was himself banged up and bloody from the rough landing. He was in no mood to coddle nervous gunners. "They're supposed to come running out of there. Dragging their asses, they're supposed to come running out of that glider and assemble! Finally they got off and I came up to the rendezvous area hauling that howitzer behind me and towed it to the section that was supposed to run it."

Already at the rendezvous point was Staff Sergeant Thurman King, Chief of the Signal Section. King was in complete charge, assembling his wire crew and radiomen, their equipment, and making all the preparations necessary for the communications of the battery. In all the excitement, it is doubtful anyone noticed that King was in considerable pain. In fact, he'd sustained several broken ribs and his chest was nearly crushed when his glider hit the ground. It was a hard landing. The field was soft, causing the nose to bury itself and the tail to rise almost perpendicular to the ground. The jeep inside broke loose from its lashings, smashing through the cockpit, where it came to rest on King and the pilot, badly injuring them both. The jeep driver was killed outright and the other two occupants were also badly roughed up in the wreckage.

Notwithstanding all this, King pulled the other men out of the glider, administered first aid, then snagged some nearby troopers, had them unload the cargo, and ordered them to get it up to the rendezvous point. When Sartain arrived he found the Signal Sergeant already coordinating the assembly of his section and organizing the men and equipment needed for forward observer teams.

A lot of guys were hurt, though most injuries were not of the scope or severity seen in the Normandy landings. Lieutenant Fellman, for example, took a nasty gash across his face, from forehead to chin. Wire Corporal Leslo Carney was one of those helping Sergeant King. Though his face was dripping with blood from numerous lacerations, Carney had already made several return trips back to gliders which were isolated by enemy mortars and machineguns to retrieve vital communications equipment. King, Carney, and Sosa would later receive Bronze Stars for their actions on the 18th of September and the days immediately following. In almost all cases these men with broken noses, cracked ribs, burst bladders, and teeth knocked out, kept right on doing the jobs they were trained to do. Some others couldn't. In one glider the cable which raised the nose through the use of a pulley system as the jeep drove forward, must have been clipped by flak. Once the glider came to a stop, the driver fired up his jeep and drove forward. When the nose came up the strain was too much and the cable snapped as he drove under it. The jeep driver was killed then and there.

Meanwhile people were asking after Sergeant Siegel. Where the hell's Siegel, they asked, anybody seen Siegel? The answer was invariably, no. It wasn't until the next day that his body was found and identified, a casualty to the small arms fire that surrounded the LZ. New to close up combat, Siegel may have exposed himself when he should have stayed under cover, or maybe he was just unlucky. In any event his wish was fulfilled, his kids would always be able to say that their father had participated in an airborne mission against the Nazis, and had given his life in the course of it.

Though no one on his glider was injured, perhaps Robert Dickson's landing was the most harrowing of all. "The glider I was in took out an antiaircraft gun with the wings on the glider," he said. "That's just how hairy it was. He had to, or be shot down. That antiaircraft gun was firing when we went in. He just headed straight for it, wrapped the wing around it. The gun was out of commission, the people left. The crew on it were women and they took off on a dead run. I'm sure they were captured but they were all women."

Manning's glider landed in good order, no one injured and his jeep evidently serviceable. He and his driver, a new replacement, made their way to a road which soon branched off in two opposite directions. The Captain made an educated guess as to which to take, but when they made the turn a squad of paratroopers concealed nearby hollered out to them that they were headed straight for the German lines. At this point they discovered the jeep had no brakes. It took a series of high speed, hairpin turns for the driver to get them started back in the direction from which they'd come.

"My first contact with the Dutch people was shortly after," Manning wrote years later. "We stopped at a small house where I saw a woman in the yard, to confirm our direction. She was very helpful and pulled a jug of milk up out of the well for refreshment. I'm not much of a milk drinker, but I will always remember how good that tasted. A short ways down the road we found the battalion CP and started out to help find everyone."

The road Manning mentions was probably the Nijmeegsebaan, the highway running from Groesbeek to Nijmegen. The rendezvous site of the battalion was along this road, somewhere just outside Groesbeek. It was really more a check-in point, one where Colonel Todd and his staff would direct the battalion men to the appropriate battery positions.

This first gun position for "A" Battery was along the mile between the Nebo Convent and the Dekkerswald Sanitarium, close to the Waal River. The convent was an imposing four story building, surrounded by gardens and finely kept grounds. The Sanitarium, an asylum for the mentally ill, also had extensive grounds in the Dekkerswald forest.

Kenneth Smith's glider came to rest very close to it. Other guys in the outfit saw the inmates, who were left unsupervised. "They let them loose and they went running

Captain Sartain with the jeep known as "Indiana Anne", November 5th, 1944. He wears a shortened pair of rubberized boots normally issued to engineers. Covais collection.

around hollering and yelling," remembered Mahlon Sebring. "I just seen them running through the woods, I didn't see the buildings. I didn't know at the time what was going on. I said something like, they're crazy, and the guy with me said, you're right!"

Another institution in the immediate area which attracted the attention of the troopers was a complex of German military hospital tents established at the BERG-MANIANUM convent, just outside Nijmegen. The facilities were being used to house Dutch women who were pregnant with the children of SS troops. These liaisons were arranged specifically to produce offspring of the SS men and pre-selected, racially acceptable, Dutch women, free from the entanglements or obligations of marriage. They would be children for the Fatherland. GIs who passed by the BERGMANIANUM facility would see its door posted with a sign reading, "For SS only." Kenneth Smith was surprised when he came across the "Baby Factory" and later commented, "I remember a German hospital there, big tents. There was a lot of women there. Hitler was trying to make a super race. They got medals for having so many babies. I forget now what that was called, but I got one of those medals and brought it home. I lost it though. The SS Baby Factory was in many ways a sort of protective custody, since most of the local Dutch population would have viewed girls who maintained such intimate relationships with the occupying Germans contemptuously.

Meanwhile, Sartain and Ragland were beginning to assess the losses. Reports were that one of "A" Battery's gliders had been forced to release its tow line early and landed fully six miles west of the LZ. Another, with its crew and trailer was missing for the present but known to be in the immediate area. Otherwise the battery had come through surprisingly well, especially given the hostile enemy presence on the LZ when the landings began.

This was directly attributable to the high level of training and combat proficiency of the men in "A" Battery and the 319th. Lieutenant Ragland was a good example. He knew his job in every detail, and his calm, unflappable character was exactly what was needed to bring the battery from confusion to readiness. "I was firing battery exec officer," he said later, "so my main duty was to be in charge of the gun position and make sure the fire direction team was set up, ready to go. The fire direction team was set up right at the gun position. After we got the guns in position, my main job was with a three or four man crew. I had to set up the map and the firing charts so when forward observers sent a mission in we could plot it, compute the data to send to the guns."

Alone among all the field artillery units which landed by glider that day, every one of the 319th's twelve guns, along with 26 of 34 jeeps, were recovered and ready for service. Of those who were in the battalion's gliders, 91% were present for duty. All this was in spite of the fact that nearly half of the HQ Battery's gliders had overshot the landing zones, coming to rest well beyond the German border. On that afternoon of September 18th, as guys in the firing batteries were unloading their equipment they could look up as eight gliders carrying their HQ Battery comrades flew right over their heads, straight into Germany. Seven officers and 42 enlisted men from this battery, including Major Silvey, were missing and presumed captured. For the next few days it would be impossible for this battery to efficiently perform the coordinating role which it normally played. During this period the firing batteries were instead handled independently, with each receiving its fire missions directly from the infantry unit it was supporting.

For "A" Battery, that unit was the 508th Parachute Infantry Regiment (PIR), particularly it's 3rdBattalion under the command of Lt. Col. Louis G. Mendez. No stranger to the 319th, Mendez was a 1940 graduate of West Point who'd distinguished

BATTERY!

himself in Normandy. In fact, for his actions at Pretot, France, on June 20th, 1944, Mendez was awarded the Distinguished Service Cross for the way he'd led his battalion in the attack. The guys in the 319th were well acquainted with the Colonel's reputation. For those in the forward observer and liaison teams, it was an honor to provide artillery support to Mendez and his men, even if that meant getting pulled into some of the hottest combat.

"Yeah, Louie Mendez was the commander of the 3rd Battalion, 508th," remembered Sartain. "I spent many and many and many a day with him. Oh yeah. La Haye du Puits, and when we crossed the Merderet River, that's when I first met Mendez, when we were in Normandy. Well, that was their first operation. The men liked him, they really did. He was not a rear echelon battalion commander. I thought he was a first class battalion commander and a first class soldier. I became very close to Colonel Mendez and his staff. The same should be said about our forward observers and the officers of the 508th's 3rd Battalion. A strong bond existed between them and "A" Battery's forward observers."

Sartain couldn't wait to get started. As soon as the battery was set up, with the guns in their emplacements, shells distributed, and wires run from the Battery Fire Direction Center, the FO teams were dispatched and he set off to find Colonel Mendez' CP. That was Sartain's style, as much as his aviator sunglasses, his pipe, or the cup of coffee in his hand. Sartain explained it this way, "I didn't hang around the battery. Once the battery was in position I didn't see any reason for me to hang around. I felt like it was more important to visit the FOs and all of that. Ragland was a good man. He had everything under control, he was low key, but he was very very effective. So, when the battery was in position I made it my business that once a day I would visit each of the forward observers from my battery. I did that religiously. I just felt like that was part of my job, to visit the FOs where ever they might be. But Todd was good about it. He let me roam. Me and Sosa, with Miller in the back with the big radio and the little radio, we roamed all over."

Sosa agreed, and remembering back to his time with Sartain, described his Captain's habits by saying, "That's why I say he's a fire eater. He wanted to be up front, with this Colonel from West Point, this little Mexican guy, Mendez."

By 1630 hours forward

Colonel Louis G. Mendez, CO 3rd Battalion 508th Parachuite Infantry Regiment. Courtesy of Jean Mendez.

275

observers and liaison teams from the 319th were placing themselves among the 508th troopers. At the 3rd Battalion CP, Mendez would have been glad to see Sartain, knowing that the Captain brought with him the artillery support any infantry required in combat. The Colonel no doubt explained to Sartain that the focus of activity was shifting from the city of Nijmegen, to highway "K," leading in a south-easterly direction out of town, skirting the German border as it ran through the village of Beek and on to Wyler. If the Germans wanted to reinforce their position at Nijmegen, and cut off the 1st British Airborne Division in the process, they would need Highway "K" to do so.

Throughout the day of the 18th, pressure from German patrols had mounted and all signs indicated that an attempt to break through in this area to secure Nijmegen and seize the high ground running from Beek to Groesbeek was likely. What was more, first contact indicated that these Germans were part of an as yet unidentified Fallschirmjaeger, or paratroop regiment, along with elements of the 10th SS Panzer Division, titled "Frundsberg" after a legendary warrior deep in the German past. Reports also showed that the 9th SS Panzer, titled "Hohenstaufen" was also in the vicinity, though making its weight felt mostly against the British at Arnhem.

This was a serious development, though most German Fallschirmjaegers weren't actually given the training to jump from aircraft by this point in the war, their elite status always made them formidable opponents in combat. Moreover, regarding the 9th and 10th SS, while both units had been decimated earlier in the summer while trying to extricate themselves from the Normandy front, even badly mauled SS Divisions had well earned reputations as fierce adversaries. Market-Garden planners were unaware that Frundsberg and Hohenstaufen were reconstituting themselves in the Nijmegen/Arnhem area, absorbing new recruits and material. Had they known, it would have given them reason to reconsider. Even if these replacements were mostly under trained teenagers, they were still well armed and fanatical in their dedication to the Nazi cause.

As afternoon slipped into night, Mendez and Sartain were up on the high ground overlooking Beek. The Colonel was explaining the situation as "A" Battery's commander surveyed the terrain through his field glasses. Taking a closer look at the village below them, Sartain spied three enemy vehicles, armored scout cars probably, and lost no time. Calling his radio operator, Bob Miller, to his side, Sartain ordered the first fire mission of the battalion in Holland at 1700 hours. Three dozen rounds of heavy explosives were fired from the howitzers of "Able" Battery and came screaming in from the west seconds later. The vehicles were neutralized.

In the fading light of early evening, still more enemy activity could be seen in the open countryside beyond Beek. This time it was infantry massing and a mortar emplacement. Sartain radioed the map coordinates to the battery and Lieutenant Ragland dropped a barrage of 36 rounds on the target. Ten minutes later another two dozen rounds were directed on a country lane leading to Beek from Persingen, another hamlet near the German border. It was infantry, apparently assembling to begin an approach on Beek and Highway K. The concentration was broken up, but it was clear that the Germans were out there in force. With night coming on, and a very limited supply of ammunition on hand, it was best to get the guns registered on a couple of fixed points while there was still enough light to do so. The next day would be a busy one. It never entered Sartain's mind that tomorrow, September 19th, 1944, would also be his 24th birthday.

BATTERY!

Part 19: "He played to his own music."

Dawn was only just breaking when, at 0600 hours, Lieutenant Gutshall called in "A" Battery's first fire-mission for September 19th. The target was infantry, probably German paratroopers, seen around a road intersection about three quarters of a mile northeast of Groesbeek. "A" Battery fired 27 rounds and the Germans were forced to disperse.

Exactly two minutes after this first barrage, Gutshall called in another. This time, 45 rounds were directed against a machine gun which had opened up on Hill 75.9, located between Beek and Wyler. The hill, which commanded Highway K and provided an excellent view of the ground around Beek, had been occupied by a platoon of "G" Company from Mendez' 3rd Battalion, 508th, on the previous night. Before the day was over it would come to be known as "Devil's Hill."

Battalion records do not indicate who the other men on Gutshall's FO team were, but they would normally have included an assisting sergeant, a radio or telephone operator, and an extra man or two. Nor do records explicitly state where the Lieutenant and his team were located. Gutshall could, for example, have placed his OP with the troopers on Hill 75.9. This would not have been unusual, since being embedded in the advanced positions or on high ground was the way the FOs did their work. The FO team could have also been in Beek, though the village was itself not situated on elevated terrain. Alternately, the Lieutenant's OP could have been on the heights of Berg en Dal. There were a number of buildings there which would have served as convenient OP locations. In fact, the roof and upper story of the Hotel Groot Berg en Dal would be used for just this purpose over the coming days. Still another vantage point from which Beek, the flood plain which extended to its north and east, Hill 75.9, and even the village of Wyler, was in plain view, was a steel observation tower constructed near the Sterrenberg restaurant. This area of Holland, known as "Little Switzerland," had been a popular vacation and honeymoon destination for years. The Dutch, who were mostly accustomed to a flat terrain with limited opportunity to survey the countryside, enjoyed the vista which the tower afforeded. Being built for observation, the tower would have made an ideal OP except that its exposed nature would naturally attract the fire of the Germans.

Wherever Gutshall and his team were, only thirty minutes passed, when the Lieutenant observed more Germans approaching from the south. Over the next hour, four fire-missions were called in succession. As one barrage would break up the enemy's formation, they would reappear somewhere else, evidently attempting to encircle Beek, or Hill 75.9, or both.

The Germans understood as well as the Americans did, that Highway K was the key to Nijmegen and the Groesbeek high ground, and they were determined to take it. While the Falschirmjaegers were infiltrating from the south, a strong force of SS, composed of three tanks accompanied by one to two hundred infantry, was seen moving from the northwest out of Nijmegen headed straight for Beek. It was now clear that the Germans were launching a first attempt to capture the village and Hill 75.9. As the panzers reached the outskirts of Beek, Able Battery threw 29 rounds of high explosives at them, but they kept on coming. If ammunition were not in such short supply, their fire would no doubt have been unceasing, but replenishment by airdrop had not yet occurred.

Sergeant Covais called in the next bombardment at 0840 hours. It was directed at Falschirmjaegers attacking Devil's Hill from the east. Though the effect was described as "excellent," the 508th troopers on the hill were just too few. They were being forced to yield ground one foxhole at a time.

The entire arc from Nijmegen, through Berg en Dal, Beek and on through Hill 75.9, on to Wyler, then circling back to Groesbeek and Mook, was now in play. The 508th's 1st and 3rd Battalions were overstretched and on the defensive in most places. At Wyler, however, Company B made a swipe for the town and occupied it, setting up roadblocks with two 57mm anti-tank guns which had been brought in by glider the day before. More salvos of artillery were meanwhile directed by Captain Sartain against the tanks and infantry which had been seen advancing earlier in the morning on Beek. This fire, together with a stubborn defense by platoons from Mendez' 3rd Battalion held the village, and by noon the SS force was reported to be in retreat. Devil's Hill changed hands three times that morning, with the Americans finally ceding it to the enemy until Company A was brought up in the early afternoon. It made a daring charge which drove the Falschirmjaegers from the crest at that time. Though the Germans counterattacked repeatedly through the rest of the day, they were never able to push the 508th men from the hilltop again.

All that morning the cannoneers in the 319th kept to their guns, responding to each call for artillery support from the 508th. Lieutenant Ragland, Sergeant Picher, and the rest of "A" Battery were completely absorbed in their work as the battle for Highway K escalated. The first report of the British tanks came about 0930 hours, when the leading elements of their armored column were sighted near Heumen, a town about five miles northwest of Mook and still some distance away. As far as Montgomery's timetable was concerned, they were already running well behind schedule.

While all this was going on, Major Silvey showed up at battalion headquarters. Since his glider had over-shot the LZ by several miles the day before, it was anyone's guess whether he or any of the other HQ Battery men who came to ground so far from the 82nd's positions would ever be seen again. At the CP Silvey told how his glider came to rest somewhere near Zyfflich, across the German border. Exiting their glider immediately, the Major and a few other men concealed themselves in the undergrowth as they watched

SS troops rounding up other members of their battery, setting fire to the gliders the GIs had landed in as they did so. After dark Silvey and his party set off to find the battalion. Eventually they made their way back to the Groesbeek area, narrowly escaping capture.

Lieutenant Connelly, the 319th's supply officer, came filtering back a couple of hours after

Captain Hawkins and Lieutinent Gutshall with a 75mm pack howitzer.

BATTERY!

Major Silvey, with a story even more hair-raising. As Connelly related to his fellow officers, when his glider made its last approach on the afternoon of the 18th, it ran into intensive anti-aircraft fire. The pilot was killed in his seat and Connelly took the controls. Somehow he brought the glider down through its last fifty feet of descent. Immediately the Lieutenant could see he was in trouble. A squad of Germans was already making their way over to investigate. He opened up on them with his carbine, but realized that he'd loaded his magazine with only four rounds. Fortunately, four rounds were enough to discourage the SS squad from coming any closer. Connelly then administered first aid to the other men in his glider, both of whom were badly wounded, unable to walk, and slipped off into the forest.

Connelly traveled all night. At one point a German soldier on a bicycle rode past him in the darkness, only a couple of yards away. Finally, while hiding in the woods outside Wyler the next morning he heard an approaching patrol. When familiar phrases of cursing in American idiom reached his ears, Connelly knew it was safe to come out. He was saved, but others were not so lucky. Lieutenant Vernon Blank, "A" Battery's XO in Italy, was captured. Some of the old "C" Battery crowd from North Africa and Italy, like Delbert Jackson and "Dirty Joe" Meagan were taken prisoner too, along with about forty others from HQ Battery. None of these men were seen again until after hostilities were over.

For now though, hostilities were far from finished. The German's increasing pressure against the 82nd's eastern and southern sectors included artillery, and at about 1430 hours, "A" Battery's position came under bombardment. Though there weren't any casualties, the barrage did drive everyone into their slit trenches for the time being. Once the shelling stopped, Colonel Todd ordered "A" Battery to displace further east along a lane leading off the Nijmeegsebaan. It was a good thing too, since the position was strafed by German fighters while the battery was packing up. No one was hit, though there were some close calls. One man's helmet flew off his head as he dove into his slit-trench. When he emerged afterwards to retrieve his helmet he found a bullet hole through it.

Displacing the battery helped to disburse the concentration of material along the Nijmegen-Groesbeek highway and took the battery away from a position which had evidently been sighted by German aircraft. The new gun position also brought "A" Battery about 3⁄4 of a mile closer to the developing battle for Highway K, bringing Wyler and its environs within better range of their guns.

By 1900 hours "A" Battery had completed its relocation. German activity beyond Beek and Wyler continued, as it had throughout the day, and several more fire missions were called to break up these formations, but as twilight came on concentrations against specific targets would begin winding down with the exception of unobserved harassing fire. Nonetheless, the 319th had fired 680 rounds since dawn, with fully 495 of that number coming from Sartain's battery. There would have been more, but as yet the battalion was limited to the ammunition it had brought with it from England. At the end of the day elements of the 508th held Beek, Wyler, and Hill 75.9, albeit with only individual companies and platoons. Given their limited strength, artillery support from the 319th would be all the more crucial when the sun rose in the morning.

September 20th opened with another attack by German paratroopers to seize Hill 75.9 before the sun had fully risen above the horizon. Almost immediately, German attacks followed against the entire front from Beek in the northeast, to Mook in the southwest, with the enemy's intention being to unite the two thrusts on the Groesbeek heights. Given the distances involved, the 82nd's positions were thinly manned and artillery support was called upon at once. As part of the 508th's defensive resource, Able Battery found itself again firing on forces of SS and Falschirmjaegers, who were reinforced with tanks and halftracks mounted with 20mm guns. Over and over, as they launched attacks on Beek, Wyler, and Devil's Hill, the Germans were punched back by the well directed artillery bombardments of the 319th.

While most of the battery's lieutenants were assigned out as FOs with individual companies of the 508th, Sartain was making his presence felt as a sort of ad hoc forward observer to Mendez' battalion where ever the need arose. Captain Manning was out there too, visiting the FO teams, coordinating their fire with the liaison officers of the battalion and the 508th's command structure. It was almost certainly Manning or Sartain who was being mentioned when one 508th officer described an example of artillery support from the 319th that morning near Wyler, in Phil Nordyke's book, "All-American, All the way."

"I was in radio communication with an artillery officer somewhere in the rear of the battalion defense position. Lieutenant Skipton stated he could see a lot of movement in the first position and he believed the enemy was planning an attack from there. I was very much excited now, and could not remember the proper sequence in calling for and directing artillery, but I told the artillery officer to look on his map and he would see a small green spot on the map about two hundred yards from Wyler and to his right. He told me he found the spot I referred to and would fire a round of smoke. We all held our breath, or at least I did, while this round was on its way. When the round landed it was right on target, and I told the artillery officer to fire for effect, but to move his fire right and left of the round a hundred yards or so. He understood what I was trying to say, and said, 'OK.' Next I heard him say, 'Artillery on its way' and could hear its deathly sound as it passed overhead and landed on target. I asked him to fire again, but was informed that he had only a few more rounds left and would hold fire until I really needed it."

Whether it was Sartain or Manning, the artillery officer in question was prudent in preserving his supply. There had as yet been no replenishment of ammunition. Notwithstanding, Germans were attacking in force and the need for artillery support could not be denied. The battery kept pumping out the shells toward Wyler, then Beek, then Hill 75.9, and dozens of points in between.

As unrelenting as the infantry attacks along Highway K were, it was also becoming apparent from the incoming rounds that the Germans had massed more artillery in the area. Determining exactly where artillery fire was coming from was always difficult without air observation, but Dutch resistance reported concrete details about the German dispositions, making counter-battery fire much more effective than it otherwise would have been.

These civilian soldiers won the respect of the Americans. As Covais explained, "There were Dutch Underground people right there with us. They wore orange armbands, I remember that. All this stuff about the French Underground is ridiculous, ridiculous, but the Dutch were right there."

Sartain agreed when he added, "We had a Dutch Underground member with us, with the 508th. They just kept us posted on everything."

German artillery was falling steadily, not only on the infantry up front, but behind them, and among the battery gun position as well. At one point Sartain was posted on the Berg en Dal heights, near the observation tower at the Sterrenberg and overlooking Beek, as he called in missions to the battery. Bob Miller and Sosa were there with him, of course, as were incoming rounds of 88mm fire. "I was up on a hilltop," said Sosa of what happened. "It was an observation post in a field of some kind. I caught a piece of shrapnel from an 88, it got stuck in my right leg, about three inches above the knee. I was scared shitless. I opened it all up and I used my first aid kit and took care of it. I pulled it out myself. It wasn't real deep, but it hurt like hell. I used that morphine and it helped the pain right away."

By late afternoon the troopers in Wyler had been forced to abandon the village. The German attacks to retake it had been savage and out of all proportion with any strategic qualities beyond serving as another roadblock on the highway. In truth, as long as Devil's Hill and the Berg en Dal Heights held, the enemy would not be able to make use of the road in any case. Beek, being closer to Nijmegen, was more crucial to the defense of the city, but in the late afternoon Mendez' "H" Company was being overrun and compelled to evacuate this village as well. The men fell back to a new line of defense on the Berg en Dal Heights. It was an excellent defensive position and one which the Germans would be obliged to take if their goals were to be attained.

The Hotel Groot Berg en Dal, being one of the most prominent landmarks up there, was becoming a focal point of defense and also an objective for the Germans. It wasn't so much a tall building, actually only two stories, but was an enormous, fortress-like structure, taking up most of a city block. Lieutenant Cook and Sergeant Covais, with Tech-Corporal Ross Marsico, a radio operator, took up residence there. It afforded a wonderful view of Beek below them, less than half a mile away, as well as all approaches to the town, but they'd been directed to save the battery's ammunition for a counterattack, unless they could determine the location of the German artillery which was pounding the 508th.

Given these instructions, Covais joined up with the crew of a light machinegun set up on a balcony on the top floor. When he commented that the hotel must have been a niceplace to stay in during peacetime, one of the machine gunners answered, 'Yeah, the

Ted Covais and James Fitzsimmons. Sartain's caption on the back of this snapshot read, "My Sergeant and a driver from the battery." Taken near or in Bemmel, Holland, November 5th, 1944. Sartain collection.

HE PLAYED TO HIS OWN MUSIC.

Heinies liked it.' But they checked out so fast they left their lunch on the tables downstairs.' The other two guys on the machinegun crew laughed as if it were some inside joke, leaving Covais with the distinct impression that they'd finished the Germans' meal for them.

When the background rattle of small arms fire started to boil up, Covais took out his field-glasses and began scanning the hillside leading down to Beek. There they were, German paratroopers in long camouflage smocks, making their way forward toward the Heights in short sprints. The GI manning the light machinegun flicked his cigarette away and said to no one in particular, "OK, here we go."

He let loose a short burst, then Covais started correcting the fire, never taking the glasses from his eyes. "Three hundred yards. Left, left, left. That's good. Right there! Now right fifty."

"I remember being on the balcony of the hotel," he later recalled, "directing fire for our machine gunners, directing fire on the Germans hopping back and forth there. Bup bup bup bup bup bup. But the mission was to get the artillery, not the infantry."

Lieutenant Cook was at another window looking at the Germans coming across the road. It was frustrating to withhold fire on a target in plain sight like this, but he had his orders. "We were not allowed to fire. They stopped us from firing because we were loading up to make an attack that night and we were getting all in position. They told me not to fire any, and so I didn't, I just watched," he said. In the waning light of late afternoon Cook could see the tracers from the light machinegun peppering the Germans as they advanced. Every so often one of them dropped to the ground, immobile. Cook continued to remember what happened, saying, "I could see the Germans coming over the hill down near the little town across the creek. Then I saw a tank come up. Pull into the rock wall there and point his gun. I knew he was gonna be shooting at me."

Cook called out to his FO team, "Let's get out of the top of this hotel!" Lieutenant Cook, Sergeant Covais, and Marsico grabbed their gear and tore down the hallway toward the stairs. All the way the hotel reverberated with the sounds of ricocheting bullets, shattering glass, and the familiar pow, pow pow, pow, ching, of American M-1 rifles.

When they reached the landing leading into the lobby, Cook could see one of Mendez' guys at a window, taking carefully aimed shots. Cook shouted to him, "Is there a basement in this hotel?"

The soldier nodded behind him and said, "Yeah, down that door there." The FO team flew down what was left of the stairs but as they swung around the corner, met with the concussion of an exploding shell from the German tank. The door to the cellar was blasted off its hinges and narrowly missed the three as they were slammed against the wall. Somebody yelled, "Son of a bitch!" then they tumbled down the basement steps in a heap. Cook, Covais, and Marsico scrambled to the exterior masonry wall and caught their breath. They were covered with a fine powder of pulverized plaster and brick dust. Fine shards of broken glass were under their collars and in their pockets. Then the distinctive sound of a German machinegun opened up, and from a much closer range than before. It was the tank, which had stopped halfway to the hotel and was now raking the building with its machineguns. "It was intense alright," said Cook later, "They shot bullets through the hotel, just ripped it up, the floor and all, right over your head. Like a buzz saw going through. I looked out the basement window and I saw the tank fire. That thing hit the building before I could get my head down."

This second blast threw the team to the floor. It seemed like the whole hotel was about to collapse on top of them, there was a deafening roar of machineguns, rifles, and explosions, then all at once it stopped. After a moments quiet, Covais looked out the window. The tank was there, even closer than he'd thought it was, but now it was on fire, with its gun pointed in some useless angle and one of the crew lying near the tread.

When the "A" Battery FO team emerged from the basement they barely recognized the hotel lobby. There were holes in the walls and debris so covered the floor that they had to step over it to walk through. Behind the building wounded men were being collected, as were the dead. But the tide of the German attack was stopped, for the time being at least.

In the relative quiet after the failed attack, Sartain instructed Bob Miller to get Sosa to a doctor so he could have his leg treated. They weren't gone long when both came back to the OP. "I went to the first aid station and they rebandaged it. Did a good job of it, no stitches or nothing," remembered Sosa. Sosa also knew that if he allowed himself to get mixed up in the stream of casualties someone else would take over as the battery commander's driver before he rejoined the outfit, so he declined the chance to get out of combat. "I don't remember whether they wanted to evacuate me out, but they wanted me to go back to the medic station, wherever that was, and that wasn't anywhere near where we were, so I didn't want to go. I just stayed with it."

Back at the battalion, the 319th turned it's howitzers to support the efforts to take the railroad and highway bridges over the Waal River at Nijmegen. To do so, "A" Battery needed to aim the guns in the opposite direction from some of its fire missions around Wyler that morning. "We were firing 3200 mills. That's a circle," remembered Sergeant Rappi of the work he and his gun crew performed that day. "We were firing backwards sometimes, when you knew where the hell the enemy was. Somebody knew about it. We were completely surrounded there until the British tanks broke through."

It took a historic and daring assault over the river in canvas boats by a battalion of the 504th Regiment, but with tremendous effort the highway bridge was taken and the British tanks crossed over. Then they stopped. The Americans were astounded and angry. After all, the purpose of seizing the highway bridge over the Waal was predicated on the relief of the British 1st Airborne Division isolated at Arnhem. Reaching them was not only the point of the whole Market-Garden operation, but it grew increasingly more vital lest all the beleaguered British paratroopers become prisoners or casualties. The Americans couldn't comprehend why the British tankers exhibited no apparent urgency to reach their own countrymen. Nor did they take kindly to the nonchalant stance of the British in light of the terrific casualties which the division suffered in Nijmegen and in taking the bridges.

Casimir Sobon was philosophic about it decades later, but still spoke with a hint of disgusted resignation in his voice. "They come up as far as we were and then they stopped to have their tea," he said. "It wouldn't be as bad, but when you know your own men are getting slaughtered on the other side, you don't stop for anything. You go. But they didn't. They had their tea. That was their way I guess, that was it."

At about the same time the bridges were being taken, an air-drop of ammunition, rations, wire, and medical supplies was released over the landing zones near Groesbeek. The drop came just in time as shortages of all sorts were already being felt. Moreover, the weather had turned sour and it was anyone's guess when another resupply mission could be undertaken. The battalion's Supply Officer, Lieutenant Connelly, immediately drove to the site and retrieved 150 rounds of ammunition. Connelly estimated that there was an additional 1000 rounds out there, but they were widely scattered and in the growing darkness it was impossible to locate the bundles, especially considering the near proximity of aggressive German units.

The whole day had seen vicious fighting in a 270 degree arc from Nijmegen in the northwest, to Mook in the southwest, where the battle had hardly been less intensive than it was along the Beek-Wyler front. At Beek the fighting went on through the night. Mendez counterattacked in the evening, with the 319th shelling the town more generously in the knowledge that some quantities of ammunition had been air-dropped. Yet German counter-attacks took most of the village back by dawn of the 21st. the 319th had done all it could, short of completely exhausting its ammunition. Indeed, 1,495 rounds were expended, 817 by "A" Battery alone.

At sunrise another fanatical attack by German Falschirmjaegers and SS pushed the remaining Americans from the village. It was now the third full day of the Battle for Beek and exhaustion was setting in. Regardless, the town had to be held lest the enemy be in a position to retake Nijmegen and the bridges before Gavin could consolidate his defenses, or unite with the German thrust on Mook to occupy the Groesbeek heights.

In spite of the limited forces available to him, Mendez had fought his battalion splendidly so far, shifting companies and even individual platoons from point to point as the Germans pressed their way forward, searching for weaknesses in the American positions. True, the 3rd Battalion, and other companies of the 508th had had to give ground, but they always took it back and never accepted defeat. Somehow though, every time Beek was taken they were forced out again. Nevertheless, Mendez had complete confidence in his troopers, convinced that they were the equal of any soldiers in the American or German forces, and now he was determined to have Beek even if it were only a pile of rubble.

Immediately, Mendez organized a three pronged attack which he believed would secure Beek for good. Company "F" attacked from the south, Company "G" from the northwest, and the survivors of "H" Company went straight back toward the village the way they'd come out.

The GIs were met with a fusillade of machine gun fire such as they'd never encountered in Normandy or so far in Holland. Spurred on by the fact that they were at the gates of their own homeland, the defense demonstrated by the SS and Falschirmjaegers was tenacious. Little or no progress was made before the Americans had to seek cover from the withering fire. Through it all was Mendez, exhorting his soldiers to keep going, modeling exactly what he was asking of them.

In support of the attack, the howitzers of the 319th hammered the Germans, who had dug themselves deep into the ruins. One fire mission after another was called, but since the additional ammunition dropped the evening before hardly replenished the requirements of the day, the batteries had to reach into their reserve supply.

For the 319th men who were with the 508th on September 21st, the courage they witnessed never left their memory. Their recollections of the Colonel were decisive and universal. Corporal Sosa, for example, said, "Mendez, he wasn't scared of a fight, he wasn't afraid of nothing! When we were in Holland, bullets flying all around us and he was walking straight up and down! He didn't even hit the dirt. He was a hell of a man I'll tell you, he was one tough little guy."

Lieutenant Cook's FO team was there as well, assigned to one of the three attacking companies. When the men were pinned down by enemy fire, it wasn't long before Mendez was on the scene urging them on. Cook looked on in awe. His later comment about the Colonel was, "He was a gutsy man if there ever was. Yes, sir! He'd walk down the middle of the road and his troops would be in the ditches. He'd say, "You gonna follow me, or you gonna stay down there like a son of a bitch?"

Sergeant Covais was almost certainly with Cook at the time, and may have been thinking of the same incident, when he said proudly, "I was with Colonel Mendez, 508th Parachute Infantry Regiment, in Holland. Third Battalion, always the Third Battalion, because "A" Battery, 319th supported the Third Battalion. That was our job." As he spoke, his memory revitalized the inspiration and excitement of his youth. With eyes alight as if he was 21 years old again, he added, "You know, as a forward observer you have to be with the battalion commander all the time. Every time he wanted direct fire Mendez would say, 'I want fire on that point and that point.' You've got to call it in, get on the phone, radio or whatever we had. We called it in. But Colonel Mendez, hey, hey, what a fighter! He was a great guy. Man, I'll tell you, this guy, it could be artillery bursting here, machineguns, he didn't care, he'd stand out there like he was untouchable! Untouchable! He was a great, great man."

With the attack stalled out on the outskirts of town, the 3rd Battalion men seemed caught in a no man's land, unable to resume the offensive, yet not in a prepared defensive position either. The Germans sensed this might be their opportunity to bust out of Beek and storm the Berg en Dal Heights. As the enemy came at them with tanks and half tracks leading the way, it looked like the 508th troopers might just be reaching their breaking point. Mendez could see the crisis at hand. "I never will forget," remembered Sartain, "Mendez looked at me and he said, 'OK Charlie, Let's go.' See, if you ever got in trouble Mendez was right there. He was hands on. He was all over the place, encouraging his troops. He was right there, right there, right up front where he was needed. We went up and the company commander had been killed. We just set up a perimeter of artillery fire around the position."

Able Battery laid down a curtain of fire like never before. The gunners worked their pieces as fast as they could and, with their help, the GIs of the 508th found the guts, grit, and stubbornness to hold on. The tide of battle flowed back and forth between the foot of the Berg en Dal Heights and the outskirts of Beek through the balance of the morning and into the late afternoon. Finally, after sustaining severe losses, the Germans started giving way, pulling back into the village, and then giving it up one street at a time. This house to house fighting, at close quarters with grenades and small arms, was brutal, but clearly the only way this town could be purchased. That the guys with Mendez kept with it through three days of combat was a testimony to their character as soldiers.

During the Battle for Beek, Captain Manning spent plenty of time around Mendez too, coordinating the fire of the 319th with the requirements of the troopers up front. When a GI who'd been assailing the German defenses was brought back badly wounded, Ed Ryan, frequently serving as Manning's radio operator, was there to witness what took place. "I remember one of the guys came down," recalled Ryan. "He had his arm up in the air and his hand was shot off. He had a bandage over it. Mendez said to him, 'How'd that happen?' Guy said, 'I don't know, it got shot off.' Mendez asked him, 'Don't that hurt?' The guy said, 'It don't bother me much.' Then Mendez told him, 'You better go to the rear.' Guy said, 'I got a job to do.' Well, Mendez said to him, 'You're going to the rear anyway.' I remember that. I was with him a lot. I thought the world of that man. He was a wonderful man, very brave."

By 1900 hours Beek was again in American hands, but the cost had been appalling. "H" Company, for example, lost two thirds of its men, and casualties in all the other companies involved were equally heavy. "It was tough. It was tough. Around that town we, the 508th, just got the hell kicked out of them. It was really a tough fight," said Sartain.

The Battle for Beek would remain a salient point in the combat history of the 508th, as well as in the military careers of Louis Mendez and Charles L. Sartain. In fact, William Lord's History of the Regiment, written immediately after the war, stated, "Notable in the fight for Beek was the splendid work done by the forward observer of the 319th Field Artillery, Captain Sartain."

For the Captain from Baton Rouge, Beek created an immutable bond between himself and Mendez, built upon mutual respect and an understanding which those who hadn't been there were at a loss to comprehend. He would always be proud of their association. It was clear that Sartain admired the Colonel's qualities of leadership, courage, and devotion to his men, but he also liked Mendez as an individual. In discussion about his service during the war, Sartain enjoyed reminiscing about the way they worked together in the field. "I had a lot of personal contact with Mendez, spent a whole lot of time with him," Sartain explained. "Things would get bogged down, and we would go to a company that didn't have one of our forward observers, you see? So we'd ease on up and I'd bring in some artillery fire," said Sartain on one occasion.

Then Sartain enlarged on the normal operations of Mendez' command structure and how he fit in with it, saying, "If the battery was gonna be in position overnight I would stay with Colonel Mendez. I had no reason to return to the battery because I would conduct night fire with the infantry. If it was a real, real slow, static situation, then, yes, Sosa and Miller and I might return, but normally I just could not sit tight around that battery."

"That's right, Louie Mendez," Sartain continued. "Most of the time, he had a back CP (command post) and a forward CP. His forward CP was right behind the com-

Bob Miller, Louis Sosa, and two members of the 508th Parachute Infantry. Sartain's caption on the reverse of this photograph read: "A dirty crew, Eh? Left to right, my radio operator and next to him my driver. Two of the best men in the army. Two on the right are our infantry." Sartain collection.

panies. The back CP would be, you know, a quarter of a mile back. You always had an advance CP and a rear CP. That was routine, that was routine infantry tactics. Generally his forward CP was out in the line, or out in the woods, and he'd have his radio operator and one or two people at his advanced CP, that's all. Very seldom was there a command post in any kind of structure. Now in Holland a couple of times he had his command post in the cellar of a residence. But the advanced CP was wherever the Colonel decided to squat, you know what I mean? It could be on the backside of a little hill, or if they had time they'd dig a pretty good sized hole and put timbering over it and all of that business. It all depended. But the advanced CP would be very, very close to the company that he'd keep in reserve, that way he would be closer to the companies that were in the line, because Mendez and the others would like to stay pretty close to where the action was."

Sosa's memory confirmed this description of Sartain's habits. "We stayed up there with the Colonel," he said. "Most of the time we were all by ourselves, nobody else in sight. Me, Miller, Sartain, Colonel Mendez and his sergeant. We'd be talking on the radio from time to time but we hardly ever saw anybody else."

Lighting his corn-cobb pipe, Sartain puffed it up and continued to talk about the command structure of the 3rd Battalion. "The rear CP was where Major Bell would be. He was the XO, 3rd Battalion under Mendez. His code name was Dingdong and he had this great big handlebar mustache, I'll never forget it. He and Bell made a good pair, good combination. The rear CP would have communication with regiment and division. Generally, nine times out of ten they would have a telephone. There'd be eight or nine people at the absolute most, in the rear CP. Major Bell, his communication people, linemen, people that would run and find a break in the wire, and a runner or two. And a liaison officer from our battalion if they had one. A lot of times I acted as the liaison officer because we only had two in the battalion. In three battalions we only had two liaison officers, you see? So I generally stayed with the third battalion and the other liaison officers would stay with the second or first battalion. But getting back to Mendez, he was something else, something else. He played to his own music."

September 21st had been a busy day back at the firing batteries too. At 0800 hours, a couple of jeeps with trailers left to retrieve more of the supplies that were dropped the night before. Not only was the supply of ammunition getting dangerously low, but rations on hand were running out as well. Each man was tossed one last K-ration for breakfast and told to make it last. Sergeant Carl Davis, Chief of Able Battery's Instrument Section, had Carl Salminen drive him out to where the air-dropped bundles lay scattered, hoping to find some wire or other useful equipment. All along the highway, British tanks were pulled into adjacent fields and their crews were brewing tea. After the first run, Carl was driving Davis back for another load when the first of several German fighter attacks along the Nijmeegsebaahn occurred. He remembered it later and said, "I was hauling air droppings of food and ammo and stuff like that out with Sergeant Davis. Then we went back for something, I can't remember what. We came to this road and the sky was all black from fires in the field. The British were cooking tea, that black tea. That black smoke there, the German planes could see that smoke from miles away. Sergeant Davis said, what are they doing out in that field! Christ, they'll have the German air force down on us! In only a minute or so a fighter plane came right through and he strafed. I told the guys, bail out! I turned the switch off and I turned the Jeep so it's off the road. There happened to be a slit trench that I dived into. That doggone plane, he made a circle around to see what kind of kills he made. He was practically upside down, this cigar smoking pilot. He had a cigar in his mouth. Oh yeah, he was that low! He was only 75 feet off the ground. He never hit us, but you could see the earth flying where the bullets hit."

When the air attack struck, Casimir Sobon was probably already on the drop zone, helping gather up the scattered bundles and load supplies into trailers. "The British, no matter where the hell they were, they had to bring their stoves out and make tea," he recalled. "Here comes the fighter planes, a squadron of planes, and automatically everybody said, aw, their Americans, nothing's gonna happen, nothing's gonna happen. Their preparing their tea and all of a sudden, when they seen the ground start to be eaten up with the bullets, then they knew it wasn't our own. Some of them got killed. But that was their way of life, that's what they had to do."

Sobon was right. This time the Germans scored hits. It was hard not to, considering the concentration of vehicles and men along the highway. At the Nebo convent at least ten British soldiers were killed and buried together on the surrounding grounds. Whatever supplies were recovered from the airdrop, it was not sufficient to satisfy the requirements of the infantry for artillery support. There was also a trickle of supplies moving up the highway from Belgium, but because the route was hardly secure, this source was as yet unreliable. Evidence of the restriction on ammunition expenditure can be seen in the comparatively low amount of rounds fired on the 21st - only 488 rounds for "A" Battery - despite the battle that raged for Beek. Still, Colonel Todd got word that there were a few 2 1/2 ton trucks of ammunition available to his battalion and he dispatched a guide to bring them up that afternoon.

The men themselves were hungry, having consumed the K rations they'd brought with them. There wasn't any more chow for the outfit the rest of that day until evening, when a meager ration from British stores was doled out. Duel Elmore thought it, "looked like a pea soup, or something like that." Whatever it was, it was disappointing in quality and quantity. There was also a small amount of captured German rations distributed, consisting mostly of crackers, sardines, canned bread, canned meat, and squeeze tubes of cheese. The guys welcomed the variety, but there wasn't nearly enough to go around.

The German rations came from one of several trains captured by the 82nd after the landing. That in itself wasn't unusual, since Nijmegen was a rail center, but what was surprising was a locomotive pulling several cars which came through Groesbeek from the city at full speed around midnight of September 17th. A running train was the last thing anyone expected to see, and so surprising was it that the 505th men occupying the town at the time, let it pass unmolested. Another train came through before dawn but was stopped before it could get beyond the American lines. There were mostly civilians on board, undoubtedly Nazi sympathizers making a desperate attempt to escape the consequences of their collaboration. They leapt from the cars and fled into the surrounding forests. A third train, stocked with food and munitions was also captured before it could pass through the division's lines, and it was from here that this first round of German rations came.

Though the train of rations and ammunition are normally described in written histories as having been captured, at latest, early on the morning of the 18th, several members of the 319th have vivid and corroborated recollections of the event itself. If their memories are at all accurate, the implication is that the German train did not attempt its run through the American lines until late on the afternoon of the 18th or perhaps sometime the next day. Though this seems unlikely, given the intensive combat taking place throughout the Nijmegen area by that time, the eyewitness accounts cannot be ignored. In the end, the mystery of exactly when the train was taken remains unsolved and the memories of those who were there must speak for themselves.

"While we were digging in we noticed a railroad track, just a little piece of railroad and we thought, well, what the hell, let's use it," said Silas Hogg as he remembered back to Holland. "We were gonna use that railroad track for a slit trench. Then we saw a train coming. Now you gotta go ahead and turn as I tell you. You got the railroad track on your right, look down to the left and you could see about a mile, two mile away and here come a train down that track. Slow, maybe ten miles an hour. Then some guy says, 'Hell, let's just take the dam train and blow it up.' So our men all got situated, the ones that were gonna take part in it. Here come that train. Finally by time it got to us it was doing probably fifteen miles an hour, and that's the fastest it ever got. So we took the train and blew hell out of the people. I helped take that train. Now we got a train. In that train was a carload of canned meat. The car next to the engine was uniforms, and the last car was grenades, what do they call them, potato mashers. I remember eating the meat, just opening the can up and taking a fork and eating the meat."

The captured train was a real boon for the guys, particularly in light of the scanty chow they'd been living on since exhausting their K-rations shortly after the landing. Though stopped and without guards, the train must still have been in some kind of running order when someone had another great idea. "We kept the car with the potato mashers and we kept the car with the meat," explained Hogg. "Then we fired that engine up again and set it going. The last thing I saw of that train was about a mile away to my left, and it must have been going 150 miles an hour because, man, it was really pulling smoke! We never did see what happened to it when it hit something, but it had to be going so fast that whatever it hit it tore it all to hell."

Ed Ryan appears to have been further down the track, among some reserve infantry of the 505th PIR when the train made its appearance. "I'll tell you what happened," he recalled. "They had some guys along a railroad track there. We were all laying along that track and here in the middle of this combat comes this train with the bell going ding ding ding. Couldn't believe it. The guy with the bazooka, he says, 'Please, nobody touch that train, I've waited for this all my life!' It was what he wanted. So he fired at it and it blew. It didn't blow as high as we thought it would, but it blew pretty good. Of course it's a steam engine and you've got to be careful around that stuff, so I didn't go right up to the train, but it was full of Kraut issue rations. They were pretty good. Most of it was hard tack and tubes of that awful Lind Berger cheese. They were taking it. I ate the hardtack. It opened up my gums and the Lind Berger cheese got in there. I wound up with a hell of a case of gingivitis. Ruined my gums."

Meanwhile, back at the uncoupled cars, the free for all continued until battalion and division supply officers took charge. Until then, GIs were rummaging through the freight train, filling their musette bags and the cargo pockets of their trousers with foodstuffs which were not part of the normal army ration. "Yeah, you better believe it," commented Harvey Rash, one of the replacements who'd joined "A" Battery after Normandy. "That doggone thing, we caught them by surprise. We went in there and helped ourselves, of course. They had some pretty doggone good food too. They had some bread, boy, you wouldn't believe, just as black as it could be. Man, you talk about something good, but it was good. Get it hot, you know, make a sandwich out of it. That's where I learned to eat that stupid orange marmalade and liked it. Orange marmalade, I never could stand that at home, but I learned to eat what they had over there, that was good. I'll tell you something else, those Germans had butter over there. Man, you wouldn't believe. It was doggone good butter too, and it wouldn't melt. Hard as a brick, but when you put it on a piece of bread, man, it was good."

Food wasn't the only thing the guys were walking away with. Carl Salminen got in on the act. "All I remember is one box car that was loaded with hand grenades," he recalled. "They were packed ten to a box, a metal box with a rubber seal on it. You could throw then in the lake and they wouldn't get wet. They made a nice container. This guy Farmer, he liked to collect souvenirs and he went to see what's in that car. He brought back three of them. I said, where'd you get those? He said, 'That boxcar over there. If you want some go and get some.' So I drove myself over there and got myself some. Yeah, I just took the hand grenades out of the box and used the box. Actually I had three or four I brought back for my close buddies."

Silas Hogg was more interested in the grenades than in the boxes they came in, saying, "We kept those potato mashers, we used them agin them, oh hell yes. See we only took enough ammunition for three days and once you run out you're in trouble. So you just go ahead and use them agin them. That potato masher, they're better than ours anyway. I know it."

Keen to explain why, Hogg added, "OK, target number one, 75 yards away. German potato masher, you could drop that right in the middle of it. American hand grenade you might get ten foot in front of it or ten foot a past it. But you throw that potato masher and you can pin point where you want it. When you're pin pointing, you want to really be careful. You could throw it more accurately and twice farther. Oh lord yes. Oh yes, and you could blow up more with it. Hell, it was just a better piece of machinery. It's just that simple."

After Supply Officer Connelly took charge of the goods, those who weren't lucky enough to be there when the train was captured got their share too. Sobon's comment was typical when he said, "Yeah, all of a sudden we got something to eat. Then the word started spreading and it came around that they blew up a German train loaded with the rations. That's what the story went around. I didn't see the train but I heard about it."

Those men who got a share, accepted the German rations with a sense of novelty, but Silas Hogg found another way to compliment his diet. "The first pheasant I ever killed in my life, I killed it with a 9mm pistol I took off a dead German," he said. "I killed a pheasant with that pistol and cooked that son of a bitch in my helmet and ate it. Heck yes, I cooked it in my helmet. I had nothing else to cook it in and I ate it too! Oh

Carl Salminen of Gladstone, Michigan. He was one of the replacements waiting at Pap's Hall when the unit returned from Normandy. Courtesy Salminen family.

buddy, when you haven't had hardly anything to eat for five days, anything tastes good. That night the FO teams of Lieutenants Cook and Gutshall were rotated off the line with Mendez' battalion and replaced with those of Lieutenants Marvin Fellman and Joe Mullen. Sartain, who'd been unofficially serving as liaison officer to the 3rd Battalion all along, was formally assigned to that position.

Casimir Sobon was assigned to Mullen's team, and he later remembered the Lieutenant as, "A young Irish kid, a real young guy. I was out with him and he said to me, 'If my old man ever knew I was fighting with the British, he would kill me.' He was a short guy, nice guy, and just as Irish as could be."

The Germans had spent their offensive power in the fight over Beek. Burned out wrecks of tanks and halftracks littered the whole area around the town from the Groot Berg en Dal Hotel to Wyler. Believing that the enemy must be in disarray, and wanting to insure that Nijmegen was out of their reach, General Gavin ordered Mendez to continue attacking northeast, out of Beek, across the flatlands along the Waal River. Companies "I" and "H" approached as far as Wercheren but there seemed to step into a hornet's nest of Germans and were forced to withdraw.

The 319th was finally able to build up its reserve and still provide artillery support. In all, 350 rounds were fired by "A" Battery on the 22nd, making it a comparatively quiet day. The 22nd was really a chance for everyone to take the first pause since landing five days before. Major Wimberley inspected the firing batteries. Written reports of the operation up to that point were furnished to division headquarters. Gas masks were collected up and temporarily stored with the batteries, until the opportunity to return them to division came along. The Piper Cub observation plane also made its appearance on the morning of the 22nd, having flown across the English Channel, France and Belgium. Piloted by Lieutenant Morgan in company with his aircraft mechanic, Sergeant Boss, the plane landed at an airstrip near Heumen. After being driven to the battalion CP to report in, Morgan was given a jeep, rations, and two men to serve as guards, and then returned to his plane.

Meanwhile, officers of the 319th took the time to exchange notes on all that had happened to them since leaving England. One rumor swept through them like wildfire. "The minute everybody got into Holland and started shooting the bull, that's when we were told that Bertsch had a stomach ache and got out of the glider and went to the hospital," remembered Sartain. "Everybody said, man, they're gonna get that bastard, they're gonna reduce him in rank and all of that. They didn't do anything to him. He was a West Pointer, so they made him a full Colonel. Oh yeah. That's correct. If it had been anyone else he would have been court martialed."

Sartain's sympathy for the average GI shone through as he considered it all in more depth. He observed, "Well, things aren't what you'd think, if you were regular army and you screwed up, you were generally moved up and later on you were promoted. Unless you did something heinous, you were taken care of, you know? But if a GI had done what Bertsch did he would have been court martialed to within an inch of his life."

As the rumor went, Harry Bertsch was made a full Bird-Colonel and sent back to the United States. He does disappear from the division's table of organization in late 1944, but whether he actually lost his nerve and absented himself from the airborne invasion of Holland, is impossible to substantiate. Nonetheless, the men of the 319th were ripe to believe the story as true and it is doubtful anything could have dissuaded them from it.

He Played to His Own Music.

On the 23rd, Mendez renewed his attacks across the flatlands east of Nijmegen, this time reinforced by tanks of the British Sherwood Rangers. Even with the extra muscle, his battalion found itself facing stubborn machineguns and an unusually heavy concentration of German artillery at certain points. In spite of this, considerable progress was made, especially along the river. Preparatory barrages and supporting fire from the 319th figured prominently throughout the day, and this time the battalion was able to meet out bombardments without the fear of exhausting its supply. In all, an impressive 1,145 rounds were fired by "A" Battery alone.

On the 24th of September the 508th re-entered Wyler. By now they'd realized that the village was the first in Germany to be occupied by the Western Allies, explaining why the Germans had fought so desperately to regain it on the 20th. It was also time for the 82nd to redeploy. Better weather had finally allowed the 325th Glider Infantry Regiment to be landed, allowing some of the more cut up battalions in the division to be relieved for a few days of rest.

Early that morning a convoy of jeeps and trailers from the battalion was sent to assist in displacing the 456th Parachute Field Artillery to new positions. When they returned, the order was given for the 319th to move as well. They were headed south, not far from Mook, the scene of heavy fighting on September 20th between the 505th PIR and German Falschirmjaegers.

In its new position along the railroad leading to Groesbeek, the 319th would now be in direct support of the 320th Glider Field Artillery, which would in turn provide the artillery back-up for the 325th Glider Infantry. As Able Battery got the order to pull up stakes late that rainy afternoon, it is doubtful anyone was sorry to leave. The battery had been strafed and bombed the whole time it was there, even as the gunners were called upon to keep throwing out the rounds continuously, day and night. Manning, Sartain, Gutshall, Cook, and all the men on their FO teams had seen enough of Beek to last a lifetime.

For those who lived through it all, the Battle for Beek would indeed last a lifetime, and then some. Beek was a turning point, after which the hope of anything short of a fight to the bitter end was gone. Beek took men to limits of their endurance. It raised them to heights they'd never thought themselves capable of, but also drew them to depths they'd prefer to forget. "I was there when some paratroopers brought in this kid as a prisoner," Covais said once, years later as he spoke about the fighting for Beek and how it left its mark on him. "He couldn't have been more than maybe seventeen, but he was wearing civilian clothes over his uniform, so he was a German soldier, I guess, I don't know. Someone said he was a sniper, a spy. Then a medic said, give him to me, I'll take him back. So they gave the medic a .45 and he walked off with this prisoner. As soon as he got around the corner we heard a shot. I ran over there to see what happened. This kid was lying in a ditch. He had the back of his head blown off. He was still twitching. I said, what happened, and the medic just said, he tried to run away. I didn't believe him. You know, we had so many of our own men killed and wounded, this guy was patching up his buddies all day and I think he wanted to get back at the Germans."

Covais reflected for a few seconds, absorbed in his memories of the battle. His eyes welled up with tears. He looked off to one side, swallowed his emotion, then continued, "Because war does a lot of things to people. You try to think rationally but you cannot in war. I mean, you're out there to kill the enemy before they do away with you, before they kill you. It's a matter of who gets that first shot in, and sometimes you have to make a decision like that. Quicker, before they get the first shot in you better do

BATTERY!

it. But many times, without any clear thinking too, because of the excitement of war, the excitement of the moment of decision, you pull the trigger or don't pull the trigger. So, those are the sights that I remember, and they're vivid ones. The suffering, the people suffering all, all over! I was a soldier. That's it. Yeah, except when you see these dead bodies, you know, then you wonder what the heck you're doing there."

319th GFAB positions in Holland, September, 1944.

BATTERY!

Part 20: "They didn't know boot-turkey."

By the morning of September 25th, time had run out for the besieged British 1st Airborne Division at Arnhem. With their armored column lingering miles away in the vicinity of the Nijmegen Bridge, on the northern bank of the Waal River, the British paratroopers had been cut off from the rest of the Market-Garden operation for over a week. Outnumbered and with their supplies exhausted, the survivors had little choice but to begin surrendering. Small groups attempted to slip through the encircling Germans. Some very few were successful, but the British 1st Airborne Division and the Polish Brigade ceased to exist as a fighting force. With their demise went the entire reasoning behind Montgomery's Market-Garden plan. From this point forward all pretense of a sudden movement that would quickly end the war came to a close, and the efforts of the invasion would henceforth be, for the Allies, largely defensive in nature.

As the firing batteries of the 319th set up their gun positions west of Groesbeek that morning, the previous day's rain eased off, but left behind a thick carpet of clouds. The weather was now sharply cooler. Everyone felt the first real taste of autumn. Activity overhead was lively, despite the gray skies, and the guys were enthusiastic spectators to dogfights between German and British fighters. At one point that morning they could see a German pilot bail out from his burning Messerschmitt and float slowly to earth where he was taken prisoner. Those in the battalion who were veterans of Italy and Normandy remarked that the German air presence was stronger here in Holland than in the previous campaigns, no doubt because they were now closing in on the enemy's homeland bases.

Intermittent shelling from the Germans had also been falling in the vicinity of the new battalion positions throughout the night. Now that it was daylight, the firing continued at a level just heavy enough to keep everyone alert to the sound of an incoming round, but posing little immediate danger. While the gun crews finished digging their emplacements and stretching camouflage netting over their 75s, orders were issued confirming the new liaison and FO assignments. Lieutenant Gutshall was sent to the 320th Glider Field Artillery to serve as the 319th's liaison officer with that battalion. Lieutenants Johnson and Procopio were assigned as liaison officers to the 1st and 2nd Battalions of the 325th Glider Infantry respectively. Lieutenant Cook was placed as forward observer with the 325th's 1st Battalion, while Lieutenants Fellman and McArthur were sent as FOs to that regiment's 2nd Battalion.

Word was also received early that afternoon at battalion headquarters that the 319th had been awarded an Oak-Leaf Cluster to its first Presidential Unit Citation. This time the decoration was in recognition of the role the unit played in the battle for Normandy. The award of any Presidential Unit Citation was, of course, a real distinction, but to be given this honor twice was something quite exceptional. If he were there when the news arrived, Sartain would have engaged in some mutual congratulations with other battalion officers. In that case, he would then have gone back to the battery to inform Lieutenant Ragland and the enlisted men of the honor. That morning, Sartain would have also gone over the new maps of the Mook area with his Executive officer. Details of a more mundane character would need to be settled with Sergeant Johnson. The closest water source, for example, and an order from Division G-4 to collect up the men's gas-masks. Chores finished, the battery was secure with all it required.

It was early afternoon by this time, and having satisfied himself that things were well established, Able Battery's commander decided to make his customary visits to his forward observers while there was still daylight. Just as he told one of the men to go tell Sosa to get the jeep, the battery telephone rang. Sartain was told it was Captain Manning, calling for him from battalion HQ. Taking the receiver, Sartain said, "Hey, what do you know!" Manning inquired if he'd be making his rounds of the observation posts. Yeah, Sartain answered, just a little social call.

Manning asked him, "Mind if I come along?" Captain Manning was familiar with Sartain's habit of visiting his forward observers each day, and as battalion S-3 he'd often accompanied Sartain on his rounds.

"Good," Sartain said, "I'll have Sosa swing by and get you."

The day before, the 325th, with which the outfit's forward observers were placed, had taken over the positions formerly occupied by the 505th PIR. Their line was an irregular semicircle defending the approaches to Mook and Groesbeek. This arc extended from the Maas-Waal Canal, west of Mook, to the Groesbeek heights, facing due east toward the Reichswald forest. Between the two flanks was the regiment's 2nd Battalion, south-east of Mook and squared off against German positions in another thickly forested cluster of hills known as the Kiekberg Woods.

Sosa first took the two Captains out to a point near the observation post occupied by Lieutenant Bob McArthur. As was routine, he parked the jeep in a protected spot and stayed with it while Sartain and Manning went the rest of the way on foot. "Things were quiet, there was nothing going on," recalled Sartain of that day. "It looked like it was going to be a quiet afternoon." McArthur's position was on a promontory south of Mook. From this vantage point, McArthur indicated the known German positions while Sartain looked through his field-glasses. At an outpost near those trees, was a suspected machine gun in the rubble of that building. Manning marked them on his corresponding map overlay. Everything was in order and, for Sartain especially, it was good to see his old Chief of Sections now serving as a very competent commissioned officer. When they were finished, Sartain ended the conference saying to him, "You're doing a great job, Tiger. Carry on!"

Back at the jeep, Sosa pulled away to the next destination. They were on the road to Mook when he told his Captains that he had something which might interest them. Sosa tapped on a German grenade box in which he was known to keep valuables. When Manning lifted the lid his face lit up. There were several hen's eggs inside. "For Christ's sake, Sosa, where did you get these?"

"Well, sir, you have to know where to look, that's all," was the driver's answer.

Sosa pulled off the road and found a discreet place to park the jeep. "I had my little Bunsen burner," he explained. "I took that with me everywhere I went. I'd just crank it up. I don't know what I used for butter, probably had some in the K rations, some kind. I just cracked those eggs open, used my mess kit to do all the cooking in. Right there in the mess kit, yeah. They tasted pretty damn good too. I forget how many eggs I had, but there were enough to go around, one apiece. I also had some coffee, Irish coffee, and I made some of that. That's it. That's it. The only thing I had was my little Bunsen burner and some coffee, and some sugar, and that's it, other than the usual equipment you're supposed to have with you."

BATTERY!

Refreshed, it was now time to check on the other FO with the 325th's 2nd Battalion. Part of this battalion's line included a position known as "Finger Ridge." This piece of high ground followed a "U" or horseshoe shape. One arm of the horseshoe protruded some distance toward the German positions within the Kiekberg Woods to the northeast. It ran alongside the main highway leading to Mook from enemy held territory along the German border, and also commanded the large expanse of open ground to its east and south. This open terrain extended all the way to the Maas River, and at the point opposite Finger Ridge that distance was not great, creating, in effect, a choke point for any movement up or down the highway from Mook. Finger Ridge was consequently of some strategic importance to both the Americans and Germans in any attack or defense in the area.

Though mostly covered in pine forest, and affording an excellent view of any approaching forces, The Finger was still an exposed location, vulnerable to attack from three sides. Lieutenant Fellman's FO team was located on the ridge with"E" company of the 325th Glider Infantry, and it was there that Manning and Sartain chose to make their next inspection.

Sosa drove up a dirt lane which led up the eastern side of Finger Ridge. It wouldn't be safe to proceed further as they would be seen by Germans in the Kiekberg. Instead, he slid the jeep behind some trees, out of sight, and said he'd wait for Sartain and Manning to return.

Even as they were getting out of the jeep, the sound of machine gun and light cannon fire was erupting from over the ridge. "Just before Manning and I got there we heard all the racket, all this commotion, so we rushed up there," remembered Sartain. The two Captains came running into the position, bent over low to present a smaller target. 20mm rounds were blasting through the trees above. Machinegun fire was snipping through the air all around. Interspersed among the trees were foxholes and slit trenches. The Captains jumped into one of the first holes they passed and demanded to know where the officer in charge was. The soldier just shook his head. He was young and Sartain could see he was very frightened. What about the FO team, did he know where they were? Again, the man couldn't help them.They got up and kept going. In another foxhole a man pointed and told them, "I think

Lt. Marvin Fellman of Pipestone, Minnesota. Covais remembered him as, "A swell officer and a swell guy." Covais collection.

297

your people are over there." Then realizing he was speaking to two officers, added, "Sir, do you know where our CO is?" Sartain and Manning exchanged glances. They noticed that none of these men were returning fire. Instead they all seemed to be huddled at the bottom of their slit trenches, overcome with inertia. Manning next got up and bounded to the adjoining foxhole, then repeated the process. Sartain followed.

Further up they noted a line of telephone wire and guessed that it might at least guide them to their forward observer. It did. Sartain and Manning tumbled into a slit-trench on the edge of the tree line. Placed at a bend in the ridge, this slit-trench was a little larger than the others. In it was Lieutenant Fellman with his radio operator. Sartain immediately wanted to know who was in charge of this position. Fellman didn't know. Besides himself, he said, there hadn't been an officer up here since he arrived the night before.

Sartain looked his Lieutenant square in the face. Fellman still had a nasty, albeit scabbed over, gash running forehead to chin from the glider landing the week before. "Well, somebody's running this shooting match, who the hell is it," was Sartain's repeated question.

"Captain, nobody seems to be in charge up here," was all Fellman could tell him. The Lieutenant then started explaining that there'd been more and more German presence throughout the day, that the infantry in the foxholes were uneasy, under increasing sniper and machinegun fire, and for the last hour or so they'd heard the sound of tanks. Pointing skyward to the 20mm rounds passing overhead, the Radio Operator added, "Now these Heinie bastards are throwing this shit at us too!" When Manning picked up the telephone receiver it was obvious the line had been broken. "God damn-it," he said, "Get fire direction on that radio right now!"

Sartain took off to assess the situation and hopefully find someone responsible for this position. Jumping from hole to hole, he found the infantrymen confused and without leadership. As he later described, "There was no NCO with them, there was no officer with them, and they were hunkered down in their foxholes. This surprised the hell out of me. I would say there was probably a full platoon or more. But they didn't know boot turkey. I mean, this had to have been the first time those kids had ever heard a shot fired over them. Had to be, because they really did not know what to do, there being no NCO or Lieutenant, platoon commander or anybody with them. Wasn't anybody there, wasn't anybody there! That's what I never could believe and nobody ever explained it to me."

When Sartain landed back in the observation post, Manning was on the radio, in a deep huddle with fire direction. He closed out the communication, turned to Sartain and asked him, "OK, Charlie, what's going on out there?"

Sartain reported that there was about fifty infantry holding this position. It was a platoon from "E" Company, but they had no mortars, no light machineguns, no bazooka, or any other weapons heavier than a BAR (Browning Automatic Rifle). There was, moreover, no apparent CO. "Johnny", Sartain said, "These kids are scared."
"Alright", Manning answered, "Let's give them a pep talk, get a few of the corporals together and get them settled down. There's got to be a few corporals at least that we can talk to."

Sartain shook his head. "I don't think so, John. And besides, these boys up here don't know what they're doing. They're pretty shook up, and if hell breaks loose, if that happens, there's no telling what they'll do."
Manning thought for a moment, then agreed that they couldn't risk leaving. He told Sar-

tain, "I want you to get a defense going, I'll get us supporting fire from the battalion."
In a flash, Sartain was gone. By this time it was clear that an outright attack on the position was on the way. Several enemy light and heavy machineguns continuously peppered the Americans in their foxholes, kicking up dust all over the place. Every so often the Germans could be seen rising up from concealment in the tall grass to spring forward or get a clear shot at the GIs on the hill, then disappear again to crawl closer. Describing what happened, Sartain later said, "Manning took over the radio and I took over reorganizing them. All this time I was jumping from one group to another. I kicked a few kids in the butt and then we were ready for them."

At first the GIs were slow to respond. The absence of leadership had left them having to shake off a strange torpor. "They were not seasoned airborne troopers," said Sartain, "You could just tell. They were frightened, you know? But you keep going among them, you keep going among them and give them a little spirit and then they start responding. We started returning small arms fire and the troops started to act like troopers. But I was lucky that I had been with the infantry enough to really know what to do. I knew how to organize primarily because I watch Mendez."

For the platoon on the ridge, the welcome sound of artillery came screaming overhead. They all knew this was their own supporting fire and that knowledge raised their spirits immensely. Explosions now erupted all over the plain across which the Germans were advancing. Given the volume of fire, the shells had to be coming from not only the 75's of the 319th, but the 105's of the 320th as well. Licking their wounds, the Germans retreated back into the grasslands they'd attacked from, probably all the way to the banks of the Maas.

The respite gave Sartain a chance to better consolidate the defense. "First thing I observed," he said, "There were no outposts. Now that's basic infantry tactics, basic common sense. You get your outposts out so no one can sneak up on you. So I got two guys to go down the damn hill and set up an outpost so we could figure out what in the hell was going on down there."

Nor did Manning lose time taking advantage of the lull. It was obvious to him that infantry couldn't hold the Finger alone. Had it not been for the artillery barrage,

One of 'A' Battery's guns in action on The Island. Sartain collection.

the position might have been overrun during that first attack, and there were bound to be more. Of course, accuracy and speed of response would be key. First he dispatched Fellman's Radio Operator and another man to repair the break in the telephone line. With Fellman filling in, Manning next had himself put in direct communication with the 319th's Batteries. Looking back, Sartain explained why, saying, "Once all the noise and everything else cleared, Manning systematically picked out and zeroed in on various concentration points. He had concentration points throughout the area. All he'd have to do is call concentration two, or concentration four, concentration eleven, you see? Manning took the radio from Fellman and really took over the artillery, and I'm delighted because Manning had a lot more savvy about artillery fire. Fellman was over in the foxhole with Manning, but Fellman was brand new."

There had hardly been time to register the battalion's guns when the fusillade of 20mm cannon fire resumed, this time accompanied by the unmistakable growl of armored vehicles. Looking out across the open plain, Sartain, Manning, Fellman, and all the other GIs at the Finger position could see armored tracked vehicles advancing towards them. At this distance, under the confusion of battle, it was difficult to identify just what variety of German armor they were watching. The Germans used a wide variety of tanks, half-tracks, and self-propelled guns. Enemy soldiers in greater numbers than had attacked before, could also be seen riding on and clustered behind the advancing armor.

The GIs readied themselves by placing grenades along the tops of their slit trenches and filling their pockets with clips of ammunition. They started firing, more to feel like they were fighting back, since even well aimed shots would have to be very lucky to hit a target at this range.

Still, the armored attacked pressed closer. One vehicle would stop momentarily to lay down a withering fire from its 20mm cannon, while the other would roll on toward the American position. Sartain went dashing from fox hole to fox hole, heartening the men to hold their ground. At first he scrambled along on all fours, but then realized this was an unnecessary precaution because, oddly, all the heavier 20mm fire was passing overhead. As Sartain put it, "These 20mm guns just kept shooting up the trees above us. I guess they couldn't depress their guns enough, but it all went over our heads. Everything they shot at us went over our heads, and there was an awful lot of it. It made a big roar, but once I was satisfied that they could not lower their guns in front of us, then I was safe in running back and forth and all of that business."

By now supporting fire from the artillery batteries was falling. There were air bursts, high explosives, and phosphorous shells going off in quick succession. No direct hits were scored however, and the German infantry was, by now, getting closer. "The grass was between knee and waist high," said Sartain of this point in the battle. "They would drop down and you couldn't see them. Sometimes we'd see a German head pop up in the grass and the whole outfit would start firing. Or then they'd give an order and jump up and all come at us. When they were close enough, then the infantry with their rifles could take care of them."

At one foxhole Sartain came across a soldier paralyzed with fear. The man was holding out his M-1 rifle to the Captain. He had a panicked look in his eyes and kept saying, "It's stuck, it's stuck. It's jammed!" Instinctively Sartain knew he had to restore the man's initiative and belief that he could help himself. "Well," he told him, "You know how to break it down. Clean the son of a bitch! Clean it, clean it!" Sartain went onto the next foxhole, but made a mental note that he'd need to check on this man. "Well, after a while I passed him again," Sartain said. "He'd broken it down and cleaned it. He was firing and he was so proud of himself. You know what I mean."

As aggressive as this second reinforced German attack was, Manning's astute preparation allowed him to pinpoint fire on the approaching armor with unusual speed and accuracy. Armor which had stopped to fire and even moving targets were showered with explosives. There was no time lost, since the exact elevation and deflection of the battalion's guns on so many points had already been registered back at fire direction.

Moreover, Manning ordered that phosphorous shells be used. Sartain later explained why this type of round was most effective. "We had the phosphorus shells to strip the German troops from the tanks," he said. "See, when it went off it scattered that hot phosphorus all over the countryside in itty bitty pieces, and it was just flaming hot. I mean, if a speck of that white phosphorous got on you it'd burn through your clothes and everything else. If it sprinkled on you it burned, man, it really burned! Manning had already established the coordinates with single gun registrations, so then the battery would just shoot on them and the battery really came through. When the infantry people took off or were eliminated, those tanks would turn around and leave because they had no protection. No, I don't think the tanks were knocked out, but once they stripped the infantry support from around the tanks, then they took off and left."

The German attack was now repulsed, but there was every reason to believe the enemy would be back for another try. Wiping the lenses of his aviator glasses clean, Sartain looked out over the open plain. There was a thin haze of smoke from the phosphorous and explosives. Dead and wounded Germans were scattered through the trampled, charred, and ground up grassland, many of them horribly burned and calling out in pain. After a few minutes white flags appeared, followed by litter bearers picking up these unfortunate souls and taking them away for medical treatment.

Sartain took the opportunity to make his way back to the OP to commiserate with Manning. He advised him that ammunition would become a problem if these attacks went on much longer. Manning made due note and said he'd renew his efforts to establish either radio or telephone contact with the 325th, along with continuing to build up his repertoire of registered concentration points. By now the telephone line was fixed. That made communication with both the 319th and the 320th more secure, but they needed to get communications going with the 325th too. Really, it was a mystery to them why no one from this regiment had appeared at the position, either alone or with reinforcements.

This conference between Manning and Sartain hadn't gone on long when the rumble of tracked armored vehicles started to rise out of the distance. Someone shouted out, "Hey, here they come again!" When they heard this, the Captains hurriedly concluded their meeting. Sartain set off for the infantry's foxholes, while Manning was already cranking up the artillery support.

The "E" Company Platoon had beaten back two attacks by now. They had confidence that they could face down another, but when they began opening fire the Germans replied with a weapon which engendered fear in even the bravest of men. It was the flame-thrower.

The German "Flamenwerfer" was, according to an early 1944 US Army intelligence bulletin, a weapon normally used against enclosed fixed positions, such as pillboxes, or for its shock value when placed with storming columns. Operated by combat engineers, the Germans were in the habit of assigning pairs of flame-throwers to infantry companies when the situation was appropriate. The apparatus consisted of two concentric rings filled with compressed nitrogen as its burning agent. Worn on the operator's back, the containers held about one and a half gallons of fuel. The nitrogen was sent through wire wrapped tubing to a hand-held nozzle, about 18 inches long, fitted with a valve and ignition trigger. Earlier versions of the Flamenwerfer utilized a battery started hydrogen flame to ignite the nitrogen, but by this point in the war most German flame-throwers used a blank rifle cartridge to set off the nitrogen agent.

When filled with burning agent, the entire weapon weighed 47 pounds and was capable of throwing its flame about 25 yards. This was not, in fact, very far. Consequently, the engineer troops who operated flame-throwers relied on being able to approach their target under cover of supporting machineguns or tanks before letting loose with their flame. In addition, once flame was discharged, the exact location of the man operating the apparatus was invariably disclosed, making casualties among flame-throwing engineers inordinately high.

There was, though, another way of employing the Flamenwerfer which did not require that the operator be placed in such close proximity to the enemy. This was the flamethrower as an agent of terror. Even the US Intelligence bulletin described the effect of the flame-thrower as "chiefly psychological." The prospect of being burned alive was simply more than most men could endure, and crews of any flame unit depended on this fact to a large extent. The German armor was still some distance out when the Flamenwerfer crews announced their presence on the field with short bursts of flame, evidently playing on the psychological impact of their weapon.

Indeed, at least one German flame-thrower had already been reported by members of "E" Company around dawn of that morning when an enemy raiding party stormed

through a portion of the Finger Ridge positions. It is possible that some of the men on the Finger with Sartain and Manning could have had a brush with it at that time. At very least it is safe to assume that rumors of Flame-throwers had already circulated among them and contributed to their uneasiness.

Whether or not the two men whom Sartain placed in a forward outpost had heard rumors about Germans in the vicinity with this weapon, they came bounding up the hill immediately when the first signs of flame-throwers appeared. "They really hustled their asses up to us," Sartain remembered. As the two threw themselves into the first foxholes they reached on the ridge, Sartain jumped up to meet them. "Get your asses back down there," he ordered, "No one told you to abandon your post!" Sartain understood their fear, but he

Capt. Charles Sartain, "A" Battery Commander

also knew that fear was a very contagious disease. "I was kind of upset about it because, unless they got personally attacked, they had no business leaving their outpost. I fussed at them and sent them back down the hill." When Sartain next looked across the field it was clear the panzers were getting rapidly closer, bringing with them infantry spitting jets of flame. Immolation would be a horrible way to die and Sartain thought, "If they ever get close enough, that's gonna be our ass."

Meanwhile, back at Able Battery's gun position, a radio call came in directly from Captain Manning. "He called in and said, there's a counter attack coming," Lieutenant Ragland remembered of that afternoon. "He said, I want you to fire in this area, and I want you to keep firing until we tell you to stop. So, I don't know how long we fired, but we had a lot of ammunition and man, those guns were getting pretty hot."

Though the air and ground across which the Germans were advancing was filled with exploding ordnance of all kinds, as well as small arms fire from "E" Company, the enemy was determined to take the Finger Ridge and kept pressing onward. Aware that they were holding an advanced point, Sartain grew concerned the Germans would try to encircle the position. Periodically he would scramble the distance up to the crest to take a look behind the ridge for signs this was happening, but never did see any attempt at encirclement.

Now the events on Finger Ridge were generating attention from other artillery battalions, and a Piper Cub from one of them made air observations. Considerable supporting fire beyond the 319th was brought in. "Oh yeah, there could have been a lot of it, there could have been a lot of it," was Sartain's comment on the role of other artillery battalions. "They brought in some heavy artillery. I know we had some 155s that were attached to the division. There could have been contributing fire from the three twentieth, there could have been, because that was a large area out in front of us. Manning would call, fire for effect, and they would just clobber the area, but that was further out, that was further out."

As the Germans came to close quarters, a furious battle boiled up involving artillery fire, machineguns, armored vehicles, 20mm cannon, flame-throwers, and any number of small arms. Dug in as they were, the GIs were protected and inflicting terrible casualties on the Germans now that they had them well within rifle range. Until that point, artillery took its toll on the enemy the whole way. "There was only one tank that got anywhere close to us. Then the flame throwers were right behind him and it was only one flame thrower that got within distance to do us any damage. If it'd gotten any closer he could have hit us, but he was about forty yards away from us and we were just out of his range," Sartain remembered. Continuing his account, he said, "Manning brought the artillery to within 75 yards of us, but he only registered one gun and only brought one gun in real close. See, he didn't want to worry about all six of them shooting. We didn't want the whole battery in on it, no, no. One shot. Then, when the targets were out further, then we used the whole battery. And they would bring in "B" Battery also. But on real, real close in shots we registered with one gun."

Calling in concentrations at such a close proximity necessarily required an extraordinary degree of coordination and skill. In a memoir written by Manning about fifty years after the event, he described how he was able to pin-point artillery fire so that it would land just beyond the foxholes on Finger Ridge. "It got down to me talking directly to Battery 'B,' under Captain Hawkins, and his Section Chief Sergeant Delos Richardson, who had been my first sergeant in Battery "C," Manning wrote. "Del and I coordinated things down to the last mil of elevation and the last yard of distance. We were able to drop the artillery rounds on the attackers within 25 or 30 yards of where we sat. We blew up two flame throwers, a few tanks, and caused a good amount of damage and confusion. Finally got things cooled off. Evidently the Germans were impressed enough to take their attack somewhere else."

When compared, some inconsistencies emerge between Manning's written account and Sartain's memory which deserve to be examined. That Manning would have insisted the closer concentrations be fired by the batteries of the 319th is both plausible and to be expected. After all, the battalion was as accustomed to Manning's manner of adjusting fire as he was with their response to his directions. The gunners of the 319th would naturally have had his trust more than those of any other unit's. Also, given the gun positions of the 319th and 320th relative to Finger Ridge, Sartain's statement that, "The shells came over from right to left, not from behind us. That's why Manning was able to get them in so close," also supports the idea that it was the 319th which conducted the close fire.

Both agree that one gun was used when the panzers and flame-throwers were at their closest. But Sartain also maintained that when single gun fire was called for, it came from "A" Battery, saying, "Manning wanted only one gun, and he wanted that gun from "A" Battery. It was brought in so close that I'm positive Manning didn't want anybody else but "A" Battery shooting those damn shells." Battalion records indicate that considerably more rounds were fired by "B" Battery than by Battery "A" during the period of the Finger Ridge attacks – 386 rounds fired by "A" Battery, compared with 627 for "B" Battery. Unquestionably, "B" Battery was more active, but these numbers could be interpreted as supporting the idea that only one gun of "A" Battery was firing during selected periods of time.

Manning, however, was very specific in his account about personally arranging this fire with Sergeant Delos Richardson. When one considers that Manning's greatest experience working one-on-one with any firing battery's chief of sections took place during the tricky fire missions at Chiunzi Pass with Sergeant Richardson, then of "C" Battery, it is understandable that he would have sought this same section chief on that day in Holland.

Whether the Germans were sending tanks, in the sense of vehicles with enclosed turrets fitted with a high velocity cannon, against the Finger Ridge position is ambiguous, even though Manning used the term "tanks" in his memoir and 319th Battalion records also describe the vehicles as tanks. Yet, Sartain did not recall, nor Manning mention, any direct cannon fire such as one would expect from attacking panzers. In this area of Holland the Germans were generously equipped with half-tracks on which 20mm anti-aircraft guns were carried, and they were in the habit of using them on both air and ground targets. Given the volume of 20mm fire directed against Finger Ridge, and the absence of direct cannon fire, it is most likely that at least some, if not all, of the enemy armor was comprised of half-tracks mounted with these guns.

With all this array of firepower directed against them, it appeared to the men on the Finger Ridge that they were fighting alone. In fact, the American command structure in the Mook area was aware that the position was under attack. Possibly Captain Manning was able to get through to the 325th's 2nd Battalion HQ, or other members of "E" Company elsewhere on the ridge may have reported what was happening. However it occurred, beginning at about 1800 hours, 325th HQ acknowledged that a full scale assault was under way. The flank of "C" Company, the next company to "E" Company's west, was described in that unit's combat journal as "threatened." Men of "E" Company who were posted at other points along the extended Finger Ridge also recorded being attacked that day. All this suggests that the attack on Sartain and Manning's position was not an isolated one, but rather part of a larger offensive operation, and that the Germans were having some success.

At 1845 hours a notation was made at 325th Regimental Headquarters stating there was a call from "E" Company that it needed help, followed later that evening by a call for ammunition to that company's right flank. "I remember ammunition getting low," Sartain recalled. "It was a bad situation. I told them all, be sure you know what you're shooting at." Though the need for ammunition remained, 325th Regimental records indicate that, at 1953 hours, a jeep loaded with ammunition was to be stopped enroute. Presumably this was not because the need for ammunition replenishment had passed, but because the road to "E" Company's position on Finger Ridge had been cut.

About this time Lieutenant Fellman came bounding into a foxhole where Sartain was reminding one GI to pick his targets carefully. The Captain was doing his best to be everywhere at once, but of course that was impossible. Sartain shouted in his Lieutenant's ear, "Fellman, get down to the other side of the OP. Tell those boys over there not to go hog wild shooting off their ammo, and make sure they keep their asses put!" With a slap on the back, Fellman was off. Sartain felt better, knowing he had one of his own officers out there, encouraging the troops with him.

The fighting was now at an intensity in which the reports of individual weapons couldn't be distinguished. Then, one German soldier got up and rushed forward. He tossed a stick grenade toward the Americans, even as he was cut down by rifle fire. Another did the same and was killed as quickly as was his comrade. It was suicidal of them to do so, but in the intoxication of battle soldiers often took risks which no sane man would ever consider.

Ed Ryan wasn't on Finger Ridge that day, but he'd found himself in the middle of plenty of hammer and tongs firefights. Describing the experience of losing one's sense of danger, he said, "When you get into that kind of combat, different people act different ways. There'd be so much fire you'd get so scared that you couldn't handle it anymore. You get scared to death, then it seemed like the adrenaline would take over. You'd get this adrenaline rush and it'd stay with you, then you didn't care anymore."

The Germans were never able to breach the Finger Ridge position, though some of them fell only yards from the American foxholes. The enemy pulled back, regrouped, and in the growing twilight hit the GIs again. "They would attack us, then settle down, then attack us again. Eventually the one with the flame thrower quit, but not until well after dark," remembered Sartain.

Everybody on the Finger Ridge felt they'd avoided being overrun by a hair's breath, and they were right. Though more fighting was expected, ammunition was low and the platoon never did get any reinforcements. Lest they be taken by surprise, Sartain and Manning knew that the men would also have to remain awake and alert, fighting exhaustion now that darkness was upon them. "All that night we could hear them out there. We'd send up some illuminating shells and light up the battlefield. You could see them scurry for cover," he said. "See, in the daylight you didn't have to worry because you could see what they were doing. But they didn't attack, no, they didn't. The Germans didn't like to fight at night, they just didn't. We found that out early." Though there weren't any further assaults, the Americans were nervous and would sporadically let loose with outbursts of fire whenever they heard noises or flares gave them a target to shoot at, but as the hours advanced closer to dawn, these incidents ceased, a gentle rain started falling, and the field became quiet.

Sartain continued his story of Finger Ridge. "They picked up their wounded and dead after dark," he said. "They never had a white flag to come pick them up, and I kept wondering why, but once it got to be daylight they withdrew. It was unreal. You'd think nothing had happened; all that commotion going on, all that afternoon and the night before."

The two Captains remained at the Finger Ridge position until late morning, by which time it was clear the Germans had no intention of renewing their attacks. Moving from foxhole to foxhole, Sartain reviewed the essentials of their defense with the individual infantrymen who'd displayed the most leadership. Before parting he'd tell them, alright, tiger, you know what to do. Carry on. Meanwhile, Captain Manning reviewed things with Lieutenant Fellman, making sure he was familiar with every pre-registered concentration point on the map and its corresponding location on the flatlands before them. Content that the situation was stabilized, they left Finger Ridge.

Back at the jeep, Sosa had a canteen cup of coffee waiting for each of them. They sat down and drank deeply, suddenly aware of how thirsty they were. Then Sartain remembered his pipe. He took it out and slowly prepared to smoke it. Manning pulled off his helmet, placed it beside him and ran his hands through his hair. No one said anything. It was obvious to Sosa that his Captains were exhausted, so he didn't ask where they'd been since yesterday afternoon. After all, from the sounds of battle which had drifted over the ridge Sosa had a pretty good idea.

When he could see Sartain and Manning were finished drinking, Sosa cranked up the jeep and drove off towards battalion headquarters. The light rain had cleared off and as he drove, Sosa noticed both Captains had fallen asleep.

As the jeep approached 319th Headquarters Sosa's passengers roused themselves. Major Silvey was already waiting outside the command tent and trotted up to the jeep as it rolled to a stop. Colonel Todd was following a few yards behind, shouting greetings. "They were glad to see Manning and me. I guess both Headquarters and "A" Battery were kind of concerned about our butts," Sartain remembered.

Inside the Command Tent, Manning and Sartain took seats at a folding table. They hadn't eaten since the fried eggs Sosa made the day before, so Todd saw to it that they were brought some hot chow. Even though the food was a strange amalgam of American, British and German rations, they felt famished and scarfed it down with great efficiency, followed by a period of debriefing. The two Captains told of the absence of infantry officers, the repeated frontal assaults, the German armor, the flame-throwers, and the way the batteries had saved the position. All the while Major Silvey took notes. Other officers and enlisted men who were within earshot, or who came by in the course of their duties couldn't help but linger and listen in.

Of course, it was only a matter of minutes before details of the Finger Ridge battle were being passed from man to man, throughout the battalion. Manning and Sartain were already held in high regard, but now their reputations soared all the more. As Sartain said, "They made a big deal out of it." The men were also projecting the pride they felt in their own accomplishments onto the two Captains. According to Sartain, "It was a high point for the men, particularly in "A" Battery. I really believe if they had any feelings about me or Manning, it increased their respect, I really do."

After the debriefing was over, Colonel Todd suggested that the two get a few hours sleep. By now it was clear to anyone familiar with the events of September 25th that Manning and Sartain's actions on Finger Ridge were something extraordinary and worthy of recognition. Colonel Todd and Major Silvey certainly thought so, and when Colonel Andy March, Commander of Division Artillery stopped in shortly afterwards, he thought so too. Todd began investigating the idea of nominating them for decorations. Decorations required corroborating written statements which then needed to be reviewed by a board of officers from outside the unit. All this would take some time and for the present Sartain and Manning still had their jobs to do.

Sixty-five years later, Sartain was still proud of, but also perplexed by what took place on Finger Ridge. "On reflection," he said, "I've never understood why there were no NCO's or officers with this group, or why once we were under attack the infantry battalion did not send reinforcements. We got absolutely no reinforcement from their headquarters. We had no contact with the infantry battalion and that just amazed me. It was like those kids were stuck out there and nobody even knew they were there. But those kids on that ridge, they did alright, they really did. Nevertheless, if it hadn't have been for Manning and the artillery, and the way he conducted the artillery fire, we couldn't have held on. If it hadn't been for Manning we never would have survived."

As far as the Germans who attacked the Finger Ridge position are concerned, Sartain remained puzzled by them as well. True, their performance at Finger Ridge displayed determination, doggedness, and even valor. But it plainly lacked ingenuity too. The attacks were poorly executed. For example, one might just look at the simplistic frontal assaults by the Germans in the face of repeated failures. Their methods had a primitive and amateurish quality suggestive of inadequately trained soldiers. Sartain's comment on them was, "I don't know who it was but I don't think it was SS because they continued their frontal assault. And a couple of them that were killed pretty close to us looked like real young kids. That's the thing I was shocked about in Holland, the German soldiers, they were just kids."

The inexperience and youth of the Germans was so apparent that, even in the heat of the battle, Sartain and Manning couldn't help also feeling pity for them. Reflecting on this years later, Sartain suddenly remembered one peculiar episode of the fight which illustrated this point. "Manning was shooting at people out there with the artillery when this kid raised up out of the grass," he recalled. "He was shooting up at us, but he was just a teenager, less than a teenager. He may have been older than he looked but he wasn't much taller than the grass he was in. I motioned to Manning, pointed to this kid and Manning realized he was just a teenager too. We called off the fire on that particular concentration. We held up fire on him, just held up the fire till I felt like he was out of the way. You know? Manning moved the fire off to other concentrations. Then that kid squatted down in the tall grass and he was gone, we never saw him again, we never saw any more of that kid again."

Why the Germans never employed anything beyond the most archaic of tactics, remained a mystery for Sartain. "I couldn't understand why they didn't try and make a flanking attack. I couldn't understand why they kept coming at us straight on. No, I couldn't understand it. I mean, they never gave up, and when they continued the frontal assault they were just artillery meat."

The failure of the Germans to depress their 20mm guns enough to bring them to bear effectively on the American position was another indication of their lack of proficiency. When coupled with the youth of some of the enemy casualties which Sartain recalled, the picture is one of what was becoming more and more common of the Germans as the war went on, under-age and under-trained troops."

After Sartain and Manning left the battalion CP, an NCO stuck his head in the command tent and announced, "Colonel, Sir, it looks like the rest of the outfit's here from England." He was referring to the seaborne element of the 319th. As with the glider invasion of Normandy, it was necessary for the heavier trucks and support personnel of the battalion to follow by land and sea. Captain Cargile and about fifty enlisted men had left Papillon Hall on September 20th. At Weymouth, England, they were loaded onto two LSTs, crossed the English Channel, and disembarked at Utah Beach. By the morning of the 22nd they were motoring across France, toward Holland. With them came eight 2 and a half ton trucks, five one ton trailers, fifteen 3⁄4 ton trucks (also known as Weapons Carriers), and eight jeeps. They also brought with them kitchen equipment, extra tentage and much needed supplies. In addition, because battalion records state that this day brought the first mail from home anyone had seen since the invasion, the seaborne element probably carried correspondence which had accumulated since the outfit left Lubenham.

When that news spread to "A" Battery, Roland Gruebling, the mail clerk, went up to battalion HQ to retrieve the correspondence, driving there in a stolen jeep festooned with a placard above the front bumper which read: "Mail Call." A little while later he was back at the battery, ready to distribute the mail and crying out, "Hey, hey, hey, we've got mail today!" He had with him a stray dog he'd picked up somewhere between Beek and Mook, named "Lydia." The guys gathered around Gruebling and Lydia as he called out their names. There were several for Captain Sartain, including birthday greetings from his parents and Peggy Lou. In all the activity of the invasion it had never occurred to him that his birthday had come and gone.

At any one of his mail calls "Grieb," as he was known, was likely to select some poor guy whose mail he'd keep placing at the bottom of his stack. He'd usually select someone who he knew was pining over word from a girl or wife and tease him. Watching him squirm with anticipation until the end, Grieb would finally say, "Oh yeah, there's five more here for Prohazka, Corporal Legg, Sergeant Jinders, Jughead or The Dago."

With only a few hundred shells fired by the whole battalion that day, the 26th of September was a chance for the men to read their letters from home, clean up, and get some rest. Many had not touched razor to face since landing in Holland and by now the higher brass were complaining to Colonel Todd about the scruffy appearance of the men. Taking advantage of the lull, water was heated up in helmets and the beards disappeared.

The 325th launched an offensive operation to drive the Germans from the Kiekberg Woods on the 27th. Batteries "A" and "B" of the 319th supported the attack. Despite all the efforts, the movement ground to a halt against SS battalions who were themselves preparing to push out of the Kiekberg toward Nijmegen.

At noon of that day, while the Kiekberg Woods fight was taking place, Sartain and Manning returned to Finger Ridge, but this time Major Silvey was with them. The battalion's XO was there to investigate for himself the events of September 25th, anticipating that the two Captains would be recommended for decorations. The party found things much the same as Sartain and Manning left them. They explained to Silvey just how the Finger Ridge battle unfolded, pointing out the German lines of approach. All the while the fighting for the Kiekberg continued, although the details were hidden in the dense forest. They could all hear the chatter and rumble of battle emanating from the forest and watch as the smoke of artillery fire came bubbling up from within, but that was all.

Later that evening a heavy rain began and German artillery was especially aggressive. Numerous high velocity shells landed around the battery positions, but none fell close enough to cause damage or inflict casualties. The 319th answered back. According to the battalion's record, "We returned five for one, as usual." By the end of the day Able Battery had thrown 788 rounds at the enemy, while Baker fired well over a thousand.

The following day, the 28th, was clear and unusually quiet. It started off with, "Field Memo #3: Salvage Air Corps equipment 1) Effective at once, parachutes and canopies will not be used for bedding or shelter. 2) All Air Corps equipment i.e. parachutes, delivery containers, etc will be turned in through channels to G4 at German camp located at the following map coordinate."

"That order didn't mean anything," said Sartain when he was later asked about it. "The crates that the guns were loaded in, that you dropped them in, nobody wanted them. But there was a pretty good market for parachutes, a very good market for parachutes. A lot of guys got parachutes and had pajamas made out of them, including me. That silk parachute, in France or in Holland, if you sold it you could pick up some good money. You'd be selling it to civilians. Sosa probably had a corner on that." In fact, Captain Sartain wasn't the only one who eventually had pajamas made for his wife or sweetheart. Roland Gruebling had a set made for his wife Jane in Milwaukee, complete with an 82nd Airborne Division patch sewn to the upper-pocket. Ted Covais had pajamas made for his wife Cathie, in Brooklyn, along with a tasseled white scarf, and Lieutenant Mullen had a set sewn up for his fiancée, Gloria in Indiana.

While the silk chutes could be collected on the battlefield, arrangements with a seamstress to have them made into clothing would have to wait until the outfit was back at its base camp. Meanwhile, on this morning, Lieutenant Mullen was sent out to the Finger

Gruebling's dog, Lydia, strikes a pose on the hood of his jeep. Sartain later said in regard to pets in the Battery, "The guys every once in a while would pick up a stray dog that they'd like. They were good at picking up all kinds of pets. You know, a guy would latch on to a dog and he'd hide it. Put him in the truck when we'd move, and the rest of the guys were pretty good about keeping it secret. I wouldn't normally have any objection if a guy would pick up a little dog, a little pet, as long as it wouldn't get out of hand. I wouldn't have had any objection to it, but if the dog was being obnoxious or causing any kind of distraction, we couldn't have that, you know? Then Sergeant Johnson would handle it and they'd have to get rid of them." Courtesy Gruebling family.

Ridge to relieve Lieutenant Fellman as FO. He did not remain there long. By mid afternoon the battalion was ordered to support the 2nd Battalion of the 508th. This battalion was placed between Wyler and Groesbeek, near the village of Voxhil. The 508th had been designated as division reserve for the previous several days and was now starting to rotate back into the front line.

Civilian reports of massing artillery and troops were indicating that the enemy was preparing another strike at the division, probably for the night of September 30th. The Reichswald forest and areas to its immediate south, much of it in the sector which the 2nd Battalion of the 508th was responsible for, was said to be harboring over 15,000 German troops and a full company of tanks. As it turned out, the night of the 30th brought no attack, though a lively counter battery duel between the American and British artillery and their enemy ensued. This was, however, not unusual and counter battery shoot outs after sunset had become routine since setting up at the Groesbeek gun positions.

While extra preparations were being made to defend against the anticipated German attack, Bob Storms and his machinegun crew learned a lesson about the Dutch people. "We set up one of our machineguns on the side of a road there because we expected a tank attack," he said. "They put one up off this one road on the corner there but nothing ever happened. Then a bunch of women and young girls come along and they were standing up on the bank. The boys all started talking, oh boy look at this and that, you know, that kind of crap. I seen the women's faces get red. So I said, 'Hey guys, hold it up, something's wrong.' Well, I went up there. I said, 'Good morning.' They said, 'Good morning.' I said, 'You speak English?' 'Oh yes, well very well!' I said, 'Pardon me.' I run down the hill. I told the guys, 'Hey shut up in front of them women. They speak better English than we do.' They said, 'What?' I said, 'Yeah! Cut the crap out.' So from then on we found out in Holland boy, they know. They speak very good English. They don't use them slang words."

On October 1st, 1944, Lieutenants Fellman and Johnson were serving as forward observers with the 508th's 2nd Battalion. It was an overcast day, with a chilled northerly wind carrying sporadic rain showers. Around dusk the Germans opened up with a fierce artillery barrage made up of every projectile from mortars to heavy artillery, and including the notorious "Screaming Meemees." Not only was the 508th's 2nd Battalion in the front line pounded, but so were its 1st and 3rd Battalions in the regiment's rear and reserve. "This time the Germans laid down their barrage in great depth," wrote William Lord in his history of the 508th. "In fact, the 3rd Battalion in division reserve near the regimental CP, was raked; by shells. The regimental CP took several direct hits. All wire communication between the front-line companies and the battalion was destroyed. After the barrage in the rear areas, all wires leading to the regimental switchboard were also cut. For more than an hour messengers and radios were the only means of communicating with the 2nd Battalion."

Years later, Lester Newman recalled the barrage which fell that night and commented, "The funny part of it was they wasn't hitting our battery. There were some tanks rolled in behind us and they set up some fifty caliber machineguns, and some twenty millimeter cannons. Boy the Germans give them hell. They were shooting right over our heads and on those guys in back of us. I'm sure glad I wasn't back there."

It was indeed a terrific bombardment; reminding everyone that even if the Germans were running out of manpower, they could still deliver plenty of firepower. Had the troopers still been in open slit trenches their casualties would have been great, but the warnings of a German offensive over the previous several days prompted everyone to dig themselves in deeper, with protective coverings built over their holes. Newman described how he and the other guys in Able Battery's machinegun section prepared theirs. "We dug a slit trench around our machinegun," he said. "It was L shaped. We had an entrance and an exit both, because it'd be pretty hard to get a gun crew out of a trench if you only had one exit. Then we would cover all but the opening and the get out place. We would take all the, you know, these cardboard, the thing the bullets would come in, they were pretty rigid and you could put, what the hell, fifty pounds of sand in them, each one of them. Then we had them on top, side by side, all the way over where you was sitting down there. They fit right across pretty comfortable there and keep any flak from coming down the hole. When they were shooting timed shots over our heads, a round would come in and blow up, and boy that shrapnel went every which way. That's why we had them ammunition cases filled with sand, to cover up our slit trench, and then just leave us a way to get in and out."

While the preparatory bombardment continued on the rear of the 508th, the Germans launched their assault on the 2nd Battalion's line. Supported by tanks and armored personnel carriers, their infantry struck with such ferocity that portions of the 2nd Battalion's lines were overrun or forced to retreat. "A" Battery's Lieutenant John Gutshall had already been assigned to the 2nd Battalion as an adjunct forward observer, with Tech-5 Harold Walz of Montrose, New York, as his radio operator. As the German bombardment lifted and their infantry rushed the 2nd Battalion's defenses, they found themselves in the middle of a very fluid situation. According to a later citation for the Silver Star which he earned that night, "2nd Lieutenant Gutshall moved to a position from which he could better observe the artillery fire of his battalion and remained in this fire swept position placing supporting artillery fire with such accuracy that two armored personnel carriers, with all occupants, were destroyed and the enemy attack became disorganized. While at his OP 2nd Lt. Gutshall was wounded in the head by shrapnel but remained at his post until forced to return to his battalion when all communications with his OP was destroyed by enemy artillery. He replaced this equipment and received first aid for his wound, returning immediately to the 2nd Battalion, where he continued to observe supporting fire."

Whether Gutshall's head wound resulted from artillery fire or some other source depends on who is recalling the incident. Back at the Able Battery gun position, Lieutenant Ragland remembered him coming back for replacement radio equipment. "That was some go round I tell you," said Ragland. "The story I got about Gutshall was that he was FO and this German come up and fired at him. The bullet went through the top of his helmet. The German thought he'd killed him, but Gutshall pulled out his pistol and captured the German. Gutshall showed us the helmet. The bullet went right through the top of the helmet, and it might have skinned his scalp but it didn't kill him. If it'd been a little lower it would have."

Harold Walz was also recognized for his performance that day. He was awarded a Bronze Star, the citation for which read in part, "T5 Walz was a radio operator in a liaison party to the 508th PIR, holding a defensive position near (censored) Woods. At about 2400 the enemy launched a determined attack with approximately 200 men supported by an undetermined number of tanks. This attack was preceded by a severe enemy artillery concentration. T5 Walz went forward as a radio operator with the battalion commander and the artillery LO. He transmitted fire direction orders for more than 2000 rounds of artillery. His initiative, courage, and devotion to duty under fire were highly instrumental in effecting the repulse of the enemy attack."

2,000 rounds of ammunition is a large amount, but a "Defensive Fire Plan" had already been distributed in anticipation of the German attack. Once it began, the 319th, along with the 86th Hertz Yeomanry, a British Field Artillery outfit now attached to the battalion, went into action. During the 48 hour period of October 1st and 2nd, "A" Battery alone fired an astounding 2,037 Howitzer rounds at the attacking Germans. Almost all of this expenditure took place between sundown of the 1st and noon the next day. The gunners in the battery remember it as a mesmerizing ordeal of continuous loading, firing, and reloading. "We was firing at will," recalled Duel Elmore. "Just as fast as you'd put one in, you'd side step and then it'd go. We burned up the slides on the gun that night that one time. I mean, they wouldn't even fire the next day. Couldn't move. It melted them off."

Sergeant Harvey Rash also remembered the artillery work the battery performed that night and concurred with Elmore. He said, "Yeah, you had to watch that. Those rascals, they get hot you know. You have to change the barrel every once in a while. As long as you can change that barrel right quick that's no problem, but some of the ammunition would get stuck, and getting that doggone round out of there is a problem. That's where you gotta be pretty careful. That was the most firepower I'd ever seen."

Orrin Miller remembered the same problems with overheated barrels that night. He later said, "The shells were so hot that the ejectors wouldn't eject them all the way. Then you had to reach in there with your hands and finish pulling the shell case out of the barrel of the gun. We actually burnt the barrels right out of our guns because we fired all night long. I don't know how many rounds, but I do believe that is what caused my hearing to be what it is today."

Miller was referring to a problem common among artillerymen as they aged. Most of those who spent any extended time on gun crews noticed some degree of hearing loss immediately after heavy bombardments like this. Though their hearing usually seemed to recover after a few days, in later life there was no question that their auditory senses were impaired.

Sometimes hearing loss could be attributed to a specific incident. As the fatigue of the night wore on, the men became punch-drunk and started to make little errors. Elmore remembered one which cost him some of his hearing. "A gun went off in my ear. I was setting the sights on it and the guy that was pulling the lanyard, he pulled it before he should have. I seen him jerk and I turned my head and missed the gun recoil. It went off in my ear. If I hadn't amoved, it'd ahit me right in the face. I come home, I couldn't hear a watch ticking. I still can't hear in my right ear."

At yet another gun, one of the cannoneers somehow neglected to properly replace the projectile in the shell casing before handing it off to the loader, who threw it into the breech automatically, without thinking. Mahlon Sebring was serving on this crew and remembered the result vividly when he later said, "It was at night, and when they went to push the shell in the gun the projectile fell out on the ground. I don't know whether the guy didn't shut the breech block quick enough or what happened, but all that was in the gun was the brass casing and the powder charge. It lit up the area when they set it off. We first thought the damn gun had had a direct hit or something, but that wasn't the case. But it kind of scares you when something like that happens because you don't know what it is for a minute."

German counter battery shelling was active too, and at times the battalion gunners were working their pieces fully exposed to this fire. "I got hit with a piece of shrapnel in the rump, but I had the fuse wrench in my rear pocket and it hit right on the wrench, so it didn't hurt me," said Orrin Miller. "That was a close call. It bruised and it stung like the devil but it didn't hurt me."

During the evening of October 1st the Germans tried to exploit their initial success in gaining much of the 2nd Battalion, 508th's defenses. Eventually their thrust started pouring over the supporting positions and threatened the 319th's own gun emplacements. "One time we was kind of scared a little," remembered Kenneth Smith of that night. "The Germans made a breakthrough. Came out of the woods and ran our troopers back, but we got called in and put a stop to it. We saved their lives really. If we hadn't have been there they would have been in a hell of a shape. We opened up direct fire and shot all of our ammunition into the woods. It stopped the Germans from coming any farther. There weren't no tanks, just infantry coming through the woods, and they had us outnumbered real bad but we stopped them. We could hear them screaming when we hit them, yelling and screaming all over the place. We could see what we were shooting, just like you'd take your rifle and shoot. We was firing the guns like that. That's the only time we ever did that. I was the cannoneer at that time with Rappi. I was loading the gun. Shooting it just as fast as we could. Then we didn't have no ammunition after that, except only 16 rounds left for our gun that was it."

After a spirited counterattack during the pre-dawn hours of October 2nd, the line was substantially restored. Then, when enemy holdouts in the 2nd Battalion's positions were mopped up over the course of the morning, it was found that the Germans left behind at least fifty of their dead, as well as four knocked out armored personnel carriers and one panther tank. In all likelihood, a good many more of their dead and wounded had already been evacuated during the night. Through nothing short of a tremendous effort, the 319th played a signature part in stopping the German thrust of October 1st. "They said that shooting that we done saved a lot of soldier's lives," Kenneth Smith proudly remembered. So prominent had their role been, that at 1230 hours, General Gavin visited the battalion CP to compliment Colonel Todd on the shooting done by the battalion during the previous night's fighting.

The 319th's reputation within the division was never higher. Even years afterward, troopers held the battalion's contribution to the fight of October 1st in high regard. "I never will forget," recalled Kenneth Smith, "I went to an 82nd convention in Detroit, and I was talking to some of the veterans about that deal, shooting direct fire into the woods. This one boy told me, you're the one who saved my life. I said, 'No I don't think so.' 'Yes you was,' he said, 'I was with that bunch running from the Germans when you started shooting.' He was tickled to death. He give me a twenty dollar bill. I wouldn't take it, but my wife did.

During these last days of September and beginning of October, battalion men noticed something new to warfare. It was the ME-262, the first and only operational jet fighter of World War Two. "Bombs would start falling or there'd be, you know, machinegun fire, then we'd hear the plane," said Covais. "It was backwards, because normally you'd hear the aircraft coming and then they'd fire."

Suddenly the men on the ground discovered they had virtually no warning of approaching enemy fighters. Silas Hogg described his first encounters with jet fighters in a manner similar to Covais, complaining, "We couldn't find out where in the hell they were coming from because they would fly over so fast. They'd drop the bomb and fly away. The bomb would go off and blast our ass all over. We couldn't find out where they were coming from. Finally some guy said, 'There they are, see them going out of sight?'

Then we found out what we was in for. Yeah, they made believers out of us."

"All of a sudden I hear this noise," was the way Louis Sosa remembered his introduction to the Jet Age. "I looked up and before I could look up they were gone. That was the first time I ever saw a jet plane. It must have been doing 300 miles an hour. They didn't attack us or anything, they just flew right over up at maybe about a thousand feet. That was something else. Damndest thing you ever saw in your life."

In fact, the ME-262 could achieve a top speed of about 550 miles per hour, far beyond Sosa's estimation. This was perhaps 20% faster than any aircraft the Allies could put in the sky, but even with this lead the German jets could still be brought down by heavy concentrations of flak. Moreover, while certainly quicker than Allied fighters, the jets did not have quite the maneuverability of the best British and American planes, neutralizing much of their advantage in conventional dogfights.

As advanced as the ME-262 was, it was still an aircraft on the cutting edge of technology and, as such, was prone to mechanical malfunctions. It also took time to develop pilots who could fly these new jets with skill, and time to train them was something the Germans had little of. In fact, the ME-262's speed was actually a disadvantage for many of its pilots because they had so little time to align themselves on their targets.

Ed Ryan was intrigued by the German jets. "I couldn't understand what they were, but I kept watching because I have kind of a mechanical mind. Anyway, the Spitfires would chase them. You could see the Spitfires going after them. Then next thing you know the Spitfire'd come back blombering. They'd blow the engine in the Spitfire trying to catch them," he said. Finally Ryan had a chance to see one of the jets up close after one crash landed, probably from an engine malfunction. Ryan approached the jet and found it fascinating. "I looked at it and it had two jets on it. Single seater airplane with two jets on it, one on each side. It went down in the middle of the street in Nijmegen. The jet was down in the street, smashed up some but the pilot wasn't hurt. He was standing there with these zippers all over his suit. I guess somebody might have been guarding him, but to me he looked like he was gonna give a lecture on the plane. He was standing there like he was proud of it."

Besides bombing and strafing, the German Luftwaffe also dropped propaganda leaflets. Members of the 319th remember them as telling the Americans that communism, not national socialism, was the real enemy. The Americans were then advised to join forces with their German brothers to defend Europe against Asiatic Communism. Covais remarked, "Sure, I thought we should keep right on going until we reached Moscow, a lot of us thought so, once we'd taken Berlin and beaten the Germans first!"

Another man in the battalion said, "I remember those propaganda leaflets. They were promising women and everything else. Come over we'll give you a good time. We used them for toilet paper. Rough but a good substitute."

In "A" Battery there were promotions for 2nd Lieutenants Fellman and Gutshall to 1st Lieutenant on October 2nd. Lieutenant Cook, who'd gained so much experience with air observation in Normandy, was detailed again to get aloft with Morgan, the pilot. There was also a demotion of Corporal Eisner of the signals section to private. "He was a good man but he got drunk and was parading down the road. When he saluted me he lost his balance. I don't know where he got his liqueur, but he was some loaded. But I couldn't have it, couldn't have it. You can't have anybody getting drunk when you're on the alert. I got back to the battery and told Sergeant Johnson to take away his stripes. Then about a month later he got them back," recalled Sartain. Considering the situation further, Sartain added, "Somebody should have rat-holed him, put him in a hole somewhere, got him off the street. The boys used to look after each other that way."

There was also a change for Mahlon Sebring. After the German attack of October 1st, Sebring found he could no longer ignore the mounting tension between himself and his Section Chief, Sergeant Jones*, which had been building since the outfit's first combat after landing. "I went into Holland in the gun section, but our chief of section, which is the sergeant of your gun section, he dug a slit trench and he wouldn't get out of it," Sebring said. "He ate in it, and we had to bring him his meals in it. He didn't even get out of it to go to the bathroom! He shit and pissed in it. See, he'd been a sergeant back here in the States. He was regular army and he'd been in five or ten years, but he'd never left the states. He being a sergeant he thought he was a hot dog, you know. Of course, we all thought we was hot dogs, but he was just a plain damn coward. He wouldn't get out of that hole, and I refused to bring his damn meals to him."

"I finally went to the Captain and I said, 'Captain, if I don't get out of this section I'm gonna shoot him. I'd hate to have that on my record that I shot one of our own men, but I don't want to be around him anymore.' That's when I got in the signal section. From that time on I helped set up the switchboard and helped lay wires to the guns."

Sergeant Jones was recollected by other enlisted men in the battery. Ted Simpson was on the same gun crew with Sebring. When asked if he remembered his Section Sergeant, Simpson immediately answered, "Yes, very much so and with not much pleasure. He was my Sergeant, one of them. Heavy set, too much, a fat guy. He's the only one I have a distinctive unpleasant memory of. The nature of the man was not utterly courageous." Simpson then recalled one particular episode to memory, saying, "I remember staying up half the night while I was on guard duty and he was there. He was trying to prove to me that the world was square. I was trying to prove to him that the world was round. You could climb up in a tree or to the top of a mountain and see the curvature of the earth. He couldn't answer that, but he kept referring to the four corners of the earth as quoted in the bible. He didn't like me much and I didn't like him much. It was mutual. Other than that I remember a big camaraderie and pride among these guys, all of them."

Most likely it was Lieutenant Ragland whom Sebring took his complaint to. As battery exec, moving men around from one assignment to another to keep things running smoothly was a common practice for him. In any case, neither Sartain nor Ragland specifically remembered Jones, or Sebring's complaint, when interviewed years later, though Sartain did observe, "That was the trouble with the replacements. Man, we'd get some real weirdoes. You'd kind of be waiting for a vacancy so you could promote one of our own guys to sergeant from corporal or PFC, up and up and up. Then we'd get these characters from the replacement units that were ahead on the waiting list. They'd come with rank, you know, and there wasn't much we could do about it."

Whether there was any disciplinary action taken remains unclear. However, since Sergeant Jones' name is not included in later unit rosters and he is not in the battery's final group photograph, there is the suggestion that he may have been transferred to another unit.

The guys in the outfit were well acquainted with fear. There were those few who tried and tried, but could never really master their dread of combat. "We had one guy," Covais later recalled, "He'd get so scared he wasn't any use to anybody, so they always kept him back at the battery. It wasn't his fault, he couldn't help it."

When a man who'd performed well in many a battle simply reached the end of his endurance his buddies were always there at his side with a cup of coffee, a cigarette, and words of encouragement. "Hey," they'd say, "it'll be alright."

An example of this can be seen in the memory Orrin Miller had of a particular man who reached his limit and could go no further. "There was a corporal," Miller said, "He was our gunner on our gun crew. He was a seasoned soldier with a lot more experience than most of us had. One time we called him for a gun mission and he couldn't come out of the foxhole. He broke down, what do they call that, battle fatigue I guess you'd call it. He just stayed right in the foxhole and shook and shook and shook. He just couldn't come out. We felt sorry for him, and compassionate. There was no ridicule. We tried to help him in all the ways we could. We offered him warm coffee and whatever we could do. We just had to call the medics and the medics had to take him away. They had to take him and send him back to the hospital. That's the first time I'd ever seen that. He had that battle fatigue."

Sergeant Jones was a different story, perhaps because of his false bravado, perhaps because he'd never faced combat before. Whatever the reason, Sebring's contempt hadn't faded in sixty years. He concluded his comments about his Section Chief by saying, "All I know is he wasn't a combat man, I'll tell you that. He was a damn coward. Anyone in our gun crew would probably tell you the same damn thing. If I hadn't got out of there I would have shot him, and I didn't think he was worth being in prison for. He wouldn't get out of his God damn hole. We had to bring him his meals. He went to the bathroom in his damn slit trench and everything. You can't take orders from someone as God damn scared as that. We were all scared. I mean if you wasn't scared you were a damn fool, but you've got to be able to be scared and function too."

That was the whole point. Still functioning while terrified, but it didn't always work that way. One afternoon in Holland, Sartain was making his usual visits to the forward observers. As Sosa drove him toward the next OP, he encountered the Lieutenant he was going to check on, walking along the road, headed back to the battalion. The man was followed by his radio operator. Sartain couldn't believe his eyes, and when the jeep came to a halt he immediately asked for an explanation. "I just can't take it any more," was all the Lieutenant could say, repeating it over and over. The Lieutenant's radio operator stood by, chewing, then turned his head and spit out a long stream of tobacco juice, but otherwise said nothing. Sartain saw it as an editorial comment, and asked him what happened. The radioman then said, "Well sir, there's been some mortars off and on all day. It kinda didn't set too well with the Lieutenant here."

"You mean you left that infantry with no artillery support," Sartain asked the Lieutenant.

The Lieutenant whispered, "I'm sorry, sir."

Sartain took a deep breath. He could see the Lieutenant was trembling, severely distressed, and at the point of a complete breakdown. The man's fear had clearly gotten the best of him. "He was in such a nervous state, he just blew his cool on that particular occasion," Sartain remembered. "Other than that, and after that, he was OK, but you see, when he was subjected to his first mortar attack it really, really shook him up. Well, it would shake anybody up for crying out loud, but you've got to learn to live with it. When I got to him he was an absolute nervous wreck. I thought he was gonna go berserk. So I sent him back to the battalion. Either that night or the next day he came up to me and said, 'Captain, I'm ready again. I'm ready now.' From then on he was OK." Until a new man could be brought up, Sartain filled in as a temporary forward observer. Decades later, Sartain thought back on the event and further commented, "I didn't report it. I should have, he abandoned his post and left the infantry without artillery support, but I never reported anybody. I think I just always thought they deserved another chance."

Once the German attack of October 1st was passed, things along the 82nd Airborne Division's front settled down. A routine of nightly air raids, bombardments, and aggressive patrolling developed, with no major offensive operations from either side. The temperate, late summer weather of mid-September was also gone. In its place a cold, constant drizzling rain falling from gloomy skies seemed to become the permanent weather pattern. So ended the first phase of the Holland campaign. Those last two weeks of September had brought more intensive and unrelenting fighting than anything the battalion ever experienced. Though the war was definitely not going in the German's favor, it was also plain they still had a lot of fight left in them. Bob McArthur summed it up well in a letter to his mother in Mississippi, when he wrote, "Last year, I made a prediction that I would be home by this Christmas. Well, at that time I didn't know what I was saying. This war here in Europe will go on into 1945 unless something drastic happens to the German people. After that, there is the Pacific war that will have to be fought, and I am almost positive that it will take more than a year after Germany falls. So you see there is no chance of me coming home for a good while yet." The GIs in the 319th weren't pessimistic about the war. To the contrary, they had no doubt the Allies would prevail, but as they were now all veterans with the hardened cynicism which comes with that status, they also knew they wouldn't be home before more hard fighting was accomplished.

BATTERY!

Part 21: "Captain, don't leave me."

The Island was the term the Americans used to describe the wedge of land located between the Waal River at Nijmegen and the Lower Rhine, or Neder Rijn as it was known to the Dutch, at Arnhem. The terrain between the rivers was distinctly different from that in the Mook-Groesbeek-Beek area, much of which was forested and had some elevated ground. By contrast, the Island was utterly flat and mostly open, with drainage canals and dykes as the only terrain features besides villages.

Once the bridges at Nijmegen were taken by troopers of the American 82nd Airborne and crossed by British tanks on September 20th, it was just this terrain which made it so difficult for the armored column to advance to Arnhem. Roads on the flat, sea level, countryside were built up; silhouetting every vehicle against the horizon from an extended distance and the ground was generally too soft for tanks to advance cross country. Consequently, once the resistance of the British 1st Airborne Division ceased about September 25th, Montgomery contented himself with holding a small area on the North bank of the Waal, covering the immediate approaches to the two bridges at Nijmegen.

On October 5th Colonel Todd, battalion staff, and the battery commanders met with the senior officers of the 508th to formulate a movement by that regiment to the north bank of the Waal. The American 508th paratroopers would be reinforcing and advancing the British defensive perimeter. "When we went back across the Nimegen Bridge to secure The Island," remembered Sartain, "'A' Battery, 319th, was to support the 3rd Battalion, 508th. Mendez said, 'I want Charlie Sartain with me', when they planned the operation, so that's how I went in on it."

The expectation was that the Germans would be present in force and stubbornly resist the 508th's efforts to advance onto The Island. For once Sartain was seized with a sense of foreboding. "I kept it to myself, but I got real concerned. The night before we left to go across the bridge I sat there in my foxhole and wrote Peggy Lou a long letter. I proposed to her, told her I wanted to give her a ring now, instead of waiting until I got home. I'd send a mutual friend the money and they could go pick it out. I never worried about living, never gave a moments thought to getting killed or whatever, except when we went across the bridge over to The Island," he recalled of his thoughts at that time. On the afternoon of the 6th, in company with a British armored unit, the operation commenced. Sartain was, as planned, crossing

The Nijmegen Bridge as it appeared from the North bank of the Waal River. The photograph was taken on October 6th, a few hours after the Battalion crossed over to "The Island." Covais collection.

with the attack wave of Mendez' battalion. "It was an assault operation," Sartain explained, "and the infantry was supporting the tanks. The tanks would go, maybe four five of them, six, seven, tanks would go and the infantry would be on each. It made a combined assault. The infantry was to clear out all the remaining German troops on that point. On that Island. They had the support of a British tank unit, so Miller and I rode on the back of a tank, you see. I rode on one tank and Bob Miller with the radio rode on the other. Sosa stayed back at the Nimegen Bridge. We came across but we didn't get shot at. Of course the island was clear at that time, but nobody knew it. It was basically a free ride. So we crossed the bridge and took a right and swept that whole island."

In fact, The Island was a significant expanse of territory and the Germans had only withdrawn from that half which lay closest to the Waal River. Perhaps they anticipated the Anglo-American advance, and did not care to bring on a general engagement. Their lines now lay more or less along the De Linge Canal, which bisected The Island. Now attached to the British 53rd Division, the 508th occupied the area just north of the town of Bemmel. The 319th, ordered to support the fire of the 90th British Field Artillery Regiment, was ready for fire missions within a few hours of crossing the Waal. Assignments of liaison officers and forward observers were made. Captain Sartain was selected as liaison to the 508th's 3rd Battalion, with Lieutenants Marvin Fellman and Harold Peters selected as forward observers. As was routine, Captain Manning led each FO to his position with the infantry, explaining to them where the enemy was, what to watch for, and what the vulnerable points were for that particular observation post.

This time "A" Battery was situated in a field of sugar beets, close to the tiny village of Boel, a couple of hundred yards from a railroad line and on the edge of a large orchard. Captain Manning described the new battalion positions when he wrote, "On the north side of the river, we were in flat farmland - cabbage patches. Where we had landed

on the south side we had been on the only hill in Holland, complete with some heavily treed areas. The new location improved the range and breadth of fire for our batteries, but left them more exposed. It also cut back on the positions for artillery observation posts."

When asked about the new gun positions, Lieutenant Ragland recalled that, "They had a big high line running right through the area, in the road, in the line of sight of our artillery.

An English officer with Colonel Todd in Holland September 1944. Captain Sartain or one of the staff officers contacted an engineer unit and had them cut down that one great big high tower. They just knocked her down so we could have a wider area to fire in."

"They told us we were gonna be there quite a while," Ragland continued, "of course, I didn't expect these other guys to dig my foxhole, they got their own foxholes to dig So I'd dug my own foxhole. I had a deep foxhole in Holland. I got some heavy timbers and covered it over, with just a place to get down in when we needed to. It might not have been a good idea though, because if the Germans had come in I wouldn't be able to get out."

Duel Elmore described the quarters of his gun crew a little differently. "Well," he said, "we put our sleeping tent in the apple orchard, oh, about 50 yards from the gun. We dug a little trench in it and put down a wood floor if we could find the wood, or hay and put it in the bottom of it. We'd dig it down about a foot deep and that would give you a little more head room."

The practice of digging out the area beneath a tent was common, but on The Island the guys were limited as to how deep they could go. It was quickly discovered that foxholes excavated more than three feet deep would fill with water because of the high water table. Even the shallowest trenches began to fill up with water whenever a rain of any consequence came through, which was frequently. "Our foxholes in Holland had water in the bottom of them because Holland's so low," Sebring complained afterwards. "So we threw brush and shell casings in them, and stuff to stay up out of the water. Well, you sleep in that for two nights and you wake up and ache all over." To compensate, ammunition crates were commonly filled with earth and stacked up around the tents, forming miniature earthenwork fortifications.

Aside from a location which offered some minimal concealment from German observation for the bivouac of the men, the orchard provided an abundance of ripe fruit.
There was evidently a variety of trees in the orchard, as the men's memories differ on what they helped themselves to. Ted Simpson remembered pears.

Sergeant Rappi agreed, saying, "I don't remember an apple orchard but I remember a pear orchard. We ate every pear that was there. They were really good pears too."

The fact was, the men weren't used to any fresh fruit in their diet and now they had access to all they could eat. Some overindulged with embarrassing results. As one "A" Battery man later admitted, "Yep, we ate fresh apples, grapes, plums, pears. Got the shits. In fact, I shit my pants, if you want to know the truth of it!"

Captain Manning's observation that the new positions were more exposed to enemy artillery was also quite correct. Within the orchard, besides digging in for sleeping quarters, the guys in the motor pool had to dig down trenches for the vehicle wheels and protect them with built up earth in much the same fashion as the men did for their foxholes. Though heaviest at night, there could be indiscriminate artillery fire at any time. A sudden shower of German artillery fell among the Able Battery motor pool one afternoon, giving Carl Salminen a close call he'd never forget. "We were in that apple orchard," he said. "We had a six by six GM truck parked there. We had to dig down the wheels on the jeep and trucks to protect the big tires from shrapnel. And that 88 hit that doggone GMC six by six when I was only about thirty feet away from it. That's one thing about artillery. If you hear them you don't have to worry about it. Boy, if you don't, well, that's another story."

Kenneth Smith was also in the orchard on that occasion, busy collecting fruit.

CAPTAIN, DON'T LEAVE ME.

His commentary on the threat of any one particular artillery round was uncannily similar to Salminen's when he said, "I was stealing some apples out of the tops of those trees when they started firing on us and hit the motor section and done all that damage. Two or three of the guys got wounded and got to go home. They were new guys anyhow; they just come into our outfit after Normandy. Those ones that got hit, it was the shrapnel that hit them. I just stayed up there in the trees till they got through shelling, then I got down. I guess I was scared, I don't know, but it didn't bother me that much really. You got to where you know whether they was gonna come in or go over. You learned how to read them, the sound of them, and you could tell where's they's a going. They just make a whiney noise. You'll know it when you hear it. The one's you didn't hear, that's the one that hits you. The ones that you could hear them, you didn't have to worry too much."

The losses from German artillery and air raids weren't heavy, but there was a steady trickle of one or two men wounded every few days. On Sunday, October 8th, for example, Mahlon Sebring and the other guys in his section were walking into the gun position after attending a religious service held by Chaplain Reid. Sebring later said of the incident, "I lost a good buddy there in that position. His name was Douglas Gregory and he was in the gun section. A few of us went to services on a Sunday, and when we got back to our gun position, just as we were turning out in front of our howitzer, an artillery shell come in. You could hear pieces of it bouncing off of our howitzer and whining. But the four of us, just turning to go underneath the camouflage net, it never touched a one of us. My buddy was over in the orchard, and he got hit. He started yelling and we went over there. He got a piece right in the elbow. I cut his sleeves up to find it and when I seen that joint I thought, boy, he's gonna have problems with that. We took him to the first aid tent and never saw him again."

Frances Tobin of Scarsdale, NY, displays a captured German vehicle identification marker, Holland, fall, 1944. Sartain collection.

A few days after this, Sebring himself was wounded. He'd only just been transferred out of Sergeant Jones gun crew to the signal section, where Staff Sergeant Carl Davis put him to work on the battery switchboard. The board was set up in a small utility building on the edge of the orchard. Inside, Sebring thought it felt great to be away from Sergeant Jones, and it felt just as good to be out of the rain and mud too. Thinking back to an abandoned train on the railroad tracks about a quarter mile away, he had a brilliant idea. "Well, there was one car with corrugated cardboard on it," Sebring explained later. "So I went over and I dragged about six inches of that corrugated cardboard back home to the command post. I put it in the corner, there by the switchboard. We had a little stove in this building. So I said, I'm gonna sleep on this cardboard. I'm sleeping in the corner tonight, damned if I'll sleep in that slit trench anymore!"

"So, I was in the CP, I'm laying there sleeping. They started shelling us and a piece come through and hit me in the hind end. I run out and jumped in a slit trench till the shelling was over with. Then the medic was going around saying, 'Is anyone hurt?' I said, 'Well I got hit in the hind end, but I don't know how bad.' He brought my boots out to me and I went back inside where it was light. It didn't go in that far, he picked it out and put a bandage on it. All I had was a big blister about four inches in diameter. He said go up to the first aid tent and they'll sign you up for a Purple Heart. I never went up there. I thought, Christ, guys get their arms and legs blown off and that's all they get. So I never went and got it, but I didn't know at the end of the war it was gonna be worth five points either."

Because Sebring's thoughts about the relative merit of wounds was common, the actual number of casualties in the battalion was certainly significantly higher than what is shown in the 319th's records. Part of the attitude came from masculine pride, but by this time even the post-Normandy replacements had seen grievously wounded men whose lives would never be the same. Respect for the way these buddies suffered pain and were maimed for life played an enormous role in formulating this point of view. Hence there was a reluctance to claim for oneself the same status if the injury was "not too bad."

Teenager Robert Dickson was another man whose name would never appear on any casualty list, but when a Luftwaffe fighter dropped anti-personnel bombs over the battery area one evening he was hit too. As he remembered it, Dickson was leaping head first into a slit trench when he felt something strike him. It was like having a hot poker jammed into his hip. Once in the safety of the covered foxhole, "I told my buddy, hey, you gotta gouge this thing out."

Dickson's friend wasn't too sure about that and answered, "How'm I gonna do it? You oughta go to the medic."

Dickson was adamant. "Well," he told him, "you got a bayonet, don't you? Then use that!" Dickson's buddy took a deep breath, then drew his knife. "I pulled my pants down and he gouged it out of my hip and put a bandage on it. I didn't get a Purple Heart over it either. That was one thing I didn't do, I didn't go to the medics and that's where I made a mistake, I didn't get a Purple Heart, but being a young boy I had a lot of pride in what I was doing."

Though certainly not always the case, the schedule of German artillery and fighter-bombers were often quite predictable. Barrages, for example, were always more frequent after sundown. There was also an enemy air raid on the Nijmegen Bridge which was so regularly scheduled close to ten o'clock each evening that it was dubbed "Bed Check Charlie" by the guys in the battery.

Still another class of aerial weapons which attracted the attention of the men in the 319th that October were the German V-1 and V-2 Rockets, the first inter-continental ballistic missiles.

Development of these Vergeltungswaffen, or so called "Vengeance Weapons," could be traced back to the mid-1930s, when Nazi leadership recognized rocketry's potential as a destructive agent. The V-1 was really a rather primitive affair, amounting to an enormous, elaborated, jet propelled artillery shell. It measured 29 feet in length and had a wingspan of 17 feet, being normally launched off a ski ramp pointed in the general direction of its intended target. Cruising at a low altitude of between 2,000 and 3,000 feet, but at a tremendous speed too rapid for conventional anti-aircraft guns to be an effective defense, the distinctive sound of the V-1's pulse style jet engine quickly earned it the nickname of "Buzz Bomb."

These fixed launch sites, located along the French and Dutch coasts, were within striking range of England's larger cities. Beginning with the first Buzz Bomb attack in June, 1944, about 10,000 of these flying missiles would eventually be hurled at London alone. Though wildly inaccurate, Buzz Bombs could produce significant damage when they did strike any populated, metropolitan area. It was, in fact, just this random nature which contributed to their psychological strength as a terror weapon. For this reason, part of the impetus for the whole Market-Garden operation was to overrun the launch sites, depriving the Germans of access to the British Isles, and restore public morale in England.

Able Battery men recognized the V-1s by their unique sound and low altitude flight. Kenneth Smith thought they sounded, "Just like a washing machine," and Lieutenant Cook remarked, "We saw plenty of them. We'd see them chugging across the air like an old steam engine. They was flying to England, unless they got shot down. There was a lot of them shot down."

Cook was right. By the time of the Holland invasion, Allied gunners and fighter planes were developing techniques to intercept and shoot down the V-1s in ever larger numbers, but they always remained a real threat, even if they exploded in mid-flight. "One of them hit right over the top of us and concussion is what really tore my ears up," remembered Dickson of one Buzz bomb shot out of the sky while it was soaring over the battery's position. "At that particular time I said something to a medic about it and he said to me, well, they'll stop ringing in a few days."

A V-1 missile must have been a terrifying object to have pass overhead, and even if intended for a target a long way off, their sound was nonetheless alarming. Orrin Miller recalled one such incident which ended most unfortunately. "We had a slit trench, foxhole dug," he later said. "We were out there brewing our last cup of coffee before the lights had to go out in the evening. All of a sudden, what were those large things they used to send over to England during the war, they make a whistling noise just like an artillery shell coming in. You could hear them very plainly. We all were jumping for the foxhole. I dove for the foxhole and caught my foot in the wires for the telephone communication. It tipped over the coffee and nobody had coffee that night."

Taking it all in stride, as John Girardin was apt to do, he started singing the popular song "Skylark" with the word "Buzz Bomb" substituted.

Oh Buzz Bomb, have you anything to say to me.

Won't you tell me where my love can be.

Is there a meadow in the mist, where someone's waiting to be kissed?

Oh, Buzz Bomb, have you seen a valley green with spring?

It didn't take long for Girardin himself to be tagged with the nick-name "Buzz Bomb" by the other GIs in "A" Battery.

V-2 rockets were a much more sophisticated device than a simple jet-propelled bomb. These 40 foot tall, single stage ballistic missiles were the first man-made objects to gain sub-orbital altitude. From a height of over 50 miles, each V-2 would plummet to earth at a super sonic speed of about 3,500 miles per hour and then detonate a full ton of explosives on impact. Being super sonic, the V-2 gave no warning of its approach the way a Buzz Bomb would, nor was there any effective defense against it. Unlike jet aircraft, or even the Buzz Bomb, V-2 rockets were really beyond the comprehension of anyone outside the inner circle of experimental rocketry at the time. "We could see the

V2s," remembered Sebring. "We could see the trail of smoke as they were going over on the way to England. Of course, we didn't know what it was until we read the Stars and Stripes."

Nor could the launch site of the V-2 be attacked from the air because, unlike the fixed catapult ramps used by the V-1, the V-2 employed a mobile launch system which required only a paved highway for its transportation. Consequently, no single launch battery of V-2 rockets was ever discovered or destroyed by the Allies. Though the ME-262 jet fighter, the Buzz Bomb, and the V-2 were all innovative and remarkably advanced weapons systems, none of them was ever produced in large enough numbers or early enough in the war to turn the tide in favor of the Germans.

With the static nature of the campaign at this point, an element of routine set in. On two occasions small groups of a few men were given 48 hour passes to Brussels, Belgium. Only six "A" Battery men were actually granted this privilege before the outfit left Holland, but the chance that one might be the next selected imparted hope to everyone in the unit. At somewhat regular intervals, the battalion was able to arrange for larger groups of men to be trucked into Nijmegen for a hot shower, a hot meal, and perhaps a picture show or even a little live music from the dance band of the 504th PIR.

The showers were especially welcome for GIs who hadn't had an opportunity to bathe since before the invasion. Between digging and living in foxholes, the mud, and the sweat of exertion, many of the men were desperate for soap and water. "I just couldn't stand it," said one "B" Battery man who was driven to extremes one day in the orchard before he got his turn to go into Nijmegen. "I took a bath. I mean when it was cold outside. I found a basin, got water and took a bath. They thought I was crazy, standing out naked in the cold, but I had a chance to take a bath and I took it. Of course, that was a little risky, but I took it anyway."

On October 17th, a four page, tabloid newspaper named the All-American Paraglide was published in Nijmegen. Some of the guys in the battalion got copies, which were eagerly passed from hand to hand. Besides the masthead was written, "This paper is made available to troops of the 82nd "All-American Airborne Division" and their families through the generosity of the citizens of Nijmegen, Netherlands. As far as we know it's the only paper of its kind in Holland. We express our gratitude and thanks to the Dutch people, whose assistance in this campaign has been immeasurable." Articles written in the paper included, "With the 82nd Airborne by glider," "82nd captures vital Nijmegen bridge in historic three day battle," "A rookie's reception," "508th 1st to enter Germany," and "Doberman pinched by MPs. Dog spy escapes fold of Provost Marshall or Panzer Pluto plays possum after MPs pinch Pinscher." One article was devoted to the exploits of the division artillery. It made specific reference to the 319th and was naturally of particular interest. Reading about the airborne invasion and the subsequent glider re-enforcement as feature stories was great, all the more since the articles were written by the troopers themselves. British and American papers at home had been all but ignoring the role played by the 82nd in the Holland invasion, so, though the "All-American Paraglide" didn't have quite the same circulation as domestic newspapers, seeing their own efforts acknowledged in print had a terrific effect on morale.

At about this same time the final phase of arrangements for soldier voting in the presidential Election of 1944, between Democratic incumbent Franklin D. Roosevelt and the Republican Governor of New York, Thomas P. Dewey, was completed. Under the Soldier Voting Act of 1942, as amended in 1944, members of the armed forces were supplied on request with franked postcards which they could send to their Secretaries of State. Upon receipt, these offices were in turn called upon to respond with absentee ballots for the troops in the field. Soldiers who failed to request an absentee ballot, but who still wished to vote, were entitled to a ballot which allowed the soldier to cast a vote in the presidential race and for any congressional seats in play for their particular state. States were then obliged to honor these Federally supplied ballots, regardless of whether the servicemen were already registered to vote in local elections or not.

Of about 12 million persons in the armed forces at the time, over 3 million are believed to have used the postcard system to request ballots. Another 85,000 were supplied with the Federal ballot because their states had no provision for absentee voting, or the absentee ballots were still enroute from the United States.

Ted Covais took an active interest in civics and clearly recalled casting his vote for Roosevelt through the absentee system. Robert Rappi and Lieutenant Fellman also say they voted for the president. Bob Storms went for FDR too, in part because his home town of Poughkeepsie was near Hyde Park, the site of FDR's estate. Robert Dickson, like many others, was just too young to vote, and John Girardin simply wasn't an American citizen.

Without doubt, Ed Ryan had the most personal knowledge in the battalion of the incumbent president. As a boy, he'd worked for him, cleaning horse stables on the FDR estate at Hyde Park, New York. "He paid me twenty cents an hour, which was five cents less than the minimum wage," he said of the experience. In later years the President stopped many mornings for gasoline at the Sinclair service station which Ryan's father owned. FDR and his wife Eleanor were remembered by him as, "The most charismatic people I ever met." In spite of all this, Ryan had no interest in the election. "They said to me, do you want a blank for an out of the country vote? I told them to wipe their butt with it. I would have had to vote communist if I did, because at the time I was all pissed off at everything. They passed out absentee ballots. Most guys didn't bother with them. What the hell, you're away from home and in combat, who wants to hear about it. I had more important things to do."

Ryan may have been exaggerating his attitude in memory, but in truth a large proportion of the guys really were preoccupied and indifferent. "We knew that FDR would be reelected, but a lot of that political news we weren't hearing too much, we were pretty well occupied," said Lieutenant Ragland in agreement with Ryan. He was one of a very few Republicans in the battery at the time, though most seem to have changed party affiliation in subsequent years. "Being from Kansas I was a registered Republican because Kansas is a republican state," he said. "People would say to me, don't you know Herbert Hoover was a Republican? Well, I'd say, so was Lincoln."

The guys in the 82nd were also able to get better acquainted with the people of Nijmegen and The Island during this period. To be sure, during the early weeks of the campaign, some of the Dutch people in the Beek-Groesbeek-Mook area seemed ambivalent toward the Americans and sometimes actually sympathetic toward the Germans. Most of the GIs weren't fully aware that they were literally straddling the Dutch-German border, among people with necessarily divided loyalties. Ed Ryan remembered the nuns at the Nebo convent running away from him and his buddies. "I got kind of pissed off at the Dutch," he said later. "They liked the British but not the Americans. It was the only place nuns would shun you. I think they thought we were going to rape them or something, but that was the furthest thing from anybody's mind." The Journal of the 325th Glider Infantry has several notations which make reference to civilians sniping at GIs in the Reithorst area, and Roland Gruebling specifically remembered that when he helped

BATTERY!

escort several German POWs through a Dutch village near there, local women came out and offered the Germans water but declined to let the Americans drink.

Now the German border was further away and the sympathies of the people were unquestionably with the Allies. Casimir Sobon later remarked,"Yeah, Holland was a good place. The people were nice. Most of them spoke English too."

Captain Manning not only liked the Dutch people, but felt great compassion for them as well. "One could not help but feel deep sympathy for the civilians, whose lives were on the line and whose properties were being destroyed," he later wrote.

Close and genuinely fond relations grew between the guys in the outfit and many of the Dutch civilians. Bob Storms recalled one family with great affection. "We went in closer to Nimegen Bridge, some town there, some city right near the bridge," he said. "I was on a side street. I dug my machinegun in and we was there a while too. I dug down in right across the street from this one house and I got acquainted with a woman in the house. She had a couple of children. All the food we got and all I could steal, I gave her and she'd cook for my crew. It was four of us and I made five. She used to cook our meals and then she'd add a little something, more like it would be at home. We'd go over there, two three of us at a time and eat. I always waited till last because I had charge of the machine gun that was my place. She was awful good. She had a beautiful home with all modern furniture like we had here in the States."

"She had a little girl. Every morning, I'd say oh about six thirty, seven o'clock; her little one would come over and want to jump right in the hole on my head. She used to holler, du baby, du baby. She was my baby. She was a little blonde. Boy, she was beautiful. She'd stay there and I'd make her cuddle up and go to sleep till it got good and daylight, then when I went over to the house and eat I'd take her back to her mother. When my men went over there her mother used to ask if she was with me. They'd say, 'Yeah, she's over there with Bob.' I used to love the devil out of that kid."

In spite of all these small fragments of normalcy, the 319th was still in a combat zone, with all the duties it called for. Once the battalion was in place on The Island, it was clear from the terrain that air observation was going to be playing a greater role than before. Considering his experience directing artillery from the Piper Cub in Normandy, Lieutenant Cook was again detailed as an air observer on October 9th.

After what he'd been through on the ground at Beek and Mook, Cook was glad for the assignment. This time flying in the Grasshopper was familiar to him and an element of fun actually began to creep into his flights with pilot Morgan. Unlike Normandy, where small fields and thirty foot hedgerows often made landing and take-offs dangerous, in Holland there was usually a strong wind blowing uninterrupted from the sea, across large flat, fields. This meant that Cook and Morgan could take off with the Piper Cub in an incredibly short distance. "We'd make a game of seeing how short a distance we needed to land or take off," Cook later recalled.

Under Morgan's urging, Cook started to try his hand at the stick more and more. "I got all of my training right there in that plane," he explained years later. "They were easy to fly and I flew right smart sometimes. I took off one time for him, and I landed one time, but that's all I did with the plane." When asked if he felt like an accomplished pilot, Cook answered, "I felt like it, but I was a far way from that."

Of course the job of air observation wasn't a lark, it was very serious business. Every time the Piper Cub went aloft there were targets to fire on. On October 12th, for example, Lieutenant Cook directed "A" Battery to fire 34 rounds of artillery against a building he identified as a German barracks, scoring four direct hits. Then, on the 15th, he guided an additional 28 rounds from Able Battery on a German command post. Again, direct hits were recorded. Lieutenant Cook recalled another fire mission he directed quite distinctly. "The British, they wouldn't get up on the front line and hit targets," he remembered, "but they said just call on down to our message center and tell us if we had any target out of range of our guns. If we did, we should call them and let them shoot at it. Well, it was just about dark one day. I was flying and I saw some gun shots across in the next town, so I called on the British to fire. They gave me a whole battalion. Their shooting was right down to the notch. I blew up an ammunition dump and that stopped the cannons from shooting."

As the battalion's Assistant S-3, Captain Manning had numerous opportunities to get in the Piper Cub and direct fire too. He later wrote about one of his experiences calling in artillery from the air. "We were given two pilots and two Piper Cub planes to use for observation," wrote Manning. "One capable pilot and one not so capable. Most of the time, I was able to get Morgan, the capable one. In the book 'A Bridge Too Far', which was written about this campaign, they mention the artillery support of one operation involving the silencing of a German 88. It was unsuccessful because the artillery response was too slow. I'll always believe it was I and the not so capable pilot who flubbed. We had been told of the specific objective and had located it on the map. Once in the air, we were the recipients of quite a bit of enemy attention. The pilot began to get panicky and I was having a hard time adjusting the rounds. He suddenly put us into a spin, and when we came out close to the ground he said we had plane trouble and must head in. The gun did not get silenced that day. The pilot told me later that he was going to insist that they equip him with a chute - if he had had one he would have used it. I wonder what he thought I was going to do without a pilot!"

During this period on The Island, the battalion, while supporting the 508th, coordinated their fire closely with British artillery batteries. Initially this was the 72nd Medium Field Artillery Regiment, then, later in the month that unit was replaced by batteries of the 90th Field Artillery Regiment. Both these units mounted large, 125mm and 155mm guns with ranges far outdistancing those the 319th could deliver with their comparatively small 75s.

Relations between the American and British at the command level went very well, in part because the antipathy so common among the GIs toward anything British was not nearly so strong or pervasive among their officers. Among the lower ranks though, that attitude prevailed and was sometimes expressed by antagonistic actions. One "B" Battery gunner, for example, later remembered with some embarrassment, "There was not an awful lot of contact between us and the British, but I do remember there was a British gun section right next to us and they would holler over to us. One guy from our side hollered over and I won't repeat what he said, it was kind of dirty, but I like the British as far as that goes."

Ed Ryan got along with the British soldiers very well and even paid visits to their batteries for purely social reasons. He was probably telling them about hunting rabbits with Stan Levit in the countryside around Lubenham, when one of their men demonstrated how he could shoot rabbits with a Sten gun. "Which is a pretty amazing thing to do," commented Ryan. On another occasion he was watching the British fire their large artillery pieces. "I'll always remember they had those big guns," Ryan said. "The officer hollered, cease fire! One of the guns was already loaded, so the gunner pulled the lanyard and yelled, 'And that's for bloody supper!'"

Being attached as they were to the British XII Corps, the 508th Regimental

Combat Team, of which the 319th was a part, was also issued British rations during the weeks they spent on The Island. Lester Newman said, "The British had better rations than we had. Corned beef, we got some of that. Yeah, we got that corned beef and it wasn't bad."

Newman was certainly in the minority. Just having tea substituted for coffee was sufficient reason for most GIs to despise the change in their diet, but there is also an underlying sense that at heart the men didn't care for the food John Bull had to offer, not so much because of the quality, but more based on the fact that it was British and they just didn't care for the British way of waging war. Among the most dissatisfied with the new rations was Mahlon Sebring. Even decades later he complained bitterly, saying, "I can't bitch on our chow other than when we was attached to Montgomery. We ate them English rations. They were terrible, terrible, and I don't like their cigarettes either. I don't think any American outfit ever should come under foreign rule!"

One component of the British ration which was controversial at the time was rum. Though traditional in the British service, there was no precedent for any regular alcohol issue in the American army. Overall, indications are that the American command structure generally declined to include rum with the British rations being issued to GIs on The Island, believing that it was bound to lead to disciplinary problems. General Gavin later said as much in his memoir, "On To Berlin." Yet Colonel Todd may have been an exception. Able Battery's own Executive Officer, Marvin Ragland, strongly implied that rum was included, at least in the 319th, when he said, "We were attached to the British army, and they served our troops. They had liquor they served our troops on a regular basis, as part of their rations, which made it different. I wasn't much of a drinker anyway, but it was kind of interesting. Of course you didn't get enough to make any difference."

Sartain's memory on this point supports the recollection of Lieutenant Ragland. He commented, "I remember the rum ration, and I don't know how far down the line it went but I think it was for everybody. The ration that I recall was enough for everybody. I seem to think they did give it to the enlisted men, those that wanted it got it, got a rum ration."

But from October 6th until Armistice Day, November 11th, when the battalion was finally relieved, there wasn't much celebrating. The whole Nijmegen area, The Island included, was still a combat zone, with air raids and artillery shelling liable to occur anywhere or anytime. Meanwhile, along the front lines just beyond Bemmel, a dreary stagnant kind of fighting ground on every day. For those in the rifle companies of the 508th, and the FOs of the 319th embedded with them, the flat, open countryside made it deadly to do anything but stay under cover in muddy foxholes, ankle deep in water during daylight hours or while there was any amount of bright moonlight at night. "I was with the infantry and every time you stuck your nose out one of their German shells would come whistling across the river," is what Sobon had to say of what it was like for those on forward observer teams. "It wasn't safe to bring up hot chow, except at night, and British rations didn't include Sternos to heat up tea to something a little bit warmer than the surrounding air temperature."

Covais recalled these days as a kind of slogging grind. There was a lot of ground to keep under watch, so at times he was sent out in charge of his own FO team, without an officer. "The jeep we used," he said, "it had a big battery pack in the back connected up to a radio with a big antennae. Usually it was me, in charge of the maps, with a driver who ran the radio, and a lieutenant or sometimes Captain Sartain, or sometimes it was just me and the driver. I remember Stelow being with me. Stelow was wire man, radio, all that stuff. These jeeps had machine guns too, on the back. Thirty caliber machineguns. We would draw a lot of sniper fire and this one driver, Fitzsimmons, he'd get on the machine gun and fire back at them. He'd be standing up there, all exposed. You bet I wouldn't do it."

As Covais thought back to what it was like being an FO, he recalled a particular day in Holland. "One time when I was forward observer," he said, "I saw a church steeple. I thought, what could be higher than a church steeple, so I go up there. I figured I had the advantage of the view, which I did, but they're no dummies on the other side either. I could see the Germans on the other side of the Rhine. As I'm directing the fire, giving the direction shots out there, they spotted me. The incoming mail started coming in, so I hightailed it out of there. I remember running down the spiral staircase and jumping in the jeep with my chauffer. See, I didn't know how to drive at the time. So the crew that I had, a couple of guys, we got into the jeep and took off. Boom boom, you could see those shells just following us, bahm, bahm, bahm, bahm, right behind us. But, we made it out of there safely."

Covais may have been using the Catholic Church in Bemmel as his OP. Battalion records specifically mention a church in Bemmel being used for just this purpose. He may also have been observing from the Protestant church just outside of the town, or another steeple in the area. Though a few miles away, the Neder Rijn would have been visible from any tower-like structure, but in any case he was almost certainly directing higher caliber guns of the British artillery, since the 75s of the 319th couldn't actually reach the north side of the Neder Rijn at most points along its banks.

With their limited range, the 319th's guns were employed instead along the front lines, principally in a defensive role against enemy patrols, mortars, and machineguns. The volume of fire delivered by "A" Battery over this period averaged about 250 rounds daily. It wasn't a very large amount when compared to the first few weeks in Holland, but it was continuous over the long period of time spent on The Island. To complicate German counter-battery fire, one gun from each of the battalion's firing batteries would be established each night in some novel location and deliver harassing fire against the enemy positions until dawn.

All the forward observers were kept busy and had their share of fire missions to direct as the weeks went by, but Lieutenant Joe Mullen appears to have been especially enthusiastic about his work. In fact, the 508th was so pleased with his service as a forward observer that Colonel Todd received a formal letter of commendation praising Mullen for his courage and efficiency in providing artillery support during the period of October 6th through the 15th. The letter specifically mentioned the Lieutenant's "cheerful" disposition whenever he was called upon to direct fire on the enemy, an action which always necessitated placing oneself in an advanced, and often exposed, position.

On October 14th, Mullen engaged in another of his exceptional artillery directing performances. During the previous night the Germans had established a new machinegun nest which compromised the positions of the 508th's 1st Battalion very effectively. That entire day the paratroopers could scarcely move within their own foxholes without drawing machinegun fire. Nor was it at all clear where the new German MG was located. At 1530 hours Mullen relieved Lieutenant Fellman at the 1st Battalion's position. When he arrived, there was a conference between the two artillery officers and others from the 508th concerning the persistent German machinegun. No one was at all certain where it was firing from, but Mullen, who'd already spent a good deal of time crawling between the lines, suspected he could make that determination if he were able to work his way close enough to the main German positions. About 1930 hours, just as darkness came on, he jammed an unlit cigar between his teeth, grabbed a walkie-talkie, and scrambled into no-man's-land. He was headed for a dangerously exposed advanced point. Even with night on his side, Mullen was dodging machinegun bullets the whole way, but once there, he found he was correct. From his advanced position, he had a pretty good idea where the new German machinegun was placed. Mullen called in a 13 round barrage from Able Battery. This quieted the Germans for a short while, but soon they were firing again. Adjusting his fire, Mullen called another fire mission from the battery. This time fourteen rounds fell just about where the Lieutenant thought they needed to go. Mullen remained at the outpost. He was every bit as close to the German lines as his own, and in danger of being overcome by an enemy patrol or, having used a radio to direct fire, a mortar barrage. Still, Mullen figured, there was a chance the Germans were simply playing possum. He was right. After over an hour they opened up again from the same location. This time he called in a 24 round barrage that really clobbered the Germans and "neutralized" the machinegun for good. It was nearly midnight before Mullen could work his way back to the American lines. All the way he drew fire, but the little Irishman with the big cigar made it through without a scratch. The next day he was nominated for the Bronze Star for Gallantry.

The campaign in Holland seemed to go on, and on, and on. By November 1st the outfit had already been in combat for six weeks, easily making this their longest time in the front lines so far. Most of the guys had reached the conclusion that they were carrying the weight of Montgomery's ill-conceived plan for the British in a static, defensive type of warfare for which airborne troops were never intended. Finally, on November 3rd, there was a definite sign that they would soon be relieved when a party of men from the battalion left for a new base camp near Rheims, France. Sartain was probably thinking about the anticipated relief on the afternoon of November 6th, as he made his rounds of the forward observers at their outposts. It had already been a few days since those five men from Able Battery left with the others for France and orders for the rest of the 319th to follow couldn't be far behind. Maybe tomorrow it would come. That would be good. The weather was really starting to get cold at night now and this damn Island was turning into a sea of mud.

There'd been a rotation of the FOs the previous evening. Joe Mullen took over for Marvin Fellman with Mendez' 3rd Battalion, 508th. Bob McArthur switched off with John Gutshall at the 1st Battalion, and Marion McGrady replaced Rodney Renfrew with the 2nd Battalion. These last two were freshly minted 2nd lieutenants, new to the outfit, having only come out from the base camp a week before.

At Mullen's OP everything was in order. The day hadn't been particularly active and Sartain didn't need to stay long. Bob McArthur's position was next in line. It was about 1630 hours, late afternoon, and as Sartain's jeep made its way to McArthur's position, whatever conversation may have been taking place between the Captain, Sosa, and his Radioman Bob Miller, came to a sudden end when a distressed message broke through the static. The voice on the radio sounded alarmed and full of urgency. Mayday, mayday, we need medics! Lieutenant McArthur's hurt bad. He needs to be evacced out of here right now!

Sosa didn't need to be told to step on it. The jeep bounced along at full speed while Miller and Sartain held on for dear life. Normally he would have parked the jeep in some concealed place, away from the OP, but not this time. Sosa drove right up to the ruin of a small shed where the forward observers had established themselves. Sartain jumped out before the vehicle came to a full stop. There was still smoke and the scent of cordite in the air from a recent explosion. McArthur's Radioman, Instrument Corporal Marvin Spoeral, was crouched over the Lieutenant, franticly trying to apply a tourniquet. As soon as Sartain knelt down beside them, he could see McArthur was very badly wounded. There was blood everywhere, McArthur's right hand was ripped half off his forearm, his left arm was torn wide open above the elbow, with fragments of splintered bone visible, and he had another serious gash across his forehead. The Lieutenant's uniform was shredded, bloody, and spattered with bits of muscle. McArthur's glasses lay on the ground with the lenses blown out of the frames. Spoeral himself was almost as bloody, and for a moment Sartain thought he must be wounded too.

"I gave him a shot of morphine, sir," Spoeral said, without raising his head. "Mortar came out of nowhere. Landed right next to him."

Sartain lifted McArthur by the shoulders and cradled him in his arms. All the while Spoeral sprinkled Sulfa on the wounds and tried to apply pressure bandages. Looking down at his Lieutenant, the Captain could see he was slipping into shock. Sartain remembered what happened next, "He kept saying, Captain, don't leave me, don't leave me! I said, Mac, I'm not about to leave you. The aid people arrived with the jeep and a stretcher and we got him out. I guess it was within five minutes and they were still trying to stop the bleeding."

McArthur was lifted on to a stretcher and placed in the back of the medic's jeep, which sped away immediately. Sartain's jeep was right behind. At the Battalion Aid Station the medical personnel were ready to get to work, doing what was necessary to keep him alive. Sartain related what happened and what he'd seen, while doctors Bedingfield and Dibble did their best. When they'd done all they could, McArthur was loaded into an ambulance and taken to Nijmegen. The 24th Evacuation Hospital was set up there, receiving wounded for the whole division. "We knew the 24th real real well. They were

Two Dutch children pose by one of the Able Battery trucks. The wooden shoes indicate that this picture was probably taken on The Island. Sartain collection.

with us in Italy and they followed us through Normandy too," recalled Sartain. At the hospital a familiar face was waiting to treat McArthur. It was Doctor Julian Hebert, who'd been ostracized by the 319th and transferred out of the unit after the Normandy landings. "When we got there they turned him over to Doctor Hebert. That was good, because, whatever you might say about him, Hebert was a good, good surgeon, and that's what McArthur needed."

Shortly afterwards, Major Silvey and Captain Hawkins joined Sartain at the hospital in Nijmegen. They all remained there until it was clear that McArthur's condition was stabilized and he'd pull through. With the good news in hand, they left and returned to the battalion. On the following day everybody in the 319th was talking about what happened to McArthur. He was, after all, one of the most popular officers in the battalion. "He looked like a tough guy but everybody liked him. He was a real nice guy," said one of the men in the outfit, whose opinion was typical of the rest.

Immediately after McArthur was wounded, a sternly worded directive was received from division HQ on the subject of looting. General Gavin was already well known for strict enforcement of rules regarding military order as it applied to treatment of civilians and their property. As preparations for the 82nd to leave Holland went into effect, quite a bit of attention was generated around this issue. One story circulated that Gavin saw a trooper on a Nijmegen boulevard with a walking cane, presumably taken from one of the numerous damaged and unoccupied homes in the city. Since Nijmegen itself was off limits, Gavin assumed the cane to be looted. If the story is true, he was probably right in his assumption.

After all, as the weeks of relative quiet dragged on, soldiers began picking up souvenirs as they found themselves around so much abandoned property. Unlike Italy, or even Normandy, the Netherlands had enjoyed a high standard of living, comparable to or above what most of the men were accustomed to at home. In short, there were things worth stealing in Holland.

One favorite item was the wooden shoes worn by many of the Dutch people on The Island. Orrin Miller found a pair which he set aside as a keep-sake. Ted Covais did too. He said," I saw them near the door of this house. Wooden shoes like for a four or five year old. A little kid, you know? I thought they were cute, so I put them in my musette bag."

Wooden shoes taken as a memento of Holland were of little real consequence, but the widespread acquisition of trinkets like this could, and did, inevitably lead to more serious pilfering. One story describing theft on what can only be characterized as a magnificent scale has been circulated over the years since the division was in Holland. Though having the flavor of apocryphal "bar talk," rumors of the robbery of a Nijmegen bank may be founded in truth.

"The dough feet were involved in it pretty heavy," Ed Ryan remembered of the scheme. "Mostly guys from the 505th and 508 th. I was curious and had my nose in it as a kind of forward observer, you might say. See, that was a humongous door on that vault. They put primacord all around it and blew it open. Guys were taking out all kinds of money in barracks bags. Some people gave me some, not much, maybe forty or fifty dollars worth. The officers were in on it at the end. They didn't want you to rat on anybody or they'd have problems, so one of Mendez' men, an officer, made a proposition. If you had enough money and you turned it over to him and you got a furlough to Brussels, he was to give you $2,500 bucks to go. This officer, he was holding the big money. So he probably had ten, fifteen thousand dollars." As implausible as this story sounds, other

CAPTAIN, DON'T LEAVE ME.

sources have mentioned that a bank in Nijmegen became the objective of some enterprising 82nd Airborne troopers as well. Considering his penchant for rackets of most any kind, it wasn't surprising that Ryan was mixed up in the caper, albeit peripherally.

As it was, orders were that within division artillery, officers would inspect the baggage of men in other battalions for illegal contraband. Officers from the 320th Glider Field Artillery would come over and inspect the men of the 319th, while 319th officers would perform the corresponding task with the men of the 320th. Captain Manning, Lieutenant Fellman, and Lieutenant Johnson were selected as the team of the showdown inspection to be held on the afternoon of November 11th.

Things began to move quickly now. Colonel Todd left for the new base camp on the 9th, and the next day Major Silvey attended a division level briefing on the new garrison in France. The 508th was to be relieved by Canadian troops on the night of the 10th. That night seems to have been the only occasion when the rum ration was unquestionably distributed to the average GI. British General Horrocks, under whose command the 508th Regimental Combat Team was serving, had been repeatedly suggesting to Gavin that he dole out the rum ration, but with no effect. Finally, on the last day the 82nd spent under Horrocks' command, Gavin received a clear order stating, "You will issue a rum ration tonight." It was probably this occasion which Ed Ryan attributed to Colonel Todd's beneficence when he recalled, "Todd heard that the British had a toddy of rum for each man, which is the truth too. He said, 'We're entitled to that.' See, Todd wouldn't let the enlisted men go without a drink. They brought it down to the battery area, a big barrel of it, and we filled canteen cups full of it. That's a pint, you know. Real rum or something. Thick. Within an hour and a half the whole battalion was sloshed down. There was nothing but medics running around with stretchers, dumping guys into their foxholes. Oh Jesus, what a sight!"

The whole of November 11th, Armistice Day, was spent preparing the battalion for the long awaited march order. There was a lot to do after so many weeks in the orchard. Tents were struck, folded up, and carefully stowed away in the trucks. Ammunition had to be dispensed with by returning excess to division ordnance. Though no one bothered to retrieve the miles of telephone wires, all the communications, surveying equipment and other instrumentation had to be cleaned and then packed up. The machine guns of Sergeant Marshall's 7th Section had to be broken down and brought back to the battery area for loading onto trucks. The howitzers themselves needed cleaning after they were pulled out of their emplacements. Once they were hitched up to the weapons carriers, heavy canvas tarpaulins were wrapped around them and tied in place to protect the guns from being spattered with mud and other debris while on the road.

During the early afternoon, Captain Donald Mongor and two other officers from the 320th Glider Field Artillery came by for the showdown inspection, searching for stolen property. Records do not indicate if any such items were confiscated, but in any case the attitude of the officers toward souvenirs was generous. No one will ever know how many pairs of wooden shoes were overlooked with a wink and a nod, and there were innumerable ways for the guys to squirrel away more bulky trophies under equipage and inside vehicles. Orrin Miller, for example, managed to secret a finely crafted horse saddle past the inspectors without difficulty. It was, he said, "A beauty."

Ed Ryan remembered that, "The only loot I had there was wine, and I drank that."

Meanwhile, the Board of Inspection from the 319th, Captain Manning as president and Lieutenants Fellman and Johnson assisting, traveled back over the Nijmegen

BATTERY!

Bridge to the vicinity of the outfit's old gun positions where the 320th was in place. By the time they were finished and on their way back to rejoin the 319th on The Island, the battalion was already formed in convoy and pulling out.

Manning's driver during this period was Clarance Janus, a Sioux Indian from the Pine Ridge Reservation and one of the old "C" Battery gang. As Manning's jeep came up to the Nijmegen Bridge, he and Janus saw a sign which the British had posted along the road. It read, "Get mobile – in plain English, keep moving!" In fact, the bridge had never been free from German observation and the inevitable artillery rounds which would result whenever vehicles attempted to cross over. Consequently, though the bridge could be used, it was never wise to linger on it.

Manning and Janus were on friendly terms, and as they approached closer the Captain said to his driver, "There is a German gunner calculating the range to the bridge right now. The shot will be on the way by the time we get on it." Janus suggested that they take a bet on that probability. Just then the first German artillery round came screaming in and exploded. "I really think Janus' foot went through the floor boards," Manning later recalled, "That Jeep took off!"

The convoy of the 319th was simultaneously approaching the bridge from the north bank of the Waal. With shells falling all around, some vehicles caught already on the bridge were racing across, and others still on the Island had pulled off the road. Everywhere men were diving for cover. One jeep and trailer from HQ Battery took a hit. Ed Ryan was riding in the back of one of the weapons carriers. He remembered watching that man get hit and tumble from the jeep behind his. "He was running behind the truck," said Ryan. "He was wounded in the foot and couldn't run real well. We held out our hands to him, but we couldn't pick him up. They never stopped the column from moving. That was bad news. His name was Seymour Englander. I don't know whether he's alive today or what."

Seymour Englander was a PFC in HQ Battery who'd joined the airborne to help support his mother at home in Elizabethtown, New Jersey. He did live to tell the tale. In fact, his memory of being wounded was sharp and detailed over 60 years after the event.

As the German barrage started coming down, Englander was riding in the back of one of the jeeps. Later he described what happened. "Our jeep gets whacked and a piece of shrapnel went through my foot like butter. It knocked me right out of the jeep. Then I remember I looked up and thought, 'Lord, I got to get home to Momma, she needs me.'" Luckily a medical jeep was passing and pulled over for the wounded man. "This medic ran up to me," said Englander. "He hit me with that morphine and I was just coasting. I remember I said to him, 'Say, Soldier, is my foot still there?' He told me, 'Don't worry, it's still there, but you're gonna need a new pair of boots.'" The medics hoisted Seymour Englander onto a stretcher in their jeep and took him away.

This final barrage was a disappointing way to end the campaign. The guys in the 319th had been fighting in Holland for 64 days and up to the last minute were still under fire, taking casualties, as they pulled out. "You know what? That whole way across the bridge and on the other side their fighter planes were strafing us," said Englander in closing. "The last thing I remember was thinking, Lord, give us a break!"

BATTERY!

Part 22: "They Must Have Made A Million Dollars!"

Though not as unfortunate as the infantry, which had to march its way out of Holland, the 319th seemed to be dogged by its share of hard luck as its vehicles made their way back down Hells Highway toward the Belgian border. At the Grave Bridge, for example, two jeeps and a weapons carrier were wrecked in a multi-vehicle pile-up involving the battalion and British trucks. In all this fracas Major Silvey was injured, as was another man from the HQ Battery. Further along there were breakdowns as the convoy crept along through a cold, drizzling rain.

At about 1700 hours on November 13th, 1944, the battalion pulled into its new base at Camp Suippes, France. A couple of hours later, once their gear and equipment was stowed away, the guys sat down to the best meal of hot chow they'd had in a very long time. After firing a total of 17,926 rounds at the enemy over a period of seven weeks, "A" Battery's role in the invasion of Holland was over.

Afterwards, Sartain inspected the men's quarters to be sure the guys were well situated. Suippes was a large and well established military installation dating from the First World War. The GIs found their digs consisted of old French barracks of two or three stories, while outside the buildings were open troughs of running water at which the men could wash. Though battalion records, and some HQ Battery men, describe the barracks as being fitted out with bunk beds, most "A" Battery men remember folding canvas cots to sleep on. Sebring's description of the quarters was typical when he said, "I don't know if the French had used it and then the Germans took it over, or what the deal was, but it was set up like an army camp. They was funny looking buildings, they were more like barns. We had folding cots that we slept on, in this one place anyway, and they had running water outside where you could go out and get water to wash with."

The enlisted men were housed six or eight per room, junior officers had more spacious accommodations and those with the rank of captain or above had private quarters at Suippes. Battery commanders and battalion staff officers were housed in individual tents, fitted out with wooden floors, a stove, and a single electric light. Sartain thought the set up was "real comfortable." Such officers also had an enlisted man assigned them to perform housekeeping duties. Sartain remembered his as, "a nondescript guy. He would come in every morning and make the bed. If you wore boots he'd polish your shoes. If you wore shoes he'd polish your boots."

It had been a long, long operation, the last several weeks of which were spent in especially muddy and inclement conditions. Everybody needed some sleep and everything needed to be thoroughly cleaned, but once those requirements were met the routine of camp life settled in. "Of course, when you get back in garrison like that, it's a bitch. You got guard duty and you got KP and all that shit. Just to keep you busy so you don't get in trouble," was Sebring's comment about Camp Suippes. He was, of course, grumbling and complaining as soldiers are apt to do, but there was a lot of truth in what he said.

There were also numerous hikes and physical workouts to keep the guys in shape. Replacements needed to be trained in the duties of an airborne artilleryman. In part, this meant they needed to be instructed and qualified as glidermen, right beside those who needed continuing flights to maintain their glider status. Captain Manning was given responsibility for these exercises. "Army regulations," he later wrote, "required that airborne troops being held in reserve must participate in some aerial exercise at least every few weeks. I inherited the assignment of running the men through these mandatory Glider rides at the nearest airport. A barracks was set up, the troops were rotated in, given so many hours of air time, and then returned to their posts."

Meanwhile, veterans were all too familiar with their duties and the dozens of picayune details which one could find themselves assigned to. For Ted Simpson his most vivid memory of this period was generated by what began as, "an everyday visit to a nearby, heavily wooded area with other soldiers on some sort of duty, most likely firewood collection. The fall now was turning from gold to brown and in lowering temperature was loosing its hospitality. Out there standing alone on a dull overcast fall day, I was at first puzzled by a network of gullies near where we were standing. It extended over many acres - gently sloped impressions in the earth that might have been rain erosion except they seemed to have a human symmetry. Then it hit me. These were the remnants of World War I trenches."

According to Simpson, the nearby community of Suippes, after which their camp was named, was, "a rather drab little French village with a strongly rural atmosphere and population - curious but not very interested in us, nor we in them. A stroll around Suippes was quickly forgettable, but to be fair we had recently come from a setting of high drama and heavy action."

Another man in "A" Battery described Suippes as, "just a little old village with a whorehouse in it." Indeed, no one remembered Suippes with any fondness or could recall developing in France the kind of close friendships which characterized the relationship between so many of the GIs and the English people. Sosa did use his command

Battalion officers, Camp Suippes, France, Autumn of 1944. Right to left back row: Major Wimberley, Lt. Colonel Todd, Lt. Ragland, Capt. Cargile, CWO Fichtner, Lt. Johnson, Lt. Kondradick . Front row, right to left: Lt. Miller, Capt. Torgerson, CWO Greene, Capt. Sartain, Lt. Mullen, Lt. Engle. Sartain collection.

of Spanish to learn some French. As he said, "You have to get along with the public, you know." But the language barrier and jaded attitude of the French toward foreign troops seems to have been enough to discourage any but the most necessary interaction.

Captain Manning's job of supervising the glider training left him with some extra time. Finding himself in a role he described as "Utility Staff Officer," he was assigned the job of finding a location for an officer's club-party house, he later wrote of his first days at Camp Suippes. "It was suggested that I investigate in Chalons-sur-Marne. Having become quite accustomed to traveling by Piper Cub, I enlisted Morgan to transport me. He was a good pilot, and one who loved to be flashy. Various times on the road to Chalons he would drop down and run along on the highway for a few yards - just to excite the populace. When we got to Chalons it turned out to be a moderate sized town with a large central square. That square took Morgan's eye - we dive-bombed it at least 15 times. We had nothing to drop - just diving in as close to the ground as possible and roaring back up and out. We did attract a lot of attention! After Morgan got tired of that, he found a small pasture at the edge of the town and landed. We did not have to worry about transportation - the Gendarme were there! After a stint in the local police office we were allowed to leave - and also given the address of a house available for the officers to rent. It always seemed that some lady in the town would show up to help us enjoy the neighborhood. In Chalons, it was Yvonne Dettling, the assistant librarian. She helped the Colonel arrange for dances and other outings."

Though Manning's mission to Chalons achieved its objective of procuring an officer's club, there were also repercussions. Evidently, Morgan's horseplay with the Piper Cub had frightened too many of the civilians in town. After all, there was a war on and many of the locals were understandably gun-shy where air raids were concerned. A formal complaint was lodged with the division. The complaint filtered through the chain of command to General March and on to Colonel Todd. While it is doubtful that Todd was the least angered by Manning and Morgan's pranks, he was still obliged to respond in some way that would satisfy the General and French authorities. A few days later, Manning was summoned to Todd's office, where he was informed that he would have the privilege of serving as the Provost Marshal in Chalons for the remainder of the time the division would be in the area. It was a thankless job, being, in effect, the Chief of Police, baby-sitting drunken GIs, tending civilian complaints, and a host of other petty but very annoying situations.

Though Chalons was a town of some size, the nearest real city was Rheims, situated a few miles up the road beyond the village. Shortly after settling in at Camp Suippes, Sartain had occasion to go into that city on some matter of military business. As he and Sosa drove along the street he noticed one building which had a line of GIs leading from its front door and extending most of the way down the block. Without giving much thought to his question, Sartain asked his driver, "Sosa, what's that?"

Sosa was perhaps a bit surprised at Sartain's innocent remark when he answered, "You're kind of young Captain, you're kind of young. That's a whorehouse."

Sartain realized how naïve his question must have sounded. "Oh good," he answered, in as blasé a voice as he could muster.

Sosa followed up with an equally nonchalant, "You want to go?"

"No," said Sartain, "I do not want to go."

Quite possibly Sartain had grown unaccustomed to the sight of GIs lining up to enter a bordello. After all, the last time the battalion would have been around brothels doing business on so vast a scale would have been in Naples and, to be sure, a lot had

THEY MUST HAVE MADE A MILLION DOLLARS!

happened since then. Such establishments were uncommon in England, where prostitutes were free to ply their trade independently, as long as they didn't make a public nuisance of themselves, but in France, houses of prostitution were a more accepted feature of the culture. Moreover, the First, and now, Second World Wars had done much to promote the sex industry in that part of the country, especially given the proximity to large, permanent military cantonments in the region. Suippes, and the neighboring Soissons, where the 101st Airborne was located, had been the sites of French bases before the war, then taken over by the Germans, and now the Americans. With large numbers of troops stationed in the immediate vicinity for years, businesses providing a sexual outlet sprang up all around.

As Sartain put it, "I never will forget it. Man, the whorehouses were back in business. We didn't have to go to Paris. Suippes, Reams, all of them had them. And the word got around. It didn't take long before everybody in the battalion knew where the whorehouse was."

"It was supervised by the army, Oh yeah. They had MPs there to kind of maintain order. See, it was better to have the men go to what was a licensed whorehouse than pick up one of these streetwalkers," Sartain remembered of the regulations balancing discipline and lust.

Yet, when asked if the military regulated the brothel in Suippes, one "A" Battery man felt certain it was not. "No, Hell no," he insisted. Though this seems unlikely, given the high profile any such establishment would have had in as small a town as Suippes, he did supply a vivid description of what went on inside. "There was a little bar of some kind in there," he recalled. "They didn't have but three girls and they were doing whatever you wanted all day long. The girls had a big steamer trunk and they'd throw the money in there, they must have made a million dollars. You wouldn't believe it unless you saw it. Sometimes there was a line two three blocks long waiting to get in the whorehouse. Damn place jammed up full all the time. That's the way it was, nothing else to do."

Quite aside from the usual bar brawls and other ordinary complications generated by pent up energy let loose through alcohol or the absence of direct supervision, the army had another very legitimate interest in regulating prostitution. This was the exposure of soldiers to venereal diseases which presented a substantial threat to the health of the troops and could, by extension, seriously sap the available manpower pool of the service. For example, during the same period in Italy, reports of the Army Surgeon General indicated that over 10% of the US servicemen were so infected. The Army's policies and attitudes toward what it termed "licentious relations" between soldiers and prostitutes had historically been ambivalent. Prior to the outbreak of war the army routinely fined and demoted men who contracted social diseases, but during the early stages of mobilization this policy ceased in hopes that the concealment of the condition and the subsequent health complications which inevitably resulted, would be eliminated.

Instead, a pro-active strategy of education and disease prevention was pursued. In the 319th any man leaving Camp Suippes was required to have with him a prophylactic kit, regardless of whether he intended to engage the services of a prostitute or not. This was not exceptional but standard throughout the European Theater at the time. In this way, men who were concerned about news of their visits to bawdy houses filtering back home, or who simply succumbed to the urges and opportunity of the moment would have no excuse for catching sexually transmitted diseases. Accordingly, if a soldier were later stopped by MPs, for whatever reason, and found to be without his kit, he would be thrown in the stockade as being AWOL from his command.

"When you signed out there was a box of condoms at the desk and they'd give you one as you left," said Sartain, explaining the system. "There were these kids in the outfit that had never been in a whorehouse, never had any kind of sexual activity in their lives. I remember this one time, little Tobin was embarrassed to take his condom, so Jess Johnson, or Gruebling, or somebody who was at the sign out book said to him, here, take this, and gave him four!"

Prostitutes were required to have frequent medical examinations by military doctors in order to practice their profession at one of the brothels regulated by the military authorities. This had, in fact, been a common practice by the army's medical corps since as far back as the Civil war. Surgeons Bedingfield and Dibble, of the 319th, were naturally called upon to make many of these examinations. Sartain well remembered the lively discussions at the officer's mess which resulted. "Bedingfield and Dibble had a real good conversation going," he said. "They were in charge of going to every whorehouse and certifying the prostitutes for being disease free. So, Bedingfield would be at the officer's mess in the morning and he would bring us up to date on his activities. Well we got two more new ones. Are they clean? Yeah, they're clean. He said all you had to do is go along one morning when he made his examinations and you'd never go back. Young, scrawny. Some of them pretty well built, but most of them just real scrawny, real, well, not worth looking at."

Although the army acknowledged and regulated prostitution, it was always a delicate issue and one which the military authorities felt ambivalent about. This was

Battalion officers. this photograph was probably taken just prior to, or during, the time the 319th was at Cologne, Germany, spring of 1945. Standing left to right: James Velasko, Richard Johnson, Marvin Ragland, George Cole, Laurence Cook, Zagradski. Kneeling left to right: Frank Kondradick, Joseph Mullen, Marvin Fellmen, Howard Fichtner, Felix Green.

especially so for the Chaplains, who felt it was their duty to discourage the moral degradation engendered by vice. Padres were known to target men whom they felt were still within the reach of redemption, as one battalion man could later testify when he recalled, "I was in one of those lines. I'm about sixteenth as far as that's concerned. Here comes the Chaplain, and out of all those guys, he ferrets me out and says, 'Let's go for a walk.' Took me right out of the line. I don't know, bad break I guess." On another occasion, one of the Chaplains interrupted what could only be described as a private burlesque show which some enterprising GIs had arranged with the girls from the house in Suippes. When the Chaplain stormed, "I want this stopped now! Think of your mothers and sisters at home, how would they like this!" the men scattered in all directions.

With all the dreary, olive drab atmosphere around Camp Suippes, anyone who could get away was glad to do so. Officers, of course, had more opportunities than the men. One morning, seeing that he had a little time to kill, Sartain spontaneously suggested to his driver that they make an impromptu trip to the French capitol. It would take a couple of hours to get there, so there wouldn't be any time to dawdle, but Sosa was altogether happy to oblige. "That was my first trip to Paris," Sartain remembered. "We weren't supposed to be there and we didn't see anything. We just dropped into Paris, circled the cathedral of Notre Dame and headed on back. We figured we had to get back to the unit before dark. So we went into Paris and came back and that was the end of our Paris trip. Just enough to say we were in Paris. See, GIs generally were only permitted into Paris for an R&R or special leave or something of that nature. It was no no for everybody else because you couldn't have all these characters running all through Paris sightseeing."

Other men were able to secure legitimate 48 hour passes. Ed Ryan got one to Paris and said of it later, "Once I was there. Committed a lot of sin too. All kinds of things went on there! I was only there 48 hours, but I'd have like to have been there at least a week." By contrast, Ted Simpson received a similar pass to the city of Chartres. He took his delight in the 12th Century Gothic cathedral in the center of the city. From a distance it seemed to float majestically above the fields of grain which surrounded it. John Girardin remembered one occasion when he went to Rhiems on army business, saying of it afterwards, "Me and this other guy, we were with Sergeant Gost. They sent us to Rhiems to pick up this truck, but it wasn't ready, so we had to wait for it. Well, they had an army wagon where you could buy coffee and bologna sandwiches. After going through and getting our sandwiches we were gonna wait for the truck and go home, you know, but we got talking to this guy. He was a reporter for Stars and Stripes."

From their jump boots and All-American insignia, the journalist knew he was talking to veterans of the fighting in Italy, Normandy, and Holland. "You fellas deserve better than bologna sandwiches," the Stars & Stripes man insisted, adding that there was lots better food at the 5th Army Headquarters mess hall. Gost, Girardin, or one of the others explained that it was off limits to 82nd Airborne enlisted men. The reporter told them, "Awe, come with me, I'll get you in. Come on, go in with me."

Accepting his invitation, Girardin and his buddies followed the journalist to the off-limits mess hall. Sure enough, the guard at the door stopped them all, telling the troopers they weren't allowed inside. "Well," said the war correspondent, "I am! I'm a reporter from Stars and Stripes. This fella here is my brother, and these two are his friends. We've come together to eat."

As Girardin recalled, the ruse worked. "He let us through and we got in there. It was the Fifth Army Headquarters mess hall, and we had pork chops, I remember that."

BATTERY!

The "A" Battery men were having a run of really good luck, first being detailed away from Camp Suippes, then the great windfall of a pork chop dinner at Army headquarters. But the night was still young, as Girardin later explained. "After that we still had to pick up this truck," he said, "But it wasn't ready, so we decided to go to a nightclub. This nightclub we went to, they had a band there, and there were a lot of people. And we drank. We drank nine bottles of champagne. We were so loaded that every time the band played a song we liked we gave them ten dollars. I do remember getting up and walking out of there and going to get the truck, but I don't remember anything after that. When I woke up I was sitting in the tail end of the truck and somebody was puking up all over me, but I couldn't move. And that's one thing I remember about Rhiems."

Gost, Girardin, and the others were awash in champagne that night. Sartain would later attest to the ready availability of the sparkling beverage for GIs out on the town when he said, "We were paid in French francs. You could go to Reams and buy champagne then for maybe a hundred francs. The franc then was a penny. Something like that, some fantastic figure."

The trio didn't come back on post until well after midnight - a good deal later than expected and quite the worse for the wear. Somebody, probably Sergeant Johnson, meted out quick discipline for those who'd had too much fun. "We had to get up the next morning and do calisthenics. Oh man! Not only me, but Sergeant Gost, he was assigned to lead the calisthenics that we did. So, what a time."

Sports were another, and probably more wholesome way GIs could passed the time at Suippes. The army encouraged these events, supplying equipment and special exemptions from onerous details for the athletes. Lieutenant Ragland was still captain of the battalion's basketball team, and when they won a tournament all ten players received a pass to Paris. The division also recruited from its regiments and battalions for football players. The plan was that there would be a grand play-off between the best team in the 82nd and the best from the 101st on New Year's Day.

Sergeant Rappi especially enjoyed the baseball games. "We got our players from every battery in the 319th, because there was that many good ball players you know, then we'd play some other battalion," he recalled. Sergeant Johnson, Casimir Sobon, and Joe D'Appolonio, along with a guy named Thomas Sowell from the HQ Battery; all distinguished themselves as talented ball players. Rivalry between the teams of various outfits was intensive, and if some of the underlying racial tension between white and black soldiers came to the surface, baseball was probably as constructive a way of expressing it as any. As Rappi said, "We played a lot of Negro ball players. Them Negro teams, they all wanted to pitch! They were fighting over who was gonna pitch against us!"

Aside from officially sponsored sports events, everyone agreed that there wasn't much to do in the Rheims area during off-duty hours that didn't involve alcohol, cavorting with ladies of the night, or some combination of both. For those who cared to participate, there was a War Bond drive within the division, with the prize of an extended furlough for the man who generated the most subscriptions, but most of the guys were of the opinion that they'd already done enough for the war effort and deserved some time away without the additional salesmanship. Inevitably, some men got into mischief. One day some very bored 319th men, with a few army air force guys tagging along, started exploring the once German, now American, airstrip. At one end were some abandoned Luftwaffe planes which attracted their attention. When one ME-109 appeared to be intact, someone had the brilliant idea of dumping some gasoline in to the tank and taking it

THEY MUST HAVE MADE A MILLION DOLLARS!

for a flight. "We got that thing wound up," remembered Ed Ryan, who seemed to have a talent for trouble. "Everybody was hanging on to the wings till he got it full bore, then we all let go, like we saw them do in the movies. But the pilot didn't know the first thing about flying a plane. We thought he did cause he was in the air corps but he didn't know anything . When he got to the end of the runway he chickened out. The plane stopped and went up on its nose. Anyway, just about then Colonel Todd pulled up in a jeep and everybody scattered."

So passed the weeks at Camp Suippes. The weather grew colder and thoughts of Christmas grew in everyone's mind as the month of November drew to a close. Men couldn't help but reflect on the year that had passed since the last Christmas in Northern Ireland. Without question, 1944 had been a year like no other. If 1945 was anything like the previous year, anything could happen.

Someone at battalion headquarters arranged for Christmas postcards to be print-

ed up. They featured sprigs of holly, burning candles, glider insignia, and an 82nd Airborne badge. The hand lettered card read, "Seasons Greetings. This Christmas greeting knows no miles, nor reckons time as some. It's borne of those remembered years and heralds ones to come." Sartain sent his out to Baton Rouge on November 27th, telling his parents, "Dear Folks, I sure wish you the very best Christmas and holiday season. I know it'll be a nice one. First, feels like this will be the last away from home. Sort of gives you something to look forward to. Things are rather quiet, and so it'll be a happy one for us."

His sentiments were very representative of how the men in the 319th felt. Obviously they wouldn't be home before 1945, but every indication was that the Germans were running out of territory and men to defend it. In the west the Americans and British were all along the

One of the Christmas cards made available to the men in the 319th to send home during the Fall of 1944. This particular card was sent by Captain Sartain to his parents in Baton Rouge. On the back he wrote: "November 27th, Dear Folks, I sure wish you the very best Christmas and holiday season. I know It'll be a nice One. First, feels like this will be the last away from home. Sort of gives you something to look forward to. Things are rather quiet, and so it'll be a happy one for us." His prediction of a quiet Christmas was not borne out. Sartain collection.

German border. In the East the Red Army had already overrun the German frontier, and within the Reich the intensive Allied Bombing campaign of the last two years had gutted the enemy's cities. With industries and infrastructure lying in heaps of rubble, there just didn't seem any way the Germans could hold on much longer. With luck the Nazis would capitulate while they still had the chance or victorious allied armies would sweep across Germany as soon as winter started to turn into spring. Just possibly, considering four campaigns so far, the 82nd might not even be called into combat again.

As Christmas came nearer, the USO organized some appropriate seasonal entertainment for the troops. Sunday evening, December 17th, featured a special event which included, according to Ted Simpson, "music, singing, dancing, laughing and hi-jinks." By all accounts it was attended by a large crowd of servicemen. Some claimed it was the whole division, and though this seems unlikely, the audience probably did number in the thousands. Lester Newman was there and was evidently enjoying the show very much. After all, "There were some pretty girls sang in it, and a pretty girl that far away from home was something to remember," he said.

"Another "A" Battery man there was John Girardin, and since records describe the show as featuring a Russian ballet, he may well have been speaking of elements of the Nutcracker Suite when he described his memory of the show. "I remember this woman dressed like a snake," he recalled. "There was this fella and she would crawl around him real slow. So, they had a bunch of officers sitting right in front there watching the show and pretty soon this non com came in and went over to them. He whispered something to an officer of quite high rank. Then another officer came down and started talking to all of them. Next thing you know they all start going out of the theatre. I remember that. We were sitting there and I said to one of the fellas, something's happening."

Lieutenant Cook was at the show too, and would have been one of those officers whom Girardin saw get up and leave. He remembered things from an officer's perspective. "Well, we was all at a show right about at Christmas," he later recalled. "There were these dancing people on their toes. What do you call them, ballerinas? Ballet, that's what it was. They stopped it right there. Called the senior officers out first, and then called the rest of us out. They told us all to report back to the barracks and then we were briefed."

Though everyone smelled a rat, the show continued for the enlisted men. Once it was over they filed out, thinking that maybe it was just a bad omen and nothing would come of it. Many men did not recall the USO show, either because they couldn't remember it, or because they weren't there in the first place. Sebring, for example, "was making doughnuts down at the Red Cross. They asked for volunteers, and I was frying doughnuts. Someone come in, they got the attention of everybody, they said, everyone report back to your orderly rooms, we've been called into battle."

By this time the guys at the USO show and other locales were filtering back to the barracks. No doubt speculation was running wild. Sebring would have been passing on what he'd been told at the doughnut bakery, but just the same, until there was some definite word, there was nothing to do but turn in for the night. After all, rumors were cheap in the army and had a way of snowballing out of proportion very easily. There was no real reason to believe this one would be any exception.

In fact, this time the rumors were quite true. While the men slept, Colonel Todd was called to a meeting of all battalion commanders at the division's artillery headquarters. There he was briefed by General Andy March on the particulars of a fast deteriorating situation in Belgium. Shortly after midnight, on his return to the 319th Todd immediately convened the battalion staff and all battery commanders, who in turn summoned their respective lieutenants and senior sergeants.

Next the news was broken to the enlisted personnel. As Ted Simpson remembered it, "We'd returned to our barracks to sleep blissfully - or so we thought! About 2 AM the lights flashed on. Our fully-clothed NCO's and officers flooded into the room announcing that several heavily armored crack Nazi divisions had surprised a weakly defended Belgian frontier and were sweeping west through the Ardennes Forest toward Antwerp."

A battery formation was called, but at least one man didn't stir. According to Orin Miller's memory, he'd "had a few drinks of beer that night, and sitting close to that stove, I just laid in my bunk and I didn't get up." As the rest of the guys assembled they stood in the dark with matted hair, rubbing the sleep out of their eyes, and looked nervously at each other. Now they knew what all the hubbub was about.

When Lieutenant Ragland approached the battery, Sergeant Johnson told the men, "Alright you guys, shut up and listen!" The battery exec was fully dressed and had apparently been up for hours already. He didn't look flustered or alarmed, but then again Ragland never did. Once he had everyone's attention he spoke. According to Sebring, the Lieutenant told them, "You guys have been in combat before. That's where we're going. You know what you have to take. Take what you want. Take what you need for combat. Draw your rations and ammunition."

That was all. The sergeants told the men to get their gear together and get back to their sections on the double for further instructions. No one who went to the supply room had ever seen such generosity from Sergeant Jinders before, as he opened the quartermaster stores to the men. It would have shamed any fire-sale at home. There were long-johns for everyone, along with British army, white woolen socks, which were heavier than the GI issue. In addition to the wool-lined sleeping bags being passed out, Carl Salminen carried off a half dozen blankets and stowed them in his jeep. Though there weren't any scarves, and there was a clear shortage of gloves and golloshes, anyone who wanted another sweater or new overcoat got one for the asking.

Orin Miller probably slept through the formation. All he remembered was his sergeant coming back into the barracks to inform him that the outfit was ready to leave. He hurriedly pulled on his jump boots and threw a few things into his musette bag. As Miller packed he glanced wistfully at the saddle he'd brought all the way back from Holland, thinking to himself that he should have shipped it home weeks ago. Now it was too late, some USO commando would wind up with it for sure.

All around him now, men were rushing everywhere, gathering up their gear, deciding what to take and what to leave behind. Sebring described how he got himself ready. "Usually you take two blankets, your shelter half, and your tent stakes. You take handkerchiefs, you take an extra pair of underwear. You don't take your duffle bag. About all you take's what you can get in that damn little musette bag. Take your cigarettes. Draw your ammunition, your grenades and ammunition. Raincoat. Just one set of clothing. Never even took an extra pair of boots. There weren't any place to keep them anyway."

"We didn't take much," recalled Rappi. "We had them big pockets on the sides of the pants and we put C rations in them because you never know when you're gonna have the next meal. We took blankets and stuff, but I don't remember having a change of underwear. The mess kit, I didn't take that either. I don't remember if I even took cigarettes."

BATTERY!

Once their kits were packed, section chiefs put the men to work preparing the battalion's guns and equipment. "We had to go over to ordnance and get our artillery pieces because a lot of our equipment, jeeps and trucks, and guns and stuff had been taken to ordnance to have work done on it," remembered Mahlon Sebring. "Hell," he added, "They hadn't even touched most of it because we hadn't been back too long. Most of our stuff hadn't been worked on yet."

Whether or not this was the reason, the battalion received a full compliment of new howitzers that night. Possibly there had been an intention to re-arm the 319th all along. Some photographs taken during the winter of 1944/45 do show 105mm guns being used. Perhaps because the battalion was not gliding into combat, perhaps because of experience gained in Holland, the decision may have been made to supply the heavier field pieces. In any event, the new guns had first to be unpacked and put together.

"Yeah, we got some new guns," confirmed Rappi when he thought back to that night. "We had to assemble them. We had to clean them all up, especially the tubes, you know. We had to get the Cosmoline out of them. I told them, you shoot one shell through there, it'll clean out that Cosmoline, but the officer, he didn't think much of my suggestion. He wouldn't go for that. He was a fly by night, I guess."

John Girardin was there too, working feverishly to help get the new guns together. As he put it, "I remember they were still in crates. They brought us guns that were still in the cases. We had to start cleaning off the doggone guns. Here we were, in the middle of the night, washing those guns down so we could put them together. They were all full of Cosmoline. Next thing I know, they told us to stop, break them down and put them on semi trucks like, then get our barracks bags and get our winter clothes on."

Sartain, meanwhile, was away as all this was taking place. "A lot of the men were on leave, so I took an R& R to Paris, but that was another mistake," he recalled of his experiences while the battalion was readying itself to leave for Belgium. "It lasted about five hours, four hours, long enough to get a shower and get all dressed up again for a night on the town. We got on the street and the sirens started with loud speakers for all men of the 82nd and 101st to return to their units. They put us in two and a half ton trucks and hauled us back. We'd just got back and the unit was already lined up. We had just enough time to put on some combat clothes and took off. That cut that trip short."

It would have been late morning when Sartain got back to Camp Suippes, he estimates after 1100 hours. The motor convoy was already drawn up, with the last of the equipment being loaded. Sartain would have no sooner changed from his Class "A" uniform to fatigues, when, at noon, the outfit pulled out of Suippes for Belgium.

The battalion was near the end of the 82nd's column, its parent 508th Regimental combat team being fourth in order of march. Accounts among the men vary as to just how the howitzers were handled and what particular sort of transportation was made available to them. Still, enough corroboration exists to conclude that, at least in part, a quartermaster transportation unit was drafted to augment the vehicles and drivers of the 319th.

Both Kenneth Smith and John Girardin said they were loaded on to, what they later described as, "these big tractor trailers, open bed jobs" and "big, open semi trailers." Another man from the HQ Battery described his transportation as, "tractor trailers with regular cattle trucks." The 508th Parachute Infantry, of whose combat team the 319th was a part, was also loaded on to these same, large open trailers. Yet, Ted Simpson distinctly remembered being loaded in a standard 2 1/2 ton truck with facing benches and a canvas cover, while Robert Rappi's memory is of riding in a 3⁄4 ton weapons carrier.

THEY MUST HAVE MADE A MILLION DOLLARS!

No doubt a variety of vehicles were used, if only because the outfit was mechanized with 1/4, 3/4, and 2 1/2 ton trucks.

The open bed trailers may have been employed for hauling both men and the new howitzers. John Girardin remembered helping to load the disassembled guns on to these large trucks, and if his memory is correct, this does lend credence to the possibility that the unit now had 105mm guns, which would have been too heavy to be pulled by a jeep.

Sosa, of course, was driving Sartain's jeep, but this time, contrary to usual practice, the windshield was up and the canvas cover was securely snapped in place. "Oh man," he said when asked about the trip to Belgium. "That was a mess! We got the call to move out, and in less than twelve hours we were on the road heading north all day long and all night. The column was stretched out for miles and miles. Everybody just heading that way, at a average speed of about, at best, at best, twenty miles an hour."

Sartain, who was sitting beside him, remembered the convoy as "bumper to bumper."

The afternoon passed into night and the guys were told there wouldn't be any stopping for hot chow, so they chewed on D-bars or ate cold K-rations if they were lucky enough to be in a sitting position. At 1600, 1800, and 2200 hours the convoy made brief halts, just long enough for the men to get out of the vehicles, relieve themselves, then get back in again. Despite the three short stops, some of the men still had to answer the call of nature during the hours after midnight, when there was no expectation of a chance to leave the vehicle for some time. This presented a problem because, packed as tight as they were, there was no way to make one's way to the back end of the truck. It didn't matter anyway, since it would have been impossible, and quite dangerous, to try to urinate off the end of the vehicle while it was in motion. The men knew how easy it would be to get pitched off the truck and be run over by a following vehicle. Left with no other alternative, miserable GIs with bursting bladders used their helmets as chamber pots. Those nearer the open end would then be handed a helmet with urine sloshing inside. If the truck had jolted through mud holes or ruts, of which there were many, much of the contents would have already spilled along the way. What the hell is this, they'd want to know, only to be told, don't ask, Mack, just dump it out, OK? Eventually the empty helmet went back to its owner, who put it back on with the rim still dripping.

As the journey wore on everyone started to become numbed with fatigue and cold. Drivers traded off when they could. In an effort to maintain a complete black-out of the column, no headlights were allowed, neither were the men allowed to smoke. "I remember being wrapped in blankets, frozen stiff in the open-ended truck," said Simpson.

Orin Miller also commented on how miserable the journey was. "That was an awful trip that night," he said later, "Riding in trucks up there, cattle trucks, you know, with the slats on them. We were all standing up, there wasn't even room to sit down in it, they loaded us up so tight. And it was cold, my goodness sakes it was cold!"

Late that night the 319th crossed the border into Belgium. The countryside in the Ardennes was full of steep, wooded hillsides which needed to be negotiated very carefully in the darkness and restrictions against lights of any kind simply made the going more hazardous. Ed Ryan described what could, and did, occur. "It was all blacked-out. They had the cat's eyes on the truck headlights, little dual cat's eyes they called them. That was quite an experience too, because if the lead truck went off the road, two or three would follow him and the whole damn bunch would go down off a cliff. So we lost a couple of trucks that way."

Around midnight the convoy entered the town of Bastogne, a "good sized town," as Sartain remembered it. The consensus among veterans of the 319th today is that the division was intended to stop there and establish a defensive line against the German advance. Lieutenant Cook remarked, "We were supposed to go to Bastogne and the 101st was supposed to go the other way, but when we got to Bastogne there was nothing happening, and they pushed us on up north. So the 101st got all the publicity at Bastogne and we missed all that."

In fact, Gavin was clear in his post-war memoir that the order from General Ridgeway, commanding the XVIII Airborne Corps, was for the 101st to hold Bastogne, while the 82nd established its positions around the prominent terrain near Werbomont. Consequently, the division did continue northward in a direction perpendicular to the German westward movement. First contact was made with the enemy somewhere about this time. Gavin's later report of this period does state that the road from Bastogne to Werbomont was cut by the Germans in the vicinity of Hoffalaise sometime before dawn. Oddly, battalion records make no mention of this, though a number of "A" and HQ Battery men clearly remember that the convoy encountered approaching German reconnaissance patrols. As one HQ Battery man recorded in his diary the, "Lead truck got hit so we had to fall back 10 miles. Lost a few men here from sniper fire."

Kenneth Smith seems to have been refering to the same incident when he said, "Yeah. When we got real close to the front and they started shooting at us, these quartermaster guys, they just took off running back. We had to get more drivers to take us up to the front. But there was plenty of guys in the outfit that knew how to drive."

Indications are that the unexpected brush with the Germans threw the convoy into some confusion, or at least forced it to backtrack and take another route of march farther to the west. John Girardin remembered passing through a crossroad and later learning that a German advancing column moved through the same road juncture minutes later. How Girardin would have known this is uncertain, but Mahlon Sebring was clearly speaking of the same incident, and may have been the source of this information when he later claimed, "I was the last road guard picked up. When they picked me up I could hear a tank column coming, and it wasn't our tank column."

The reaction of the quartermaster drivers reflected the growing atmosphere of chaos and even panic among the rear echelon and less highly trained American troops in the face of the German breakthrough. "We didn't have much information," commented Lieutenant Cook of the growing disarray which the column began to encounter. "That was the most confusing thing there ever was in the world. We'd be going down the road and we thought we was going to the front. Then we'd meet a column of trucks coming with soldiers in them. We asked them where were they going and they said, going to the front! So we's all mixed up, we didn't know what we was doing." Even Colonel Todd was in the dark. Lieutenant Ragland recalled speaking to him during one of the brief halts. "I think a lot of people were lost. I know when we first got into Belgium, I remember Colonel Todd saying, 'Well they want us to go into position on up in there somewhere. I don't know anything about it or what we're gonna run into, but we'll go set up.'"

The leading elements of the 319th finally rolled into Werbomont at about 0620 hours on the morning of the 19th of December, though the balance of the battalion did not finish arriving for another four hours, probably due to the backtracking caused by the brush with the Germans the night before.

They must have made a million dollars!

By that time the rest of the division was already in the assembly area, having arrived throughout the previous evening and night. Werbomont wasn't nearly as large a town as Bastogne but it was a logical place from which to organize a defensive perimeter for the division. The town occupied an important road juncture and was situated upon high ground leading down to the Salm River several miles away, beyond which the German advance was encircling a stubborn American resistance near the Saint Vith crossroads.

It was not until later that morning that their howitzers reappeared, somehow fully assembled. As Girardin put it, "I don't know if they had some guys put the guns together, but later on we got our guns." While the battalion collected itself, Colonel Todd and battery commanders reconnoitered the area and received orders to set up the batteries where they could reinforce the fire of the 456th Parachute Field Artillery.

At 1130 hours the battalion moved out, taking up positions outside Werbomont. The day was turning sharply colder and a light snow started. Setting up the gun emplacements was a miserable task in winter weather like this and the men were already exhausted, but finally the howitzers were laid, foxholes dug, and the 319th settled down for the night.

That evening "A" Battery fielded 136 enlisted men and seven officers. As had been the case in Holland, there was Captain Sartain in command, with 1st Lieutenant Marvin Ragland as his executive officer. Other members of the battery's officer corps included 1st Lieutenants Laurence Cook, Marvin Fellman, and Joe Mullen, all experienced officers with a history of service in the battery. There was also Irving Gelb, a 1st lieutenant from Headquarters Battery, a native of New York's Hudson Valley who'd worked in Albany for the city's water department, as well as 2nd Lieutenant Rodney Renfrew, a relatively new replacement from Coshocten, Ohio.

All this time Colonel Todd, Major Silvey, and senior officers from other outfits in the 82nd were learning the scope of what had been taking place in the Belgian Ardennes. Code-named Wacht am Rhein, Hitler's plan was to make a lightening thrust through Belgium and in so doing separate the British and American armies from each other. The Germans would then go on to capture Antwerp, depriving the Western Allies of an essential port of supply. Ideally, the British to the north would be completely cut off and forced to capitulate. Just possibly the Germans would inflict enough casualties to drive the British and Americans out of the war. If successful, the Germans would then be able to shift their entire military resources to the east and forstall the catastrophe which would surely result if the Red Army overran Germany. In any event, the plan was desperate and the achievement of its goals were, in reality, always remote. Whether the American command facing the German offensive fully comprehended the enemy intention is unknown, but the challenge of reestablishing a secure front out of the current disorder was quite enough in itself. While the staff officers and battalion commanders poured over maps, the GIs in their foxholes climbed into their sleeping bags. Few of them had had any sleep for two nights and despite the thoughts of what was to come which preoccupied them, they finally settled into a deep slumber. Though they didn't know it, tomorrow would be their first full day of the Battle of the Bulge.

BATTERY!

Part 23: "Ass deep in bullets."

That night the snow started coming down heavily, settling as a silent, white blanket over everything. When the guys awoke on the morning of December 20th, six to eight inches of fresh snow covered the ground. "We got in there in the position and woke up the next morning with three feet of snow on top of us," recalled one "A" Battery man years later. "It got rough out there that first night. That's the way it was. Cold. The boys was mad. Some of them's mad, some of them's scared too. Especially the new ones that haven't had that much experience."

Even if this man was exaggerating the snowfall, he probably wasn't overstating the mixed emotions of the "A" Battery veterans. They anticipated the danger which waited for them in any combat mission, while the replacements, yet to experience their first time under fire, had their own apprehensions of the unknown and what their response to it would be. On this morning, however, there was one more element in the air which added to the ordinary tension of those who knew they were going into action. Previously the Germans had always been on the defensive – fighting stubbornly, to be sure, but at a time and place of the Allies choosing, with massive air support and training which honed the readiness of the men to a sharp point. Now the enemy had the initiative. They had burst through the American lines and were pressing their advance aggressively, spearheaded by some of their best equipped SS divisions. Rumors of overrun positions and surrenders were already filtering back, punctuated by reports of an atrocity in which about one hundred American prisoners were said to have been machine-gunned in an open field near the Belgian village of Malmedy. News of the Malmedy massacre, as it was quickly named, was spreading like wildfire through the American ranks. Not only did the story confirm all the Allied beliefs that the Germans, and most especially the SS, were capable of the most extreme brutalities, but the event did much to feed the growing conviction that the enemy deserved all they got and would only be defeated when utterly annihilated.

At mid-afternoon the "A" Battery kitchen truck straggled in from Suippes. Soon the guys were lining up to have their canteen cups filled with coffee, thankful for the first hot refreshment since they'd left France. Then word came down that the battalion would be displacing again. The battery commanders went forward with Colonel Todd to scout out new positions during the last hours of daylight. When they returned the men were instructed to pack up the howitzers and head out for the small village of Goronne. To reach their destination the battalion convoy, under the command of Major Silvey, needed to travel about twelve miles to the southeast, much of it through mountainous terrain and dense pine forests over winding roads, where they went into position about midnight. The countryside wasn't anything like Baton Rouge, but it would have reminded the Appalachian contingent in "A" Battery of the east Tennessee and north Georgia hills they called home.

This movement was a part of the larger advance of the division to establish a line of resistance through which the troops in the Saint Vith pocket could retreat, or from which a counteroffensive against the Germans could be launched. On its left flank, the divisions positions faced eastward, along the Salm River from roughly Trois Pons, past Grand Halleux, then Vielsalm, and as far south as Salm Chateau. From there the division's lines made a 90 degree turn to run along the formidable Their Dumont ridgeline. Now facing south, perpendicular to the direction of the German advance, the line continued as far west as Frature, another crossroads village on the road leading north, back up to Werbomont. That portion of the line held by the 508th was at the point of this finger and thrust furthest out into the bulge in the American lines. Goronne itself lay in an open expanse about one thousand yards north of the Thier Dumont Ridge and a few miles to the west of Vielsalm. An important objective for the success of their offensive, Vielsalm offered bridges across the Salm which could support the German's heavy Panzer tanks.

Having set up the battery positions along the road about a mile northwest of Goronne, the 319th was only in place a couple of hours when communications were received from the 508th's headquarters that only its 1st Battalion was in line. Due to a shortage of motor transport, the rest of the regiment was covering the distance from Werbomont by making a forced night march. Accordingly, Colonel Todd ordered that the security perimeter be doubled up with additional outposts to guard against German infiltration and overly inquisitive patrols. These posts were probably manned by personnel drawn from the motor pool and other extraneous men who could be spared, Sartain later suggested.

Where ever the manpower was found for the extra posts, the consequences of sudden, direct contact between the batteries and the enemy would be very serious, especially given the unsettled state of affairs. To complicate the situation, English speaking German soldiers, masquerading as GIs, doing all they could to disrupt the response to Wacht am Rhein were known to have insinuated their way behind American lines. Concern over these methods of German subterfuge was palpable, and it was thus no surprise that a message from the battalion intelligence officer to all batteries warned that, "All personnel must be on the lookout for Germans in American trucks and tanks. The Germans are known to be using American vehicles marked with "Z." They may be using other types of marking as well. All suspicious vehicles must be challenged and its occupant's identification thoroughly checked. All personnel will be especially watchful at night and will challenge all persons and vehicles in the vicinity of their positions, especially sentinels on duty. Proper ID must be established before they pass."

Meanwhile, during the early evening of December 21st, liaison officers and forward observers from the 319th were sent to the 508th. Lt. Eskoff was placed as liaison officer to the regimental headquarters. Lt. Torgerson was liaison to the 1st Battalion. The 2nd Battalion's liaison officer was Lt. Peters, and Lt. Gelb served as liaison to the 3rd Battalion.

Among them went the forward observers with their team of assisting sergeants, radio operators, and spare men. Lt. Cook went to the 508th's 1st Battalion, holding positions along the Salm from north of Vielsalm to Salm chateau. Lt. Valesco was assigned to the 2nd Battalion, while the 3rd Battalion received Lt. Mullen and his crew. These battalions were posted from the river at Salm chateau, along the Their Dumont Ridge, and beyond to a tenuous link with the 325th on the division's right flank.

Notwithstanding such warnings, the Goronne location was still a quiet one for the present. As Sergeant Rappi remarked, "We were sitting there waiting for them to come over that hill so we could start shooting at them, but nobody showed up." Once they had themselves dug in, small parties of men took advantage of the calm to drive weapons carriers up to the pine forest north of the gun emplacements. They were in search of logs to cover over their slit trenches but discovered the forest was littered with strips of aluminum dropped by Allied bombers to confuse German radar and anti-aircraft fire during their bombing runs. At least one battalion man gathered up these strips and fashioned them into ornaments to decorate a little Christmas tree he set up beside his slit trench.

Although the 508th made contact with only outlying German patrols during those first 36 hours, this was certainly not the case beyond the regiment's left flank, up the Salm Valley, where fierce fighting was already taking place between the 504th and 505th against the 1st SS, "Adolph Hitler" division. At Trois Pons the 505th fought tooth and nail to prevent the enemy from crossing the Salm River in force. Meanwhile, in the area around the town of Cheneux the 82nd's paratroopers were out to avenge the Malmedy massacre and tore into the Germans in a fight which involved hand to hand combat among the enemy's armored vehicles. As Ed Ryan put it, "The 504 surrounded the place and killed every nit whit they could lay their hands on." Meanwhile, to the right of the 508th, in and around the towns of Frature and Regn, the 325th Glider Infantry Regiment was engaged in a struggle to prevent the division from being outflanked from the southwest. Soon reinforced by a battalion of the 504th, the airborne troopers found they were facing elements of the 2nd SS Panzer Division, known as Das Reich. Holding a front which extended over twenty-five miles, the 82nd was already facing at least two strong SS Panzer Divisions, with the prospects that still other enemy forces were about to make their presence known. It was, from end to end, a thinly defended line, but one which had to be occupied if the GIs being encircled at Saint Vith were to reach the safety

Sergeant Rappi's gun emplacement and crew. Included are Kenneth Smith, Russell Sykes,and Gunner Corporal Vic Buinowski. This photo is believed to have been taken on December 27th, 1944. Looking at a copy of this photograph, Rappi said, "This must be the Bulge. There's snow on the ground and we've got a camouflage net over the top of us. You can see the gun sticking out from under the camouflage. There's Lappert, he was from the Upper Peninsula. And Buinowski's there! And Sykes is there. He's got his helmet on, screwed right on. And that kid that I sent to the infantry, I don't know what his name is. It looks like there's a Lieutenant there, he's got bars on his helmet. Kenneth Smith's in there. I'm there, I look dirtier than hell. I'm the only one without a helmet." The officer is probably Lt. marvin Ragland. Sartain collection.

of the main line of resistance.

At mid-afternoon on the 22nd of December the 319th was finally called into action. From their observation posts on Their Dumont Ridge, forward observers could see a heavy column of armored vehicles accompanied by infantry moving north along the road between Joubieval and Jou-due. Together with the 456th Parachute Field Artillery, the battalion let loose its first salvos in the Ardennes.

Gavin himself recalled what happened in his post-war memoir. "All the artillery we could bring together was brought down on the column. It inflicted tremendous damage, scattering the Germans through the woods on both sides of the road."

Sergeant Covais was probably with Lieutenant Mullen's crew on their Dumont Ridge. He may well have been thinking back to this fire mission when he remembered helping direct a barrage on an armored column in the Belgian Bulge. "We fired on them," he said. "They went off into the woods, trying to hide, but we hit them hard and I don't remember seeing any of their tanks ever come out of there."

As was later established by patrols, the column the battalion fired on was a part of the 9 th SS Panzer Division, Hohenstaufen, which the 82nd had fought in Holland scarcely six weeks before. Hohenstaufen's panzers were now feeling their way northward, up the west side of the Salm River, hoping to gain the Thier Dumont ridge and ideally seize the bridges at Salm Chateau and Vielsalm before the Americans at Saint Vith could be withdrawn over them. When they emerged from the shelter of the forest after daybreak on the 23rd, the 319th was called on to hit them again. In one of that morning's fire missions, Able Battery shot 46 rounds of high explosives, directed by Lieutenant Gelb from his observation post on the Thier Dumont Ridge. The battery destroyed at least three of the German's armored vehicles, which could be seen belching fire and black smoke against the snow covered landscape.

At 1230 hours Captain Manning took the opportunity to now register the battalions guns by using a solitary building about 1000 yards beyond the Thier Dumont ridge as his point of reference. This registration was especially important since it was the first recorded use of the new VT (Variable time) Proximity Shells by the 319th. Also known as the POZIT shell, these rounds had been developed by the Johns Hopkins University Applied Physics Lab in collaboration with the British. Tested with good effect against German V-1 rockets, the VT shells were only just now coming into general use

Staff Sergeant René Picher (standing) and David Stelow, late January, 1945, near St. Vith, Belgium. Covais captioned this photo "The comfort of a campfire in winter." Covais collection.

as a way to deliver more deadly airbursts over the heads of infantry.

Air bursts were not themselves a new feature of field artillery by any means, having been achievable all along through timed fuses. This method was, however, crude and often meant that shells could explode far too high, scattering their fragments over a wide area and diluting their concussion blast with little effect. Through the use of an embedded micro-transmitter, the POZIT shells permitted highly accurate airbursts at a pre-set height of two, four, or ten meters above the target. The result was, as Sartain said, just "terrific." "If you shot the regular shell the dispersion might be too far above you, but these were something else. Man, they could really do some damage, very effective. I don't think the Germans had anything like it."

Notwithstanding all this, the VT shells were still experimental and subject to malfunction. Sebring explained what he recalled about problems with proximity shells. "The thing that we did have trouble with in the Bulge was what they called them radar shells," he said. "Most fuses are set by hand, but these were some type of a new fuse that made me think they had a liquid in them. They had fuses that, when they got close to something they'd go off, but if we had trees or infantry digging in we had air bursts over our own people. When we fired them in the Bulge they might go off after they go out of the gun for only four, five hundred yards. The closest we had one going off was like two or three city blocks after it went out of the muzzle of the weapon. Something about the cold weather and the fuse."

Sebring remembered right. The first generation of POZIT shells were prone to detonate prematurely if trees, a building, or a hill were close by as the shell traveled along its trajectory. Rain, or wet and snow covered ground might further confound the shell's micro transmitter. From their gun positions on December 22nd, Thier Dumont Ridge could have presented just such interference. Evidence that this is exactly what happened is indicated by a comment Ed Ryan made about being on the ridge that day. "When the first Pozits came over," he remembered, "They didn't tell us. It was raining and those things exploded right over our heads." If some of the battalion's Proximity shells were exploding as they passed over the ridge, it would explain why the firing batteries displaced a little further southeast, on a knoll closer to Goronne, early that evening. From the new vantage point the guns could obtain a clearer field of fire over a low area on the ridge between them and a large proportion of their targets.

On the morning of December 23rd, a letter of Christmas greetings was received at Battalion HQ and passed on to the individual batteries. In the face of what was fast developing into a battle of colossal size, the holiday message struck many as a distraction. As Sartain later said, "Every once in a while we thought about it, but we were too busy protecting our butts."

At this same time the last remnants of GIs from the Saint Vith pocket were crossing over the Salm and into the safety of the 82nd's lines. As the pieces of the 28th, 106th, and 7th Armored Divisions passed through the 508th's lines and the batteries of the 319th, it was alarming to see these men who'd been presenting the Germans with a stubborn, often heroic rear-guard action for over a week. "They just looked like they had gone through hell," Lieutenant Cook recalled. "They got shot up and a lot of them got surrounded. They finally got out, but they come in with sacks around their feet and everything else. They were a pretty rough looking bunch. Oh yeah they were."

Wanting to press their advance, the Germans were close upon the retreating Americans heels. At mid afternoon another column of German panzers was spotted, this time creeping north, up the west bank of the Salm River, below Salm chateau. Immediately the battalion let loose with a shower of 200 shells which left more vehicles burning and destroyed. Ed Ryan remembered what happened to one in particular, saying afterwards, "I could look into the valley and I saw a tank go into a little barn. We fired on it with one of them POZIT shells and it blew the barn away but it left the tank sitting there naked." As the afternoon went on, the 319th fired continuously. Nearly 300 more rounds were dumped on the same area as before, blasting tanks, vehicles, and infantry as they probed the approaches to the Salm Chateau bridges and Thier Dumont Ridge. Then, at 1400 hours, Lieutenant Peters directed "A" Battery in a 108 round barrage against German artillery which could be seen setting up near the east bank, between Vielsalm and Salm Chateau. Effect from this mission was described as "good," with the enemy's guns being "neutralized."

Other fire missions were called in by an unlikely source. One corporal Manger of the 508th, while on patrol two days before was stranded behind German lines when his jeep broke down. Removing the jeep's radio, the trooper concealed himself in a nearby copse of trees and transmitted reports of enemy movements until his batteries gave out. When Manger observed the bridge between the villages of Petit Langlier and Prove Deux being repaired by German engineers, he called in artillery fire from the 319th. Though the barrage did not demolish the bridge, it halted the German advance. At another point that day, Manger transmitted his observation of the SS armored column, saying, "Tanks are rolling by. 50 yards apart. Two columns of panzer grenadiers are marching down the road at close intervals. The column seems to be of battalion strength." Manger was eventually taken prisoner when he, after nightfall, brazenly inserted himself among a column of German infantry as they marched toward the American lines. The corporal was discovered, but the German probe was stopped for the present.

With the 7th Armored and other troops now safely within friendly lines, serious consideration had to be given to the 82nd itself. The division's extended position, while offering good terrain for defense, was over-extended in relation to the American units on its flanks. Contact with those hard pressed units was tenuous and there was a very real possibility that the division could be encircled in much the same way the 101st was already bottled up at Bastogne. Something had to be done to place the division in a more secure area, with a shorter defensive line. Finally, Ridgeway and Montgomery, with Gavin's grudging acceptance, decided that the 82nd should pull out and reestablish itself about ten miles to the northwest. Over the protest of many in the 82nd, who prided themselves on never relinquishing ground once taken, orders were issued for a withdrawal over the night of the 24/25th of December.

Colonel Todd was summoned to 508th headquarters at dawn on the 24th and briefed on the upcoming rearward movement. Major Silvey, meanwhile, visited each of the firing batteries, informing the officers of what, in general terms, was going to happen and warning them to be prepared. This also meant that the half dozen Christmas turkeys thawing outside the kitchen truck had to be packed away for another day.

At 1230 hours Silvey and the battery commanders were summoned to division artillery headquarters, where General Andrew March briefed the assembled officers on the withdrawal. "All the artillery battalions in the division were represented, so there were maybe two dozen of us, all majors and captains," Sartain remembered. "They got us together and we got a pretty good explanation of the situation. There was a big map that showed us where we were and where we were going. March gave each of us areas where we were gonna withdraw to. We were told that we were just gonna straighten out the line, but that's when we could see it was no little adjustment, no, uh uh. We'd never had to give up that much ground and we were all upset about it. Hell, it was a major retreat."

Then General March began to explain how the withdrawal would be conducted. Except for a skeleton force to hold the Germans at bay, the regimental combat teams would begin pulling out immediately after sundown on Christmas Eve, leaving one platoon from each infantry company to serve as a screening force for the retreat. The 508th, being the most extended, would have the farthest to go, about seven miles before it reached its new position. Sartain's battery was singled out to remain in place until the last possible moment, providing a mask of covering fire to slow down the German advance and keep the infantry from being overwhelmed. It was, without doubt, a position of honor, but disengaging in the face of an aggressive enemy was always an exceedingly dangerous proposition. Sartain's recollection of the choice of his battery was, "We took it as a matter of fact, just one of those things, but I honestly think they chose us because we were so dependable. They figured they could count on "A" Battery to hold the fort down while the rest pulled out." Before the meeting was adjourned, General March informed those present of one last, ironic detail. The pass word for the night of the withdrawal would be "Final Edition."

While all these meetings were taking place, Chaplain Reid arrived at the battalion from division artillery headquarters. It was, after all, both Christmas Eve and a Sunday. At the same time the guns were being registered on new targets, he held a brief Protestant mass behind each battery position. Meanwhile the Catholic men who could be spared were given permission to walk into Goronne and attend services with the local parishioners at the village church. Whether Protestant, Roman Catholic, or even Jewish, the juxtaposition of worship against a background of rumbling artillery and a world immersed in the slaughter of war must have been striking.

Perhaps on the pretense that they intended to join in the Catholic mass, Mahlon Sebring and "Killer" Kane went into Goronne in search of inspiration of a different kind. Operating on the military intelligence that there was a liquor store in the village, the two "A" Battery men reconnoitered and located their objective. Sebring remembered it clearly, even decades later. "It was a cubby hole of a building with a hundred and fifty, two hundred bottles of booze," he said. Mahlon and his buddy were looking for cognac. They'd never had it before, but were somehow convinced it would be ideal to warm them through the frigid nights. "We got a quart of Cognac, but we argued with the guy about the price. He wanted something in the neighborhood of 14 dollars for the damn stuff. We knew we were supposed to pull back, we'd already been told that. So I told him, well shit, the Germans will have it tonight, and they won't be paying you anything for it!"

Along with his religious services, Chaplain Reid distributed some Christmas parcels from the folks back home. In Able Battery, Joe D'Appolonio received one from his mother with sticks of pepperoni sausage inside. Joe remembered sharing it with his buddies, then tucking the remainder in his trouser belt. "It just oozed in there for a long time and left a heck of a stain," he later recalled. Sebring and Kane came back from Goronne just about then and joined in the exchange of delicacies. "We passed that cognac around so everyone had a shot of it," he said, adding, "You know, after you've got a bottle, you got a lot of friends."

Amidst the warm camaraderie, Ted Simpson found a quiet place to himself. It was typical of him, this sort of introspective, solitary behavior. Wrapped in his own thoughts, Simpson tried to write a quick letter. Years later he wrote of the moment, "I remember sitting on a hillside with all those wonderful white trees around me, trying to compose a letter to my then girlfriend and feeling very sorry for myself, stuck there at Christmas eve and lamenting the fact that I wasn't there with her, or she with me. It was relatively silent. I was thinking, my God, what a crazy place to spend Christmas Eve." Simpson's chance for private reflection could not have lasted very long. As if aware of the division's pending withdrawal, the Germans were already starting to gather on the opposite bank of the Salm, as well as to the south of Thier Dumont, in preparation for a crossing. Battalion records show steady and considerable firing by the 319th beginning at 0800 hours that morning, mostly against targets close to the bridges at Salm Chateau and Vielsalm. A good proportion of these fire missions were directed by Lieutenant Cook, who was by this time occupying an OP in the upper floors of a commercial building in Rencheux, directly across the river from Vielsalm. For example, he directed 118 rounds against vehicles just outside the town. Any signs of the German troops he knew now occupied the town would provoke another such salvo of high explosives.

The other forward observers and liaison officers were busy too. These fire missions included, for instance, Abel Battery's concentration at 1140 hours against infantry and a machinegun in a 57 round barrage directed by Lieutenant Peters. 106 rounds were expended by Lieutenant Valesco at 1120, wrecking a set of anti-aircraft weapons at the village of Greavay, on the west side of the Salm near Salm Chateau, while Captain Manning dumped another 111 rounds against an enemy command post in a small building in the same area, scoring direct hits.

There were numerous other concentrations fired that day, but it should not be inferred that the artillery punishment was a one way street. In fact, at mid afternoon a storm of enemy shells came screaming into the 319th's positions in and around Goronne. The German artillerymen were evidently searching for the American guns which were doing so much damage. Duel Elmore remembered this barrage well and later observed, "You could hear the rounds hitting the ground, but they didn't all go off. You could hear them hitting the ground and that's when you hit the fox holes. Well, you're only thinking of one thing, getting down as low as you can."

Ted Simpson later told of the experience of getting mixed up in one of these counter-battery duels. "You hear the shells coming in," he explained, "That deadly warble. You know they're coming right at you. You wait, praying at the bottom of a muddy, shallow hole, digging with your hands. A totally helpless feeling. Finally, after twenty-plus minutes, both units firing at each other as quickly as possible, it's over. You wait and wait. It's over. You got them or they ran out of ammo. You climb out, look to see who's gone or injured, then start firing again."

Even if some of the German shells were duds, plenty of them were quite alive and deadly. One exploded in a barn where "B" Battery had its switchboard set up, seriously wounding one man with shrapnel. Another shell made a direct hit on one of "A" Battery's 3/4 ton weapons carriers. The vehicle wasn't with the rest of the motor pool. Instead it was parked at the battery gun position where it was being used as an incidental utility truck. Sebring was well acquainted with it. "We'd dug a hole for the switchboard the day before," he later explained. "It was maybe, you know, ten long by six feet wide and four feet deep. Anyway, I asked Sartain if I could take a weapons carrier to get some logs and cover it over and he gave me permission. We got it done and were just hooking the wires up to the switchboard when he came back. I asked him if I should take the truck back to the motor pool and Sartain told me, just leave it there for now, we can take care of it tomorrow. Well during that bombardment the next day that weapons carrier got hit right in the radiator. Blew it all to hell. When I came out of the hole I saw it burning and thought to myself, I wonder if I'm gonna have to pay for the damn thing."

By now the plans were settled on how the 508th Regimental Combat Team would disengage. Immediately after sundown the main body of troops was to evacuate their positions and begin their withdrawal northwest, to the new defensive line in the vicinity of Froidville and Erria. During this movement the screening platoons and Sartain's battery would hold the Germans back until at least 0200 hours on Christmas morning. All communications were to be by runner because of the need for radio silence, and elements of the 307th Engineer Battalion would be careful to blow bridges and fell trees across the roadways after the last Americans passed.

Huddled over a map, Manning and Sartain drew up a list of several predetermined targets such as bridge sites, road junctions, and other locations, where the enemy was likely to pass. The battery would begin laying interdictory fire on these coordinates at irregular intervals from 2300 hours onward, but until then, the guns were to withhold fire in order to surprise and further confuse the Germans when bombardments did resume. When asked if he recalled receiving instructions, Lieutenant Ragland answered, "Oh yeah, well I was firing battery exec. Captain Sartain told me, here's what's gonna happen, the battalion is gonna start moving out but we're going to stay here in case we're

"A" Battery men digging in during the Bulge campaign. They are, from right to left: James Rossati,Sgt. James Russell, David Stello, Lieutenant Marvin Ragland, Calvin Pouncey (?), Roland Gruebling, and Stephen Palmisano. Courtesy Gruebling family.

needed to fire on the enemy if they start coming in all of a sudden. The rest of our battalion is gonna pull back." Finally, prior to their ultimate withdrawal, the screening forces at Rencheux and on Tier Dumont would assemble at Goronne before continuing up the road to Erria. Sartain was to be notified of this development ahead of time. Theoretically the battery would have sufficient time to hitch up its guns and be well on the road before the first Germans entered Goronne.

For this scheme to work, everything had to take place just as intended, but Sartain knew as well as anyone that chaos and confusion were an inevitable part of every battle. "I decided to go ahead and reconnoiter our route beforehand," he recalled. While there was still light he told Lieutenant Fellman to get a weapons carrier with a crew of road sentries ready. Since there wouldn't be any laying of telephone wire that night, Sartain suggested taking some of the men from the signals section. The sentries followed Sartain and Sosa back to the new position at Froidville, where they turned around and started leaving men at key locations. "On the way back to the battery we dropped off a man at every point you could make a wrong turn. I followed them and was satisfied we had it all in order."

Darkness came and, as planned, HQ and "B" Batteries of the 319th, along with most of the 508th, started off. They had a long way to go. The weather, which had been hovering just below freezing, rapidly dropped to about 20 degrees Fahrenheit, leaving a glazed snow pack which crunched under the feet. The cloud cover cleared off too, revealing the start of a cold, star filled night with a rising moon. There were other objects in the night sky as well. Occasional parachute flares were being fired by the Germans to illuminate the American's movements, whom they now surmised were falling back. Every ten minutes or so the flame of a German V-1 rocket could also be seen arcing its way across the night sky as it traveled toward London or Antwerp.

For the present "A" Battery remained silent, even though lively firefights were flaring up along the whole of the 508th's outposts. Small parties of Germans were attempting to cross over the partly blown bridges at Vielsalm and were pressing their way forward from a foothold on the west bank they had established above Salm Chateau. With the skeleton force that was holding the positions, Lieutenant Cook's driver, Carl Salminen, was pressed into service hauling wounded men from the front lines to Goronne and then coming back for more. When tanks and half-tracks mounted with 20mm guns started lining up hub to hub at Vielsalm, clearly intended to cover a crossing in force, Cook received permission to open up on them. From 2100 to 2140 hours, "A" Battery pummeled the tanks with over eighty rounds of high explosives until they reversed gears and faded back into Vielsalm's rubble strewn streets.

Teenager Robert Dickson was also called upon to make a run back to the Froidville position that evening. As he later recalled, "That particular afternoon we had a gun knocked out. It was just out of commission, and we had a truck out of commission. It wouldn't run. Lieutenant Fellman said to me, 'Robert, take this crew and go to our pull back position.' He said, 'You come immediately back.'" Dickson makes a clear reference here to the weapons carrier destroyed during the afternoon bombardment, but he also introduces the question of one of the battery's guns being, as he said, "Knocked out." While the exploded weapons carrier is duly notated in battalion archives– even down to 1531 hours as the exact time it was hit - there is nowhere any specific record of destroyed guns. Nor did Sartain or Ragland have any memory of this when interviewed. Yet Dickson isn't alone in his recollection. Duel Elmore volunteered that there were two guns disabled, and on further inquiry added that they were not left behind.

BATTERY!

This converging testimony suggests that there was, indeed, at least one gun disabled, or, as Dickson put it, "out of commission." That the gun was worth retrieving, and could still be pulled by a weapons carrier, as Lieutenant Fellman instructed Dickson to do, advances the conclusion that, whatever was wrong with it, the gun was not destroyed. Quite possibly the gun had sustained some sort of repairable damage during the afternoon barrage, or even later in the day. There may have been some other cause, but in any case it was deemed best to remove the gun and its crew early to expedite the battery's final withdrawal later that night.

So, as Dickson explained, "I started out. I don't know exactly what time it was but it was after dark. I don't know how far it was but it was quite a ways. I drove a three quarter ton and pulled a gun crew. I was told to go to a position we were to back up to and then return. I left the crew and I headed back." Along the way Dickson would have passed retreating members of the 508th making their way by motor and foot toward Erria. He would have also passed GIs from the 307th Engineers preparing demolitions for small, incidental bridges, while roadside trees at selected choke-points were having sticks of dynamite strapped to their trunks with explosive primacord.

At 2300 hours, just as "A" Battery was scheduled to begin its series of interdiction fires, the American positions opposite Vielsalm at Rencheux, and along Thier Dumont ridge came under a storm of German artillery and mortar fire. Around Goronne the standard artillery shells were mixed with "Screaming Meemees," or the familiar Nebelwerfer rockets. Working their howitzers in darkness, intermittently illuminated by the flashes of their pieces, the "A" Battery crews systematically worked the seven prearranged targets. All the while the German artillery kept firing in return. At no other time during the unit's service did battalion records ever admit to so large a volume of enemy fire as on this night. As Colonel Todd's report later stated, "They stepped up their artillery fire to a point far greater than at any time before. For every round that Battery "A" fired, the Germans retaliated. They had our range but were slightly off in deflection. Consequently they inflicted no damage."

The barrage signaled the start of the German's all-out attack. With the men of the 508th's screening force hunkered down at their dug in positions, the 9th SS Panzer crossed its best unit over the river at Vielsalm. This was the 19th Panzer Grenadier Regiment, an outfit said to have been recruited from ethnic Germans in the Black Sea region and known for its courage and discipline under fire.

The German guns firing on Rencheux switched to smoke shells for their last few salvos. As the ear splitting roar of artillery explosions ceased, receding into the night, Lieutenant Cook peered into the smoke but could see nothing more than the GIs could from their foxholes on the edge of the village. Then, through the haze and darkness, they could all hear a maniacal yelling as the Germans came running toward them. Everybody opened up with whatever they had. M-1 rifles, light machineguns, Browning Automatic Rifles, carbines, and finally hand grenades were all used freely. Cook saw the situation was desperate and telephoned the battery. Beginning at midnight and continuing for fifty minutes, the Lieutenant called in five fire missions of ten rounds each, in addition to the scheduled and continuing interdictory fire. In many places the enemy was driven back, mown down by machine guns and rifles or blasted by the "A" Battery artillery, but not everywhere.

The screening platoon from company "A" of the 508th at Rencheux was having a particularly tough time of it. Germans were infiltrating their perimeter and filtering into the village behind them. Cook's driver, Carl Salminen, was guarding the doorway to the building from which his Lieutenant was still calling in artillery. Even though Salminen described himself as "hard boiled," the growing whirlwind of small arms fire was starting to get to him. When Carl heard someone burst into the other end of the building, he aimed his carbine and called out for the pass word. In response to "Final," Salminen heard, "Edition!" it was an instrument man from the battery who'd been out repairing a broken telephone line. As he tore past Carl and up the stairs to where Cook was directing fire, he blurted, "The Germans are all over the field out there!"

Salminen later remarked, "He was scared, boy, he was running. It's a good thing he had the pass word because I'd have had to open up on him. He would have been dead."

Over an hour of fighting at close quarters had now passed and the SS Panzer-Grenadiers were reinforced by tanks which had crossed over the partly destroyed, and now repaired, bridge at Vielsalm. The screening platoon at Rencheux was about to be overrun, surrounded, and annihilated. Lt. Col. Thomas Shanley, Executive Officer of the 1st Battalion, 508th and in charge of this force, knew his orders were to hold on until 0200 hours, but a decision had to be made immediately. Salminen seems to have been present when Shanley gave the order. "We left on Christmas Eve from the front roughly about one thirty in the morning when the Colonel took the last call," Carl remembered. They said, 'You got to stick it out.' He said, 'I'm hanging up, I'm leaving this area. We're getting trapped by the Germans.'"

Shanley got word to Cook that it was time to call in one last series of fire missions from "A" Battery and then bug out for Goronne while he still could. Accordingly, Cook called for four more concentrations. As before, they would each be ten or fifteen rounds fired over a five minute span of time. "The Captain in charge told me they were pulling out," Cook remembered decades later. "I was up on the upper side of the town where the Germans were fighting, just coming over but I knew it was time to leave. It got too hot. Yeah, they were coming right on in."

Cook and his men piled into his jeep, taking with them the field phone and maps as they left. Carl Salminen was at the wheel and remembered the other passengers besides the Lieutenant as Staff Sergeant Carl Davis and another, unidentified radio operator. According to schedule, everyone in the screening force was to fall back to Goronne at 0200 hours, and it was now almost that time. As the jeep sped through what was left of Rencheux, they passed 508th troopers making for the rear, others engaged in sudden gun battles in the streets, and even the German soldiers who were already of the attitude that the town was theirs to occupy. Carl later described driving past some of these panzer-grenadiers. "On our way out of that town I looked up and I could see three black helmeted guys looking over the bank," he said. "They were German regulars, they weren't Americans, and they could have shot us right there. If they would have hollered Merry Christmas, I would have hollered back. That's how close they were, but they let us go. Oh yeah, they were right on top looking down on us."

Just about this same time Robert Dickson was returning with his weapons carrier from Froidville. He'd long ago passed by the last of the 508th's main body as it made its way northward and left behind him small parties of engineers busy with the finishing touches on their demolitions and roadblocks. Now, as he crossed over a small bridge at Abrefontaine and drove closer to Goronne, Dickson could clearly see the flashes of artillery, even if the engine of his weapons carrier drowned out the sound of small arms fire up ahead. Still most of a mile from the town a figure hailed him from the roadside. Dickson drew his truck to a stop and a very cold, tired looking infantryman stepped up to

Dickson's truck. The man had an M-1 rifle slung over his shoulder and wore a wrinkled, mud spattered overcoat. "Soldier," he said, "where are you going!" Dickson explained that his battery was set up in a field, just up the road a piece. "Well, you boys better get gone," the soldier warned. "You better tell them to move out. We're pulling back. I'm the tail end, the rear guard of the infantry."

Over the idle of the engine, Dickson could hear machinegun fire coming from the direction of Goronne and recognized most of it as German. "He pointed down the road," remembered Dickson. "It was real dark."

Then the infantryman said, "Do you see that object? That's a German tank. There is tanks down that hill there behind me."

Though the exact sequence of events around Goronne that night is muddled, Dickson's personal memory of the scene was vivid as he continued his story of what happened. "I saw them. I could see them through the dark. They were just down under the hill there. So I told him, well I see them but I'm just a man. I can't go out there and tell the Captain we gotta move, but since you're an infantryman he might listen to you. You go with me and talk to my officers and tell them what the deal is." The lone sentry climbed into the truck with Dickson and they proceeded down to "A" Battery's gun position together.

The battery was already in a state of unease when Dickson drove up with the 508th trooper. As Sartain described it, "I couldn't get anybody on the radio as the radio silence had not been lifted. And nobody had sent me a courier either. I don't remember how long we were waiting, but I remember thinking it had been too quiet for too long." To complicate things, the sound of automatic weapons from the direction of Goronne was getting steadily closer. Even men on the Battery's security perimeter had been catching glimpses of Germans off in the distance, advancing across snow covered fields. Sartain questioned the infantryman, asking him to indicate on his map where those German tanks were. The man studied the map for a moment, then pointed, "here, and here too." Without being told, Ragland knew what to do. He took the coordinates and ordered the battery's five howitzers to fire on them. Three rounds from each gun, target, tanks and personnel. It was 0230 hours, Christmas Day, 1944.

Plainly unhappy with the situation, Sartain said to no one in particular, "Well, ain't this a bunch of shit. They're supposed to let us know when to pull out of here!" He then decided he would have to go up to the front and see for himself what should be done. Turning to his Executive Officer, he gave Ragland last minute instructions. "Now, if the Germans do get in here be sure and pull the safety switch on all the guns. Tell everybody on the gun crews to pull the safety pins on the guns real quick. That way if the guns are captured and they try to use them they'll just fall apart. The tube will slide clear off." Sosa and Sartain's Radioman, Bob Miller, were already set to go with the jeep idling. Sartain and the foot soldier climbed in and they were all gone in to the night.

Up on the road leading out of Goronne, Sosa dropped off the infantryman and turned the jeep toward the village. The screening force under Colonel Shanley should have been assembled there already, well ahead of any German advance. However, as the jeep got closer it became obvious to Sartain that Goronne was already disputed territory. Through his field glasses, he could see tracers from machineguns were zipping back and forth within the village and GIs were pulling back, setting up makeshift defensive positions outside of town. To make matters worse, Sartain could see the tank Dickson and the 508th trooper had warned him about. It sat there, motionless, but no less threatening for the lack of movement. Moreover, he could hear the deep rumble of massive diesel engines. That could only mean that more panzer tanks were on their way. If the Germans broke through and advanced past the gun positions on this road, his battery and probably most of the men in it would be captured.

With the jeep momentarily stopped, Sartain threw radio silence to the wind, took the walkie-talkie from Miller and spoke into the mouthpiece. "Marvin, this is Sartain," he said, "get the hell out of there! Pack up and get those guns out of that field in a hurry. I'll wait here and alert you if anything comes this way, but get your asses up here now!"

Meanwhile, at the battery, march order was given, and not a moment too soon. Knowing they'd be leaving at any moment, the gun crews had already packed away everything they could possibly dispense with beforehand, but just as the order was received the stakes were raised. Joe D'Appolonio recalled that, "You could see the firing coming in. You could see the red flashes of the artillery. Then we started getting small arms."

Sebring remembered it too. "All at once bullets started coming through our camouflage net at the gun position," he later said. "I told the guys, when the bullets start coming like that let's get the hell out of here! So we had to hurry and do our march orders real quick."

Sergeant Marshall always kept one man from the security section at the battery gun position. That man knew where each of the machine guns were posted and ran off to notify them at once. When asked if he had a memory of getting the news to evacuate the position, Lester Newman, part of Marshall's crew answered, "Yeah, I remember that, you bet I do. We almost had to run. They told us we were surrounded and, boy, we all packed up and was all ready to go and get the hell out of there! That march order, when you have to get out of there, that happens pretty fast, and nobody drags their feet either." Then Newman paused, as if placing himself back in the moment, and added, "Actually, everything happened so fast I can't remember being frightened."

It could not have taken the battery more than thirty minutes to get completely loaded, hitch up the guns, and vacate the position, Sartain later estimated. It probably required considerably less time than that, judging by the memories of the men who were there that night. They had done this so often, under so many circumstances and conditions, that they worked automatically and ingrained habits were difficult to ignore, even in this most extreme situation. John Girardin's experience is an excellent example. "They told us to get out of there! We hitched up the guns and threw everything in our trucks," he said. "We had these camouflage nets over these guns. So we removed the camouflage net and put it in the truck because you can't leave anything behind. Well, the doggone net fell off. We were already moving, but I told the driver to stop, I don't know why. I got out and ran back for it. The funny thing is, it always took two men to pick those nets up, but I picked it up myself and put it back on the truck. Everybody was hollering at me! I mean, it was a stupid thing to do anyway."

Quickly forming up in convoy, Abel Battery started pulling out of the Goronne position at precisely 0300 hours. Lieutenant Ragland was in the last vehicle with Robert Dickson, having told him, "You bring up the rear. You know where you been in case we get split up." Glancing back over their shoulders at the now empty gun emplacements as they drove away, the guys could see just how close it had been.

As Girardin later said, "I don't think we were gone five minutes before the Germans had that whole area covered with machinegun fire."

When the column met Sartain at the road he felt enormous relief seeing the trucks turning away from the Germans and toward safety. "We were very fortunate that the Germans were not in hot pursuit," he remarked afterward. Nevertheless, the last few trucks were sprayed with a desultory fire from automatic weapons as they climbed onto the road to Froidville. Most of the men saw tracer rounds flying by and heard approaching German tanks. Both Sebring and Dickson remember seeing one of the panzers standing in the road behind them, not so very far off.

The battery had escaped, but just barely. Though they weren't home yet, the worst of the immediate danger was behind them. Most men in the battery remembered the final minutes at Goronne as at once frightening and confusing. Even the unflappable Sosa, who prided himself on never losing his composure, sounded disoriented in his summation of the night. "We had a helluva time getting out of there," he said. "There was a lot of firing going on. I was in my jeep and I was moving, but frankly I can't tell you which direction I was moving in, north, south, east, or west. Hell, half the time I couldn't tell if we were on a road, or a bridge, or anything else."

The convoy sped away toward Abrefontaine on the Lienne River, a tributary of the Salm about four miles away. "We got to that bridge and they were just about to blow it, but they didn't," remembered Robert Dickson. After what was evidently a short conversation with some demolitions engineers, Able Battery crossed over to the northern bank and continued toward Froidville. That seemed in order after all, they thought, the engineers were keeping the bridge intact until they got safely over to the other side.

A short distance further their way was blocked. Large pine trees along the road had been felled, alternately from one side and then the other. An exhausted Duel Elmore remembered being jolted awake from a dead sleep and asking what was going on. Some kind of roadblock, he was told. A number of men got out to investigate with flashlights. "At first we thought that maybe the Germans had done it and they were booby trapped," said Girardin. "Then I remember them saying that our engineers had knocked them trees out for our purpose."

Whoever had done the job, the trees somehow had to be taken away before the vehicles could go any further. The whole convoy first had to be backed up some dozens of yards, then, as Newman explained, "We had to get out of our trucks and a bunch of us pick up that tree and get it off the road." Even with a couple of dozen guys lifting, it was hard to get a good hold of the pines with their long nettled branches. Given that there were several downed trees, this was going to take a long time, and meanwhile the battery was in a highly vulnerable position. Then someone had the idea to just winch it out of the way. Fortunately, a truck near the front of the column had one affixed to its front bumper. It took some maneuvering, but the truck was brought forward and rapid progress was made.

In all it took a little more than a half hour to get all the trees pulled away. As the last vehicle went through, a gang of men pulled one of the trees back in place, as if to shut the gate behind them.

Like jumping hurdles at a track meet, "A" Battery now met another obstacle, but in this case a welcome one. It was friendly troops with a tank and several vehicles. Though these GIs welcomed the battery into their lines, they immediately raised a question. Sebring recalled the conversation. "They said, 'How'd you get across that bridge?' We said, 'We drove across it.' They said, 'Hell, it's mined!' Well, if it was, it didn't go off. That's all I can say."

The whole issue of how the battery had gotten through revived suspicions about German infiltrators posing as everyday GIs. Dickson's memory was that, "We found out the bridge was supposed to have already been blown but wasn't. We thought they were about to blow it when we were there, but that was the bridge that the Germans was in charge of, they had got American uniforms and didn't blow it."

Whatever the case was, the convoy started up again on the last leg of its displacement to Froidville. It was about 04:30 hours when they arrived, worn out, cold and dog tired.

Girardin recalled everyone dropping out of the vehicles in a stupor. Then Sergeant Johnson came around. "Well, just lay down and go to sleep, we're not even gonna set up the guns," Johnson told them.

Rappi dropped where he stood, in the snow with a shelter half pulled over him. He "slept like a log."

Another man simply remembered, "There was a barn full of hay nearby. I didn't even go up there to the gun section, I just crawled up in the barn in that hay and got warm. I didn't care, I thought if I was going to freeze to death they can go ahead and shoot me."

Yet adrenaline kept some of the other guys from sleeping. Exhausted as they were, they quietly shared cigarettes and talked about what had happened over the last two days. "We didn't have nothing to eat," remembered Girardin. "The only thing we had around there was a bottle of French moonshine. What the hell do they call it, they had a name for it. It's a moonshine more than anything. It was homemade or something like that. I remember the guys were passing that around and I drank of it. It was so cold it was going down like water. So we slept there in our sleeping bags and the next morning when I woke up my lips looked like somebody had put a blow-torch to them. That's how strong that stuff was."

While all this had been taking place, Lieutenant Cook and his FO team went through an adventure of their own. Rolling into Goronne at about the same time "A" Battery pulled up stakes, Cook made his way down to their last known position. "I got the relief from firing and I come back down to the CP," explained Cook afterwards. "It was where the whole battery was, but our battery had moved out, and the infantry had it then. It was an infantry post then. I was the only jeep up there and since they didn't know I was up there, headquarters didn't report it, we like to have got it full force right there from our own people. The captain who was in charge there sent me back up to the road to see what was going on, but when I got up there bullets were flying every which a way, and I came back."

The captain Cook refers to was probably Colonel Shanley, who, satisfied that "A" Battery was hitched up and already on its way, must have informed the Lieutenant that he might as well try to catch up with his outfit. After all, there wouldn't be any more fire missions until everyone was back at the new line near Erria anyway. "So I got my jeep and my radio operators and assistant operators and everything. We started out down that road and there was just tracers and machinegun bullets flying right alongside of the jeep." Luckily for Cook, the 19th SS Panzer-Grenadier Regiment was satisfied at the time to consolidate its position at Goronne and regroup before resuming its advance up the highway. Consequently, they seem to have been firing up the road, into the darkness, guessing by sound alone where Cook's jeep might be.

Even with no headlights, Salminen was driving toward Froidville as fast as he could. Fortunately, over the previous few days he had shuttled wounded troopers back to aid stations along this section of road numerous times and so had a good idea of where he was. At Abrefontaine, Cook remembered, "We hit the bridge at full speed and it was fine, we got through it some way. We did hit something on the bridge but didn't nothing explode. We couldn't figure out what it was because we couldn't see. You just see a faint outline of the road."

Glad to be putting some distance between themselves and the Germans, Cook, Salminen, Sergeant Davis, and the Radioman continued at top speed until they ran headlong into something very large lying in their path. It was the single pine tree which "A" Battery had pulled behind itself when it passed through this point perhaps an hour earlier. Everyone was thrown forward, but owing to the thick evergreen boughs no one was hurt beyond some bruises and bumps. True, the jeep was stalled out but, except for a rammed in grill, undamaged. Most of all, the scene was spooky, utterly silent and utterly dark. Getting out and inspecting the situation, it was evident that there was no way the four of them could pull the tree out of their way. Then someone said, "This is it, we better burn the jeep so the Germans don't get it." The Radioman started pulling the radio from the back but then let it drop, already stepping away. "He took off like a ruptured duck," remembered Salminen. "He was scared I guess."

Then Davis told Carl, "Come on, let's go."

Salminen was sure that if they abandoned the jeep none of them would ever get home alive. "Sorry sergeant," he said, "Have a Merry Christmas, a good one. I'm taking the jeep!"

Cook's voice hissed in the darkness," Ain't nobody going nowhere!" They all looked at him. He knew they were waiting for his decision. Salminen had a point; the jeep was probably their best bet if they had any chance of getting back to the battalion. Cook looked all around, and then he thought he could see a way out through a small clearing down an embankment from the road. Of course, with an obstruction like this, that would be a logical place to sow mines. Be that as it may, there was no real choice. Salminen said he knew this section of road. If they could only get the jeep down the embankment, he could easily drive back up on to the roadway further up. Observing the felled pines and brush resting between the road and the field, Carl then suggested he could safely drive the jeep down there. "That'll act like a steel spring mattress," he said with confidence.

"Alright," said Cook, "let's try it." Taking out his flashlight, the Lieutenant told the others, "Once Salminen gets down there, I'm walking through that field and y'all are going to be right behind me. Now let's go."

Salminen's idea for getting the jeep down the steep embankment worked. Now Cook found himself gingerly placing one boot in front of the other, glancing up from time to time, but mostly searching the ground in front for any sign of irregularity or disturbance. He'd seen what happened when someone stepped on a mine. If they were lucky they were killed outright, if they weren't they bled to death with their legs blown off. When interviewed decades after, Lieutenant Cook's recollection of that night was etched in his mind by the intensity of the experience. "I didn't know whether it was a mine field or not," he said, telling his story slowly. "I thought maybe they might have had that thing mined. Well that would have gotten us all right there. I walked in front of that jeep and led them until we got back to the road on the other side, around that spot, through a field. I didn't know whether I was going to get blown up or not but I went through there. I knew I had to do it, but, oh yeah, you're scared all right."

Though from a different perspective and with a different selection of details, Salminen remembered getting the jeep through the possible mine field too. "I put her in four wheel drive," he said. "I just let her go down the bluff and landed out there and I crossed a big field. I knew the roads in the area so I knew where to go around this big curve. Then I picked up the guys. I told them, 'You want a ride, or what.' There's German tanks, three of them behind us! We couldn't see them because it's dark, but we could hear them. Anyway, after Cook got in the jeep he said he'd put me in for a Bronze Star for saving the jeep and probably saving their necks. I said, we'll talk about that later, but right now we're gonna get the hell outa here. And that Bronze Star, I never saw it."

With great relief in the knowledge that they'd once again cheated death that night, the four "A" Battery men proceeded on. Before long the jeep came around another curve. In the sudden light of a parachute flare they could all see that a tank sat in the roadway up ahead, its barrel pointed directly at them. Cook turned to his driver and said, "Now what are we gonna do, now that you're in charge." There was, fore sure, a touch of sarcasm in what Cook said, but he'd also grown to appreciate Carl's steady nerves in dangerous situations.

"We're going forward, cause if we make a false move now they're gonna open up on us. No matter who they are, American or Germans or who," was Salminen's answer.

With that the jeep went forward, ever so slowly. As it crept closer to the tank, they could see that its .50 caliber machinegun was following their advance, ready to dispatch them at the least sign of trouble. From somewhere in the darkness a voice shouted, "Just keep it slow, Mack, and don't try anything funny."

In the glow of a distant flare, Lieutenant Cook, Sergeant Davis, the Radioman, and Salminen became aware that there were GIs all around with weapons trained on them. Then the same voice called out, "Alright asshole, cut that engine."

Carl switched the jeep off and, except for the sound of a far off machinegun, it was quiet. The 319th men sat still, then a corporal with a grease gun stepped into the road and told them to get out slowly, with their hands up. As soon as their boots touched the ground, the four were immediately surrounded. The colt automatic pistols were snatched from Cook and Davis's holsters, then they were all grabbed by the scruff of the neck and brusquely pushed off behind the tank.

Sergeant Davis asked, "Hey, what's this all about," and was promptly told to shut the hell up.

"We're asking the questions here," barked the Corporal.

"Yeah," said another GI, "We've already shot two of your sauerkraut friends. You wanna see'em?"

When Davis protested, saying, soldier, you're making a big mistake, someone threw him against the back of the tank and demanded to know who won the 1942 World Series. Unfortunately for Davis, he didn't follow sports.

"Don't follow freakin baseball? What the hell kind of American are you?"

Cook, Davis, Salminen, and the Radioman exchanged looks. These strange GIs were desperate and wild eyed, glaring at them over beard stubble and through breath which stank of cigarettes and coffee. Before any of the 319th men had a chance to speak, someone stuck one of the confiscated colt automatics in Salminen's face and snarled, "What'd mammy Yoakum do with the Yoakum berry bush!"

Disoriented by the inane question, Carl could only answer, "Huh?"

"You heard me," the man repeated, "Yoakum berry bush!"

Salminen had to think fast now. "Look," he said, "you guys got this all wrong. We're GIs just like you fellas". But Carl's hint of Scandinavian accent only enraged the man holding the pistol to his nose.

He howled, "This one's a Kraut for sure!"

Then another man gave his own opinion, adding, "Yeah, these guys sound more like Krauts all the time. Let's just shoot'em all right now."

A three way argument erupted between the 319th men, the infantry who wanted to shoot them as spies right there, on the spot, and those who thought they should ask a couple of more questions first. Cook could see the situation was getting out of hand. If he didn't act quickly they would all be shot as German infiltrators. Mustering his loudest, most commanding voice, he bellowed, "Y'all better know this, if any one of my boys is harmed I'll have all your asses up on charges!"

It worked. The crowd of GIs went quiet, then a Staff Sergeant stepped up to Cook and said with a thick Southern accent, "Lieutenant, tell me what town you're from."

"Santa Fe, Tennessee. That's in Jackson County," Cook told him.

"Uh huh," said the Staff Sergeant, who seemed to be the only one who'd kept his self-control. "Tell me what other towns there is around there."

"Well," answered Cook, "there's Bloomington Springs, Flynn's Lick, Pine Lick, Nameless."

"That's enough Lieutenant. I'm from Flynn's Lick and I got family in Nameless too, so I reckon you're alright."

The Sergeant explained that he knew Cook was a local boy when he heard the Lieutenant's accent. "I'll still have to see your military ID, sir." After verifying their identification, the Sergeant returned Davis and Cook's pistols to them, apologized for the inconvenience, and finished by asking them how they ever got over the blown bridges. "We drove over," Cook answered, "It felt like we drove over some mines but didn't none of them go off."

The Sergeant from Flynn's Lick told Cook, "That bridge was supposed to get blown and it wasn't. Some of your outfit came through here a couple of hours ago. They went over that bridge and it sounded like they talked to some suspicious GIs, that's why my boys were a little rough on you. We figured y'all were Krauts for sure."

Cook then asked if they'd really shot two German infiltrators.

"Sure we did," he was told.

"Anyway," remembered Carl, "we got the third degree. They'd shot two Germans because they had American uniforms. They didn't know that we were up there. So anyway after we got our searching and they were satisfied that we were Americans, we got out of there and went down the road to sleep at some farmhouse. Pretty soon the 82nd MPs came. They said, 'You guys can't sleep! You gotta get moving.' He says, 'Five minutes and the German tanks will be here.' So that's the way it went. Like I say, there was only one time I was ever scared, and that was Christmas Eve. That was close. I prayed that I'd live to see morning."

Everybody in Sartain's battery was exhausted, but after the hot meal which was supposed to have been served out the day before was fed to the men for their Christmas breakfast, it was back to work. New forward observers were detailed: Lieutenant George Cole to the 508th's 1st Battalion, Lieutenant Richard Johnson to the 2nd Battalion, and Lieutenant Rodney Renfrew of "A" Battery with Mendez' 3rd Battalion. There was also a visit from General March just after 1100 hours, during which the performance of the battalion on the previous night was without doubt reviewed in detail.

Given the serious and complicated nature of what had transpired, Colonel Todd wanted to review the events too. Sartain recalled the meeting and said, "Colonel Todd later told me that it was the responsibility of either the liaison officer or the forward observer with the 508th to tell me when they were pulling out, but no one told them either. There was no coordination. The infantry went off and left us. Everybody withdrew, but no one told "A" Battery and we were kind of pissed off about it, frankly. I was supposed to pull out right ahead of the last remaining infantry company. They would be the rear guard, and none of that happened. So when it was all over with, Gelb and Cook, probably Mullen, were all called in to a rap session with the Colonel about not letting me know that they'd pulled out." "Well Cook had a good answer," he said, 'Colonel, I was ass deep in bullets. I couldn't worry about anybody else.' Well, I can understand that because once we got reassembled Cook was telling us about how they fought a rearguard action. You know, Cook was a good man, he was not a bullshit artist, he was accurate and didn't exaggerate things, so when he told you something, you could make book on it."

Christmas Eve would remain one of the salient points in the collective memory of "A" Battery. In the course of preparing this book, I several times heard the words, "Did your dad ever tell you about how we had to retreat when we were in the Battle of the Bulge?" Veterans would raise the event as a point of conversation, but often with a hint of caution in their voice, as if sounding me out. Before they spoke frankly, battery men would first inquire whom I had spoken to and what they'd said about that night. At the heart of all this was the sense that the battery was let down by someone, somewhere. The night of the 24/25th of December was still controversial. Sartain's comments were typical of the rest of the battery. He said, "I am firmly convinced that the infantry pulled out and left us and didn't tell us. We were left high and dry. And when I say high and dry, I mean high and dry!" Although I tried to determine the objective facts, some points will almost certainly remain unresolved. What Robert Dickson finally said of the episode is probably as close to a consensus as will ever be achieved. "We were the forgotten battery in a holding position on Christmas Eve night. That's the way it was, and I'll never forget it."

"Zemo"
57 Halleran ave
Lawrence, Massachusetts

Joe Mullen
Kent land
Indiana

Steve Palmisano
2232 Adams Pl.
Bronx, New York

BATTERY!

Part 24: "Like a puffed up hen."

With the division now collected along its new defensive line, the understanding throughout the 82nd Airborne was that they'd made their withdrawal and, as far as they were concerned, there would be no more backward movements. The new positions around the Froidville area were well selected along an extended hill mass reaching back to Werbomont but there was little time for acknowledgment of the Christmas holiday.

Despite this, "A" Battery gunner Ted Simpson found a few minutes to write home to his parents. His letter read, in part, "Today is December 25th, Christmas Day. I am using V-mail, not through choice but because where I am that is all I have. I cannot tell you where I am except that I'm in Belgium. You probably have been reading or know why. In most ways the spirit of Christmas is totally lacking. True, where I am sitting, Peace on Earth, Good Will to Men seems a bit out of place. Even though it is not the way I would choose to spend Christmas, it is not completely empty of pleasure. We are in a very pretty section, we're alive and it has some aspects in keeping with the Christmas spirit. Most of all my thoughts are completely at home with you and I am aware that there are many ways that this must be a harder Christmas on you, Mom and Dad, than for me."

Pretty countryside notwithstanding, Simpson's letter didn't describe the more serious duties which were occupying him and other men in the 319th much of that day. The first job was digging gun emplacements into the frozen ground. It was backbreaking work with picks and shovels, made all the more tedious by the thick blanket of snow, but experience had proven that such precautions were absolutely necessary. Then, in anticipation of rigorous German attacks, parties of men started cutting logs out of the nearby forests. These timbers were then dragged over to the guns and fashioned into covered shelters to protect the howitzers and their crews from air bursts of artillery. To top it all off, camouflage netting was stretched over the entire emplacement. In fact, all this olive green, raw earth, and timbers would be quite conspicuous against white fields of snow until a light overnight snowfall finished the disguise.

As time allowed, the guys started looking after personal comfort. Lester Newman described what it was like for the battery's machinegun crews as they established their security perimeter. "The guys would start by ripping up the cartons that the bullets come in," he said. "We built us a fire, then a couple of the guys would run around out in the fields looking for something to burn. The funny thing is, we was never warned about that. Somebody asked me once if the Germans couldn't zero in on that smoke. That's true, but they never zeroed in on ours."

Some disagreement exists today among "A" Battery veterans over whether fires were allowed in their fixed positions and no doubt the practice depended a great deal on the circumstances of each location. More unanimous is the memory of using hay as an insulating agent. At the Froidville position there were haystacks which dotted the immediate area and were put to good use. Duel Elmore, John Girardin, Rappi, and Kenneth Smith all described taking straw from barns and haystacks to use at the bottom of their foxholes and dugouts, typically covered by tarpaulins.

Like a Puffed up Hen.

At late-afternoon, Christmas Day, before the battery men had a chance to test their new sleeping quarters, the outfit's cannoneers were called to their guns. Forward outposts of the 508th spotted a company sized formation of Germans making their way up the road from Abrefontaine, toward the village of Odremont. At 1730 hours the 319th opened up on them. The barrage caught the enemy in the open. It was an ideal opportunity to exploit the destructive potential of POZIT shells. After 41 rounds had exploded among the unprotected enemy, Paratroopers from the 508th reported a "heavy casualty effect," leaving the German column scattered.

A short while later, at about 2230 hours a spirited night attack was launched against the 508th's lines in the vicinity of Erria. The attacking Germans were members of the same 19th SS Panzergrenadier Regiment which Lieutenant Cook and the screening force had faced on Christmas Eve. Comprised of two battalions of infantry reinforced by four halftracks, the enemy rushed the defenses of the 508th's 1st Battalion repeatedly until well after midnight. A furious firefight took place in the darkness and the 319th backed up the paratroopers by saturating the ground with over 2,000 rounds of artillery fire. The SS Panzergrenadiers were obliged to withdraw. In the morning the snow covered pastures in front of the 508th's foxholes were littered with German helmets, weapons, and pieces of equipment. There were also a large number of dead who had either been killed during the fighting or, having been wounded, died of exposure to the cold during the night. Covais remembered watching through binoculars as enemy trucks came out under a flag of truce early in the morning. "They were picking up their casualties and loading them on these trucks. It was eerie because when they picked them up you could tell they were all frozen solid, frozen stiff, truckloads of them," he later said.

There was also enough of a break in the weather to allow for air strikes against the Germans for the first time since the battle had begun. Bob Storms was posted with his machinegun crew on the outskirts of the battery position and remembered what happened when the first American fighter-bombers appeared. "The day that fog lifted," he said, "oh my God, we seen this plane coming. At first we thought it was a German but it

Members of Able Battery pose together for a group photo during the Bulge campaign. A variety of headgear is seen, including the hoods Captain Sartain had made from GI blankets. "If Gavin had come by and seen those guys with their headgear, it would have been my ass," remarked Sartain later. Covais collection.

was a big P-38, that's what it was. He was headed right at us. I was right out in the open with my gun and my men. He fired at us and hit the breechblock on our fifty caliber. He nicked it a little, not bad. The minute he'd shoot, you could see smoke come out from the guns. We all ducked and soon as he went by we throwed up a flare. He seen the flare and then he flipped his wings. He almost got us, he could have wiped us right out."

Storms was probably fired on by some of the same aircraft which caused friendly-fire casualties in the 508th and other American units that day. Regrettable as these losses were, once the airmen oriented themselves to the location of American and enemy forces, the toll exacted on the Germans was of a vastly larger magnitude. From his machinegun nest, Storms could watch the destruction taking place about a mile to the south. "When that fog went up they had our planes up there by the thousands. The Germans, the roads were packed with them, guns and men and tanks. We couldn't stop them no more, but our guys seen them and oh my God, what a turkey shoot. That was the worst. You never seen anything as bad as that. They really got them on the road and oh they slaughtered them. It was nothing but bodies and equipment. Everything was blowed up, you couldn't believe it, that road was just terrible."

Over the following few days the front lines along the 82nd Airborne's positions were relatively quiet. The Germans were regrouping, accumulating their forces for another push against the division's defenses along the northern shoulder of the Bulge. Consequently, fire missions were limited to targets of opportunity and harassment of German positions. Sebring remembered being at observation posts with Lieutenant Mullen at this time as his radio operator. Always a firebrand, Mullen would quickly grow bored and restless. "'I gotta have some action, I gotta have some excitement! Let's get things going here,'" Sebring remembered Mullen saying. "Shit, he'd tell them he seen tanks coming, but there wasn't anything coming. We had to go through what was called fire direction center. They'd say, what's the target? He'd always lie and say, advancing infantry, tanks, something like that, but hell, you couldn't see a damn soul out there." Lieutenant Mullen was also proud of his skill in directing artillery fire. On one occasion he boasted, 'I can hit a damn dime out there. You just show me the dime and I can hit it.' "I don't know whether he could or not," Sebring remarked, "but one time there was a German come out of a building to take a shit. Lieutenant Mullen said, 'Boy, I'm gonna burn his ass.' I actually believe he hit that shell six foot in front of that guy. I'm not sure, but when that cloud lifted there wasn't no one around. It looked like he'd dropped it right under his hind end."

For the 508th, this period called for constant and aggressive patrolling along their front. Part of these duties involved taking prisoners to determine which enemy units opposed them, what their strength and intentions were, as well as their morale. Because of his penchant for keeping himself up front with the infantry battalions, Sartain had some first –hand experience with this practice. "What really used to give the infantry, and Mendez, and all them a red ass was this S 2 back at regiment," he said. "He'd have nothing to do but call up and say, get me a prisoner tonight. Then they'd have to go on a night patrol and get them a prisoner. Well sometimes they'd bring two of them back. So what they'd do is just keep one of them at battalion headquarters. That way, when that S-2 called again for a prisoner they'd send the other one up."

Being regularly assigned to "A" Battery's liaison officer with the 508th's 3rd Battalion, Sergeant Covais had a clear memory of these captured Germans. "Young guys," he said of them. "But the Germans were good fighters, I've got to give them credit. They were the best equipped, and initially they were the best trained, especially the SS. The SS were fanatical, just fanatical! The rest of the Germans, in the end, were young boys, older men, younger boys anyway. We could see they were inexperienced and frightened themselves, like any young boy I would think. Sad looking, very sad." Captain Sartain was around the same prisoners at 3rd Battalion Headquarters, and he agreed with Covais' observations, saying, "We could tell if they were SS because they had on the SS cap and all that business and the regular German troops were dressed in the typical German military attire, you know. We could tell, and we could tell the attitude of the SS when they were captured. They were rebellious. The attitude of the regular Wehrmacht that was captured or surrendered was so docile. But the SS never changed their attitude. They were really hostile."

About midnight of December 28th the SS demonstrated their hostility in no uncertain terms. By this time the 9th SS Panzer Division was able to consolidate itself along the 82nd's defensive line, with the same 19th Panzergrenadier Regiment still facing the American 508th. Unlike most German units, this outfit seemed to favor night attacks, and this time they had their entire regiment assembled for the assault.

Throughout the afternoon there were growing signs of German activity, especially opposite the positions of Mendez's 3rd Battalion at Erria and Villettes. For example, at 1811 hours Lieutenant Renfrew, the "A" Battery FO with this battalion, sighted "vehicles and personnel." The battery fired twenty rounds with good, if not spectacular, effect. Shortly afterwards there were more sightings: infantry digging in, more personnel, provoking more fire missions from both batteries of the 319th. At 2300 the German attack began in earnest and Sartain's battery was called on to pummel what was described as a "sortie in force" with just under 100 rounds of high explosives. Fire missions continued all night and into the following day as the Germans first took, and were later driven out of the villages of Erria and Villettes. The 508th's 3rd Battalion, personally led by Colonel Mendez, worked hand-in-glove with the 319th throughout the morning to retake the lost ground and hold it. Able Battery was especially prominent during this phase of the battle. Lieutenant Renfrew, for example, directed five consecutive fire missions from 0910 to 1054, with the targets including mortars, personnel, and tanks.

An "A" Battery gunner loads a shell into the breech of a 105mm howitzer during the Bulge. Note the scope mounted on the side of the gun. It was used to correct the orientation of the howitzer in relation to a pair of aiming stakes placed some yards behind the trail. Covais collection.

The 319th, along with a battalion of heavier 155mm guns, blasted not only the enemy's attacks and fixed positions, but most significantly their troops while still assembling in preparation to renew the offensive. To quote Colonel Todd's report of the battalion's actions that night, "One of our observers spotted a battalion of Germans casually strolling around with rifles slung. The fire placed on this battalion virtually wiped it out, according to the statement of a prisoner of war. Again that night, we placed fire on a counterattack believed to consist of a company of Germans, but prisoners taken revealed that the supposed company was actually a regiment preparing for the attack. Our fire caught them completely unprepared and put an abrupt end to their plans. In some of the German companies, prisoners of war stated as few as seven or eight men remained. In one company only one man went uninjured." German reports admitted afterwards that the 1st Battalion of the 19th SS Panzergrenadier Regiment ceased to exist as a unit. The rest of this organization was a shattered remnant of what had been the best fighting force in the 9th SS Panzer Division.

By the time the smoke settled shortly before noon, the 319th had fired about 1,500 rounds since 2300 hours the previous day. In his post-war memoir written for his family, Ted Simpson wrote, "That night we air-mailed practically everything we had toward them, unbroken, hour after hour, until dawn. The breech blocks of our guns, which were smoking and left open to receive fresh shells, became so hot that they froze. We had to pee on them to unfreeze the metal, open the block and keep firing. Finally, when it was over and "Cease Fire" ran down the line, each gun crew, totally fatigued and totally deaf from the continuous explosions, fell into sleep. It took several days to regain hearing but the German advance had been stopped cold by a valiant infantry and these tiny pop guns firing six abreast for ten to twelve hours nonstop."

On the 28th of December, with the line of defense stabilized, air observation with the 319th's piper cubs was re-established. "We had the bulldozers come in and make strips for us where we could take off and fly," Lieutenant Cook remembered. "That snow was piled up higher than the plane was. You could see the planes coming in and going down in the snow and coming out the other end."

Cook was the most experienced officer in "A" Battery where air observation was concerned, so it came as no surprise that he was once again assigned to this job. Though Cook acknowledged that air observation duty brought with it a dry and comparatively safe place to sleep at night, winter flights in the unheated Grasshoppers were dangerously frigid to the point where they had to be kept to a limited duration. He explained, "It was hard going. We'd fly an hour, then I'd sit at the stove for an hour with my feet ahead of me, getting them thawed out, then we'd go back up for another hour."

In fact, it was during the afternoon and evening of the 28th that the cruel easterly wind of an Arctic front sent the temperatures in Belgium plummeting to depths that would mark this winter as the coldest in decades. Some sources put nighttime temperatures below -20 degrees Fahrenheit, and though this is difficult to substantiate, there is no question that the period from December 28th to the middle of the next month was one of acute and extreme cold. For the troops living outdoors, in the field, whether American or German, the suffering became intense.

There was already a shortage of adequate winter clothing throughout the 82nd Airborne when the campaign began. In part, this was because the division had only been taken off the front line in Holland five weeks earlier. In December of 1944, the consensus was that if the 82nd participated in another mission before the close of the war in Europe, it would surely be an airborne drop deep in Germany and not until sometime in the spring. As a result, the 82nd had low priority in the overburdened supply chain to receive winter clothing. These factors were all exacerbated by the haste with which the division was rushed to meet the Wacht Am Rhine offensive.

Among the airborne GIs, scarves and gloves were the exception. Rubber gollashes were theoretically waterproof but were ill fitting, and generally not adequate to the hard services which combat called for. Shoe-packs, a rubberized shoe with a six inch leather cuff and felt insoles were the only bona fide winter footwear designed by the army but these would not appear until the end of January.

The Germans, with three winters of combat against the Russians already under their belts, were both more experienced and better clothed to meet the battlefield environment. Their troops were liberally supplied with a quilted parka, trouser, and mitten combination, which was reversible from snow white on one side to assorted autumn camouflage patterns on the other. These uniforms were superior to the GI issue in that they were both warm and offered concealment as well.

Though cautioned against wearing any articles of German uniform, the Americans in the 82nd picked up pieces out of necessity.

One of them was Covais. As he explained, "One night I was up with Mendez when they brought in these prisoners. They all had on white camouflage uniforms and mittens with a trigger finger. We didn't have anything like that, which was stupid, stupid. So I pointed to the one and took his mittens. What could I do, my hands were freezing and he didn't need them anymore."

Ed Ryan was in a position to observe this practice of appropriation first-hand and recalled, "People were taking those white uniforms off the prisoners. Guys would look for anything white to wear, but I never found any bed sheets or whatever, always a dollar short or fifty cents late I guess. That was a dumb thing on our part, that we didn't have any of those camouflage jobs. You stand right out against the snow in them battle greens, but they didn't give us Jack."

Some GIs were clearly angered by the lack of forethought and the degree to which those in front line foxholes felt exposed and conspicuous is difficult to overemphasize. Covais felt like "a sitting duck" against the snow and remembered being driven to a ludicrous extreme. "We had no camouflage, no white camouflage whatsoever," he recalled bitterly. "The Germans did, but we did not. So I found this thing in a farmhouse, like a lady's nightgown or something. I put that on, but then they started shooting at us and I kept tripping over it. It was too long and I kept tripping! I thought, I'm going to get myself killed this way, so I got mad and tore it off and that was the end of it."

As for overcoats, many men in the 82nd left Suippes without one or discarded them during the first week of fighting. This was particularly true of forward observers, wiremen, radio operators, or any others who needed to be up with the infantry and highly mobile. Covais, for example, tossed his aside because he found it too bulky when climbing the steep, wooded hillsides of the Ardennes or dodging enemy fire.

As Lester Newman said, "They were warm and they were nice, but they weren't an infantryman's dress. Them guys had to get up and move, but as long as you were just setting around a gun crew they were alright."

Even those men who served as cannoneers or drivers found the GI overcoat could be an encumbrance. It was, "thick, and once it got wet, took a strong man just to carry it," is how one "A" Battery driver put it. Bulky or not, as temperatures approached zero, those who had overcoats buttoned them to the throat and were glad to do so.

Other men began modifying their coats. Ed Ryan described what he and some 508th infantrymen did to theirs, saying, "The Krauts had really long overcoats, so guys started doing like the Krauts did, you sew a skirt on the bottom of that coat so it will be down close to the ground. Otherwise snow and water and everything can come up beyond your knees. You take a piece of cloth that you can get from somewhere, an old pair of pants or whatever, about a foot wide or more, and sew it on to the bottom. That'll keep the water and snow and everything away from your knees, keep it down below."

Lieutenant Ragland's memory is that he relied on one of the government issue raincoats which, if not warm, at least cut the wind. Ragland also recalled how the battery men were suffering for lack of warm headgear and how Sartain responded to this problem. "The men had knit caps they could put on underneath the helmet," he said, "But they didn't cover your ears or anything. Then Captain Sartain, he got a hold of a bunch of these wool army blankets, and what he did is have somebody cut them like a big scarf. It kept your neck and ears warm. He issued them to the guys in 'A' Battery. I don't know what you'd call them, but they were wide enough to cover your head, come down over the back of your neck and cover your ears before you put your helmet on."

When asked about this, Sartain remembered it clearly. "We were near a small village and in one of the houses I saw a sign where the lady took in sewing," he explained. "So I gathered about 15 blankets from Harold Jinders in supply and the lady made us enough scarves and hoods for the battery. It was a hood. She cut it and sewed it on the top and put it on the edge and it came down just below the back of; your neck. They could put that on, then they could put their wool knit cap on and then put the helmet on and the neck was kept warm, you see? But as for General Gavin, he was a stickler for regulations and if he had ever seen one of these he'd have raised hell. I kind of worried about it."

It was obvious to Sartain that his men needed more protection than what the quartermaster could supply. Having blankets cut up into some sort of ad hoc headscarves was, without question, against regulation. Nonetheless, his decision to do so was consistent with the attitude that officers at the battery level knew best what their men needed --army regulations be damned. He probably had the cowls made in Froidville, having had battery business to conduct at the battalion CP located there. Evidently, Covais was with Sartain, either when he contracted for the head-covers or picked them up. Desperate for some sort of warm

Lt. Ragland, Lt Gelb and Capt Sartain in the Bulge 1945.

layer suitable for combat conditions, Covais paid the same woman to take his wool lined sleeping bag and alter it to his specifications. He later described the makeshift coat this way. "My body was cold, really cold because I had no overcoat, no, I did not. I had the sleeping bag and what I did, I had a Belgian woman, a seamstress, cut my sleeping bag into a short coat. Really, the sleeping bag was a jumper. Sleeveless, to keep my arms free. So, she made this thing for me and it worked. It kept my upper body torso warm and that saved me."

"I had one made too," said Sartain when the subject was raised during one interview. "It was made by the same lady that made the scarves. The only two that I knew that did it was your daddy and me." In fact, the idea was not unique to Covais and Sartain. Staff Sergeant Rene Picher also wore one of the sawed-off sleeping bags while others in the battery – if not in the battalion and division – probably did too. Commenting further on the topic of sleeping bags as extemporized winter clothing, Sartain then added, "We'd have to hide them if Gavin was gonna come because he'd have considered us out of uniform and accuse us of desecrating army equipment. But everybody had to improvise. I wore a pair of knee high boots stuffed with hay during the Bulge. He would have reprimanded me for that too. He wore GI all the time."

Sartain's comment here about hay in his rubber engineer's boots touches on the most serious problem which the bitter weather presented, namely, frostbite. In all, the army's post war medical corps reported that losses of front-line troops due to cold weather injuries in northwestern Europe– principally frostbite and trench foot were in excess of 70,000 men during the winter of 1944/45. This was the equivalent of one full division during each month of cold and wet weather. Moreover, a disproportionately large number of these losses came from those units such as infantry and combat engineers where the opportunity to take preventative measures was least likely and least affordable to the war effort. Many of the men who were evacuated to aid stations never returned to duty, while those who did were highly susceptible to a recurrence of the condition.

Trench foot, or Immersion foot as it was sometimes termed, resulted when the men's feet were left wet for days on end in cool, chilly weather. The condition didn't require very extreme cold at all and was aggravated by snug footwear such as the Jump boots which were so prized among the American airborne forces. In fact, the paratroop Jump boot could hardly have been a worse design from the standpoint of preventative foot care in inclement weather. Its sewn soles and seams leaked in water. The leather construction of the upper became easily wet and was slow to dry. In addition, wartime studies of the American army's shoes revealed that, in comparison to other nations, United States servicemen were routinely issued shoes which were too small, with no allowance by size or lacing to accommodate extra or heavier socks in winter.

The socks themselves were found efficient. They were sized too tightly, especially around the ankles, and their wool content was judged to be too low to provide adequate thermal qualities when wet. To further complicate the problem, enlisted men and officers alike were given little – if any – instruction in the importance and techniques of foot hygiene, nor did military commands think the issue one worth emphasizing.

The end result was that American rates of cold injuries to the feet were several times that of other armies. The British, for instance, had comparatively insignificant rates of trench foot during the same period, even though they had been wading through mud and water in Holland since Operation Market-Garden in mid-September. Why? The answers included a wider and more generously cut shoe which allowed the wearer to flex his feet and had room for extra socks, socks made of 100% wool, and the fact that a daily supply of clean, dry socks was routinely provided whenever battlefield conditions made it possible to do so.

In addition, the British enforced a strict policy that all men remove their shoes once each day, change their socks, then, if practicable, elevate and rub their feet to discourage swelling and promote circulation. Though GIs were recommended to do the same, men in combat zones were disinclined to carry through with the suggestion unless directly ordered to do so. Of course, such precautions were a low priority or even preposterous for GIs who were preoccupied with staying alive long enough to see the next day. Even a simple changing of socks was problematic, especially for American troops who were either required to cope with the numerous lacings of their canvas leggings or of the airborne Jump boot. Men also found that, once removed, rapid swelling of the feet made putting their footgear back on difficult and uncomfortable.

Frostbite was an even more acute danger than Trench foot. Resulting from frigid temperatures and greatly enhanced by any wet conditions, it shared with Trench foot the symptoms of swelling and aching pain, but also involved destroyed nerves, blood vessels, and capillaries to any exposed or wet surfaces. Flesh would first turn grey and pasty, and then actually freeze. Numbness was a warning sign that hands or feet were becoming frostbitten. As Silas Hogg later warned, "Let me tell you something, when your shoes has froze so tight to agin your feet that you don't know whether you got shoes on and you got to look down and see, you're in pretty bad shape."

If body tissue was affected in this way there was a real danger of permanent harm or even gangrene setting in. When this happened, amputation of toes or feet was a very real probability.

As the incidence of trench foot and frostbite escalated, directives were sent to all units in the division that a system of preventative measures be instituted. In the 319th, Colonel Todd called a meeting of the battery commanders. Doctor Bedingfield was present and explained the situation to the officers. "Todd told us it was the responsibility of the battery commanders like me, or Ragland, to see that there were foot inspections," said Sartain. "First we got supplied with heavy socks. Then Bedingfield went around to the battery commanders, but in combat it was too dangerous to pull everybody together at one time for an inspection. You had to kind of take it easy. So we had to leave it up to the sergeants to check their guy's feet. Then you'd go by every gun section, one at a time and the Gunner Sergeant would report that he had done it."

In spite of the foot inspections, men tortured by freezing feet were apt to take reckless measures which were dangerous, such as exposing their feet to the heat of a fire or immersing them in warm water. Rapid warming of frostbitten extremities, particularly if accompanied by rubbing, leads to hemorrhaging of the blood vessels in the afflicted areas. Unfortunately, it was also the most common way by which uninformed soldiers tried to warm their feet or hands. Robert Dickson had his own experiences watching the consequences of such measures on another member of "A" Battery. Dickson said, "I got my feet frozen, and a friend of mine even lost his feet there in that snow and ice that winter. His feet just froze. He was so miserable he put his feet in warm water. He didn't know how warm it was. I said, 'Don't do that, you can't tell how hot it is.' He said, 'I've got to warm them.' I had mine in snow and ice water trying to warm them up. That was the most miserable place I'd ever been in my life. My feet to this day get cold on a cold morning. I hate snow."

As the late December and January cold continued, losses throughout the division from cold injuries were as high as battle casualties. During the month of January, for example, the 508th PIR lost a total of 413 officers and men from enemy fire, but it also lost 385 evacuated sick. This nearly equal number was composed almost entirely of frostbite and Trench foot cases. The 319th, though an artillery outfit and in a better position to prevent and treat cold injuries, also lost more and more men in this way. Given the losses due to cold, division doctors were reluctant to evacuate men without clear justification. Casimir Sobon appears to have run into resistance when he reported himself as a cold injury one day in January. "One morning I swear I got frozen feet," he later recalled. "So I went to the aid station and the guy says, 'What's the matter?' I says, 'I got frozen feet.' Then he asks me, 'What makes you think that?' I said, 'I can't feel my toes, what the hell do you want me to say!' 'Oh, OK,' but the doctor didn't even bother looking; he had the aid guy do that. He told him, 'Put the Sulfa drug on it and go back, come back tomorrow.'" Sobon was eventually evacuated to a hospital in France and then spent several weeks more at a facility in England. "They put me in a ward with everybody that had frozen feet, amputees and all that. I've had trouble with my toes and legs ever since."

Being from New York State's Adirondack Mountains, Orin Miller probably had as much prior experience with temperatures well below zero as anyone in the battery. He put that knowledge to good use, but also saw how other men's lack of familiarity with such harsh conditions placed them at a disadvantage. "The first thing I did is take my boots off and throw them away," he remembered. "I just kept my overshoes. My mother had sent me six pair of silk socks. I would put a pair of silk socks on and would put my army socks on. Then I would tear up a blanket into strips about two inches wide. I would wrap my feet in those strips like a bandage, right up to my knees. Then I would take those heavy British socks that they gave us and put that right on over the top to hold everything in place. Every time I had a chance, I would fill my overshoes with hay or straw in the amount that I needed, and then put my feet into that. You had to wash and dry your socks every day if you possibly could, change socks every day if you possibly could. That's the way to avoid gangrene, gangrene, and gangrene. I never had frozen feet over there, but a lot of people didn't know enough to do that, particularly the people from the South, they didn't know how to handle themselves."

Although Miller's strategy for foot hygiene was more elaborate than most, his practice of discarding his Jump boots in favor of overshoes, or galoshes, seems to have been general among all but those who had to keep moving with the infantry. Overshoes were apparently widely issued to the men in the battalion in both the canvas topped and full rubber styles before leaving for Belgium. Designed to be worn over the service shoe or Jump boot, the galoshes fastened by four metal clips which were easily closed, even with cold or gloved hands. John Girardin preferred the full rubberized version over the canvas topped overshoes because they kept his feet drier, although not as warm. Most men seem to have agreed with him, but in either case wearing overshoes without boots was very commonly practiced.

This was contrary to their intended use as well as military directives. "The important part about wearing your boots with your issue gollashes was that if you were ever taken prisoner you had your foot wear with you, you see," explained Sartain of the policy, "because if you were ever taken prisoner you were probably going to end up barefoot."

The practice of insulating feet with hay or straw was universal and not confined to enlisted men. Battery commander Sartain stuffed his boots with hay, as did his Executive Officer, Lieutenant Ragland. "My feet were so cold that I put straw in the bottom of my boots, set my feet in there and packed straw all around my feet. I wobbled along like an old duck, but my feet never got cold," he recalled later. Sergeant Rappi, Carl Salminen, and every other man in the battery who was in a position to do so lined their galoshes with straw too.

Sebring described the whole process in detail, along with some of the unforeseen consequences. "I'd take and find a barn and I'd try to find hay chaff or straw chaff," he explained. "I put some in my boots, and then I put my foot in it. Then I put some more of that stuff in so I had insulation all around my feet. Of course it was chaff, chowdered up chaff. Get some of that all around your foot and it actually insulated your foot about as good as it could get. Then we'd dump it at night and try to put fresh stuff in in the morning and go all day with that. In fact, I got hog lice by doing that because I was using straw that come out of a hog pen or something."

Aside from frostbite and Trench foot, other health complications included a powerful and very painful dysentery. At first the cause was obscure. For sure, men had had dysentery before, but the sharp pains which accompanied these spells was frightening. Eventually it was determined that the condition was caused by the habit of melting frozen canteens on campfires, causing tiny shards of aluminum to flake off into the drinking water.

Aluminum dysentery came on very quickly. Bundled as the men were, in long johns and two pair of trousers, along with other layers of clothing or equipment, there were many embarrassing accidents. The mummy style sleeping bags were an especial problem. Their heavy zippers had a tendency to freeze on the coldest nights. If there was an urgent need to drop ones pants or a fire mission was called, the only recourse was to urinate on the zipper to melt the ice from the inside. "I honestly don't remember how we

Chow line in the Bulge. Covais collection.

cleaned up clothes, underwear and sleeping bags after these accidents and I'm not sure I'd tell if I could. I do remember there were no laundries in the Ardennes," Simpson later revealed.

With the opportunity to wash their bodies or clothing virtually nonexistent, anything approaching normal hygiene was impossible. Collars and cuffs of clothing became black with a layer of dirt and sweat. Washing uniforms in gasoline seemed to cut the grime, but the chance to do this only came at infrequent intervals.

The intense cold also had a wearing effect on the soldiers' morale, making the long winter nights seem like endless periods of misery. At times the temperature made it nearly impossible to sleep. The men huddled together, fully clothed in their sleeping bags. Those who were not on gun crews, such as the guys in the machinegun section or those out with forward observer teams often didn't have access to dugout shelters. When that was the case the GIs had to find more primitive ways of finding shelter through the night. Bob Storms remembered one way this was done. He said, "You get two, three guys, you each got a blanket or two, and you dig a hole in the snow bank. You go in there and you's all cuddle up with the stuff you got and you plug the hole up. You could sleep like a log, but you just wish no Germans come around while you're sleeping."

The stress of the weather converged with the disturbing sights of the battlefield. Veterans of Italy, Normandy, and Holland were shocked by the slaughter they saw in the Ardennes. Indeed, the emotional echo of what they witnessed seemed to grow as they approached their elderly years. Storms' voice broke and the tears flowed freely as he said, "We lost a lot of boys just freezing to death. You'd see them in the morning, what ever position they was in. The graves guys would come around with a big ten wheeler. They used to pick them up, load them, and dump them in a big heap till they thawed out. If their mothers ever knowed that it would've been terrible."

Years afterward, Ted Simpson wrote of standing in miserable breakfast chow lines. Everyone was dirty and disheveled, with eyes stinging from smoke and fatigue. "Just to trigger our appetites, all the soldiers from our division or others or German units who had not made it through the night were neatly stacked, frozen stiff beside our chow line. They 'slept' in olive drab, plastic sacks, hiding from us their shattered bodies. A neat hole through the head, back or stomach. Legs gone from a land mine, frozen to death, shattered by fragmentation, arms still frozen askew or legs or faces. GI's in the food line looked and then quickly looked away. Not as curious as you might think. They saw it day after day. One saw the same thing out in the field. Frozen faces, imploring hands and arms stuck into space, missing body parts, not buried yet lying peacefully in the fields. Some alone, some in groups where they had been ambushed."

Clusters of dead Germans who had been ambushed, as Simpson mentioned, or mowed down in the cross-fire of combat or caught in the open by artillery were generously sprinkled through the hills and forests. Some were prisoners, shot in retaliation for the Malmedy massacre and for which the 82nd held a deep grudge against the SS. While not witnesses themselves, many of the 319th men interviewed for this book heard of prisoner executions. Sebring maintained that it was an unwritten policy never to take SS men prisoner. In his memoir, Captain Manning wrote, "War brings out the worst in all of us. While I was traveling with the paratroopers, we captured six German prisoners. The captain of the paratroopers interrogated them and then assigned two men to escort them to the rear. The two escorters were back with us within a half hour – 'Sorry, Captain, they tried to escape and we had to shoot them.'"

Covais may have come upon the scene of one of these executions one night. He was marching with a line of 508th men, moving silently through a dark as pitch pine forest, muffled in deep snow. Then the woods opened up into a small clearing. Covais, glancing first to his left, then right, realized he was walking among bodies aglow in reflected moonlight. "They were dead Germans, thirty or forty of them, maybe more, I don't know. They were laying all close together, side by side. Their arms and legs were all intertwined with each other, frozen and sticking up in the air," he said. Covais had to stop and observe the scene for a moment. He took in the silent field, the crescent moon, and the frost covered faces with open mouths gaping. For the rest of his life, Covais would say there were some things from the war which he remembered "like they happened yesterday." This moonlit clearing in the Bulge was one of them. "At the time I assumed they just got caught in the open in a cross-fire, but thinking back, I don't remember them having any equipment on, whoever they were."

As fatigue and the ghastly sights of the battlefield were compounded by the cold, nerves began to fray. "You talk about cold, I been so damn cold I couldn't talk hardly so you could understand," claimed Sebring later.

Fortunately, the most even tempered and imperturbable men in the battery helped pull the rest through. Ted Simpson later commented on the stabilizing influence of one "A" Battery veteran, saying, "I have very strong and not very pleasant memories about the Bulge. You were frozen to death and you were under counter battery or you were called on a fire mission till you were gaga and deaf. Girardin was the guy who could put a friendly twist on that in the morning. He was the guy that always kept his balance. He wasn't tempted to be frightened, depressed, or anything like that. He was always pretty sunny."

While griping was the GIs prerogative and normally a healthy way to vent the frustrations of army life, excessive complaining was also an indicator of more serious unease and could sap morale contagiously if left unchecked. Lieutenant Ragland saw the signs and was astute enough to intervene one day when he heard Sebring complaining about the cold in a particularly bitter and persistent way. It wasn't typical of Sebring, who usually maintained a cheerful demeanor. Sensing that he needed to distract this man from his train of thought and help discharge some of his anger, Ragland stepped up from behind and ground a ball of snow in his face.

Maddened by the insult, and unaware of who had interrupted him in mid-complaint, Sebring roared, "God-damn you!" he was in a blind rage. He leaped at his antagonist and the two wrestled, rolling in the snow until Ragland finally said, "Alright Seeb, cool down now, cool down." The pair were out of breath and panting by this time, but more importantly, Sebring felt a lot better. He was his old self again and even smiling when Ragland offered his hand to pull him to his feet.

There were over 800,000 American troops who fought in the Battle of the Bulge, and the ways in which desperate men worked their way past the point where simple determination failed were as varied as the number of men in the Ardennes that winter. In confidential tones, Sosa shared the lengths to which one 508th man was driven. "There was one of them guys," he said, "one of the infantry guys, he got fooling around with his first aid kit and give himself that shot of morphine. It's a strange thing about this morphine. It was colder than hell, zero weather, but after he got through with that shot he said he wasn't cold anymore. You understand what I'm saying? He said he wasn't cold anymore."

Others found escape by refocusing their thoughts. Sebring demonstrated this strategy well when he described how he coped with the urge toward despondency. "When it was the roughest," he said, "to get my mind off of it I'd think, what is the first thing I'm gonna do when I get home, hit the old U S soil. I'd think, I want to say thank you to that special guy, and then what's it gonna be? A steak dinner, am I gonna get a Hershey bar? A stiff drink? It sounds crazy, but if you can get your mind off of where you're at and what's going on, jus for a little bit, you feel better. That seemed to work for me. It's not all in the head, but a lot of it is."

LIKE A PUFFED UP HEN.

1944 came to an end, and to be sure the Germans didn't get the wrong impression, the New Year was brought in with an artillery serenade from every battery in the division. Still in position at Froidville, the 319th had been engaging in defensive, harassing fire since the last German attacks on the 28th. Now it was January 1st, 1945. Unquestionably, the Germans would not be able to forestall their defeat for more than a few more months, no matter how many secret weapons and surprise offensives they might muster. On the Eastern front the Soviet armies were already chewing their way through German territory, while in the west, American, British, and French forces were all taking positions on or across the border. In Belgium, the great Wacht am Rhein offensive had clearly ground to a halt. American troops were preparing now to open a counter-offensive which would drive the enemy back into Germany and beyond.

On the morning of the 1st, word came down to battalion headquarters that battery commanders and field officers should be present for an expected visit from General Gavin, General March, and their chiefs of Staff. With everyone standing outdoors at the battalion CP, Gavin and March first spoke with approbation of the battalion's conduct during the prior two week's fighting in the Ardennes. Then the Campaign in Holland was raised. "I had no idea of a Silver Star until Manning and I, and Gutshall were called front and center. Gavin pinned it on us, saluted us, and stepped back. It was a fancy deal, but it was quick," remembered Sartain.

The formal recognition for the awards involved reading the citations for their meritorious actions. The military and personal partnership between Manning and Sartain, with all the talk of tanks, flamethrowers, and calls of "Fire for Effect," was strengthened by the acknowledgment of what they had accomplished outside of Mook a few months earlier.

With the ceremonies finished, everyone returned to their duties. Colonel Lindquist, Commanding Officer of the 508th, was apparently present at the gathering. He afterwards requested that Colonel Todd bring him out to the two firing battery gun positions, where he inspected the emplacements and thanked the gunners for their recent work. Sartain, meanwhile, must have resumed his observation activities among the infantry as, among other fire missions that day, he is recorded to have directed 39 rounds against enemy personnel with "excellent" effect.

January 2nd saw the distribution of a New Years turkey dinner. Unfortunately most of the meal was frozen solid and inedible. Even Rappi had to pass on the turkey, which was unusual because, as he said, "I was young then and I could eat any damn thing when I got hungry."

At about this time Sartain was once again drawn into an open confrontation with one of his superiors. This time it was Major Wimberley, the Battalion S-3. As operations officer, Wimberley was called upon to adjust the fire of the batteries in response to the instructions of the forward observers. But the Major's textbook approach to this role had been a point of growing frustration among these front-line artillerymen. The FOs all agreed his methods were unnecessarily protracted at a time when their exposed positions placed them in the greatest danger. Dissatisfaction over this problem had been building since Normandy and on this afternoon in January of 1945 it finally came to a head.

Sartain described what happened. "I was with Mendez, and Mendez said, 'We're having trouble with "I" Company. Go see what the problem is and tell me.' So I go up to I Company. There was a machinegun that was giving them all kinds of fits. The company commander said, 'This is where we think it is and we gotta do something about it.' Well, they didn't have a FO and it was a static situation. There was a bunch of little trees in front of them. They had sacks in the trees. The Observer would crawl up the tree, hide behind a sack, and direct either mortar fire, or in my case it was artillery fire. Of course every once in a while bullets would go through one of the sacks, so you just hope it's not your sack."

While they did provide a brief period of concealment, these sacks, whether they were blankets, or shelter tent halves, offered no protection whatsoever. As soon as the first artillery round came whistling toward them, the Germans knew they were under observation and would begin systematically raking each hanging sack with machinegun fire. Eventually they would pick the right one and blast the American FO from his perch. It was all a matter of whether the American artillery observer could zero in before the Germans eliminated him. In either case the issue would be decided within seconds.

Sartain and Miller crawled out to the observation tree, then the Captain scrambled up through the branches and took position behind one of the hanging sacks. As he peered from behind with his field glasses, Sartain could plainly see the believed location of the German machinegun. Checking the spot against his map, he called the coordinates down to Bob Miller. Sartain's radioman raised the battalion fire direction center on the walkie-talkie and relayed the command.

"It hit where I thought it would land, where I wanted it to land," said Sartain. "I told them, left one hundred, up one hundred, fire for effect. Fire direction comes back and says, we're giving you two hundred left and three hundred over. That was Major Wimberley, he always doubled, you know, just second guessing the forward observer. So I repeated my command. I'm calling down to Miller, who's on the ground with the radio, and he's giving it to fire direction. 200 right. 100 over. Fire for effect!"

The German machine gunners were already working their way across the tree, punching holes through each hanging sack in turn. Just as Sartain dropped from the limb a cluster of machinegun rounds tore apart the blanket he'd been concealed behind.

Sartain was already aggravated by Major Wimberley's insistence on rigid procedure when he hit the ground, but when he looked up and saw the shredded sack hanging where he'd been just moments earlier, he was livid. He grabbed the walkie-talkie from Miller's hand, punched the button and called into the microphone, "I want to know who's the son of a bitch running fire direction." There was no answer. Of course, it was a rhetorical question. Sartain knew exactly who it was, but, having now raised the issue he wasn't willing to let go. He repeated the demand. "Tell me who is the son of a bitch running fire direction!"

Corporal Frank Motyka receives communication over one of the EE-8 Field Telephones used by Able Battery. A 105mm Howitzer is seen in the background. Covais collection."

LIKE A PUFFED UP HEN.

There was dead silence, then Major Silvey's voice came through the speaker. "Charlie," he said, "the Colonel wants to see you." At this point Sartain may have realized that he'd gone too far, after all, insulting a superior over the radio and before an audience was a serious matter. Thinking quickly, he reasoned that a little time to calm down might be in order. Citing the gathering darkness, Sartain requested that he be granted permission to return to the battalion CP first thing in the morning. After another pause Silvey answered that first thing in the morning would be alright.

Early the next day Sosa drove his Captain back to the battalion headquarters. On the way Sartain went over the previous evening's events in his mind. Sartain knew there would be some consequence to his outburst; at very least, he would receive a formal reprimand, at worst, if Wimberley insisted, there might be a court martial. Sartain had clearly stepped over the line of insubordination excepting that he hadn't spoken directly to Major Wimberley or used his name. Anticipating how a court martial would unfold, Sartain reasoned that this might just be the technicality he needed.

There was also the problem which generated the incident in the first place. Sartain knew he had a legitimate complaint and reasoned that this could work to his advantage. This was probably the best opportunity he would have to gain a hearing, and besides, the real issue here wasn't so much his possible insubordination but rather Wimberley's dangerous habit of dragging out fire adjustment.

Major Silvey was expecting him and already approaching Sartain as he got out of the jeep. "Charlie," he said, "you're in big trouble."

Feigning innocence, Sartain asked, "Why am I in big trouble?"

Silvey's answer was immediate. "You called Major Wimberley a son of a bitch."

Sartain raised his technicality at once and answered, "No, I didn't call Major Wimberley a son of a bitch. I said whoever's running fire direction was a son of a bitch."

Silvey could see immediately what Sartain was doing. In fact, he admired the bravado of the Captain's defense. Nonetheless, Sartain would still have to answer for his actions. "Well," the Major said, "the implication was that you were talking about Wimberley."

"Alright Major, we'll leave it at that," answered Sartain, conceding the point.

By now they had walked to the battalion command tent. Silvey told Sartain to wait outside while he told the Colonel he was there. It took a while before Silvey came back out and told Sartain that Todd would like to have a talk with him now.

Inside Colonel Todd was seated at a portable desk covered with military paperwork, a canteen cup of cold coffee, and a mess kit lid loaded with cigarette butts. The scene may have reminded either, or both of them, of the day Sartain had first entered his office at Fort Bragg two and a half years before. A lot had happened since then. Sartain saluted, then was told to sit down in a camp chair.

Todd asked him, "Sartain, what the hell is this all about? Major Wimberley is very upset and now I've got a mess to straighten out."

Sartain explained to his commanding officer what took place the day before. Thank God he could talk frankly with Todd. Then Sartain added, "Colonel, I lost my cool, but let me tell you one thing. You can check with any FO and they will tell you Major Wimberley is constantly second guessing them, constantly! He's not giving them what their asking for. He's interjecting himself in it and he is putting these FOs lives in serious jeopardy. Check with any forward observer, check with fire direction, check with anybody in the unit and they will tell you he is not following the commands they ask for. What they're doing is having to recorrect for what he is giving them while looking at a damn map back in the dugout when he hasn't the faintest idea what is going on. Wimberley has never ever been beyond battalion level. He has never been to an infantry battalion. He has never been in the vicinity of an infantry company commander, much less the FO position. Colonel, don't take my word for it. Check with any FO and see what they say."

Colonel Todd listened closely, then held up his hand. "Alright," he said, "I'll look into this. In the meantime I'd like you to stay around the CP and I'd appreciate it if you didn't say anything about this to anyone else."

Sartain thanked the Colonel, saluted, then left. Later on he sought out John Manning. At times like this Sartain wished he had Manning's ability to never speak afoul of anyone, no matter how much they deserved it. The two talked quietly about the whole controversy. They agreed that Sartain was right to be furious with Wimberley, but had also placed himself in a very precarious position by voicing his anger in the manner he had.

Later that afternoon Major Silvey called for Sartain to come to Todd's tent again. "I thought I was getting shanghighed out of the outfit," he recalled of his thoughts at the time.

To the contrary, after Sartain had saluted and taken a seat, Silvey told him, "The Colonel has checked with all these FOs and every one of them backs you."
Sartain felt not only relieved, but vindicated as well. Clearly there would not be a court martial, nor would he be transferred out of the battalion. With renewed confidence, he suggested that the episode could be a valuable learning experience. The comment was ambiguous, leaving exactly what that lesson was and who it would benefit open to interpretation. There was quiet for a minute as Todd and Silvey concluded that Sartain just wasn't going to give an inch. Then Colonel Todd spoke up. "You going to apologize to Wimberley?"

Sartain said, "Colonel, I will explain to Major Wimberley that it was nothing personal and that I didn't realize it was him." Sartain was again choosing his words carefully, taking pains to avoid telling Todd that he would actually apologize.

"Well, try that," said Todd, evidently resigned to the fact that an outright apology from a young officer of Sartain's pride and outspoken nature was unlikely.

"So I go in to Wimberley and he's like a puffed up hen," recounted Sartain of his audience with the Major. "See, Wimberley had an exaggerated view of his ability. I really wanted to tell him off then and there, but I said, 'Major we had a little misunderstanding. I had no intention of hurting your feelings or insubordination.' He said, 'Well, you apologize?' I said, 'If that's what it will take.' He didn't answer me so I saluted and turned around and walked out."

Sartain thought it was all very similar to the day back in North Africa, when Colonel Bertsch summoned him to his quarters after the Goldfarb trial. On that occasion the Colonel had berated him and no doubt expected an apology from such a junior officer, but Sartain just wasn't going to kow-tow to someone he didn't respect – regardless of rank, not Bertsch, and not Wimberley either. "No more was ever said, but I'll tell you what, the FOs from then on were never harassed." By now, in his recollection of events, Sartain had built up a head of steam and seemed compelled to go on. He continued to emphasize his point as if presenting a closing argument before a judge. "See, the longer it takes to get the fire on the target the FO is exposed! Exposed! No question about it.

LIKE A PUFFED UP HEN.

Our forward observers then had enough experience directing fire to know whether 100 yards right or left 50 yards right or left, 200 or a 100 was gonna do it. Textbook is that you gotta bracket it. You go 200, then you go 100 to get it on the other side. Then you'd go over, over, over, under, split the difference. Right left split the difference. Right, left, split the difference. Well these FOs got to where they could say left 100, fire for effect, and they were right on the button. Then they could get down out of a tree or a church steeple or out of an open window. You know?"

"Probably if I hadn't been battery commander, have already gotten my Silver Star, Air Medal, all that humbug, probably if someone junior to me had pulled that they would have been court martialed," he said, "Mullen or Gelb, probably anybody but me. Maybe Hawkins could have gotten by with it, but anybody except somebody like Bubb Hawkins or myself would not have gotten by with it. That was it. That was the end of it. Manning then took over fire direction from that point on."

Sartain's memory was riled up by his discussion of the confrontation with Major Winberley. There were more controversial issues surrounding the employment of Forward Observers which then came to mind. "One time I had to get Colonel Mendez to issue an order that the artillery FOs would not go with the point group," he began. "The point is the squad that leads the first of the troops out of the position. A lot of time these infantry fellas would want the artillery observer to be the first man out for everything. They just wanted them way up there with them. But a FO was of no use to anybody if they got pinned down. I had to go to bat for a lot of them because the infantry commander would put them out on the point where they had no business being. They didn't have any business but to stay with the company commander. Instead they would put them up with the leading element of the company, put them up on the point, you know? Once the firing starts then everybody had to take cover and the forward observer couldn't do anything. See, if they'd stayed back with the company commander, then he could point out targets and get to an observation point and direct fire. If they're right up with the leading element, they get pinned down quick and if an artillery FO got pinned down he was of no use to anybody."

By now Sartain seemed satisfied that he'd made himself clear. He rested, then stuffed his pipe with Captain Black, lit it, and concluded, "Well, the Colonel did tell me to watch my language over the radio. You know how it is, you get carried away and you cuss, but you really shouldn't, you shouldn't."

Carl J. Salmonsen
Route #1 Box 60
Rock, Michigan

BATTERY!

Part 25: "Better than a wooden cross."

On January 2nd, 1945, orders were distributed through the 82nd Airborne that the division would soon return to the attack. That evening Colonel Todd called a meeting of his staff and battery commanders to outline the coming offensive. The first stage would be to take back the ground surrendered on Christmas Eve. In this advance the 508th PIR would be held in reserve until the final assault on Thier Dumont Ridge, the key to the territory west of the Salm River. This released the 319th from direct support of the 508th. Instead, the battalion was directed to temporarily reinforce the fire of their sister Battalion, the 320th Glider Field Artillery.

The 319th displaced on January 4th from its Froidville positions to a location outside the much fought over village of Erria. The town- or what remained of it- had been pretty well blasted apart by the battalion's own fire missions on the 25th and 28th of December, not to mention the fierce gun-battles that were waged through and around it. Signs of the fighting were everywhere in such concentration that hardly a square yard was unscathed. As the battery was getting settled in at Erria the men were fortunate enough to be served a hot meal. "We always wanted something hot, coffee or even just plain hot water, we didn't care," remarked Sebring. In this case there really was hot coffee and chow. With both mess kit and tin cup in hand, Sebring found a convenient spot to sit. "I sat down on this log and was setting there eating. Then I raised my canteen cup up to take a drink and when I went to set it back down I saw where it had melted through the snow. I thought, 'Christ, there's a swastika!' I was sitting on a frozen German. I reached over the other way with my gloved hand and brushed the snow off. There's his face, all froze stiffer than a poker, and I'm sitting on him."

American artillery participation in the approach toward Thier Dumont was restricted. The mountainous and heavily forested terrain through which the 319th and other units of the division were obliged to pass, compounded by the heavy blanket of snow and inadequate roads, necessitated the use of tracked jeeps, known as Weasels, to deliver supplies, including artillery shells, in any quantity. Consequently, resupply was problematic. Just the same, both batteries were kept busy throughout the period. At one point the battalion began a routine registration of its howitzers, using a farmhouse as its benchmark. According to the unit's Operations Journal, "After three rounds were fired, considerable enemy activity was observed. Three volleys were quickly placed on the target with the result that 34 Germans decided they had had enough and surrendered to our infantry."

By the morning of January 7th the division was ready to move on its objective. The battalion was supposed to have been moved to the vicinity of Abrefontaine the previous afternoon to support the attack, as was the usual procedure. An advance party was sent to prepare the new position but the group came under an intensive barrage from German artillery. "We got caught up there on that hill and, man, they really had us zeroed in. Airbursts in the trees and all that business," remembered Sartain.

The site had to be abandoned quickly and another one, this time near the village of Foss, selected instead. All this delayed the timetable of the displacement. Consequently, the move took all night during some of the coldest weather of the entire winter. Sartain's Floridian driver, Louis Sosa, thought the sub-zero temperatures were beyond belief. "We pulled up in the bivouac area and I couldn't find a place to lay down," he recalled later. "There wasn't space in the truck or anywhere, so I had to lay down in three feet of snow. God Damn that was cold!" Then Sosa saw something which magnified the unreal quality of the night. "Some guy, he was one of these tobacco chewing hillbillies, you know what I'm talking about, he was just smiling and laughing and dancing around. He just laid right down in the snow like it was nothing. Didn't bother him a bit, but it tickled the shit out of me to see that. I thought, damn, this guy's not human!"

The effort to retake Thier Dumont was scheduled to begin at dawn. According to the plan, the assault would be led by a battalion of the 505th on Rencheux and the entire 508th Regiment against Thier Dumont Ridge itself. Mendez' 3rd Battalion would lead the way. He would strike the ridge at its western end and, on gaining the crest, swing south toward the village of Compe to meet any counterattack from that direction. The 1st Battalion would be right behind and was to clear off the northern slope of the ridge, working its way toward the heights overlooking Rencheux. The 508th's 2nd Battalion's job was to fill in the gap created between the 1st and 3rd Battalions when the latter turned south. 2nd Battalion would then continue along the crest, clearing off any German resistance it met. If things went as planned, each Battalion of the 508th would be reoccupying the same ground it had evacuated on Christmas Eve.

No one was under any illusion that the attack on Thier Dumont would be easy. True, the much vaunted 9th SS Panzer Division had been replaced by the 62nd Volksgrenadiers, but if not an elite formation, this unit was by no means substandard. The Volksgrenadiers were liberally armed with machine-pistols, machine guns, and an ingenious hand-held anti-tank weapon known as the Panzerfaust, forerunner of today's rocket Propelled Grenade. The Germans also occupied excellently prepared defensive positions. They were thoroughly dug in, with a network of deep bunkers and entrenched defensive points all along the slopes. Thier Dumont also provided an unobstructed view of the valley stretching from Abrefontaine, through Goronne and Rencheux, all the way to Vielsalm. This terrain was, moreover, mostly open and would provide scant cover for any attacking force.

To augment their punch, Mendez' 3rd Battalion was reinforced by four M-36 Tank Destroyers and five Sherman tanks. The 1st Battalion was also assigned three Tank Destroyers as well. These armored vehicles were equipped with massive, 90mm guns designed to penetrate the steel plates of the German Mark V "Panther" and Mark VI "Tiger" tanks. The M-36 was, however, lightly armored by comparison, with a turret which was not enclosed but open to the air. All this was intended to reduce weight and make them faster than the German heavy tanks, and they were, yet their thin skins left them vulnerable if their first shot didn't hit the target. Indeed, the common strategy among American tank destroyer crews was to get in that first shot and, if they didn't score a bull's eye, head for cover.

At first light the division was on the move. Wending their way through Abrefontaine, the columns immediately attracted the attention of German observers on Thier Dumont. Enemy artillery started streaming in and there were casualties even before the assaulting troops reached their jumping off point.

Once everyone was in place, the men huddled close to the ground, blowing warm breath into their fists and wishing the attack would just get started. Temperatures hovered around zero and seemed disinclined to rise any higher. They could stay where they were and freeze to death, they reasoned, or get the attack moving and perhaps survive. At that moment a preparatory barrage by the 319th, supported by a couple of other artillery battalions, opened the ball. Everyone knew from experience that as soon as the barrage lifted it would be their turn, so the moment the sound of outgoing artillery slackened, the tank destroyers revved up their enormous Ford V-8 engines and the attack on Thier Dumont began.

"G" company was in front, with Colonel Mendez, his immediate staff and the liaison team from the 319th in tow. Following in the next waves were "H" and "I" Companies, with the Shermans and Tank destroyers interspersed among them. There was about a half mile of mostly open pasture to cross before reaching any cover at the base of the ridge. To complicate things, the ground was covered in a thick blanket of snow, making the advance even more daunting.

Immediately the slopes of Thier Dumont bristled with fire from automatic weapons. What was more, cleverly concealed 88mm guns and tanks started hurling their high velocity shells into the 3rd Battalion. One of the tank destroyers was hit immediately and burst into flames, then another got nailed and exploded in a similar fashion. The fire was murderous. 3rd Battalion men were falling individually and in groups all over the field. One "G" Company man was decapitated by an 88 shell. His buddies swore he ran a few more steps before his headless body dropped into the blood spattered snow. Still the assault wave continued on. It was a race against time, since to stay in the open meant certain death. They were at once running for cover and running straight into the German positions. Seeing the location of one of the enemy 88s, a "G" Company bazooka-man with a shattered, bloody left arm and shoulder, raised his weapon and fired, scoring a direct hit against the protective shield of the German gun, driving off its crew.

The five American Sherman tanks were now mixed among the attacking 3rd Battalion men, but they were taking their losses too. One of the Shermans was already disabled by a mine, three others were knocked out by direct hits from German 88s. As part of the 319th liaison team with Mendez, Covais, a radio operator, and the liaison officer ran to keep up with the Colonel. Periodically his command group would drop to the ground at some relatively protected spot before bounding forward again. At these points Covais and the liaison officer would check their bearings and try to call in fire on targets which they could

Best buddies, Covais and Gruebling, Becco, Belgium, January, 1945. Covais wears the woolen liner of his GI sleeping bag – shortened and with slits at the sides for his arms. Covais collection.

see. In his last conversation about his war experiences before his death, Covais finally let loose of one memory which he'd kept bottled up since the attack. "I looked up from my map," he said. "There was this wounded paratrooper. He was trying to crawl away when one of our tanks ran over him. He wasn't far from me. I never told you about that. There's a lot of things I've never told you."

After the wooded foot of Thier Dumont was reached, the fighting changed to a thousand individual battles from tree to tree. German potato mashers and American pineapple grenades were being tossed freely. Tommy guns dueled with machine-pistols, and Mauser rifles were matched against the M-1 Garand. Even Panzerfausts were fired at close range. Their rockets slammed into trees and exploded with massive detonations.

By the time the crest of Thier Dumont was secured in late-afternoon, the evergreen forests were littered with the dead, the wounded, and smoking wreckage. Just in the 3rd Battalion's area, Mendez and his men counted about 95 dead Germans and took another 119 as prisoners of war. In addition, trophies of the 3rd Battalion included, three 88mm guns, one 75mm infantry howitzer, one half-track, two mark IV tanks, five 75mm anti-tank guns, and six other assorted vehicles, but the price paid was high. In "G" Company alone, which had started the day with more than 100 men, there were only 33 present for duty at nightfall.

Meanwhile, as the 3rd Battalion was storming the western end of Thier Dumont, the 508th's 1st Battalion was advancing across the valley, past Goronne and on to the Northern slope of the ridge. Lieutenant Eskoff of the 319th's Headquarters Battery was assigned as their liaison officer that day. His team included Ed Ryan as his radio-

man and Sergeant Henry Broski as his assistant. Eskoff had instructed the two to remain behind - he would go forward with the infantry and call for them when he reached a good point of observation.

The pair were hunkered down, waiting for the order to join their Lieutenant. They could hear the three tank destroyers assigned to the 1st Battalion approaching from the rear. The M-36 was a loud beast with massive engines which could be heard at quite a distance. As the tank destroyers came into view, a German panzer concealed behind a copse of evergreens emerged from its cover. It fired, narrowly missing the lead tank destroyer.

Suddenly, Ryan and Broski found they were caught

Ed Ryan and William Bragg in Belgium January 1945.
Ed Ryan Collection.

between the American tank destroyers and three or four German panzers. Shells were screeching past them, sometimes only a yard or two over their heads. Every time one of the tank destroyers fired its huge 90mm gun they were pounded by the muzzle blast. Then Eskoff's voice came over the radio, telling them to hustle up to the infantry position. "He wanted us to come out there where he was with the infantry," explained Ryan. "So I carried that radio equipment up a hill in a wide open space. The country there was an upward slope, wide open. I'm carrying all this stuff through that snow with Kraut tanks shooting at me and the tank destroyer is behind me, shooting back at that Kraut tank. You could hear those shells going right past us. Eskoff thought it was quite a thing, so he put me in for a Bronze Star, but it's the old story, you had a job to do and you did it."

Ryan and his buddy both received the Bronze Star for gallantry. His citation read: :"Edward R. Ryan, Technician Fourth Grade, 319th Glider F. A. Battalion, for heroic conduct near Goronne, Belgium. Technician Fourth Grade Ryan, while serving with Command Liaison, and although dazed by concussion, continued to operate the radio which enabled the Liaison Officer to coordinate and direct fire upon the enemy strong points and gun emplacements. When the leading elements of the attack were pinned down by direct fire he carried the radio across approximately 600 yards of open terrain to bring communication to a place from where the LO could better observe and direct friendly artillery fire on the enemy positions which were holding up the advance of the infantry."

When Ryan was interviewed for this book, he was asked about his matter-of-fact attitude toward the decoration. Didn't he feel some pride in receiving the Bronze Star? "Well," he answered, "it's better than getting the wooden cross."

Thier Dumont was retaken, and with it all the ground the division had given up on Christmas Eve, but there was little sense of elation over the victory. Casualties had been very high and it was a race against time to collect the wounded before they all died of exposure. That night Covais was at the point of hopelessness. What he'd seen during the attack disturbed him deeply, he was physically exhausted, and succumbing to a penetrating cold like he'd never felt before. The night of January 7th came to represent a watershed for him in his war experiences.

"Well, let me say this," he said sixty years afterward, "I saw a lot in the Battle of the Bulge. It was really a tough experience for me. I saw more people get killed and I had more close calls than, I think, just about anybody. You suffer, after a while, from mental depression. You're so fatigued with cold, from the misery you see that inside you're being tortured. You're being ripped apart mentally. You reach a point where you don't realize what you're really saying or what you're really doing. Speaking frankly, I was so sick of the war, so sick of everything. You just want to end it all. It was so cold! Bitter cold. Bitter cold."

Covais told how he stood, shoulders hunched, leaning against a tree, trying to drive the last few days' events from his mind. The eerie, moonlit field of dead Germans, the wounded soldier crushed under tank treads. It was no use, he only shivered and stared blankly ahead. He had lost the feeling in his feet a couple of days before. Just as bad were his hands. They were filthy and numb, with infected bleeding cracks at every joint, making each movement of his fingers painful. A wave of despair rose up within him. Thinking back to that night, Covais said, "I was so cold that I didn't care if the Germans shot me, captured me, I just wanted to end it, and the thought crossed my mind that maybe it was a good time for me to take and put the gun, my .45 automatic to my head. I was so disgusted, maybe depressed too. When you feel that way it demands a lot out of human resources, human effort to maintain your strength. You know, I used to think I would never do that or think about that, but I came close to it that night."

He had already unsnapped his holster and was pulling out his pistol when he thought he heard a voice speaking to him. It took a few insistent calls before he realized the sound was not his imagination. "Hey you, hey Sergeant! You want to warm up? Come On in."

The voice came from under the tarp of a parked jeep which Covais had been unaware of. Following the directions of a beckoning hand he made the several yards in a sort of daze. "Get in," the voice continued, "Come on, get out of the cold." Covais looked inside. There was a candle stub burning in the corner and a guy in the back, pumping up a Coleman stove. "Shut that tarp up behind you there, would you?" He said.

Covais unslung his carbine and took off his pistol belt. He got into the passenger seat and mumbled, "It's so cold."

The GI, who by now was placing a flaring match to the wick of the stove, answered, "You can say that again." The man looked up, smiled, then continued, "I fell asleep waiting for the Colonel and the stove ran out. If I keep that tarp over the back and really run this thing it warms up pretty good in here. I seen you out there and thought you might like to get out of the weather."

Staring at the growing flame, Covais voiced a scarcely audible, "Yeah."

The GI resumed, "You're one of the guys from the three nineteenth, right? I've seen you around with your Captain, the one with the southern accent."

Covais asked, "Aren't you Mendez's driver?"

"I'm the Colonel's driver, right." With the flame taking hold the man continued, "That was some hairy shit today, man oh man! But the Colonel pulled us through. Well, you might as well make yourself comfortable. What's your name, Sarge. Where are you from?"

"Uh, New York. Brooklyn."

"No Kidding. I'm from Pittsburgh. That means we're practically neighbors in this man's army. What did you say your name was?"

"Covais."

The soldier cupped his hands around the stove and asked another question, "You married, you got kids?"

Covais answered, "Yeah, married. No kids, not yet." His voice was still monotonous and trancelike, but the questions were reminding him that he had a home, and a wife, and a name.

"Oh, that's nice. That's nice. You're a lucky guy, Kovack."

Rooting through a metal storage box, the driver added, "I mostly raised myself, so the guys in this outfit are like family to me. Now, if I remember right, there's still some Sanka around here."

After a little while the inside of the jeep really was warming up. Covais's hands and face were beginning to get some sensation back in them but his feet were still numb. It occurred to him that he should get his wet boots off. "Hey, can I stay here for now?"

"Sure, make yourself at home Sarge. Get one of those blankets over there and stay for a while. I'll get this coffee going and we'll be just fine. Maybe you got some smokes?"

"He was the Colonel's driver," Covais said years later. "He didn't know it, but he saved my life. I was so glad to be there. See, I felt the warmth, and feeling the warmth from that little stove I was saved. I felt the life come back into me. Then the warmer I felt the further away the thought left me, about killing myself."

The next morning Covais woke up with a start. It was already light, and through the windshield he could see the rest of the liaison team talking to a cluster of 3rd Battalion officers. That was good. What was better was that his feet and hands were warm for the first time in a week or more. Even his jump boots were drier than they'd been in a long time. Covais also noticed how alert and clearheaded three hours of deep sleep left him. He later recalled, "Instead of thinking about death I was thinking about staying alive, and that felt so good." The driver was gone, off somewhere, so he laced up his boots and pulled his gear back on. Before he left, Covais placed every K-ration packet of smokes he had on the seat.

Over the next few days the 82nd consolidated its regained positions on Thier Dumont and along the Salm River, with the 319th delivering steady support in driving out the last German holdouts. Much to the relief of the entire division, the 75th Infantry Division took the 82nd's place in line at 0200 hours on the morning of January 11th. Movement to the designated rest area didn't start until 1000, and at mid-afternoon the 319th's motor convoy arrived in the vicinity of Becco, Belgium. Becco was a small dairy farming community situated on a hilltop not far from Spa. "B" Battery men were given billets in the village homes, while The GIs in "HQ" Battery were pleased to find themselves quartered at the chateau of a local Baron. Most of Battery "A" was lodged at a nearby country hotel, but a substantial portion were also assigned to billets with Belgian families.

Part of "A" Battery's Instrument Section was directed to stay at the dairy farm of the Jules Masson family on the outskirts of Becco. The group included Sergeant Covais and Mahlon Sebring. Two or three other instrument section men were there too, probably Jimmy Rosati and Felix Ferrante or Orin Miller. When the truck deposited them and their gear at the Masson's doorstep they were a rough looking bunch. A week or more of whiskers bristled from their tired faces and none of them had washed since leaving France, their uniforms were rumpled, caked with mud, and more than a little tattered. All this did nothing to inhibit the hospitality of the Massons, who were more than happy to have a crew of rugged American airborne soldiers under their roof.

The GIs felt simultaneously elated at being in a real home and awk-

Mrs. Masson. Covais, Sebring, and a few other men from "A" Battery were billeted at her farmhouse near Becco, Belgium, for several days in January, 1945 . her husband later wrote to Sebring's fiancé, telling of a pleasant visit with their American GI houseguests. Covais collection.

ward about the burden they knew their presence must place on these Belgian civilians. Notwithstanding, Mr. Masson was clearly proud to have the soldiers as houseguests. He lined up his family, introducing each in turn. They were a middle-aged couple with two children - a 17 year old son and a daughter a few years younger. His wife was a pleasant, dark haired woman with a round, welcoming face. She wiped her hands on her apron before offering one in greeting. The Masson's daughter kept close to her mother, obviously excited and a little frightened of the Americans. The son was a fair haired boy who took after his father in appearance and grinned broadly as he shook each soldier's hand as firmly as he could. The family spoke only a word or two of English, and when Sebring apologized for not speaking any French, Mr. Masson protested with nationalistic fervor, "No, no, no, Belgique! Belgique!"

Sebring later recalled the conversation and commented, "Of course, I didn't know what they was saying, I said they speak French but they said, no, Belgian. I don't think there's much difference, but I don't know that for a fact since I don't speak either one."

While father and son turned to go upstairs, Mrs. Masson motioned to the men that they should take off their boots and outer clothing right where they stood. Her daughter disappeared, then returned with a sheet on which they all dumped their filthy uniforms. Meanwhile the lady of the house set large basins of water on the cook-stove to heat up. With a few towels brought to the kitchen, Mrs. Masson pantomimed to the soldiers that they would be left alone to wash up and shave.

After a little while had passed the guys were cleaner, but this first, cursory sponge bath only removed the surface layer of grime. Presently the Masson's son brought back their boots and golloshes with the mud scraped off the soles, while mother and daughter took away a large pile of dirty clothes to be laundered. As they ventured into

The Masson home near Becco, Belgium. Covais, Sebring, and a few other men from Able Battery were lodged here during janaury, 1945. Sebring collection.

the main house the guys found that Mr. Masson and his son had brought a couple of mattresses down from the upstairs bedrooms. A few of the men could sleep there while two more followed Mr. Masson upstairs to what was apparently their son's room. Here too the mattress had been placed on the floor so that one man could sleep on the mattress and another on the box spring.

In the style typical of the Belgian Ardennes, the Masson home and barn were attached by connecting kitchen and dairy processing rooms. Though he'd been raised on a farm in Michigan, it was an arrangement which was quite unlike anything Sebring was familiar with. "This family had a great big two story brick building," he remembered, "and on one end of it there was something like ten or twelve cows. They kept the cows in during the fighting so they didn't loose any of the cattle. The next room you went in was the separating room where they separated the cream from the milk. That separating room had a red tile floor and was scrubbed three times a day with a bristle brush on hands and knees. Then the next room you went in was the kitchen. You couldn't smell that cow stable in the kitchen even though it was all in the same building."

Over the following days Covais, Sebring, and the others cleaned themselves thoroughly, got haircuts and shaved their faces smooth. They slept a lot. Mrs. Masson laundered and mended all their clothing. Whenever he could get away from his farm chores, the Masson's son would seek out the soldiers and watch whatever they were doing with great interest. There were, after all, weapons to clean, maps to sort and organize, along with optical equipment, aiming circles and other instruments of the field artillery trade to look after.

"They were awful nice people," remembered Sebring. "We tried to make a good impression and offered to help out around the farm, but they wouldn't let us. They didn't want you to do anything, even though we could have helped them quite a bit. They said, 'No, you rest.'"

The guys still walked into Becco to get their meals from the mess kitchen, but aware that they'd pretty well taken over the Masson home, they never failed to bring back extra foodstuffs for the family. Oranges, for example, were an item the Belgians had not seen in years. The Massons ate them with delight, skins and all. Other eatables, such as chocolate bars, were either saved or pilfered for the Massons. Though the GIs were refused when they asked for coffee to bring back with them, the Mess Sergeant was willing to let them have the grounds. Mrs. Masson spread the grounds on a cookie sheet and dried them on her cook-stove. The next morning the aroma of coffee filled the farm-house for the first time in years. At night the GIs and their Belgian hosts sat together, playing cards, smoking, and listening to the radio. Mr. Masson would harvest tobacco from the guy's cigarette butts to fill the bowl of his smoking pipe.

One night there was a special treat when Sebring had a great idea. He explained later what happened, "I used to write home and tell them to send me popcorn. The lady made butter, and so I told her I needed a kettle that I could set down on the fire and some butter. I popped some popcorn. I don't think they'd ever seen it before. When it really started to popping I looked around and they was jabbering back and forth with each other and motioning. I took the lid off and of course it come flying out about three foot high. They thought the house was gonna blow up! We popped a bunch of popcorn and I put melted butter on it. Boy, they thought that was alright."

Naturally, whenever you have four or five airborne soldiers as houseguests there are bound to be impositions. Tromping around in their clumsy Jump-boots, the men were unused to living in these civilized conditions. One morning Covais kicked over a chamber pot. He tried frantically to clean it up but without towels he couldn't do much. Finally, mortified with embarrassment, Covais had to find Mrs. Masson and ask for her help. "That poor lady," he said years later. "I felt so bad about that, but I didn't mean it, it was an accident."

On another occasion, Sebring brought an M-1 rifle upstairs to the boy's bedroom. From the window he began shooting at a target he'd placed in a tree some distance away. Mr. Masson and his son observed the fire with a pair of captured German binoculars, commenting on Sebring's accuracy and having a good time. What Mrs. Masson and her daughter thought of the sound and gunpowder smell of live rifle fire in the house is not recorded.

During this time there was also the usual army business to attend to. Battalion staff was directed to submit written reports of the 319th's operations during the previous month to division artillery headquarters. Religious services were held by Chaplain Reid and one officer from each battery went to corps headquarters to exchange money from French francs to Belgian currency.

On January 15th the men of the 319th were treated to a series of special events. First was a visit from a Red Cross Club-Mobile at Becco. These were single Decker buses operated by the Red Cross, fitted out with machinery for making coffee and doughnuts. In addition, some simple amenities for sale such as chewing gum, cigarettes, magazines, and American newspapers were also available. Record players with a selection of 78 rpm recordings were also part of the standard equipment and served as a way of calling attention to the Club-Mobile's presence. The whole idea was to offer some of the atmosphere of home normally provided at Red Cross clubs to troops who were either stationed too far from major cities or were resting from front-line combat.

Each Club-Mobile carried three Red Cross girls and a male driver. The girls were, in reality, carefully selected. All were college graduates, single, and at least 25 years old. Applicants were carefully screened for their personality traits, charisma, and interpersonal skills, with emphasis placed on their ability to be friendly and appealing, yet not seem seductive.

Despite its clear notation in battalion records, none of the men interviewed recall the visit specifically. One possible exception was Ed Ryan. He may have been referring to this occasion when he recalled a Club-Mobile visit which didn't go so well. He said, "Those women came down there and wanted stuff from the Mess-Sergeant, flour, sugar, whatever, and coffee too. Well he said to them, 'You know, I have this stuff for the troops and I run short when I give it to you.' This one woman raised all kinds of hell. They got in quite an argument and so he told her to go to hell. She said she's going up to see the General. He said, 'Oh yeah? Be sure to mention my name!'"

Later that same day a shuttle of trucks took men to an outdoor mobile shower facility. Typically these were a trailer truck fitted with a long pipe to which a series of nozzles were attached. Having stripped, two men stood under each with a piece of soap when hot water was turned on for 90 seconds. This was followed by a second rinsing blast a few minutes later. Handed a new set of underwear, the men toweled off and put their old uniforms back on. On returning to Becco, the dance band of the 504th Parachute Infantry gave a 45 minute concert, rounding out what had been a most unusual day.

The next day, January 16th, the battalion was shown a movie, possibly one belatedly produced by the Medical corps about the dangers and prevention of Trench foot. Before the film was started there were a number of announcements. The first was a precaution against theft. Whether the directive was generated by the complaints of Belgian civilians with whom the men were billeted, or by reports of soldiers taking "souvenirs" from abandoned homes is not clear. But looting of evacuated civilian property had been persistent since Normandy, and what was made clear was the policy of the army toward any such activities. The other issue which arose in the announcements that day concerned interaction with German civilians. In short, the order was that there would be none tolerated of any kind. Anticipation that they would soon be crossing the border into Germany must have generated this announcement by headquarters. Several reasons were at play: crimes against civilians, the potential of German partisans operating behind American lines, and the question of whether GIs of German extraction might go in search of relatives.

Over the following few days the battalion continued its rest and recuperation, and a few men From "A" Battery were even fortunate enough to receive 48 hour passes to Paris. By the 20th though, rumors were afoot that the 508th Regimental Combat Team, of which the 319th was the artillery component, would be returning to the front. Confirmation of this story was made when officers from the division headquarters inspector general's office searched the men's belongings for "looted and stolen goods." Then, at 1700 hours, the formal order to pack up for a movement the next morning was issued.

At daybreak on January 21st the battalion men left their comfortable quarters, and those who'd been fortunate enough to stay with Belgian families found the leave taking was surprisingly emotional. In some cases the ladies wiped tears from their eyes as the soldiers said goodbye. Parting like this reminded the men of the mothers, sisters, and wives they'd left in the States. For the instrument section guys at the Masson home, a genuine affection for their hosts had developed. "Nice people, nice people," was how Covais fondly remembered them over sixty years later. Mrs. Masson presented him with a small photograph of herself and another of her son, while Sebring was given a photo of the family home as a keepsake. In return the GIs left any articles of warm clothing and blankets they could spare, along with a collection of cigarettes, rations, and other sundries for the family which had treated them so kindly for the last ten days.

The battalion reassembled itself in Becco, cleaner and more rested than they'd been since leaving France nearly a month before. Liaison officers and forward observers were assigned out to the 508th and left to join the infantry. From "A" Battery, Lieutenant Gelb was made liaison to the Third Battalion, with Lieutenants Renfrew and Fellman sent to the First and Third Battalions respectively as FOs. It was at 1230 hours, that the 319th left for the front lines. Though Captain Manning and the battery commanders had already scouted out the new gun positions, it still took several hours to reach the sites and place the howitzers.

The convoy crossed over to the east bank of the Salm River, then continued to the vicinity of Diedenberg, Belgium, not far from St. Vith. "A" Battery's new position was located near an abandoned farmhouse situated on the back of a long ridgeline. It was a nice spot, protected and affording some shelter as well. Though the snow was deep, a recent artillery barrage had left the slope pockmarked here and there with shell craters, exposing the bare earth underneath. By the time Sartain and an advance party of men from the instrument section set up the battery CP in the house, it was late afternoon. Putting together the telephone switchboard, sweeping the area for mines, and establishing the security perimeter would take a little while. In the meantime Sartain sent Sosa back for the rest of the battery.

Sweeping for mines had become a particularly critical task as the Americans began again following up on the retreating enemy. The Germans were always clever at anticipating where the GIs were likely to encamp or take up positions and they salted those areas generously with a variety of these explosive devices. When mines were detected along the slope leading to a copse of pines, no one was surprised and the spot was marked as off limits.

By 1700 hours the battery's guns were in place. Since the sun was already setting, the gunners worked to get the howitzers laid and the signals men were busy running telephone wire while there was still some daylight. At the house, Motor Pool Sergeant Holman approached Sartain, telling him that all the guns were unhitched and the trailers unloaded. Where, he asked, "Did the captain want him to park the dozen or more trucks which constituted the battery's transportation?"

Sartain indicated to Holman that there was an area in the nearby pines where the trucks could be camouflaged from the view of enemy aircraft. "I went all through there with Sosa and it looks good, but be careful now, we found some mines in that field, so stay clear of them." Holman gave him an axle grease salute and turned toward the waiting trucks.

Driver Robert Dickson was in the lead vehicle, a 3/4 ton weapons carrier. Sergeant Holman stuck his head into the cab and told Dickson that he should drive toward the copse of pines over yonder. Holman didn't bother to get in, instead he perched himself on the running board and held on as Dickson set the truck in motion. The little convoy circled the perimeter of the mined field in a wide arc. Holman was pointing at the entrance of a firebreak road which he wanted Dickson to drive down. The weapons carrier was just turning into the lane when there was a massive explosion.

A mine had gone off directly underneath the Motor Pool Sergeant. Witnesses later said that he was hurled far into the air and then, when he hit the ground there was a second detonation. Holman had landed directly on top of another mine.

Everyone at the house immediately looked up, already knowing what must have happened. Sartain turned to the men closest to him and called, "Come on!" Sebring and a couple of other guys jumped into the Captain's jeep as Sosa drove full throttle up to the site. Even in the gathering darkness it was immediately apparent that the worst had taken place.

"The thing about it," said Dickson later, "we knew there was mines there. He was on the fender, right over the right front wheel, pointing me where to go. We were trying to park them trucks in among some trees when it hit the mine. It was really a big explosion and it blew him all to pieces. I was driving the truck but I didn't have a thing touch me."

That Dickson escaped unhurt was nothing short of a miracle. "We thought the guy driving the truck that Holman was riding on had a broken neck because he went up against the canvas top," recalled Sebring, who was as amazed at the driver's luck as was everybody else. The only other casualty was Private Ed Marsee, of Kay Jay, Kentucky, who caught a stray piece of shrapnel and was lightly wounded.

It was Holman's fate which was so shocking. When Mahlon Sebring rushed up to the scene with Sartain and a few others, he saw a ghastly sight. According to Sebring, "The first two or three trucks back had parts of him pasted all over their windshields. His drivers, they just went ape shit, they just went crazy. We had to slap the shit out of one guy, just to get him out of it. He was just like a banshee Indian, you couldn't shut him up, he was just nuts! You get a guy like that, grab his hands the guy might not calm down, but if you slap him up side his face it brings him to sometimes."

In the twilight battery men were collecting around the wreckage. Sartain kept demanding, "Where is he, God damn it, where is he!" Except for blood splattered trucks and two smoking craters there was no sign of Sergeant Holman. With every passing second the chances of finding him alive grew slimmer. Then Rappi saw something in the snow and reached for it. "I can remember picking up his boot with his foot still in it," he remembered when interviewed, then declined to say more about it.

It was clear now that Holman was gone. "Somebody get a mattress cover," said

BATTERY!

Sartain quietly, "the rest of you get these trucks put away. We'll see what we can find." "Zemo" Zermanski, the battery medic, was tending to Marsee's wound, applying Sulfa. Dickson, if somewhat stunned, was intact, but was taking Holman's death hard. A motor pool driver since he'd joined the outfit, Holman had been Dickson's sergeant the whole time. He told Sartain that he wanted to help in the search.

The 21st of January, 1945, would forever mark the end of Robert Dickson's youth. He explained the change, saying, "That was a hard job to do but it had to be done. We couldn't leave him there. It was a lot of pieces of him. I don't remember how many pieces but we put them in a mattress cover; that was something that would hold it. I remember picking up one hand with part of an arm which would have probably been about a foot long. In other words it was blown off about his elbow. Picking that up was hard to do. It was the hardest thing I ever done in my life, but it, well, I'll just say it'll make a man out of you. When a person can do that, they can do anything."

Sartain, Sosa, Sebring, Bob Miller, and Robert Dickson gathered up what they could, but finally it was too dark to continue the search until it was daylight again. "We got most of the body then and there, what we could find, but all we could find were two legs below the knees, maybe a hand," said Sartain.

As they sealed up the mattress cover containing what could be found of Jesse Holman's body, Sebring recalled a conversation he'd had with him in Becco a few days before. They were discussing news that some few of the men, specially selected for time served and circumstances at home, would soon be sent back stateside. "I got a letter from the Supreme Allied Commander today," Holman told him.

"Eisenhower?" Sebring asked.

"No, my wife," Holman answered, "She said, 'When you coming home, Honey?'"

Now Sebring thought bitterly to himself, "He's coming home, but not the way you expected." Later he said of the Sergeant's death, "I've often wondered what was ever told to the guy's wife. He never suffered any pain, I'll tell you that."

In the morning Sartain, his Radio Operator Bob Miller, and Sosa returned to the scene. In daylight it was, if anything, even more appalling. Here and there, among the bushes and pine boughs were tiny fragments of blood soaked cloth and human tissue, but nothing large enough to make a difference. It was a good thing, Sartain thought to himself, that the other men didn't see this. "We went back the next day to be sure we had gotten all of it," he explained, "but we just could not find where the rest of his body landed. Of course, we were kind of afraid to go up on that hill after that. It really did

Ted Simpson in a Class "A" uniform photo. Simpson collection

shake everybody up, especially since we couldn't find his body. It was totally mangled, it was horrible. It was horrible, oh yeah."

Finally there was nothing else to do. Sartain placed the sack of remains on the hood of his jeep and the three took what was left of Jesse Holman to a casualty collection point. They left him with others who hadn't survived the previous day, got in the jeep and drove back to the battery.

Having been with the outfit from the earliest days at Camp Claiborne, Louisiana, Holman was well known to every man in the battery. More significantly, he was immensely popular. Everyone remembered Holman's broad grin of teeth stained with tobacco juice, his hearty laugh, and manner of talking with his hands. "He was a real happy fella like, always smiling kind of," is how one battery man put it. He and First Sergeant Johnson had tussled in numerous wrestling matches and others recalled his capacity for a good time when off duty.

Kenneth Smith may have been speaking for them all when he later commented, "Everybody loved Sergeant Holman."

For the rest of their lives there was a nagging sense for the men involved that, had they done something, anything, differently, Jesse Holman wouldn't have been killed. If Sartain had told him to place the motor pool someplace else, or if Robert Dickson had only driven his truck a few more inches to the left or right. Sosa spoke to this feeling when he was later asked about the incident. "The thing about it is," he said, "I was already all over that place with my jeep, scouting it out with the Captain. You understand what I'm saying? I walked all up in that area but I didn't get anything. Then Sergeant Holman, bless his heart, Sergeant Holman got blown all to hell and gone. He was regular army. He was a pretty nice guy, kind of rough around the edges, but a nice guy. He never got to retire."

Holman's death took on a tragic quality larger than his own life, perhaps because of his genial nature, or maybe because the end of the war seemed to be looming

Always Time For A Poker Game, Becco, Belgium: Guys in the outfit take time out for a quick poker game while in reserve at Becco, Belgium, January, 1945. Sebring Collection.

just over the horizon. Assessing his attributes decades afterward, his Captain commented, "Jesse Holman was our motor pool man, was our Motor Sergeant. He kept all our vehicles running. He would lead the seaborne sections, the cooks, and the seaborne guys after things had settled in. There was thorough grease on him from head to foot, him and his assistant, Corporal Legg, they were real grease monkeys with out a doubt. But Jesse Holman was ok, he really, really, really was." Then, thinking back over the whole episode, Sartain finally summed it up by saying, "I wrote a lot of letters to families when guys were killed or when they were seriously hurt, but the hardest letter I ever wrote was for Jesse Holman."

All that next day the guys in "A" Battery were gloomy and pensive. The usual cracks and Wisenheimer remarks were absent. Some of the men kept to themselves, while others were seen in pairs, talking in serious, hushed tones. Ted Simpson recalled feeling like the war would never end. He'd still be on a gun crew in a hundred years if an anti-personnel mine didn't get to him first, he thought. Sebring was typical in his description of the mood when he said, "Your mind keeps going back to it. You try to put it out of your mind, but you can't. You go to chow and you sit down. Then as soon as you're alone your mind comes back to it."

Sartain and Ragland discussed the situation into the night. They knew that not only Holman's death, but the way he was killed was having a harmful effect on the entire battery. As bad as he himself felt, Sartain also knew it was incumbent on him as battery commander to break this mood and restore the morale of his men. He swallowed the last of his coffee, zipped up his sawed-off sleeping bag, and walked out to the guns where they were bivouacked.

"It was cold," remembered Ted Simpson of that night. "it was miserable. It was just one of those times when you didn't know what was coming tomorrow. I was getting together my bedroll and ready to climb into the sack when Sartain came up. He sat down and just chatted frankly, not demandingly at all, just supportively. How you getting along, where you from, that sort of thing. Very one on one. It was one of those warm and friendly conversations. I didn't really know the guy very well so everything he said was illuminating to me about him. It was a friendly, warm, encouraging few minutes with him before he moved on to somebody else. I think he was calling on a variety of people spread out over this hill top where we were bedding down. It was an upbeat conversation with me, very pleasant, very positive. Comforting is the way I would describe it. That's one of my memories of that Captain. My thought at the time was, how come he can spend so much time with me? I'm just one of many, many guys around there. Yet by God he came up and set down and we had a couple of minutes together and it was just really wonderful. It made me feel good, and then he went off. Quite a guy."

At Diedenberg the 508th Regimental Combat Team was operating independently of the 82nd Airborne, reinforcing a stalled offensive launched by the 7th Armored Division. German artillery, much of which had been assembled for the opening phase of Wacht am Rhein, and was still in place, was very active. For this reason numerous concentrations were fired against these enemy batteries while the 319th was emplaced at Diedenberg. "A" Battery alone fired 391 rounds on the 22nd, for example, and another 355 the next day. The outfit was also relieved on the 23rd, left the Diedenberg position early in the evening, and by 2245 hours was back in Becco where the men were told to return to the quarters they'd occupied before the move.

The Masson family was happy to see their GI friends return. That is, all except Sebring who had been on one of the last trucks out of Diedenberg and arrived at Becco later than the others. "There was some pretty long faces," Sebring recalled, "but when they saw me coming up the road, they ran out and hugged me and kissed me."

Sometime on the evening of the 26th Jules Masson penned a letter to Mahlon Sebring's fiance', and later wife in Michigan. He wrote:

Mademoiselle Kerr, You'll be a little surprised to see this letter, although you probably won't be able to understand it. At present we are boarding some American soldiers and your fiance' is one of them. I must tell you to begin with, that we have only praises for all the soldiers who are staying with us. They have been able to give an account of good manners, and your fiance', and of the things you have been able to do. We have passed some very pleasant days in their company and will regret seeing them leave. What do you wish I tell you in this letter? For the moment, in Belgium, we have certainly had enough snow and the last winter of war has been harder than the preceding ones. But we do not loose confidence and we hope that it will soon put an end to all our trials. It is the dearest wish of this family that your plans work out as you intend them. Please receive kindly, mademoiselle, our kindest wishes, Jules Masson.

A considerable amount of warm feeling must have developed between Sebring and this Belgian family to prompt Mr. Masson to write this letter. Similar letters were probably written to the families of the other men who stayed with them. The feeling was returned by the Americans, whose sympathy for the Belgians grew stronger as they were in the Ardennes. It wasn't only that the Belgians displayed more appreciation for the GIs than the French, but they also seemed to be suffering more. "The Belgians, they really had it hard on that Bulge though," Sebring commented afterward. With a lingering trace of anger in his voice, he added, "A lot of times you'd go into a house and when there weren't anyone around you'd go out in the garden and there they laid, all shot. When the Germans left they'd shoot them. And for no reason, they're civilians! They thought they'd been helping us, you know. A lot of Belgians killed in that Bulge."

On arriving at Becco Sartain issued his promotions to fill the vacancy left by Sergeant Holman's death. "When I made Legg Motor Sergeant I had a little static among the battery officers. Everybody had their own favorite but Legg was the next in line, he was Holman's Corporal. That's what my policy was for any promotion. If I'd have promoted someone over him, that would not have been good for morale," he said.

A distribution of Stars & Stripes newspaper was made and the Special Services Officer was directed to pick up films and a projector at artillery headquarters. Records do not indicate whether these were some of the 16mm versions of Hollywood films which were made available to the armed forces or if they were educational shorts produced by the government. In any event, this second stay at Becco did not last long. On the 26th Colonel Todd met with battery officers to inform them of their role in the division's coming offensive, intended to carry them into Germany. A reconnaissance of the new positions was made and, on returning, orders issued for the men to have everything packed and ready before they turned in for the night.

Everybody was up well before dawn on January 27th. At the Masson farm there was a round of handshakes, hugs, and farewells. This time it was clear that the outfit wasn't coming back. At 0630 the battalion pulled out of Becco for good.

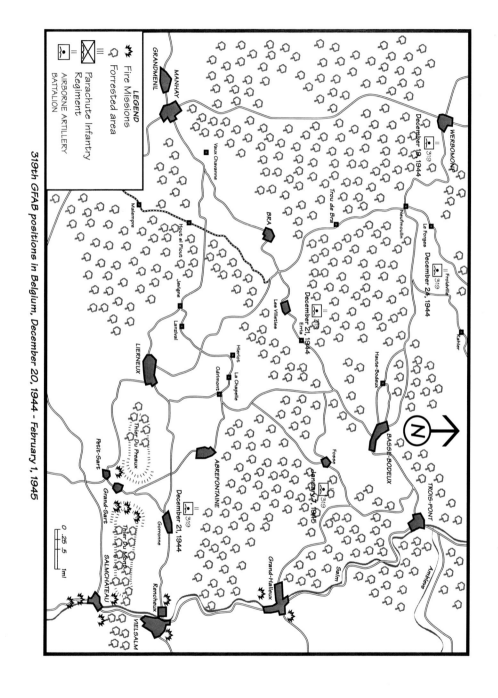

319th GFAB positions in Belgium, December 20, 1944 - February 1, 1945

LEGEND

- Fire Missions
- Forrested area
- Parachute Infantry Regiment
- AIRBORNE ARTILLERY BATTALION

GRANDMENIL

MANHAY

WERBOMONT

December 19, 1944

Froidville

Le Forges

Neufmoulin

December 24, 1944

Cahier

Vaux Chavanne

Trou de Bra

BRA

Malempre

Haut al Plout

Jevigne

Lansival

Les Villettes

Ernia

December 21, 1944

Haute-Bodeux

BASSE-BODEUX

LIERNEUX

Hierlot

Ouhimont

La Chapelle

Thier Du Preaux

Petit-Sart

ABREFONTAINE

Fosse

January 3, 1945

TROIS-PONT

N

Grand-Sart

Gorronne

December 21, 1944

Salm

Grand-Halleux

Amblere

SALMCHATEAU

Thier Du Mont

Rencheux

Grand-Halleux

VIELSALM

0 .25 .5 1ml

BATTERY!

Part 26: "A Bang up good job."

The 319th crossed over the Salm River at Vielsalm and continued on to Wallerode, a town near Stavelot, Belgium, where new positions were established in support of the 376th Parachute Field Artillery.

Stavelot was also now a staging area for the division, with all the logistical support one would expect at such a facility. The battalion's supply officer was therefore directed to report to the division quartermaster for an issue of waterproof ponchos, mittens with inserts, and most significantly, the long awaited shoepacs with felt insoles. Remembering how much they'd suffered with frozen feet in jump boots or wobbled around in galoshes stuffed with straw, the guys were glad for the change of footwear. However, there were unforeseen consequences. Released from their constricting jump boots the men's feet rapidly swelled. Over the next 24 hours there was a lot of exchanging of shoepacs for larger sizes. Then, as the men's feet began to recover the swelling subsided and another round of musical shoepacs ensued. Notwithstanding all this, the shoepacs were a significant improvement, albeit two months late in their issue. Had the division gone into the Bulge with shoepacs, thousands of cases of Trench foot and frostbite would undoubtedly have been prevented.

A platoon of the 740th Tank Battalion was attached to the 319th and designated as Charlie, or "C" Battery while the outfit was at Wallerode. These tankers were armed with 105mm guns, mounted on a tank chassis. The 740th, known as "The Daredevils," had entered combat the previous November in Sherman tanks with attached assault gun platoons. Elements of the battalion were assigned to various units of the 82nd Airborne Division beginning in late December and quickly gained a reputation as the kind of tankers the airborne troopers like to fight beside – aggressive and eager to tangle with the Germans. In the case of this new "C" Battery, the 740th platoon with its self-propelled guns would simply serve as another battery of stationary artillery.

Notified that the battalion would revert back to direct support of the 508th PIR, forward observers were assigned out to the 508th at noon on the 28th: Lieutenant Cole to the 1st Battalion, Lieutenant Zagrodski to the 2nd Battalion, and from "A" Battery Lieutenants Joe Mullen to the 3rd and Lieutenant Fellman as liaison to the artillery of the adjacent 87th Division. Captain Manning, meanwhile, took the job of liaison officer to the 508th's Regimental Command.

On the 29th the 508th again moved out with the 319th following close behind. As with the movement against Thier Dumont Ridge, the 508th would be held as reserve until the Germans were fully engaged. To complicate the advance, the winter weather, which had moderated somewhat since the middle of January, came roaring back to life making the movement through blowing, drifting snow all the more arduous.

Manning's Sioux driver, Clarence Janis had a time keeping the jeep going as he and his Captain kept apace with the advancing 508th. At intervals Manning set up relay stations, trying to maintain contact between the advancing infantry and the 319th. Ed Ryan was one of Manning's radio operators during these last days of January. He remembered, "Janis would be in the jeep, waiting on Manning." "He looked just like Sitting Bull. He'd have a blanket over him and kept feeding twigs into this little campfire on the floorboard between his legs."

The pleurisy Ryan had contracted in Italy was coming back after six weeks of winter combat. "I finally was spitting up blood and had to stop. Captain Manning told me to set up a relay station, so that's what I did. Sat there in a snow bank for a couple of days."

Sometime during this same movement Covais had another one of those close calls which hammered home the capricious line between life and death. He was with the 508th's 3rd Battalion – as either part of the liaison or the forward observer team. The day was blustery and cold, with a wind which blew snow up the sleeves and down the collars of everyone's clothing. He knew it would be another miserable night if he had to spend it outdoors. After sundown the temperature would plummet and he'd be up all night in an ice and mud foxhole. An abandoned and unheated building would at least be dry and out of the wind, but there was no guarantee such accommodations would be available.

The column Covais trudged along with was leaving the road and going cross country. Some yards ahead a jeep was idling in the snow and as he walked past it a familiar voice hailed him. "Hey Kovack! Thanks for the smokes."

Covais paused. He remembered the voice as that of Colonel Mendez's driver, the jovial soldier who'd saved him when he was at the point of despair on Thier Dumont Ridge. "Don't mention it," Covais said when he stepped up to the jeep.

"Come on, get in. I'm headed up to where you're going," said the driver. "Why don't you get the hell out of the cold."

The driver was right, the day was frigid and Covais' first impulse was to climb in, but something stopped him. Sure, the road had been cleared, it was a secured road, but experience had taught him that adjacent fields were a favorite place for the retreating Germans to sprinkle mines unpredictably, like the one that had blown Sergeant Holman apart the week before. Moreover, there had been snow on most recent nights, so any signs that mines had been placed as the enemy withdrew were now hidden. "Naw, I'd rather walk. If I get warm now I'll really freeze tonight."

"OK, suit yourself," the driver said with a smile as Covais stepped away.

Immediately, another man asked if he couldn't take that empty passenger seat and got in. A few minutes later, after slogging through only fifty more yards of deep snow, an explosion blasted the air. Covais threw himself to the ground, then, looking back, it was immediately apparent that the Colonel's jeep had indeed struck a mine. Covais ran back to it. The vehicle was still upright but perched at a strange angle with its underside smoking and twisted. Mendez's driver was sitting up on the ground beside it with a couple of guys leaning over him, alright but stunned and pretty badly shaken up. The man who accepted the seat Covais had just declined was still seated in place but with pulses of blood spurting from the right side of his head. A medic ran up and tried to apply a pressure bandage to his wound. In his last few seconds of life the stranger gazed directly at Covais with a look which seemed to ask, "What did you know. Why didn't you tell me!" Then his expression turned from panic to a vacant stare. "It was just what I was afraid of. That guy didn't make it, he did not last long. It could have been me, but when you're in war these are the things that happen," Covais later observed.

At the villages of Holzheim, Medendorf, and Eimerscheid the 508th finally caught up with the retreating Germans. 319th gunners went into action. According to their Operations Journal, "heavy casualties" were inflicted on enemy infantry as it retreated out of Holzheim and four 88mm guns were destroyed in the same vicinity.

BATTERY!

When the outfit rolled into Honsfeld, Belgium, on the 30th, a disagreement arose between the 319th and an infantry regiment from the 1st Infantry Division over who had clearance to occupy the buildings in the village. Just what decision or compromise was reached is not clear, but battalion records indicate that only the Headquarters Battery remained in the town. All three firing batteries apparently took up new gun positions along the road leading out of Honsfeld toward Lanzerath.

German units were desperately trying to reconstitute their lines before the Americans pushed across the border into Germany, so there was no real opportunity to take advantage of indoor shelter anyway. Frequent fire missions were called throughout the day on January 30th. One enemy battalion found itself caught under such a concentrated and accurate artillery barrage from the battalion's Honsfeld positions that it was forced to surrender en masse. Prisoners later told the Americans that they had no choice, being unable to retreat or attack without being annihilated.

The dawn of January 31st was a murky morning with low clouds, fog, and freezing rain. Under orders to advance northward, the 508th's 2nd and 3rd Battalions were just about to cross the border into Germany when they were suddenly struck by a combined infantry and panzer counterattack. With the dank, foggy air muffling all sounds, the German tanks and Panzergrenadiers seemed to materialize out of the mist. A furious close-quarters fight ensued.

When the 319th's forward observer radioed for artillery support the call came just as the battalion was hitching up the howitzers for another displacement, but the cannoneers sprang to their jobs and again laid down a terrific fire. In the first barrage of 135 rounds, one of the panzers, a Mark VI Tiger, was knocked out, as well as two personnel carriers. The Germans fell back, regrouped, then came on again. The batteries resumed their bombardment and another Mark VI tiger was hit. By now there were numerous casualties inflicted on the attacking infantry and a large proportion of the German armor was destroyed. It seemed the German attack was broken up. Colonel Todd ordered Charlie Battery to stay in place and be at the ready to deliver fire while Able and Baker Batteries displaced to new positions. While this movement was underway, Captain Man-

Receiving instruction from Battalion Fire Direction Center in the vicinity of the Siegfried Line, February, 1945. Lt. Ragland is listening on the field telephone. At left stands Lt. Cook. Sartain collection.

ning, liaison officer with the 508th spied a force of approximately 300 Germans with supporting armor massing for another attack. Once again the artillery fire was called in. The next 183 rounds were so accurately placed that the German assault never got started. As the enemy quit the field, they left many casualties behind, as well as a third tank of undetermined type whose crew was seen abandoning the disabled panzer for safety.

February 1st and 2nd, 1945, were quiet, with no firing from Able Battery. Though orders had been issued to relocate the battalion to Loshiemergraben, directly on the German border, no suitable sites to place the guns could be located without first having the engineers prepare the hilly and heavily forested ground with bulldozers. This position was established at mid-day on February 3rd and was more or less directly where the American 99th Infantry Division's lines stood on December 16th, when the German Wacht Am Rhein offensive began. The 319th's Batteries were placed in clearings within a vast, silent pine forest, with the border less than 100 yards to the east. Other units were moving ahead of the 82nd now and there was no firing for a few days.

Before the battalion left for Loshiemergraben the first step in what would ultimately end in the disbanding of "A" Battery and the 319th Field Artillery as it had existed from the outbreak of the war took place. In accordance with War Department policy, and with the end of hostilities in Europe in sight, a very few selected members of the outfit were to be sent back to the United States on Temporary Duty Assignments. In the 319th the first officer to go home was Captain Manning.

"Every battalion got to pick a man to send back home," explained Sartain. "Manning was picked because Manning had been through the mill. He deserved it. He'd had that bad accident in Normandy and he was a favorite of the whole battalion, he really was. I was part of an earlier discussion about it with Colonel Todd and I recommended Manning. All the battery commanders and upper staff of the battalion were in on it too, but the final decision was left up to Todd and Silvey."

It all happened very quickly. The news was delivered to Manning quite suddenly on February 2nd, during the lull which settled in once the Germans were driven back into their Siegfried Line defenses. He came back to the battalion CP, where he was given his official orders by Colonel Todd, who congratulated him, adding that Manning had earned the assignment. As modest as he was, Manning still wasn't about to argue the point if it meant going home to the Hudson Valley. He took his papers, then immediately started packing up his belongings. That night there was an impromptu farewell party for the Captain. "We all had a good drink or two. Goodbye, hugged everybody," recalled Sartain.

The next morning Manning left for division headquarters at Malmedy, where he received orders to proceed to Le Harve, France, and board a transport for New York City. As he traveled homeward, Manning must have reflected back on the three years just passed. He'd seen Louisiana, North Carolina, most of Europe and a good piece of North Africa as well. Gathering stones in the Algerian desert for Colonel Bertsch. Taking command of "C" Battery and seeing it change from a collection of misfits into the 319th's best outfit. The battles along the Italian mountain tops, Naples, and the Volturno River. There was Ireland and England, and the Normandy invasion, which was at once terrible and majestic. Manning may have thought back on the still aching injury to his right hand and shoulder. There was the invasion of Holland and the 24 hours spent fighting off tanks and flamethrowers on the Finger Ridge near Mook. There were also the memories of the Bulge, Christmas Eve and the bloody attack on Thier Dumont.

Intermixed must have been thoughts about the men and boys he'd come to know, heroes, a lot of them, and a few, like Colonel Bertsch and that drunken fool, Lieutenant Warren, who'd have to reconcile their actions with a higher authority. Some wouldn't be coming home ever: Sergeants Seagle and Holman, Lieutenants Fitzgerald, Carey, and Simpson. He hoped he didn't forget them easily. Would the friendships he'd formed endure? Colonel Todd, Hawkins, Cargile, and of course Sartain. With so much to think about, it was good that New York was so far away.

There were corresponding thoughts among those left on the Belgian/German border. Probably no one was more aware of Manning's absence than Sartain. "I missed him, I really did," said Sartain as he looked back on his time in the battalion after Manning left. "We were very, very close all the way through and he was the one guy I could talk to, you know? We developed sort of a bond. I don't remember anybody else in the 319th who had the bond that I had with Manning. Hawkins and Cargile were close too, but I doubt like Manning and I were. Manning was, how shall I say it, a formative influence in my military career, and working under him was a privilege, it was one of the high points for me. It was a crying shame that Manning didn't get his majority while he was with the battalion, you know what I mean?"

As it was, the business of war continued. Bubb Hawkins took Manning's place as assistant operations officer for the battalion and Max Torgersen moved into command of "B" Battery.

Though officers and men occupied their time constructing log covered bombproofs in the forest near Loshiemergraben, there was also time to explore the surrounding woods. Scattered here and there were signs of the fighting that swept through this area the year before. Small parties of men would walk forward through the forest, far enough to say they'd crossed over into Germany. Joe D'Appolonio and a few friends from "A" Battery did this one afternoon. "We were walking through and we got startled because we thought we saw a guy," he later recalled. "It was a German soldier, but he had been shot and killed instantly. He had been doing number two. Never fell forward, just, that's it. This guy, this German soldier had a corn pipe in his mouth. We reached down and pulled out the pipe and his teeth and everything came out. That's how old the body was."

Other men found the chance to steal away from the gun position for other reasons. Kenneth Smith, for example, had developed quite a reputation for gleaning any foodstuffs in the battery vicinity which might be unguarded. For sure, his talent for foraging was notorious since the days in Naples when he was brazenly lifting hundred pound sacks of flour off British supply trucks. This particular afternoon he had a couple of buddies in tow as he explored the area in search of eggs, chickens, or any other unchaparoned eatables.

Smith and his crew were standing by a roadside, discussing their next move. Meanwhile, a long column of 2 1/2 ton trucks was crawling past, each loaded with troopers of the 517th Parachute Infantry Regiment, an independent airborne outfit which jumped into southern France the previous August and had been more or less fighting in the 82nd's neighborhood since late December. As the trucks bounced along, splashing mud and slush, a voice called out, "Kenneth, Kenneth! It's your brother!"

Smith looked up, in time to see a GI leaning out of one truck, waving his arms wildly. The man looked like every other GI – tired, whiskered, bundled up in disheveled winter clothing. Smith didn't recognize the man, yet the stranger again yelled to him, "Kenneth, it's me! It's your brother!"

Smith called back," You ain't my brother. I ain't got a brother over here."

A BANG UP GOOD JOB.

"It's me, it's Pig!" the GI insisted. His truck was already pulling ahead.

"Sure enough it was my brother Kyle. He was in the 517th Paratrooper outfit and he'd just come overseas. That was his nickname. That's what we called him, Pig," explained Smith.

Kyle Smith remembered back to that unlikely meeting decades later and said, "So help me God I can see it yet today. I seen Kenneth standing there on the side of the road. I don't know where the hell he came from. He was standing there on the side of the road and I came by at five or ten mile an hour and well God damn! That's Kenneth!" Kenneth Smith began running after the truck, caught up with it and the two began their visit even as he jogged along side. "It so happened the truck stopped," Kyle continued. "I got off and we had a little reunion."

"He looked, I don't know, like somebody else standing there in the snow, all covered up from head to toe, not with snow but with clothes to keep warm. If he hadn't been so tall I wouldn't have recognized him. How in the hell did he get in them gliders being that tall, I never could understand that neither!"

Once Kyle jumped down off the tailgate, the two brothers exchanged a vigorous handshake, followed by a bear hug. Kenneth informed his older brother, "You know your sister got married, don't you?"

Kyle answered, "No, I haven't had no mail for seven months."

Thinking back on the conversation, Kyle Smith remembered, "We agreed right then and there that if we didn't like that guy she married we was gonna throw his ass out when we got home. Well, she married the nicest guy you could get; she got a real good guy, so we didn't have no trouble."

Kenneth's Able Battery buddies had caught up with him by now. One of them had a camera and suggested that the Smith brothers should pose together, which they did, arms draped over each other's shoulders. "Hell no, I couldn't reach his shoulder, what are you talking about! Probably around his waist," corrected Kyle who, at 6'4" was still at least four inches shorter than Kenneth.

Top Sergeant Jesse Johnson supervises the distribution of hot chow from a pail during one of the brief rests at some point in the drive on the Siegfried Line. Sartain collection.

BATTERY!

Kyle continued his narrative of the impromptu meeting, saying, "I had a tripod thirty caliber and a carbine. Kenneth said, 'Hey, let me help you carry that up to the front line tonight.' I said, 'No, you're crazy, you ain't gonna do that.' He said, 'No, let me help; you. I ain't got nothing to do back here now anyway.' I wasn't about to let him do it, but God damn if that night I wished a hundred times I'd had him with me. I kept falling down. I fell down so many times hauling that thirty caliber up them hills. I said, 'God I wished I'd have let Kenneth help me carry this stuff up here tonight.' It's just like yesterday, I can see it all now."

Kenneth Smith visited his brother Kyle at his frontline machinegun position the next day. When he returned the day after for another visit he learned that Kyle had been wounded by German machinegun fire in a failed attack on the enemy stronghold known as Hill 400.

The self-propelled guns of the erstwhile Charlie Battery returned to their parent 740th Tank Battalion and on February 6th the 319th traveled back to Abrefontaine for a very brief rest. Along the way they passed once again through the heartbroken Belgian towns of Vielsalm, Rencheux, and Goronne. The guys passed by Thier Dumont ridge and other ground which had been fought over so much during the previous six weeks.

At Abrefontaine the men were comfortably quartered with townspeople or at a chateau on the outskirts of the village. After a hot meal and a night's rest they spent their time cleaning and repairing equipment, vehicles, and personal gear. Some of it was simply used up and had to be replaced. Another item which was replaced was the 319th's radio codename. Now they were to be redesigneated as "Andy Red."

The outfit had hardly time to get settled in when march orders were received and early the next afternoon they were moving back over the same roads they'd traveled since mid-December. With the first real thaw since the middle of December, the February 8th movement was reduced to a slow slog through mud, slush, and ice. The road network in the Hurtgen area may have been adequate to the pre-war requirements of civilian use, but under the weight of tanks and other military vehicles, multiplied by the vast volume of this traffic, the highways quickly came apart in this weather. Truck after truck sank up to the axels or deeper, while engineers cut ad hoc lanes through the forest in an attempt to by-pass the worst of the quagmires. Efforts to tow and winch stuck vehicles from the mud required enormous expenditures of time and manpower, leaving everyone's patience exhausted. Even so, long periods were spent at a standstill for the convoy while these jobs were accomplished.

Driver Robert Dickson was attempting to negotiate one of these temporary roadways when his weapons carrier came to a grinding halt, like a ship run aground. "I had my truck hung up on a stump," Dickson confessed. "I had a little old dinky kind of a little old saw like thing and I was laying under the truck in mud and water and slush, trying to saw that stump off. A buddy of mine was just standing out there watching me. He had been under there and then he had got out. I could see this man awalking down through the mud, he was just slopping along and I didn't think nothing about it. He got up right even with the truck and my buddy didn't say a word. He said, 'Soldier, what are you doing under that truck?' Of course, you know how I felt in that snow and water and slush. I said, 'Any stupid idiot that could ask a dumb question like that ought to be shot dead!' He didn't say a word, he just walked off. I got out from under there and my buddy said, 'You know who that was?' I said, 'I really don't care.' He said, 'That was General Gavin.' When I heard that I said, 'General Gavin? I'd just as well to shoot myself because I'm in trouble!' It wasn't fifteen minutes, and I had the stump cut off and laying out there on the ground, here he come back. I told my buddy, 'Well, here's where we find out now.' We didn't normally have to salute in combat, but boy, when he walked down through there I popped one to him. He said, 'Soldier, relax! You fellas are doing a bang up good job. Now go about your business.' He just kept walking. You talk about getting a good feeling, I got it!"

Dickson's experience wasn't unique. In fact, by the end of the war most GIs in the 82nd Airborne seem to have come away with their own personal Gavin story. All were aware that he'd started out a buck private, enlisting in the Army as a 17 year old orphan. His youth and physique mirrored their own and the GIs took vicarious pleasure in their General's unspecified, but clearly sexually charged relationship with the glamorous actress and singer, Marlene Dietrich.

Gavin never forgot his enlisted roots. Rappi remembered him coming into the Paget Arms pub in Lubenham. "Sure," he recalled, "he used to come in our beer hall. I don't remember talking to him, but he'd come in there and drink beer with us."

The General's habit of carrying an infantryman's M-1 rifle was not only a ruse to conceal his rank from snipers, but also another way he identified with the average dogface. Gavin wasn't afraid of using his rifle either. Ed Ryan remembered being in the middle of a firefight in Normandy. "I looked over, there's Gavin shooting away with the M1." Meanwhile Casimir Sobon described Gavin as, "A good man. Gavin was a GIs general. I seen him right up on the front lines with a rifle, talking, 'How's everything?' He had a guy that was working with him, his aid or whatever he was, was a real fat guy. Gavin was Slim Jim. He would be running all the time, and the other guy would be puffing, trying to keep up with him."

It was true, Gavin did have a reputation for being seen all over the battlefield and especially where ever the fighting was toughest. Sartain testified to this when he said, "Any time there was a problem, he was right there. Gavin was right back, right back, if there was a trouble spot any where on the front, Gavin was there."

Covais' encounter with the General contained all the elements of a classic Gavin story, including his ability to appear anyplace, at any time. "In the Battle of the Bulge me and General Gavin met," Covais later claimed with pride. "I saw the General walking out of the woods, on to the path I was walking on. It's General Gavin, Slim Jim Gavin with his M-1 rifle slung on his shoulder. Well, the Germans were behind us, right? Nobody knew where the Germans were and the fire was getting close to our lines. I said to him, 'Hi there, General. You know, it sounds like those shots are coming from

Rows and Rows of Dragon's Teeth: The Siegfried Line as it appeared to members of the 319th in February, 1945. Covais collection.

the rear.' Gavin said, 'Yeah, it sure sounds like it, Sergeant. I'm gonna go find out who they belong to. I'll check into that.' That's the only conversation we had. He was a good man, he came up the hard way. Came up from the ranks.''

Typical of the attitude toward their General was Robert Dickson's comment when he later stated, "I didn't know of a man in that division who didn't just love him to death. In my opinion, that guy was the best general in the whole army!''

On the afternoon of the 9th the 319th pulled out to take a position at the infamous village of Hurtgen, Germany. On the way it passed through a section of the recently breached Siegfried Line with its concrete pillboxes and miles of "Dragon's Teeth" tank obstructions. If any of the Americans felt like they had chased the Germans back into their defenses behind their border, the sight of the Siegfried line fortifications would have made them wonder if pushing them further wasn't going to get a lot tougher. More ominous was the village of Hurtgen and its namesake forest.

The United States Army had been feeding one division after another into this meat grinder of machinegun nests, mine fields, bunkers, and booby-traps since mid-September. As a sort of natural extension of the Siegfried Line, the fifty square mile Hurtgen was deemed a necessary objective in order to skirt the most foreboding of the man-made defenses. Yet the dense coniferous forest, rugged terrain, and paucity of roads or open spaces of any kind neutralized the American superiority in armor and in the air. It was ideal for a dug-in and experienced defender, which the Germans certainly were. The Hurtgen Forest was also judged to be the most direct route to seize the dams spanning the Roer River, the last natural obstacle before the Rhine. If the Germans held possession of the dams they could release the water and make the otherwise docile Roer uncrossable for weeks or even months.

Such was the army's logic at the time, but casualties began to mount quickly. By the time elements of the 82nd Airborne Division came on the scene in the first days of February, 1945, most of the Hurtgen Forest had been taken, but already at a cost of over 30,000 casualties. With enemy losses of no more than half that number, the wisdom of securing the Hurtgen at such an expenditure of lives became a hotly debated issue and the battle remains controversial to this day. "The brass insisted they wanted to take the Hurtgen Forest, but their ego was the real point," opined Sartain on the question. "I remember stopping at the edge of the Hurtgen Forest and looking over at the town of Schmidt. Half the trees were blown off at the top. It was an unbelievable sight. Fallen trees, stumps anywhere from 3 to 10 feet, all the result of intensive artillery fire. Man, there must have been a lot of it.''

The 319th took over the positions of the 460th Parachute Field Artillery, a part of the 517th Regimental Combat Team, on the outskirts of Hurtgen, while the battalion's command post located itself in the cellar of what Colonel Todd's report later described as the only intact building in the area. The 517th had gotten its nose well bloodied a few days earlier attempting to take Hill 400, and was now being replaced by the 508th.

In fact, the 508th, in tandem with the 505th, was already on the attack. It's 2nd Battalion drove forward nearly a mile on the morning of the 9th, but, like the 517th before it, failed to break through the curtain of extremely dense minefields, overlaid with heavy mortar, machinegun, and small arms fire. "We ran in to the remnants of a German paratrooper regiment and it was a real dog fight," commented Sartain. There were numerous casualties, including Lieutenant Valesco, wounded while serving as liaison officer to the 2nd Battalion.

That evening the 508th's 1st Battalion was given the order to make a night attack. Carl Salminen found himself assigned to take the forward observer up to the front. Salminen explained how he got the job, "The jeep driver, this Italian guy, he broke down. I don't know if you would call it shell shocked, but I mean he was just wild. Like I say, he was just really scared. He left the jeep and says, 'I'm not going back no more!' He was crying and hollering. He was screaming, and jumping on his belly and everything else. So the motor pool sergeant that replaced Holman, Sergeant Legg, he says, 'Well Carl, looks like your gonna have to go.' I said, 'That's my job, driving,' so I went. "A" Battery's Lieutenant Rodney Renfrew was the officer given the forward observer's assignment. I took this young lieutenant from the signal team up front with his radio operator and telephone operator. Observation officer, a 2nd Lieutenant. Real nice guy, real young guy," continued Salminen as he remembered back to that night in February. "All I had to do was drop him off."

When the attack started at 0200 hours, Company "C" was in the lead, with Lieutenant Renfrew in tow. It advanced through belts of mines of every description: shoe mines, box mines, S mines, booby traps, and "Bouncing Betties," a variety which was spring loaded so as to jump a few feet in the air before it detonated. At the base of Hill 400 the men were met by the combined fire of no less than six German machineguns. Lieutenant Renfrew called in fire missions but it was no use. In the darkness it was impossible to adjust the concentrations accurately and "C" Company could go no further. While these men laid down as much covering fire as they could muster, Companies "A" and "B" made a flanking attack on the hill and finally took it sometime around dawn.

In the darkness and chaos of the night battle, it took some time for Salminen to make his way back to the battery. At about 0430 hours he pulled into the gun position, flecked with mud but otherwise intact. Carl hadn't had a chance to report himself returned when Sergeant Legg walked up and asked him, "What did you do with that Lieutenant?"

"What are you talking about," answered Salminen, "I took him out where I was told to take him."

"Well, he's dead," was the offhand response.

Carl was taken aback. "Go on, you guys gotta be kidding me!"

"No," Legg answered, "He is dead. He stepped on a box mine."

The message had just come in from the battalion CP where a transmission from Renfrew's radio operator in a garbled and addled voice was received. Over reports of

Gun Section near Hurtgen, 1945.

machinegun and rifle fire heard in the background, details beyond the fact that he'd exploded some sort of mine were sketchy. When Sartain got the news he immediately told Sosa to crank up the jeep and headed out to see for himself what happened.

They took the jeep as far forward as they could. The fight for Hill 400 was still in full swing and there were flashes of tracers and artillery silhouetting the twisted, devastated trees which surrounded them. Sosa had just stopped to get directions from some 508th men when the survivors of Renfrew's team appeared. It was his radioman and wireman. They looked like they'd been roughly handled, with blackened faces and a strange, wild look in their eyes. "Where's Renfrew?" asked Sartain.

"He's killed," the radioman said in a dissociated manner.

The answer didn't satisfy Sartain, who immediately demanded, "What do you mean! What did you leave him for!"

"I don't know, sir, he pulled a tripwire. It was a big explosion. He didn't move and there was shit going on all over the place. We didn't know what to do! Now he's dead, now he's dead. I'm sorry, Captain Sartain, I'm sorry!" The words tumbled out of the Radioman in a panicked sort of way, as if only now realizing fully what had taken place. The Wireman, who'd been silent up to this point, came apart. He started bawling and fell to his knees with filthy hands hiding his face in shame.

Sartain was livid. "You don't leave a man out there like that!" he hissed. "He could have been alive, but you two clowns left his ass! You don't ever do that, you should have brought the body with you!" Sartain glared for a moment, then added, "Now you both are coming with us. We're gonna see if we can find him."

The 508th Paratrooper who'd been giving Sosa directions, spoke up, contributing, "Captain, I suggest you leave it for tomorrow. That trail is loaded with booby traps. Things are still pretty confused out there and in the dark someone else is liable to get killed. We'll find your Lieutenant in the morning, but right now, sir, I don't recommend it."

Sartain thought a moment, then said, "Alright." Then, turning to Renfrew's team he added, "You two get in the jeep, we're going back."

"Man, I ate his butt out," said Sartain later of the incident. "His crew were all late replacements and they were very, very upset, all of them. One of them was so shook up I don't think I ever let him go back out with another FO again. But Renfrew, he was a nice kid and a very good little forward observer. It was a real shame what happened to him."

Hill 400 was the last remaining German stronghold west of the Roer. The next day the 508th advanced all the way to the banks of the river, ending the Battle of the Hurtgen forest.

The battalion displaced its batteries to a position near the German town of Brandenburg early that same morning. As expected, the Germans had released the waters from the reservoir and it would be some time before a crossing could be considered. For the present the 319th had to be content with numerous fire missions of harassment. "A" Battery alone expended over 350 rounds in this way on February 11th, for example, and another 596 on the 14th, firing at no target in particular. The enemy was there, of course, and made their presence known by frequent artillery and mortar fire but otherwise stayed out of sight and concealed.

Having a flooded river between the two combatants did much to ratchet down the level of tension for everyone, even if precautions against small, dislocated bands of Germans remained a threat. Still, there was a relaxation of vigilance.

A BANG UP GOOD JOB.

As was always the case under circumstances like this, men were apt to go exploring if they had a few hours to themselves. Some took the opportunity to inspect German defense fortifications up close. Ted Simpson seems to have wandered off the beaten path one day and found himself alone in a solemn and strangely peaceful setting. What he saw and did there was still a vivid memory five decades later when he recorded it in writing. "I remember one morning inspecting a knot of German corpses ripening in the sun along a hillside. One soldier with a very large hole in his head was facing upward toward me with his arms stretched outward from his side. His uniform was torn open with his wallet edging out of the pocket. Who could resist? Gingerly, I pulled it out, mindful of booby traps. There were the usual cards and notes. Also was a lovely small photo of his pleasant wife and three pre-teen boys and girls smiling upward toward me. Had I been older and sensitive enough at the time, I would have copied his name and address, taken the photos and returned them to his wife with a brief and kind-hearted letter, skipping the gore, but informing her gently of our meeting. Had I done this, she would at least have known what had happened, where he was and when I wrote. Is it better to know? I'll always wonder. But I don't think so."

Most men were not so given to contemplation as Simpson was. Bob Storms, by comparison, had not lost his talent for escapades which danced just beyond the edge of military discipline whenever circumstances allowed, and this business of waiting along the Roer River was just right for mischief of the Storms variety. "After things got kinda quiet, we was way out from the battery up near the edge of a woods standing guard by ourselves," he recalled later, succumbing to his weakness for storytelling. "I think there was five of us altogether on the machinegun. I used to let two men go at a time, goof off or go where ever they want to go. So Arthur Brodelle and I, we went out one day. Man, there was snow up to your neck. We went down the road and we seen a little tavern. Some woman and her daughter was running it. We had a couple, two, three beers and took off. Then we heard a vehicle coming up the road. We ducked in the snow bank so they wouldn't see us. It was one of our halftracks. It stopped there at the tavern and three guys went in. I said to Brodelle, 'Hey, he didn't take the rotor out.' See, you didn't have no keys in that truck. All you got is a throw switch on all them trucks. If you take the rotor out, then nobody can steal it."

Brodelle probably recognized another one of Storms' brilliant capers being hatched, but didn't let on. He simply said, "So what."

It was already too late. Storms told his buddy, "I'm going back and see what that is."

"So I walked back there," he continued. "It was a halftrack and it had a turret on it. It had four fifties and a 37mm anti tank gun in the middle. It was from the anti-aircraft outfit for shooting down planes. I looked over in there in the tavern and those guys were busy kidding with the woman and girl."

Nudging Brodelle in the ribs, Storms said, "Oh boy, this is for us!"

Brodelle knew better. The vehicle was one of the half-track mounted anti-aircraft guns of the 80th Anti-Aircraft Battalion, several of which were a part of the 508th Regimental Combat Team. "Stormsy, let's get out of here," Brodelle advised.
Like a runaway train, Storms was carried away by the opportunity and answered, "No, no, no, I'll bet this will start!"

"So I throwed the switch and seen the ampmeter jump. I told Brodelle, 'Get in. If you don't I'm gonna leave you.'"

Even as he climbed in, Brodelle protested, "We're gonna get in trouble."

418

BATTERY!

"The hell with it, we're taking her," declared Storms. He was overcome with the joy of unauthorized acquisition, laughing as they drove off. Looking behind them Brodelle and Storms saw the three GIs burst out of the tavern, running after them, trying in vain to recover their stolen half-track.

"We took it up there where my machinegun was. Boy, I didn't have no trouble for a week and a half getting anybody to stand guard, I'll tell you that. Everybody wanted to stand guard. Even the officers come up and looked it over. Well the word got around that it was there. Finally the Captain send word that they were coming to pick it up. He told them anti-aircraft guys that we just found it along side of the road. He told them we didn't know where it come from. That's how he passed it off. We got away with it. Anyway, I didn't ask too many questions, I was just glad to see them go without getting in trouble. But boy, we had some fun while it was there," concluded Storms with satisfaction.

Other men in the outfit were having fun too. For those who weren't city-bred, hunting for fresh game was one pastime, especially given the forested surroundings, an abundance of deer in the area, and the fact that everyone was armed to the teeth. Robert Rappi and Carl Salminen both tried hunting deer with their carbines and, both found the weapon inadequate. Salminen fired nine times at one deer and gave up, but Robert Dickson and some friends took a more heavy handed approach. "When we were in Hurtgen Forest we were trying to get anything fresh to eat that we could get," he said. "We got a thirty caliber machinegun, set it on a jeep and went deer hunting and we killed a deer too. Of course that deer was easy to kill. We cut loose with that jeep running and cut him down with that 30 caliber machinegun. Brought it in and had the cook cook it, so we had fresh meat while we were there."

Sebring went hunting as well - in his case with an M-1 rifle picked up off

the battlefield, and bagged a different kind of trophy. "A bullet went into the differential on Captain Sartain's jeep. Locked the gears up in the rear end. That ended the deer hunting," he admitted.

When asked, Sartain remembered the incident and added his perspective by saying, "Yeah man, there was a lot of deer around there, but I didn't like them deer hunting right on our front yard. See, these deer would run over in our direction and these crazy bas-

Aggressive Gun Crew: Ted Covais captioned this photograph of one of Able Battery's howitzers "Aggressive Gun Crew!" in his album. The view was taken sometime during the late winter of 1945, in the vicinity of the Siegfried Line. Covais collection.

tards were still shooting. It was dangerous, you know? I thought, we gotta put an end to that, that's foolish, so I wound up making them quit shooting deer."

Not all supplements to army rations were wild game. Since the region along the Roer River was newly occupied, it was sometimes possible to come across hogs or even cattle. Duel Elmore remembered what happened when livestock like this was brought into proximity with the battery. "We butchered some animals," he recalled. "There was three or four of us who knew how to do it. Country boys, they knew how to do it. I did a hog and then some more boys butchered a beef. They had it killed and hung, and quartered in 15 minutes."

Elmore may have been remembering a particular beef which played an essential role in one of Sartain's favorite wartime memories from this period. "I was going down the road with Sosa," he said. "I looked over to the right and there was this nice little steer tied up to a tree. I guess the steer weighed probably about four hundred pounds. Nice looking little steer. Young steer. So I radioed the battery and they sent somebody over to get it. They tied a rope around it and led it back. They slaughtered it. OK. So my friend Armand Butler from the 320th, I called him the next morning and said, 'Butler, what are y'all doing? Why don't you come on over and have supper with us tonight.'

So he showed up and said, 'You know, the damnedest thing happened to me the other day. I was going along the road when there was this steer. My driver and I were able to catch it and we tied that damn thing up to a tree. I hadn't been gone an hour and a half and when we came back for it somebody stole my damn steer!' Just about that time the guy walked up to us from the kitchen and he said to Butler, 'Sir, how would you like your steak?'"

On the 19th of February, word was received that the 82nd's mission was finished and that it was time for the division to be sent back to France. In accordance with the order the guys in the 319th were told to be sure they recovered all salvageable mate-

Members of "A" Battery enroute from Aachen, Germany, to Camp Suippes, France, about the 22nd of February, 1945, bringing an end to the Bulge/Siegfried Line fighting. Covais stands at right with hands on knees. Behind him is Frank Tobin and to his right stands Sgt. René Picher. Covais collection.

rial before leaving their positions. They were also directed to expend all surplus stores of ammunition. Consequently, the battalion fired over 1,300 rounds on that day, at nothing much in particular. Four extra trucks were secured and, at 14:00 hours the outfit pulled away from its Brandenburg emplacements.

The arrangement was for the battalion to proceed to Aachen, Germany, the first major city to be taken by the Allies. Once there, about one third of the outfit would continue by motor convoy back to Camp Suippes. The rest of the outfit was to board freight cars and make the trip by rail.

Having been assigned to the motor convoy, Lieutenant Cook placed a request with Colonel Todd to make a side trip to locate his brother Spencer's grave in Holland. "That's where my brother got killed," Cook later explained. "He was in the Canadian army. He was too old to get in the air force in the American army, they wouldn't let him in, so he went to Canada and joined the air corps up there. He was five years older than me. We were pretty close though. He went to England and flew big bombers over Germany until the night he got shot down over this little town in Holland. I took my section in the jeep, we went up into Holland and found a man that used to live in the United States. He was the only one who could speak English. He took us all around and showed us where my brother was buried and where the plane landed. The plane come right over his house and like to hit it. The Germans left the crew, they left them dead there, but the town people took them to the cemetery and buried them in a row. He was buried with two or three Germans. After a while they moved him to another place, to a Canadian burial ground, but he's still there."

Once the motor convoy was underway, the rest of the outfit was packed into boxcars and left the Aachen train station at 1730. Altogether it would be a 36 hour journey, with numerous unexplained stops along the way. Though the freight cars were cold and not very comfortable, the knowledge that each mile carried them further from the front lines went a long way toward compensating for any lack of creature comforts. In the dim light of Coleman stoves the guys slept, played cards, smoked cigarettes, and congratulated themselves at having survived another campaign. Orin Miller was lucky enough to be posted as a guard in the car loaded with the men's barracks bags. "That was a good trip," he recalled. "I just climbed up on the barracks bags and went to sleep. I enjoyed that trip very much."

Once the train came to a stop at Reims, everybody piled out. It was not yet daylight, actually 0430. Standing around in the chilly pre-dawn air, rubbing their eyes, yawning, getting their bearings and waiting for trucks which would bring them to Camp Suippes, they became very aware of how clean all the rear echelon personnel looked in contrast to themselves. Off to one side of the platform was a Red Cross refreshment stand with hot coffee, doughnuts, and other snacks to welcome the men back after over two months of winter combat. Clusters of men wandered over, then came back with paper cups of coffee and a surly disposition. "Hell, we thought it would be free after all the fighting we'd been through," complained Sebring.

The army's official ending to the Battle of the Bulge is given as January 25th – with all other operations after that date along the Siegfried Line and Roer River being regarded as separate actions. But the GIs in "A" Battery never made this distinction. For them it was all just "The Bulge."

When Ted Simpson wrote down his wartime experiences in the 1990s, he stated, "Fifty years later I still do not care much for snow, frozen woods, or unexplained mounds on the frosted white ground." His words summed up the lasting impression which the

A BANG UP GOOD JOB.

Battle of the Bulge had on all who were a part of it. While participation in the D-Day invasion is so often described in terms which suggest exhilaration mixed with pride at being part of something so magnificent and daring, memories of the Bulge are invariably expressed as a frozen crucible, a passage which tested each man's endurance and left its imprint deep within the individual. The men emerged from it more hardened than from any previous campaign. Conversations with those who were there leave one with the impression that much is left unsaid, perhaps because words are inadequate, perhaps because such memories are best left alone.

In all, over 800,000 American troops were engaged during the battle. Approximately 75,000 became casualties, of whom about 20,000 were killed. Over 20,000 were accounted for as captured or missing. It was the largest land battle fought by the United States Army during World War Two.

Estimates of German casualties in the failed Wacht Am Rhein offensive range from 60,000 to over 100,000, with another 100,000 taken prisoner. The German gamble to drive a wedge between the western Allies and sue for peace had failed. Instead they had suffered an enormous loss of life and materiel. Never again would they be able to field such a large army or mount offensive operations on any significant scale.

Some of Mahlon Sebring's buddies: Asa Morris of Griffin, Georgia, Orin Miller of Massena, New York, James Thousand, of Ithaca, New York, and Harry Kerr, of Anderson, Indiana. Sebring collection.

BATTERY!

Part 27: "He bawled like a baby."

Back again at Camp Suippes, the tired soldiers of the 319th were quartered in the very same barracks they had left the previous December, two and a half months before, in such haste. It seemed like a long time, yet not long enough for all that had happened since.

After a brief opportunity to take a hot shower and a hot meal, followed by some sleep, the entire enlisted cadre was loaded onto trucks and dumped off in Paris. Most men remembered it as a 48 or 72 hour pass. All agreed it was brief, but as one battalion man explained the time could be stretched out if one stayed up all day and all night.

Paris was indeed quite different than London. GIs immediately noticed the wider avenues, the ever-present bicycles, and the odor of perfume. While many of the men visited the usual Parisian landmarks: the Eiffel Tower, Napoleon's Tomb, the Arch de Triumph, And the Louvre, not surprisingly, much of the entertainment involved large amounts of alcohol and sometimes feminine company of easy virtue.

In any event, a few days later trucks returned to Suippes carrying the same guys they'd brought, restored if not altogether rested. Military routine was reinstated, replacements appeared, and a dozen or more men in "A" Battery volunteered to attend jump school.

There were also vacancies created in the battalion as more men were granted detached service in the United States. In Able Battery this meant significant changes among the senior NCO staff when 1st Sergeant Jesse Johnson received orders for stateside service. Staff Sergeant Rene Picher, the battery's chief of sections since Bob McArthur received his field promotion during Normandy, was advanced to fill Johnson's post as first sergeant.

"Oh yeah," remarked Sartain later of the change, "Picher was a good guy. He was slight, he was an itty bitty guy, he didn't weigh 130 pounds, but he commanded everything he was around, I'll tell you that."

Jesse Johnson had been with the battery from the beginning at Camp Claiborne, Louisiana, when the 319th was reactivated in early 1942 and months before anyone had ever heard of paratroopers or gliders.

Ted Simpson could have been speaking for anyone when he said of Johnson, "I remember him as first sergeant of all first sergeants. He was strictly a pro, very much a pro soldier. Not with a strong personality but a man who was not anything but duty driven. Straight arrow. Yes sir, no sir, three bags full sir."

As battery commander, Sartain and his "Top Sergeant" inevitably worked in close consort managing battery business. "Jesse Johnson handled many details that were never brought to my attention. He gave me a lot of suggestions but never until I asked for them. He was an old line regular army guy and a very good 1st sergeant," Sartain remembered later with respect.

Johnson meted out punishments and kept the whole battery under tight control. "He wouldn't take any stuff off of anybody," commented the Battery's Executive Officer, Marvin Ragland. "The story goes that he floored some guy who got out of line. That straightened him out in a hurry. I don't think anybody seen it, cause I don't think you're supposed to do that."

Silas Hogg was one who'd served under Johnson from the start. He was the object of his strict discipline on numerous occasions, but he also recalled the 1st Sergeant being both the dispenser and recipient of military justice. According to Hogg, Johnson was involved in a lively crap game at Camp Claiborne when Colonel Bertsch discovered the gamblers. "There was about fifteen of us in a big game," Hogg recalled. "And the Colonel walked in and there we were. He busted Johnson down. He got busted flat assed to a private, in front of everybody! The Colonel busted him, but he didn't take his stripes. He didn't change his barrack, he didn't change anything, he just changed his money. Just money. He told him, 'Alright Sergeant, you are now a private, but you still carry on your duties as a first sergeant.' And that's exactly what he was. Then every month he got one rank higher until he was back at 1st sergeant's pay again. That's the way it was. Nobody questioned it."

Tough as he was, when the day came for Johnson to leave, the departure was surprisingly difficult for him. He'd always been six feet, two inches of unbending military authority. Respected by all and feared by many in "A" Battery. As the Top Sergeant came to the "A" Battery barracks to say his farewells, a cluster of men gathered around him, especially the old crew, many of whom now held sergeant and corporal rank themselves. Johnson said, "I'm going back but I hate to leave you. I hate to leave you guys! I hate to leave you but I got to go." Then, before he turned away they saw something they'd never seen before. Johnson's eyes welled up with tears, then he broke down and the emotion flowed freely.

"He bawled like a baby," remembered Rappi, who was among those saying goodbye. "He'd been in the army quite a while, just got married before we left the states and had a child that he'd never seen."

Another man who got orders sending him home was Bob Miller, Manning's, and later Sartain's radio operator. A native of Chicago, word was quickly received back at the battery that Bob Miller was killed in an automobile accident just days after returning to the Windy city. "You know, I've always regretted that I never put him in for a Bronze Star. Miller went with me everywhere I went and he deserved it, he really did, but I never thought to put his name in. Now I wish I had," commented Sartain with some sadness.

Sosa would have agreed. "He was a pretty good man, that Robert," Sosa said later. "He got hit twice. I heard that he got killed in an automobile accident. I felt bad about that. After going through all that crap, then he comes home and gets killed in a car accident."

Captain Manning, meanwhile, had arrived at New York City after more than a week's voyage on the Atlantic. As soon as he could get clear of army red-tape, Manning made his way to Grand Central Station, where he bought a ticket on the Erie line home and telephoned his wife. He hadn't heard Marge's voice since before leaving for North Africa. Hurriedly, Manning told her she could expect him in a few hours. It all seemed like a dream.

Since leaving Middletown, New York, three and a half years before, Manning had accumulated more baggage than he could carry alone. "I found it necessary to carry some bags some distance - put them down - go back for the rest and portage them on ahead - go back – etc," Manning later wrote. "I finally got on the Erie train at Hoboken for the ride home. It seemed so tranquil and welcoming to ride up through Tuxedo, Monroe, Chester, and Goshen. Finally I arrived in Middletown to find that the station was no longer in use. I was dropped off in the middle of the rail yard. Marge was there. Home and love at last!"

Some of the men who'd been taken off the line during the Bulge with frozen feet returned to the outfit. Others, like Casimir Sobon, would remain in the hospital for weeks or months longer. Meanwhile, Lieutenant Bob McArthur, formerly Able Battery's Chief of Sections, and who'd been so grievously wounded in Holland was still in the midst of a long, long recovery. In one letter home he expressed gratitude for the care being given by the hospital staff. "The American people should really get down on their knees and thank God for the medical corps," he wrote. "This medical corps can do anything. You can have a nose or ear shot away and they'll make you a new one. I've seen some men come in here shot all to pieces and they make brand new men out of them."

Most of the time hospital life was uneventful for McArthur and the other men in his ward. Occasionally there was some amusement, as when Ole Miss, McArthur's alma mater, upset Mississippi State. "There is a boy here in the ward that went to Ole Miss when I was there. There is also a State man here too and when Ole Miss beat State we like to have run him out of this ward. You know State was supposed to have beat Ole Miss," he wrote to his mother.

Nevertheless, McArthur could hardly wait to get back to Mississippi. On March 6th, 1945, he told his mother, "Tell Grandmother that it won't be too long until she can cook me that ham and eggs and biscuits for breakfast." His yearning to get back home was so strong that McArthur made his feelings known to one of the higher ranking officers one day. According to McArthur, "A Major came in the ward a few days ago and gave me a 'Purple Heart' medal. I told him that he could have it back. All that I wanted was for my arm to get well. I told him that as far as I was concerned, he could take all of my ribbons, medals, battle stars and everything else if he would just let me go home, but I know there is no chance."

With the outfit back at Suippes, men started packaging up the souvenirs they brought back with them from Belgium and Germany for shipment home. However, these items were not restricted to German helmets, pistols, or other military trophies. The fact was that a large amount of what could only be described as stolen civilian property was also among the goods being brought back. Indeed, the scale and extent of looting by Allied soldiers in Europe during the war may have been more serious than has been generally acknowledged. When Carl Salminen said, "You think that the Germans were confiscating stuff from people's homes, Americans done that stuff too," he was speaking to what had evolved into a serious embarrassment for the military authorities by the end of the war.

Theft of non-military goods from civilians, whether allied or enemy, was in violation of the conventions of war. That soldiers would sometimes loot or commit other crimes against civilians and their property is not a surprise. It has been a part of warfare since the beginning of time, but what causes altogether decent young men to plunder? The social psychology of war posits that, out of psychological necessity arising from the stress of killing, enemy combatants and, by extension, civilians, become progressively more dehumanized. This mental defense takes place so that violence can be perpetrated with minimal distress. The anarchic and chaotic setting of the battlefield further serves to erode normal social inhibitions against conduct which would otherwise be thought immoral or at least improper under other circumstances. Moreover, exposure to trauma and violence has a demoralizing influence on soldier and civilian alike, with the axiomatic result that the soldier repeatedly brutalized by combat becomes more apt to vent his experiences through actions he might previously have considered beneath him. Sartain's observation on these phenomena was that, "The average GI was prone to loot. I saw it as a breech of military discipline and of human nature as well, but there was a natural tendency to loot."

Even though it is difficult to quantify, the overall impression gained from interviews and battalion records suggests that looting gained acceptance and became more widespread with each passing campaign. Oddly, this took place despite the fact that the most easily accessed avenues of depersonalization of the enemy, such as race, religion, or even class differences, were largely absent in the European theater. After all, the French, Dutch, and Belgians were allies and a very large proportion of the GIs were themselves of either Italian or German extraction.

Although the first prohibitions against looting seen in battalion records do not appear until the later part of the campaign in Holland, members of the 319th recalled ransacking the homes of Italian fascists in Naples, evidently to the delight of local mobs. "I think they were looting from Normandy on," commented Sartain. "Some guys would go into a house in France and send the silverware home. If I could figure out who it was I'd make them take it back. We had to put an end to it because these people were supposed to be on our side." Theft in Holland ranged from the ubiquitous and inconsequential pair of wooden shoes to the legendary bank heist described in Part 21 of this book, and was probably made easier by the fact that the unit's return to its base camp was by land, not by sea.

By the time of the winter fighting during 1944-45, the taste for plunder seems to have grown in direct proportion to the war weariness of the men. Instead of calling themselves liberators, a joke began circulating in the outfit that they had become "looterators." Sartain's commentary suggests that there was also a growing degree of apathy on the part of the officers. "We'd take a house to billet and these characters would strip the house, or houses that were vacated. I mean, we used houses where everything was just left, like the people were gone to church, you know? If they occupied an empty house it was totally looted. I couldn't do anything about it. I tried to put an end to all this looting, but they'd hide it, wrap it up and send it home."

If battalion records are an accurate indicator, looting of homes appears to have been more pervasive in Belgium than Holland, and to have continued with enthusiasm once the German border was crossed. Nor does it seem that most soldiers who helped themselves to plunder made much distinction between Belgian and German property. Ed Ryan stated without apology that he took what he wanted and that nationality made no difference to him. Sartain thought men who looted didn't make any distinction between friend or foe because they were not primarily motivated by revenge. "One time when we were in Belgium the incoming artillery got so bad we thought the world was coming to an end," recounted Sosa of one example which may have been typical. "We were in this house and got down in the cellar. When the firing was all quieted I heard this clock start chiming. I forget what time it was. I said, 'God damn it, this baby's going home with me!' So I went up there and got it and carried it out of there. You better believe it. That's all I wanted. It's a pendulum clock. It sits on the mantle piece. I've still got it and it still works."

Huddled in the cellar during the bombardment, Sosa felt like his world was coming to an end. He felt certain that his time was up, but when the barrage lifted the chiming clock signaled that he'd been given a reprieve and maybe his lifespan wasn't over after all. That clock may have represented this idea, though he might not have been consciously aware of it or articulated it in those terms at the time. Whatever the reason, vengeance does not seem to have been foremost among his motivations.

When asked if his war experiences taught him anything profound, Sosa's retort was, "It's hard to learn any good lessons when you're getting shit on and shot at! Did you hear what I said? Well, that's the way it is, getting shit on or shot at."

To be sure, Sosa was right. Participation in war was not edifying but instead degrading. Living in often filthy and always unhygienic conditions for weeks or months, the constant fear and fatigue of combat, the specter of death and destruction all around, and the sight of innocent civilians driven to acts of debasement, all converged to erode ideals and gave birth to profound, disillusioned cynicism. Ted Covais entered the service as a bright-eyed 19 year old whom neither smoked, drank, nor swore. "I would stand up if I heard the national anthem on the radio," he said of those days. By the winter of 1945 much had changed. This transformation from idealistic lad to jaded veteran is illustrated by his answer when he was asked about his participation in looting. Covais confessed, "Initially, no, I didn't take things, but I did in the Battle of the Bulge, I did manage to get some silverware and other things out of this house. I found out that this lady's husband was an SS Offizier. I think I found that camera there and I acquired it, confiscated it, however you want to put it. I figured he had no right to own it, and I had the right to own it. That's when I got the silverware, German silverware. Heavy stuff that we had for years. The spoons were enormous, the knives were big. I confiscated it. I did some looting maybe, you might consider it that. It was a stupid thing to do. It was not proper and I don't feel right in my spirit about it."

Covais talked casually about the camera for a few minutes more. It was a 120mm Voigtlander viewfinder with a leather case and tripod. Then he felt compelled to return to the subject of looting. "You know when you want something you're not thinking rationally," he explained. "When you want something you don't care how other people feel. I felt more like, you robbed all these people of their masterpieces, of museum pieces, paintings and artwork and statuary and all that. Millions! I figured they deserved not to have it. I felt I had the right, maybe not morally, but I had the right to do it. I wanted to show them who's the real master. I'm the master. Now I'm sorry about all this, all these things."

The volume of unauthorized souvenirs being presented for shipment at Suippes was large enough to attract Sartain's attention. "There were some things I tried to put a halt to about shipping home," he said. "I issued an order that I, or one of the officers, had to inspect and initial every package going home. We alerted the mail clerk and told him they had to bring the package to me unwrapped so it could be OKed. Then the guy would supposedly mail them." Nonetheless, most officers were, if not themselves complicit, at least willing to turn a blind eye toward plundered civilian property. It could never be returned to its rightful owner anyway.

While the rest of the outfit had been so eager to get to Paris, Sartain's desire to go there was nil, remembering that the last time he'd been to that city it was interrupted by the German offensive in the Ardennes. "No way I was going back there!" he recalled. Instead, the Captain stayed at Suippes, taking care of battery business and planning to take his leave when the outfit got back.

As it turned out, it was almost mid-March before Sartain's chance came up. This time his strategy was to get as far from the seat of the war as possible, as quickly as possible. In company with Captain Bourgeois, Sartain gave his destination as the far flung New Hebrides islands, off the coast of Northern Scotland.

HE BAWLED LIKE A BABY.

When the day came, the Captains got into army trucks which carried them to the English Channel, where they took a transport over the water. They were together with several other officers from division artillery. As Sartain remembered, "There was me and Wilson Bourgeois from the 319th. Then there was Captain Kneckt from the 320th, and Paul Brock from Pensacola, and some guy named Martin from the 320th too.

Once in England, the party boarded a train to London where they would transfer to another continuing on to Scotland. "We were supposed to change trains in London," Sartain recalled, "but we went into a pub to wait and somehow we missed the train. We were supposed to be going off the coast of Glasgow but we didn't make it. Of course, your leave didn't start until you got to where you were going, so we checked into the Strand Palace Hotel instead. The Red Cross got our bags back and we stayed in London for I don't know how many days, a couple of weeks anyway."

The Strand Palace Hotel, while not quite on a par with the Savoy located across the street, was still a London landmark. In decades past its signature brown and gold trimmed awnings and staff uniforms were elegant. By 1945 though, six years of wartime economy were putting a tarnish to the old brilliance. Just the same, it was still one of London's best hotels when the American artillery officers checked in.

While the Captains and Lieutenants were all apparently chums, the fact was that one of them was fast growing tiresome to the rest. Sartain later explained the situation. "There were five of us, you know," he confided, "but Martin was from Texas, he was a real Texas A and M man, and you know they've got a real attitude. He was just shooting his mouth off like most guys from A and M do. He was obnoxious. He was a braggart about his sexual exploits and he just wouldn't shut up about how he was gonna find him some female company. That bastard was all hat and no cattle. So we said, 'Well, were gonna fix him up, we're gonna brand him. We're gonna brand him!' So we told the hotel staff that he was a Chaplain, a Methodist minister or whatever. We said he took his cross off so he could find him a date, get him a little bit of you know what. We told the staff they'd need to watch out for him. Well, that frustrated any of his attempts to make contact with any females there." Sartain slapped his knee, laughed and added, "yeah man, he couldn't understand why he was having so much trouble. I mean, there wasn't a woman in that hotel who would say a word to him if he begged them. We got tired of hearing about his conquests and that was the reason we put the quietus on his fun."

The reality is that there was no shortage of Lieutenant Martin's sort of "fun" in wartime London – particularly if one was willing to pay for it. With millions of soldiers in England at any given point in time, several hundreds of thousands of whom were within easy access to the city; London became a Mecca for prostitutes, especially given the relatively lax British laws pertaining to sex trade workers. In fact, recently released Scotland Yard archives reveal that the issue was of grave concern to army officials. US Army Headquarters in London pressured the British government to pass measures which would make the jailing of so-called "Piccadilly Commandos" easier. One army legal consultant was quoted as complaining that, "There are far too many prostitutes, their behavior is far too blatant, and the impression created on the American troops and their 'mommas' at home is bad."

It was, of course, a two way street. Martin's intention to exercise his libido to the fullest could have been more typical than exceptional. In the meeting between American and British authorities, London metropolitan police rejoined that prostitute seeking GIs, "many of them worse for drink and quarrelsome until the early hours of the morning" greatly aggravated the situation. Regardless of responsibility, the atmosphere created, particularly at locations like Piccadilly Circus and Coventry Street, was a real public nuisance.

Sartain himself remembered being pestered one afternoon as he left the Strand to do a little sightseeing with Captains Knecht and Bourgeois. "I'll never forget when we were in London," he said. "Wilson Bourgeois and I were standing by the hotel, which was just two blocks from Trafalgar square. So he said, 'Let's walk down and see what's going on.' Well, on the way we must have been propositioned by three or four prostitutes. Yeah, yeah, right outside of the Strand Palace Hotel, right outside of the Savoy. Bourgeois said to the first one, 'How much?' She said, 'Two pounds.' Well that would be about eight dollars. Next one propositioned us, she said four pounds. Then the next one that propositioned us, she said eight pounds. So Bourgeois pulled his billfold out and pulled off about two pounds and gave it to her. She said, 'What's this for?' He said, 'That's for talking to me.' A pound note was worth four dollars and three cents."

At Trafalgar Square the trio admired the heroic monument to Lord Nelson and got acquainted with a delightful pair of Canadian Red Cross girls. "They really had

a routine," remarked Sartain of the meeting. "It was a very strictly enforced rule that the Canadian Red Cross girls had. They could never go anywhere alone. Regardless of what they decided to do they had to have a companion. Which was good advice." The girls walked about the square with the airborne officers, at one point stopping to feed the pigeons while Bourgeois snapped a photo to capture the moment.

There were other sights in London for the GI tourist. Covent Garden was the location of a large dance hall which booked some of the best Big Bands that side of the Atlantic. Piccadilly Circus, while famous for street walkers, also featured the Eagle club, an establishment run by the USO. The Eagle was intended to cater to homesick GIs by replicating an American Diner. As such it offered a menu of hamburgers, hot dogs, french fries, milk shakes, and Coca Cola, all complete with a jukebox.

Mostly the glider officers spent their time at the

Captain Sartain and Captain Knecht of the 320th Glider field Artillery, while on furlough in London, March, 1945. Sartain's caption to this photo read: "Feeding pidgeons at Trafalgar Square. Don't know how those girls got mixed up in it!" Sartain later explained that they were Canadian Red Cross nurses. Sartain collection.

Strand. There was really little reason to leave. After all, a sumptuous restaurant, a bar of imposing proportions, a constant stream of colorful, often attractive guests, and any number of social functions made it a complete world of entertainment in itself. As with any establishment of this sort, the Strand hosted wedding receptions. When they noticed the wedding of a British officer getting under way the airborne officers were not above crashing the gate. "There was a big crowd of people going in so we just followed in with them," Sartain said. The American artillery officers had a little food, a drink or two, and cut in on dances with invited guests. As the newlyweds shook hands in the receiving line, Sartain invented a story that they were old chums of her husband from the Sicilian campaign. "Oh yeah, we put it on right. We had a good time and I still don't know who the groom was."

In the Strand's restaurant the five officers established themselves at a favorite table which they occupied every evening until well after midnight, filling the seats with new friends. "After the war somebody handed my daddy fifty dollars he said I gave to him at the Strand. I didn't remember lending anybody fifty dollars but I guess I must have," admitted Sartain.

In the end the party was over. It was check-out time at the Strand for Sartain, Bourgeois, Knecht, Brock, and the hapless Martin. "The final bill came to something like 800 pounds sterling, or about $3,300," remembered Sartain. "So we called a meeting, everyone had to cough up about $900. We had to go to the bank and cash checks just to get out of the hotel." As they emerged on to the street with their bags the officers heard the roar of hundreds of aircraft. Looking up, they saw the flotilla of Operation Varsity, the parachute drop on the Ruhr and the last airborne operation of the war passing overhead.

While Captain Sartain was in London, back at the battery Kenneth Smith had an unexpected visitor. It was his brother Kyle, who'd been in a hospital in England since being wounded near Hill 400 the previous February.

"They were getting ready to send me to the repo depot and I didn't want to do that," explained Kyle, "so next morning I went AWOL. I knew where Kenneth was at; I knew where the 82nd was at. I went out to the airfield and I asked these pilots, 'I want to go to Rheims. Are any of you guys going to Rheims, France?' This one guy said, 'Well just about all these guys are gonna be going in the morning with equipment.' I said, 'Can I get on the plane?' He told me, 'All you have to do is climb on there and you're in.'" Kyle Smith's determination to stay away from a replacement depot was not unusual. It was the bonds between buddies who'd trained and fought together that made the experience of war bearable, and those sent to "repo depots" after recovering in hospitals were routinely assigned to any outfit which needed replacements, regardless of the men's unit of origin.

Because Kyle had gone AWOL just days before the scheduled launch of Operation Varsity, hitching a ride to the airborne encampments around Rheims was easy. "I found the 82nd and I knew where I was going. Found Kenneth and we talked and had another reunion for a while," recalled Kyle, who'd learned that his regiment was scheduled to go in with the Varsity invasion force. He knew it was important that he get back to his outfit if serious consequences of his improvised furlough were to be avoided. "I said, Kenneth, I don't know where my outfit's at. Let's go up to your Captain and see where my outfit's at. So we went on down to the Captain's office and told him the situation."

At battery headquarters, the two lanky Smith brothers probably received an audience with Lieutenant Ragland, who asked Kyle, "Have you got your orders?"

"No," answered Kyle, "I left them back there where I was when I went AWOL."

Ragland said, "You don't have no orders?" realizing suddenly that he had a serious situation standing before him he turned to the other Smith brother and ordered, "Kenneth, you go down to the motor pool, get a jeep and get his ass out of here! We don't want nothing to do with him!"

"So that's what Kenneth done, he drove me down town someplace. He let me out and we said goodbye," Kyle recounted. Kenneth's brother eventually made his way back to the 517th, arriving just as the outfit was formed up and moving out.

During this period at Camp Suippes the battalion's men were ordered to report to the supply sergeant and be measured for new service uniforms. A short time later each man turned in his Class "A" Blouse and received a much shorter jacket in return.

The new uniform was a loose fitting, hip length jacket of dark olive drab wool, inspired by the British battle-dress jacket in use since 1940. GIs had first seen these jackets being worn by British soldiers in North Africa, then Italy, and liked the cut. By the fall of 1943, during the occupation of Naples, men in the 319th, and no doubt other units as well, were having their Class "A" service tunics shortened into a kind of imitation American battle dress of their own. At about that same time, army air force personnel in England were lobbying for the development and issue of a similar uniform. Then, when Commander-in-Chief Eisenhower was seen sporting a custom tailored version himself, the momentum to devise a jacket of this style for general issue was all the more appealing.

Introduction of the "Jacket, Wool, OD, M1944" coincided with the issue of the new olive green combat uniform of 1943. As it was originally envisioned, the "Ike Jacket," as it came to be known, would be used in accord with the quartermaster's new layering principle. The jacket was intended as a field uniform, to be worn in combat conditions. It was sized large to accommodate a wool sweater underneath in colder weather and was supposed to be worn under the m1943 Field jacket. In fact, this was never done and today veterans find it difficult to believe that the Eisenhower jacket was ever expected to be utilized in this manner.

The first issues of the Ike Jacket, actually manufactured in England, were made in the late Fall of 1944, but it was not until the 82nd Airborne was finally given a respite from front line duty in early spring, 1945, that there was an opportunity to issue the Eisenhower style to the 319th. And what happened to the men's old service blouses? There is a possibility that they were altered to an Eisenhower-like jacket at about the same time. At least one man interviewed for this book held a vivid memory of this. According to Mahlon Sebring, "Originally we was issued what was called a blouse. That was your Class "A" jacket, which was fingertip length. We turned them in to the orderly room and I don't know where in the hell they took them to, but I don't think we were without them for a week and they were back. They cut them down to Eisenhower jackets. Yeah, mine's all been cut down. Some guys got new ones, I guess, but very few of us, most guys got cut down. It was cut down from a Class "A". I don't know who done it."

Sebring's recollection notwithstanding, no other evidence has surfaced to corroborate his statement that this was done in any organized, systematic fashion throughout the 319th, or even "A" Battery. Just the same, examples of uniforms altered in this way do exist. For example, in addition to his Ike Jacket, John Girardin still had his unaltered

He Bawled Like a Baby.

Class "A" tunic when he was sent home in December, 1945. At Fort McCoy, Wisconsin, he did have it shortened to the Eisenhower style before proceeding home to Rockford, but this was months afterward and a continent away. Moreover, numerous photographs show the new pattern Ike Jacket in use from March, 1945, onward, but not shortened Class "A"'s.

Whatever the case, issue of new uniforms to the entire battalion set off a flurry of activity attaching glider wings, ribbon bars, and unit citations with great precision. There was a scramble for needles and thread as chevrons, overseas bars, and division patches were sewn on. Each man did his best, "Unless you've got a girlfriend or you can talk to a French woman," Sebring interjected during one conversation.

Some men in Able Battery, like Duel Elmore, made a small business at this. He later explained it in some detail. "I got into the tailor business, pressing pants and did some sewing, you know, buttons, all this and that. You'd get fifteen, twenty-five or fifty cents, maybe. Didn't have a machine. Had an iron and an ironing board but that was it. I used parachute thread most of the time to sew the patches on with. You get those parachutes, you know, they got strings with nylon and then on the inside, there's silk thread. You take that outside off and inside you can get the thread out of it and it sews real nice."

The parachute shroud lines which Elmore referred to had other uses as well. Some men braided the lines into trouser belts, often with a mixture of white and olive worked together to create a smart pattern.

Best buddies Robert Dickson and Carl Salminen in their new "Ike" jackets, Lubtheem, Germany, May, 1945. Courtesy Robert Dickson.

Other men began using the shroud lines as laces for their jump boots. There were a variety of lacing patterns, each of which carried a certain esoteric élan. It was all another way of calling attention to an article of uniform which the guys knew set them apart from the average dog-face, the average GI. As Covais later put it, "We were proud of wearing the boots because that's the symbol of the airborne, although we were Gliders we were Airborne anyway."

Bob Storms went into detail about the cult of the jump boot when he said, "Sometimes you'd sit by the hour polishing them up, and then smear them up and polish them again. You'd get layers of it on there. Just shine like a mirror. We spent more time polishing our boots than anything else. Our boots used to be like glass. That was one thing we were really proud of. You could see us coming a mile away with them boots. Boy, we went to town. That was our pride and joy."

Between polished jump boots with parachute laces, belts made of braided shroud lines, their glider wings, unit citation, and the insignia of the vaunted 82nd Airborne Division, the guys in the 319th cut a dashing figure in their uniforms, and knew it.

Corporal Bob "Stormsie" Storms served in Sgt. Marshall's Machinegun Section throughout the war. He claims to have held the rank of "Acting Sergeant" during his entire time overseas. Covais collection.

Ted Covais described the meticulous effort which most of the men put into their appearance. "We all creased our shirts. A crease here and a crease there. We didn't have to do it, not everybody did it, but we creased it with the iron, we pressed the iron. We kept ourselves clean and neat." Looking at a photograph of his buddy, Roland Gruebling, he continued his dissertation on the pride he and his friends in Able Battery took in their uniforms. "Grieb was always a sharp dresser," Covais said, "and Tom Ludwick too, but The Grieb, he loved to dress. He was impeccable, immaculate. We all were, as a matter of fact."

So passed the month of March, 1945. At Camp Suippes, the men of the 319th rested, absorbed replacements and some, like Lieutenant Cook, even wrangled furloughs to the French Riviera for a chance to relax in real style. For those left at Suippes the demands were light.

The guys took some ease in being able to read about the Varsity Jump in Stars & Stripes, instead of taking a direct part. It was, in fact, the largest single days airborne drop of the war, with over 16,000 British and American troopers dropped east of the Rhine River at one fell swoop. Everywhere the German armies were in retreat, and while there were pockets of resistance, these were isolated and increasingly unusual. Generally the Germans' ability and will to fight was melting away as the warmth of another spring swept over the European continent.

Finally, during the last days of March, the outfit was notified that it should be in readiness to move out – not as an airborne operation, but by motor and rail transportation. The guys were headed into Germany for the last offensive and, while confidence was high, they all knew from experience that going into combat was never something to take lightly. Covais remembered his thoughts at the time. "I figured, well, the Germans are in a desperate position. We're gonna be fighting them again and the Russians are coming from the other side. They're gonna be desperate." Even if that were the case,

HE BAWLED LIKE A BABY.

over the past eighteen months the enemy had thrown everything they had at the 82nd and every time come away worse for the effort. Now, as far as the gang in the 319th was concerned, they were going in to be present for the closing act of what had been a drama of the highest magnitude.

Carl J. Salmonen
Route #1 Box 60
Rock, Michigan

W J "Web" Bearing
12 v Whyel Avenue
Uniontown, Penna.
"Good Luck - always"

T. O. Simpson
4664 Pershing Ave.
St. Louis, Mo.

BATTERY!

Part 28: "A bunch of crazy assed guys."

When the motor convoy of the 319th reached Cologne on the evening of April 2nd, it was directed to the Mungersdorfer sports stadium. The men were told to go inside and pitch their tents on the soccer field, which they did, finding it a delightfully civilized way to make bivouac, something like camping on a golf course.

In a briefing at Div Arty headquarters, Colonel Todd learned that the 82nd Airborne was relieving the 86th "Blackhawk" Division. A large, if beleaguered force of over 300,000 German troops were encircled in the portion of Cologne east of the Rhine River. The division was ordered to clear out remaining pockets of German die-hards still holding out on the west bank of the Rhine and insure there was no enemy break-out in that direction. As Lieutenant Ragland would later remember, "We were on one side of the Rhine, and the Germans were on the other. In fact, they told us that each unit better have alert people out watching in case the Germans tried to cross over." Eventually the shortage of supplies and rations would catch up with the Germans and force them to capitulate.

Until that time, Todd's battalion would be reinforcing the fire of the 320th Glider Field Artillery, which was itself supporting the 325th Glider Infantry Regiment. This was a change. Since Normandy the 319th had been an integral part of the 508th Regimental Combat Team. With the break-up of the combat team after the Bulge, the 508th was now part of the XVIII Airborne Corps Headquarters and the 319th became an independent artillery battalion once again.

In the morning a reconnaissance was made by Todd and his battery commanders, with locations in the Nippes borough of Cologne selected for the new battery positions. At mid-day, as the batteries were wending their way toward the city center, they started to pass pockets of damage from years of aerial bombing. These desolated areas became first frequent, then more and more widespread until one burned and shattered neighborhood bled into another. The GIs gazed out from their vehicles with mouths agape, trying to comprehend the landscape around them. Intact structures were no where to be seen and many streets existed only because bulldozers had pushed paths through heaps of wreckage. The guys in the outfit had been through bombed and damaged cities before, but nothing compared to this vast sea of devastation.

Ted Covais was still in awe of the scene decades later. "Cologne was completely decimated. I mean Obliterated! I don't know what you want to call it, but gone, just gone! Rubble, rubble, debris all over the place, amazing," is how he put it.

As Germany's fourth largest metropolis and a major industrial center, the ancient Roman city of Cologne had been the destination of no less than 262 bombing raids since 1940. The first 1,000 plane bombing raid conducted by the Allies was directed against Cologne on the night of May 30-31, 1942, and the bombardments continued until the last attack on March 2nd, 1945. By the spring of that year, it was estimated that fully 90% of the structures in the central city had been destroyed or sustained extensive damage. About 20,000 citizens were killed in these raids, and the pre-war population

A BUNCH OF CRAZY ASSED GUYS.

of 800,000 had shrunk to about 150,000 souls, many sheltered in basements without electricity or running water. Inexplicably, the magnificent 13th century cathedral at the city's center remained standing despite having received at least fourteen direct hits from Allied bombers, its twin spires standing watch over a boundless expanse of destruction.

When the location selected for the battery's howitzers was reached, the men found it little more than a wide spot in the ruins. John Girardin's memory of the site was, "We cleared off enough to set up the guns, but where we made camp there were houses half torn down and half blown up. We were actually dug in the rubble of buildings."

By late afternoon Able Battery was set up and ready to receive fire missions. Sartain and Ragland had the battery personnel gather in an enormous bomb crater. It may have been blown by one of the "blockbusters" dropped on Cologne, as the crater was large enough to contain every man in the battery below surface level. The men were reminded that there would be no fraternization with German civilians, advised against exploring buildings for souvenirs, and warned against booby traps.

Near midnight word was also received that the railroad contingent of the battalion had arrived from Aachen and a party was dispatched to guide them to the new positions. A liaison team under Lieutenant Bourgeois was sent to the 325th, and preparations were made to resume air observations.

Just about this time, Girardin had an unexpected guest. John Pesivento had grown up with Girardin in Rockford, Illinois, but hadn't seen him since 1942. Now Pesivento was a rifleman in the Blackhawk Division. "They were moving in as we was moving out," Pesivento said when asked about the visit. "When I saw the patches I went to my CO and said I would like to visit a friend of mine who's in this outfit. He gave me permission and I went to their headquarters."

Thinking back on scenes such as this one of Cologne, Covais later said, "Row on row of homes destroyed. Cities destroyed. I mean completely obliterated! There's a lot of stuff out there that people don't realize. Entire families just disappeared, just by one bomb! Entire families were obliterated. Everything. it's a shame. For what? To what purpose or end? Everything is annihilated. Everything is destroyed! Property damage into the millions, into the millions, you know? The absolute destruction of the war. My God." Covais collection.

BATTERY!

At the 319th CP, Pesivento presented himself and explained, "I'm from the same town as John Girardin." The people at battalion headquarters were suspicious. They asked him a lot of questions while someone else got "A" Battery on the telephone. "I was put under scrutiny. They got somebody who really knew John so they were sure that I was from the same hometown, that I actually knew this guy, and wasn't infiltrating. Then some guy came and drove me with the jeep out to where he was."

Pesivento had only just seen combat - now he was surrounded by some of the most battle-hardened troops in the European theater. "The impression I had was that they were seasoned veterans. They were a tough bunch; I mean they had a lot of experience, a lot of battle experience. Of course, they were nice guys, but you could tell they weren't afraid of anything," he remembered of the crew at the Able Battery gun position. Lieutenant Ragland asked Pesivento a few more questions, then pointed toward one of the howitzers.

Remembering back to that day, Pesivento described Girardin as he approached the battery's gun position, "He was in a gun emplacement. It was a dugout. There was a cannon of some kind, it was dug down and I think they had a camouflage net over it. I was carrying full gear, helmet, and my rifle. When I got near him he looked at me and didn't recognize me. He jumped down in the hole and he started checking the sights."
"I said, 'You think you'll hit it, Scope?'" he looked up and said, 'What?' He'd never heard that before in the army. See, his nickname at home was Scope. His father they called Scopella, and John, we called him Scope."

Girardin enjoyed the visit from his hometown buddy and said, "He heard we were there so he came and looked me up. We had a hot meal together. Then he took off, but man, it was good to see him."

The next day a forward observer team led by Lieutenant Gelb was directed to establish an Op at a riverside factory. Covais was with Gelb as his assistant. Sebring was there too as the radio-telephone man. They picked their way carefully down the deserted streets, now and then passing burned out tanks or piles of broken masonry from which floated the odor of decay. GIs at checkpoints advised them, "You're clear here, Mac," or "Watch out for snipers up ahead." The constant rumble of artillery, accented by distant bursts of machine gun fire provided a constant background score.

At a stop along the way, idle curiosity prompted Covais to walk over to one of the dead Germans who still littered the streets. "It seemed like a young guy. Only this one was all maggots and everything else, just a mess, just a mess. You know, maggots, after you're dead a while, they eat you up, eat the flesh," he said. The man's overcoat and uniform lay about him, flung open and ripped apart. No visible wounds, concussion could do that. Seeing the impression of a wallet in the man's tunic pocket, Covais investigated. "I think there was a photograph of children and a wife, or maybe a girlfriend, you know, one of those things," he recalled in an oddly distant voice. "Sad, so I put it back. I think that should stay with the body. Taking that would be an invasion of privacy."

When the forward observer team reached the factory situated on the west bank of the Rhine they discovered it was a Ford Motor Works facility. The irony of occupying a factory which bore the name of one of America's quintessential success stories was not lost on them as they explored the grounds. By this time in the war many GIs had noticed that a large portion of the trucks the enemy used were of the Ford variety, identical to those made in the United States. Now they could see why. The Ford plant was massive, occupying a promontory on the river bank and featuring buildings several stories tall. In

A BUNCH OF CRAZY ASSED GUYS.

fact, it was the most intact cluster of structures for some distance in any direction.

It is unlikely that any of these GIs knew Ford's international branch had been making automobiles in Germany since 1925 and at this cologne plant since 1931. After the rise to full control of the government by the Nazis two years later, close and constant cooperation between Ford headquarters in Dearborn, Michigan, and Hitler's regime in Berlin continued. Throughout the 1930s, while most American corporations were distancing themselves from the German government, Ford remained amenable to Nazi war aims.

Once the US entered the war, a state of suspended collaboration took hold. Because the parent company in Michigan held a 52% interest in its German subsidiary, the company was placed in trusteeship by the German courts in 1940. Dearborn's share of the profits was then directed to an escrow account, pending an assumed resumption of business when peace was restored. Meanwhile, Dearborn's hand-picked head of the Cologne works, a Herr Schmidt, known to be an active and enthusiastic supporter of the Nazi Party, stayed on as its executive because of his political allegiance.

Direct involvement by Dearborn with its subsidiaries continued as least as late as the summer of 1942, when it facilitated contracts between the Wehrmacht and Ford factories located in Vichy France. German Ford produced a variety of military vehicles for the Wehrmacht, the SS, and other military organizations of the Nazi government. To meet its contracts, as many as 2,500 slave laborers mostly Russians, French, and Belgians, toiled at the Cologne site during the war years, and the factory actually doubled in value over that time. In fact, one 1945 army report described the Cologne Ford works as an, "Arsenal for Nazism."

Though the army air force did designate the factory as a target on several of the many bombing runs conducted over Cologne, to the airborne troopers the facility seemed remarkably free of significant damage. Whether there had been deliberate efforts to spare the Ford facility in response to the influence of the Ford family in Dearborn has never been proven, but suspicions that this was the case arose quickly and have persisted to this day. Certainly the relatively undamaged condition of the plant in relation to all the rubble which surrounded it left that impression.

That Dearborn Ford regarded its subsidiaries within the German Reich as an

Covais, Gruebling, and "Webb" Gearing pose beside a German Panther tank near the Cologne Cathedral, April, 1945. The sign on the tank says "Booby Trapped." Speaking later of knocked out German tanks, Sartain remarked, " I cautioned my men to leave them alone." Covais collection.

important part of the Ford family, worthy of any protection it could muster seems clear in any case. By war's end Ford had already received from the Nazis and Vichy French several hundred thousand dollars in compensation for damages caused by Allied bombings. The auto producer still sued. In 1965, a seven million dollar claim for damages caused by Allied bombings was initiated, despite the fact that most of the value of property destroyed came from material intended for the German military. In the end Ford was eventually awarded $1.1 million in damages.

There were several groups from the 319th at the factory during the next week. One was from Headquarters Battery, a liaison crew under the command of Captain Gutshall, with communications man Ed Ryan, his buddy Sergeant Broski, and a couple of other guys. Lieutenant Gelb's forward observer team was rotated sometime that week with another under Lieutenant Fellman, and there may have been other teams from "B" Battery as well.

Sartain came by, it being his habit to visit every forward observer every day. He remembered the position at the Ford Factory, "We would look across the river and in a similar building was the German OP. We'd make a nasty sign to them and the bullets would come through the window. We'd duck down. Then they'd make a nasty sign and we'd shoot back at them."

While the Germans were happy to pick off individual American soldiers – especially artillery observers - with sniper fire, it was obvious that they avoided targeting the buildings themselves with artillery or other high explosives which could bring down the structures and cause irreparable damage.

Bob Storms' experience certainly reinforced the idea that the Ford buildings were off limits to German heavy ordnance. His machinegun crew was set up in a concealed position near the Ford works, at a cemetery just back from the riverbank. They were vulnerable to enemy fire there, but exploring the facility, he discovered that being inside the factory itself offered relative safety. "You went in that factory you could do anything you wanted. You could go in there; start a fire, cook meals and everything, nobody ever fired a shot at that factory. The Germans right across the river, they never fired a shot at you. But you go across the street to another building they'd shoot the hell out of you," insisted Storms.

Secure in the knowledge that they were reasonably safe; the 319th men at the Ford factory explored the facility whenever they had free time. For those who'd worked on assembly lines back home, it was a strangely familiar environment. Naturally a spirit of liberation took hold. Socket wrenches, sets of metric micrometers, and other tools found their way from employee lockers to GI musette bags.

Others had more ambitious goals. "I remember the Ford factory," said Ed Ryan. "They had those Fords on an assembly line, new Fords. Actually what they were was like a 37 Ford with a four cylinder engine. The assembly line was I suppose five hundred feet long. That part wasn't hurt. These Fords were sitting there, so we got one off the line and we got gas and put it in it and fired it up. We went for a ride in it. The damn thing broke down about three four miles down the road, so we did what I always wanted to do, we pushed the damn thing off a cliff and left it there."

Other men filtered into the administrative chambers. Snooping around one office, perhaps Herr Schmidt's, Lieutenant Fellman found a gold plated cigarette holder in one desk drawer and pocketed it as his personal souvenir of Cologne.

At another office Covais seated himself at a secretary's desk and found his own prize. "There was a typewriter I got out of the Ford motor works in Cologne Germany that I remember. I took it because I never owned a typewriter of my own. All my life I wanted a typewriter, and although it was an old machine it seemed sturdy. It had the German alphabet and a key to make the SS symbol. It was a Rheinmetall make or brand, Rheinmetall. It was huge, huge; it was heavy, but old fashioned with the manual return, the handle, boom boom."

As Covais carried his trophy out of the building and stowed it in Lieutenant Gelb's jeep, he never knew his typewriter was made by the principle manufacturer of the Germans' MG42 machinegun, as well as artillery pieces, bomb fuses, and numerous small arms components. In his mind at the time was an opportunity to get back a little of what the war had kept him from, and from him. "I boxed it somehow, and I shipped it home," he said. "Would you believe it? I don't remember what it cost me to send it home. Maybe it didn't cost me anything, I don't even remember. But it was a stupid thing to do. Dumb, because it was just a heavy thing. I used it for many years, and then I got rid of it."

Mahlon Sebring was there too. He ran to investigate when someone called to him, "Hey Seeb, come on down here, they're breaking into the safe of the plant!"

"We spent two days trying to get into the safe," he recalled with amusement. "I didn't actually take part in it but I stood there and watched them a while. A bunch of crazy assed guys! They had torches and everything, but they never did get it open."

In spite of treasure hunts, there was also legitimate work to be done, and the Ford factory offered a fine vantage from which to get it accomplished. "My observation post was there at the Ford Motor works. Up on the top, on the roof, that's where it was," said Covais of the spot years later. "I had a piece of sheet metal that I hid under. I could see across the Rhine River and could see the cathedral was on my right, on the right side. I had my field-glasses and from that point I directed fire across the Rhine River on the German positions."

To make sure the Germans stayed bottled up in the ruins of the city, aggressive patrols were sent across the Rhine every few nights by either the 504th PIR or the 325th GIR. Invariably these raids would need diversionary and supporting barrages or, a covering barrage while the party broke off contact and recross to the west side of the Rhine. The 325th, for example, sent a company across the river on the night of April 6-7th, and the 319th provided some of the supporting fire for this operation. Many of the targets included suspected sites of German Nebelwerfer "Screaming meemees." Others were simple targets of opportunity, as when enemy vehicles or personnel were sighted moving among the ruins on the other side of the Rhine.

Even with the rooftop OP, pinpointing German positions concealed among the battered structures was difficult. This was particularly true of the Nebelwerfers, which had been easy to locate in Italy from the smoke trail which their rockets left. Now these rockets used a smokeless propellant which was all but invisible. However, air observations were established and greatly aided the location of targets.

This duty was now especially hazardous because of the high concentration of anti-aircraft batteries gathered in and around the city. Indeed, the piper cub was thoroughly peppered and forced down and on April 15th. Pilot Morgan and Captain Hawkins were both wounded – the latter in his posterior. "When he got out of the hospital Hawkins would always be asking if you wanted to see his war wound," Sartain recalled with amusement.

In the interim life at the gun position settled into a routine. Firing was steady at about 150 to 200 rounds per day, mostly targets of opportunity. It wasn't a large amount, so the guys had a little time on their hands. Most tried to make themselves as comfortable as possible in the rubble. Settled in among the wrecked and damaged buildings, those who knew carpentry cobbed together wooden tables and chairs. Those who knew some plumbing couldn't help fiddling around, trying to get some running water, and those who thought they had some knowledge of electricity knew there had to be a way to get the lights back on.

Robert Dickson, Orville Farmer, and a few others tried their hand at being electricians with mixed success. "These buildings we were in, they were pretty much tore up," Dickson recalled. "We was trying to light up one room. We'd already had it blacked out, but then we found a high line that was hot, so we wired it into an old meter box. We knew there was electricity in it even though the building was blown apart. Well, when we hooked it up we lit up about three blocks and immediately somebody hollered, 'Lights out, lights out!' We had to break the lights off in a hurry. We just had to run, grab the wires and jerk them loose and of course we got shocked and knocked right off the second floor, but we got them off. And we never would admit who done it."

Kenneth Smith found the situation ripe for his foraging talent. "We found a wine cellar," he said proudly. "Got all the wine we could drink. Champagne too. Found a cheese factory and got all the cheese we wanted."

Other troopers in the area found a V-bomb supply depot with containers full of pure alcohol, which fueled these bombs. According to Lieutenant McNally at division artillery headquarters, "After that there was a considerable amount of drinking of this new drink, promptly labeled "V-bomb juice." I never tasted it but heard it was good with tomato juice."

Lieutenant Joe Mullen wrote home to his girlfriend, Gloria that he wanted her to "try a Blood & Guts, & a Buzz Bomb, & a Nebelwerfer. They'll really knock you silly, the last 2 anyhow. The B. & G. is tomato juice, salt, pepper & gin mixed for a hang over."

Two New Yorkers; Frederick von Hassel of Queens, and James "The Nose" Rosati of the Bronx. Rosati played "the GI" in the skit titled Jivin' in France. Of him Sartain later commented, "He was a real cut-up, a real cut-up. he was something else." Covais collection.

Early on the 12th, the 319th received orders to displace to Hurth, a Cologne suburb located about seven miles west of the city. Much of the area on the Allied side of the Rhine was served by an electric power plant there, and with repeated calls by the moribund Nazi government to carry on the war through acts of sabotage, it was naturally considered a prime target. The battalion's orders were to guard the power plant against die-hard Nazi partisans.

During this duty the battalion was housed in private homes in Hurth. To some of the men's surprise, many found that living among the

A BUNCH OF CRAZY ASSED GUYS.

German people was more congenial than they expected.

Kenneth Smith's comment was, "Actually, I liked the Germans as much as I liked anybody. They were nice people. I didn't have too much to do with the people in Holland, only the time we was up there in combat. I didn't care for the French. I didn't care for the English. I didn't like the Italians, that's for sure. I'd say the Germans probably were the people I liked best. They was more like us."

Initially, many of the Germans were apprehensive of the GIs, regarding them with a mixture of fear and distain. After all, these uninvited guests were conquering enemies who's behavior couldn't be predicted. Many of the Germans had also lost property and family members to the war. The thought that they were now sheltering those who played a role in their fate was difficult to put aside. Yet, as the days passed and the GIs reveal themselves to be mostly homesick young men, these emotions softened.

One Headquarters Battery man spoke about these unexpected phenomena when he said, "We moved in with this little German woman, she was the only one who lived in the house and she didn't like us. In fact, she hated us at first. Then she started bringing us stuff for breakfast like eggs and milk and stuff like that. When we left she was our friend."

Meanwhile, security for the power station was established. It was a sprawling complex; with transformers spread over dozens of acres. One of the guys from Headquarters Battery was a career sailor by the name of James Horatio Jones. Still in the habit of answering, "Aye, aye!" to orders, he'd come to the 319th by a circuitous route which somehow involved being torpedoed in the North Atlantic. Since his navy rating was as an Electrician's mate, Jones was called in to inspect the facilities.

Ed Ryan remembered what happened. "I was with Lieutenant Procopio and Jones. Supposedly he knew what the hell he was doing. Of course, we were only going to see if the power plant was in working order, but Jones decided to fire up the whole thing. Holy shit, all kinds of stuff started sparking and popping all over the place. See, the Krauts had that thing shut down for some time, so when he turned it on the insulators

The men of "A" Battery enjoy a unit banquet and variety show, April 16th, 1945. Though colonel Todd, major Silvey, and Major Wimberley were invited, the affair was otherwise reserved for members of Able Battery alone. Covais collection.

weren't up to snuff. Anyway, it scared Procopio pretty bad – which was funny - but it scared me too!"

Warnings of acts by agent's provocateurs against the power station were well founded. The anti-Nazi Mayor of Aachen had just been assassinated and sporadic, if not widespread, acts of violence against occupying forces were being reported. According to battalion records, late on the night of the 13th, three individuals wearing American uniforms approached a checkpoint near the power station and, when challenged, ran. One was shot dead, presumably providing evidence that the group were, in fact, Nazi saboteurs. Shortly after this incident a black sedan drove up to another checkpoint. Inside were four persons uniformed as American officers. When challenged by the guard the automobile quickly changed direction and sped away. Though they may have been part of the vast "werewolf" program which the remnants of the Nazi government threatened to launch, no other attempts were made to gain access to the electrical plant.

At 0230 hours on the 14th, news of the death of President Franklin D. Roosevelt was received at battalion headquarters. With it came instructions that a battalion formation would be made at 1000 hours that day, during which one minute of silence would be observed. The report was a shock to the average GI. Due to the strict censorship which had always surrounded the subject of FDR's health in the press, few of the men had any idea of his fading condition. They'd left home with the Roosevelt administration in charge and fully expected to return home to it again. Indeed, most of the men had little recollection of any other chief executive than the cosmopolitan Roosevelt. The rest of the battalion left Hurth to occupy other Cologne suburbs a couple of days later, but Able Battery remained in place, living in town and guarding the power station.

All in all Hurth was a pretty good arrangement for a combat zone. Everyone slept dry, with a roof over their head, while the mess staff used the cafeteria in a municipal building to serve out hot chow from the kitchen. Covais remembered it and said, "We had pretty good quarters at Hurth. There was a mess hall and everything. We had a map in the back of the room with the American flag on one side, and the battalion flag on the other side. This was a map that I used to keep track of the allied advance in Germany on. It was pretty big, maybe a four by two, maybe something like that. I used to mark that all out in red pencil, the front lines so everybody could look at a glance and see how far we have advanced."

The early spring weather was delightful, and regardless of "werewolves," the danger of contact with the enemy was small. The men's baggage even came up with their Class "A" uniforms and personal gear. It was almost like garrison duty at the base camp.

Access to the men's barracks bags and municipal cafeteria gave rise to a uniquely festive idea. "I don't remember how it got started," recalled Sartain, "but we decided that we would have a banquet, and that the officers and top NCOs would serve the troops. It was a totally enlisted man's function, totally. They organized it, set it up, and did the program, had it printed, all of that. Officers had nothing to do with it."

In the time leading up to the gala event there was much to do. In addition to musical entertainment, a selection of theatrical skits would be performed. There was also the matter of food. As much as possible the battery cooks were determined to find some special, or at least unusual, foodstuffs as a departure from the standard army rations. A special requisition was made for cans of GI beer. There was already cheese from the cheese factory. Inquiries also revealed that a Cologne area ice cream factory was among the buildings being guarded by division personnel. In view of that an expedition was made to procure an amount sufficient for the battery.

The banquet was scheduled to begin at 1730 hours on April 16. That afternoon the men put on their Class "A" uniforms as if it were prom night, checking that brasses and jump boots were polished to perfection. As the guys filed into the cafeteria they found places set with a mimeographed program listing the menu and schedule of entertainment. Taking their seats and perusing the list of delicacies, the guys couldn't believe their eyes. Nor should they have.

Looking over one of the blotted, blue ink mimeographs years later, Sartain explained, "They say here the menu is roast chicken, mashed potatoes with giblet gravy, cream corn, whole tomatoes, hot rolls with butter. That's a fantasy, that menu and all was just a fantasy. It's a joke. We didn't have that kind of a menu, they just got carried away when they did it."

There were also place cards for each setting on which one of the battery clerks, Gruebling or Munger perhaps, had typed phrases and mottos such as "Our Boss" or "A man of few words." If their significance has been obscured by the intervening years, at the time any man who'd been serving in Able Battery would have understood their meaning. "They read them out loud, they swapped them around," said Sartain. Even though it was an exclusively "A" Battery function, Colonel Todd, Major Silvey, and Major Wimberley were invited and took their seats with the battery. The aroma of hot food was filling the hall. Bob Carte, a tall West Virginian known to take a drink under social pressure, stood up and called the room to attention. Tonight Carte was the Master of Ceremonies. After he dedicated the occasion, Able Battery's officer's and NCO staff started carrying the meals from the kitchen, delivering two at a time to the privates, corporals, and section chiefs. Someone distributed cans of GI beer and, after a quick benediction, the banquet began. "That's right," said Sartain as he thought back to the banquet, "the officers served the food. Whoever cooked it up put it on plates and we served it."

Except for the beer, the meal was standard GI fare with one notable exception. "We had ice cream, I remember that," swore John Girardin.

There was also music. "In the corner of the room was the biggest damn player piano I ever saw in my life," Mahlon Sebring recalled. "It was a beautiful piano, but the Germans had piled about a foot of stuff around it so it wouldn't get damaged. Well, we had a few guys that could play the piano, so they uncovered it and

Two views of Roland Gruebling as he appeared in his role as "The French Girl" for the skit known as "Jivin' in France" during the Able Battery banquet in Hurth. Courtesy Gruebling family.

played it. We had one guy, I can't think of his name, but he was pretty good on it. We had a couple of guys that could play accordions too. I guess they found accordions in Germany somewhere and fortunately they knew how to play them."

Aside from these amenities, something more singular was in the air that night of April 16th, 1945. It was hard to avoid thinking back to all the events since landing at Casablanca. Now being here, together in Germany, participating in what were clearly the closing acts of the war imbued the occasion with extra meaning. The gesture of appreciation

During the variety show, William Lucas, of Thornton, Arkansas, provided music from his fiddle, while Talmage 'Sam' Glenn, of Virginia, played his guitar. Both photos courtesy of Helen Glenn.

by the officers toward the rank and file seemed to say, "Thanks guys, we couldn't have done it without you," in a voice that was loud and clear.

Once the ice cream was finished the tables were pushed aside to make room for the theatrical portion of the evening's entertainment. Carte got back up and announced that "Glenn &Luke" would now serenade the battery.

Virginian Tallmadge Glenn was a virtuoso on the steel guitar, and he'd added the lively tone of his strings to many barracks evenings in the past. William Lucas, of Alexandria, Louisiana, had his fiddle too. Together the two played a series of Country and Western songs to the delight of their audience.

Harold Walz and Bill Forsythe then acted out a humorous scene titled "The Jerks." All the while the pair was accompanied by the unnamed soldier at the piano, who kept pace in much the same way he'd seen done with silent movies as a young boy. Sartain was both surprised and impressed by the man's talent. "I forget who it was, but he could just make a piano talk," he later remarked.

For the third act, "Gruebling & Company" performed a pantomime titled "Jivin' in France." The routine opened to a slovenly army cook played by Covais, smoking a cigarette, dressed in a sleeveless undershirt and knitted cap. He was peeling potatoes into a basin between his knees. Soon the army cook was joined on stage by Jimmy "The Nose" Rosati. Rosati was a natural born comedian, whose expressive face communicated every ribald thought which crossed his mind. The guys were already chortling among themselves. Then, from a side doorway, Gruebling skipped in, dressed to the nines in a women's skirt and pastel colored sweater, purse swinging from one hand. It was "The French Girl." The hall erupted with whistles and cat-calls. One guy in the back row howled like a wolf.

The theatrics which followed were in the finest traditions of Burlesque. "There wasn't any real plot," laughed Sartain, "But the skit was hilarious! Rosati was a cut-up, a real character, and Gruebling was dressed up like a woman. I don't know where he got the clothes, but there he was with a skirt on and a blouse with a false brassiere. He sang and he strutted around, making like he was singing, straightening his brassiere up and all that foolishness. He was good!"

When Sebring was asked about the sketch, he remembered it immediately and agreed with his battery commander. "They put on quite a skit. Gruebling had a mop on his head like you mop the floor with and he had softballs for breasts. Yeah, Gruebling done quite a job. They got a lot of laughs out of that one," he said.

Glenn & Luke provided another musical interlude until the fourth act in which Lieutenant Joe Mullen starred as the protagonist in a skit titled "Tyler's Clip Joint." Again, the exact plot has been forgotten, but clues suggest that it involved Mullen sitting for a trim, only to walk away with a nearly shaved head as the bungling barber attempts to "even things up a bit."

The fifth and final act involved Gruebling and a bevy of beauties dancing a French cancan to the rockus delight of the crowd. Hairy legs were thrown toward the ceiling and derrieres were shaken, all in choreographed unison.

Sartain said of it, "There were four or five of them and they were all dressed up like women. They look good too, but Gruebling had the prettiest legs! Yeah man, that was some party."

By this time most all of the battery was standing, many gathered around the piano player. With sweat beading on his forehead, he'd broken into a boogie-woogie beat reminiscent of Hoagie Carmichael.

"It surprised everybody because he was a guy that never ever opened his mouth or said anything. He got on that piano that night and took the house down," Sartain said.

Reflecting back on the banquet, Sartain later spoke with pride, "You know that banquet that night was just for "A" Battery. We purposely didn't invite anybody else, any officers from the other batteries or anybody else. It was strictly an "A" Battery function. That's why "A" Battery was so closely knit. I don't know what the rest of the battalion thought about our party, but we did it and the men did it all, put it together."

During the week following the banquet "A" Battery, and the rest of the battalion as well, was detailed to sweep the outlying neighborhoods of Cologne for weapons and all articles of Nazi regalia.

According to Lieutenant Ragland, "They had us divide up into teams of about four or five people. They gave us a printout written in German and we went house to house knocking on the door. We'd show them this print out and it said they were to hand over anything about Hitler or any weapons they had. Some of them just came to the door and read that and said they didn't have anything. Well, in that case we didn't go in the house and search. I think they were so used to having Germans come and if Germans said something you'd better do it."

Ragland seems to have taken a gentle approach with the natives. Lieutenant Cook's memory was similar. He recalled that the men with him were well behaved, courteous, and also asked the residents for extra articles of clothing for displaced German civilians. Other groups were clearly more aggressive.

Ed Ryan's team from Headquarters Battery was probably representative of this style. "We called that a screening party," he said later. "That was quite a thing. You had a jeep with a fifty caliber machine gun on it, towing a 75 howitzer, and any number of grenades. We'd go around banging on the door of these houses. Getting in to look for

German propaganda and one thing or another. With all this armament on the jeep we were hoping that somebody would shoot at us so we could knock the house down but it never happened."

Some of the Germans greeted the Americans with at least an outward appearance of affability, others were openly hostile. Lieutenant Ragland gave examples illustrating each response when he spoke about the search parties. "I know this one place we went to this lady come out with this case of German bayonets. The box had been opened and there was, I don't know, four or five left in there. For some reason or other one of those didn't make it to headquarters. It ended up in my footlocker," Ragland explained. "Then, at another place this guy had a real fancy over and under shotgun and rifle, I guess you'd call it. He banged it against the door jam and broke off the stock and handed us the rest of it."

Most men remember going into the homes regardless of whether the Germans surrendered their contraband willingly or not. The searching parties looked in closets and emptied drawers. Carpets were rolled back to check for evidence of loosened floorboards under which weapons could be hidden. If photographs of sons or husbands in uniform were displayed, any swastika or overt Nazi insignia was torn off before handing the portraits back to the family.

Sergeant Rappi thought the exercise hardly worth the effort and was left feeling ambivalent about it all. "Yeah, I remember going around to these homes," he said, "But we didn't find many weapons. Somebody probably found some, but we didn't find any guns hardly. Anything that pertained to the military we had to take, like the uniforms, they had to take them. This one old lady started crying because it was her son's I guess. Maybe he died in the war and she wanted something to remember him by. I don't know why we had to take it because that navy uniform wouldn't hurt anybody. I didn't really care for that job."

All manner of weapons and regalia were collected, with a lot of smaller items destined to become souvenirs. Aside from Lieutenant Ragland's bayonet, John Girardin found a nice flag, for example, and Covais set aside a Brownshirt's dress dagger for himself.

Other items were too large for GI pockets, as Sebring remembered. "By the end of the day we probably had three or four truckloads of crap we picked up," he said. "All kinds of guns. We even picked up what was called an elephant gun. The paperwork with it said elephant gun anyway. It took two men to shoot it. One man stood about two foot from the muzzle and rested it on his shoulder. The other guy aimed it. I could pick it up and aim it just for a short period of time all by myself, but this damn barrel was about two inches around and six feet long. A hex barrel. You didn't hold that and aim high."

In the end, truckload after truckload of uniforms, flags, armbands and copies of Mein Kampf were hauled out and tossed in a colossal heap. Added to it were rifles, shotguns, muskets, pistols, swords, bayonets, and at least one elephant gun. Lester Newman described what happened, saying, "We brought it all back to our battery and threw it in a pile. It was about fifty foot in diameter stacked up there about four foot high. Nothing but guns that we took away from them. All them guns got burned up. Everything. Everything that had to do with the Nazis, we would take, bring it in and throw it on the fire and burn it. We took all their favorite guns, and boy there's some of them guns that were really classic. They were pretty upset, but they couldn't do anything about it. They had to put up with it. "

A large proportion of the Able Battery men were from rural areas, familiar with guns for hunting and by tradition. Watching a small fortune in perfectly good firearms go up in smoke wasn't easy.

As Newman went on to explain, "I wished I could have gotten some of them guns home, I'll tell you, but there was no way. Our outfit wouldn't let any of them go. I'd liked to have brought my dad home one but there was no way of getting it home. You could steal it out of the pile but you couldn't get it home, they wouldn't let you send it. And you couldn't take it with you to different places. You'd have to leave it. We was warned if we catch you with it you're in trouble, so I didn't want to get in that fix."

Getting in that fix didn't deter everyone. During these closing days of the war there were those who carefully disassembled longarms and shipped them home. Even Sartain succumbed to the opportunity, albeit unsuccessfully. Remembering back to one billet, he recalled, "The GIs that were living in the building where I was were up in the attic, in a attic bedroom. They kept messing around. There were some loose planks and they pulled up one of the planks and there were some rifles in there. Guns, shotguns. I was so naive. There was one gun, double barreled, over and under, that was a 28 caliber rifle and basically a sixteen gage shotgun. It was a beautiful weapon. Broke down, over and under, with the rifle on top and the shotgun on the bottom. It was really a masterpiece. I should have kept it but I left it up there. Then I got to thinking about it and I said to myself, you know, I want that damn thing. So I went back to the house, went up to the attic and its gone. I don't know who got it. One of our guys got it. I had to sign approval for all these guys to bring these things back home, but who ever got that I never had to sign for it because I was waiting for it. Oh man, yeah, and I would have taken it. For that piece I'd have pulled rank on him."

On the morning of the 28th of April the 319th was on the move again, destined for the town of Wiedenbruck, north of Cologne. The battalion was to travel with the division across the northern plains of Germany, cross the Elbe River, and advance as close to Berlin as possible before meeting the Soviet Army approaching from the east. Their time at Cologne had been unlike any other mission. Hardships of campaigning were light, and contrary to their expectations, they found the German people oddly similar to themselves, complicating their attitude toward the enemy.

As the outfit pulled out, the "A" Battery guys noticed a young woman on a bicycle, trailing the motor convoy. It was the girlfriend of one of them. She trailed the convoy for several miles, but fell farther and farther behind. Finally she accepted that following where they were going was impossible. They could see her standing her bicycle by the roadside, waving goodbye.

Part 29: "This is risky business."

The 319th's time at Cologne brought the issue of close contact between American soldiers and German civilians to the forefront. From early on in the war, the Army anticipated there would be an extended German occupation and gave considerable forethought to the question of just how military government should be conducted when that time came. Experience in Italy had already shown that occupation of beligerant states was often a difficult task which needed to be handled delicately. There the civilian population was clearly in sympathy with the Allies; regarding them as liberators instead of conquerors, but how the more ardent Germans would react to the presence of American GIs among them remained to be seen. The single element military authorities were sure of was that interaction should be kept to a minimum and limited to strictly necessary affairs.

One Army circular distributed among troops in the 82nd Airborne described the policy in these terms, "Do not associate with Germans. Conversation will be limited to the minimum necessary for transacting official business. Visits to civilian homes, dining with civilians, and barter or trading with civilians is prohibited except when specifically authorized in the dispatch of military duty. Troops are prohibited from leaving their bivouac area except on official business. Sightseeing and souvenir hunting invite unnecessary casualties. No German children or adults will be allowed in bivouac areas, mess areas, or billets. Food, fuel, and living necessities will not be given to civilians by troops. All troops should understand that while we are not entering Germany as oppressors, we nevertheless are conquerors. The Germans must bear the consequences of the war they have brought to the world. Every German shares the responsibility of allowing Hitler and his Nazi party to begin this war. Hence, we only open routes of propaganda and sabotage aimed at another war if we allow even normal American friendliness to exist with the German people."

This was, in fact, the stance taken as early as the fall of 1944, when US forces first crossed the border into Germany. Generally known as the "nonfraternization policy," the prohibition against interaction with Germans was difficult to enforce. Most men, and many officers, simply didn't see the necessity. A large portion of the men had German backgrounds and found the civilians to be amiable company. With the war coming to an end, when Germans had something the Americans wanted, and could offer something in return, there was simply no compelling reason to maintain strict segregation.

Problems surrounding the interpretation of the non-fraternization order arose almost immediately upon crossing the German border. For example, during the final weeks of February, 1945, while the battalion was in place along the Roer River, enforcement of the regulation was already lax.

One day Sartain received a call on his field-phone from First Sergeant Johnson. "Captain, we've got this German lady here who says she's making schnapps for us and I don't know what to do about it," he asked.

THIS IS RISKY BUSINESS.

"Why," Sartain answered, "What's the problem?"

"Well," Johnson continued, "We're not supposed to fraternize, sir."

Sartain already knew about the arrangement. Dehydrated potatoes from the battery mess were being distilled into homemade vodka. As he later explained, "See, we would take these freeze dried potatoes to the lady next door and she'd make schnapps for us. She probably had some of it working already. So I told Jess Johnson, you don't have to fraternize. Just bring your stuff to her and let her make it!"

"OK," said Johnson, "That's what I wanted to find out."

"So they loaded her up on all this powdered, dehydrated potatoes and she turned it into schnapps. I didn't see it as a problem at all," Sartain concluded, having evidently determined that distilling schnapps from government rations lay within the boundaries of official business, necessary to the dispatch of military duties.

The rules were, of course, directed primarily against sexual contact between soldiers and German women. Germany at the closing days of the war and during the occupation which followed was ripe for interaction between American soldiers and German girls. The GIs were in a position of power, young, lonely, well-fed, and liberally supplied with all sorts of goods which had been unavailable to civilians for some time. The local girls were young and lonely too, but also hungry and powerless– except in one important respect.

The Army had been in this situation before. Italian occupation saw an alarming explosion of venereal disease among military personnel. This, as well as other complications of contact between the sexes, such as sexual assaults, marriages and children, was something the military wished to avoid through strict enforcement of the non-fraternization policy.

Sartain thought the average GI complied but Sergeant Rappi's attitude was quite possibly more typical, "They didn't mind us fraternizing until we got to Germany," he said. "Then they used to fine you fifty five bucks. Fifty five dollars! I said, put it on my tab."

Certainly, given the access to willing girls, violating the non-fraternization order was seen by many GIs in the 319th as a problem only if they were caught. Bob Storms remembered the details of one illicit liaison he and a buddy had in Cologne. "I took off late one afternoon and I met a girl," he remembered. "Way over in a field there was a house. I went over there with one of my buddies. Her and her girlfriend, we met them and we had a lot of fun. Then one of them looked out the window and said, 'Hey, there's lots of soldiers coming.' I looked out and there were MPs and stuff checking everything. The girls said, 'You go by the back window, when you hear us yell, jump out the back window and run like hell.' So they got dressed and when the MPs come to the door they opened the door they screamed and hollered and everything. Me and my buddy, we jumped out the back window. We run like hell. I fell down in a bomb hole crater. There must have been a little shrapnel around. I cut my arm but that didn't stop me from getting up and running like the devil. After that I stayed where I belonged. Boy that was a close one."

The contemplative Ted Simpson described the bleak days which 319th men found in the fall of 1945 while occupying Berlin, but the same relationship was already in place and flowering in Cologne the previous spring. Simpson wrote, "The Frauleins were just as deprived, hungry and comfortless as their brothers, fathers and mothers but with a very special commodity to sell - usually for cigarettes or silk stockings. Warm male underwear, GI-Issue sweaters, toilet articles, candy bars, and K rations were equally negotiable. These girls were frequently beautiful, savvy, bright and falsely cheery with a flirtatious, flattering approach to often uncultured GI's and certainly a knowledge of how a soldier, lonely and far from home, in need of warm, pleasant, feminine attention might be cared for. I noted that their male, German counterparts were too tired and/or defeated to care much about them."

On the afternoon of April 9th, Captain Sartain was summoned to Colonel Todd's quarters and told that a 319th man from Battery Headquarters was in the division artillery guardhouse, having been arrested the night before. When he inquired after the details, Sartain was told, "Well, it's a rape case. Major Silvey is investigating it right now, but for the present, that's all I know, except that he specifically asked for you as his defense council."

Representing soldiers in trouble was nothing new for Sartain. After all, he'd been doing this ever since the Goldfarb case in North Africa, but the question of his qualifications had recently come up after he successfully defended a paratrooper charged with rape. The man was clearly guilty, yet Sartain suddenly turned what should have been an open and shut case into an acquittal. Sartain spoke about the trial years later and said, "One guy from either the 504 or 505, I forget what his name was, assaulted a German woman. He told me he didn't do it. Well that's the normal story. They tried him by General Court Martial. The victim was kept outside of the courtroom for all the stuff that didn't pertain to her, and then she was called in to testify. The defense asked her a bunch of questions, this, that, and the other, then they submitted her to me. I had a hunch that she was scared, so I took a chance. The key to a good defense lawyer is to know when to ask your questions. I asked her, 'Is this the man that raped you?' I pointed if that was him and she said no. Honestly, she was scared. I'm convinced she was just too scared to follow through on it. So they found him not guilty and he was guilty as sin. Well the court martial turned him loose. So Colonel Moss, who was the Division Judge Advocate, when it was over with and all, we were walking out and he says, 'Sartain, you kind of took a chance there, didn't you?' I said, 'What did I have to lose? If she'd have said, yes, that was him, well, that was what he was already being tried for. I thought, there's nothing to lose because they're gonna hang his ass anyway.' See, I had a pretty serious suspicion that she was scared shitless and was gonna say no and that's exactly what happened because the way she testified, and it was pretty bad, she never looked at him. So I just figured she didn't look at him for a reason, she didn't know what he was gonna do. You know, the Germans, they didn't know what the hell was gonna happen to them if they crossed one of the Americans. They just didn't know."

"A few days later Moss called me in and said, 'Charlie, you're not a licensed lawyer are you? You don't have a law degree?' I said, 'No sir, I don't.' He said, 'Well you know you can't represent these fellas in these General Court Martials without a law degree, unless you're particularly requested.' Sure enough, day or two passed or a week passed and Colonel Todd told me, 'You've got a message here for you from some guy in the stockade.'"

The guy in the stockade was Private Paul Blake*, a 27 year old truck driver from Oklahoma who'd been assigned to the battalion as a replacement just before Normandy. Much of that time Blake had been detailed out to a division quartermaster unit as a truck driver and had only recently returned to the 319th's Headquarters Battery. When Sartain interviewed him, Blake said, "I want you to represent me."

"Well have you told the Adjutant General about it here?" Sartain asked him, remembering his conversation with Colonel Moss.

THIS IS RISKY BUSINESS.

"Yep," answered Blake. "He said the only way you could represent me is if I asked for you. So, I'm asking for you."

"OK," Sartain nodded, "Let's go."

Over the next few days Captain Sartain familiarized himself with the details of the case against Blake. He was charged with violation of the 93rd and 96th Articles of War – in other words, rape and disregard of the non-fraternization order. Sartain spoke to his battery commander, Captain Eskoff, and a couple of other 319th officers who were acquainted with the accused. He also read through Major Silvey's report, part of which included a sworn statement by Blake describing the events of April 8th, 1945, which led to his arrest.

According to Blake, he'd been tracking down a break in a telephone wire in one of the Cologne neighborhoods when a German woman approached him and asked if he'd like a drink of wine. Blake said he would and was told to follow her to her apartment nearby. There Blake, the woman, Theresa Muller*, and her husband Albert drank wine, listened to the radio, and conversed amiably for some time. At one point, Mrs. Muller sent her husband out to find cognac, leaving the two alone. Blake propositioned her and they proceeded to the sofa. There they were discovered by Mr. Muller when he returned with two American MPs, who unjustly arrested him.

The Judge Advocate would, of course, present a different version in which Blake pulled out a pistol and ordered Mr. Muller out of the apartment. Blake was attempting to force Mrs. Muller, at gunpoint, to have intercourse with him when he was arrested.

Whether or not Blake's statement was truthful was secondary to Sartain's task at hand. As he saw it, "He had the right to a Defense Council. My job was to defend him and a defense lawyer gets his client off."

The trial opened on April 13th. Because of Sartain's unlicensed status, 1st Lieutenant Robert P. Catch was the head Defense Council. Sartain served as assistant and actually handled the case, as requested. Charges against the accused were read aloud and he pled Not Guilty to both. 1st Lieutenant Alston R. Law served as prosecutor.

Law began his case by first calling Sergeant Major Wisecarver of the 319th's Headquarters Battery to the stand. Wisecarver was questioned about the posting of the non-fraternization order, testifying that it was circulated twice – first in February, 1945, at which time it was read aloud at a Headquarters Battery formation, and was again distributed in late March, just before the unit left France for Cologne. At that time the order was given to the section chiefs who in turn read the directive to their men. The order was, in addition, currently posted on the Headquarters Battery bulletin board, Wisecarver added. All this was intended to demonstrate that Blake should have been fully aware of the nonfraternization order.

Wisecarver further testified that the copy of the order shown to the court and identified as "Exhibit A" was not identical to the one he remembered posted on the battery bulletin board. Sartain raised this as a point of objection, asserting that there was thus no evidence that "Exhibit A" was ever posted. Though the objection was sustained, Law had clearly succeeded in establishing that Blake was aware of the nonfraternization policy and Sartain declined to cross examine the witness.

Captain Wilson Bourgeois, Blake's battery commander was next called to the stand by the prosecution. Law ascertained through his questions that Private Blake had no explicit authorization to be away from his post, in Cologne, checking communication wire.

BATTERY!

Sartain cross examined and asked, "When the line goes out, is it customary for the men to get your permission to go out and check that line, or is it their initiative to go out and check the line themselves?"

Bourgeois answered, "It is on their own initiative." Having provided sufficient grounds for Blake to have been in Cologne without direct orders, Sartain had no further questions.

The plaintiff, Theresa Muller, was now called as a witness. Speaking through an interpreter, in the regional Kolsch dialect, Mrs. Muller described herself as a housewife residing at 42 Kieferstenstrasse. According to her story, she'd been walking through nearby Barbarossa Platz on the evening of April 8th when an American soldier in a jeep motioned for her to approach him. The soldier, identified as Private Blake, asked her for wine. Mrs. Muller pointed to her nearby apartment building and communicated that Blake should follow her. "I thought the soldier was thirsty and I told him that I had wine at home. Since I knew that my husband was at home I took him along. I did not think that the soldier would have the wrong idea, otherwise I would have brought him a glass of wine down to the doorstep," she said.

Theresa Muller continued her testimony, "When I came upstairs the soldier was thirsty and I gave him a glass of wine. We made a conversation with the soldier as good as it was possible. I gave him an old pistol as a present. The pistol was in no working condition. My husband had found the pistol in a parcel of my brother-in-law's. He was very glad to get the pistol. I also gave him a picture postal card of Cologne. Then he took his pistol and shot into the ceiling. Then I told my husband I would take him back down into the street and I told him that it was time for him to go. When I came to the entrance of the house he came towards me. He took the pistol out of his pocket and molested me. I ran up stairs again and he followed me. He took me at the arm. He tore my dress at the sleeve and he pushed me against the wall. I tried to get him out of the house but he closed the door. I could not get him out of the house. When he came upstairs again he again took his pistol and told my husband to get out of the room. My husband went downstairs and called the police. He pushed me and I fell on the couch. He had his pistol in his right hand and he was laying on me. He forced me to take my underwear off. A few minutes later my husband returned with the police. The police took the pistol from him and took him away."

When Judge Advocate Law asked Mrs. Muller, if Blake lay upon her body, she answered, "I can no longer recall that. I was too nervous. All I can say is that he opened his pants. He had his pants opened and his genital parts were hanging out."

It was a tough opening for any Defense Council. Sartain could see that there was little use disputing Blake's violation of the nonfraternization order, but somehow he would have to reframe the rest of this story into one in which Blake was entrapped by either an unfaithful wife, or was the victim of a premeditated plot by the Mullers to ensnare an unsuspecting American in a rape charge.

Sartain asked if Mrs. Muller's husband was in the room when she brought Blake home and was told that he was. "Did you drink wine together? Did you laugh and joke?" he asked.

"Yes, we laughed a bit."

"Did you laugh when the pistol was fired in the room?"

"No," she said. "Then I was afraid."

Frau Muller denied that she had offered to procure cognac. "The word cognac was not mentioned?" Sartain asked, and was again told no by the witness. Since cognac was an important part of Blake's alibi, Sartain asked Theresa Muller a few other questions, then suddenly returned to the issue once more. "Did you ask your husband to get some cognac?"

"No," she answered, "We had no cognac. We had only two bottles of wine in the house."

In his cross examination, Sartain's search for more details about the incident did not open any opportunities for him to discredit Muller's story. She appeared quite certain of the course of events up until the alleged assault. In fact, the more information which was revealed, the worse Blake's intentions appeared.

Finally the members of the court asked her if she was in the habit of inviting GIs up to their apartment. She answered that she was not in that habit and only coincidentally had two bottles of wine to share. "I thought it was permitted to bring him in," she said. "We are glad the Americans have come to Cologne. If I had known that it was not permitted, I would not have called him in."

Theresa Muller was excused and her husband, Albert Muller next took the witness stand. He gave his name, address, and described himself as an unskilled laborer. Prosecutor Law then asked him if anything unusual happened at his home on the night of April 8th, 1945.

"Yes," he said, "My wife came to the house at about seven o'clock together with an American soldier. She told me this man was thirsty and to give him a glass of wine. I gave him a glass of wine. I told him to sit down and we conversed as well as we could. The soldier did not know German and I did not know English. We conversed as well as we could with signs and motions of the hands. Then suddenly he got up. He heard a noise on the street and he went towards the window and he took out his pistol and took the safety off. As far as I could understand he wanted to see if anyone approached his car. Then he put his pistol back in the holster and we continued to talk. The day before, I had done some housecleaning in that apartment and I found an old pistol which is no longer in working order, which had belonged to my brother in law. I told my wife we would give him that pistol so that we would not have to turn it in. he was very glad to get that pistol and said he would keep it as a souvenir. Then my wife also gave him a few picture postcards of Cologne. I gave him a second glass of wine and then he took his pistol out and a shot went off into the ceiling. Apparently he did not have the intention to shoot, but the pistol went off because the safety was not on. I believe that is so because previously, when he went toward the window, he had taken the safety off and had not put it back on when he put it back into the holster."

"What did you, your wife, or the accused do when the pistol went off?" asked Law.

Muller answered, "We were all frightened when the shot went off. My wife said, 'I will bring him down the street so he leaves.' I mentioned to my wife that you can see how careless people are because he could have just as well hit somebody. My wife took him downstairs but then she came back up again together with him and she told me he did not want to go. He motioned me toward the door. There was a radio there and he made as if I should go. I understood him that he wanted me to turn off the radio and the radio was on at that time. I turned the radio off but when I turned around he drew his pistol and pointed it to me and said to go out. Then I went downstairs and called the police. The police car was driving up and I called to them and then two of those police went up with me to the apartment. They found the soldier bent over my wife. My wife was lying down and the soldier was kneeling over her. And she had her panties off. That is all I could see. He had his pistol in his hand. The police took the pistol away from him and arrested him. They took him away. That is all as far as I know."

Prosecutor Law then asked Muller, "Did you hear anything from that room before you entered it with the police?"

"Yes," Muller answered, "My wife was calling me. She called for help. She called out 'Albert, come and help me!' and when I drew the curtain back she said, 'Look here, he has a weapon.'"

This brought an end to Law's questions. Sartain approached the witness and began asking his own.

"Did you laugh and joke with the accused?"

"We conversed together and we laughed because we could not understand each other well."

"Did you think the soldier nice and well-mannered?

"Yes I thought he was a nice man and even after the shot went off as well."

Sartain now asked just what happened when Blake came in the apartment. "At first he placed his helmet on the couch and kept his pistol belt," Muller recounted, "Then he removed his pistol belt. He just opened the buckle and the pistol belt fell down, the pistol fell down to the floor and my wife picked it up and gave it back to him."

A few more questions followed, then Sartain asked, "Are you sick or were you sick on the night of this incident?"

"Yes, I'm sick. I do not go upstairs very well. That is also the reason why my wife brought the soldier down and why I did not bring him down myself. That is also the reason I was home while my wife was out for a walk."

"Do you understand English?" Sartain asked.

"Yes but I only understand a few words. I can understand "yes," "okay" and a few others."

"You said that after you gave the pistol to the soldier the soldier was definitely glad to get the pistol and said he would keep it as a souvenir. How did you understand that?"

"He took the pistol and asked, 'For me?', And I answered, 'Yes.' He put the pistol in his breast pocket and then took it out several times and laughed about having it. He often mentioned that this was such a small pistol while his was a large one," Muller added.

Hoping to establish that there was a friendly atmosphere in the apartment, free of intimidation, Sartain inquired if Frau Muller laughed after the shot was fired.

"Yes," said Muller, "I believe my wife laughed after the shot went off, and the soldier asked me whether my wife was laughing at him."

In all, the answers didn't leave Sartain much to hang his hat on. The husband and wife's stories corroborated each other, were consistent, and were rich in detail. Unless he could find some flaw in the Mullers' story, Sartain would be limited to damage control.

Staff Sergeant Bert C. Erkes, Battery "C", 74th Field Artillery Battalion, was now called as a witness. After being sworn in, the prosecution asked him to recount the events in question.

"Staff Sergeant Tolbert and I was out on patrol to inspect the guards up that street and seen this parked jeep without a driver," Erkes began. "So we stopped to see whose jeep it was. Sergeant Tolbert was driving and he parked across the street from the jeep, and went across the street with a flashlight to look at the jeep." Erkes described how Albert Muller came out of the doorway, approached them, asking if they were military police. On being told they were, he urged Erkes and Tolbert to follow him upstairs.

"So I said to Sergeant Tolbert, 'let's see what's cooking up there.' When I got to the door the impression I got, I thought the woman must be having a baby, putting together the way the thing happened and the sounds she was making and sounded like."

Erkes went on to describe how he and Sergeant Tolbert discovered Blake, loaded pistol in hand, atop Mrs. Muller. As Blake stood up they took the weapon away, placed him under arrest, and escorted him out of the building.

Law pressed for further information about Theresa Muller's condition, saying, "Did you notice whether she was calm, quiet, and cool or was she excited?"

Erkes answered, "Well, up to the time when the man got off her she was bawling but I cannot truthfully say what she was like from then on because I was not interested in her."

"Will you tell the court what you mean by 'bawling'?"

"Well," said Erkes, "She was just naturally crying. You can tell whether a woman is really crying or just putting it on. She was scared apparently."

"Was she really scared?"

"Yes," responded Erkes.

The prosecution declined to question the Sergeant further. The testimony was damning, leaving a clear understanding that Blake was committing a violent assault upon Mrs. Muller when the MPs came into the room.

Again Sartain had little to work with. Though questions were likely to bring out more incriminating details he still had to try something. Sartain first asked the witness to describe the layout of the apartment.

"To the best of my recollection it was two rooms. One was a large one and the other one where the couch was a small one and there was a blanket between the two rooms in the door," Erkes answered.

Sartain then went on to explore the possibility that it was too dark for Erkes to really see what was going on. Erkes testified that though he was not sure of the light source, he could definitely see the accused and Mrs. Muller once the blanket was drawn back.

This was exactly the sort of answer Sartain wished to avoid. Changing tack, he now asked, "Did you make any noise at all while you were going up to the apartment?"

"Just knocked on the wood going up the steps."

"Of what material were the steps made?" Sartain asked.

"Wood, I think," was the reply.

Whether Sartain was hoping to suggest that Erkes could not have heard any cries of distress while ascending the stairs is not clear, but this was evidently not a subject he wished to pursue for the present. He declined to continue his cross examination.

Major Silvey next testified that he was the investigating officer appointed by Colonel Todd. The major confirmed that Exhibit "C," was indeed Private Blake's sworn statement, and when asked if he had interviewed the Mullers, said he had. Silvey was asked by the court what Theresa Muller told him and he answered, "She said she and her husband had liked the accused and she did not want to press charges against him. She did not want to cause trouble with the American forces."

This closed the prosecution's case. It was now Sartain's turn. He declined to give an opening statement, instead Sartain called his first witness, Captain John Eskoff, commanding officer of Headquarters Battery.

As Sartain questioned his witness the answers revealed that it was Eskoff who proffered charges against the defendant. Sartain then asked him, "During the time you have known the accused have you been able to form an opinion about him?

"Yes, sir," answered Eskoff, "Because I used him quite a bit in Camp Suippes, and he was a pretty good soldier as long as I knew him. We put him in the liaison section when we reorganized the battery with the idea of making him a liaison corporal."

Satisfied that he had at least obtained a positive character reference, Sartain concluded his questions. The Judge Advocate now cross examined Captain Eskoff, leading him to agree that since Blake was a member of the HQ Battery it should follow that he was aware of the non-fraternization order.

Eskoff was about to be excused when Sartain said, "I have no further questions of the witness, but I do object to that last insofar as it is a conclusion that he was instructed concerning the subject of non-fraternization. I do not object to the fact that he must have been present in the battery, but I do object to the conclusion that he must have been notified."

The court had to agree and the objection was sustained. Sartain felt like the trial was shifting, if not in his favor, then at least in a direction which would benefit his client regardless of the final verdict.

Feeling the momentum, Sartain next recalled Captain Bourgeois to the stand. As the former battery commander, Bourgeois was asked during what periods Blake was with Headquarters Battery.

"He was with the battery after we came back from Normandy for about three weeks. He was then sent on detached service with the division quartermaster. Soon after that we went into France. He again returned to the battery shortly after we went up to the Bulge and has remained with it until now," responded Bourgeois.

"With reference to character and efficiency how would you rate his character?"

"Excellent," was the answer. The prosecution declined to question the witness and Bourgeois was excused.

Lieutenant George Cole was next to account for Blake's character.
"He was my FO driver during the Bulge campaign. He is quiet but very reliable. He always performed his duties, not only to the best of his ability, but exceptionally well," testified Cole.

Sensing a chance to capitalize on a friendly witness, Sartain pressed Cole, "As a member of the FO party you did not hesitate one minute to send him out on any job, is that right?"

"Not a bit," said Cole. "I knew when I sent Blake out he would always do an excellent job."

Sartain knew he'd racked up another positive characterization of Private Blake and stated that he had no more questions. Judge Advocate Law certainly did though. After preliminary questions, Law asked Cole if he knew why the accused had been sent back to the 319th.

"No," said Cole, "I did not."

"You never found out?" Law shot back, clearly insinuating that there was something left undisclosed.

"No one told me," answered Cole. "I thought perhaps he had been a member of the battery on detached service."

Law tasted blood and would not let the issue rest. "But you did not attempt to find out anything about this man's record before he came to you?" he asked.

"It is not customary to ask a man about his previous experiences," Cole demurred.

Prosecutor Law felt satisfied. The idea that Blake's prior service with the quartermaster battalion had been something less than sterling was raised in the court's mind. For now he had no further questions.

Sartain called PFC Albert Jamieson of Headquarters Battery as a witness. Jamieson testified that he was aquainted with Blake in civilian life as a truck driver, knew him as a man of good character and a responsible employee. "At that time it was my opinion and the opinion of everybody I knew that the accused was of high character."

"Is your opinion of the accused the same now as it was then?" continued Sartain.

"Yes, Sir," Jamieson answered.

At this point Sartain rested his defense. He'd been unable to refute the charge that Blake violated the non-fraternization order. Neither could he do much to contest the specific assault charge, but Sartain had done much to mitigate any questions surrounding Blake's conduct as a soldier. Clearly Prosecutor Law knew something incriminating about Blake's time with the Quartermaster outfit which he might try to expose, but Sartain reasoned that if he could keep this information out of the trial, he might still be able to win a light sentence.

Blake was brought before the court and informed that at this point he could exercise one of three options. He could take the stand and testify on his own behalf, in which case he would be available to the prosecution and the court for any questions which were deemed apropoe. He could submit an additional sworn statement, orally or in writing, which the court was at liberty to take into considerationor disregard as it saw fit. Lastly, the defendant could remain silent. After affirming that he understood the choices, Blake was informed that the court would recess for five minutes while he commiserated with his Defense Council.

Though it is generally not advisable for accused persons to testify in their own trials, Blake informed the reconvened court that this was just what he wished to do. Whether Sartain advised him to take this action isn't clear, but he must have felt some confidence from the testimony of the witnesses he'd called.

Sartain later remarked on his own thoughts about defendants testifying when he said, "I did not want any of my people to take the stand unless their record was without a blemish. You know, unless you are satisfied they'll be a good witness and can't be messed up."

Perhaps Sartain believed that the direction of the trial had changed in Blake's favor. Perhaps he felt that there was simply nothing to lose. Perhaps Blake was convinced of his own innocence and felt he could convey this fact to the court if only given the chance. Whatever the reason, it was now Private Paul Blake's time to give his version of the events.

Blake took his seat, identified himself, and was asked by Sartain, "Private Blake, will you relate to the court the incident which occurred on the evening of 8 April, 1945, in your own words."

"We received word that somewhere there was a line knocked out," recounted Blake. "I went out to check the line. I was checking the line and I noticed this woman standing there and she motioned for me to come over. I went across the street to see what she wanted and she asked me if I wanted some wine. I told her I did. We went to her apartment and when we got up there she had two bottles of wine. She poured me out a drink of wine and turned on the radio. Then she showed me some pictures of Cologne. We talked a few minutes. She gave me a pistol, a small pistol. Then her husband came in. I was preparing to leave when she brought up the subject of cognac. She sent her husband out of the room and I took it that he went to go get the cognac. When he went out the room I asked her if I could get in her pants. She said nothing and laid down on the couch. I took my web belt off and my jacket and laid them on a table in the middle. I took my pistol out of my holster and put it in my back pocket. She laid down on the couch and pulled up her dress, but she did not take her pants off. I laid the pistol on the couch and kept pulling my pants down. Then all of a sudden I heard a commotion in the other room and about that time she started screaming. When she started screaming I heard her husband coming through the other room. He was saying something but I could not understand just what. The MPs burst into the room and hollered for me to get up. I had the pistol in my hand when I got up and was pulling up my pants. The MP grabbed me by the arm and held my arm behind me, and I gave him the pistol. Then they took me down to their Headquarters."

"What caused you to take the pistol out of the holster? Why did you not leave it in the holster?" asked Sartain.

"I did not know at what minute he would come back into the room, and this is risky business," Blake explained.

Private Blake's testimony painted the picture of a flirtatious hausfrau who invites an airborne soldier home for drinks and perhaps more. Sending her husband off to search for cognac was the opportunity for the two to hurriedly consummate their attraction. If a loaded pistol was in Blake's hand, who could blame him - a jealous husband was due back at any moment. Sartain had no further questions.

The Judge Advocate began cross examining Blake. Who were the other two men who were with him on the wire detail? How long had he been assigned to the liaison team? Was the Muller's apartment on a main thoroughfare?

Other questions revealed that the neighborhood was badly damaged by bombing. The streets were "littered with debris" and the buildings themselves "mostly demolished," not really habitable, though people were living in them.

Finally, Law asked Blake how it was he took out his pistol and fired it. "After she gave me the pistol she wanted to see mine and see how it worked. I took it out of the holster, stuck it up in front of her and fired into the wall," he said.

Judge Advocate Law now asked where Blake had been during the time he was not with the 319th and was told, "The rest of the time I was on detached service with the 407th Quartermasters."

Seeing this as Law's first step in bringing up the incriminating data about his client's prior service, Sartain immediately exclaimed, "I object to that question!"
When the objection was overruled, he came back immediately, insisting, "The accused may be questioned only as to the facts concerning the things he is charged with and not to any other facts."

The court was unmoved, explaining that such questions were admissalble to establish the defendant's credibility and allowed the Judge Advocate to continue.

Law asked Blake his status in the quartermaster unit at the time he was returned to the 319th and again Sartain disputed the inquiry. "I object to this questioning!" he persisted. "The matter about which the prosecution is questioning the accused has nothing to do with the charges in this case."

THIS IS RISKY BUSINESS.

Law offered his reasoning, saying, "If the court please, we are trying to show whether the drawing and shooting of a pistol was playful or whether it was probably habitual on the part of the accused."

Sartain's objection was once again overruled. The Judge Advocate was allowed to proceed. He went right to the point and confronted Blake, "Were you not, in fact, in the guardhouse?"

"One night, sir," Blake admitted.

Law then asked, "What were you in the guardhouse for?"

At this juncture Sartain had a pretty good idea of what was going on. Good-soldier Blake was sent back to the 319th because he'd probably pulled a pistol on someone while with the 407th Quartermaster Battalion. If Law were allowed to make this information known to the court, all Sartain's efforts to establish Blake's good character would be for naught.

"I will again object to this line of questioning!" Sartain exclaimed. "My objection is, sir that the prosecution is introducing facts which are not in proper evidence and I object to any testimony along this line. If this testimony was concerned with infractions which resulted in former convictions it could be introduced, but there are no facts to show that any of the accused acts resulted in former convictions. In other words, he must have stood a trial before a court and unless he had been charged and tried before a court I do not think it is proper evidence. Prosecution is attempting to impeach the witness and he should lay a predicate first for that. The testimony that he is trying to show or bring out should be brought out through some other source than this."

Reviewing this case decades later, Sartain commented on his objections. "See, you've got to lay some kind of foundation that the guy had this habit. The fact that he was not court martialed was not important in itself, but the Judge Advocate had to have some kind of evidence that the guy was guilty of a similar action on at least one or two other occasions if he wanted to ask these questions."

When the court requested that the Judge Advocate explain how he could question the witness concerning prior misconduct, he was stopped short. Sartain had blocked his efforts to reveal what may have been a most incriminating piece of evidence at every turn. "I will withdraw the question to save further argument," the prosecutor finally said with resignation.

The trial was all but over. Prosecutor Law asked the court for a continuance so that he might call up other witnesses but was refused. The court had heard enough of the whole sordid affair. In the end Private Blake was found guilty of both charges and sentenced to five years at hard labor.

"All those good witnesses didn't do him much good, did they," commented Sartain thinking back on the sentence. "Five years. Well, it could have been a lot worse. You know, molestation of civilians, General Gavin would have none of it. None of it. Anybody that would mess with a civilian was court martialed. As battery commanders we had to stay on top of all that conduct, and we did. But generally I think the GIs were pretty well disciplined. There was not that much of those shinnanigans, but I was assigned to defend some knuckleheads of that type."

Word of the verdict quickly filtered back to the battalion. In Headquarters Battery the consensus was that Blake never had a chance. "Those MPs were against us to begin with," complained Ed Ryan when asked about the court martial afterwards. "They were anti airborne because we got more money and dressed better." He was also convinced that Blake was innocent. "I know damn well she lied about it," he said bitterly.

"Blake was in my section. He wasn't the boastful type or anything. I know he didn't do anything like that. They court martialed him and he didn't do nothing. It was a bad deal on some of that rape bit anyway because some of these women would claim that GIs did it when they didn't. Krauts, particularly, they'd try to lump something on a GI just through hatred."

Despite Ryan's assertion, when Sartain was asked about German women falsely accusing GIs, he held a different opinion. "No," he said, "I don't think so at least I never heard that, no. I don't have any recollection of that. Most of it was consensual. A lot of it was consensual, a lot of it. The guys made friends with the family and these girls probably thought they were gonna get something, and a lot of them were pretty loose to start with."

Sartain went quiet, trying to find an adequate closing to an unfortunate series of past events, then spoke. "You know, there were a lot of cases they had to dismiss because civilians would not testify. They were scared, and of course the GIs knew that. A civilian woman was not gonna testify against a GI. They were scared and they didn't want to cross that bridge."

Was Frau Muller entrapping Blake, or was she just fabulously naïve? Did Paul Blake intend to force himself, or did he actually think he was being invited into a tryst while the cuckolded husband was out? The language barrier must have complicated communication and wine has never been known to sharpen judgement. Whether what happened between Private Paul Blake and Theresa Muller was consensual or not will never be known for sure, but what is clear is the desperate condition of the civilians and the attitude of entitlement to sexual access which many GIs felt toward German women in 1945. When these factors converged with the general degradation of wartime conditions for all parties, cases like this were too often the sad and inevitable result.

Some of the Battalion Headquarters staff, Taken at Epinal, France June 1945. Front row left to right : Capt. Hawkins, Capt. Cargile, Major Silvey, Colonel Todd, Major Whimberley, Capt. John Connelly, Capt. Wilson Bourgeois. Back row left to right: CWO Felix Greene, Capt. Eskoff, Lt. Harold Peters, Doctor Howard Dibble, CWO Howard Fichtner.

BATTERY!

Part 30: "You couldn't use any sympathy."

After leaving Cologne the 319th moved rapidly with the rest of the 82nd Airborne north and east. Those looking at a situation map could see this movement both cut off German forces in Denmark and blocked any direct Soviet thrust into Scandinavia. The focus of attention now became the relative positions of the western Allies and the Soviets at war's end. In this competitive atmosphere it was determined to advance the line as far east as possible short of Berlin, to contain the Communists' sphere of influence. The convenient allegiance with the Soviet Union against a common enemy was disintegrating faster than the Nazi regime in this vast geo-political game of musical chairs. Indeed, the Germans were quickly becoming the odd-man-out.

Again the division was placed under British command. This was a development which was met with some antipathy, reinforcing the attitude among the 82nd men that they were once more supplying the backbone for another British operation. Notwithstanding, German resistance was weak and unenthusiastic. Firing by the battery was minimal and often interrupted since the rapid advance of Allied troops kept pushing the front lines beyond the limited range of the battalion's 75mm howitzers.

By the 29th day of April, the 82nd received orders to make an immediate crossing of the Elbe River at Bleckede, enter Mecklenburg, and continue driving south-east toward the city of Ludwigslust. When the division arrived at Bleckede, they found British and Canadian soldiers preoccupied with looting the town. Civilians were evacuated in anticipation of German artillery directed against the crossing troops and the 319th established gun positions near the nearby village of Alt Gorge.

The 505th PIR was ordered to spearhead the assault, paddling its way across the Elbe at 1am on the morning of April 30th. Meanwhile the 319th would be reinforcing the supporting fire of the 376th PFAB during the crossing with a covering barrage. Little resistance was encountered by the 505th troopers, but later in the day an unusually heavy German artillery barrage was directed on the crossing site, interrupting the work of division engineers who were laying a pontoon bridge. The battalion was directed to meet this with counter-battery fire. Soon the bridge was complete and the division's units began streaming across the Elbe to the east bank.

The 319th itself crossed over in the late afternoon of May 1st, making a rapid advance toward the village of Haar. By 1800 hours the battalion's new gun emplacements were established. The front was advancing too quickly to avoid hitting friendly troops, so no firing was done from the Haar positions. In fact, if they didn't know it by now, the 319th had already fired its last angry salvo.

May 2nd, 1945, dawned with the familiar rumble of artillery and small arms fire peculiarly absent. Looking around them, the GIs in Able Battery saw a beautiful spring morning. The countryside was a mostly level plain of rich, black soiled fields and forests, dotted here and there with farmhouses or villages. Some of the buildings were brick and many had thatched roofs, but amidst the chaos of war all were still meticulously kept.

In spite of the pastoral setting, by noon the outfit was again displacing – this time further east to the town of Hof Heidhof. The battalion was barely in place at this latest position when it was suddenly ordered to Karenz, another five miles further east. As the battery loaded up, word was circulated that they should not be alarmed if German troops were encountered on the way. Large numbers of prisoners were expected enroute. This confirmed a rumor which was circulating since the night before that the opposing German 21st Army Group had surrendered to General Gavin.

Hardly had the outfit started traveling along Highway 191, really just a lane and a half of pavement flanked by trees, when the "A" Battery men passed a strange sight. Ted Simpson later described it as, "German soldiers, fully-armed, coming toward us on ancient wooden carts pulled by trucks or oxen. The passengers were a unique and amazingly cheerful lot of singing, waving soldiers freely drawing on homegrown bottles of schnapps, vodka or whatever. Many soldiers were accompanied by poorly clad and equally drunken farm women. All smiling, waving to us as they headed for the rear and away from the Russians."

Then a long, unending column of soldiers was spotted up ahead. At first the guys could not make out details. All they saw was an undulating, greenish-grey mass moving toward them. It was the color of German uniforms, distinctly different from the olive and brown tones of GI clothing.

Standing in the open bed of one of the battery's trucks, Orin Miller would never forget the sight. "I can still see it," he later said. "A straight line of men coming down through there, all German soldiers. They gave us orders not to shoot, they said they surrendered and it was over with. We had them all pass by us. My goodness sakes, I can still see that day."

The spectacle was immense. Though accurate records of the type the Germans were used to keeping were impossible at this point, the consensus is that about 150,000 members of Lieutenant General Kurt Von Tippelskirch's 21st Army Group had

An 82nd Airborne trooper stands guard over members of the surrendered German 21st Army near Ludwigslust, Germany. Courtesy Dayton Edie.

BATTERY!

The man perched on top of the rifles is holding an MP44. This weapon was the prototype for the AK-47 and all other "Assault Rifles" used to the present day. Courtesy Leonard Linton family.

surrendered en masse to the 82nd Airborne. With them, and to some extent intermixed, were perhaps another 100,000 extraneous military personnel and civilian refugees. Von Tippelskirch's soldiers were fully armed, still under military discipline and largely intact. They were instructed to remove themselves from the roads and deposit their weapons in neat stacks, then proceed to the rear.

Because of the large numbers involved, all this would take time. This is why some veterans of "A" Battery remember the Germans as fully armed and mechanized, while others recall them as having no weapons or vehicles. John Girardin's memory was of whole disarmed battalions marching past him, three or four abreast, several dozen yards from and parallel to the road.

Robert Dickson's recollection was different. He said, "I never will forget that. They had their tanks, they had their weapons, they had everything. That was really strange. We knew the war had to be over or it wouldn't be happening."

Like Dickson, all found the experience of being immersed within so large an enemy force bizarre and even unsettling. For German and American alike, years of intensive training and psychological trauma had conditioned in each a violent reaction to the mere sight of each other's uniform.

Mahlon Sebring gazed at the scene around him and thought, "All these Germans going one way with their guns loaded and all of us going the other way. Boy, if someone gets trigger happy it's gonna be a mess."

When Lester Newman was asked if he remembered the surrender he replied, "Sure, I was in on that. We were in the truck, our gun section there, following another truck ahead of us. All of a sudden we had to stop. These Germans come marching, I mean right past us. They had their guns, their weapons, and everything. I thought we were

Heaps of weapons and equipment surrendered by members of the German 21st Army. Some of the helmets have various patterns of camouflage paint applied to them. Courtesy Leonard Linton family.

You couldn't use any sympathy.

being surrounded and taken over. Then I seen a bunch of them up ahead of us just go off to the side of the road and throw their guns away. I thought at the time, boy, I wish I could get away with taking one of these for a deer hunting rifle."

Actually, many of the GIs had souvenirs in mind, jumping down from their trucks to scoop up dropped pistols when Germans didn't simply place them in their hands. Roland Gruebling was ecstatic. He'd been shipping captured pistols home for some time, but now he'd struck the mother lode.

Captain Sartain was in on it too, acquiring a Walther PPK and a Lugar. "It was quite a sight," he remembered. "They were lined up, man, just as far as the eye could see, as far as the eye could see the Germans were coming and throwing their rifles in a pile. Piles of helmets, everything. They laid all their weapons in stacks. Lord, the stack got so high, then they made another one. It was stack after stack after stack of rifles and pistols."

Smaller, unattached and less disciplined units started simply dropping their arms as they walked along. Abandoned vehicles and equipage littered the roadsides. Yet 82nd Airborne troopers said later that some of the Germans initially shook their heads and pointed behind them, toward the Soviets, when first told to throw down their arms. Others remember English speaking officers suggesting that the Americans give them fuel for their tanks and join them against the communists.

Fighting the Russians held some appeal for many 82nd men. Ted Covais was one of them, "Because we'd only have to fight them in twenty years. I thought we should have taken Berlin and then gone right on to Moscow, that's how I felt at the time."

Louis Sosa addressed the issue of the Red Army as the principle object of fear among the Germans when he remarked, "There was a long line of them, trying to get away from the Russians and we just let them come through. There were a lot of civilians with them too, a lot of civilians. They didn't want to go through the Russians because the Russians would probably kill them. Sometimes there'd be a tractor towing trailers behind them with civilians riding on them. The Germans are intelligent people, but the damn Russians back in them days, they were uncivilized and uneducated."

There was truth in what Sosa said. Escaping capture by the Soviet Army was a powerful motivating force for German soldiers and civilians alike. The Russians' reputation for harsh treatment of those German prisoners they didn't shoot was a long held fact of life on the Eastern Front. For any German soldier, surrender to the western Allies was infinitely more appealing than misery and probable death at the hands of the Red Army.

For civilians, and most especially women, the fate which waited for them if they fell into Russian hands filled them with terror. A significant portion of the Red Army of 1945 was composed of men from remote regions of the Soviet Union. Some came from cultures which were essentially tribal, with more akin to a world which was, by comparison with western Europeans, several hundred years in the past. Few of these soldiers were familiar with the hallmarks of modernity in the 20th Century, such as electricity, indoor plumbing, the telephone, or any notion that the women of a defeated foe are not a conventional prize for the victor. Indeed, the Russian proverb, "Hunt first the enemy, then his woman." Seems to have been the attitude of most of the Red Army.

Compounding this mind-set was the spirit of revenge with which the Red Army entered Germany. Rape was seen by many of its soldiers as justified -- a legitimate means to inflict revenge against an enemy who had not only occupied their "matushka Rossia" "birth country" in a cruel, ruthless, manner, but who had also devastated the nation and caused the deaths of as yet uncounted millions of their kinsfolk. Consequently, wholesale rapes of German, Austrian, and Hungarian women, as well as Russian and Polish slave laborers, were reported as soon as the Red Army crossed the border into Germany and its ally, Hungary. Simply put, rape was another way to dishonor the enemy by defiling his wife, daughter, sister, or mother.

How pervasive the use of rape was as a terror tactic of the Red army remains controversial and difficult to quantify. Since the war, German women have largely remained silent on the subject, but even in the most supportive of environments, rape victims are frequently reluctant to come forth out of shame, trauma, or fear of retribution. For those living among the perpetrators as a conquered people, silence was really the only choice. Some atrocities were almost surely exaggerated by the Nazi propaganda machine to prop up public resistance, but far too many well documented cases of mass rapes exist to dismiss. Today estimates of victims range from hundreds of thousands to as many as two million. Whatever the number, the threat of rape at the hands of Soviet soldiers for German women, and savagery against the entire civilian population, was a real and substantive fear during the closing months of the war.

Wading through so many thousands of prisoners and refugees slowed the progress of the 319th's convoy, but by mid-afternoon of May 2nd the guys started setting up their howitzers in Karenz, correctly surmising that this would be the last time. Even as they dug slit trenches and worked to lay out the guns, Germans continued surrendering themselves with annoying frequency, politely asking to be directed to the nearest prisoner stockade.

Among the surrendering troops of Tippelskirch's army were two regiments of Hungarian Hussars. Mounted troops and horse drawn equipment were not unusual on the eastern front but always struck GIs as a surprising anachronism.

Ed Ryan certainly thought so when he recalled seeing them. "It was a marvel to watch," he said. "They came hiking down the road, a couple of hundred of them. A lot of their horses were white. They were in military order, all leading their horses by the bridle with their carbines stuck in this scabbard on the side of their saddles. That was quite a surrender you know. They surrendered with the horse and the sword and the sheath and all the rest of that stuff. It was like something you saw a hundred years ago. Of course, they did the surrender right. I mean it was done by the numbers. Done the way the book says."

The Hungarians stacked their arms and proceeded further to the rear where Roland Gruebling was posted. When their mounted Colonel rode up to him, Grue-

Roland Gruebling with the crew of the same Soviet tank. He wears his trademark Army Air Force shoulder holster and is handling two German Army Mauser rifles. Courtesy Gruebling family.

You couldn't use any sympathy.

Sgt. Ted Covais poses with a Soviet officer in front of his tank, May 2nd, 1945. Note the sickle insignia painted on the right front fender. The tank itself is an American M4 "Sherman" -- one of thousands provided through the Lend-Lease program to the Red Army. Usually remounted with Russian made guns for consistency of ammunition, about 30% of Soviet tanks were of this variety. Covais Collection.

bling relieved the officer of his sword and pistol, mounted his horse, and escorted him to Captain Sartain's command post. The Colonel presented himself to Sartain and requested permission to bivouac his men and horses in an adjacent pine forest. His horses were, he said in very broken English, "Kaput."

Sartain had no objection, and seems to have taken the whole incident nonchalantly. In any event, when interviewed for this book he did not remember his audience with the Hungarian Colonel. "I honestly don't remember him, I don't," he admitted, "but what I do recall is that several of the guys wanted to ship those horses home. They were riding those damn horses all over the place. They had a good time, those that wanted to ride those horses, but I didn't give a damn about a horse. I'd ridden my last horse at Fort Sill." Sartain thought about the Hungarian cavalry some more, then added, "I don't know how many German surrendered to us but there was a distinction between the average German and the Polaks that were forced to fight with them or the Hungarians. As soon as the hostilities were over we had to place a guard on them so they wouldn't go out and kill Germans, you know what I mean? Get even with them."

The battery remained at Karenz throughout most of May 3rd, but many of the men were busy organizing the chaos around them. There were hundreds of abandoned vehicles and thousands of pieces of discarded weaponry to be collected. More urgently though, the quarter million German prisoners and refugees needed to be sorted out, then herded westward and beyond Russian hands. According to the Germans, Soviet troops were hard on their heels and only a few kilometers behind.

In fact, the 82nd had been preparing its men since late April for a link up with the Red Army. On April 29th, while collecting at Bleckede, members of the division received a leaflet called Russian Army Uniforms in anticipation that once the Elbe was crossed, contact could happen at any time. All through May 1st and 2nd, pathfinder groups from the 82nd remained on the lookout for signs of any Soviet presence. Then, during evening retreat on May 3rd another pamphlet was handed out, this time titled, "When you meet the Russians."

It was already too late. All day long on May 3rd members of the 319th and other units in the division had been making contact with Soviet troops.

BATTERY!

This was first true in the battalion for the liaison and communications men who were posted with infantry units. Covais and Gruebling were with their liaison team among the 505th Parachute Infantry near the village of Grabow, about five miles south of Ludwigslust on May 3rd. By mid-day the stream of German prisoners and refugees had pretty well stopped in their immediate area and, like a lot of other GIs that day, they started scouring the roadsides for binoculars, unusual weapons, and pistols, especially Lugars. Then a passing paratrooper told them there were Russians up ahead. Curiosity demanded they snag a jeep and investigate, besides, maybe they could trade some of the cognac they'd found for vodka. Sensing a photogenic moment, Covais grabbed his Voigtlander camera and they were off.

Once the two had driven about a mile they noticed what appeared to be American M-4 Sherman tanks up ahead, parked to one side of the road. These Shermans didn't have the familiar white star of American armor. Instead their turrets were festooned with slogans crudely painted in the indescipherable Cyrillic alphabet. Some had hammers, sicles, and other symbols suggestive of the class struggle painted on their fenders. They were part of the Soviet 8th Mechanized Corps. Clusters of Red Army soldiers wearing padded tanker's helmets were gathered around these steel fortresses. They started shouting and waving as soon as Covais and Gruebling got close enough to be recognized as American GIs. As he slipped the Voigtlander into his field jacket pocket, Covais remarked, "I don't think we can trust these guys."

The Russians were certainly friendly, and enthusiastic, pressing past each other, trying to be first to shake hands with the Americans. The two GIs were escorted to the tanks, where a lively conversation ensued, albeit completely beyond the understanding of any of the participants. Then the hatch of the nearest tank opened and a man climbed out. He jumped down to the ground with the agility of a cat. Immediately the other Russians grew quiet and stepped out of his way. As he walked toward him, Covais could see he was small, dark skinned, with distinctly oriental features. He wore a fur hat of curly lamb's wool on which were perched a pair of goggles. There was a woolen pullover blouse under his wide leather belt, breeches and highly polished riding boots.

Anyone would have recognized him immediately as an officer. Gruebling held out a pack of cigarettes. The Russian withdrew one, admired it for a moment, and then smiled broadly. One of his men struck a match for him. The officer then said something to a tank crewman, who ran off and returned with a bottle and three glasses. Generous servings of Vodka were poured. The Russian held his up and exclaimed, "Roosevelt!" It was the first of several toasts to FDR, Stalin, Truman, America, and the Red Army, drunk from glasses made from the bottom portions of wine bottles.

After accepting another cigarette the Russian pointed to Covais' Sergeant Chevrons, turned, and motioned for the American to follow him. "Their Lieutenant was a Mongolian, a little guy, and he wanted me to go inside the tank, which I did," Covais recalled later. "He started showing me the dials and gauges. They were all in English, American writing. He kept saying, 'Panzki Americanski, Panzki Americanski!' But I didn't trust them, no, no, you can't trust the Ruskies, so I answered back, 'Shove your nanutski up your kaputski!'"

The tank was one of 450,000 vehicles furnished under the Lend-Lease program to the Soviet Union during World War Two. In fact, approximately one third of tanks used by the Red Army were of this variety, most refitted with Soviet made cannon to accept their ammunition.

When Covais and the officer climbed out of the tank they could see Gruebling

You couldn't use any sympathy.

involved in a lively dialogue with several Russian crewmen. They were examining a German rifle, passing it back and forth. Covais took the camera from his pocket and gestured that they all pose for pictures together. Gruebling stood with the tankers, Covais with the officer, then they snapped the shutter, shook hands and left.

Other members of the 319th and "A" Battery were making contact with the Russians that day. Two guys from the Headquarters Battery got picked up at a Russian roadblock while searching for trophies and another tried to disarm a Russian officer whom he mistook for a German. Carl Salminen was driving a forward observer or liaison team between the outfit and the infantry when he drove into one of the small villages beyond Ludwigslust, just as the Russians were pillaging the town. "First thing I know we're kind of surrounded by Russians with their Tommy guns, their machineguns. We figured, we better get the heck out of here! They were like a bunch of animals!"

Guys in "A" Battery were strongly discouraged from exercising their curiosity about the Russians by visiting until things settled down. Of course some men in the battery were apt to take such advice as a challenge.

Two in "A" Battery who balked at the restriction were Silas Hogg and his best buddy, fellow Kentuckian Olden Tilford. "Get this," said Hogg, who was eager to tell the tale. "They told us that there's a good chance that we'd run across a Russian soldier that afternoon and to watch ourselves real close. I told Tilford, I said, 'Tilford, fuck this. Let's beat them to it, let's go find them.' And we took off right across the lines. We found them, every one drunker than a fiddler's whore. Every one drunk. After we got through looking at them we looked at each other, shook our heads and said, 'If that's who we got to fight we ain't got no problem.'"

When Ed Ryan was asked if he remembered his first direct contact with the Soviets, an unsettling series of memories came to mind. "They were pretty violent you know," he began. "I was going up a road with another guy in my section. These people were coming down, refugees. A Russian came up to us. He spoke pretty good English. He said, you better get out of here because we're gonna have some fun. So we did, and boy they started putting mortars right in that column of refugees. What a terrible mess. People were screaming and hollering all over the place. The horses climbed up on back of each other and all."

Barracks buildings at Wobelein. Covais collection.

BATTERY!

Ribald events were frequently the hallmark of Ryan's stories, but this time he seemed genuinely troubled by what he remembered. "We had a place there where some of the civilians came through," he continued. "It was like a peninsula where these Krauts would come into our lines. They thought they were getting into our lines, but then they would go out the other end and they were right in with the Russians again.

These two female prisoners at Woebbelin may have been among the factory workers producing nazi regalia in the Reiherhorst compound. US Army signal corps photo.

Boy oh boy, some of them had a bad time. Them Russians were doing the old rape bit. Grabbing women out of the lines. One guy said to me, 'Want one? There's a good one, I'll get her for you.' I said, don't bother. Jesus. They were screaming for help and all the rest of that. The Russians believed in that rape and all the rest of that shit, at that time anyway. Oh yes."

Ryan was quiet, then he spoke again. There was clearly more he wanted to get off his chest. "You know, those people lost their homes and everything they ever owned. They were starving and everything else. But the Russians hated the Krauts for what they did to them, so that was it. Well, you couldn't have done anything about it anyway, even if you wanted to. In those cases you've just got to push those people past you. You can't use any sympathy, it'll only pile up on you."

As disdainful as it was for the average GI to stand by while outrages were committed, the chance for open conflict with the Russians had the potential of erupting into a bloody international incident. This was especially so considering the ubiquitous presence of automatic weapons, pistols, alcohol, and bravado. Nonetheless, there is evidence that armed confrontation between Americans and Russians did occur.

Bob Storms was probably referring to one such episode which took place on the night of May 3-4, in Grabow between troopers of the 505th Parachute Infantry and Russian soldiers. "The first night we were tangled up together we had a lot of trouble," explained Storms. "It started with the town women. The Russians went through there and thought they could do what they wanted with them, but half that town was ours. We had a gun battle but it was hushed up pretty fast. It was ten years and a court martial if you talked about it, even with your own men. They hushed that up so big hardly anybody ever knowed about it. Oh yeah. Them Russians was rough, they was rough, I'm telling you. I was glad we didn't have much to do with them."

"A" Battery and the rest of the battalion remained at Karenz until the afternoon of May 4th, when they were displaced again. By 1800 hours Headquarters and "B" Batteries were located in the village of Alt Krenzlin, and "A" Battery occupied the neighboring village of Neu Krenzlin, with Major Silvey appointed as Military Governor

YOU COULDN'T USE ANY SYMPATHY.

for the area under the battalion's control. Since there was no longer any organized German resistance, the posting was one of occupation duty. Even if there was no need to set up the howitzers, the 319th's men were kept busy. It was necessary to determine if German civilians were Nazi party officials, members of the SS, or soldiers in mufti trying to avoid being taken as prisoners of war. Attention had to be given to refugees and displaced persons who needed direction to appropriate collection points. Searches for possible hidden stores of arms and ammunition were conducted and there was still an enormous amount of abandoned military material to be collected.

At about this time it became widely known that a concentration camp had been discovered a few miles north of Ludwigslust. Pathfinders from the division had first located the camp on May 2nd, though the true liberation didn't take place until the next day. Only then were the gates opened, allowing those prisoners who were still ambulatory to join the stream of refugees and German soldiers fleeing the Russians. Trucks and medical personnel also arrived on May 3rd, but it was too late for hundreds who lay dead in open burial pits, stacked in heaps or scattered around the compound, and lying in the crude barracks.

Woebbelin was a satellite camp of the large Neuengammen concentration camp complex at Hamburg. It was built over the previous winter to accommodate prisoners evacuated from more extensive camps in Poland, but which were being steadily over-run by advancing Soviet forces. Drawing its designation from the nearby village of the same name, Woebbelin was actually two camps. The original and smaller camp was begun in September of 1944, under the supervision of Luftwaffe Commandant Willibald Scherer. This facility, known as Reiherhorst, was of somewhat substantial construction, with electricity and basements for at least some of the buildings. Once Reiherhorst was completed it became the barracks for the slave-labor work crew which began building Woebbelin.

Some half dozen barracks buildings, a kitchen, and the lazarette – a sort of combination hospital and latrine comprised Woebbelin itself. All this was placed within a stark treeless parade ground and surrounded by a double barbed wire enclosure fitted out with watchtowers at each corner. Photographs indicate that the barracks buildings were built in a herringbone pattern in relation to each other and diagonal to the sides of the wire

enclosure. This arrangement offered the greatest field of fire between the barracks from the towers. Outside the wire were located barracks for the SS guards, storehouses, and sundry utility buildings.

Though made of brick, the barracks at Woebbe-

Dead bodies inside one of the barracks at Wobelein. Covais collection. lin were poorly constructed of inferior materials and left unfinished. The floors were bare earth and the doorways and windows were open to the weather. Inside was a scaffold of slightly milled, green lumber. Two tiers of bunks were then fashioned by stretching barbed wire across the framework.

In mid-February, 1945, Woebbelin took in its first compliment of about 700 political prisoners. Many of these individuals were French, Dutch, or Belgians who had run afoul

Partly consumed bodies in the open cremation pit at Wobelein. Covais collection.

of their Nazi occupiers as members of trade unions and socialist or communist inspired organizations. Some were suspected of resistance activities, others were simply deemed incompatible with Nazi ideology. Only a minority were Jews. At least one was a Catholic priest. The majority were probably Poles and Russians whose status as prisoners of war or slave laborers pulled them into the vortex of the concentration camp system. The facility was not an extermination camp and thus did not include gas chambers or crematoria. Instead, Woebbelin was intended to serve as a labor and detention camp. Some prisoners, for example, were put to work at a bakery in Woebbelin village, and others were almost certainly utilized as a labor source in Ludwigslust and other nearby locations.

As German occupied areas shrank to nothing over the following ten weeks, the population of the camp swelled in excess of 4,000. Overcrowded, the already weak inmates were given inadequate shelter and little subsistence. Deaths rose from about 100 per week to several times that number as the infrastructure supporting the camp collapsed. When reconnaissance teams of the American 8th Infantry and 82nd Airborne Divisions finally arrived on May 2nd there were about 3,500 living prisoners confined behind the wire. Hundreds of bodies were strewn about the camp and hundreds of others had already been deposited into burial pits, the victims of starvation and disease through sinister, monstrous disregard.

Reiherhorst had, by this time, been reorganized as a labor camp for female prisoners. Women held there were kept at work sewing flags, banners, and other Nazi cloth goods in a factory located on the premises. Indications are that living conditions at Reierhorst were marginally better than at Woebbelin itself, in any event the sleeping bunks are known to have been wooden boards and not barbed wire.

Most of the Woebbelin prisoners walked or were taken away from the camp on May 3rd, but a substantial number remained, mostly to receive critical medical attention. Throughout that day and the next, more living prisoners were carefully moved to army hospitals as their conditions stabilized. The dead were left as they'd been found, and would remain there to confront the townspeople of Ludwigslust.

Sartain had also made an impromptu investigation of the site with Sosa on May 3rd, having smelled as much as heard about it. He found the compound locked up and guarded by division MPs while medical personnel tended to the survivors. "The medicswouldn't let the average GI go in," he explained. "Wouldn't let us give them anything. When I went to see it with Sosa, a lot of the inmates were still there. It was horrible. I didn't get to go inside but I walked along the wire. All these people were lined up. They were going crazy, hollering and putting their hands through the wire to touch you. They wanted to hold your hand and all of that business. I was pretty well shook-up to see it, all of us were, but we'd been instructed what to do when we ran across something like that. They had to have immediate medical attention before they put anything in their stomach, so we knew not to mess with them. Even so, they kept pushing us to let them out. But we didn't. We followed division and immediately a medical unit showed up. Immediately."

When he got back to the battalion there was already a lot of talk about the concentration camp. The next day a directive came down that as many of the men should have an opportunity to see Woebbelin as possible. "I was all for it, I wanted them to see it, I really did," remembered Sartain.

Thus arrangements were made that the next day, May 5th; each battery would

One of the living dead at Wobelein. "Everybody was sad. Nobody was smiling. Happy, yeah, in a way, but they had been through so much," said Covais as he thought back to attempts he made to talk to the prisoners. "Few were alive, and those that were alive were like skin and bones, just barely alive." Covais collection.

take its turn going out to the site. Lieutenant Ragland remembered the directive as a suggestion. Strictly speaking it may have been put in those terms though strongly encouraged. In any event, other units of the 82nd were also sending their men to tour Woebbelin at about this same time.

Carl Salminen's memory was that in "A" Battery, "We had to go. No ifs and buts about it, we had to go. The orders were that we had to go and see it so you'd always remember what the Germans did."

At mid-afternoon "A" Battery all piled into weapons carriers for the ride to Woebbelin. Lieutenant Ragland had First Sergeant Picher remind the men that feeding or physical contact with the prisoners would be regarded as a court martial offence. Though some avoided the trip by design or chance, most all of the battery was there and curious to view for themselves the worst crimes of the Nazi foe. Kenneth Smith, Ted Simpson, Carl Salminen, Joe D'Appolonio, Sebring, Bob Storms, Covais, Lieutenant Ragland, and several dozen others all climbed into the trucks.

They passed first through Ludwigslust, which appeared to be an attractive town of about 5,000 inhabitants, with a beautiful baroque mansion at one end of the town square and a church at the other. The town was also intact, having been the intended and achieved objective of the division since crossing the Elbe.

Though they knew they were being taken to see some sort of atrocity site, their spirits were high - after all, the weather was beautiful and the war was over as far as anyone could tell. The formal surrender of the Germans was all that remained. Then, a couple of miles after clearing the northern outskirts of Ludwigslust the guys in the convoy noticed a foul odor

Men of the 319th were among the first to enter the camp after its SS guards left.

wafting through the air. A short distance further they could see why. Just a dozen or so yards from the roadway was the outermost perimeter of barbed wire. It encompassed what seemed the most desolate cantonment they'd ever seen. Craning their necks to get a better look, the GIs first thought they saw small piles of abandoned clothing here an there along the fence line. Then they realized there were astonishingly thin bodies inside the rags, looking remarkably like frail puppets which had dropped in place when their strings were cut.

The convoy followed along the road, parallel with the compound boundary for some distance, then turned into a wooden gate and came to a stop. By this time any conversation was silenced and men started getting out of the trucks. Some wrinkled their faces in reaction to the suffocating odor which enveloped them. Close to them a GI truck was unloading food and medical supplies. A few pathetic souls in striped clothing hovered around the truck or could be seen walking very slowly in the background.

Before wandering off in small groups or individually, the "A" Battery men stood there and tried to take in the scene. The six or eight buildings, the silent parade ground, and empty watchtowers were like a colossal crime scene.

"It was quite large, a large camp and it didn't smell very good. It had a sweet smell, like death. It gave me an eerie feeling," remembered Covais in a conversation he had about the camp many years later.

"Eerie" was exactly the word which came to Mahlon Sebring's mind as well,

You couldn't use any sympathy.

while Kenneth Smith described Woebbelin's first impression on him as "just kind of spooky."

Finally small groups of troopers started out by walking to the area where some of the weakest survivors lay on stretchers, being fed intravenously, while others sat patiently waiting for medical attention. These were the remaining survivors of Woebbelin. The majority were those whose health was most precarious or others who had elected to stay, perhaps because the camp now offered some security in a very turbulent and still dangerous time. By May 5th this could still have numbered a hundred or more. Ragland remembered that for many of these individuals, "About all they could do was move their eyes."

Covais described them this way, saying, "They were all dressed up in black and white vertical stripes. I would say every one of them had dysentery and typhus, stuff like that. They were thin, and bony. Their cheeks were all sunken in. Their arms were like sticks, they had no flesh on their arms or legs. Half dead. They were starving. They were just skin and bones, completely emaciated."

Reviewing his memory, Covais recalled human details which he'd tried to keep at the back of his mind for years. "I talked to these people, Popolski, Russian, even some of the women," he said. "Everybody was sad. Every body was sad. Nobody was smiling. Nobody was grinning, nobody was rejoicing. Happy, yeah, in a way, but they had been through so much."

One of the medical crew remarked to the guys that if they really wanted to see some sights they ought to take a look at the barracks buildings. They all started off in that direction. Halfway there Bob Storms turned on his heel and went back to the trucks, then a few other guys followed him.

The barracks buildings looked ominous and unexplainably dark considering how they sat unsheltered in the open compound. Each had a number – 57, 58, 59, and so forth painted on the outside in enormous numerals. There were a couple of MPs posted at the doorway to each barrack and at one a medical team was moving about, searching for survivors. When they stepped up to the first building most simply poked their head inside for a quick peek. The stench of death and disease kept all but the most

Citizens of Ludwigslust digging over 200 graves for victims of the Wobelein camp in the town center. Sartain collection.

BATTERY!

Freshly buried dead in the town center at Ludwigslust. During the East German communist regime, the crosses were removed. Today they have been replaced with flat memorial markers. Sartain collection.

curious from going any further. Those who did took a few cautious steps inside, turned around before they'd gone far. On the way back they gingerly picked their way between and over corpses, puddles of excrement and blood. The so-called barrack was a single, cavernous room with a few brick support columns inside for the roof. The only other construction was the tortuous beds of barbed wire.

Ed Ryan was with the Headquarters Battery group that afternoon and saw the barracks too. "The bunks they had there, they used barbed wire for the bottom of the bunk. Then you stretch your blanket over that and let it bite on you. That's how nice they were to people," he later said bitterly.

There were people in there – more dead than alive, and in many cases it was impossible to easily distinguish one from the other. Some lay in the aisles or on the dirt floor, others lay on the wire, often in their own waste, or that of someone lying above them.

"What was bad was these people begging for food and you didn't dare give them any," one "A" Battery man said with sadness about the few who held up their feeble, birdlike hands or begged to be given some morsel. A few murmured words of encouragement knowing that was all that could be offered.

Another HQ Battery man later said, "I remember one face in particular. The guy was sitting up against the post and he had died and he was just sitting there. He was just a rack of bones. Most of them, they were just skeletons almost. It just don't seem possible that anybody could be that mean to people."

One of the sergeants, probably Carl Davis took out a camera. Folks at home would never believe this if they didn't see the pictures, he thought.

Covais continued on to the next, and the next, and next barracks after that. Between some of them a few lonely victims of starvation lay scattered about. When he passed the corner of one building Covais suddenly found himself staring at what was the most hideous thing he'd seen since leaving home. "There were a lot of bodies, naked bodies on the ground about four, five feet high, stacked up outside the buildings," he remembered. "These bodies were just exposed like cordwood, just stacked up on top of one another in any grotesque way or manner, fifteen or twenty at a time. Just thrown there like it was garbage, like garbage. Well, they say all's fair in love and war, but this was a vicious crime."

The Lazarette, where the dead had been accumulating for some time, was an especially gruesome station on this macabre journey. Corpses inside this structure were said to have been so plentiful that the first liberators were unable to push the door completely open. After this came the cremation pit. Located at a back corner of the compound in what had once been a quarry. The ashes and half consumed bodies there exposed still more atrocities.

The final destination in the tour of Woebbelin was a series of burial pits in the pine woods just outside the wire. Lieutenant Ragland remembered, "One huge grave that had a lot of bodies in it. They hadn't covered it up yet. I was really shocked. You know, we heard about things, but until you see it you just don't believe it."
The sight left John Girardin reeling. "What got me was the way they were stacked up. They weren't just thrown in there, they were stacked. Like they wanted to put more in there, more bodies in there. That's what I remember."

Even though photographs of prisoners in other concentration camps were already widely seen by members of the division before crossing the Elbe, everyone who went to Woebbelin was overcome by the indescribable crimes all around them. "I was appalled," Covais later said of what he witnessed. "All this mess, the injustice that was being done, it was unbelievable. All this inhumanity towards these people."
At this point many of the men had had enough and went back to the trucks. Several decided, among them Lieutenant Ragland, Covais, and Salminen, to cross the railroad tracks and inspect the women's camp.

New prisoners were being transferred by the SS to Reiherhorst as late as the morning of May 2nd, immediately before the guards vanished. By May 5th at least some female prisoners were still confined to their quarters, probably for medical reasons.
Whatever the justification, both Covais and Salminen remembered them as still locked in their basement barracks, clamoring for relief. "There was a grating," recalled Carl. "As you'd walk by it, the women were hollering, 'We need help, we need help, help us, help!'"

Covais once remarked that the women prisoners in that chamber seemed to have been driven to insanity. There was nothing they could do, and in any case, the scene was far too heart wrenching to linger. ·

Moving on, the GIs found the factory. It was a large room with what seemed like three or four dozen industrial sewing machines. All were black metal with the name "Singer" emblazoned in gold. Bolts of cloth and rolls of machine embroidered insignia were left. Black, white, and red were the only colors. Covais walked over to a large pile of flags ready to have their final binding sewn on. Lieutenant Ragland joined him and they each took one as a souvenir.

"They had the women sewing the swastika flags and all that stuff," recalled Covais. "I confiscated one. It was a big banner and I had it for years, but the thing stunk. It smelled awful! I washed it and the smell would not leave the banner. I don't know what happened to it. I think my wife threw it out or something, got disgusted and didn't want anything stinking that much."

Shock was already turning to disgust and anger by the time everyone reassembled at the trucks. Some of the guys cursed the Germans, others were quiet and still trying to make sense of what they were just exposed to. For the first time since anyone could remember, Bob Storms had nothing to say. He sat alone, looking like he'd been weeping. More than anything else, they all now knew what they'd been fighting for. A fury to confront the German people rose within the GIs and had to be satisfied.

The next day the citizens of Ludwigslust were trucked out to Woebbelin and forced to confront the reality of what lay just outside their town. MPs funneled the Germans through the camp, at places maneuvering them into positions from which they were forced to step among and over bodies. Some of the "A" Battery men were there to see the procession.

Ted Simpson later wrote of the, "Respectfully dressed women weeping at the pits contents. The men, hats in hands, properly solemn. It was as if the entire exercise was a complete surprise to the village's occupants and yet for years, the death stench of Woebbelin had permeated the area for miles around."

Simpson shared this widespread belief of American soldiers that the local Germans were fully aware of what had been going on at Woebbelin, and that the camp had been there with their sanction for a long time. Few, if any, understood that the prison had actually been there just ten weeks, or considered that there was little or nothing the citizenry could have done about it. In a sense, totalitarianism had turned the entire nation into a prison. Moreover, during the time that the camp was in operation the Germans were in fear for their own lives, preoccupied by either death from Allied bombings or the approaching Russian Army.

In the final analysis these mitigating circumstances were inadequate to excuse the culpability of the Germans. That the people of Ludwigslust and surrounding villages did not know about the camp is inconceivable. An unpardonable violation of humanity was taking place under their noses, with at least their passive collusion. Woebbelin was, after all, in plain view, just yards off the main road between Ludwigslust and Schwerin. Some area inhabitants later admitted that from a distance they saw bodies being carried to the burial pits. Prisoners worked in the area's towns and as recently as April of 1945, the SS was screening motion pictures for the local residents in one of the buildings at Reiherhorst.

Sartain put it most succinctly when he said, "You could smell it miles off. That's why we got pissed off with the neighbors who said they had no idea it was there."
Reflecting back on the whole question of German complacency, Covais later complained, "You know, when we went into Italy nobody was a fascist. When we went into Germany, nobody was a Nazi. They denied knowing the existence of the concentration camp. They said they didn't know anything about it or that it even existed. They were very adamant about that but, I didn't believe them, of course not, no. They said, 'Oh, it is all propaganda. We would never do anything like that.' But somebody did, right?"
All that day the citizens were forced to handle the corpses of over 200 victims with their bare hands. The remains were carried out to trucks and brought to the town square. "Our revenge was making them dig the graves," said Covais.

On May 7 the 82nd Airborne Division conducted funeral services for the deceased prisoners. Most of the citizens of Ludwigslust, captured German officers, and several hundred members of the division attended the service. The US Army Chaplain at the service delivered a eulogy which pointed out to the Germans that, "Within four miles of your comfortable homes 4,000 men were forced to live like animals, deprived even of the food you would give to your dogs."

During interviews for this book, it is fair to say that most of the veterans were at some point overcome with emotion as they relived their war experiences. Woebbelin

YOU COULDN'T USE ANY SYMPATHY.

was the most common juncture in their narrative at which this happened. When Bob Storms was asked what he saw at Woebbelin he suddenly choked up. Through tears he explained, "I couldn't go through. I tried, I'd seen a lot but I couldn't go, I couldn't go through. I'd get so far and just couldn't take it. I still get shook up. I guess you never get over it."

BATTERY!

Part 31: "We don't swim naked in Louisiana."

The day following the burial of the Woebbelin victims in the town square of Ludwigslust, all hostilities in Europe ceased. The war against Nazism was won. Hitler had already committed suicide on April 30th, while the 82nd Airborne Division was crossing the Elbe, and over the following week events rapidly brought the Third Reich to a conclusion.

For the men in the 319th, official news of the end came as something of an anticlimax, the war having been finished in their sector since the surrender of Von Tippelskirch's 21st Army Group on May 2nd. Just the same, the urge to look back on the two years since landing at Casablanca was irresistible at a time like this. With it, came memories of dead and wounded comrades who had not been fortunate enough to see the journey to its end.

Some of the men may have felt a vague sense of disorientation or even emptiness once the first cheers of elation had been released. When highly stimulating circumstances come to an end this is often the case, especially when these circumstances involve danger and fear.

Covais seemed to be speaking about this effect when he said, "We were happy of course, but there was no hysteria, there was no outburst of gladness, of laughter, not in the field anyway. All that came after. When the news broke out it was calm, it was quiet, and there was a sigh of relief. I think we were relieved that we made it through alive."

With the cessation of hostilities searches of local homes for weapons or fugitive SS and Nazi party members continued. Lieutenant Mullen was in charge of one search crew which flushed out a belligerent SS officer. The man resisted interrogation, but Mullen had just seen the work of the SS at Woebbelin and had no patience for him. "I was just helping an SS officer remember some things & he had some hard jaws," is how Mullen later explained the broken knuckle of his right hand in a letter home.

Ed Ryan and Milton Sussman were part of another search party. "Outside of Ludwigslust we were doing a screening, a shake-down of Kraut houses," Ryan later said. "We come around the corner and these Russian civilians were hollering that someone was shooting at them. We come up to this house and there's a Kraut upstairs with a Schmeisser. We didn't want to go in because they could roll a grenade down the stairs on you, but he must have jumped out the window. We couldn't figure out where the hell he went. Then Sussman says, 'I know where he is. He's in the outhouse.' So we tipped it over and there he was. We checked his arm and his blood type was tattooed there, so that meant he was SS too."

Like Mullen, Ryan had been to Woebbelin and seen what was there, while Sussman himself was a German Jew who'd narrowly escaped to the United States with his life. Neither of them had any sympathy for the SS.

"We took that prisoner to this Limey camp up there and they asked us, who hit this man! We told the Limey that he fell out of the jeep. He said, 'I don't believe that,'" Ryan finished.

Screening German homes for fugitive SS and Nazi party members were the last serious actions that the 319th troopers were called upon which involved any real risk. In "A" Battery, Orin Miller said, "They more or less didn't pay much attention to us there for about a week and a half, two weeks after the thing was all over. We just moseyed around and did what ever we wanted to do, no reveille and retreat, none of it."

Many of the usual details of military decorum were relaxed and duties reduced to a minimum. After all, everyone felt they deserved a rest. One HQ Battery man wrote of this period in his diary that it was, "like being on vacation." But with time on their hands and a good deal of motorized transportation at their disposal, GIs exploring the countryside were bound to get into mischief.

In one case, Sosa was on the prowl for anything worth foraging and came across a wine cellar. "One time I was running around in my jeep," he explained, "Seeing what's happening and I found a warehouse with wine in it. So I, there's a word for it, I looted it. I brought a barrel back to the battery and set it up there right out in front. We helped ourselves."

A guard was placed on the warehouse, but the arrangement was an opportunity begging for exploitation. Robert Dickson remembered it well and said, "The Germans had the best wine there was and there was a lot of boys got stewed on that stuff." Clearly having foxes guard the henhouse wasn't working out. Perhaps too much of the delayed celebration which Covais alluded to was taking place. In any event, after a few days Able Battery was taken off this detail. There was still a lot of wine in western Mecklenburg though and the men were rather thirsty.

Robert Rappi took to patrolling the surrounding area with Motor Sergeant Legg in a 2 1/2 ton truck. At one place they found an enormous hogshead of wine. Proud of their forethought to have on hand the means to haul such a prize, they loaded the over-sized barrel in back and brought it to the battery.

This time the outfit became sufficiently inebriated to attract the attention of one of the battalion's staff officers. From Rappi's words, it may have been Colonel Todd himself. "Then the Old Man came around and took an ax to the barrel of wine. I don't remember who it was but it wasn't Sartain," he said with regret.

"That's right," agreed Dickson when asked about the incident, "I remember we all got drunk, then an officer came along and took an axe to that barrel, but not before we got a lot of stuff out of it."

When he heard about it sixty years later, Sartain was amused but protested that whoever took an axe to the barrel, it wasn't him. Then he added his comment on the possibility that a barrel of wine was kept at the battery bivouac in the first place, "Could have been, but if they did they kept it a secret. I didn't see it. There were a lot of things that they kept secret and I didn't know about. They had a lot of secrets among themselves." Battalion brass was not at all happy about enlisted men who overindulged, but Mahlon Sebring recounted one episode in which intemperance by the "A" Battery guys was met with understanding and concern, at least by their battery commander. "We'd run on to a bunch of alcohol. Well, there was a lot of guys really sucked that alcohol up and got in bad shape. Captain Sartain was afraid they'd drink straight alcohol and kill themselves, so the guys were cutting it half and half with grape wine. Well, we had one formation where I was the only one in our section who showed up. When I reported our section all present and accounted for, Captain Sartain said, 'Are they still all Breathing?' I told him, 'They were when I come out here.'"

Sartain's tolerance for the men's excesses may have stemmed in part from the fact that the officers were having their own share of drinking parties. Frequently these

BATTERY!

involved social visits between the officers of the 319th's batteries or with those of the 320th and other outfits.

Lieutenant Cook remembered the "A" Battery officers riding back to camp from these parties in a commandeered German sedan which lacked brakes. In order to stop the automobile it had to be skillfully run into a wall, tree, or some other stationary object. "Charlie was good at that," Cook remembered of Sartain's driving ability at these times.

If the Able Battery guys could lay hands on large quantities of free alcohol, their access to confiscated vehicles of all kinds, but particularly German military motorcycles, was even greater. As Lieutenant Cook put it, "At the end of the war you could just pick one up in a ditch. The road ditches were full of them. Bent wheels, blown out tires, out of gas or something. Take two or three and put them together and you'd have you a motorcycle."

Lester Newman claimed that there were so many discarded German army motorcycles lying around after the surrender that, "All of us in the battery had one, everybody that could ride one. John Girardin had a German motorcycle, so did Sosa and Tom "Jughead" Ludwick. Kenneth Smith found one for himself and tore it up learning how to ride it."

Having selected his own abandoned motorcycle, Lieutenant Cook used his position as battery motor officer to have it put into top running condition. "I got it rebuilt and it rode pretty good," he remembered, then added, "the Motor Sergeant painted it up with GI colors and even put a little star on it. I rode it for a long time and then gave it to one of the sergeants."

Sebring found one for himself and remembered it in detail. "After the war," he said, "for at least two weeks I don't remember doing anything except screwing around with this motorcycle I found. It was a shaft drive motorcycle but it didn't have a battery in it. I knew where there was a German ordnance truck, so I went back there and found new tires that would fit it, and tubes. I found a brand new engine for it. Then I found a big case about two foot long. It must have had, I don't know how many batteries in it, but they were each about the size of a K ration box. All of them hooked together may have made something like 24 volts. I took two of them and hooked them up to that motorcycle. They were dry cell, so they weren't something you could charge back up, but they would start the motorcycle and run it for two, three days. Then I'd throw them away and hook up two more. I had a lot of fun with that motorcycle."

Talking about the motorcycles they acquired, if only for a week or two, it is easy to see that each of the guys loved and took pride in his own personal transportation, but without question,

Robert Dickson found the best motorcycle of all. "We were going house to house, me and another boy," explained Dickson of how he found his trophy. "I told him you search the lower floor, it was a barn, and I'll take the upper part. Well, I found an American made motorcycle with ten miles on it. It was an Indian motorcycle. I got that thing out of there and took it to Colonel Todd. I said, Colonel, look what I've found! Can I keep it? His answer was, 'You can keep it if you want to and when we get to a certain point I'll help you ship it home, but you can't ride it now because you'd be burning government gas.'"

Dickson packed the Indian into the battery mess truck, which he was responsible for driving at the time. In the 1940's the Indian brand motorcycle was recognized as the fastest being made, consistently chosen by those in competitive racing. The company had begun manufacture at its Springfield, Massachusetts, factory in 1902 and quickly earned a reputation as the most desirable vehicle among motorcycle enthusiasts. In the years immediately before the outbreak of World War Two, Indian was producing the Scout, a 750cc bike, and the Chief, which featured a huge 1,200cc engine capable of reaching speeds in excess of 100 mph. Both displayed the Indian headdress emblem of the company on the gas tank.

It is not clear exactly which type young Dickson found, but he must have been beaming as he showed off his brand new Indian to friends in the battery. Naturally, he couldn't wait to take it on the open road, but if that was ever to happen he'd have to resist temptation and follow Colonel Todd's instructions. "Well, suspense was killing me," Dickson admitted later. "I decided I was gonna ride it anyway. I got on the German autobahn highway and run a hundred miles an hour with it. I had a thrilling ride, but the MPs took it away from me. They got my Indian motorcycle. Boy it was a big motorcycle, it was a shiny dude!"

Of course all this riding of motorcycles required gasoline and there was no private source to be had. Sebring's explanation of where he got fuel for his motorcycle was, "Stole it off the jeeps. Each jeep had five gallons in a can strapped on the back." When asked if the army didn't have something to say about that, he added, "Probably they would if they knew it."

Other men were more brazen. "We used American gas to travel with," recalled Lester Newman. "They didn't care for it but they didn't really say anything. I'd just go down to the motor pool down there and fill up with gas when it got empty and go all over hell."

Given the intersection of alcohol and motorcycles, needless accidents began happening. "You just have no idea what a bunch of young guys get into," remarked Sebring. Remembering one battery man who impaled himself on a barbed wire fence, he added, "he got cut all to shit."

Another man in "A" Battery broke his leg riding the cycle which Girardin lent to him, while, according to Ed Ryan two other men in the battalion were actually killed in racing accidents. "Yeah," he said, "we had motorcycle races on the quarter mile cinder track behind a school. Everything went fine until a couple of guys got killed when they went up against the wall. Well, that stopped that shit. I was doing some of the same thing too with them. It would have been my own fault."

But motorcycles weren't the only transportation expropriated by the men. During that first week of May, 1945, chow time at the battery mess would see an astounding assortment of civilian cars, Hungarian cavalry mounts, carriages, and every German vehicle from motorcycles with sidecars to scout cars assemble.

In the spirit of the time, Sosa picked up a German military Volkswagen for his own private use. He enjoyed the novelty of exploring the area in an enemy automobile all his own, judging it to be a bit, "short on horsepower, but a good little utility car." Then, while on one of his foraging expeditions, searching for something useful like another wine cellar, he discovered a Mercedes Benz automobile hidden in a barn. The Mercedes was beautiful – white with brown leather interior. Sosa considered trading it on the spot for his army Volkswagen, but looting of civilian property on this kind of conspicuous scale was not tolerated. Still, he reasoned, there had to be some advantage to be gained in such a find as this. "It had leather seat-covers," he said later. "I wanted the covers for my jeep. So I ripped them off and took them out. Then I took the radio out of it too. I just helped myself. I was thinking, fuck them Germans."

BATTERY!

Once he got back to the battery Sosa wired the radio into the dashboard of his jeep and covered the vinyl GI seats with genuine leather. Sartain's driver was pleased, but there was still something missing. Then creative inspiration took hold. "I made a piece of metal and I joined the front of the front fender clear down to the bumper. I painted them green, then I put on one side two stripes for me and on the other side I put two bars for the Captain." When Sosa stood back to admire the work he was sure there wasn't another jeep customized like this in the whole United States Army.

During this first week of peacetime there was still a great deal of contact with the Soviet troops encamped just a mile or two away from the "A" Battery guys at Neu Krenzlin. Though the Russian soldiers' rough reputation had preceded them and most GIs were cautious, they were also enormously curious. So were the Russians. Fortunately, there were enough men in the battery from Chicago, Cleveland, Pittsburgh, and Milwaukee who spoke some version of Russian or Polish to made communication possible.

Mahlon Sebring's remark that, "We were glad to see them because we knew when we did the war would be over," was representative of the average GI's attitude at this time.

However, nearly all found the Russians company grew tiresome rather quickly. For example, Robert Dickson said, "I really didn't care to be around them very much. Most of them was big cognac drinkers. They were pretty overbearing people on top of that. A lot of guys said that when they was around them they were pretty nice people, and I guess they were, but they was a percent of them that it was just kind of their way and nothing else."

Most battery men were remarkably consistent in their comments. In spite of their own drinking, virtually all remembered the Soviets as drunk and undisciplined. "Drunker than skunks," was a term heard several times during interviews. One GI freely admitted that the average Russian soldier's tolerance for liquor far surpassed that of the American soldier, estimating that it took two to five times the amount of alcohol to bring the Russian to a stupor. Kenneth Smith simply dismissed the Russians as, "a bunch of dumb clucks."

While Americans seemed fixated on accumulating cameras, binoculars, and pistols of all kinds, the Russian soldier was even more compelled to collect wristwatches, and if GIs wouldn't readily trade their timepieces for vodka, they frequently became belligerent.

Others were struck by the ragged appearance of the Red Army soldiers in comparison to themselves. "They had hero medals all over them," said Sebring, "but I don't think any two had the same damn uniform on. It was the biggest ragtag bunch of individuals I ever met, and compared to us they were dirty. We were dirty, but they were much more sloppier than us."

Sebring's reference to "hero medals" is a clue that he came across members of a Soviet Guards Division. Such units were designated as specially trained shock troops in the Red Army and each member wore with pride a medal signifying that he was part of one of these elite outfits. This particular unit may have been the 5th Guards Cossack Division, an organization known to have been in the Ludwigslust Area at the close of the war.

Visits between GIs and Soviet troops brought other differences between the two armies to light. Red Army units were, for example, in the habit of taking any of their vehicles which were expected to be parked more than a day and mounting them on blocks to relieve stress on the tires and springs. The practice was emblematic of the value placed in the Red Army on equipment and supplies over human life – exactly the opposite of the frequently wasteful Americans who would gladly expend massive amounts of firepower to save the life of one of their men.

The presence of women in the soviet ranks was particularly surprising to the Americans. Though approximately 350,000 females saw duty in the United States military during the war, their service was restricted to clerical, nursing, and aviation duties, usually at some distance from combat zones or stateside. In the Red Army, by contrast, about 800,000 women served, often in combat. Russian females could be found in nearly all front line roles, but especially as snipers, drivers, pilots, machinegunners, and as members of tank or mortar crews. Sometimes Russian women were organized into separate female battalions, but just as frequently they were integrated directly into mixed gender units – a practice never adopted by the United States or any of the other western Allies.

Despite the novelty, few GIs and none of the 319th men interviewed for this book described the Russian female soldiers as anything like feminine or attractive.

"Some of the Russian women, they looked like they weighed two hundred pounds," remarked Ed Ryan. "It must have been awful cold where they came from because their uniforms were that padded stuff, but if they got the uniform off they weighed 120."

Notwithstanding all this, a few men alluded to awkward amorous encounters. One Able Battery cannoneer confided, "Oh boy, there was some big ones. I went up against one of them. She was a whole lot bigger than I was."

Even Bob Storms, who was never displeased to find female companionship, was intimidated and found the Russian women too aggressive for his taste, saying, "Boy, I'll tell you, them Russians, they were rough. They had their women with them and they were rougher than the men. They were big women. They come over there and wanted to fool around with us but I stayed away from them!"

Among Russian soldiers, and most especially with their officers, GIs also noticed an obsession with security and secrecy. At the same time their Russian counterparts no doubt regarded the relative openness of their American allies as naïve and foolhardy. Amidst the guarded attitude, fraternization and celebrations continued among the front line veterans of both armies, even if the camaraderie was superficial.

319th officers were among those who received formal invitations to have dinner with their Soviet counterparts encamped nearby. Given that he could speak Russian, Captain Eskoff of HQ Battery was an especially welcome guest. These dinner parties always featured repeated toasts in which glass after glass of vodka, wine, or cognac were consumed. Anyone found to have even a swallow left in his glass would be met with a chant of, "Pey do dna!" or "To the Bottom!" These gatherings generally included sumptuous meals obviously drawn from supplies of the local German population. The music of accordions would soon initiate the classic Cossack dance with each leg alternately thrown out from a full knee-bend position. The dance was normally beyond the reach of Americans, but when Eskoff was able to perform the Soviet officers went wild. They would cheer and propose another round of toasts.

Inevitably the fragile allegiance between the Americans and Soviets broke down altogether. There was simply too much suspicion and competition to sustain any illusion of friendship. "Then the freeze came," is how Sartain described the breakdown. "Man, when I say the freeze came, I mean we were told that we were not to even tell the

Russians hello. Nothing!"

The orders which were suddenly issued canceling all further dinner parties between groups of American and Russian officers or impromptu visits between enlisted men was the start of the cold war. Sartain never could see the wisdom in this policy any more than he could the non-fraternization order with German civilians. Both struck him as arbitrary and counter-productive. Until the final collapse of the Soviet Union in the early 1990s, the state of unabashed hostility would go on.

"We were invited to a supper but the word came down very quickly that we could not go," Sartain continued. "No fraternization with the Russians. Some of the guys didn't get the word and went. They danced on the table and all that humbug, but there was nothing to it, it was all friendly. Why our military could have been so off base, it just didn't seem right."

Aside from GIs, Red Army personnel, German prisoners of war, the local civilians, and the liberated inmates of Woebbelin, there were also an estimated 60,000 Displaced Persons within the area of the 82nd Airborne's operations during the first weeks of May, 1945. These Displaced Persons were individuals whom the Nazis had taken as slave laborers to work on farms and in industry throughout Germany. Just feeding and sheltering all these DPs, as they were commonly called by GIs, was a monumental task for the military government. German prisoners of war were put to work. With the added labor, bakeries in villages were directed to produce bread around the clock, German and Hungarian army horses were slaughtered for the meat, and Allied military rations were distributed.

Despite the best of efforts, it was going to take some time to process and repatriate all these unfortunate people. They hailed from nearly every European nation overrun by the Germans. Each day thousands of DPs were interviewed and categorized according to their nationality. Then, as transportation became available, they were sent to their homelands by train or truck: the Dutch back to Holland, the French to France, and so forth. No one knew what to do with the approximately 1,200 Italians. Since the Communists tended to see most DPs as Nazi cooperatives at some level, many of the Russians, particularly those of Ukrainian background, dreaded being returned to Soviet hands. It was pitiful to see them being forced onto trucks pointed east, all the while begging with the British and American soldiers to let them stay.

American soldiers were free in the meantime to associate with DPs. Quite a few members of the 319th did so, especially those who could speak foreign languages. In "A" Battery, for example, Corporal Stanley Bichefski was a member of Bob Storms' machinegun crew. He spoke fluent Polish and on the afternoon of May 16th approached Corporal Storms, saying, "You know Stormsy, there's a farm over the hill there. They got a lot of slave labor and they're all Polaks. Would you go over there with me? I don't want to go alone."

Storms readily agreed. He was already in the habit of allowing any two members of his crew to "go and goof off or whatever," and that afternoon would have been his and Bichefski's turn anyway.

"So we went over there," remembered Storms. "Them people weren't prisoners no more. They were all on their own on this farm. Boy, Bichefski was right in his glory, talking to them. They played some kind of card game and man, we had some kind of whiskey they made out of potatoes and stuff. I started to get drunk, I'm telling you. Oh was it strong."

Storms could feel a powerful drunk coming on, and experience had taught him that once his intoxication passed a certain point he couldn't predict what would happen. For the present though, he still had enough of his wits to tell Bichefski they needed to get back to camp.

Bichefski had seen Storms under the influence and knew he could get out of hand, but was reluctant to leave, so he made a proposal instead. "Let's stay a while. You see that black haired girl over there? I want to make her. Don't worry, I'll take care of you."

"You gonna get me back to camp?" asked Storms with a thick tongue. He was already slipping out of reach.

Bichefski assured him, "I'll get you back to camp. Man, she's gorgeous! I just got to see if I can make her."

"So he's in the card game and I guess I really got drunk," continued Storms. "Next morning I woke up in a bed with something curled up against my back but I don't remember nothing. I reached over behind me and felt this long hair. So I turned over and here was this girl, this black haired girl. Oh my God what'd I do!"

A few minutes later Bichefski came in the room. He had a sour look on his face. When Storms asked him what happened, he was told, "You got drunk and puked all over yourself. She took you outside to the horse trough and washed you off and put you to bed. I come in three times but she had your 45 and told me if I came near she'd shoot me. I spent all night outside and couldn't even get in here!"

Bichefski was somewhere between crestfallen, furious, and love-sick, but there was nothing for it. The two were already hours overdue. Sergeant Marshall probably already had men out searching for them, hopefully he hadn't reported them as officially absent yet. "We made it back just in time. The outfit was all packed up, ready to go. They were waiting for us. Everything was packed up, all our equipment. Boy, we were lucky," concluded Storms as he took great pleasure in another good story told.

Whatever the facts, on the morning of May 17th the battalion was being re-moved to Lubtheen, a town about twenty miles closer to the Elbe. After two weeks without the pressure of combat the battery was relaxed, so getting the outfit rolling was taking longer than usual. Maybe some guys in the battery were dragging their feet, really waiting for Storms and Bichefski. In any case, First Sergeant Picher was kicking asses, delivering the unwelcome news that the party was over. It was back to the army way, reveille, retreat, and on the double.

Like a lot of other guys, Lester Newman wanted to take his German motorcycle with him. But all these distracting personal vehicles the men had accumulated were a nuisance by now. When Newman approached Sartain and asked permission to load his motorcycle onto one of the outfit's trucks, the battery commander bristled and showed a rare example of pique at one of his men. "No, no, no!" he shot back. "You can't take that with you. We aren't gonna haul all that stuff around. If you want another motorcycle when we get where we're going, then find yourself another motorcycle, but you're not taking that one."

As it turned out, nobody took their motorcycles to Lubtheen. "HQ" and "A" Batteries were distributed among residences in the town itself, while "B" Battery ended up billeted in Quassel, a village a couple of miles to the north. Sartain recalled how personnel from division artillery headquarters rode down the streets with him, pointing at homes and indicating with drawn fingers how many men should be assigned to each. The unit was replacing another field artillery battalion, which reported the local houses as safe and already screened for weapons and forbidden contraband, though occasionally fugitive SS men or other Nazis still turned up. Major Wimberley was appointed Military Governor and the outfit settled in for occupation duty.

Once billets were assigned, Sartain inspected the area and was surprised to learn an indoor swimming pool was located in the town center. "I went to check out the pool," recalled Sartain. "When I went into that building I was absolutely totally shocked. There were men and women in the pool together swimming buck naked. I saw it with my own eyes. There were unisex showers and unisex bathrooms. I asked a native and they said there was nothing unusual about that. Well, we don't swim naked in Louisiana, so we took over the pool and that was the end of it."

After the battalion arrived in Lubtheen, word circulated quickly about the indoor swimming pool. Many of the men in the 319th were rustics who had never seen a facility of this sort and probably a small minority had ever been swimming in one. In any case the water was immediately full of GIs in their skivvies, the local custom for nude bathing being something strange to American sensibilities. Of course, the German civilians were all gone by then, and the guys remained unaware of the former bathing arrangements.

Sosa thought the water was far too cold to enjoy, but Robert Dickson felt differently. "We really lived it up," was his enthusiastic comment.

Although the Germans were compliant with the military government and relieved to be under Anglo-American occupation instead of the Soviets, some of the Lubtheen natives balked at being turned out of their homes to make room for the GIs. Sartain remembered one incident connected to this issue. "The residents were evicted, so to speak," he recalled. "They went to the mayor and complained. The mayor made an appointment to come see me. He spoke very broken English. I just looked at him and said, 'Thank you,' but he kept talking. I said, 'Thank you' again, and he kept talking. Then I said, 'Kaput.' That was the end. He saluted and walked out."

Part of occupation duty included regular patrolling of Lubtheem and its surrounding villages. The military government and local German Burgomasters had reestablished order by this time, in no small part due to the classically German predilection for following authority without question. This cultural trait helped make the transition go more smoothly than expected, but circumstances were still unsettled. With some frequency, all manner of situations arose which needed to be decided or otherwise disposed of.

To keep a lid on things, details of battery men were engaged in running round the clock motorized patrols or manning roadblocks. Storms, for instance, was told to take a jeep with a couple of guys and make a circuit twice each evening through a series of small villages which were without any GI garrison. "I'd go there and listen to their troubles and stuff. If it was anything serious I'd have to come back and turn them in to the captain and he took care of them from there on, but most generally I took care of it," he explained.

The role seems to have agreed with Storms. He saw these impromptu hearings as an opportunity to reintroduce a little justice into what had become a most cruel and unfeeling world. "We held a session each night like a judge and jury. The boogie master, or whatever they called them, it's like the mayor of the town, he always wanted to be the big shot, but I was over him. He was trying to be too strict on them. I'd set most of the people free. In wartime you've got to give a little and take a little."

Policing and patrolling went along on schedule as the 319th Glider Field Artillery Battalion remained in Lubtheen through May and into the first few days of June, 1945. Toward the end of the month a formal battalion parade was made through the town. "I don't remember what the reason was, but they were prone to do these things," recalled Sartain. The occasion was likely connected to news that the battalion would shortly be leaving Germany to return to its base camp in France. On this day the guys assembled in their Ike jackets with ribbons, glider wings, and Presidential Unit Citations displayed. Aside from highly polished Jump-boots, they wore their helmet liners without the steel pot and carried their folding-stock carbines slung over the right shoulder.

We put on a real show, our fancy class as and all that," was Sartain's memory when asked about the Lubtheen parade. "I was at the head of the battery and Fellman brought up the rear. We gave your daddy the battery guidon to carry. I don't know why we picked him, but he was taller than most of the guys and of course we couldn't pick a midget for that job."

More of the battalion's most senior NCOs left for the United States at about this time under the policy through which Captain Manning and Sergeant Johnson had left earlier in 1945. None of these soldiers who had been sent home were discharged, but just being stateside again made all the difference. Among these fortunate men appears to have been Staff Sergeant Carl Davis of Mansfield, Ohio. One of the original regular army cadre around whom the battalion was reactivated in 1942, Davis was thought of as the unofficial historian of the 319th, and may have been the mysteriously unnamed sergeant who took the hundreds of snapshots which Captain Sartain and others inherited copies of. Quiet and unassuming by nature, Davis had refused a battlefield commission during the fighting in Normandy, knowing that to accept such would necessarily cause him to be transferred outside Able Battery. For Davis, leaving the battery was too high a price to pay to become an officer. Thurman King, another Ohio native, replaced Davis as chief of the instrument section.

Everyone understood that while Germany was out of the fight, there was still the war in the Pacific to win. This issue was a constant topic of conversation among officers and men in "A" Battery. Most were of the opinion that the outfit would be granted a 30 day leave at home while the division was in transit and preparations were made to send the 82nd Airborne to Japan.

Lieutenant Joe Mullen expressed his views on the subject in a letter written to his fiancée Gloria, in Indiana that spring. "I only hope that I get home to see you on my way to the Pacific," he wrote in regards to the opportunity for the couple to get married. "If I don't I'm afraid it will be '47 by the time I get home. That's entirely to damned long to suit me." Next, in a letter dated May 9th, he commented further on the question of what would happen, writing, "I imagine it will be 3 or 4 months before I go anyplace, which is alright with me cause I figure each day over here is one less day in the Pacific."

Mullen's speculation about plans for the division now that the war in Europe was over was typical. Indeed, the subject was on the tongue of everyone in the battery and time seemed to drag for the men. All their thoughts were now directed toward home and the loved ones they'd left behind. With the war finished, being separated felt all the more onerous.

On May 29th Mullen penned another letter to his bride to be, betraying both his boredom and longing. "Good morning beautiful!" he wrote. "Or am I wrong in presuming it is morning as you read this? It is now 11:45 pm and I've just finished playing bridge all evening. I really expend a great amount of my time trying to get to be a half decent bridge player, but doubt like hell if I'll ever make it. I've got a pair of pajamas made from parachute silk which I'm going to send to you tomorrow. I hope you like them, they are rather revealing I imagine. I just told Lt. Larry Cook, a friend of mine, about the nightie and he says there isn't any use in wearing anything the first night as it doesn't stay on long anyhow. Sounds interesting. I wonder why not? Hope you're finding more to do than yours truly. I'm not doing any thing but eating sleeping & occasionally a few drinks. I'm going through a drink that just won't wait. Well Darling let me know how you're getting along."

Thankfully, preparations to leave got underway quickly. The 319th was to be replaced in Lubtheen by the British 92nd Regiment and some of their officers were already afoot, making arrangements for the changeover. The howitzers were readied for shipment and all field uniforms were turned in for replacements.

This time the instructions were to leave all the battery's used clothing at a former Luftwaffe airfield near Ludwigslust. The facility had been home during the war to a night fighter unit, as well as the 54th "Greenhearts" Jagdgeschwander, intercepting British and American bombers on their way to Berlin. For several months in 1944 a contingent of Finnish Air Force pilots was even stationed there, receiving training in night fighting tactics from their German allies. In the first days after the German surrender the airfield served as a collection point for displaced persons and liberated Soviet POWs. GIs also found the airfield to be a favorite tourist stop, giving them the opportunity to pose in the cockpits of derelict German Messerschmidt's and Focke-Wolfe fighters.

On one of the last days before the outfit pulled out, Sosa received directions to take the discarded clothing from "A" Battery to a collection point at the Luftwaffe airfield. "The captain gave me a map. Said, 'You go to this airstrip right here an unload the jeep and the trailer,'" remembered Sosa. "When I got there I figured there'd be somebody there, but there wasn't. It was an abandoned airstrip, and there was not a soul in sight. Nobody around, no guards, nobody, but there was a pile of mostly cloth goods. Underwear, blankets, some uniforms, all kinds of stuff. It must have been thirty feet high and at least a hundred and fifty feet in diameter. Laying out there all by itself, no guards, no nothing. Can you believe that?"

Apparently, by the time the battalion was ready to leave Lubtheen the Soviet POWs were gone, as well as the DPs and American guards. Sosa knew instinctively that he was looking at a small fortune and needed only to seize the opportunity. Sartain's driver knew the situation in Mecklenburg was still very fluid. Everybody not in the US or British military was in dire need of clothing, whether they were Displaced Persons or part of the local German population.

"All that big pile of stuff laying out there for the taking. Somebody was going to get it, I thought it might as well be me," is how Sosa described his thoughts at the time. He later claimed to have sold some of the clothing on the black market for $5,000. Though the amount seems exorbitant, the enterprising Sosa freely admitted to black market dealings and fortunes were in fact being made in the subterranean economy of the time. "They needed clothing, so I sold a bunch of it. Two trailers worth," he said unapologetically. Whatever the truth, Sosa clearly regarded the sale as one of his greatest entrepaunurial accomplishments.

By noon of June 3rd the first contingent of the 319th departed by rail for France from Hagenow, Germany. The next morning, at 0530 hours, the balance of the battalion followed by motor convoy under the command of Captain Cargile. Three days later the 319th closed in camp at a colossal, and as yet unfinished, tent city near Laon, France. It was the afternoon of June 6th, 1945. One year to the day since the glider attack which had brought them fighting across Europe.

BATTERY!

Part 32: Don't fence me in.

Camp Chicago lay just outside the village of Marchais, about eight miles south of Laon, France. It was one of the "American City" camps concentrated in the region surrounding Reims and used as staging areas for operations directed into western Germany since the fall of 1944. The names of cities in the United States had been selected for these camps because such designations would provide little military intelligence from which the Germans could predict where new divisions were being assembled. Moreover, the use of familiar city names – Chicago, Pittsburgh, and so forth, was thought to have a reassuring psychological effect on young GIs.

For the guys in the 319th the first order of business after three continuous days in railroad cars or trucks was a visit to the hot showers which Camp Chicago offered, followed by a hot meal. German POWs attended to everything. Seemingly under no guard whatsoever, they prepared and served the meals, collected laundry, policed the grounds, and did it all with great efficiency. Everyone was in high spirits, eagerly anticipating events which would start the journey homeward and end in demobilization.

At the next day's formation the men were informed that there would be a division review on June 9th, so they needed to get everything from uniforms to equipment in tip-top shape. The news was greeted with groans and grumbling. Admonishments followed from the Sergeants that there would be silence in the ranks.

"They told us it was for good old Jim Gavin, but we didn't want to review for anybody," said Sartain. "Every time some big shot came around, we had a review. Every time we turned around we had another review and it gave everybody the red ass. We weren't happy with any of them. You had to get all dressed up, all slicked up, and we just didn't want to do it."

The men were also instructed that a free copy of a government publication titled "82nd Division Summary of Operations in the World War," could be picked up at the Orderly Room for the asking. The book was an official history of the Division's actions in World War One, prepared by the American Battle Monuments commission, complete with a series of topographical maps of the Western Front tucked into an inner sleeve. Whether the idea was officially suggested or not; the guys universally began using the books to collect autographs of their buddies in anticipation of their discharge from the army.

"Some of us was real close to one another," explained Sebring. "We just went around at the mess hall and handed them around. We'd say, 'I want you to sign this.'" Peacock blue ink flowed from fountain pens as guys wrote their names and home addresses in the margins, sometimes with nicknames or cryptic messages like "Remember the Foxhole" added for effect. One of the guys from the Deep South wrote, "Come by for fried chicken!" in every book he signed. Coincidentally, the New York Times was reporting the arrival of the first wave of men to return home from Europe. Among those being processed at Camp Kilmer, New Jersey, was almost certainly Sergeant Davis.

For the first time in years, the prospect of leading a civilian life, far away from the Army had become real. But even while there was a preoccupation with getting home, an inkling of concern was growing in the private thoughts of many. Lurking on the fringe of each soldier's eager anticipation was a growing question: What will it be like when I try to explain the war to people who weren't there?

Friendships started to take on a different and more profound meaning as men considered the changes which were about to take place. The only other people who knew what they'd been through were soon to be gone, dispersing back into their prewar civilian lives. As he reflected on the camaraderie he shared with others in the battery, Covais later spoke about this bond, saying, "You develop a fond affection for them, for your fellow soldiers, because they know, and you know, what you've been through. They become like your brothers. You're all together. You've got to be all together as a team because if you don't, you're dead, you're lost."

The most popular topic of conversation continued to be the Army's new point system governing who would be eligible for discharge and who would be retained, perhaps including redeployment to the Pacific theater of operations, a real possibility since the war against Japan was raging as fiercely as ever. Introduced on May 12th, 1945, the program was developed in part from surveys of troops asking what criteria should determine a man's suitability for discharge. GIs and sailors agreed that overall length of service, length of time spent in combat, wounds, and children at home, should be the determining factors.

Everyone had an opinion, but most felt the criteria selected were essentially fair. The President even voiced his endorsement of the Point System, telling Congress on June 1st, "The Army's system for selecting the soldiers for release to civilian life represents a democratic and fair approach to this most difficult problem." Truman went on to state, "It embodies the principle of impartial selection that we applied in drafting our citizen Army and that we shall continue to apply in meeting the manpower requirements of our armed forces until Japan is defeated."

The Point System allotted one point for each month of service and another for each month overseas. Five more points were awarded for each combat operation. For those in the 319th who'd landed in Africa, this meant Sicily, Italy, Normandy, Holland, the Ardennes, and Central Europe. Each wound was worth another five points, as was a Bronze Star or other decorations. If you had a wife at home with kids, that was an additional twelve points for each child.

"I had 83 points and you needed 85," recalled Rappi. "If I'd have had a purple heart I'd have come home earlier, but I didn't draw no blood."
Rappi's memory was correct - the threshold number which made men eligible for discharge in perhaps two to five months was set at 85. This meant that a sizable proportion of what was considered to be the old timers of the battalion -- those who'd landed at Casablanca in 1943, were just short. They described themselves as "83 Pointers."
John Girardin, for example, had 83 points, as did Gruebling, Plassa, all the guys that came from Fort Sheridan just after Christmas, 1942. "I don't know why," Girardin remarked years later, "I was in as long as anybody, but a lot of it depended on what age you were, if you had family, if you were married, you got points for that."

Few if any replacements who had joined the outfit after Italy would have accumulated enough points unless they'd been wounded, decorated, or had children at home. But some of those who had shed blood were equally out of luck. For example, the German shell fragment Sebring was too embarrassed to submit for a Purple Heart in Holland did him no good. "I was ashamed of it, getting hit in the hind end," he confessed. "But it ended up being worth five points."

On the morning of the 9th, after much polishing of brass and replacement of worn equipment, Able Battery and the rest of the 319th took its place in the sequence of the division's review. It took time to assemble the whole division, and all that standing around was tedious, but finally the battalion stepped off. The troopers paraded down the airfield which the 82nd used at Marchais to conduct parachute and glider training. It was a vast open area, so all the individual battalions could be seen marching in close order, Field Officers in front, followed by the national and battalion colors, then the rank and file. Jeeps and weapons carriers pulling howitzers followed every battery. When it marched past Slim Jim Gavin mounted on the reviewing stand, each unit gave a sharp "Eyes Right!"

Besides the battalion and regimental colors, every battery or company had its own guidon. Able Battery's was a swallow tailed pennant, horizontally bisected into red and white fields, denoting artillery. The upper half displayed the numeral "319" and in the lower field the letter "A."

On June 9th Sergeant Covais held the guidon for the battery, as he had been doing in unit formations since before Normandy. The job was one in which he took particular satisfaction. "When they needed a flag holder, man, I volunteered for that," he declared proudly. He thought back to battalion and division reviews before Eisenhower, Ridgeway, Gavin, and others, and then added, "When you pass in review with the guidon, you got to dip it. I studied these guys at West Point a little bit. I saw them do it and I liked what they did, so I emulated them. When it came time to dip the guidon, man, I stood out there and shwooosh! See, you got to be a little bit of a copy-cat if you're gonna do it right. You've got to copy the experts, or attempt to anyway."

Once the division's units had passed and taken up their places in formation, all the colors were assembled before the commanding General. Gavin saluted them from the reviewing stand, which was draped in red, white, and blue bunting. He addressed his victorious Airborne troopers, congratulating them on another mission well done. Their

The men of "A" Battery, 319th GFAB march in formation through Lubtheem, Germany, May, 1945. Sgt. Covais carries the Battery's guidon.

record was unequaled, and as a reward they would have the distinction of occupying Berlin.

Though being chosen to represent the United States Army at the German capitol was, as Sartain admitted, "a pretty big deal," most men in the 82nd greeted the news with limited enthusiasm. The High Point men just wanted to go home and would hopefully already be gone anyway. As far as the Low Point guys were concerned, it was an honor, but if they were going to Berlin it was probably because the Army needed a tough outfit to keep the Russians in line.

Following the June 9th review the 319th was given several days of light duty. Some of the men visited area tourist sights such as the cathedral at Reims or Joan of Arc's birthplace. Others visited nearby battlefields of the First World War. Though surface litter had been picked up and the shell blasted earth was overgrown with grass and wild flowers, the trench systems were still deep and distinct.

At this juncture First Sergeant Rene Picher, the little French Canadian received his orders to return home to Springfield, Massachusetts. In his place Staff Sergeant Albert "Heinie" Hein, the Battery's Chief of Sections and, according to Sartain, "A very reliable soldier," was promoted to First Sergeant. Hein was thirty years old, married, and had already done a hitch in the service when he re-enlisted in 1942. "He was in the regular army," remembered Robert Rappi, who succeeded Hein as Able Battery's Chief of Sections. "They made them officers and Sergeants faster than us guys coming out of the woods, but he was a pretty good guy and I liked him." "

"A" Battery's Supply Sergeant, Harold Jinders also left for home. Another regular army man, Jinders had been with the battalion since reactivation. Whether it was a typewriter, a size 38 Extra Long jacket, or a pair of rubberized engineer's boots, if you needed something Jinders knew how to get it. Neither did Jinders treat you as if

The men of "A" Battery, 319th GFAB march in formation through Lubtheem, Germany, May, 1945. Lieutenant Fellman is seen bringing up the rear of the column. All photos from Sartain collection.

BATTERY!

Captain Sartain addresses the men of his Battery, June, 1945. this may have been one of the last occasions he had to speak to "A" Battery as an intact unit. Soon he and the other High Point men were sent to the 17th Airborne to become "A" Battery, 681st Glider Field Artillery Bn. Sartain collection.

he were personally responsible for cutting the War Department's budget, as most Supply Sergeants were apt to do. Old timer John Girardin commented on Jinders' generosity when he said, "He was a good Supply Sergeant. You know, sometimes I'd go down and ask them for something and they won't give it to you, clothing, shoes, things of that sort, but he was always good about that. For me he did anyway. Anytime I went there he always gave me what I needed."

Sartain's observation on the Sergeant's good fortune was, "Jinders was picked for two reasons; he was a good man and he was probably the oldest man in the battery. You got to give Harold Jinders credit for being the granddaddy of everybody."

Before he departed, Sartain and Jinders had a long conversation, reminiscing over all that had happened since the Captain's assignment to the battery as a newly minted 2nd Lieutenant in September of 1942. Jinders had watched Sartain grow as an officer from the day he showed up to his current status as probably the most respected Captain in the battalion. As the two parted, he asked Sartain, "Captain, can I do anything for you when I get back to the States?"

"Yeah," Sartain answered, "send Peggy-Lou some roses."

Sartain started to pull out his wallet for cash, but the Supply Sergeant refused to take any payment to pay for the flowers, protesting, "No, I'll be glad to. I'll send her some roses."

Jinders kept his word, but the best of intentions often go awry. Sartain explained later how that axiom held true in this case. "So when he gets to the states he orders a dozen red roses for Peggy Lou, and he sent it to her with a card that said, 'I love you, Charles.' Well she didn't know who in the hell Charles was. Back home in Baton Rouge everybody always called me Lenton, see? Not until I got home and we started shooting the bull I said, did you get some roses one time. She said, 'I sure did, and I always wondered who sent them!'"

"The Sergeants really ran the show," Sartain affirmed in a later conversation about the NCOs in his battery. "When we had a vacancy I was a very strong proponent of making the appointment. I mean, when we had a Corporal that got shipped or injured or was no longer with us I made a PFC a Corporal, or made a Corporal a Sergeant. I had a very strong feeling about that. And "A" Battery was terrific because of the NCOs and the personnel. The officers could screw it up, and fortunately we didn't have any officers that really messed up, but the backbone of "A" Battery was the personnel, the rank and file personnel. I guess I had the right attitude to work through them and with them. The men knew that. I was very fortunate, very fortunate."

Lieutenant Ragland expressed the same sentiments on this subject when he said, "I'll tell you, we had excellent Chiefs of Sections. Of course in any military organization you got to have good officers, but the key personnel are the Sergeants and Chiefs of Sections. If they have a good crew they're the ones that get things done."

A couple of days after the June 9th review, Colonel Todd called a meeting of the battery commanders. Everyone arrived full of expectations that they would be learning the details of the mustering out of the battalion. Todd informed them that the 319th would shortly be relocating from Camp Chicago to Epinal, a small garrison town near the Swiss border. Over the coming weeks, he explained, the High-Point men, which included most of the personnel in the outfit, would be transferred lock-stock-and-barrel to the 17th Airborne Division, staying in France while the rest of the 82nd would move on to its occupation of Berlin.

For Sartain, the big news was that once the transfer to the 17th Airborne was made he would be moved to battalion staff, ostensibly as the Battalion Athletics Officer, while Lieutenant Ragland would be given command of "A" Battery. The announcement came as a shock to Sartain. As far as he was concerned, Athletics Officer was a joke, a crock, and everyone knew that. There were already too many officers on battalion staff.

He lingered at Todd's quarters after the meeting was adjourned, seeking clarification. "Colonel, I really want to go home with my battery," pleaded Sartain.

Todd listened closely. He'd already anticipated Sartain would feel this way. "Well, Charlie," the Colonel told him, "Even if you stay with the division and go to Berlin there won't be an intact battery to go home with anyhow, since most of the men are being transferred. I understand how you feel, but I want to get Ragland promoted before we go home. Giving him command of your battery is the only way I can do that."

At first Sartain left feeling short-changed, convinced he'd been rewarded with a trivial position in the battalion. As days passed however, he came to comprehend the Colonel's decision. "When Todd gave the battery to Ragland I didn't know how to handle it," Sartain admitted later. "I can appreciate it now, and I really feel like Todd was trying to give me a rest, but for sentimental reasons and everything else at the time I really wanted to come home with the battery. Instead I came home as Athletics Director. When I look back over it now I can see it was the one way Todd could get Ragland's promotion. And Ragland was a good CO, he richly deserved it, he really did."

As jarring as the news may have been, for the present "A" Battery was still Sartain's command. A few days later, following a final series of qualifying glider flights at the Marchais Airfield, the 319th was loaded on board a train for Epinal, some 200 miles southeast of Laon. At the station the men were trucked to an old French cavalry installation known as Caserne Bonnard. The facility was said to have been constructed about 1870. It featured a large number of two story, white washed stone barracks for the enlisted men, surrounding an expansive parade ground. Some of the guys thought their quarter's resembled horse stables, which some of them were. Officers were quartered in small houses on the base which had once been the homes of French officers and their families.

Epinal itself lay in the foothills of the Vosges Mountains, nestled among hills mostly covered with tall pines. All in all the countryside resembled the North Carolina piedmont where Fort Bragg was situated. The Moselle, a small river by American standards, flowed from the Vosges, curling around a park at the town center, in which the division band was already giving frequent concerts.

Since virtually all camp duties were the responsibility of German prisoners, as had been the case at Camp Chicago, the guys quickly settled in to a leisurely routine, part of which involved daily trips to the Moselle for a swim.

"There was a certain place where you could go swimming, like a swimming hole, like a public thing," remembered Sosa. "You'd come running and take a flying jump into it. Well, that river came out of the mountains so that water's colder than hell too. Yeah man, we just jumped in that river buck naked!"

Soldier life for the troops went on this way for about a week when, on June 20th, the men in the 319th were scheduled to assemble for group photographs of the individual batteries. A kind of bleacher arrangement had been constructed for this purpose, allowing an entire battery to be photographed with four successive rows of men. Those in front would be seated cross-legged on the ground. Behind them were another row sitting on a bench, then a standing row, and finally a rear row at the back, standing on another bench. The men filed into position, one row at a time. Placed at the center of the battery was Captain Sartain, flanked by his officers and First Sergeant Hein.

After the photographers were finished, the entire battery was drawn up at attention to one side of the field. Sartain stepped in front of the men and, turning toward Hein, told him, "Sergeant, have the men stand at ease." The order to be at Parade Rest was

Captain Charles L. Sartain, Jr.,stands with the men of "A" Battery, June, 1945. Sartain Collection.

given. With his hands clasped behind his back and signature aviator sunglasses shielding his eyes, Sartain stood in front of his battery. There was complete quiet.

Ever since Todd had given him the news, Sartain knew he would have to address the battery for the last time sooner or later. This seemed like the right moment. "In a few days," he began, "Most of us will be leaving the 319th for the 17th Airborne. The rest of you will stay here with the battalion and go on to Berlin." There was an uncharacteristic pause, then Sartain resumed. "Lieutenant Ragland will be taking over command of this battery at that point. I know, because I think I know all of; you pretty well, that; you will show him the same respect and performance you have always shown to me." The Captain took a few steps to the left, then to the right. From behind his sunglasses he studied the faces. "Because this may be our last, my last opportunity to speak to you all together like this, I want to make it clear to each and every one of you just how very much it has been an honor for me to serve as your battery commander. A privilege."

There was another, longer pause. Seconds passed, Sartain appeared to swallow hard. He turned his face away sharply as if looking at something far off on the horizon, then glanced momentarily downward. The guys in "A" Battery had never seen their Captain at a loss for words before. Then, with the slightest suggestion of a quaver in his voice, but looking his men straight in the eye, he concluded his farewell. "I'm honored to have been part of YOUR youth. I'm honored by the courtesy you've shown me. Good bye and God bless. Now carry on."

Sartain turned on his heel and walked off. As he did, he could hear first applause, then a round of three cheers from his men. "You have no idea how much we thought of Captain Sartain," remembered Mahlon Sebring when he was asked about the occasion. "It was really a sad day when he said he was leaving."

Interviews conducted for this book show that Sebring's opinion of Sartain was shared by virtually everyone. "He was a fine fella, Captain Sartain. Yes he was. Everybody thought the world of him," said Lieutenant Cook of his battery commander."

Others had similar things to say. Louis Sosa, Sartain's driver throughout the war and someone who probably got to know him as well as anyone, asserted, "He was a stand up officer, first class all the way down the line. A fire eater, that's what I called him."

Both the popularity and edge which Sosa described was acknowledged by Lieutenant Ragland when he said, "As far as I know everybody liked Sartain, maybe there's a couple of higher officers who felt differently, but that's because he wasn't afraid to stick up for the men, and he wasn't afraid to speak up to the Colonels and Majors."

Ted Simpson went into more detail when he was asked about his battery commander. "Sartain had a softness about him that was really quite unusual and yet he had a very magnetic personality," he said. "He was the one guy that I think I was most drawn to of anybody. Not because I was a Corporal and he was a Captain, but just because he was a wonderful person. Sixty years later I still think he's a wonderful, wonderful guy."

The affection the men in "A" Battery had for Sartain was fully reciprocated by him, and as tough as it was, saying farewell to them was the first, but hardly the last time he would choke up when "A" Battery became the subject of conversation. As we neared the conclusion of our interviews Sartain reflected back on that day after six decades were gone by. He said, "I remember addressing the battery for the last time, telling them goodbye. I hated to leave the battery. I felt like I was a part of them, you know? I did a pretty good job of containing my emotions, but it was very difficult for me, very difficult, so I couldn't say much. I just thanked them. It's very difficult for me now to talk about these things without getting too emotional. I just can't do it. Therefore I don't do it."

Sartain sat quietly in his chair, absorbed in his own thoughts. He repacked his corncob pipe, lit it and continued to reminisce. ""A" Battery of the 319th was a very, very important part of my early life, it really was, and now, having aged, when I talk about things I get very sentimental. It's difficult for me to keep my composure when I talk about things I dearly love, you see. And "A" Battery was really something else. I didn't realize it was as special as it was until the damn thing was over with, but looking back over the years I understand that now."

Over the following few days' events moved rapidly. There was much paperwork to process and details to attend to in advance of the transfer. Not knowing just what things would be like once they left the battalion, each man took care of personal chores. Souvenirs were shipped home, farewells were spoken. Kenneth Smith wrangled a pass to visit his brother Kyle in Nancy, about thirty-five miles away, leaving with him an extra pair of jump boots and all his French currency.

At one point Colonel Todd found himself among an informal congregation of GIs from his battalion. Climbing on to the hood of his jeep, Todd delivered a rousing, spontaneous goodbye and good luck. Considering his more than jovial mood and reputation to willingly take a drink now and then, some of the guys nudged each other knowingly.

The GIs were in a celebratory state of mind, calling out good natured barbs to the Colonel, laughing at his jokes, and cheering him on. He was, as one of them said, "A damned good man," after all. When Todd noticed one of his men holding what was clearly not a cup of coffee, Todd pointed to him and called out, "I thought I told you never to drink on duty. Well, you're not on duty now, so let me have some of that!" The soldier handed his mason jar up to the Colonel, who took a long and exaggerated gulp of the contents. "My God," he exclaimed, "How do you drink that!" According to Ed Ryan, who was one of those gathered around the jeep, "The soldier held up his hand, expecting his drink back. Instead Todd told him, 'I'm not finished!' and drank the rest. The men went wild."

On the morning of June 23rd Able Battery assembled together for the last time. Trucks were waiting to convoy the transferred men south to the town of Neufchateau, base camp of the 17th Airborne's artillery battalions. The High-Point men separated themselves from the others. Best buddies said good-bye. There was a flurry of firm handshakes and bear-hugs. Those leaving included Captain Sartin, Lieutenant Ragland, Lieutenants Cook and Gelb. Ted Covais, Kenneth Smith, Bob Storms, Casimir Sobin, Eddie Ryan, and Louis Sosa as well. They amounted to about a third of the battery. Then the loaded trucks pulled away. Sebring's memory was that those left behind felt a little lost without what amounted to the heart of the battery. Among those staying behind were Lieutenants Fellman and Mullin, Robert Rappi, John Girardin, Roland Gruebling, Mahlon Sebring, Ted Simpson, Orin Miller, Lester Newman, Robert Dickson, and Carl Salminen.

When the High-Pointers arrived at Neufchateau, they learned that they were now designated "A" Battery of the 681st Glider Field Artillery Battalion. As much as possible, the command structure of the old 319th was preserved. Colonel Todd and Major Silvey were still in command, except now of the 681st. Ragland had charge of Abel Battery.

Most of the guys felt indifferent about the new designation, assuming that it was merely a matter of paperwork. "I didn't care," remarked Kenneth Smith. "I didn't give it a second thought. I just wanted to go home."

Sartain felt the same way, saying, "It didn't make any difference to us, being in the 17th Airborne for administrative purposes, but the bad part about it was that we had to get the 17th Airborne badge, the talon of the eagle, put on our uniforms. We just didn't like that, but we had to. They issued them and they expected everybody, officers and enlisted alike, to do it."

A controversy immediately developed over this issue. Men who had trained and fought with the 82nd since 1942 maintained that being told to remove the insignia they felt so much pride in was unacceptable. For them, the order to sew on the black circle bearing a gold eagle's talon was simply an outrage. Ed Ryan was still indignant over this when he was interviewed in 2007. "Yeah, some chicken claw," he griped. "We were pretty disgusted about that. Those people never did anything and here we got to wear their plumage. Had to put that 17th on there and leave it on."

Ryan's attitude was rather typical of the mind set among the old 319th men. But the widespread belief that the 17th Airborne in general and the 681st Glider Field Artillery in particular, were rookie units with no combat experience to their credit was quite mistaken. The 17th Airborne Division was actually a highly trained outfit, having been established early in 1943, though it did not arrive in England until the end of August, 1944. Consequently, the division was logistically unprepared to participate in Operation Market, the Airborne invasion of Holland just a couple of weeks later.

Finally, the 17th Airborne, with the 681st in tow, were rushed in to help stem the German advance in the Ardennes and saw its baptism of fire during the first days of January, 1945. Their fighting spirit was certainly not lacking. In one action alone, the struggle for control of "Dead man's Ridge," the 17th sustained over 1,000 casualties. In March of that year the 17th Airborne Division, in tandem with the British 6th Airborne, executed Operation Plunder, the Airborne component of Operation Varsity. Casualties were again heavy for both paratroopers and glidermen when numerous transport aircraft were shot down or seriously damaged over the drop and landing zones. In spite of this, all objectives were taken and a very successful crossing of the Rhine River was accomplished within one 24 hour period.

All in all, during the five months from January to May, 1945, the division racked up 45 days in combat. During this time it sustained 1,314 men killed in action and another 4,904 wounded. In addition, the "Thunder from Heaven" division's troopers were awarded an impressive number of decorations for bravery, accumulating, for example, four Congressional Medals of Honor – one more, in fact, than the 82nd garnered. The 681st, under the command of Lt. Col. Joseph Keating, participated fully in all of the 17th Airborne's combat operations. Twenty-three members of the battalion were killed in action — one of whom received a Silver Star.

To what extent the High-Pointers became aware of their new division's record is unclear, but orders to replace the 82nd Airborne patches with those of the 17th continued to be met with considerable hostility. A compromise was finally settled on when the High-Pointers were told they should wear their 82nd Airborne patches on the right shoulder. Today it is customary for US Army personnel to wear the insignia of the first unit with which they see combat at this location on their uniform, and the practice appears to have originated with the transferred 82nd men in 1945. "So we switch the 82nd from the left to the right and put the shit-hook on the other side," commented Sartain. "We called that the shit hook, that's right. I hated having to wear that. I really wanted to

BATTERY!

take it off."

This new policy helped to neutralize the hard feelings, but the attitude of the transferred men remained resistant. Evidence indicates that they did comply insofar as sewing 17th Airborne patches on to their Eisenhower jackets, but few, if any, seem to have bothered applying the new insignia to their shirts or other sundry uniform items. Sartain, for instance, left the 82nd Airborne patch which was displayed on the breast of his leather A-2 jacket undisturbed, while photographs taken weeks after the transfer to the 681st show High-Point men as still displaying the 82nd insignia on their shirts. Indeed, there is no evidence that the talon was ever applied anywhere except to the men's formal service uniform.

Thinking the issue was settled, and wishing to see a demonstration of uniformity in the ranks, Major General Miley, the 17th Airborne's commander, held a division review a few days later. When the 681st passed the reviewing stand the old-timers saluted with their fingers crooked inward to imitate an eagle's talon. After the review Colonel Todd summoned all the officers to

Members of the 319th's Battalion softball team playing baseball while a crowd of soldiers and French civilians look on. "I was the Athletic Officer of the Battalion," said Sartain. "If that wasn't a crock! I had to keep the guys going with athletics, baseball, whatever we did. We had a good time. We didn't have anything to do but train and do calisthenics. From two in the afternoon till two the next morning they didn't have anything to do. It got real boring. Everybody put on a little weight." The catcher is Milton Goldfarb, the "B" Battery man whom Sartain defended in North Africa – his first trial as a guardhouse lawyer. All photos Sartain collection.

his office and reprimanded them harshly.

Sartain was hugely amused by the whole stunt. "Yeah man, we gave them the claw," he recalled, "But Todd put an end to that business in a hurry. He told us, 'Cut all that crap out!' But we didn't give a damn; we were ready to go home."
The transferred men persisted in expressing their attitude about the whole situation, albeit surreptitiously. "We still saluted with our fingers like a claw," said Sartain with pride, "But we only saluted ex-319th people with the "Claw" because we had to be extra careful about that. We didn't want to get in any trouble; we were on our way home."
Once all the hoopla over division patches was settled, life in both the 319th and the 681st Glider Field Artillery Battalions took on a relaxed and unhurried pace. With a choice of England, Switzerland, Paris, or the Riviera, many of the troops left on weeklong furloughs, and since a soldier's furlough didn't officially begin until he reached his destination, few exercised urgency while traveling.

If they'd chosen the Riviera, Nice was designated for enlisted men, while Caan was reserved for officers. Whatever the men did, all considered it a well deserved vacation. Some would have visited the perfume capitol of France at Grasse, and doubtless acquired a bottle of Channel No. 5 for their wives, mothers, or best girl at home. Others went swimming in the Mediterranean, though servicemen were prohibited from visiting the topless beach. Most were content to lounge about, drinking beer at outside tables, and enjoying the scenery.

"Nice. A big nothing to see there but women," remarked one of the High-Pointers, while low-point Lieutenant Joe Mullen wrote from Caan on June 29th, "I'm enjoying a 7 day leave at the Riviera on the beautiful blue Mediterranean. The only thing bad about it," he complained, "is the GI food that these people can't cook."

There was meanwhile little, if any extensive training going on at Neufchateau. Neither Kenneth Smith, Storms, Ryan, nor Covais could recall any instance of the new

Covais captioned this photo "The Big Four" – in this case, right to left: Roland "The Grieb" Gruebling, Tom "Jughead" Ludwick, Albert "Smash" Lewis, and Ted Covais, enjoy a cup of coffee at the Mess hall at Camp Chicago. Courtesy Gruebling family.

BATTERY!

battalion or the new "A" Battery ever actually assembling for drill and maneuvers.

In the absence of strenuous military training, athletics became the only structured activity to occupy the men's attention during daylight hours. Naturally, the Army encouraged sports activities as a way to keep the men fit and work off some energy through a safe outlet. As a result, football, basketball, and baseball teams were all organized at both the battalion and division level. One game or another was held nearly every day and members of winning teams were rewarded with week long furloughs to Nice or Paris.

"As athletic officer I had to keep the guys going with athletics, baseball, whatever we did," remembered Sartain. "We had a good time. We didn't have anything to do but train, do calisthenics and then everybody, from two in the afternoon till two the next morning; they didn't have anything to do. It got real boring. Everybody put on a little weight."

While bats, gloves, and balls were all supplied by the military, no provisions had been made for maintenance of the sports fields and equipment.

Sergeant Arno Mundt poses at a signpost at Camp Chicago showing which direction, and dhow far, each man would need to travel to get home. Courtesy Rita Mundt.

Just the same, as Athletics Officer this was part of Sartain's responsibilities. After making some casual inquiries he came up with a resourceful solution. "I had to cut the grass on the baseball field," he explained, "So I went to the hospital and told the nurse, 'Look I need some lawn mowers.' She said, 'Come meet me at such and such a time.' I had to sign for them. I forget what I signed, Joseph A. -- something crazy, some Lieutenant. Sosa and I put those lawn mowers in the jeep and never brought them back, but we kept that grass cut like it was a major league ball park."

With so little to do, and having mixed emotions about leaving the battery in the first place, Sartain had to restrain himself from drifting back too often. "I visited with them a lot. Watched some of their exercises, but I tried to stay out of the battery operations once I left. I appreciated the fact that it was Ragland's turn, but he was a very bashful man and never had much to say, so I didn't want to overshadow him or cast a presence."

Sartain respected that there was always a learning curve, something Ragland later described as a period of "adjustment," when ever a man takes on new responsibilities. Assuming command of "A" Battery, 681st GFAB, presented such an experience for Ragland, who now found himself in charge of a battery of his own, many of whose personnel were unknown to him, all within an unfamiliar battalion and division. "Captain Sartain had such a way of being battery commander that it was a hard job to replace him," Ragland later explained. "I had been with other senior officers before but he was the best. He just knew how to take care of people."

Ragland's very different command style was an adjustment for the men as well as their new battery commander. His quiet and unassuming nature, which was distinct from that of the colorful Sartain, was a change for men who may have been used to a more authoritarian presence and a lot less free time. With wartime restrictions relaxed and a generally triumphant spirit in the air, there were bound to be some problems. After one of his High-Pointers ran afoul of some MPs in a Neufchateau bar, Ragland was given advice from Colonel Todd. "The higher brass told me I should take hold of the battery and watch out after those men. Make sure they don't get in trouble."

When he was Sartain's Exec, Ragland had normally been responsible for affairs within the battery. Now, dealing with external matters between the battery and outside authorities was a duty which he was new to. "Well, I'll see what I can do," was Ragland's rather indifferent response to his superior.

If Ragland seemed detached from battery operations, it may be that he was just emotionally and psychologically fatigued after two years of combat. "Burned out" is how he has described his own state of mind at this period in time. "I was just worn out. I think all of us were getting kind of wore out by then," he supposed when I discussed the period with him later.

In fact, many of the guys were showing signs of the same combat weariness. Being in danger of exposure to battle had always reinforced the men's self-control, but with that pressure removed, and following the breakup of the old battery, many felt unsettled. Some seemed unable to shake a general malaise. Though finally able to relax, others felt strangely numb, or to the contrary noticed that their emotions were more difficult to modulate. Judging from the body of anecdotal sources, a significant number, though probably a minority, externalized their disoriented feelings through liquor, women, gambling, or fighting, sometimes in combination.

All this anticipation produced the most nerve wracking, yet boring of situations. Even Sartain succumbed to the tedium, "In one poker game in Epinal I dropped about sixteen hundred bucks. I lost it to Wimberley or someone else I didn't like.

Nurses of the 24th Evacuation Hospital holding oranges while on a chow line at their facilities near Verdun, France. Sartain collection.

BATTERY!

All in big British notes. Boy, it made me mad," he said.

Alcohol was the most frequently applied tonic for the insufferable limbo of waiting and waiting. Officers had easier access to hard liquor than enlisted men, and exercised this privilege freely. Drinking socially during card games or commiserating among themselves had always been customary when off duty, but now the practice seemed more widespread. Commenting on this time, Lieutenant Joe Mullen wrote, "About the only outlet over here is a jug, & some of us do that every twice in a while."

Among the 681st officers at Neufchateau and those back with the old 319th at Epinal, parties were also held in conjunction with army nurses from nearby hospitals. Some of these social gatherings took place at a medical facility outside Verdun. Attended with great enthusiasm, the merrymaking there must have become particularly rockus on at least one occasion. Serving as an ad hoc driver, Ed Ryan claimed to have helped pull Captain Hawkins and Colonel Todd out of one late night Verdun bash in which there was, "puke on the floor and nurses dancing barefooted."

In another case, Lieutenants Joe Mullen and Marvin Fellman were involved in a serious jeep accident while driving back from a party, also in Verdun. Mullen was so badly injured that he never was able to return to duty. On July 30th he wrote home from a hospital in Nancy, describing what happened. "I was pretty well loaded the nite I got put in here and don't remember anything for the first week. That was due to a crack in the head and not whiskey. I'm glad I was loaded as I don't remember the wreck. I got told that they had to lift the jeep off of me to get to me. Naturally I was some place I wasn't supposed to be when it happened. The Lt. who was driving and went to sleep, has to pay for the ($265) damage. He's gone to Berlin as he didn't get much banged up. No one did but me. No rest for the wicked. I'm a good boy, or so the nurses tell me."

Bob Storms spoke in some detail about this urge to break loose, discharge pent up tension and forget unsettling emotions. His was probably the most thoughtful commentary on the subject when he said, "You know, they can say what they want about drinking and raising hell in-service, but if you stayed in camp and minded your own business you never lasted. You'd go crazy. You had to drink and raise hell or you'd go out of your mind. I had all I could take. I had enough of being hurt and everything else, so I drank. No, no, you can't stay and worry about your wife and kids because if you do you're not going to go home -- not like you was. It's no good that way, you'll go nuts. Some of them went right off their rocker and I don't know if they ever straightened out. For what we seen on the line and seen in the death camps, and seen all over, you know it's hard to take that stuff."

Of course, the great majority of contact between the officers and nurses was of a much more mild nature. After someone produced a grill, frequent cook-outs became popular. On one occasion even General Andy March and Chaplain Bill Reid from 82nd Airborne Artillery staff joined the gathering.

These afternoon picnics offered Sartain an opportunity to showcase a proper Louisiana barbeque as best as circumstances would allow. "I cooked barbeque on that charcoal grill with those nurses from the 24th Evacuation Hospital," Sartain remembered. "You dig a hole, get your charcoal real hot and put your grill over it. I did it all, well, 90% of it. None of these other guys could cook - they didn't belong to the Boy Scouts and all that foolishness. Yeah, man, we had tenderloins and pork chops. I made a barbeque sauce out of ketchup and I forget what else. They couldn't understand it, they loved it! I was considered a coon-assed cook. Coon-ass, that's a low class Cajun."

Aside from barbeques, the officers spent many evenings visiting with the nurses in

Don't Fence Me In.

Verdun. "The 24th was with the division right through and we got to know the nurses real well. We first met them in Normandy. After the war was over, in France, we used to make what we called "The Verdun Run" every night to their barracks. Well, we didn't have any business being there so the gals had to sneak us in. One time we didn't know what the guard situation was and we had to spend the night. Finally they snuck us out in a delivery truck the next day. There was one gal I had a lot of fun with, a redhead from St. Louis. She was a good sport. We had some wild parties, we had a good time, but I behaved myself. I was kind of faithful to Peggy-Lou, I really was, and I'm glad I was." In his memory, Sartain always associated the song: "Don't Fence Me In" with the Verdun Run. "It was our favorite song," he said. "I remember us all out there on the veranda singing, "Don't Fence Me In." We were all sitting on that portch looking out over the nurses all taking sunbaths. There must have been a hundred of them out there in their

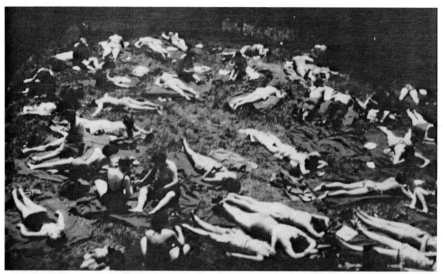

Nurses of the 24th Evacuation Hospital sunning themselves on a tennis court near their quarters at Verdun, France, summer of 1945. "We used to make what we called the Verdun Run every night. That was us leaving to go to the nurses in Verdun! That's where all those nurses are where you see them taking their sunbath and all of that. All those nurses laying out there in their skivvies. That was a good experience, a real educational experience." Sartain collection.

skivvies."

The song was a number one hit in the States during the previous winter, after Bing Crosby recorded a hugely popular version with the Andrews Sisters in September, 1944. It is likely that the nurses had a phonograph on which they played a 78rpm recording of the recent release. Largely written by Cole Porter, the song perfectly captured the desperate yearning for rest and home, far away from Europe and the awful events that took place there.

> Oh, give me land, lots of land under starry skies above,
> Don't fence me in.
> Let me ride through the wide open country that I love,

BATTERY!

Don't fence me in.
Let me be by myself in the evenin' breeze,
And listen to the murmur of the cottonwood trees,
Send me off forever but I ask you please,
Don't fence me in.
Just turn me loose, let me straddle my old saddle
Underneath the western skies.
On my Cayuse, let me wander over yonder
Till I see the mountains rise.
I want to ride to the ridge where the west commences
And gaze at the moon till I lose my senses
And I can't look at hovels and I can't stand fences
Don't fence me in.

Final photograph of 'A' Battery, taken in June, 1945, before the high point men were transferred to the 17th Airborne division.

Top row, Left to right: Kenneth Smith, Billy Cadle, Norman Dwyer, Eugene Varner, Russell Tyler, Robert Dugger, Lloyd Cattell, Hildure Madison, Norman Beyert, William Kennedy, William Lucas, Francis Siler, Harold Mell, Flag, David Stelow, John Sievwright, Louis Sosa, Brown, John Spicer, Arthur Brodelle, Thurman King, Alex Peto, Lester Crooke, Flavious Carney, Thomas Legg.

Second row, left to right: Lester Newman, Leslie Niemi, Joseph Tatreau, John Girardin, Edward Spencer, Charles Grigus, Calvin Hightower, Arthur Forsman, Morrisey, Leroy Miller, Frances Tobin, Leroy Samples, Willie Hall, Charles Youngblood, Arno Mundt, Paul Massie, Frederick Van Hassel, Leslo Karney, James Jones, Robert Dickson, Ernest Schilson, Harry Kerr, Rogers.

Third row, left to right: George Romanus, John Thomas, Herbert Gost, Stanley Bichefski, Jack LaHue, Marion Litchfield, Theodore Simpson, Oscar Fields, Clovis Thompson, Fred Fitzke, Duel Elmore, Milton Susman, Albert Hein, Charles Sartain, Irving Gelb, Marvin Ragland, Laurence Cook, Marvin Fellman, George Nederoscik, William Forsythe, James Gwaltney, Mahlon Sebring, Victor Buinowski, Robert Rappi, Calvin Pouncey, Talmage Glenn, Arthur Pease, Harold Walz, William Bonnamy.

Bottom row, left to right: Donald Kane, Raymond Smart, Robert Carte, H. Harvey, Otto Porche, Vernon Edge, James Russell, Louie Wall, Silas Hogg, B. Carpenter, Charles Shaw, Roland Gruebling, Ted Covais, Thomas Ludwick, Ercie Holcomb, Severino Scarsella, Robert Storms, James Fitzsimmons, Warren Jones, Barney Brighton, Louis Doherty, Richard Millard, Howard Dearwester.

BATTERY!

Part 33: "The get-out-quick-line."

The entire month of July passed in seeming slow motion, waiting for something to happen when, on August 6th, 1945, the first Atomic Bomb was dropped on Japan, followed by another on the 9th. Over the following several days it became clear that no one, even under the worst chain of events, was going to have to see combat in the Pacific. Everyone, whether in the 82nd or 17th Airborne, breathed a sigh of relief.

By this time the 82nd Airborne was already in Berlin, the old 319th Battalion having gone with it. When Sartain and the other High-Pointers left them, the original "A" Battery received a large influx of low-point personnel from the 681st. The event came to be known as "The Big Switch."

Sebring recalled that the old battery men felt forsaken and left behind. "We felt," he said, "kind of lost without Sartain. He took good care of us."

The GIs transferred from the 17th Airborne were alright, just regular guys but, with the exception of Lieutenant Fellman, all the officers were new. Accepting new officers was harder.

According to Sebring, "When you got in new officers you never knew what would take place. The ones that took over had just come over from the states and we didn't like them telling us what to do. We weren't in the mood."

A fortnight after the Japanese surrender, the 681st found itself loaded on to another train of forty and eight cars. This time the destination was a holding camp outside the French Mediterranean port of Marseilles. Marseilles looked like it would be the last stop on this side of the Atlantic. During these final days there was another round of paperwork and chores, some of which involved accounting for, and turning in all vehicles, weapons, and equipment. Before surrendering his jeep to the motor depot, Sosa took the radio and leather seat covers out and sold them to another driver for $50.

After three years of build-up, enormous quantities of material were being collected and left behind. Ed Ryan recalled what he saw. "I went down to turn in a truck to this place where they turned in the rolling stock," he said. "It would be a mile of trucks and a mile of tanks and stuff like that where they turned them all in. I never saw anything like it in my life."

Before the guys could leave Marseilles, Sartain was called on once more to come to the defense of one of his men. Though they had been warned to stay out of trouble, Corporal Bob Carte was implicated in some incident which landed him in the guardhouse. Evidently the offense was serious enough that he was scheduled for a General Court Martial, but if that happened Carte would not be on the ship home and would face a trial at a great disadvantage.

Sartain heard about Carte's predicament when the Corporal requested him as Defense Council. As Ragland remembered it, Sartain came to see him one morning with some advice, "You're battery commander," began Sartain. "Do you know that you could go to the Colonel and have him pardon Carte so he could go home with us? Because if he isn't pardoned he can't go home with us. He's been with us from the beginning. He was one of our better soldiers! He's never given us any trouble, and it sounds like he was just in the wrong place when this thing happened."

Sartain may have been stretching the truth a little bit. After all, Carte did have a reputation for getting mixed up in things that "weren't his fault," even though the incidents were never terribly serious. In any event, neither officer wanted to see him left behind at this critical juncture.

"So I did," recounted Ragland, I went to the Colonel and sure enough we got him off. It worked out alright. "I wasn't aware of the situation, of the legal aspects, but Captain Sartain, he was an attorney and he knew all the regulations. He clued me in on it."

At last the big day arrived. The 681st Glider Field Artillery, along with the other High-Pointers transferred from the 82nd to the 17th Airborne, assembled at the docks in Marseilles. As the guys detrained, hefting their barracks bags over their shoulders, they eyed a large transport ship of the type they had traveled on before. It looked a lot like the Santa Rosa which brought them to Casablanca, except that it was larger. That was a lifetime ago.

Before boarding, the men were drawn up for a visit with the paymaster, who settled his accounts with each of them in turn. What with sporadic paydays and accumulated credits, most of the GIs walked away with a good deal of cash in their pockets. Best of all, they were paid in United States dollars for the first time in years. Since GIs are always paid in the currency of the country in which they are stationed, this could only mean one thing – they were really, really, really going home.

The day was September 6th, 1945. Their work in Europe was done.

The ship waiting at the dock in Marseilles was the SS Wakefield, hull number AP-21. Displacing a little over 24,000 tons, she was 705 feet long, with a beam of about 86 feet, and able to cruise at an impressive 24.5 knots. Originally constructed in 1931 as the SS Manhattan for the lively transatlantic trade of the time, the ship was operated by the

Seven members of "A" Battery strike poses for the camera. Louis Sosa is pointing to five Overseas Bars on his sleeve – indicating two and one half years overseas service. The man with his hand on his left hip is Motor Pool Sergeant Tom Legg. Sartain collection.

BATTERY!

United States Lines as one of several luxury passenger ships. Through the 1930s, Manhattan made a regular run between New York and Hamburg, Germany, by way of ports in Ireland, England, and France. After one crossing of the Atlantic in less than six days the Manhattan was truthfully advertised as "the fastest cabin ship in the world."

But with the outbreak of hostilities in Europe, the resulting collapse of the transatlantic passanger trade, and anticipated American involvement in the war, Manhattan was chartered by the War Department as a troop transport for a period of two years and renamed the SS Wakefield. When an onboard fire nearly destroyed the vessel in 1942, the navy purchased the ruined ship from the United States Lines and completely rebuilt her interior. The new Wakefield, designed to carry 6,000 soldiers and their equipment, re-entered service in February, 1944. With a crew of nearly 800 accompanied by a police force of 60 Marines, Wakefield had already made over twenty transatlantic round trips by September, 1945 and earned the nickname of the "Boston and Liverpool Ferry" from her crew.

On this trip the Wakefield was to transport nearly the entire 17th Airborne Division – about 8,200 men in all, through the Straits of Gibraltar, westward all the way to Boston. This was, of course, about a third more men than the ship was intended to carry and would make for an especially crowded voyage.

One of the crew, a coastguard's man named Walter E. Lafferty, remembered life on the troop transport bringing new soldiers to the war in Europe and then returning with wounded men or German prisoners. "It would take the best part of a day to load the soldiers and their gear as we usually carried about 7,000 soldiers. While we were loading, the ship's canteen would be open and they could buy candy and stuff. Cigarettes were free," he later said.

According to Sartain, unit organization started melting away when the personnel of the 681st stepped on to the deck after ascending the gangplank. Officers were separated from enlisted men and the batteries were broken up as GIs were assigned to cabins. They filed down steep, ladder like staircases, passing mess halls that had once been beautifully appointed dining rooms along the way, continuing down to decks well below the water-line. Though Wakefield still retained the elegant outline of a luxury passenger ship, living quarters on board were decidedly spartan.

"We were kind of stacked in there like sardines," commented Lieutenant Cook.

Crewman Lafferty described the accommodations this way, "The army personnel 'quarters' were bunks five high with a narrow aisle for access. The only one who could sit up-right was the top man. The latrine arrangement was a series of out-house like holes over a galvanized metal trough that was constantly awash from a large pipe at one end and a slope to the drain at the other. When the ship rolled you could get your fanny washed unless you were quick."

It must have been near sunset when the Wakefield shoved off from the pier. Thousands of men swarmed the decks, elated at actually being underway. A sense of joy, relief at knowing they'd survived the war unscathed imbued everyone's spirit. There was also the satisfaction at being part of the army's most decorated combat division. As darkness fell, the lights along the coast remained bright until they disappeared behind the horizon. On the ship the lights also remained on, just as things had been before the war, lending a festive atmosphere to the scene.

Without the threat of torpedoes from enemy submarines, the Wakefield sailed directly toward the Straits of Gibraltar and on into the deep water Atlantic. Since there was no longer any need to sail an evasive, zigzag course, the GIs were told they could expect to reach Boston in as little as eight days. There was also no prohibition against smoking, so the men all indulged their considerable appetite for tobacco.

Sartain in particular remembered enjoying this peacetime pleasure. "Oh, we had a good time," he said of it. "It was nice. I could sit on the deck, smoke my pipe and not worry about it. It was fun, but there was no liquor, no, there wasn't any liquor for sale on the boat."

In fact, despite Sartain's statement to the contrary, a lively commerce began immediately on leaving port and some of it involved alcohol. Crewmen offered bottles of liquor to soldiers which they had smuggled aboard at hugely inflated prices.

"Most of the thing with sailors was buying booze off them," explained Ryan. "They'd have it in their locker. They'd get $25 for a bottle. Same bottle would be $6 in the States."

GIs retailed souvenir pistols in return. According to Sosa, sailors would, "give their left nut for a Lugar." Sailors liked other pistols too -- the Walther P-38 in particular. "Hey, we got a hundred bucks apiece for them," crowed Storms later. "I sold two on the ship and then I brought one home. I think that's the only thing I had left when I come home was one P-38."

Most features of life on the Wakefield were otherwise much the same as they

John Girardin disembarks stateside after nearly three years overseas. He returned home to Rockford, Illinois, was back on his job and married a few weeks later. Courtesy Gruebling family.

had been on the Santa Rosa coming over and, for that matter, on the Dickman in late 1943 as well. With so many on board the ship and the weather mild as it was, the men took turns rotating between sleeping on deck and in the jam-packed, stuffy cabins below. Two meals were served per day to chow lines which never quite disappeared, but ran continuously around the clock. The men ate standing at counters and the food itself was all dehydrated and quite unappetizing. For the first few days, and in rougher seas, seasickness meant decks had to be hosed down every few hours. "I didn't get sick because I had kitchen duty all the way coming back," remembered Lieutenant Larry Cook. "It's when you don't have anything to do is when you get sick."

Feeding 8,200 men of the 17th Airborne Division every day, twice a day, was a massive operation. "I kept the chow line coming," continued Cook. "That was a big job because there were thousands on board, so there was always a chow line."

Army cooks were evidently stationed in various gallies to do their part in the preparation of so much food. But given the mild contempt which soldiers and sailors held for each other, it is not surprising that there were arguments. The mess sergeant of HQ Battery, Alvin P. Larrieu of New Orleans, Louisiana, had a reputation as a temperamental cook.

"Larrieu, his famous words were always, 'Get out of my kitchen!'" began Ed Ryan as he recounted one of his memories of the Wakefield. "Anyway, I hung right there down in the mess hall with Larrieu most of the way back. Well some chief petty officer started giving him a hard time, so he said, 'Get out of my kitchen!' This petty officer said, 'I won't get out of your kitchen.' Larrieu said, 'You get out of my kitchen or I'll throw you out!' So right away this guy ran for help. He got some sort of a naval officer. Meanwhile, Larrieu got hold of a first lieutenant. They met head to head down there and this rank thing started going right on up until it got to the General. When it did the General lost because the captain is in charge of the ship when it's at sea. So you had to take their shit for a while."

The lieutenant may have been Larry Cook, although when asked about the incident sixty-five years later, he supposed genially, "Could have been, but as far as I remember I just got along with everybody."

To help relieve the tedium, movies were shown in the mess halls. Still, the combination of boredom and the large amounts of cash in the men's hands gave birth to problematic pastimes. Aside from drinking, there was a substantial amount of gambling. Blankets were spread out in every nook and all over the decks for crap games. When asked if he saw any gambling on the Wakefield, Sosa exclaimed, "Oh man! Around the clock. You could see them all hunched up shooting crap. But for the first time in my life I won money gambling, can you believe that? I've always been a loser but I picked up about eighty dollars in a crap game.

Sosa was lucky, but many, many more GIs lost money, particularly to those who had honed their skill at throwing dice to a razor's edge.

Sartain found the whole gambling situation disturbing. "Professional gamblers were taking advantage of these novices." He later complained of how difficult it was to watch without intervening. "These kids had saved their money, didn't have any thing to do with it, no place to spend it, and then lost all of it on the damn ship coming back. I wanted to put a stop to it but I was advised by Colonel Todd not to. He told me, 'Charlie, stay out of it. It's none of your business.'"

"Talon," a single sheet 17th Airborne Newspaper, was distributed daily. Each issue featured up-to-date articles from the wire services, with a heavy emphasis on boxing matches and the up-coming World Series. The men were also kept abreast of the distance remaining to Boston: September 8th 2,861 miles, September 10th 1,663, on the 12th 655, and by the 13th less than 200 miles.

Finally, and as predicted, the SS Wakefield rolled into Boston Harbor on the morning of September 14th. "All the boats in the harbor were blowing their whistles," remembered Sartain. "All the boats in the harbor were shooting all this colored water up in the air, red, white, and blue. It was quite a celebration."

Notwithstanding whistles and fountains, as they drew closer to shore, it became clear there was no brass band or delegation of grateful, cheering civilians ready to welcome the GIs at the pier. From the ship the men could only see a rail spur with waiting passenger cars. The scene struck Lieutenant Cook as a bit disappointing, especially given all the hubbub in the harbor. Nevertheless, Cook had always believed he would make it home alive and now it was only a matter of hours, maybe minutes before he would feel his homeland under his feet. In spite of his impatience, it had taken most of the day to load everyone on the Wakefield and it would take nearly as long for the men to disembark. Finally it was the 681st's turn to go ashore. Military formalities like closed formations and saluting relaxed and then gave way altogether as the men's civilian identities started to reawaken. When Lieutenant Larry Cook set foot on American soil he couldn't help but kneel down and kissed the ground.

The train took the men to Camp Miles Standish, a 1,500 acre installation forty miles south of Boston, just outside Taunton, Massachusetts. Many thousands of American, Canadian, and even Australian troops had left for Europe through this camp. Both Italian and German POWs were housed there. Now it was turned into an enormous reception center for returning soldiers.

After detraining at Camp Miles Standish the men were guided into a massive receiving hall where Red Cross girls served refreshments. "They gave us milk and doughnuts. The milk tasted good and the doughnuts were kind of tough, but they were OK," recalled Sartain, adding, "they had coffee too but it was Boston made coffee which wasn't that good."

This reception hall was primarily a facility from which soldiers could place toll-free telephone calls to their families, informing them that they were safely arrived in Boston. The hall was fitted out with dozens upon dozens of telephones lining the walls. Some men stood in lines and others sat at long tables, sipping coffee or chugging milk as they waited for an unoccupied phone.

"Everybody could grab a telephone and call home. It was well, well managed," recalled Sartain approvingly.

Sosa called Tampa. Covais made a call to Brooklyn, Ryan made a call to his parents in Poughkeepsie. Others called Iowa, Tennessee, Indiana, and West Virginia. "I placed a call to Peggy Lou at the Shreveport library where she worked," Sartain remembered. "Then I called my mother. When I called Peggy-Lou at the library they didn't want to connect me with her. They asked me who I was, so I told them, 'Its Lenton Sartain.' If I'd have told them Charlie Sartain they would have had no idea who it was. So they said, 'Oh, just a minute!'"

That night the guys were fed a turkey dinner with all the trimmings. Everyone was restricted to the base and only allowed to go to the Post Exchange, but nobody cared about that. In the morning they were assured that the next day trains would begin taking them from Camp Miles Standish to processing centers at the army facility nearest their home. On the 16th the trains were there as promised. Every few hours another one pulled away, carrying with it more of the guys and leaving behind a dwindling remainder. In the impatience to get home, and with everyone so weary of being in the service, farewells were limited to a quick handshake devoid of sentimentality.

Kenneth Smith boarded a train headed for Camp Benjamin Harrison, outside Indianapolis. Sosa got on another for Camp Blanding, Florida. Covais, Storms, Ryan, and all the other guys who'd come from the now closed Camp Upton three years before shouldered their barracks bags and climbed aboard a train for Fort Dix, New Jersey. "We all knew then where our discharge was going to be," Sartain said. His was one of the last trains to leave that day. "I was loaded up on a train to Hattiesburg, Mississippi, with an air force canvas suitcase and a barracks bag. We had a bunch of people from Tennessee on the train too, so they stopped in Nashville. Then I got to Hattiesburg where

BATTERY!

Camp Shelby is."

Once at Camp Shelby, Sartain could have marked time waiting to be processed and formally discharged, but when it became clear this could take as long as a week, impatience overtook him. He obtained a ten-day furlough, bought a bus ticket for New Orleans and called home to inform his parents just when he would arrive. Shortly before his 90th birthday, Sartain thought back to his homecoming. He said, "When I got into New Orleans my daddy was there at the bus station to meet me. I didn't know he was gonna be there. He was a little short guy but he looked about the same to me. It was a home coming, oh man; we hugged and had a nice visit. Then he rode with me on the bus to Baton Rouge. We got in around nine o'clock, nine thirty. I remember going up the front steps and Bessie Landry, who was a nosy, nosy lady, opened her back porch and she hollered, 'Hello Lenton! Welcome Home!' Bessie was a real 24 hours a day busy-body. I started to ignore her, my daddy punched me. I said, 'Hello Bessie, how're you!' Of course, my mother cried but I was just glad to see them both, it was real nice. The three of us stayed up kind of late that night. Somebody'd been rat-holing my packages from home for a while, so it was the first time I had Louisiana coffee in some time. So that was it."

Sartain stayed at home one day, then got on the night train for Shreveport to see his girl, Peggy-Lou. "Oh brother, it was really good to see her. She was at work when I got to Shreveport but she left work early and never went back to the library. She quit, that was her last day."

After a few days Sartain returned to Camp Shelby to complete his discharge. As the sweethearts parted he began what would become a lovers' tradition between them. "I'd kiss her on the cheek, then kiss her on the other cheek, then kiss her on the lips. Then I'd say, 'That's a bracket. That's the bracket, Honey.' Later on I bought her a bracelet with the word "BRACKET" engraved on it," he remembered fondly.

Sartain's comment to Peggy-Lou was a reference to the field artillery practice of "bracketing" a target in order to find its range. Once a target was bracketed the command, "Fire for effect!" was given.

At the very same time, all across the country other members of Sartain's old battery were arriving at their discharge processing centers. They were subjected to a series of interviews and examinations. There were numerous forms to be filled out, one of which enrolled discharged servicemen into what was popularly known as the "52-20 club," a government stipend of $20 per week for one year.

Kenneth Smith was typical of most GIs as he was being processed at Fort Benjamin Harrison, outside Indianapolis. "We went through a line," he said later. "People that wanted to sign up for disabilities and stuff like that go this way, if you want to go home go that way. I wanted to go home so I got in the get out quick line."

GIs knew that claiming any sort of disability would initiate a series of medical examinations and documentation which could take days or weeks to complete. Few had the patience, even if they did have legitimate, but undocumented, wounds or injuries. Among artillerymen this was apt to include loss of hearing, or ringing in the ears. Others had bum knees, residual effects of malaria, or tiny fragments of shrapnel in their flesh.

At Fort Dix, medical personnel encouraged Bob Storms to stay on for dental treatment. "They wanted me to stay and fix my teeth because I never had good teeth and I never got them fixed in service," he explained. "They wanted me to stay another month or two, get my teeth fixed and get all straightened out. I said, I wouldn't want to stay another day if I don't have to. I'll let my teeth get fixed when I get home. I gotta get out of here. I had, well I had seen so much I just had to get out. I enlisted for three years and I pulled it right to the day, right to the day."

Once he arrived at Camp Blanding, Florida, Louis Sosa discovered that there were stateside GIs willing to pay for certain items of clothing. The short style, Eisenhower jacket which soldiers returning from Europe wore was much in demand, but most sought after of all were Jump boots. "I remember when I got back to Camp Blanding I sold all my extra uniforms and stuff. I had an extra pair of brand new jump boots. Boy, those guys were like to have a fight over who was gonna get them," Sosa recalled.

Where ever they were being processed, GIs with souvenir pistols or other firearms were required to provide adequate paperwork accounting for each individual piece, signed by their commanding officer. Failure to do so would make these items liable for confiscation. Sartain, for example, carried a permit signed by Colonel Todd listing both his Italian Berretta and his German Walther. Not surprisingly, so-called USO commandos were known to try and separate particularly desirable items from their GI owners. But these combat veterans with silver wings, six battle stars, and unit citations on their chests were disinclined to be intimidated under these or any other conditions.

Ed Ryan described one such incident at Fort Dix. "They had all kinds of things going on there. Everybody wanted out but the compliment there at Fort Dix wasn't too great. In fact, they wanted to make things as tough for you as they could. I remember one guy from the 505th, he had a chrome plated Mouser. Well he showed it to this Lieutenant on the way out. The Lieutenant said, he was from Fort Dix too, he said, 'I'll keep that.' The guy said, 'You will not, I killed somebody to get it and I'll kill you to keep it.' Scared that guy right out of his boots, but they were all scared of us because we were a tough outfit."

As had been the case at Camp Miles Standish, soldiers being processed at regional discharge centers were also subject to quarantine. Ted Covais' wife, Cathy, knew he would be arriving at Fort Dix sometime on September 16th. Together with his older brother Jack and his wife, she traveled the next day to New Jersey from Brooklyn, beside herself with anticipation at seeing her husband after nearly three years.

At Fort Dix there were hundreds of people inquiring about their beloved soldier relatives. Every few minutes another happily discharged veteran with a "Ruptured Duck" sewn to the right chest of his jacket was welcomed into the crowd of civilians by handshakes, hugs, and tears, and then carried away by families and friends.
Cathy hoped that reunion would be only a matter of minutes, but after expending quite a bit of time standing in lines and waiting for answers, she learned that this would not be the case.

"Yes, there was a Sergeant Salvatore Covais here, and, no, they couldn't see him."

"Why?"

"They were very sorry but he was still on quarantine."

"Couldn't we just look at him through a window? Wouldn't that be alright?" she pleaded. The answer was a firm, no.

The three left disappointed but reassured. Cathy returned to her basement apartment. Under wartime conditions, she'd been lucky to get the flat and furnished it completely with money from her job and what Covais sent home from his army pay. A few months earlier he received photographs of the rooms and a key in the mail from her.

She later recounted what happened next. "A couple of days later, it was about six o'clock in the morning and I was lying in bed wondering when is he coming, when is he coming?" she recalled. "All of a sudden I hear my door jiggling. I looked up and, the way I remember it now, all I could see was those big army boots. I thought to myself, oh my goodness, it's him! About a half hour later my brother-in-law Jack came knocking at the door. He was doing that for about a week to see if Sal was home. I thought, bad timing, knocking on the door now! But we let him in. Then we went over to my mother-in-law's house. Everybody got together and we had a beautiful dinner, and that's how our life began."

Ted Covais was now a civilian again and reverted to his given name of Salvatore. For a few weeks he tried to get people used to calling him Ted, but the idea never would stick. Though he left behind the nickname and uniform of army life, picking up civilian mufti had its complications. Cathy noticed that he had changed. Her husband who'd left home as a wholesome nineteen year old, was now a heavy chain smoker. He sometimes swore now, in the way that most people do but which would previously have been unthinkable for him. Sal had no interest in attending church. And though he'd been an avowed teetotaler before the war, he now drank socially.

Of greater concern were the nightmares. These would usually begin with increasingly frantic, but indecipherable muttering. Then the thrashing would start. Sometimes Covais would suddenly sit bolt upright, shouting in his sleep, "What's that! Who's there! Watch out, watch out, watch out!"

On the worst nights Cathy would switch on the lights to see Sal curled in a ball with his arms shielding his head as if trapped in the bottom of a foxhole during an artillery barrage. He would be howling in some strange terrified and animalistic voice. At first it was frightening for her, but in time she learned that by gently repeating to him, "It's OK, Honey, you're home now. It's OK." She could calm him down. In the morning he'd usually have no recall of the dreams which terrorized him.

There were other things. Sal, the erstwhile Ted, was now uncharacteristically sentimental and apt to shed tears at holidays or anniversaries. Crowds could make him edgy and sudden noises bothered him in ways they never used to. On one occasion he and Cathy were walking down a Brooklyn sidewalk when the backfire of a taxi cab sounded. The noise startled her, but it sent him diving for cover on the concrete. Another evening they were visiting with friends, drinking coffee, eating cake, and smoking cigarettes, as couples did in those days. At the sound of a slamming door Covais threw himself flat on the floor. Then he got up, slapped the dust off his slacks, and apologized. The whole thing was a little embarrassing, but explained as a part of what was then popularly known as being "Nervous in the Service."

Covais wasn't alone in having a prolonged period of nightmares. Lieutenant Joe Mullen returned to Kentland, Indiana, and was dogged by the same problem. As an ironic consequence of his jeep accident, Mullen actually beat everyone else home, arriving at a Michigan hospital in August, 1945. Joe and his fiancée Gloria carried through with the wedding plans they'd made over the course of dozens of letters, even though he was still partly paralyzed and recovery was slow. He experienced many of the same effects of combat fatigue as Covais and other guys from the old 319th. "My mother said he would wake up in the night screaming and sweating, though he wouldn't talk about it. That went on for years," said his son Michael.

Marvin Ragland came home to Hutchinson, Kansas, but was in his own troubled state of mind. "When I came home I just wouldn't talk about the war at all. My mother and stepfather, they're both gone now, but they never knew that I got a Purple

Heart or Bronze Star while I was in Normandy. I never did tell them, I never did show them, and now that they're gone I kinda wish that I had. I was just depressed. Burned out. But I think it just kind of wore off and took care of itself.

When Ragland considered how he worked out of the gloom which beset him since the end of the war, he said, "I was home about two weeks. I had relatives in California, so I went out there. I was on the west coast during my basic training and I kind of liked it. I stayed for about six months, then I came back home and started working at Sears & Roebuck. My wife was working there. She wasn't my wife then, so we always tell everybody that we got each other at Sears & Roebuck with a money back guarantee. We never had to use the Guarantee."

Lieutenant Larry Cook, on the other hand, wanted very much to tell those around him about all he'd seen. When he got home to Santa Fe, Tennessee, he would sometimes start to talk about the war but his experiences seemed somehow beyond communication. In any case, people didn't appear to be interested or would change the subject. "After a while I just stopped talking. Since then I haven't talked about it much. I hardly ever talk about the war but I think about it," he said.

Each returning soldier handled his transition to civilian life differently. Ed Ryan, for example, took a taxi to his parents' home from the Poughkeepsie bus depot. That afternoon he bought two bottles of Scotch, drank one and passed out sometime before he could finish the second. Others turned inward, moving quietly through their homecoming.

When Kenneth Smith stepped off the Greyhound bus in his hometown of Washington, Indiana, there was no one to greet him. His brothers were all in the service and he knew his mother was ill at home, being cared for by his sister. Smith understood all this, but it was the way he walked through Washington's streets completely unnoticed by anyone that got to him. After a short reunion at home Smith decided he'd go downtown to the shine shop where he had passed so much time before the war. Surely there he would receive an enthusiastic hero's welcome back from the war.

Instead, he was inwardly crestfallen when the barber simply remarked, "Hello Kenneth, where you been?"

Given the disappointing response, there seemed nothing left except to get a job and begin the routine of workaday life. A few days later he took a factory job in town, and then Smith traded away his souvenir German pistol for a basketball.

Whatever the homecoming each soldier received, peacetime lives were resuming all across the nation. The imperturbable Corporal Louis Sosa returned to Tampa. He had driven Captain Manning and Captain Sartain through six battles and six countries, now he gave himself a chance to rest. "When I got home, for a year I was a man about town," he said. "I was a playboy. I bought me a car, bought some clothes, and I was a playboy. I got the girls, got everything, for a whole year I didn't work a lick. Then, after a year, I said, well I'm ready to settle down now, find me a job or do something, and I'm gonna get married."

Meanwhile, in Europe, the low-point guys had been doing occupation duty in Berlin since August. Before the war the city was said to have been the world's sixth largest metropolis, but in the fall of 1945 it was quite possibly the world's largest heap of rubble. The 319th men were housed in what had formerly been an SS barracks. The brick building stood in one of the scattered fragments of relatively undamaged neighborhoods in the American sector and was remarkably intact. Officially their duties involved a lot of guarding of supplies and facilities, management of the German civilians, and civil administration. However, much of the reason for their presence was clearly to act as a counterbalance to the Red Army on the city's eastern side. As had been the case the previous May in Mecklenburg, the Russian military assumed a confrontational posture. Every day there were incidents which tested the limits of cooperation between the Allies and some of them turned violent.

For instance, Robert Dickson recalled being mixed up in a fire-fight between 319th troopers and Russian soldiers when the latter were caught pulling up railroad tracks in the American sector. There were hundreds of altercations between individuals as well. In a conversation with the author in the mid-1980s, Roland Gruebling remembered being posted as a sentry on the American end of a bridge which spanned a canal dividing the two sectors. A Russian soldier approached him brandishing a pistol and demanding his watch. According to Gruebling, a scuffle erupted. He shot the Russian and dumped his body into the canal. Other men told of off-the-record killings, which took place nightly in the ruined streets of Berlin, and though carrying a weapon off-duty was forbidden, after several GIs were found dead everyone armed themselves.

The black market economy flourished, with cigarettes, Lieca cameras, food of any kind, and sex being the principle commodities in demand.

John Girardin remembered this lively black market trade, saying, "I tell you, it may have been against army regulations to sell anything to the Germans, but that was all black market. You figure we only paid fifty cents or a dollar for a carton of cigarettes and you could sell them for ten dollars. That was a lot of money in those days, not like it is now.

The Berliners impressed most of the GIs as friendly but pathetic. They were underfed and poorly clothed, eking out a life from the cellars of ruined apartment buildings by trading watches, cameras, or any other valuables for food or cigarettes. Most seemed cowed and frightened of Allied soldiers. The exception to this was young women who learned quickly that their companionship could buy them a meal and protection. The luckiest of these found employment with the army as performers for the entertainment of troops, laundresses, secretaries, or nurses. Under these circumstances, it isn't surprising that so many of the 319th troopers in Berlin found German girlfriends to spend their off-duty time with. "I've got a picture of one," recalled an "A" Battery man. "She was an acrobat and I got acquainted with her taking her home after shows. It happened that she lived in the American sector. I've got a picture with her here. My wife, one time she saw that picture and asked me about her. She said, 'Who was that woman anyway!' I told her, 'Don't worry about her, she ain't no where around.' She was an acrobat and boy you'd be surprised at what she could do. The only thing is she never could teach me how to dance. She tried to teach me but I couldn't learn."

As the summer passed into autumn, more and more of the guys in Berlin had enough points to be discharged. The first group left on October 29th from Leharve, France, aboard the SS William A. Graham. Among others, it carried Roland Gruebling, John Girardin, and Robert Rappi. These men were processed at Camp McCoy, Wisconsin, and discharged in late November.

Like those who'd come back with the 17th Airborne Division in September, these men picked up their civilian lives where they had left them. Gruebling was reunited with his wife, Jane, and resumed his job with Borden Dairies, delivering milk to stores throughout the Milwaukee area.

John Girardin returned to Rockford, Illinois, but collected his $20 weekly stipend for only a few weeks. After passing the month of December and its holidays at home, he returned to his machinist job in January, 1946. While Girardin wasn't plagued by nightmares, the reflexes of a front-line soldier took some time to settle down, as they had for others. "I would walk down the street sometimes and somebody might open a garage door that squeals, like a bomb falling, and I would find myself on the ground," said Girardin later, "That's about the only thing."

Sidna, Michigan, in the state's Upper Peninsula, was Staff Sergeant Robert Rappi's destination. Because his father worked as a game warden, the family home was deep within the Michigan forest, near a fish hatchery. On the day he returned, the final leg of Rappi's journey included a long walk through the quiet woods. While he was still some distance from the house, Rappi's dog, a bay retriever named Trigger, started barking as if a stranger was approaching. Rappi called out, "Hey Trigger, what's the matter boy, don't you remember me?" The barking stopped immediately. On hearing his voice, Trigger bounded forward, leaping into Rappi's arms, wagging his tail, and licking his face.

A second group of men from the 82nd Airborne who were qualified to go home was ready in early December. In the 319th this group included those who'd been replacements to the battalion from about the time of the D—Day invasion onward. Mahlon Sebring was among them, as was Orin Miller, Robert Dickson, Carl Salminen, Ted Simpson, and Silas Hogg. Before these soldiers were sent on their way they were addressed by General Gavin, who requested they remain in Berlin until the entire division was sent home later in the month.

Sebring remembered the formation clearly. "There were 1800 of us and the General told us, he said, 'If you'll stay with the division I guarantee you I'll take you home on the Queen Mary. We're gonna march through New York, and when that's done I'll get you right out to your separation centers.'"

Ted Simpson thought about the proposal. Ending his war with a rousing parade up New York's fifth Avenue, led by Slim Jim Gavin, and cheered on by throngs of adoring citizens was appealing. On the other hand, the prospect of being home in Saint Louis for Christmas with his family held more sway. Simpson elected to bug out while he could.

Sebring was suspicious from the start. "Yeah, yeah, once you get us back in \we're hooked till I don't know when," he thought to himself.

The voyage back attracted one problem after another. To begin with, it was impossible to procure a troop transport in Leharve due to a dockworker's strike. At the last moment an available Liberty ship was located in Antwerp, Belgium, allowing the men to proceed, but once beyond the Eng-

January 6th, 1946, parade down 5th Avenue in New York City, shows General Gavin marching at the head of his Division. Covais collection.

BATTERY!

lish Channel the ship sailed directly into a late season hurricane.

"We took one rough ride home," remembered Orin Miller. "You would stand on the ship and it would roll, and you would start to look for the sky but all you would see is that great big swell rolling up there twenty or thirty

The 319th Glider Field Artillery at the New York parade. Covais collection.

feet. Every rivet in that ship would just shake and shiver. It was just terrible. There was one day we never even progressed a mile ahead. We were pushed backwards. My goodness sakes, people were all sick on the ship. We had broken arms and broken legs from when they got thrown out of their bunks. It was one mess."

So heavy were the seas that the Liberty ship actually started to break apart. Crew and passengers were alerted to this when the coffee, which was made from fresh water ballast, tasted salty from taking on seawater. Three men were washed overboard and GIs were finally forbidden to venture on deck on pain of a court martial. Finally the ship put in to the Azores, where it waited out the storm and received repairs. No one left the ship, but the guys on board did enjoy fresh bananas for the first time in years. On December 31st, 1945, the Liberty ship entered New York harbor. It had taken nearly three weeks to cross the Atlantic and, needless to say, no one made it home for Christmas.

Doris Day singing "Sentimental Journey" played on the ships public address system as it came to rest at the pier. After disembarking these men were brought by rail to Camp Kilmer, New Jersey. Sebring had pulled himself through some of the toughest hours in the war by preoccupying his mind with thoughts of what he would do when he made it back to American soil. Now he had to make that decision in reality. "On the way to the mess hall we went by a PX," he recalled. "I went in there and I bought a Hershey bar that weighed about a pound. I wanted to eat it then but I thought, no, they promised us a steak dinner, but after the steak dinner I'll be too damn full to eat the Hershey bar!"

Processing of this contingent of men seems to have gone more swiftly than with the first two groups. Quickly discharged at Jefferson Barracks, Missouri, Ted Simpson found himself enjoying a hearty meal in Saint Louis. "My final wartime recollection is having a celebration dinner with Mother and Dad in a local restaurant. I was still arrayed in all the 82nd paraphernalia with decorations and battle trapping. They were impressed. I was so proud. Home safely, but this time as a man, fully grown by the experience."

Robert Dickson also reached his discharge center at Jefferson Barracks on January 3rd. Two days later he stepped off a bus at his hometown of Belleville, Arkansas. Contact by mail had been inconsistent over the previous six weeks and no one was expecting him or, for that matter, really knew where he was.

THE GET-OUT-QUICK-LINE.

"When I hit the states all I could think about was getting discharged and getting home," he remembered. "I got off of a bus about a quarter of a mile from where I lived. Walked that quarter of a mile home and I just talked to my mother and dad a little bit. My wife was teaching second grade two miles away in the town of Havana. I told them I'd see them later and I hit the road. I walked that two miles because I didn't have no other way to go. I walked in on her in the school room out there. I just opened the door to the back of the room and she looked up there and she couldn't move. Kids jumped up there and turned around and said, 'A soldier! A soldier!'"

Robert Dickson and his girlfriend Dorothy were married a month later in a double ceremony with another returning serviceman and his girl.

At the same time Dickson was receiving his discharge in Saint Louis, the Queen Mary was entering New York harbor with the balance of the 82nd Airborne Division, 8,800 men in all. A large banner decorated the side of the ship, bearing the division's insignia and the words, "The All-American Division." It was a noisy welcome with sirens and horns blowing the entire way past the Statue of Liberty and up the Hudson to the 50th Street pier where the Queen Mary docked at 11am.

There were several hundred cheering civilians and an army band waiting at the docks. General Gavin and General Andy March, who'd preceded the division to New York a few days before, were there too. With them, was the city's newly elected Mayor William O'Dwyer. Speaking through a loudspeaker at the troops who packed the decks, O'Dwyer called out in his Irish brogue, "New York is just waiting to tear you apart!"

An honor guard composed of two platoons from the 325th Glider Infantry, wearing white ascots and web gear came down to the pier. They stood in formation as the division's 56 piece brass band descended the gangplank playing "Eastside Westside."

New York had seen other GIs returning home for the last six months. Indeed, on this day a total of 28,700 soldiers on nine different vessels arrived from Europe. What was different though was that this was the vaughnted 82nd Airborne Division and they

John Manning poses with his wife Marge, the wife of Norbert Tamms or Herbert Gost and Cathy Covais, January 6th, 1946. Covais collection.

were carrying their weapons on their shoulders –the first returning division to do so.

The troops were immediately trained to Camp Shanks, a large installation on the Hudson River in Orangetown, New York, and given three day passes. Meanwhile, all dress uniforms were dry-cleaned and all web equipment turned in for new replacement items. Gavin had promised that they would finish their military service by parading up 5th Avenue, and they would do just that. As he told the New York Times, "We walked all over this damn world and we're gonna walk all the way."

On the morning of January 12th, 1946, the men were roused early, inspected, and taken to Washington Square in lower Manhattan, where they assembled. The skies were overcast and the streets were wet from an overnight rain which had only just stopped falling.

The victory parade was scheduled to begin at 1pm sharp. General Gavin was at the head of the column of some 13,000 soldiers, led by the 82nd Airborne Division but augmented by members of the 13th Airborne and numerous other units. The weather was turning dryer with a northerly wind, but colder as well, and as the head of the column stepped out the first patches of clear blue sky appeared overhead.

Swinging on to 5th Avenue it was immediately clear that the sidewalks and buildings were thronged with spectators. Indeed proud citizens, especially discharged members of the 82nd, had traveled to New York from all across the eastern United States. The sidewalks were packed four, five, and six deep, while every window, ledge, and rooftop was occupied by onlookers as well. Among the crowd were uniformed servicemen and women of all kinds, sailors, marines, gold-star mothers, discharged veterans, wounded soldiers, and every element of humanity which could be imagined. Hundreds of thousands had poured into the city that morning. Estimates of the total crowd varied from a conservative 2 million to as high as, according to the Police Commissioner, 4 million.

Gavin marched at the head of his division and each point he passed went wild with cheering. His helmet was set at the slightest bit of an angle but the chinstrap was pulled tight. Behind him marched his men, nine abreast, with rifles and carbines slung over their right shoulders, left arms swinging in unison with a perfect cadence.

As the column moved toward Madison Square, the cheering could be heard to roll up 5th Avenue, echoing like some tidal wave. It could also be seen in the form of an advancing blizzard of white ticker-tape fluttering down from every window and rooftop.

Seeing the formation approaching, one wounded trooper in the crowd rose up on his crutches and called out to those around him, "That's old Slim Jim, he's a hard coal man from Pennsylvania!"

Aside from the troopers themselves, every one of whom faced sternly ahead, Gavin also was backed up by 34 Sherman tanks, 12 tank destroyers, and 18 105mm howitzers drawn by weapons carriers, 21 jeeps, 12 armored cars, and numerous other military vehicles of all varieties.

As the parade marched uptown the sun shone more and more strongly. Ticker-tape clung to the flagstaffs and colors. The men, particularly those in the front ranks of each unit, were soon festooned with confetti, kicking along ever growing clumps of it as they passed each block.

Squadrons of mounted police escorted the column and kept crowds at bay, but in the vicinity of the New York Public Library at 42nd Street the press of people was too great. One man in the crowd was stepped on by a horse and badly hurt, while six women are reported to have fainted.

At 66th Street a contingent of First World War veterans of the 82nd, many of them wearing remnants of their Doughboy uniforms, saluted their contemporary counterparts as they marched by. When a Times reporter asked one of them for a comment, he was told, "That was us 26 years ago, now we're the old guys."

There were three brass bands as well, whose martial music stirred the crowds, but were apparently too widely placed to prevent a large portion of the column from marching in silence except for the tramp of Jump boots on pavement or the roar of mechanized vehicles. Given that the procession took over two hours to pass, hoarse crowds grew quiet when bands were absent, lending a solemn air to much of the parade. This was, as it turned out, the only criticism heard all day. At 53rd Street one man in the ranks couldn't help but yell to the crowds from the corner of his mouth, "Come on and give out, the war's over!" Another was heard to reprimand the spectators by telling them, "What's the matter with you folks! Let's go here!"

The number of bands was, as suggested by the New York Times article which appeared the next day, far too few. "New York crowds do not give their loudest without music," said the Times. The comment of one policeman corroborated this view when he was quoted saying, "They came here to cheer these kids, but they need the brass stuff to touch them off."

Among the multitude lining the city's 5th Avenue were Sal Covais and his wife Cathy. They'd known about the parade since reading about how the Queen Mary arrived on January 3rd. On this morning they took the subway from their Flatbush Avenue apartment in Brooklyn and joined those awaiting the column's approach. Covais had with him his souvenir Voigtlander camera, fully loaded with film. As the parade came nearer, Sal could hear the military music and his heart began to quicken. A part of him wished

Left to right: Norbert Tamms (in uniform), Sergeant Herbert gost, Sergeant Sal "Ted" Covais, and Major John R. Manning, posing on 5th Avenue after the division had finished passing in review. Covais collection.

he were in the ranks again, holding the guidon perhaps, or calling cadence. Then, as the column came nearer, he could see his General at the head. "That's him, that's him, that's Slim Jim!" he told his wife and pointed. Then Sal opened the Voigtlander and extended the leather bellows. He raised the camera above his forehead and started taking pictures.

As the first group of troopers marched by, Sal turned to say something to his wife but noticed a familiar profile in the crowd a few feet away. When the stranger turned to speak to a woman beside him, Sal swore he recognized the man as none other than Captain Manning. "Hey Captain Manning, hey, its Covais! Sergeant Covais!" he yelled. It was indeed him, only dressed in civilian topcoat and fedora hat instead of olive drab and a steel pot. He wore one black leather glove on his right hand.

Manning looked up and said, "Ted, for Christ's sake!"

The two men stepped toward each other and slapped shoulders. Covais knew not to offer a vigorous handshake as Manning's own hand was still healing from the glider crash in Normandy. Wives were introduced "Cathy, Marge Manning. Marge, Cathy Covais. Ted was a sergeant in my battery. Can you believe it?"

Then, as if the coincidence weren't enough, two more "A" Battery men walked up. It was Sergeant Gost from Manhasset, Long Island, and Private Norbert Tams, who'd put on his uniform and come down from the Bronx for the parade.

The sun was fully out by now as the four Able Battery men stood together, watching the 82nd Airborne Division march by. Finally the 319th was passing. They all cheered wildly and searched for familiar faces in the ranks of their old outfit but couldn't recognize anyone. By this point very few of the original men who'd fought with the division in Italy, Normandy, or even Holland were still with it anyway. In the 319th, only the most recent replacements remained, the rest of the outfit being made up of transferred men from the 17th and 101st Airborne Divisions.

Then people around them started pointing to the sky. Manning, Covais, Tams, and Gost looked up to see a two mile long stream of C-47 transports in four tiers, each pulling a glider behind it. Shielding their eyes from the sun, each of them gazed up in silence and, sensing they'd never see this sight again, thought about how beautiful it was.

Finally the procession reached the reviewing stand at 82nd Street where Gavin joined Mayor O'Dwyer, New York Governor Thomas E. Dewey, and Acting Secretary of War Kenneth Royall. Each unit dipped its colors and gave a sharp eyes right as it went by. Two blocks further the troops were loaded into army trucks and taken back to Camp Shanks.

Gavin's pride was obvious to all. "I think the boys did a wonderful job," he said later when asked if he was satisfied with the show.

"We met accidentally, believe it or not," said Covais afterwards as he reminisced about the day. "Captain Manning and his wife, and this guy Tams, a Jewish fella, and a guy by the name of Gost. Don't ask me in the world how that ever happened. It's a big city with hundreds of thousands of people watching the parade, maybe a couple of million people. Amazing."

The four "A" Battery men stayed until the last ambulance had gone by. Fifth Avenue was covered with ticker-tape. The marching formations and rumbling tanks were gone. It was quiet, except for the incidental sounds of street sweepers, pedestrians, and traffic on nearby streets. They stood on the sidewalk talking for a while, but once the excitement of the parade faded they seemed to be searching for things to say to each other. The war was over and they weren't soldiers anymore. Finally one of them said, "Well, I've got to get going here." There were handshakes, left-handed in Manning's case and they all went home.

Mahlon C. Sebring.
Tecumseh, Michigan

James L. Gwaltney - ted always.
Lots of luck
Marshall,
Box #353 North Carolina

Frederich von Hassel
110-15-176 St
Jamaica N.Y.

BATTERY!

Part 34: "It wasn't their water fountain to start with.

Though he was home, Sartain was technically still in the service, and would be until he'd used up several weeks of allotted furlough. This didn't mean that he was required to be in uniform, but in the fall of 1945 there was little in the way of civilian clothing to be had at any price. "When I first got back, I wore my uniform with my jump wings on it," said Sartain. "Of course my daddy was very proud and all of that business, but I had to be in uniform then because you couldn't buy clothes. Suits were not available. When they started coming in I went to my regular man here, the Varsity Shop. As soon as that 40 came in, he pigeonholed it for me and I got a suit."

Peggy-Lou and Lenton proceeded with their wedding plans through the weeks of October and November, 1945. Sartain stayed much of this period in Shreveport, spending time with his fiancé and getting to know his future in-laws better. It was a different world from his comparatively middle-class upbringing in Baton Rouge and some of what he saw did not appeal to him. "Shreveport was something else in those days," Sartain remembered. "My information is that it has changed, but at that time either you were rich or you were poor. There was no middle ground in Shreveport. The rich were very rich and the poor were very poor."

During the previous few years Sartain had seen tremendous sacrifice, courage, and suffering – the best and worst of human nature. Moreover, his intolerance for unjustified inequity had been sharpened by his military experiences. In comparison, much of Shreveport society impressed him as pampered and superficial. He knew in his heart he'd never feel comfortable there. "They were raised with money, I mean oil money, big money, and they were a bunch of spoiled people, they really were, but Peggy-Lou was a cut above the Shreveport crowd," he later observed.

Lenton loved Peggy-Lou intensely and in the interest of happily married life, this meant that he'd have to cozy-up to her parents. They were nice enough people, but their expectations would have to be handled with care. "The only trouble I ever had with Peggy Lou's daddy was that he was bound and determined I was gonna come to Shreveport to practice law. I really had to be very careful, very nice, and explain to him, 'Pop, I was born and raised in Baton Rouge. I'm going back to Baton Rouge. I'm gonna practice law in Baton Rouge, I'm gonna die and be buried in Baton Rouge.'"

"Now Peggy Lou's mother was something else and I made sure I made peace with her early. She was very social conscious – a good mother, but very social conscious. She insisted that Peggy-Lou go to Stevens College her first year because that was what society demanded. So Peggy Lou went to Stevens against her will, stayed one year, then came back to Shreveport, went to Centinary, then started her third year at LSU. When I met her, Peggy Lou had clothes, shoes, shoes for her clothes. You can't believe what she had! But Peggy Lou always had her head on right. I'm just real proud of her."

The wedding was planned to take place at the First Methodist Church in Shreveport. Saturday, December 1st, 1945, was the date selected by the bride. When Sartain heard this he realized it conflicted with a football game between LSU and Tulane. "Oh man, that was a big deal in those days!" said Sartain, "nowadays it doesn't matter much because Tulane doesn't have much of a team, but at the time it was momentous." Sartain made an urgent call to Shreveport and the nuptial was changed to Friday, November 30th. "People told us it was bad luck to get married on a Friday because its hangman's day, but we didn't care."

Aside from the usual array of relatives and family friends, Peggy Lou and Sartain sent invitations to all the officers from the old 319th who were stateside; Colonel Todd, Major Silvey, Ragland, Manning, Hawkins, Torgersen, Bourgeois, Cargile, and others, as well as Armand Butler from the 320th, and Chaplain Bill Reid from division artillery. There were, on the other hand, three whom he very deliberately declined to send invitations to. "I was very conscientious about who I invited," he recalled. "I didn't invite Bertsch, I didn't invite Wilcoxson, and I didn't invite Wimberley either. I don't regret that I didn't invite them. I guess I let my prejudice be shown."

The fact was that Sartain still harbored considerable resentment and anger toward these three individuals. He regarded them as imperious and pompous fools, lacking in intestinal fortitude. In his opinion they had treated the common GI with disrespect. Because they were remiss in their responsibilities as officers, Sartain believed they had placed the lives of the men under them in needless jeopardy. It was all beyond Sartain's capacity for forgiveness. Over the last three years he'd been forced to demonstrate some deference toward these officers, but now that obligation was lifted.

This was an aspect of Sartain's military service which he hadn't shared with his parents – after all, there was no need to. However, there was one more act which remained to be played out in the struggle between Bertsch and Sartain. Since the 319th's days at Camp Claiborne, Colonel Bertsch had been romantically involved with a Baton Rouge woman who was coincidentally acquainted with Sartain's mother. The Judge explained the situation to me this way: "Every time she got a letter from Bertsch, or my mother got a letter from me, they would talk on the telephone and compare notes. Well, after the war they got married. I came home one day and mother says, 'We got a call that Harry Bertsch was in town and wanted to visit with you. Call him at this number.'"

Sartain ignored the message. On the following day there was another call from Bertsch and once again Sartain declined to reciprocate. Manners being what they are, disregarding Bertsch's calls left Sartain's mother in an awkward position with her friend. "My daddy got kind of upset," Sartain remembered. "He came up to my room and said, 'What's the matter, son?' So I told him, 'Pop, Bertsch was yellow, just plain yellow, and the whole time I was in his command he never spoke a word to me in courtesy. I'm not going to call him back.' He said, 'OK, that's OK; just explain it to your mother.' I did, and I never did return his call. I hope he got the message."

Though it would be hard to overestimate the depth of Sartain's feelings regarding Harry Bertsch, after this incident his anger toward his former battalion commander lay dormant for decades. However, reviewing his military service with me during my research for this book plainly reanimated those emotions. One day, as was my habit, I called Judge Sartain for clarification of one detail or another. "Did I tell you I had a dream last night about Bertsch?" he asked rhetorically. "Yeah, I dreamt that I was asked to give a speech commemorating the dedication of a building in his name at Fort Bragg. Joseph, I woke up in a rage, a rage! It was hard for me to get back to sleep." I observed that Bertsch still got under his skin after all these years. We had a good laugh about it. "Well Judge," I told him, "you'll get the last laugh."

Marriage of Captain Charles Lenton Sartain, Jr. to Margaret Louise "Peggy-Lou" Huddleston, on November 25th, 1945. A number of officers from the 319th and 320th were present. Col. James Todd stands fourth from left, followed by Armond Butler of the 320th, Chaplain Reid, Wilson Bourgeois and Capt. Cargile. Sartain stands behind his bride's left shoulder. Sartain collection.

The day before the wedding everyone gathered at the Captain Shreve Hotel in Shreveport. There was a rehearsal dinner, followed by an enthusiastic bachelor party. By this time most all of Sartain's buddies from the 319th who would be at the wedding were already checked in at the hotel. It was the first time they'd been together since landing at Boston and the urge to revive old habits was impossible to contain. "There were quite a few adult beverages that night, quite a few," Sartain admitted later. One antic in particular stuck in his memory. Being the airborne troopers that they were, someone had the inspiration of jumping from the second floor balcony down to a sofa in the hotel lobby. Everyone, except the hotel staff, thought this was a brilliant idea, most appropriate given their military record. Sartain recalled them all chanting together in old minstrel style as each took his turn jumping, "Get up, hook up, stand in the door. We's a member of the 504!" It was tremendous fun. "We'd kick him on the ass and he'd jump off the balcony on to the couch. I don't think we hurt the couch, but everybody had to jump off the balcony. Peggy Lou's mother was worried sick that all this crowd of mine was gonna show up the next morning drunk. We were worried particularly about Bourgeois because he looked drunk even when he wasn't. But it was good."

November 30th was a clear day in Shreveport, but chilly as the guests arrived at the church on Texas Avenue at the top of the hill. The church itself was spacious. It needed to be as there were many guests and a large wedding party of eight bridesmaids

IT WASN'T THEIR WATER FOUNTAIN TO START WITH.

and groomsmen. Armand Butler, Sartain's friend since their ROTC days at LSU, and whose goose had gone loose in Naples, was the Best man. "I would have preferred something smaller," said Sartain later, "but husbands have no say in wedding plans, you know."

Sartain was in uniform as he and his bride exchanged vows. The Sartain family's Episcopal priest from Baton Rouge performed the ceremony together with the minister of the First Methodist church. In hindsight, Sartain wished that he'd asked Chaplain Reid to perform the service but the idea did not present itself at the time.

"After the wedding there was a reception at Peggy Lou's mother and daddy's house. Everybody was there, everybody was there," he recalled.

Late that evening Peggy Lou and Lenton were driven by her father's driver, Luther, to the Shreveport Railroad station where they, along with several other members of the wedding party, caught the Illinois Central's night train for New Orleans. Once aboard, the newlyweds locked themselves in their compartment, refusing to see anyone until they all arrived at New Orleans in the morning.

For the two LSU alumni, following their wedding with a game against their arch rivals was a great way to start their marriage. "Tulane had a star player named Kellogg, I remember that, and we beat his fanny!" said Sartain, whose memory was evidently correct. Records indicate that the LSU tigers shut out the Tulane Green Wave that day in a score of 33 to 0.

Following the victory over Tulane, the newlyweds checked into the St. Charles Hotel, along with several of the wedding party. The celebration continued, but when Peggy Lou and Lenton finally retired that night there would be little rest. "They knocked on the door all night, Johnny Isles and Armand butler. They kept telling room service to send us ice water and ice all night long. Then they tried to chain our luggage to the pipes in the room so we couldn't leave. After a couple of days of that foolishness, Peggy Lou started to get annoyed. We had to sneak out of the hotel one morning and take a cab to the train station and go to Biloxi. Both of us had had enough, you see."

The Sartains found their way to an old ocean-front hotel. Given the disruption of the normal resort economy by post-war conditions, they were the establish-

Mr. & Mrs. Charles L. Sartain, Jr. on their wedding day. They later had two daughters, Charlotte and Lynn. Sartain collection.

ment's only guests, but after the confusion of the previous few days the chance to quietly spend time together suited their preference. The proprietors were an elderly couple who took the youngsters under their wing. For the first time the Sartains were able to enjoy each other's company alone and without interruption.

Lenton and Peggy Lou came back from their honeymoon and moved into a third floor apartment in downtown Baton Rouge. She found a job working in the LSU law Library, while he started classes for his law degree when the spring semester began. In the meantime, life was good. "We kind of lived it up," Sartain remembered of this period. They bought a BRAND NEW Plymouth coupe and several months later purchased a house of their own on Castile Avenue with a veteran's .04% mortgage. "When I got home in 1945 I had $8,700 in my bank account. Now $8700 in 1945 when I got married was a hell of a lot of money. We bought a wedding ring, we bought a house, and we bought a car. Well, in about a year and a half I didn't have any money, I was broke and I was still in law school. We went through it man. We even had a maid named Louise for crying out loud. We took her everywhere. Peggy Lou was raised right, but what we needed a maid for I don't know."

As budgets grew tighter, Sartain signed up with the army's Inactive Reserve. "There were about thirty of us," he recalled, "we met once a month, doing problems with maps, things like that. It was a waste of time, really. Regardless of its military efficacy, the reserve offered a stipend of $70 per month. This did help with the household budget. In addition, Sartain learned that by declining a major's commission in the reserve he would be eligible for a $400 bonus as a field officer. Lenton discussed the situation with his wife and, considering he had no aspirations of staying in the military, made the decision to remain a captain and collect the money.

By taking summer school classes, Lenton graduated JD from LSU in June, 1948, fulfilling his lifelong ambition to practice law. He immediately opened an office in Baton Rouge with Joe Baynard, another young attorney. When I asked him if going with an established law firm wouldn't have been advisable, Sartain answered, "No, because all they were paying young lawyers was 115 per month. We thought that if we were going to starve to death, we might as well do it by ourselves."

According to Sartain, in those days he did, "anything and everything," in his efforts to find work in his chosen field. For starters, he picked up some work with the firm of Huckabay & Daspit, with whom he'd interned before the war. Sartain also ventured into publishing. The idea came to him while researching land titles for local subdivisions at the courthouse. Research of this type was necessarily limited to courthouse hours, which excluded nights, holidays, and weekends. Much more convenient would have been a book of the subdivision maps in his office. Sartain teamed up with his friend, Bob Mundinger, and together they produced the Sartain and Mundinger Map Book, a compendium of all the subdivisions in the East Baton Rouge Parish. "We sold eighty of them. All the law firms bought them. I think we sold them too cheap. Then we did one for Shreveport, then Mobile, Alabama, and lost our ass on that one."

Like the other discharged GIs in "A" Battery, Sartain was busily pursuing his personal life and career. But events in Korea pulled the United States into a very hot version of the Cold War he'd seen begin in Germany five years before. American involvement began in the summer of 1950 and in March of the next year Sartain's entire Inactive Reserve unit was called up. When our interviews turned to his re-activation, I gained the impression that Sartain did not welcome the order to re-enter the army. I commented about this and Sartain agreed, "I was not, I was not, I didn't think I should have been recalled. At the end of World War Two they discharged us on the point system and I thought they should recall us on the same point system."

The last time Sartain was at Fort Sill, he was a newly minted 2nd lieutenant during the summer of 1942, now he was back again. This time he was able to qualify as an airborne artillery instructor, so he and Peggy Lou could at least be reasonably certain he wouldn't be sent overseas. They rented an off-base house in Lawton, delightfully situated alongside a peach orchard. Life in the Lawton house would have pleasant memories for the Sartains. Sundays usually featured guests for breakfast that'd also been reactivated from the Baton Rouge unit. Their first daughter, Lynn, was born at Fort Sill in November, 1951, and even though the Oklahoma weather always seemed either too hot or too cold, there was good fishing at the nearby lake.

The great majority of the officers at the artillery school were veterans of fighting in the pacific or Europe. Some of them were even airborne troopers who'd participated in Normandy, Holland, or the Bulge with the 82nd and 101st. For these men there must have been a strong group nostalgia for past glories. Sartain may have felt this way as well, but at least one effort to recapture those times clearly held no appeal for him. "Colonel Donnelly was head of the department of gunnery at Fort Sill and he was the CO of the 376 during the war," Sartain recalled. "He called me in and said, 'Charlie, we're gonna go to that airstrip at Fort Sill and we're all gonna make a jump.' I said, 'Well, be my guest.' He said, 'What's the matter?' I said, 'I'm just not interested in that anymore. I'm married, I've got a daughter, and I'm happy.' So they went ahead and I didn't even go watch them, but I heard that they jumped in a twenty five mile an hour wind and half of them got sprained ankles and broken limbs, so I was glad I wasn't with them. I didn't have any more desire to jump. To me it was all over with."

The whole episode illuminated Sartain's growing disenchantment with the military. During the war his experiences with high-handed superiors had taught him that caste and station were frequently more valued than skill and bravery under fire. Memories of Bertsch's promotions, for example, in the face of his incompetence still rankled. Now, several years later, Sartain saw many of these same systemic injustices rearing their ugly heads again, and with little recognition from the service as compensation. "I got fed up with the army deal. When I got recalled I gave up my law practice and sold our house. I had two years date of rank on all of the other captains in the instructional unit I was in at Ft. Sill. Three of them while I was there, were promoted to major over me. I got lost in the shuffle. If I had not gotten recalled I probably would have gotten my promotion to major in the reserves, the active reserves. But I got recalled and then at Fort Sill they didn't take care of the reservists, they really didn't. They really didn't care. That was alright because I knew I was gonna give them seventeen months and I was gonna get out. Which is just what I did."

In September of 1952, Sartain was discharged from active service. He declined to remain in the army reserve. "I didn't want anything to do with the military I was kind of browned off. But I made a real mistake," he said in retrospect. "I could have had a nice pension and all that business, but I was mad at them, so I left."

Back home again, Sartain began rebuilding his law practice. He rented space at the offices of Dodd, Hirsch, & Barker. It was an established Baton Rouge law-firm with important political and commercial ties. After all, Dodd was a former Lieutenant Governor of Louisiana and Hirsch handled all the legal work for the state's largest labor unions. "Bill Dodd was a real easy going guy, but he never did anything as far as I could tell. He sat in his office all day and talked long distance with his cronies around the state.

I think he was trying to get elected Governor," Sartain recalled. "Aubrey Hirsch was a fine fellow, real good lawyer and he represented all of the labor unions in Baton Rouge. He was a very, very good labor lawyer. I made some contacts while I was with that firm. They stayed with me when I opened my own office. Not labor people, but individuals. I was very fortunate because it gave me time to get my feet on the ground."

Sartain worked with the firm for nearly four years while he built up his own practice. The firm was, according to Sartain, "a good group but they were labor oriented. They represented all the labor unions. Well, my inclination and interest was totally opposite. I didn't care about getting called at eleven o'clock or midnight to get some guy out of jail who'd just poured sugar in his boss's tank, you know what I mean? I didn't want any of that because I didn't want some drunk bastard calling me at three o'clock in the morning to get him out of jail. That happened to me one time. Telephone rang, it was about two thirty in the morning, this guy says, this is so and so and I belong to such and such local. I'm here in jail. Come get me out. I said, 'Well, you stupid son of a bitch, if I was to come get you they'd put us both in jail at this hour of the morning. I'll see you around eight thirty.' I did, I saw him about eight thirty, got him out and that was the end of that. I was on his nonfrienship list but I didn't care."

It was during this period that Peggy Lou hosted her own daily cooking program on Baton Rouge television. "She just had the right personality for it and she really loved to cook," Sartain told me with pride. "When she was a girl her mother would never let her in the kitchen to boil water! Then she got to be a real authority on cooking. After the birth of their second daughter, Charlotte, in 1953, the demands of raising two small girls forced her to quit the program.

With a growing family and growing law practice, the Sartains moved to a new home – actually the old overseer's house located on what had been the McInnis plantation during ante bellum times. The girls enjoyed life there with numerous animals. Charlotte remembered adopting an orphaned calf and feeding it with a baby bottle. Lynn remembered both sisters receiving pet goats one year. "There was a goat phase, then we had a chicken phase, but we almost always had a horse or two," she said.

Sartain remembered the chicken phase with a bit less fondness. "Charlotte fell in love with them," he said. "They were dwarf chickens, the size of doves. They laid eggs in the ivy patch and then we had little bitty hens running all over the place. Trouble is they'd get up in the tree by our bedroom window and cackle all night long."

The couple remained active in community affairs. For years they headed their church youth group and every year helped out with the Kiwanis Club Christmas tree fundraiser. "These Christmas trees would come packed in snow on a railroad car," remembered Lynn. "They'd unload them at Memorial Stadium. We'd play in it and have snowball fights. That was the only snow I ever knew."

In 1955 Sartain also went into partnership with Rolfe McCollister, a new graduate of the LSU Law School. Aside from sharing their alma mater, the two were also veterans of World War Two and Korea. In the latter conflict McCollister was, like Sartain, also awarded the Silver Star for gallantry.

Sartain had actually first made his new partner's acquaintance while being legal counsel for the North Baton Rouge Journal, a local newspaper owned and published by McCollister. The new firm prospered through the 1950s, eventually taking on a third partner, John Smiley.

"I loved the practice of law, but I got really tired of being a lawyer, I really did. I was going back to the office on Saturday mornings, Sunday afternoons, just to catch up with my work. I was in court two full days a week. It got to be a real real hassle," remembered Sartain as we discussed his decision to run for a judgeship in 1960. The idea had been a growing ambition for some time, when he was approached by members of the Louisiana Bar Association asking him to consider seeking election as judge of the family court in East Baton Rouge Parish. Sartain accepted the offer after discussing the suggestion with his wife. On November 10th, 1960, he was sworn in as judge of the family court.

The family court was located on the first floor of the courthouse in Baton Rouge. It handled everything related to juvenile delinquency, as well as all domestic matters. These latter could include divorce proceedings, child custody suits, domestic violence cases, and a multitude of other family oriented situations which called for adjudication. With the opening of his first session, Sartain's goal of becoming a judge was finally realized. What was more, being in a position to positively influence the life of youngsters headed in the wrong direction was especially appealing to him, having been involved with youth groups since his own adolescence.

The importance of his responsibilities as a judge was a duty Sartain took very seriously. It had been that way as an officer during the war and was that way now as a judge. There was, however, a fly in the ointment. From his elevated seat at the bench, Judge Sartain watched as the citizens of the parish entered his court seeking redress for their grievances. But, as had always been the case in Louisiana, the court was segregated, with one side reserved for whites and another for "coloreds."

Despite Sartain's upbringing in a fully segregated culture, there was something about this which was deeply troubling. For him, a segregated courtroom must be inherently flawed. After all, how could the halls of justice really function if their fundamental rules of operation were so blatantly partial? Sartain pondered the question, knowing that taking action against segregation might have serious ramifications, regardless of how much it eased his sense of decency. "When I got to be judge that changed my attitude," he later explained to me. "My gut feeling was that when I put that black robe on like God almighty, I had to be open-minded and I had to be fair. People would come in and the bailiff would have whites sit on one side and blacks on the other side. I thought, we are in a court of law. You know that's wrong, that isn't right. So I was not gonna separate the races in the courtroom, I was not gonna do it. I told my bailiff when somebody comes in the courtroom they should take their seat where they wanted to. He got upset and quit, which was OK with me. I would have fired him anyway."

Having made the leap, there was no turning back. Moving forward was the only real choice. Sartain recounted his next action, saying, "Then I created a little stir when I personally took the "White Only" sign off the water fountain in the hall in front of my courtroom. It was an affront to anybody walking down the hall, you know, so I took it down. I had to use a screwdriver and a hammer to do it but I took the damn thing down, took the white only sign off the fountain."

News about the fountain and Sartain's unorthodox courtroom habits spread quickly. Nothing like this had ever happened since reconstruction at the East Baton Rouge Parish courthouse, or at any other courthouse in Louisiana for that matter. Most whites were scandalized by what had taken place, but some inwardly supported the stance which Judge Sartain took. "Fred Blanch, my buddy I was raised with, he came down and said, 'Sartain, what in the hell are you doing!' He was OK with it, Fred was a good man. He felt like I did. But the other judges up stairs were kind of upset about it. I said, 'I took the sign off of that water fountain.' He said, 'You know, you've created a little stink.' I said, 'Look, y'all handle the upstairs, I'll handle the first floor down here,'" Sartain remembered and added, "I think some of the white ladies downstairs were uptight about it too. The ladies in the record room across the hall had an absolute fit. I knew that but I just felt like, well, it wasn't their water fountain to start with."

For sure, Sartain's measures to desegregate his court weren't taking place in a vacuum. As a well educated, southern professional, he would have been well aware of the growing pace of civil rights actions through the 1950s. School desegregation efforts in Little Rock, Arkansas, resulting in the 1954 Supreme court decision of Brown V. Board of Education, boycotts such as that organized against the public transit system in Montgomery, Alabama from 1955 to 1956, lunch counter sit-ins like that held in Greensboro, South Carolina, in May, 1960, and the Freedom Rides being held throughout the south during the spring and summer of that same year, would all have been prominent news stories which Sartain could not possibly have been unacquainted with. Given the focus of the movement on legal challenges to discriminatory laws through the courts, Sartain would have been particularly attentive to these issues as a lawyer and then elected Judge.

The subject of discrimination was simply the most controversial and divisive issue in the south since the Civil War. Dodging the question would have been the expedient political, social, and professional thing for him to do. Instead Sartain faced it head on by taking down the "Whites" only sign above the drinking fountain and desegregating his courtroom. In effect, he was publicly declaring his alignment with the Civil Rights movement.

This had not always been the case. Indeed, we are all prisoners of our background, and Sartain's attitudes toward race relations were representative of his time and origin. "In the world I was raised in, if a black was walking on the sidewalk towards you he'd step off the sidewalk and let you pass. My parents expected them to step off the sidewalk," Sartain told me as we talked about his childhood.

"Well," he continued as he remembered his early life on France Street, "our next door neighbors were a black family with two children, two boys. When we got together on the corner lot, which was vacant, to play baseball we just played baseball. We didn't have any trouble at all. Baton Rouge was black on one street and white on the next street, you know? Some of Baton Rouge was all white, but there were a lot of very mixed neighborhoods."

The white consensus of the day was that the races were, and had always been, distinct and separate. Segregation was not only the law, but also a natural part of the social fabric of the south and there was no reason not to accept this or expect anything to change. It was, if such could exist, a sort of benign racism, emphasizing a paternalistic sense of superiority over virulent hatred.

Sartain had grown up with and been inculcated with all these attitudes, and he carried them with him into the service. to be sure, John Manning seems to have been amused by Sartain's southern style. Manning would sometimes playfully imitate his friend's accent, while Sartain himself remembered that Manning pinned a magazine portrait of Lena Horne over his bunk as a practical joke. Later, when he was recalled for the Korean War, Sartain viewed the first stages of integration of the army with skepticism. Though the subject was clearly a sensitive one, he spoke frankly with me about his attitudes at the time. "My upbringing and everything was totally contrary to it, totally contrary," he said. "I thought that blacks should have their own schools, their own military units, and I really believed it."

It Wasn't Their Water Fountain to Start With.

In the mid-1950s Sartain was persuaded to affiliate himself with a local chapter of the White Citizens' Council. Formed in direct response to the 1954 Supreme Court decision against school segregation, chapters of the WCC sprang up across the Deep South over the following year. Membership quickly reached beyond 60,000, but unlike some other segregationist organizations, there was no negative stigma attached to those who belonged to the WCC. To be sure, the council met openly and enjoyed the participation of prominent members of every community where it held a chapter.

As an up and coming lawyer in Baton Rouge, already with an eye on becoming an elected Judge, Sartain understood the value of building a strong network of social and professional contacts. While he was with Hirsch, Dodd, and Barker, Sartain made the acquaintance of Jared Y. Sanders, Jr., the son of a former Louisiana Governor and himself both a state representative and senator, as well as a member of the United States House of Representatives from 1934-36 and from 1940-42. He was known throughout the state as an aggressive opponent of "The Kingfish," Louisiana governor and Senator Huey P. Long. In the 1950s, J. Y. Sanders, Jr. was a powerful figure in the Louisiana Democratic party during a time when, as Sartain put it, "If you weren't a Democrat in Louisiana you didn't even get to vote!"

Under Sanders' tutelage, Sartain was encouraged to cast his lot with the Baton Rouge WCC. "I have regretted it ever since," said Sartain in an uncharacteristically apologetic way. "I thought he was looking out after me, but he led me astray on that. Thinking back over it, once I got involved they were so anti-black it just rubbed me the wrong way. I felt very uncomfortable around those people."

Between 1955 and 1960, as the demands of African-Americans for equal rights gained momentum, Sartain engaged in a lot of soul searching. In all likelihood, by the time he ran for judge of the family court, he already knew his heart on the question. Nonetheless, he could not be open about the conclusions he'd reached privately. "I got elected basically as a segregationist," he told me, "but that was the only way you could run in those days or you couldn't get elected dog catcher. If you hinted you were pro desegregation they'd skin you alive here, they really would!"

Having removed the sign above the water fountain and prohibited the segregation of the races in his courtroom, Sartain became the object of local civil rights leaders eager to see more substantive changes. They lobbied him constantly. He shared their views and already intended to hire black probation officers. But as sympathetic as he was, Judge Sartain also knew well the reality of Louisiana in 1961.

Being familiar with the black leadership in Baton Rouge, Sartain requested to meet with them. The Judge explained at this meeting that he needed some time, eighteen months, perhaps two years to prepare the way. "I was determined to hire black probation officers," he recalled. "So I did, but I had to wait about two years to do it until after I had talked to every Boy Scout troop, every Sunday school class, every high school in the city, till I thought I was personally strong enough to withstand the storm. I hired two black probation officers and then later on I hired another one. By the time I left the family court it was about forty percent integrated."

Because he knew there would be a backlash, part of Sartain's plan to integrate the family court included going about it without attracting undue attention. In fact, he specifically asked the editor of the Baton Rouge Morning Advocate to keep the news of his hiring the first black probation officers out of the paper. Years later, when his daughter Charlotte was having difficulty establishing a program for disadvantaged teen mothers, she asked for his guidance. Sartain's advice referred to this strategy when he told her, "What you need to do sometimes is fly under the radar, do it quietly and people will come around."

Despite what anyone in the white community thought, the reasoning behind the hires of black probation officers was twofold: First, the positions had always been withheld from them, so correcting that situation was justifiable on moral grounds. Also there was the simple fact that the largest portion of the youths coming before Judge Sartain, were black. Warnings and admonishments expressed by white probation officers were, if not resented, then apt to fall on deaf ears.

"Curtis Johnson was my first hire," said Sartain as he looked back over the decision. "I hired him because he could take a little black kid, slap him on the back of the head and tell him to go home and behave. If you'd have a white probation officer do that you'd have a civil war on your hands. But a black probation officer could do it."
When I spoke to Curtis Johnson he remembered feeling both proud and apprehensive. "That first day was really exciting," he said, "and when I got home I had a lot to tell my wife about. I held my head high. I was cordial, nice to everybody, even though some would not speak to me."

It was clear to Johnson that not everyone was happy about working with a Black probation officer and their resentment was overtly expressed. Johnson remembered one episode which brought the racism in the court to a confrontation. He told me, "Some members of the staff, one lady in particular, would use the n word in my presence and I brought that to Judge Sartain's attention. He said, 'Well OK, I'll talk to her.' I picked up from his expression that he was gonna tell her not to do that again. A month or two after another staff member made the same comment. I went back to Judge Sartain again. This time he was really upset. He said he really wanted to support me and cut this kind of thing out."

Sartain had been in these situations before. Honest, hard working people – whether soldiers or civilians – needed to be defended when he was in a position to make the difference. It was the right thing to do. "As I remember," Johnson told me, "he brought it up in a staff meeting. It was very, very quiet. He came down on everybody. Judge Sartain was really upset, his face was all flushed and red, he was really really angry. He said that he wouldn't tolerate it, that we should cooperate with Curtis and work closely with him. 'He's a good Probation Officer. He has come from a good school and he's gonna be of great service to us. He is gonna work with the black kids here and try to prevent them from being sent to LTI (Louisiana Training Institution).'"

If it was not already clear, Sartain made it so. There was no place for racism in the court. There never had been, and if that meant that the habits of generations needed to change, then he would lead the way. Change was indeed in the air. Curtis Johnson was only the first of several Black probation officers to come, slowly Transforming what had been an intransigent animosity into mutual respect.

"Curtis turned out to be a terrific probation officer. I put him on a stipend later to go to LSU to get his master's degree in social work. After that he went to Southern Methodist University and got his doctorate. So now he stops by every time he goes by here. He comes in and we have a visit or we'll holler and wave at each other. Yesterday he stopped and waved at me not to get up. I got up anyway, went to the door and he had his wife with him, you know, just to tell me hello."

There was an obvious measure of pride and affection in Sartain's voice as he told the story. It was also clear that he viewed what he'd done as one of his best accomplishments and wanted to say more. "Then I hired a black lady," he continued. "Gladys

IT WASN'T THEIR WATER FOUNTAIN TO START WITH.

Robinson, she's got her PH. D. now too and they're both on the faculty of SMU. I'm very proud of hiring the first two black probation officers. I've been very, very proud of them because they've gone on, they've gotten their Ph.D.s, both of them, and they've done really well. They're good people. They give me credit for giving them the opportunity to move up the ladder, but I don't deserve all of the credit. A lot of it goes to them and a lot of it goes to my staff because they were ready and supported it."

When I called Dr. Johnson to ask about his time with Judge Sartain the first words out of his mouth were, "I have a lot of respect for that man." We talked for over an hour about his days at the Family Court and events in his life since then. Toward the end of our conversation we discussed the change in white attitudes and he commented, "My attitudes changed too. You know, coming from a segregated world created in my mind certain kinds of hostility and also some inadequate feelings. I think Sartain helped me with that because he often recognized that I had a lot of built up anger. During our sessions regardingthe probation dispositions he would remind me, in a kind way, that white people were not all evil. Some were good, just like some black folks were good and some bad. But the most important thing Sartain taught me was to depend upon the Bible for the solution to any problem and, being a Christian, that helped me a lot with my anxiety about intergration."

In reviewing these events with the Judge, he always maintained that his actions were primarily generated by pragmatic considerations, though I found this explanation unsatisfying in this story of personal transformation. It was then, and remains now, difficult for me to understand why he was so reticent about the principled stand he took, except perhaps out of modesty. As we concluded our conversation about the changes in race relations during his lifetime, he finally said, "I think the progress that has been made now has been phenomenal. Black employment has upgraded and I thoroughly agree with that all, I really do. It's much better now the way it is. Nowadays, Baton Rouge is just a model for integration. We have a black mayor and he's a good man, so is our chief of police. But I wasn't a crusader. I never have gotten out on street corners and all of that foolishness, it's just that there isn't any reason why an individual, black or white, can't be treated with respect."

Sartain remained judge of the family court until 1966. During that time the juvenile program in Baton Rouge drew national and even international attention as a progressive, trend setting plan for the care of adjudicated minors. According to one 1964 newspaper article, the Family Court was "considered a model in the entire south and has been visited by jurists, probation officers, court corrections experts, law enforcement officers, and others from all over the United States and many foreign countries." Sartain remembered one of these visitors in particular when he said, "I had a Japanese guy come visit the family court and we had him to supper one night. Every time Peggy Lou would walk out of the room he'd stand up."

The Baton Rouge program was already unusual when Sartain began his tenure. It, for example, already had a judge dedicated to juvenile matters instead of temporarily assigned to this post. But after Sartain became judge he also created a "Community Advisory Committee" made up of important individuals representing the varied facets of Baton Rouge society. It was an integrated group which met monthly to discuss ways in which the court, civic groups, and the private sector could promote positive alternatives for troubled kids. There was also an expansion of the court's staff. The number of probation officers increased from four in 1960 to 12 by 1964.

Serving as judge of the family court was rewarding but, considering the pace of changes and growth which took place, the work was all consuming. And given the Judge's compassionate nature, family court affairs often had a way of spilling over into the Sartain home. When I spoke to Charlotte about those years, she said, "On a few occasions I distinctly remember Lynn and I looking out our bedroom window because some teenager with her little suitcase was knocking on our door. They looked so pitiful. There were all kinds of people coming to our house looking for help, so I didn't think it was weird. There'd be a knock and then you'd hear, somebody is here to see Daddy." Judge Sartain began to think about a new arrangement. "I liked it alright," he said, "but it got really tiresome. Boy. Real, you know, messy stuff. I'd had all the domestic squabbles I could take. I was either gonna go back to practicing law or run for the court of appeals."

In 1966 an opportunity to do just that came around. Feeling his chances were good, Sartain ran for the unexpired term of a deceased judge and was elected to the 1st Circuit Court of Appeals in June of that year. "When it was time for somebody to run for court of appeals I was head and shoulders above everybody. I'd kept my contacts. I'd hired my two black probation officers by that time, then we'd hired two more, so I was in solid with the black vote, you know. The guys that were gonna run against me, I told them go ahead and run. I got elected with opposition. First to a two year term of un-expired vacancy, then secondly to a full twelve year term. It got to where they couldn't anybody run against me."

Over the following fourteen years Judge Sartain continued his judicial duties and supplemented them with a full schedule of activities in community and church affairs. He was a member of the Masonic Order and a founder of Acacia, an associated fraternity. The Sartain girls, Lynn and Charlotte grew up to marry lawyers themselves – a situation which the Judge jokingly complained about when he told me, "Too many damn lawyers in the family. We need some plumbers! Sink gets clogged up, nobody knows what to do."

Lenton and Peggy Lou moved again, this time to a home on Harrell's Ferry Road, a good distance outside of the city of Baton Rouge. The site was situated on a 33 acre property which featured a pond and marsh. Sartain thought the location was perfect to dabble in his pastime of training Labrador Retrievers for hunters. The sport of duck hunting was one which Sartain had first been exposed to in college. Now he found the hobby -- both the hunting and culinary preparation of these birds more pleasurable than ever. What was more, he enjoyed considerable success training retriever puppies. Andy, Jocko, and Pooh-Bear being among the most memorable. Sartain brought his trained Labs to field trials throughout the south and sold them to duck hunters across the United States.

Though these years as appellate court judge passed without the controversy of his family court days, there was, however, one ruling which brought Sartain head to head with his lifelong friend and fellow judge, Fred Blanche. Sartain and Blanche had led parallel lives in many respects: they lived in the same neighborhood as children, and attended the same elementary school. The pair went to LSU together and both served in the army during the war. Afterwards they attended LSU law school, graduated together and worked as attorneys in Baton Rouge. In 1960, Sartain and Blanche were both elected to judgeships.

All this had served to reinforce their friendship, even though things hadn't started out that way. "Fred Blanche lived down the street from me and across Douglas Street," Sartain told me. "I would walk from my house, go down to what we called

IT WASN'T THEIR WATER FOUNTAIN TO START WITH.

Griffith's Corner and take a left and go to school. It was about a five or six block walk down Government Street. Well, one day Fred Blanch met me at the corner and whipped up on me all the way to school. He took my lunch money. Then he did it again the day after that. So I developed a stomach ache the next day and my mother had to walk me to school. We walked by Fred Blanch and he just gave me the look, you know."

Some family members remember Mrs. Sartain giving young Fred a thrashing. Whatever happened, for a boy of perhaps ten years old, young Lenton faced the choice of having his mother walk him to school under her protection each morning or confronting his tormentor directly. The first choice was safe but temporary and humiliating—the second frightening and honorable, but required courage. Knowing he couldn't outfight or avoid Blanche, Sartain elected to reason his way through. During recess time on the playground, Lenton boldly walked up to Fred and demanded to know just what it was he had against him.

Blanche was taken off-guard by Lenton's direct style. Moreover, there was a kind of logic to the question which provoked Fred's immediate respect. The erstwhile bully was disarmed and could only reply, "Alright Sartain, you're my buddy. Anybody that whips up on you let me know." It was perhaps Sartain's first act as defense council – in this case, his own. He was successful and from this point forward the two enjoyed a remarkable friendship.

Years later, Blanche was a trial judge and Sartain now held a seat on the appellate court. It was only a matter of time before one of Blanche's rulings came before Sartain on appeal and was overruled.

Sartain took delight in telling the rest of the story. "I came back to my office after lunch at the City Club," he said. "My secretary says, 'Judge, I have a message for you from Judge Blanch, but I think I got it wrong.' I said, 'What's that.' He said, 'It says, don't walk down Government Street without your momma.'"

Those years spent in the court of appeals brought a wider variety of cases before Sartain than he had seen at family court. One of these which remained prominent in Sartain's memory, for instance, was the case of "Sparkle," the baby elephant. Sparkle was to appear as a Republican mascot, part of the 1968 presidential campaign. The elephant met an untimely end while lodged with a Baton Rouge veterinarian and fervent Republican. In the ensuing trial, the doctor was found negligent – principally because the elephant ingested poison left within reach of his trunk. Though Sartain issued a dissent, the decision was reversed on appeal. Whether the GOP would have carried Louisiana in 1968 had Sparkle lived to throw his weight into the race will never be known. In any event, the local election went to Independent candidate George Wallace.

Shortly before Christmas, 1978, Judge Sartain announced that he was retiring at the end of the year. According to an article which appeared in the State Times of November 23rd, Sartain stated that though he wanted to take this step early enough to be able to enjoy his retirement, the decision was "not a hasty one, nor an easy one." The article went on to say that Judge Sartain would continue to serve in an ad hoc role for trials as needed. It also reported that Judge Fred Blanche would be taking a seat at the Louisiana Supreme Court. The article delineated the parallel lives and professional careers of the two jurists, going on to describe them as being "noted for their remarkable sense of humor." –Sartain jokingly speculated whether the Supreme Court is "ready for Freddy!" His final statement to the newspaper was, "To have served this parish and the state as one of the collective judges for the past eighteen years is a privilege that just cannot be expressed in words."

BATTERY!

Before leaving, Judge Sartain announced that he intended to treat his fellow jurists to a thank-you meal. He arranged for a duck dinner to be served at the library of the court of appeals in New Orleans. "I had about twenty killed ducks in my freezer that I shot at the duck camp," he said. "I cooked them up, put them in a big Dutch oven. Peggy and I brought the ducks to New Orleans and we really put on a spread for them. So that was my swan song down there, a duck dinner." During the course of the meal, one of the judges asked Sartain if he was aware of the limit on ducks. "Six," he answered. "Yeah, these are six. I just cut them up different!"

Retirement did not mean leisure. Judge Sartain took a seat on the panel of the 4th Circuit Court of Appeals in New Orleans. He shared the panel with Judge Lawrence A. Chehardy, long time Assessor of Jefferson parish, on New Orleans' southern side, and Judge Jim Garrison, former District Attorney for New Orleans and controversial investigator of the assassination of President John F. Kennedy.

"The three of us, Sartain, Garrison, and Chehardy, we were a panel on the Fourth Circuit Court of Appeals," Sartain remembered. Considering Garrison's reputation, I was compelled to ask the Judge about him. "Garrison was quite a character," he answered. "I knew him real well. Quite a guy. He had been out of the practice of law for years when he got elected to the court of appeals, which is OK. He didn't know his details when it came to law, but that didn't make any difference because he had a good law clerk; he was very, very good. He would wait for me to make my views known and then he would concur, but I don't think he really ever knew what I was saying."

The Sartains took a second apartment downtown on royal Street in a section of renovated slave quarters. "We really went New Orleans," he said of his time in the Big Easy. "We had a walk up apartment on Bourbon Street, you know, and we went all over on foot. Peggy Lou made a lot of friends, little old ladies in the neighborhood that had apartments. Then the girls would go down on weekends. That would be their base to operate from, see? They say that once you got that New Orleans blood in you, you got to go back. I enjoyed my New Orleans stint, I really did but in my opinion I think once you leave New Orleans you ought to stay gone.

Though he may have felt ambivalent about some features of the city itself, Sartain always enjoyed trying something new, moving on to higher achievements. Life in New Orleans afforded him the opportunity to exercise this quality in himself and observe New Orleans politics close up at the same time. In a state known for colorful politicians, the city did its best to uphold the tradition. "It's a different world down there," he once remarked to me, further observing that, "as far as folks in New Orleans were concerned, every other spot in Louisiana – including Baton Rouge -- was nothing but a rural back-water."

After several years in New Orleans, Sartain grew tired of writing opinions and listening to attorneys argue points of legal minutia. He pined for the old days of being a trial judge, listening to the testimony of witnesses and watching the individual courtroom performance of combating lawyers. After all, that was where the real action was. Sartain left the 4th Circuit and began to take assignments in the Lafayette and Lake Charles area. "I covered all that part of the country. I wouldn't serve on any court of appeals that involved Baton Rouge cases. I just didn't feel like I could look over the local judges. Just stayed clear of them."

This final phase in Judge Sartain's judicial career may have been his most enjoyable. He was by then an experienced and highly respected member of the judiciary, the pressure to build a practice or be elected was past, and he was again hearing cases in a southern Louisiana setting which he was at home with.

In late 1984, Judge Sartain was called on to preside in what would become a landmark case in archaeology and its relationship to the heritage of Native Americans. The case originated in the 1968 discovery of a burial site of the Tunica tribe on private property along the east bank of the Mississippi River by a local Louisiana treasure hunter. Leonard Charriers was searching for the grave of Cahura-Joligo, a wealthy chief of the Tunica tribe killed in an attack by Natchez Indians in 1731. Over the following two years, Charier unearthed an enormous number of artifacts from the graves of over 100 Tunica interned at the location during the mid-18th Century. The artifacts included not only items of indigenous manufacture, but hundreds of pieces of European trade goods. The collection encompassed Muskets, brass bells, glass beads, cooking vessels, Delft pottery from Holland, stoneware from the Rhineland, bras buttons, smoking pipes, eating utensils, kettles, and knives, to name but a few. The relic hunter unearthed what was arguably the greatest single cache of European/native American trade goods ever discovered, and the finest archaeological site in the lower Mississippi Valley. Unfortunately, he was looking for treasure and had little or no interest in the historical significance of the site itself. In his digging, Charier employed scant regard for the site as either a grave, or a historic place worthy of preservation. Moreover, he used no archaeological methods, resulting in the loss of irretrievable historical information.

By the time Judge Sartain arrived on the scene a considerable legal brawl had erupted involving the Tunica Tribe, Leonard Charier, the landowners, and the State of Louisiana. "The trial was held at the West Feliciana Parish Court House in Saint Francesville, which is a very beautiful old town," Sartain told me. "You know, they buried their people in a circle and they buried their muskets with them. It was a very interesting case."

At the heart of the legal issue was the question of whether society's interest in preserving and studying Native American archaeological locations, including any human remains found within them, superseded the claims of modern tribal descendants.

In March, 1985, after a trial of several months, Judge Sartain ruled in favor of the Tunica Tribe. His fifteen page opinion stated that "While the relinquishment of immediate possession may have been proved, an objective viewing of the circumstances and intent of the relinquishment does not result in a finding of abandonment. The relinquishment of possession normally serves some spiritual, moral, or religious purpose of the descendant/owner, but it is not intended as a means of relinquishing ownership to a stranger." In other words, however old, such sites remained the graves of ancestors of members of current day tribes. Treating them as simple abandoned property was as good as accepting a form of grave robbery.

Judge Sartain's decision was sustained by the Louisiana Supreme Court and ultimately served as the foundation for the Native American Graves Protection and Reparation Act of 1990, signed into law by President George H. W. Bush. Since then, the Act has been responsible for the repatriation of thousands of artifacts and remains to their tribal origins, yet it has become a controversial issue among archaeologists. In the case of the Tunica Treasure, as it came to be known, the connection between the remains and current day descendants was clear and nearly within living memory. At some of the earliest, and thus most important archaeological sites where the remains discovered predate any indigenous population by thousands of years, that lineage is often murky, if it exists at all. When NAGPRA has been invoked in these cases the Act has been seen by historians and others as a hindrance to research. Today the artifacts exhumed by Leonard

BATTERY!

Charier have all been returned to the Tunica people. Selected items are on display at the Tribal Research Center and Museum in Marksville, Louisiana.

Though he did preside over a few more cases, the Tunica Treasure trial really marked the end of Judge Sartain's active career. Later that year, the Sartains, along with daughter Lynn, her husband Len, and daughter Charlotte traveled to England. Judge Sartain's last visit to London had been his stay at the Strand in March of 1945, forty years before. At one point a Londoner, overhearing their American accents as they toured the city's streets and seeing a man of the right age, approached Sartain and asked him if he'd been in England during the war. When Sartain answered that he was, the man removed his hat and told him, "Thank you, Yank."

The incident generated a good deal of talk among the vacationers about his experiences in England during those years. Someone suggested that they travel to Market Harborough and visit Papillon Hall. Sartain was at first reluctant but then acquiesced. In a rented car they made the trip, but drove past the old estate when nothing looked familiar. In Lubenham they stopped at a gas station, where they were told that the house had been torn down years ago, but a Mrs. Hewes and her son lived on the grounds and might welcome a visit.

Following the directions they were given, it was now easy to recognize the entrance to the old estate. "The two gatehouses with the cherubs, where the men put the knit caps on the statues were still there," Sartain recalled. The Judge and his family drove up the lane to what had been the stable building. Since 1944 it had obviously been remodeled into a residence. Mrs. Hewes told them it would be altogether fine if they wished to look around. "When they were finished, wouldn't they come in for a cup of tea?"

The manor house was indeed gone. Only the foundation and a large rubble filled cellar pit remained of the once regal building. As he strolled around, Sartain began to recognize features like the artificial pond, the horseshoe shaped drive, and what remained of the gardens.

Afterwards they all returned to Mrs. Hewes' cottage where they enjoyed a cup of tea with her. Early in the visit, Sartain introduced his family, the Sartains from Baton Rouge, Louisiana. "Captain Charles L. Sartain?" Mrs. Hewes asked. When told yes, she walked to a sideboard and drew several slips of paper from an antique pewter teapot. Mrs. Hewes told Sartain that men of his battery had left these notes to him over the years.

"When we heard that we like to fell out," remembered the Judge. "There were four or five notes that the fellas had left for me. They said they knew I'd be by sooner or later. If Peggy Lou and Lynn and Charlotte weren't there, no one would ever believe it."

The whole experience contributed to a growing willingness on Sartain's part to finally talk about his wartime service. Before the trip to England, the Judge's time in the 82nd Airborne was rarely spoken of in the Sartain home. Occasionally someone would call and ask for "Captain Charlie," but this was not often. "Until I was an adult, we never talked about it, it was just too hard for him, and if it did come up he never gave us girls any details, said daughter Lynn. "He would give us short answers and tear up. Then he had five grandsons and that changed it all."

Charlotte agreed that having grandsons went a long way toward opening Sartain up to talk about the war. She told me, "When Sam, our oldest was in the fifth grade they were studying World War Two, I asked Pop, 'Will you go and speak to his class?' He said 'No,' so I had to work on him for two or three weeks. Finally he said, 'ALRIGHT.' Momma and Daddy went to Trinity Episcopal school. They brought a box of photos, his leather jacket, his medals, and some other things. They asked him all kinds of questions and he answered them honestly. Momma told me that once Pop got going he did well. When he'd get too choked up to talk Momma would take over and start to show the kids ration books or something like that until Daddy composed himself. The teacher called afterwards and told me it was the most amazing experience her class ever had."

Judge Sartain began doing the same for his other grandsons, but he never did warm to the idea of formal speeches or newspaper articles. When we talked about his preference of keeping his military service in the background, he explained himself further by saying, "Yes, I've been very protective of that, I'll be frank with you. I have personally declined to speak because when I get into it I get too emotional. I have just kind of safeguarded the military aspect of it. Even during the campaign the first time. They wanted to run an article about it. I told them, 'You've got a copy of my discharge that says I was 82nd Airborne, Silver Star, Air Medal with Clusters, Order of the Bronze Lion medal, and Six Campaign Stars, well that's it. That's it.' So the editor of the paper called me. He said, 'We've got to do something about this, you know, there's not too many guys around anymore. We want to do a feature on you and Normandy.' I said, 'I can't do it. I really don't want to.' If I've got a peculiar hang up about it, so be it."

Both Sartain's daughters attributed his preference away from public appearances and involvement in veteran's organizations to modesty, and a strong conviction that many who deserve to be recognized go unacknowledged. From my long discussions with him I am inclined to agree. One reason I support this view is that I had several extended conversations with the Judge about "A" Battery before he made the first passing reference to his Silver Star. Because of his reticence, even some friends of many years whom I spoke to were surprised to learn of the decoration when I interviewed them. If she were to ask him why he felt this way his daughter Lynn thought her father would have said, "I did what I did, what many people did," and leave it at that.

After fully retiring from the court, Sartain was free to devote his time to his three passions of family, community, and church. It was his grandchildren, after all, who were able to pull him out of silence about the war years, and they continue to be the highlight of his life today. Participation in activities of the Episcopal Church and its associated organizations received much of his attention too. Judge Sartain's long involvement with the Masonic order remained strong and continues. "I'll tell you, I really enjoy my Masonic work," he once told me. "I am a coach in the Masons with each degree. They take that first degree and then they come and visit with me. I coach them on what they have to learn and then they stand an examination at the lodge and then they take the next degree. You've got certain memory work that you have to pass before you can take the next degree. That's all memory, it's not written anywhere. There's a little codebook that keeps you up to date, a recitement book, but my coaching at the lodge has really meant a lot to me and I enjoy it."

The Scottish Rites Childhood Learning Center of Baton Rouge is a nonprofit organization, sponsored by the Masonic Scottish Rites lodge. It focuses on the needs of children with speech impediments. As a past president of the center and chairman of the fundraising effort to build the facility, Judge Sartain has found the whole experience tremendously rewarding, with especial pleasure taken in seeing the work first hand. "We've got a beautiful little center out there," he said. "Our assistant professor, Doctor Mendoza from LSU is doing a terrific job for us and we've got our two graduate students from the university each semester. Then you watch these four or five year old children come in. We've got a pair of twins now that remind me of Charlotte's twins, they're four years old. When they came in neither one spoke a word, they just motioned what they wanted. Now they've got them talking to one another. It's something. We have them coming in with different speech impediments and then we have a little graduation ceremony when they graduate. We have their pictures on the wall. We've got them all. We call it our alumni association."

For years since the opening of the center, Sartain has made a practice of visiting two or three times a month to observe firsthand the work being done. "I just like to go by and watch the children come and go. It's a real rewarding experience to watch these little kids come in and then watch them develop, it really is. It's one of the few things you can do for charity and see the results of your effort."

The Sartains moved into a Baton Rouge retirement community in late 2003. During my first visit there I was fortunate enough to meet Peggy Lou. She was a gracious hostess who impressed me as enjoying the recitation of stories every bit as much as her husband. "Daddy will tell you that there wasn't a person in the world Momma couldn't talk to," said Charlotte. Peggy Lou Sartain passed away on May 18th, 2006, of congestive heart failure. "She died a very peaceful death," Sartain told me. "I was with her when she passed away."

Today Judge Sartain lives by himself but certainly not alone. There are visits nearly every day from Lynn, Charlotte, their husbands, or one or another of his grandchildren. Tuesday afternoons are reserved for a standing poker game with old friends. "He's all about attitude," Lynn told me. "If he's not feeling well he'll just tell you he has a bad attitude, which even that is sort of having a good attitude about it."

When I asked one friend of Sartain who had known him over fifty years if the war might have had any effect on him, I was told, "I'm certain it did. But I never saw it -- not in a negative way, other than appreciation. There is no chip on his shoulder." Charlotte made the same observation, and also suggested that her father's time in the service developed his talent for leadership. We talked a while longer, then she returned to the subject and said, "If I had to sum him up, I would say it's his gentleness and integrity and sense of humor. Pop has an innate sense of right and wrong. I call him, well; Daddy is one of those Southern Gentleman in the sense of a gentle man, which he truly is."

When I last visited with the Judge, we talked about all the things he'd seen and the changes during his lifetime. I made the observation that working with me on this story was perhaps his last action as battery commander. What did he think? Sartain took out his pipe, repacked it with Captain Black tobacco, lit it and, having considered the question fully, spoke slowly. "Other than my parents, wife, children, grandchildren, and son-in-laws," he said, "I can truthfully say that the best thing that ever happened to me was my days with "A" Battery, the 319th, and 82nd. Even though it was sixty-five years ago, there is never a day that I don't think about those days. It just means more and more. "A" Battery was a special group, every last one of them. To feel that I had their respect is a cherished memory. Now there's a lot more behind me than ahead, but when I think about it all and say my little prayer, I just thank goodness."

As we concluded our interviews I had one more question of Judge Sartain. We had been discussing current events ; politics, Afganistan, and the recent economic difficulties. I asked, "Judge, do you think the nation has lived up to the sacrifices made by you and the other men in the battery?"

Sartain's answer was immediate and came without hesitation. "The country's

IT WASN'T THEIR WATER FOUNTAIN TO START WITH.

gonna do alright," he said. "I'm optimistic. I don't have any reason not to be. Whatever crisis wwe have, the country will do what's right. I can relax over that, I realy can. The youth today, the present young generation, if called upon they'll come through. My only problem with them is tattoos. Other than that I think they're gonna do just fine."

The Author with C. Lenton Sartain at his home in 2006. Covais collection.

BATTERY!

Part 35: Epilogue. I remember everything.

Immediately after my father's funeral in June, 2004, I returned home to hang the frame displaying his portrait, medals, and airborne insignias on the wall in my office. I had, of course, been aware that he was in declining health for some time, and this knowledge imparted an urgency to learn about his military service while it was still possible. Just the same, at the time of his death I was only starting to comprehend his wartime experiences. There would be no more conversations with him now. I took out the few paltry cassette tapes I had of him describing the photographs in his album or answering questions about the war, and started listening to them. The voice, the accent, the tendency to repeat phrases or emphasize particular words was all unmistakably his, but this time it sounded different. Maybe it was that I was listening differently, knowing that there would be no more after this.

I began to transcribe the recordings. For some time I had been toying with the idea of writing an article documenting my father's service in the 82nd Airborne. Starting this project seemed timely, and this particular activity of transcribing the taped conversations was a way to connect with him, while my sense of loss was fresh. It was important, of course, to make an accurate record, but the sound quality was poor, so I had to listen to every word with care. In doing so I discovered much which prior casual listening did not reveal. There was a poignancy, a depth of thought and emotion, as much in what was left unspoken in the pauses, as in what was actually said.

There were also a number of my father's personal documents which I brought back with me: his parents' naturalization papers, his discharge certificate, and newsletters from the 319th Veterans' Association among them. Reading through the Association directory I recognized names I'd been transcribing, seen written in captions on the back of photographs in my father's album, or which I remembered hearing him mention at one time or another. My focus then became the effort to capture some greater understanding of him and the historic events he'd lived through by speaking with those who'd been there with him at the time.

About forty years had gone by since the contact information listed in the Association directory was collected. How many of these men could still be living and at the same address? In fact, more than one might have thought, and over time I was able to locate about 25 members of Captain Sartain's Battery. I did gain insights into my father's life, but in doing so I found myself in the presence of a much, much larger story.

When I contacted these veterans it was often on the strength of my dad's service with them that they were so willing to talk with me. They usually didn't remember him, but I was obviously the son of someone from the old outfit and that was enough. Typically, I would be warned that they were "old" and "didn't remember much," only to have several hours of conversation and memories follow, sometimes with prompting, but more often as if some long withheld reservoir of experience was being released.

Like any collection of persons, some were naturally more talkative than others – not out of any unwillingness to speak, but rather from varying degrees of extroversion

EPILOGUE. I REMEMBER EVERYTHING.

and expressiveness. Often wives could be heard in the background or would join their veteran husband on the telephone, occasionally punctuating the conversation with an "I didn't know that!" or "You never told me about this." During a few of these interviews I could distinctly hear the ticking of a clock, symbolically underscoring the passage of remaining time.

In most cases the interviews were conducted intermittently over a period of years as the writing progressed and follow-up questions came to the fore. Genuine friendships developed, creating a cadre of adopted grandfather figures for me. Sadly, too, about half of the men whose stories this book is built from have passed away or are no longer in a position to engage in meaningful conversation since the research for this project started.

As I got to know them as individuals, I became interested in their post-war lives. I'd seen firsthand the ways that my father's service never completely left him, and suspected this must also be true for others.

What happened to them during the intervening years from 1946 to the present? When I asked John Girardin what he had done since the war, he answered quickly and without hesitation, "First of all, two years after I was discharged, I got married to a wonderful woman. I had four children, four boys. That's how I spent the next fifty years - working, raising my kids, going on vacation with my wife and children. She passed away about five and a half years ago. Otherwise, that's about all I did."

Girardin clearly enjoyed reviewing his military service in the 319th with me. "It feels good that I had a chance to tell you things," he once commented. Though there was a substantial amount of memories and stories he recalled clearly, Girardin was still troubled by how much he had forgotten. "You know," he said, "I look at these photos and a lot of it I don't even recognize at all, like I was never there. I was there, but I can't remember anything. It's sad because I'd sure like to remember all those fellas. It hurts me not to remember all this. I tried and tried, but I can't." Today John Girardin lives in his hometown in Illinois. He remains physically active and consistently cheerful in his demeanor.

Orin and Pauline Miller had six children whom they raised on the family farm near the Canadian border. When asked if the war had occupied his thoughts since returning to his northern New York home, Miller's answer was, "No, I more or less put it out of my mind. It might have been had I not just come home and got married, but my job was waiting for me at Alcoa, and things worked pretty fast at that point. I didn't have time to relax and didn't think about all of those things."

Despite this, family members remembered that Miller consistently refused to watch movies or television programs about modern warfare. "He wouldn't stop us, but he'd get up and do something else," reported his daughter Mary. Miller later told her that though ambivalent at first, he felt relieved after being interviewed. "I think it felt good to

John Girardin

him that somebody wanted to hear about it. It gave him an outlet." Orin Miller passed away on March 28th, 2007.

A similar course of events took place for Kenneth Smith. "I just came home, got a job, went to work and got married," he said. The Smiths had four sons. For over twenty-five years he worked for the town of Washington, Indiana, and then took a position at the nearby Crane Ammunition Depot. He retired in the early 1990s and moved to Florida, where he lives today with his wife.

Though still living in Tampa, Louis Sosa was a very private individual with an unlisted telephone. Learning that it could be possible to contact his driver, Sartain suggested that he might, as a retired jurist, have some success obtaining Sosa's telephone number. He did, and called Sosa preliminary to my interview with him. It was the first conversation between them since the day they boarded the SS Wakefield at Marseilles. "I was surprised, very pleasantly so," commented Sosa of the unexpected telephone call. "I just got done talking to him. He's a pistol, that guy."

The ever-so-tall Kenneth Smith in Normandy posing in front of the "Paratrooper Wall".

I learned that through the GI Bill, Sosa obtained a single engine pilot's license immediately after the war. For years he enjoyed flying piper-cubs of the sort he'd seen used for artillery spotting in Europe. "That piper cub really flies itself, it's wonderful," Sosa said. Around 1970, he went into the used car business, in Tampa, Florida. At the time he was contacted for this book, Sosa was in the final stages of emphysema, from which he died in 2005.

"I have two children," Sosa told me proudly when I interviewed him, "a boy and a girl. We all live right here. We stay together. My wife and I, we've been married fifty seven years! It gets better all the time."

When I commented that he sounded devoted to his family, Sosa answered, "Oh yeah, I'm real strong about family because without family you're nothing, nothing at all. That's the way I feel. Family is all of it."

Bob McArthur, the author of letters quoted in previous chapters, who received a battlefield commission and was grievously wounded in Holland, returned home to become the Chief of Police of his hometown of Marks, Mississippi. He married and had one daughter. About 1970 he died of carbon monoxide poisoning while on a stake-out of a suspected crime scene.

Lieutenant Laurence Cook stayed in the Army Reserves after he was discharged from active service, eventually achieving command of a tank company. Looking back over his military career, Cook observed, "I think "A" Battery was a top notch outfit --

best unit I was ever in."

For several years following the war Cook operated a Western Auto franchise in his hometown. Afterward he worked for the local telephone company. He has one son and lives today in Tennessee with his wife Diana and their two Yorkshire Terriers, Mandy and Macy.

Ted Simpson also reentered the Army briefly as a reserve officer but left the military just before the outbreak of war in Korea. He took up a career in advertising and raised a family. He currently divides his time between Florida and a summer home in France.

Though the predominant pattern was for the discharged men from the battery to immerse themselves in work, married life, and children for the next fifty years, this transition was by no means effortless or universal. Some found the suddenly unremitting responsibilities of civilian life difficult to assume after years in the military. As Covais put it, "You're used to three squares a day, everything taken care of, and then all of a sudden you've got rent to pay." Others felt the same way.

"It was kind of hard to get started for a while," admitted Robert Dickson when interviewed in 2005. "When I came back I was just out of high school. I thought about college, but I thought I couldn't make it if I went to college so I didn't even go. I bought a small farm right off. It wasn't very big, it was a hundred acres. I got to having a little problem and I got up one morning and told the wife I was going to California."

Dickson having a family with two small children to support, found work with the United States Navy at Port Chicago, just outside Oakland. He continued working there and sent money home until the end of the Korean War, at which time he migrated to employment in the oil fields of the south-west. In time Robert returned to his family in Arkansas. "I came back home and went to work for a friend in the poultry hauling business. After that I built me some chicken houses and raised poultry and cattle for thirty five years."

My habit in these interviews was to ask the "A" Battery veterans if there was something which was permanently changed in them from the war. Dickson thought about this question and answered, "It was quite an experience for me overseas, I'll tell you it was. It was an experience that I'll never forget. It's a thing that will make every kid grow up. When I went in the service the war was going on and I wanted to do my part. I wanted to get in and of course I got in and I grew up in a hurry. I think that made a man out of me."

Was there anything else, I asked? There was. "We had so much Spam over there I still can't even stand to look at it, much less eat it," he added. "It got to where it just turned my stomach to even look at it. That's one thing I never allowed, Spam in my house. I don't

Ted Oliver Simpson in 2011.

want it around me! I've got a neph-
ew who's got a store not too far from
here. One day I went in there and he
was eating his lunch. I saw what it
was, I said, 'Dave, I'm leaving.' He
said, 'Wait a minute. What's the matter?' I said, 'You got Spam right there.
I don't want to look at it.' He knew
how I felt about Spam. That's the way
it is, and I couldn't eat it if I wanted to.
I'm not even gonna try."

Robert and Dorothy Dickson
live today on their farm in Arkansas.
They have four grandchildren and three
great-grandchildren. "Fortunately I'm
in fairly good health. I might not be tomorrow but I am today. I'm in pretty
good shape. I've got a three hundred
acre farm and a hundred head of cows
I'm taking care of. That's something I
like to do," he concluded with enjoy-
ment in his voice.

As time passed, Dickson's
desire to reconnect with some of his
buddies from the old outfit grew. With

Robert Dickson at Thier DuMont, Belgium.

the advent of the internet and the help of a grandchild, he was able to find the telephone
number of one of his friends in the battery motor pool. "Sergeant Legg was quite a guy,"
Dickson told me. "I finally got a hold of him in Virginia and I talked to him briefly but
I couldn't understand what he was saying. His wife took the phone and she said he has
had a stroke. He can't talk plain at all. I told him, I said, 'Sergeant, listen to what I've
got to say,' and I talked to him a good little bit. I said, 'I'm gonna write you a long letter.' The minute I hung up I sat down and wrote him a letter. The next thing I knew I got
one back from his wife. She wrote me and she said, 'I'm very sorry to have to write this
letter. Thomas was reading your letter and I walked in the room and he was sitting there
holding your letter in his hand, dead.' Maybe, I wonder, if my letter caused him to have
a heart attack or what. It made me want to just quit trying to get a hold of anybody."

Robert Dickson's contact with Sergeant Legg at the time of his death may not
have been entirely coincidental and was certainly not unique among battery men who'd
formed strong bonds. My father, Sal Covais, and Roland Gruebling, for example, were
the best of buddies throughout their time in the service. Over the following decades they
kept in close touch. Christmas cards were regularly exchanged. With their wives they
traveled to each other's homes for occasional visits and had telephone conversations at
least once or twice a year. In late February, 2002, my father couldn't shake the idea that
he needed to give his buddy Rollie a call. On Saturday the 23rd he phoned Milwaukee.
Gruebling's wife Jane answered and informed him that his friend had passed away that
very morning. The news left him feeling gloomy and alone. "The Grieb, what a great
guy, what a great guy," I remember him saying to me that afternoon. Oddly, my father
received a similar telephone call from Judge Sartain a few hours before his own death in

2004. For so many of these men their experiences in the war represented the pinnacle of their lives, all that followed paling in comparison. Never again did they feel as physically vital, so totally alive and so fully engaged in the elementary struggles of life and death. Nor did they experience friendships again of the same quality and intensity they'd known before, when death walked among them all. Later, as more and more of their spans in the material world began drawing to a close, one could imagine them feeling the need to communicate with their buddies one last time as they prepared to cross over to reassemble on the other side.

One of the qualities which my father found so appealing about Roland Gruebling was his gregarious and cheerful nature. His son, Lance, speculated that his father's exposure to so much human suffering served to accentuate this feature of Gruebling's personality. "I think it humbled him," Lance told me as we discussed the influence of the war on his father's life. "I think he also sympathized with the people, Dutch, Belgian, and German, all of them. It made him even more of a people person than he already was. He got along with everybody."

Jane and Roland Gruebling had two sons. Lance remembered his father spending a lot of time with his boys in the outdoors, duck hunting or fishing for walleye and musky on northern Wisconsin's Eagle Lake. Family camping trips were a particular pleasure for him, as was coaching the local Cub Scout baseball team.

After he retired from Borden's Dairy, Gruebling occupied his time by selling sportsman's fishing boats and supervising a launching ramp on Lake Michigan. As Lance said, "He had a lot of fun with boats and people." Gruebling died in 2002 at age 84.

Like almost every other veteran I interviewed, Ed Ryan was married soon after coming home from the war. As he recalled, he met his future wife on a blind double-date with another ex-serviceman. "I decided I wasn't gonna go steady with any woman," remembered Ryan, "so I'm lying on the couch in the living room one night and I hear stones hitting the window. I went out to see what it was. I look out and my wife is out there. She said, are you gonna take me out, or what! She was after me. We were both 23 or something like that. Sarah DelSanto, My little Ginzo sweetheart."

Roland Gruebling with Shag.

After purchasing a utility truck from his new father-in-law, Ryan and his bride hired themselves out as movers. She would drive while he did the heavy lifting. Later on Eddie worked as a fuel-oil furnace mechanic, but on the weekends the Ryans participated in numerous automobile races throughout New England and New York. "We went everywhere," he said. "She helped me all the time." Though they nearly went broke promoting racing events, Sarah and Eddie went on to have two daughters whom they raised in a 19th Century farmhouse a few miles from FDR's estate at Hyde Park, New York.

Of all the veterans I interviewed, Ed Ryan's memory was perhaps the most remarkable. When I first asked if I could speak with him about his war experiences, he told me, "I remember everything. What do you want to know?" he wasn't exaggerating. Time after time, Ryan would recount a story complete with the first name, last name, middle initial, and home town of every principle character involved. Invariably, every detail I was able to double check was corroborated. For sure, Ryan's stories were often among the most ribald and graphic, on occasion making me blush with embarrassment. A few of them were outrageous to the point of being unsuitable for in-

Ed Ryan

clusion in this book and, while I thought that some of the details must have been embellished, I could never prove this to be the case. Despite the fact that his attitudes were often socially unpopular by contemporary standards, never once did Ryan apologize or equivocate. Despite his grumpy, intolerant veneer, I soon came to recognize a generous, if highly opinionated soul who gazed back fondly on the memories of his youth. Ed Ryan was unforgettably endearing. He died on March 23rd, 2010. I will miss his phone calls very much.

For all his gregarious nature, Bob Storms was unquestionably one of the more emotionally turbulent of the "A" Battery men I interviewed. Speaking with him, it became clear that his bubbling spring of comical stories masked a deep well of still painful and heartbreaking memories. At four or five points in our conversations he broke down when recalling either the human suffering he witnessed or the gentle kindness extended toward him. As his wife Betty explained, "He gets upset when he talks about these things."

She was right. My question to Storms of how the war has stayed with him brought a response which began and ended in tears. Just considering the idea over-

whelmed him. "I don't know . . . I can't . . . it gets me sometimes to talk about it. I'm sorry I do that, but I can't help it," he finally blurted out between sobs. Once Storms regained his composure, he tried to complete his thoughts. "Them women, their husbands died, their sons died. They'd take you in, they'd feed you, they'd give you clothes their husband's wore to put on while you took a bath. They'd cut your hair and make you look human. So I like to treat everybody the best I can and I'll help them, almost anybody."

Bob Storms worked during the immediate post-war period for Central Hudson electric company, then for years operated heavy equipment, such as cranes and bulldoz-

Robert Storms

EPILOGUE. I REMEMBER EVERYTHING.

Arno Mundt skydiving.

ers. He and his wife Betty had two sons and retired to Florida in 1988.

As with many of these veterans, Storms took the opportunity of the interview to look back on his life and describe the aspects which have endured through the passage of decades. "My dad had a farm and I learned to ride horses before I could walk. I got throwed many, many many a time. I used to climb on anything, wild or otherwise, and I could ride it. I had a blind pony at one time. Blind as a bat, but I could jump that pony three four feet with out tripping him. Oh yeah, I used to be quite a horseman. But I'm not that boy anymore. I miss my horses more than anything and I'd still love to try to ride. I just love horses; that's all. To me that's better than people."

At the time he was interviewed, Storms went on to describe his day to day life. "Like now, I don't got nothing to do. I go down to the farmer's market and buy two, three crates of tomatoes. I got a little table out here; I sit out front and sell tomatoes. I make a few dollars. And I got plenty of tomatoes to eat for myself. You know, my friends come, the neighbors come, I give them a quart of tomatoes, they think that's a big thing. They call me the Tomato Man."

Bob Storms died on July 27th, 2008. In anticipation of this event, he told me, "I've already made arrangements to get cremated. My wife says, 'What do you want me to do?' I says, 'Throw me out on the front lawn, back lawn, flush me down the toilet – I don't care what you do, whatever makes you happy. Just be happy and take care of yourself.'"

Casimir Sobon summed up his experiences in Sartain's Battery with jaded simplicity when he said, "Well, it was fun, an experience . . . well no, not really." He divides his time today between New Jersey and Florida.

Robert Rappi took off his uniform but couldn't shed the wanderlust in his soul. After spending a couple of seasons in the northern Michigan woods logging with a crosscut saw, he left home for Oregon in a 1939 Chevrolet he'd bought with money left over from his discharge. Oregon was nice, but when Rappi heard of jobs available at a sawmill in the wilderness of the Alaska territory, he couldn't resist the call." It seemed like I come home when I got here. I been in a lot of places in the world, you know, and none of them really struck my fancy. But when I come up here I felt really like I belonged here," he said when I spoke to him.

For an outdoorsman like Rappi, Alaska in 1951 was a dream come true. The mountains were majestic, hunting and fishing were unequaled, and the pressures of civilization remote.

After having a couple of sawmills burn out from under him, Rappi found work as an engineer on a surplus LST, delivering heavy excavation equipment to logging camps up and down the Alaskan coast, instead of tanks on hostile beachheads. In time Rappi became skipper of the vessel and later piloted a tugboat hauling logs.

Rappi never did marry or have children. When I interviewed him at age 88, he doubted he ever would. "The girls don't want an old guy like me," he explained. "They want them young and spry." Though he still enjoyed watching the Chicago Cubs on Television, Robert Rappi continued to live in his adopted home. He became a proverbial Old Timer in an Alaska where few could remember the days before statehood. "I go out for coffee in the mornings with the old crowd, but there's strangers around. The old crowd is kind of gone."

Robert Rappi died on November 28th, 2010, just as the final corrections for this book were being made. "He lived life on his own terms," observed his niece, Yvette, after she scattered his ashes into the bay outside his adopted Alaskan home of Seward.

Once he came back from California in 1946, Marvin Ragland followed a lot of other discharged officers from the 319th and joined the National Guard. It wasn't his idea – in fact, rejoining the military was the farthest thing from his mind, but after receiving a telephone call offering him a position in a local Hutchinson, Kansas, field artillery unit which was being reactivated, he reconsidered. "I told them, 'Oh, I don't know. I'll give it a try but I may not stay long because I'm kinda burned out.' So they brought me in as a captain and it didn't take me long to find out that most of the men and officers that were there were veterans. We really had a good outfit and for some reason I stayed 18 years in the Hutch unit of the National Guard. I didn't plan on staying that long," he said.

Though he never was commissioned a captain in the 319th, Marvin Ragland achieved the rank of major in the 130th field Artillery and retired from the Kansas National Guard in October, 1965. He had, in the intervening years taken a job with the Postal Service as an accounting clerk, maintaining the financial records of several area post offices.

It took time, but Ragland's unsettled feelings about the war became more quiescent as the years passed. In 1954 the local newspaper interviewed him for a story commemorating the tenth anniversary of the Normandy invasion. Ragland talked about this during one of my conversations with him. "The reporter was asking me about jumping into Normandy," he said. "I told him that the division started out in Africa, then Sicily and Italy. But when they put the article in the news the guy wanted to make it more exciting I guess so he added a

Marvin Ragland with his military medals display.

bunch of stuff that wasn't true. I was really upset. He put in the paper that I jumped into Sicily and jumped into Italy before we come to Normandy and all that stuff."

Ragland preferred to let the issue alone rather than stir up a hornet's nest of clarifications with persons who simply could not understand. "I didn't tell anybody any different, but I was ashamed because it wasn't true."

Every tenth anniversary of the battle for Normandy the local paper would approach Ragland again. He'd usually acquiesce to an interview, but only with reluctance. He later spoke with me about the acceptance which slowly grew over his status as a publicly recognized veteran of the war's most decorated airborne division. "For a long time I really didn't care too much about even talking about it," he said, "but after so long a time it started to loosen up. Since my kids have gotten bigger in the last few years they've started asking questions and I've had a chance to talk to different organizations in town. I tell them, 'Well, I can tell you who I was with and where I was at, but I won't go into anything about the combat, fighting or anything. I've tried to forget all that.'"

Like nearly all of the "A" Battery veterans I spoke to, Ragland's post-war life revolved around his wife and family. He spoke in some detail about the importance his domestic life had for him, saying, "It just seemed like we were meant to be together. We hit it right off and a year later we were married. Wanda and I had an ideal marriage. We had a thing going that worked. She did what she wanted to and I did what she wanted to. We were married almost 57 years and we had three kids over the period. It got so we would know what each other were thinking, we'd always agree on everything, we always did everything together. Now that she's gone I don't know what to do."

Work on this book re-established contact between Ragland and Sartain, and the anniversary of D-Day became a regular opportunity for them to talk over their time together in "A" Battery. On June 6th, 2011, they had a long telephone conversation, reminiscing over events on that same date sixty-seven years before. It would be their last. Marvin Ragland passed away five days later, on June 11th.

Carl Salminen returned home to Michigan's Upper Peninsula and literally married the girl next door. Zerilda and Carl had known each other since childhood and

Carl Salminen

became husband and wife in 1947. Over the coming years they had two children. During most of that time Carl worked as a truck driver and parts manager. After his retirement, he and Zerilda enjoyed traveling to craft shows throughout northern Michigan, selling crafts which they made together.

I found Carl Salminen to be surprisingly friendly when I called him during the summer of 2004. This was good, considering that he was the first "A" Battery veteran I contacted. Someone less welcoming might have easily swayed me from calling any others, but Salminen's openness encouraged me to continue. Sadly, when Salminen died the following December, he was also the first of the veterans interviewed for this book to pass away.

Salminen was exceptional in that he not only seemed psychologically unscathed by his war experiences, but actually enjoyed talking about them. Virtually every other man interviewed for this book still had the disfiguring imprint of the war on his character in one way or another, until the very end.

According to his wife, Silas Hogg was plagued by nightmares of the war for his entire life. "Silas didn't sleep well," she told me. "He'd yell and scream in his sleep about combat. I learned that you didn't touch him when he was having a nightmare or he'd hit you. In fact, I al-

Silas Hogg fishing.

ways told the children and grandchildren, don't touch him, don't touch grandpa if he's asleep."

Post-traumatic nightmares are not unusual, but ordinarily this symptom will recede over time. This was true for Joe Mullen, Sal Covais, and others, but in Hogg's case they remained severe, frequent, and unrelenting for decades. So much so that Hogg sought the help of Veteran's Administration psychiatrists, who eventually recommended that he make a trip back to the battlefields of Europe, where he'd fought. Silas and Emma did just that and for two years the remedy worked, then, without warning the nighttime flashbacks of combat came roaring back. "I went back to the psychiatrist and told him about it. He said, we did all we could do, sent you back where it happened. I said, 'You didn't send me nowhere, I paid my way there and back.' Well, anyway, you took our advice and went. I said, 'That's right, I did. It hasn't helped any. They're coming back, all of them.'"

When he was interviewed for this book in August, 2006, Hogg spoke candidly about his nightmares. "Like last week," he said as he described one, "there were three of them on one side the fence and I was on the other. They'd already kicked my carbine away from me, all I had was a knife. I killed all three of them with the knife. Of course my bed was cut all to pieces. That's a funny dream, ain't it? Well it's actually not funny, it's a nightmare. I try to place where that happened. I can't place where that happened, but I know it did. Them nightmares are not funny at all."

Shortly after his discharge Silas Hogg married a local eastern Kentucky girl, then rejoined the army in 1947. He remained in the military for another 23 years, seeing tours of duty in 39 countries around the world. After achieving the rank of Master Sergeant, he retired with his wife, Emma, and two daughters to Texas in 1964. He died on July 10, 2007.

Silas Hogg was a remarkable man. Though limited in formal education, his recitations of the events he'd lived through were insightful and betrayed a keen intelligence. Moreover, there was never any question that he was being both sincere and genuine when he expressed his views, even when they were controversial. His was a brusque and often combative style, which was strangely balanced with respect. The re-

Marvin Fellmen at his 90th Birthday.

sult was refreshing in its honesty and candor. Hogg spoke to this at the conclusion of our interview when he said, "Now, I've led you through a lot of country and I know that a lot of that you don't want to believe, but that's your prerogative. Believe what you want to what I told you, every word is the truth." I believe him.

Marvin Fellman was probably the only officer from the wartime organization of "A" Battery, who marched in the victory parade up Fifth Avenue in January, 1946. After being discharged from active service he returned to Pipestone, Minnesota, where he assisted in operation of the family store. Later he went back to college and entered into the field of accounting. He also joined up with the Minnesota National Guard, in which Fellman was given command of a battery of the 151st Field Artillery of the 47th Infantry Division. He was on active duty through the Korean conflict as an instructor. Eventually Marvin Fellman was placed as commandant of the 47th division's garrison and retired as a Brevet Colonel in 1974. He has four daughters and lives today with his wife Rene in Minnesota.

Fellman's best friend, Joe Mullen came home to Kentland, Indiana, and his bride, Gloria. After working briefly for a seed company, he was hired by Kraft Foods, traveling the country and marketing their products. Later he took a position as an auditor with the Indiana Board of Accounts. Joe and Gloria had two sons. According to Michael Mullen, his father was plagued with headaches and back problems as a result of his 1945 jeep accident for the rest of his life. He passed away in 2001 from Parkinson's disease.

"My father never talked much about the war," said Mike Mullen, "but as I got older he started to tell me a few things, sometimes funny and sometimes tragic, but they would not be terribly graphic." Mike had the feeling that there was much left unspoken, lying just beneath the surface. "My mother told me he was terribly upset about some of the things that happened. One time he confided in her that during the Battle of the Bulge he'd killed a German soldier at close quarters who was only sixteen years old. He was himself only nineteen when this happened. Another time we were sitting in a bar having a beer. I was underage of course, but that didn't matter. It was during the height of the Viet-Nam war and I remember I told him I didn't understand what it was all about, but I had an offer to go to West Point after high school. I asked him, 'Dad, should I get involved?' He got really very thoughtful, looked at me and said quietly, 'No. Don't go if you don't have to.' That's all he would say. As it turned out, I failed my physical anyway."

During his time in the army, Mahlon Sebring swore that if he survived to come home he wouldn't work for three full months. Just the same, when I asked him what he did after he was discharged he answered, "I got married, then I had to get a job!" Wedded to his fiancé Clara five weeks after coming home to Tecumseh, Michigan, Sebring took a position at a local factory producing air conditioning compressors. The work became a lifelong career of developing, engineering, and testing compressors for every variety of air conditioning from domestic window units to massive systems designed for industrial use.

In the meantime Mahlon and Clara had three children – two sons and a daughter. They lived briefly in Rockford, Illinois, and then Sebring took a job establishing a new compressor plant outside Bristol, Virginia, in 1975. "Up in Michigan I belonged to a volunteer fire department," he said, commenting on how well entrenched in his home community he had been. "When we moved down here I didn't know anybody, so it was kind of quiet around here for a while, but now we know plenty of people. This is a good place to live."

Mahlon and Clara still live in Virginia. They have seven grand and six great-grand children, with a seventh on the way. "Since I retired I don't do much other than mow the lawn. When I feel like it I go down in the basement and do some woodworking," he explained. Sebring enjoys producing pieces of furniture for his home, as well as other woodworking projects. For a while he had fun making wooden statues of Uncle Sam. "I made a bunch of them," he said. I buy a cedar fence post and sand it down, give him a top hat and arms, then I paint a face on it." When General H. Hugh Shelton, former commander of the 82nd Airborne Division and Chairman of the Joint Chiefs of Staff addressed Sebring's local chapter of an airborne veteran's group, he bought two Uncle Sams for his home. "We invited him to one of our dinners and damned if he didn't come," Sebring said proudly. "Later on I saw him at Bragg during All-American week. I asked him if he still had the Uncle Sams and he told me, 'He's on duty where I live, he's standing on the front steps of my house.'"

As with the others, I asked Sebring how the war has stayed with him. "That's hard for me to say," he answered, "but if there's a chance this country will ever get in an-other war like that again, we should think about it first. You just can't believe how bad people can get hurt. It changes lives in so many different ways. We lost over 400,000 in World War Two and you never know what some of those people could have done with their lives."

Attracted by the brotherhood of airborne troopers, Sebring has been a frequent attendee at the 82nd's yearly All-American Week at Fort Bragg, North Carolina. All veterans of the division, from World

Mahlon Sebring.

EPILOGUE. I REMEMBER EVERYTHING.

War Two to Operation Iraqi Freedom, are welcome at this event. "They have an old timers division review and they wanted all the old timers to be in it. So I went down there," said Sebring as he described the event held in 1994 to me. "All at once your dad walked past me and I saw he had on a 319th crest. I said, '319th! What the hell are you doing here?' He turned around and said, 'I was in the 319th, "A" Battery.' I said I was too. He said, 'What's your name?' I said, 'Sebring.' All at once we recognized each other. He grabbed my hand and we marched that day side by side."

When I asked my father if he remembered the chance reunion, he told me, "Sure, Sebring came up to me and he saw I had the 319th insignia on. Hey, you're from the 319th? I said, 'Yeah, I'm from the 319th, and I'm from "A" Battery.' He says, '"A" Battery? I'm from "A" Battery too!' 'You're from "A" Battery -- I'm from "A" Battery. What's your name?' 'Sebring. Sebring? Sebring? I know you. I know you, Sebring, I'm Covais! Hey!' The bubble lit up. It was maybe 45 years later, over forty five years. You know, when you haven't seen a guy for a long period of time, you just pass each other. Boy, it was good to see him again."

To be exact, it had been 49 years since the day the high and low point guys were separated at Epinal, France, so there was a lot of catching up to do. The next morning Sebring and Covais had breakfast together at the 319th mess hall. "Believe it or not," Sebring said, "the 319th kitchen has won a whole lot of awards of the whole United States Army. You ought to see the trophies all along the back wall. I asked them, 'Where the hell did all the trophies come from.' They said, 'We have the best kitchen in the whole United States Army!' I said, 'Is that so? Well show me some of the food!'"

Only one man I contacted declined to participate in an interview. It was the medic, "Zemo." I forget just how I was able to locate him-- after all, he'd changed his last name since the war to a noun which was suggestive of his role treating wounded soldiers. When I first called him he was startled and reluctant to say anything much beyond asking how I'd gotten his telephone number. Somehow I convinced him I wasn't dangerous, and after taking my contact information he told me he would phone me back in a few days. "I found your father's name in an autograph book I have here," he said to me when I answered the phone, "so I must have known him." While he was cordial, Zemo

Lester Newman

also was evasive. I sensed something was wrong and asked if our conversation made him uncomfortable. "It upsets me too much to talk about these things," he admitted. "In fact, I've been depressed ever since you first called. I'm not in good health you know, and talking about this isn't good for me. I wish you success though and hope you can understand."

About a month after this conversation I received a package in the mail containing his autograph book. Inside were the signatures of Ted Simpson, Robert Rappi, Kenneth Smith, Louis Sosa, Mahlon Sebring, Bob Storms, Silas Hogg, Ted Covais, and dozens of other now familiar names. Zemo had mentioned that he might do this, since his children were hardly aware of his war experiences and in his opinion I would have more use for the book. Still, there was no letter enclosed and I had the impression that in a larger sense Zemo was closing the book on the war for good, so I left him alone. When contact with the mysterious Zemo was next attempted several months later, it was learned he had passed away.

The lives of the 319th's staff officers after World War Two were as varied as those of the enlisted men. Colonel James Todd, the battalion's second, and very popular commanding officer, continued to be a favorite among the discharged veterans. Ed Ryan remembered encountering him at an early reunion. "After the war," said Ryan, "the first reunion, in New York City, Todd pulls up in front of the hotel with suitcases full of booze. Says to me and another guy, 'I know the war's over, but will you help me get these bags up to my room?'" They did and according to Ryan, "All the mixers were charged to Todd. Another big, big party."

Marvin Ragland remembered visiting Colonel Todd and his wife sometime around 1990 at his home in Tahlequah, Oklahoma. He is since believed to be deceased. Major Jerry Wimberley, with whom Sartain locked horns on, more than one occasion, transferred to Military Intelligence shortly after the war. Following a posting at the Pentagon he was stationed in Vienna, Austria, and remained there for a two year tour. According to Sartain, he is believed to have committed suicide sometime in the 1960s following his retirement from the military.

Major Frederick Silvey returned to San Antonio, Texas, where he operated a successful music business for many years. According to his daughter Silvia, he died of a heart attack in 1987, shortly after watching a television showing of "The Longest Day" on the 43rd anniversary of the D-Day invasion.

Colonel Harry Bertsch, who was poorly remembered by every last man interviewed for this book, is known to have served as a United States military advisor to the Philippines from the late 1940s until 1951. He retired from the army in 1954, when he went to work as an operations analyst for Corvey Engineering, a defense contractor. Bertsch retired to Bellaire Bluffs Florida, where he died on January 13, 1982.

After he was transferred out of the 319th, little is known of what happened to Major James B. Wilcoxson – possibly the only officer of his rank ever forced out by a petition of the enlisted men under his command. Sartain believes he stayed in the army until retirement. Sometime around 1970 he received a letter from Wilcoxson, stating that he was planning to write a history of the battalion. "I never answered his letter," said Judge Sartain bitterly. "He wrote me a letter and instead of starting it Dear Charlie or Dear Lenton, he started it off Dear Captain! Well, that's bullshit you know. He retired and was living in Lawton, Oklahoma, near Fort Sill. I don't know what ever happened to him."

Much more pleasing was the contact between Sartain and Colonel Louis G. Mendez, the former commander of the 508th's 3rd Battalion, in the mid-1980's. The Regimental Association was holding a convention in New Orleans and Sartain was eager to attend, although judicial obligations in Baton Rouge made this impossible.

"The convention was still going on," Sartain remembered. "So I called and I left a message. About an hour or two later he called and he said, 'This is Louie Mendez, I have a message with this number. Who am I speaking to?' I said, You're speaking to Charles L. Sartain.' He said, 'Artillery?' I said, 'Yes.' So we had a forty five minute phone call. That was really, really something. He was such a terrific combat commander, but he never made brigadier and he should have. I always wondered what had gone wrong. I just think somewhere along the line he ruffled some feathers."

Mendez's wife, Jean, agreed with Sartain's assessment that her husband's outspoken nature did little to further his career in a 2009 conversation with me. She also believed that the peace-time army was simply not ready to accept a Hispanic as a Brigadier General. Whatever the reason for his failure to advance beyond the rank of colonel, Mendez continued to serve in varied and distinguished capacities. Immediately after the war he taught at the Infantry School at Fort Benning, Georgia, and then served as United States Military Attache' to Spain. He later commanded the 4th Cavalry Regiment of the 1st Cavalry Division in Korea. "Every man in the fourth cavalry in Korea was made to get a GED (General Education Diploma) while he was in command," his wife told me with pride. Mendez also served in the war histories division of the Army General Staff and as secretary of the Organization of American States' Inter-American Defense Board. When he retired in 1970 he was both a graduate and on the staff of the Industrial College of the Armed Forces. Colonel Mendez was also a graduate of the Command and General Staff College. In addition, he earned a Master's Degree in International Relations from Georgetown University.

After leaving the army, Mendez pursued his lifelong passion for personal edification through learning. He entered the Department of Education as National Director of

Salvatore "Ted" and Cathy Covais

the Right to Read Program and later served as Chief of the department's Vocational and Adult Education Branch when he retired in 1985. Colonel Mendez died on September 19th, 2001, after suffering a stroke. He was survived by his wife, their 12 children, 22 grandchildren, and 5 great-grandchildren. He is buried at Arlington national Cemetery.

Captain John Manning continued to work his family's agricultural supply business in Johnson, New York. Despite a disastrous fire in 1952 which left him badly burned, Manning rebuilt the operation into a large wholesale establishment in the years that followed. In time he branched out into construction and then real estate appraisals, an occupation which Manning pursued successfully for the rest of his life. He and his wife Marge had one son.

John Manning remained active in community affairs throughout his life, holding positions of responsibility in the area Chamber of Commerce, the Lions club, Kiwanis, and other service organizations. He served as Chairman of the local town planning board, as well as the Minisink Valley School Board, and as president of the Mid Hudson Real Estate Appraisal Society. In the 1990s, Manning became involved with the Port Jervis, New York, chapter of the 82nd Airborne Association, through which he renewed contact with Ed Ryan and Bob Storms.

Manning and Sartain maintained their friendship through the years, with several visits back and forth. First the Mannings came to Baton Rouge in the 1950s, and made a trip together with the Sartains to New Orleans for a proper Mardi gras celebration. Later, in the autumn of 1969, Sartain and Peggy Lou spent time in New York City where the Judge took a class in Judicial Administration at New York University. Manning drove to manhattan and brought the Sartain's back to his home near Middletown. "It was before 1970, 1969, something like that, after I'd been elected to the court of appeals and I took a course at NYU. One weekend Peggy Lou and I took off to visit with Johnny and his wife. He came down and got us from the hotel on Washington Square and drove us up to his home in Orange County. I thoroughly enjoyed the ride up there. It was a beautiful old home; big, big house, well maintained, with a well in the courtyard where you could pull you up some cool water. He drove us by West Point, then we went to a spot where you could overlook the Hudson," Sartain remembered.

About ten years later the Mannings returned to Baton Rouge. During their stay with the Sartain's they all visited the historic town of St. Francesville, Louisiana. According to Sartain, "Manning got a big kick out of taking a tour of all the old homes. Every home he visited, his was older. His place in New York was a pre-Revolutionary War home, you know."

Unfortunately, John Manning died in October, 2003, before he could be interviewed for this book. During our conversations concerning Manning, I asked Sartain about the last time they were together. "That would have been in 2000," he said. "Johnny came down here alone because this was after his wife had passed away. She was just a delightful person, and Manning himself was a terrific individual. We had a nice visit." Judge Sartain's high opinion of Manning was obvious, and when I asked him just what it was about him which generated such regard the Judge told me, "John Manning was a good man and we were buddies. But more than that, Joseph, he was my idol, boy, he really was. He was just a good guy and I learned an awful lot from him. I miss him, I really do."

My father, Sal Covais never realized his dream of moving to Washington State. It was an idea which had taken hold of him as a teenager in the Civilian Conservation corps but which the vicissitudes of life never allowed. Instead, he had children – two daughters and a son, myself. He began selling life insurance and in the 1950s moved out of New York City to Long Island. When his brother Jack died in the mid-1960s, Covais took over his subsidy music publishing business. By 1972 he had moved his family to Florida, where he continued in business and dabbled in real estate.

By the 1980s Sal and Cathy Covais found a renewed faith in God. It took a long time to recover from the disillusionment which marked his post-war life, but this reborn faith sustained him in his later; years.

As time went by my father grew more and more involved in commemorating his fellow veterans of World War Two. For a long period he marched in every Memorial Day parade, often wearing a paratrooper's jump suit, until he no longer had the strength to walk the distance. "Those guys got killed out there. When I march on Memorial Day,

Epilogue. I remember everything.

I march for them. For them, not for me. I wear the uniform proudly, for them. What ever insignias I have, I wear for them. But they paid the price, they didn't make it back," he once told me.

It became Dad's habit to scan the obituaries and attend the funerals of perfect strangers who had been, after all, airborne brothers in arms. A few times he met other troopers who did the same.

My father's reputation as an emotional man who wept easily at anniversaries or holidays was a bit of a legend in our family. Indeed, we jokingly called him "cry-baby" at these times, not understanding all he'd been through. On one occasion in the mid 1970's, after he'd welled up with tears on reading some sentimental birthday card, I asked him, "Dad, this crying thing, have you always been this way?"

He stopped what he was doing, paused, and answered, "No, only since the war. I think I realized there were things in life worth crying over."

At the time, though I sensed his statement was something profound, I was too young and inexperienced to understand. Since then, what he said has stayed with me through the years, revisiting me over and over as questions I've considered in conversation or rumination. What is worth crying over? What is worth dying for? What really counts in this life? My father seemed to know those answers though he paid dearly for that knowledge. In some absolute way, I can now see this book has been my own attempt to answer those questions.

Regretfully, I only took the opportunity to record a few informal interviews with my father before his death. During one of these conversations I realized that he was no longer speaking to me. Cognizant of his own mortality, he was addressing some as yet unknown and perhaps unborn future audience. "I'm proud that I went through the 82nd Airborne," he said in a voice trembling with passion. "I'm an airborne trooper, and I love this country. If the country called me again I would go back again, I would do that, I would do that. But I cannot begin to tell you; really, I can't put three years into three hours. I can't describe all the things that I've seen. As you can see, I am an emotional person when I think of these things. There's so many things that go on, that you experience, and either you forget them or you don't want to remember them. So, Folks, if you're listening to me, pardon me, I'm doing the best I can. I love you all and God bless you. And God bless the United States of America."

Bibliography

Author's Collection

Correspondence with Author, 2004-2010:
- Robert G. Dickson
- Marvin Fellman
- Mrs. Talmadge Glenn
- Marvin L. Ragland
- Robert G. Rappi
- Edward Ryan
- C. Lenton Sartain
- Ned B. Smith
- James D. Stanard

"Court Martial Transcripts." US Army Office of the Judge Advocate General. Alexandria, VA.
-First Lieutenant Harry Warren (real name withheld), November 17, 1943 and March 6, 1944.
-Private Paul Blake, April 13, 1945.

Burbidge, Barbara. "A Brief History of Papillon Hall and Photographs." Unpublished letter, December 6, 2007.

Combs, Roland J. "Letters to family." 1942-1944.

Davis, Carl L. "319th Glider Field Artillery Battalion (World War II) Directory." Distributed by the 319th News Service.

Glenn, Talmadge. "Letter to his father." November 27, 1944.

Gruebling, Roland. "Letter to employees at Borden's Dairy in Milwaukee, WI." June 23, 1944.

Linton, Leonard. "Kilroy was Here." Unpublished manuscript, 2004.

Manning, John R. "Untitled Memoir." Unpublished manuscript, 1991.

McArthur, Robert. "Letters to his mother." 1943-1944.

Mullen, Joseph W. "Letters to his wife, Gloria Blanke." 1944-1945.

Mundt, Arno. "Untitled Memoir." Unpublished manuscript, 1994.

BIBLIOGRAPHY

Simpson, Theodore O. "WWII: How One Boy Grew." Unpublished manuscript.

US Army. "Headquarters 319th Field Artillery Battalion, Training Memorandum." Unpublished. July 6, 1943.

Individual Deceased personel File for Willam Siegel

Individual Deceased personel File for Rodney Renfrew

National Archives and Records Administration, College Park, MD.

"Battalion Casualty List." 319th Glider Field Artillery Battalion, July 26, 1944.

"General Orders." 82nd Airborne Division, 1943-1946.

"Unit History." From the collection WWII US Army Operations. 319th Glider Field Artillery Battalion .
-September – October, 1943
-June – July 1944
-September – November 1944
-December 1944 – February 1945
-April – June 1945.

"Unit Journal." 319th Glider Field Artillery Battalion.
-September – October 1943
-June – July 1944
-September – November 1944
-December 1944 - February 1945
-April – June 1945.

"Unit Journal." 325th Glider Infantry Regiment. September, 1944.

"Unit Journal." 505th Parachute Infantry Regiment. October, 1943.

"Unit Journal." 508th Parachute Infantry Regiment. September, October, and December, 1944.

Maps

Army Map Service. "Boscotrecase. Italy." First Edition. 1:25,000. Washington D.C.: Army Map Service, 1943.

"Sarno." First Edition. 1:25,000. Washington D.C.:
Army Map Service, 1943.

"Castellamare Di Stabia." First Edition. 1:25,000. Washington D.C.:
Army Map Service, 1943.

Michelin. "Battle of Normandy, June-August 1944." 1:250,000. Michelin, 1947.

US Army Corps of Engineers. "Cherbourg." Second Edition. 1:250,000. London:
War Office, 1944.

"Durbuy." Second Edition. 1:50,000. 1943. Washington D.C.: US
Government Printing Office.

"Jessenitz." London: War Office, 1944.

"Lubtheen." London: War Office, 1944.

"Nijmegen." Second Edition. Washington D.C.: US
Government Printing Office.

"Malmedy." Second Edition. 1:50,000. 1943. Washington D.C.: US
Government Printing Office.

"St. Saveur." 1:25,000. 1943. Washington D.C.: US Government Printing Office.

"Ste. Mere Eglise." 1:25,000. Second Edition. 1944. Washington D.C.: US
Government Printing Office.

"Vielsalm." 1:50,000. Second Edition. 1943. Washington D.C.: US
Government Printing Office.

Newspapers and Magazines

319 News.
  -Issue no. 19, November 1970
  -Issue no. 15, April 1969
  -Issue no. 20, December 1971.

325 Glider Tow Line.
  - Summer 2005
  -Winter-Spring 2005.

The All-American Paraglide. "21st German Army Surrenders to 82nd Division."
May 1945.

The Intelligence Bulletin. "How Paratroops Clear Fields for Gliders." June 1944.

BIBLIOGRAPHY

Life. "Atlantic Convoy." July 27, 1942.

"Battle of Chiunzi." October 18, 1943.

New York Times. "82nd Set to March Full Parade Route." January 3, 1946.

"82nd Airborne gets Noisy Welcome." January 4, 1946.

Quitman County Democrat. June 30, 1994.

State Times. "Family Court." March 22, 1964.

"State Appeal Court Judge Sartain to Retire Dec. 31." December 23, 1978.

Talon, 17th Airborne Division Newsmagazine. WSA Voy. 28, S.S. Mariposa.
    September 12, 1945.

Berger, Meyer. "City Hails the 82nd in GI Tribute." *New York Times.* January 13, 1946.

Kilburne, Clara. "They Jumped into History, D-Day Experiences Lead to Friendship
    between Two Paratroopers from Reno County." *Hutchinson News.*

Perlmut, David. "Holocaust Survivor, Camp Liberator Retells Experiences in Germany.
"   *Charlotte Observer.* May 5, 2003.

Reeves, Joseph R. "Untitled." *Field Artillery Journal.* March 1946.

Salton, George. "Sharing Painful Memories Reveals Many Unexpected Connections."
    The Forward. November 7, 2003.

Schwarz, Benjamin. "The Real War." *The Atlantic.* June 2001.

Treanor, Tom. "Glide into Death." *Colliers.* August 5, 1944.

Online Databases

Hull Number. <www.hullnumber.com>.

HyperWar. <http://www.ibiblio.org/hyperwar>.

West Point Association of Graduates. <http://www.westpointaog.org>.

Oral Interviews

Cook, Laurence. Telephone interviews. 2005-2010.

Covais, Salvatore J. Telephone and personal interviews. 1965-2004.

BATTERY!

Curry, Quentin. Telephone interview. September 1, 2004.

Dappal, Joseph. Telephone interviews. 2008-2010.

Dixon, Robert G. Telephone interviews. 2004-2010.

Elmore, Ethred Duell. Telephone interviews. 2004-2008.

Fellman Marvin R. Telephone interview. March 5, 2005.

Girardin, John. Telephone interviews. 2004-2010.

Gonzales, Frank. Personal interviews. 2005.

Goodspeed, James. Telephone interview. January 2, 2010.

Gruebling, Lance. Telephone interviews. 2004-2010.

Hogg, Sylas. Telephone interviews. 2006 – 2007.

Hogg, Emma. Telephone interview. June 9, 2010.

Kilgore, Lynn. Telephone interview. August 12, 2010.

Knecht, Edward. Telephone interview. January 12, 2007.

Lentin, Leonard. Telephone interviews. 2007.

Manning, John R. Jr. Telephone interviews. 2007-2010.

Mendes, Jean. Telephone interviews. 2008-2010.

Miller, Orin G. Telephone interviews. 2005-2007.

Mullen, Michael. Telephone interviews. 2004-2010.

Newman, Lester. Telephone interviews. 2005.

Pesivento, Richard. Telephone interviews. 2006.

Pollard, O. Miles. Telephone interview. August 22, 2010.

Provenza, Charlotte. Telephone interview. August 18, 2010.

Ragland, Marvin L. Telephone interviews. 2005-2010.

Rappi, Robert G. Telephone interviews. 2004 -2010.

Jones, Sgt. (real name withheld). Telephone interviews. 2005.

Ryan, Edward. Telephone interviews. 2007-2010.

Salminen, Carl. Telephone interview. July 1, 2004.

Sartain, Charles L. Jr. Telephone interviews. 2004-2010.

Bibliography

Scarsalla, Servino. Telephone interviews. December 2009.

Sebring, Mahlon. Telephone interviews. 2004-2010.

Silvey, Sylvia. Telephone interviews. 2005-2007.

Simpson, Theodore O. Telephone interviews. April 2006.

Smith, Kenneth. Telephone interviews. 2004-2010.

Smith, Kyle. Telephone interviews. 2005.

Smith, Ned. Telephone interviews. 2005-2006.

Sobon, Casimir. Telephone interviews. 2006-2010.

Sosa, Louis. Telephone interviews. 2005-2006.

Stephens, Lowell. Telephone interview. October 3, 2005.

Storms, Betty. Telephone interview. June 8, 2010.

Storms, Robert. Telephone interview. January 21, 2006.

Published Works

German Military Dictionary. Mt. Ida: Lancer Militaria, 1944.

World War II: Infantry Commanding Officer Narratives. BACM Research. CD-Rom.

508th Parachute Infantry Regiment. "57 Days in Holland and Germany with the 508th Parachute Infantry." <http://www.508pir.org>.

Adams, Jonathan E. *The Operations of "A" Company, 508th Parachute Infantry, 82nd Airborne Division Near Rencheaux, Belgium (Ardennes Campaign) 22-25 December.* US Army Maneuver of Excellence. <https://www.benning. army.mil/infantry>.

Alexander, Mark J. *Thirty-Four Days in Normandy in 1944.* . US Army Maneuver of Excellence. <https://www.benning.army.mil/infantry>.

Alley, Herman L. 1997. *"Soldiers."* 505 Parachute Infantry Regiment. <http://www.505rct.org>.

BBC News. "Prostitutes Preyed on US Troops." <http://news.bbc.co.uk>.

Baumer, William H. and William O. Darby. *Darby's Rangers: We Led the Way.* New York: Ballantine Books, 1980.

Beevor, Antony. *The Fall of Berlin 1945.* New York, Penguin. 2003.

Cailloux, Lucien. 2000. *With the Artillerymen of the 82nd Airborne Division: "All American" in December 1944*. Centre de Recherches et d'Informations sur la Bataille des Ardennes. <http://www.criba.be>.

Cambell, James A. "From VJ...Mental Disorder Following Discharge." *Psychiatric Quarterly,* vol. 20, no. 3: 375-380.

Child, Paul W., ed. *Register of Graduates and Former Cadets of the United States Military Academy, Eisenhower Centennial Edition*. New York: Association of Graduates, USMA, 1990.

Dawson, W. Forrest, ed. *Saga of the All American*. Atlanta: Albert Love Enterprises, 1946.

Gavin, James M. *On to Berlin: Battles of an Airborne Commander 1943-1946*. New York: Viking Press, 1978.

Gohmert, Roland L. *A Parachute Infantry Battalion in the Attack of a Fortified Position*. US Army Maneuver of Excellence. <https://www.benning.army.mil/infantry>.

Hennessy, Jefferson. 2005. *The Legend of the Tunica Treasure*. The Hennessy Chronicles. <jeffersonhennessy.blogspot.com>.

Home of the 508th Airborne Chapter 82nd Airborne Division Association, Inc. "Regimental History: 508th Parachute Infantry Regiment (1942 - 1946)." <http://www.red-devils.org>.

Hutto, James C. *World War II Memoirs January 31, 1923 – December 6, 1993*. 508th Parachute Infantry Regiment. <http://www.508pir.org>.

Kissane, Joseph. *WW2 Memoirs*. 508th Parachute Infantry Regiment. <http://www.508pir.org>.

Le Febvre, Henry. *Operations of the 2nd Battalion 505th Parachute Infantry (82nd Airborne Division) in the Withdrawal from and Recapture of Keer-Du-Mont Ridge, Belgium, 22 December 1944-7 January 1945*. US Army Maneuver of Excellence. <https://www.benning.army.mil/infantry>.

Lewis, Kenneth. *Doughboy to GI: US Army Clothing and Equipment 1900-1945*. Bournemouth: Norman D. Landing Books, 2002.

Lewis, Robert. 2001. *Ford Germany Under the Nazis*. Car Keys. <http://archive.carkeys.co.uk>.

Lloyd, Pen. *The History of the Mysterious Papillon Hall*. Leicester: Duplitype, 1978.

BIBLIOGRAPHY

Lord II, William G. *History of the 508ᵗʰ Parachute Infantry.* Nashville: The Battery Press, 1977.

Louisiana Court of Appeal. "Elephant, Inc. v. Hartford Acc. & Indem. Co." Animal Legal and Historical Center. Last Updated September 10, 2010. < http://www. animallaw.info>.

Lowe, James B. "NADDAB The First Successful Airborne Operation, 1943." M.A. thesis, Louisiana State University and Agricultural and Mechanical College, December, 2004.

MacDonald, Charles B. *The Siegfried Line Campaign.* Washington, D.C.: Center of Military History, United States Army, 1963.

Madison, James H. "Wearing Lipstick to War: An American Woman in World War II, England and France." *Prologue,* vol. 39, no. 3 (fall 2007).

Masters, Charles J. *Glidermen of Neptune: The American D-Day Glider Attack.* Edwardsville: Southern Illinois University Press, 1995.

McCann, John P. *Passing Through: The 82ⁿᵈ Airborne Division in Northern Ireland 1943-44.* County Down (Newtownards): Colourpoint Books, 2005.

McEnroe, Sean. "Painting the Philippines with an American Brush: Visions of Race and National Mission Among the Oregon Volunteers in the Philippine Wars of 1898 and 1899." *Oregon Historical Quarterly,* no. 104.1.

McNalley, John V. *As Ever, John: The Letters Of Colonel John V. McNalley To His Sister, Margaret McNally Bierbaum 1942-1946.* Fairfield: Roberts Press, 1985.

Merridale, Catherine. Ivan's War: Life and Death in the Red Army, 1939-1945. New York: Picador, 2006.

Miller, Donald L. *Masters of the Air: America's Bomber Boys who Fought the Air War against Nazi Germany.* New York: Simon and Schuster, 2006.

Nab, Adrie and Cissie Plattel-Berben, eds. *Liberation of the Betuwe: Operation Market Garden.* Translated by Adrie H. Nab. Huissen: Herdenking Bevrijding Overbetuwe, 2004.

Nigl, Alfred J. and Nigl, Charles A. *Silent Wings Savage Death: Saga of the 82ⁿᵈ Airborne's Glider Artillery in World War II.* Santa Ana: Graphic Publishers, 2007.

Nordyke, Phil. *All American All the Way: The Combat History of the 82ⁿᵈ Airborne Division in World War II.* St. Paul: Zenith Press, 2005.

Pauwels, Jacques R. "Profits uber Alles! American Corporations and Hitler.» *Labour/ Le Travail*, (Spring 2003). <http://www.historycooperative.org/journals/llt/51/ pauwels.html>.

Pierce, Robert. "The Airborne Field Artillery: From Inception to Combat Operations." M.A. thesis, U.S. Army Command and General Staff College, 2005.

Pierce, Wayne. *Let's Go! The Story of the Men who Served in the 325th Glider Infantry Regiment.* Chapel Hill: Professional Press, 1997.

Pitkin, Thomas M. "Airborne Clothing and Equipment." *QMC Historical Studies.* No. 5 (February, 1944).

Plebanek, Frank A. "18 Months in 'E' Company 325 Glider Infantry Regiment 82nd Airborne Division June 1944 to December 1945." Ontario: Self-published, 1993.

Reeves, Joseph R. "Field Artillery in the Ardennes." *The Field Artillery Journal,* (March 1946):   138-184.

Roquemore, Frank U. *The Operations of the 2nd Ranger Battalion in the Htjrtgen Forest, 6-8 December, 1944.* US Army Maneuver of Excellence. <https://www.benning.army.mil/infantry>.

Ryan, Cornelius. *A Bridge too Far.* New York: Simon and Schuster, 1974.

Sackenham, Bill. "Belgium – Ardennes, Battle Of The Bulge" from *Bill Sackenheim, A Success Story.* 508th Parachute Infantry Regiment. <http://www.508pir.org>.

Smith, Graham. *When Jim Crow Met John Bull: Black American Soldiers in World War II Britain.* London: I.B. Tauris & Co Ltd, 1987.

Sokolova, Alyona. 2005. "American Aid to Soviet Union, or Unknown Lend-Lease." *Vladivostok News,* April 13. Free Republic. <http://www.freerepublic.com>.

US Army Quartermaster Foundation. "Army Clothing History." Last modified March 25, 2007. <http://www.qmfound.com/army_clothing_history.htm>.

The Wartime Memories Project. "The Womens Land Army." <http://www. wartimememoriesproject.com/ww2/womenslandarmy.php>.

Wiegand, Brandon T. *Index to the General Orders of the 82nd Airborne Division, in World War II, First Edition.* Creighton: D-Day Militaria, 2003.

Wills, Deryk. *Put on Your Boots and Parachutes: The United States 82nd Airborne Division.* Leicester: Deryk Wills, 1992.

BIBLIOGRAPHY

Wiltse, Charles M. 1965. *Medical Service in the Mediterranean and Minor Theaters.* Internet Archive. <http://www.archive.org>.

World War 2 US Medical Research Centre. "307th Airborne Medical Company Unit History." < http://www.med-dept.com>.

World War II Troop Ships. "1945 Troop Ship Crossings." <http://ww2troopships.com>.